ANCIENT
JUDAISM

MAX WEBER

ANCIENT JUDAISM

TRANSLATED AND EDITED BY

HANS H. GERTH AND DON MARTINDALE

THE FREE PRESS, *New York*

COLLIER-MACMILLAN LIMITED, *London*

Collier-Macmillan Canada, Ltd., Toronto, Ontario

Library of Congress Catalog Card Number: 52–8156

FIRST FREE PRESS PAPERBACK EDITION 1967

CONTENTS

Preface   ix

PART I—THE NATURAL AND CULTURAL BACKGROUND OF ANCIENT JUDAISM

I. *The Social Structure and its Setting*   3

   1. Prefatory Note: the Sociological Problem of Judaic
      Religious History   3
   2. General Historical and Climatic Conditions   5
   3. The Bedouins   10
   4. The Cities and the Gibborim   13
   5. The Israelite Peasant   23

II. *The Gerim and the Ethic of the Patriarchs*   28

   1. The Plebeian Strata   28
   2. The Pre-Exilic Metic   32
   3. Herdsman and Peasant   36
   4. The Ethic in the Time of the Patriarchs   49

PART II—THE COVENANT AND CONFEDERACY

III. *The Social Laws of the Israelite Legal Collections*   61

   1. The Laws as an Index to Social Development   61
   2. Social Law of the Israelite Collections   70
   3. The Berith   75
   4. The Yahwe Confederacy and its Organs   77

IV. *Warfare and War Prophecy*   90

   1. Holy War, Circumcision, Nazarites   90
   2. The Nebiim   96
   3. Nabi Ecstasy and Prophecy   102
   4. Changing Forms of Prophecy   105

V. *Social Significance of the War God of the Confederacy*   118

1. Uniqueness of the Relation of Israel to its God   118
2. The Nature of the War God   124
3. Social Reception of the War God   130
4. Non-Yahwistic Cults   139

PART III—PRIESTHOOD, CULT, AND ETHICS

VI. *Cultic Peculiarities of Yahwism*   149

1. The Sabbath   149
2. Baal and Yahwe: The Idols and the Ark   154
3. Sacrifice and Expiation   162

VII. *Priests and the Cult Monopoly of Jerusalem*   169

1. The Levites and the Torah   169
2. The Development of the Priesthood and the Cult Monopoly of Jerusalem   174
3. The Fight of Yahwism against Orgiasticism   187

VIII. *Forms of Israelite Intellectuality in the Pre-Prophetic Era*   194

1. The Israelite Intellectuals and the Neighboring Cultures   194
2. Mesopotamian Culture Relations   201
3. The Yahwistic and Elohistic Intellectual Traditions   205

IX. *Ethics and Eschatology of Yahwism*   219

1. Magic and Ethics   219
2. Mythologies and Eschatologies   225

X. *Intercultural Relations in Pre-Exilic Ethics*   235

1. Substantive Content of Jewish Ethics   235
2. The Ethic of the Decalogues and the Book of the Dead   250
3. Economic Ethic   252
4. Charity   255

PART IV—THE ESTABLISHMENT OF THE JEWISH PARIAH PEOPLE

XI. *Social Psychology of the Prophets*   267

1. Political Orientations of Pre-Exilic Prophecy   267
2. Hellenic and Judaic Prophecy   270

3. Established Authority versus the Prophets   271
4. Status Orientations and Inner-Political Attitudes   277
5. Social Context of the Prophetic Message   278
6. Psychological Peculiarities of the Prophets   286

XII. *The Ethic and Theodicy of the Prophets*   297

1. The Prophetic Ethic   297
2. Eschatology and Prophets   321

XIII. *The Pariah Community*   336

1. The Development of Ritualistic Segregation   336
2. The Dualism of In-Group and Out-Group Morality   343

XIV. *The Exile*   356

1. Babylonian and Egyptian Exiles   356
2. Ezekiel and Deutero-Isaiah   364
3. The Priests and the Confessional Restoration after the Exile   380

PART V—SUPPLEMENT: THE PHARISEES

XV. *Sects and Cults of the Post-Exile Period*   385

1. Pharisaism as Sect Religiosity   385
2. The Rabbis   391
3. Teaching and Ethic of Pharisaical Judaism   400

XVI. *Judaism and Early Christianity*   405

1. Essenism in Relation to the Teachings of Jesus   405
2. Increasing Ritualistic Segregation of the Jews   417
3. Proselytism in the Diaspora   418
4. Propaganda of the Christian Apostles   421

Notes   425

Map, Location of Historic Places   462

Glossary and Index   463

1. Subjects   463
2. Persons   478
3. Places and Countries   483

I

PREFACE

The essays on Ancient Judaism appeared originally in the 1917–1919 issues of the *Archiv für Sozialwissenschaft und Sozialforschung*. They represent decades of study of Mediterranean antiquity and the great world religions.

Max Weber's untimely death in 1920 prevented him from rounding out his studies with an analysis of the Psalms, the Book of Job, Talmudic Jewry, early Christianity, and Islamism. Marianne Weber, his widow, published *Das Antike Judentum* as volume three of Weber's *Gesammelte Aufsätze zur Religions-soziologie* (Tübingen, 1921). In presenting the essays "almost unchanged in their original form," she observed: "A sovereign and resigned calmness toward his personal fate characterized Max Weber. Perhaps he would say now as often before: 'What I do not achieve others will.'"

According to Weber, the world historical importance of Judaism is not exhausted by the fact that it fathered Christianity and Islamism. It compares in historical significance to Hellenic intellectual culture, Roman law, the Roman Catholic church resting on the Roman concept of office, the medieval estates, and Protestantism.[1]

Considering himself a relative amateur compared to historical specialists, archeologists, Egyptologists, and Old Testament scholars, Weber does not claim to have unearthed new facts. "It would require more than a lifetime to acquire a true mastery of the literature concerning the religion of Israel and Jewry. . . . We entertain but modest hopes of contributing anything essentially new to the discussion, apart from the fact that, here and there, some source data may be grouped in a manner to emphasize some things differently than usual."[2] This emphasis, a genuine theoretical contribution, is sociological. New relations are perceived between old facts when Weber brings the varied talents of jurist, economist, historian, linguist and philosopher to the task of integration.

---

[1] See below, p. 5.
[2] Footnote 1, p. 425 below.

The first volume of Weber's sociology of religion, *The Protestant Ethic and the Spirit of Capitalism* (1904–5) [3] occasioned one of the great debates in modern intellectual history.[4] Having developed the thesis that the puritan middle-class man of conscience was a casual factor in the rise of modern industrial capitalism, Weber tested his hypothesis by comparative studies of China and India.[5] These Eastern civilizations, while possessing many favorable factors, did not develop industrial capitalism. They buttressed Weber's contention that Puritanism had to be included among the necessary and sufficient conditions for the emergence of modern capitalism.

Thus, the questions of *The Protestant Ethic* form one of the themes of Weber's *Sociology of Religion*. However, as his studies in religion progressed, Weber increasingly saw industrial capitalism as only one typical development of the West. In the introduction to the book edition of *The Protestant Ethic*, written just before his death, Weber subsumed the development of modern capitalism under a more general Occidental process of "rationalization." He found parallels in Western music, based upon a system of notation, standardized instruments, harmonic chord and counterpoint composition which also appeared to him peculiarly "rational" in structure. He traced other parallels in Occidental painting and architecture, as illustrated by such things as perspective and the use of the Gothic vault as a means of distributing stress and roofing spaces of all sizes. In Western thought Weber noted the primacy of the rationally defined concept, the systematically arranged universe of discourse, the mathematical "proof" (the legacy of Athens), the "experimental demonstration" (the Legacy of the Italian Renaissance) as uniquely constituting Occidental science. The Importance of Calvinism for science as for daily conduct is found in its force for emancipating man from magic and ritual.

In place of magical ritual western man has developed rational bureaucracies of vocationally specialized men in ecclesiastic, political and economic organizations. Modern capitalism, for Weber, is best understood as a rational structure based upon capital accounting and the productive organization of formally free labor for the sake of the enduring profitability of competitive private enterprise. Western Culture—its actors and symbols, its types of organization—are assessed in subtle polarities of "rational-irrational."

[3] Tr. by Talcott Parsons (New York: 1930 and 1948).

[4] Cf. Hans and Hedwig Ide Gerth "Bibliography on Max Weber," *Social Research*, vol. 16, n. 1, March 1949, pp. 70-89.

[5] Max Weber, *The Religion of China, Confucianism and Taoism,* tr. by Hans H. Gerth (The Free Press: Glencoe, Illinois, 1951).

In his sociology of religion Weber brought into focus the two major interests of his life work: (1) The problems of reason and conscience, of enlightenment and ethical responsibility in the face of capitalism which he called with Adolph Wagner "a system of masterless slavery." (2) The tension between rational and irrational processes in world history.

In this concern with man's reason and freedom Weber stands in the tradition of German Liberalism which at all major turning points of modern intellectual history reassessed the legacy of Jerusalem, Athens, Rome, and North Alpine antiquity. Lessing, Herder, and Hegel with their intellectual concern with early Christendom were part of the first "wave." Goethe's Suebian country parson speculates about ethical universalism and ritualistic particularism in early Judaism.[6] The Napoleonic generation enthusiastically hailed the storming of the Bastille. Hegel's theological writings were anything but "theological," as Georg Lukacs has recently shown.[7] The "Young Hegelians" of 1848, Ludwig Feuerbach, Karl Marx, Bruno Bauer, and David Friedrich Strauss followed suit and in turn were superseded by Nietzsche. Feuerbach displaced the "priestly lie" theory of enlightenment philosophy by interpreting religion essentially as a wish projection of needful and suffering man. Marx combined this with social historical determinism:

"Religious misery represents at once the expression of and the protest against actual misery. Religion is the moan of the oppressed creature, the heart of a heartless world, the sense of senseless conditions. It is the opium of the people." [8]

Finally Nietzsche attacked the Judeo-Christian tradition with the tools of his depth psychology and the concept of "resentment." [9]

Weber stood between the two towering critics of modern western culture, Marx and Nietzsche, dealing simultaneously with Marx' attacks on the world of capitalism as irrational "wage slavery" and an "anarchy of production," in which man is compelled to alienate the

[6] "Zwo wichtige bisher unerörterte Biblische Fragen zum erstenmal gründlich beantwortet Von einem Landgeistlichen in Schwaben," *Goethe's sämmtliche Werke* (Stuttgart und Tübingen, 1854), vol. XIV, p. 269 f.

[7] *Der Junge Hegel Ueber die Beziehungen von Dialektik und Oekonomie* (Wien, 1948).

[8] "Zur Kritik der Hegelschen Rechtsphilosophie," *Aus dem literarischen Nachlass von Karl Marx und Friedrich Engels,* ed. by Franz Mehring, 4th ed. (Berlin, 1923), vol. I, pp. 384 f.

[9] Cf. his *Genealogy of Morals,* First Essay, esp. sections 8, 10, 14. See also Max Scheler, "Das Ressentiment im Aufbau der Moralen," *Vom Umsturz der Werte* (Leipzig, 1919), vol. I, pp. 45-236.

truly human, and with Nietzsche's attacks on Democracy and Christianity, on rational and ethical universalism.[10] Weber rejected Marx and Nietzsche although he learned much from both. He remained a liberal on the defensive, a nationalist in the ice age of imperialism, a humanist desperately holding on to the legacy of Kant and Goethe with their affirmation of rational man's dignity and freedom, a politically astute thinker seeing only bleakness ahead.

Choosing science as his vocation, Weber took his stand for sober, rational enlightenment rooted in the Socratean ethos of intellectual integrity. He felt that nowadays prophets are singularly out of place. He concluded his lecture on "Science as a Vocation" with Goethe's answer to the question, what shall I do? "Meet the demands of the day." [11] Weber understood his *Sociology of Religion* as a scientific work aiming at insight rather than edification. "The fate of our times is characterized by rationalization and intellectualization and, above all, by the 'disenchantment of the world.' " [12]

Critics and zealots have doubted that one can do valuable work on matters religious unless one can at least write on the basis of what Rudolph Otto and Schleiermacher termed the experience of "the holy." This requirement would have made the development of comparative religion inconceivable from the time of Max Mueller to the present. Max Weber refused to reveal his inner experiences, rarely spoke of such matters, and referred to himself as "religiously unmusical." The reader will look in vain for theologico-philosophical assertions such as Paul Tillich's: "Religion lasts as long as man lasts. It cannot disappear in human history, because a history without religion is not *human* history, which is a history in which ultimate concerns are at stake." [13]

Men close to Weber disagree in their estimations of him. In his obituary essay Robert Wilbrant called him a *homo religiosus*. Paul Honigsheim appears to agree, urging "If anyone is entitled to be brought into the neighborhood of Luther, it is Max Weber." [14] But Karl Jaspers memorialized his friend at his bier as *homo philosophicus*, meaning a wise man not assured of possessing the ultimate truth. "He who has the final answers can no longer speak to the other as he

[10] On Nietzsche's influence on Weber's generation see Karl Jaspers, "Nietzsche and the Present," *Partisan Review,* Jan., Feb., 1952. no. I, p. 19.

[11] From Max Weber: Essays in Sociology, tr. by H. H. Gerth and C. Wright Mills (New York, 1946), p. 156.

[12] Ibid., p. 155.

[13] Paul Tillich, *The American Scholar*, vol. 15, no. 1, p. 103.

[14] Max Weber: "His Religions and Ethical Background and Development," *Church History,* December, 1950, vol. XIX, no. 4, p. 23.

<u>breaks off genuine communication for the sake of what he believes</u> <u>in</u>." [15] This corresponds to Weber's own contention that <u>all logico-</u> <u>theological systems of belief eventually demand the "sacrifice of the</u> <u>intellect</u>." [16] Weber's last words were "<u>the true is the truth</u>." [17] They were a final affirmation of his dedication to man's reason.

There is no evidence that Weber adduced theological propositions to make the contingent meaningful. He attributed his own success in academic life to chance, fortune, or "good luck." In his last lecture, "Science as a Vocation," he described Goethe's position as "purely inner-worldly" and presents it as his last judgement on his own ethical commitment. He displayed an inner-worldly, stoic attitude in the face of death, and comforted relatives sorrowing for a suicide by endorsing the right and freedom of man to choose a preferable death by his own hand. He felt sympathetic respect for highminded Confucian statesmen of his own day who preferred to die in dignity by their own hand rather than to go on living a shameful life. And when World War I ended with the defeat of the Central powers and the downfall of the Romanovs, the Hapsburgs, Hohenzollers and other princely dynasties, Weber remarked that "Confucsian rulers and generals indeed knew how to die proudly when Heaven was against them in the high gamble [sic!] of war and human destiny. They knew better how to die than their Christian colleagues, as we in Germany know." [18] He had advised the Kaiser, before his flight to Holland, to seek death in no-man's land.

Weber shared the attitudes of the stoic philosophers of ancient Rome and of humanists like Montaigne, Hume, and Nietzsche. His essentially humanistic, rather than theological, attitude is most clearly evident in his attitude toward death. He knew that no redemption religion approves suicide, "a death which has been hallowed only by philosophies." [19] He could agree with Montaigne following Seneca "Living is slavery, if the liberty of dying be away. . . . For a desperate disease a desperate cure. . . ." [20] Weber was profoundly impressed by Tolstoy, the artist and "repentant noble." But he held that "under the technical and social conditions of rational culture, an imitation of the life of Buddha, Jesus, or Francis seems condemned to failure for

[15] Karl Jaspers, *Der Philosophische Glaube* (München, 1948), p. 61.

[16] Essays, *op. cit.*, pp. 154, 352.

[17] Marianne Weber, *Max Weber Ein Lebensbild* (Tübingen, 1926), p. 711.

[18] *The Religion of China, op. cit.*, p. 208.

[19] Essays, *op. cit.*, p. 356.

[20] Works of Michael de Montaigne, ed. by Hazlitt, Vol. II (Boston, 1862), pp. 9, 25.

purely external reasons." [21] Modern culture has developed its own ironic contexts negative to the possibilities of the good life and a meaningful death. Even Tolstoy could not imitate Jesus in a railroad station, or die without newspaper reporters as watchmen. Nevertheless, he viewed Tolstoy as a great challenging figure of his time and intended to write a book about him.

The question of a meaningful death, Weber thought, was the "keynote of Tolstoyan art." [22] Tolstoy had decided that neither art, science, nor social progress could give meaning to life. Hence death had no meaning. "The peasant, like Abraham, could die 'satiated with life,' "[23] having rounded out his organically prescribed life cycle. For ancient man the organic relation between society and nature still obtained. Once cultural development and urbanism emanicapted man from nature, he found himself with an unlimited horizon for developing cultural values. Devoted to the perfection of an all-rounded self the cultured man is increasingly unable to subjectively incorporate even the objectively available culture. Goethe was the last *Homo universale*, and even he in but a qualified sense. Thus every advance of culture seems to condemn man to an ever more "senseless hustle in the service of worthless, self-contradictory, and mutually antagonistic ends." [24] This is the humanistic rather than the religious search for the meaning of life.

Weber's humanism affords contrasts to what has since happened in Germany in the fate of European Jewry under the Nazi heel.

Weber was neither an anti-semite nor an equally dangerous philosemite. Meyer Shapiro's judgement is, we think, accurate: "His whole nature was firmly set against Nazi barbarity and anti-semitism." [25] To stress this point is especially necessary since Werner Sombart in his highbrow anti-semitic tract *The Jews and Economic Life* (1911) sought to "out-Weber" Weber by arguing the false though popular thesis "Puritanism is Judaism." In this work Weber covered Sombart's work with charitable silence and refuted in efficient brevity its major contentions. [26]

---

[21] Essays, *op. cit.*, p. 357.

[22] *Ibid.*, p. 139 f., see also p. 356 f.

[23] *Ibid.*, p. 356.

[24] *Ibid.*, p. 356.

[25] "Max Weber's Politics," *Politics*, ed. by Dwight MacDonald (New York, February 1945). Cf. also "Max Weber's Politics, a rejoinder," by H. H. Gerth, *ibidem*, April, 1945.

[26] See, however, his *Wirtschaft und Gesellschaft* (Tübingen, 1921), pp. 349 ff., 352 ff., and his *General Economic History*, tr. by Frank H. Knight (Glencoe, Illinois, 1950), pp. 358 ff.

As regards Weber's attitude toward Zionism we may be permitted to quote extensively from a letter he wrote in 1913:

"Judaism and especially Zionism rests on the presupposition of a highly concrete 'promise.' Will a prosperous colony, an autonomous petty state with hospitals and good schools ever appear as the 'fulfillment' rather than as a critique of this grandiose promise? And even a university? For the meaning of the promise lies on a plane altogether different from the economic goal of colonization. It would seem to lie in the following: Jewry's sense of dignity could feed on the existence and the spiritual possession of this ancient and holy place—just as the Jewish diaspora could build its dignity on the existence of the kingdom of the Maccabees after their war of independence against the empire of the Seleucids; as Germandom all over the world could build its dignity on the existence of the *Deutsche Reich,* and Islamism on the existence of the caliphate. Germany, however, is, or at least appears to be, a powerful *Reich,* the empire of the caliphs still covers a large territory—but what at best is the Jewish state nowadays? And what is a university which offers the same as others do? To be sure, it would not be irrelevant but it could hardly compare to the ancient Temple.

What is chiefly missing? They are the Temple and the high priest. Were they to exist in Jerusalem all else would be secondary. Certainly, the pious catholic also demands the church-state, however small. Even without it, and in that case more readily, he gains his sense of dignity by realizing that the politically powerless pope in Rome is a purely spiritual ruler of 200 million people. This rule amounts to infinitely more than that of the 'king' of Italy, and everybody knows it. A hierarch of 12 million people in the world—who amount to what, after all, Jewry happens to be—that of course would mean something truly great for Jewish dignity, regardless of personal devoutness. But where is Zadok's sib? Where is an orthodoxy to obey such a hierarch? According to law, what orthodoxy could grant this hierarch even one tenth of the pope's significance? The pope's authority is effective in every diocese and parish by virtue of the *disciplino morum* and his universalist bishopry more than by virtue of the relatively irrelevant infallibility. Where is nowadays the opportunity to establish anything comparable? The true problems of Zionism would seem to me to touch only here upon those values that concern the dignity of the Jewish nation. This sense of dignity is firmly knit to religious prerequisites."

This letter, addressed to E. J. Lesser, was a follow-up to an "important discussion." Marianne Weber states that Weber granted the possibility of colonizing Palestine but failed to see in it "a solution for the internal problems of Jewry." [27] Like Friedrich Schiller on the eve of Jewish emancipation in his lecture on *Moses' Mission,* Weber, on the eve of the Rathenau murder, might have said: "the nation of

[27] *Lebensbild, op. cit.,* pp. 477 ff.

the Hebrews must appear to us as a world-historically important people and all evil that is usually ascribed to this people, all efforts of wits to belittle it will not prevent us from doing it justice." [28]

Weber basically accepts Eduard Meyer's and Wellhausen's 'higher criticism' of the biblical texts although he disengages himself from their overall views and constructions. He makes use of literary form analyses when he distinguishes, e.g., in the Song of Songs pastoral love songs, courtly love songs, and heroic warrior songs and sees in these materials the scanty legacy of a rich literary tradition of kingly and possibly pre-kingly Hebrew life. He characterizes the Joseph legend as a work of art, a skillful short story of a practiced writer; the Servant of Yahwe theodicy in Isaiah 53 as the poem of a religious intellectual who in Babylonian Exile constructed a theodicy of suffering. He employs iconography in his interpretation of the images of God held by the prophets. Not committed to any special theological tradition and ready to learn from all of them, he avails himself of methods that in specialized theological traditions would seem to contradict one another. Thus, Johann Gottfried Herder even depreciated the psychological study of the prophets as a "useless art . . . since times have changed so greatly." [29] J. Ph. Hyatt in his *Prophetic Religion* (1947) follows Herder's judgement, so do Bentzen and Ivan Engnell.[30] Weber with due caution against overconstructing scanty source materials nevertheless discusses psychological aspects of the prophetic experience and characterizes the prophets as "ecstatic men" alternating between withdrawal into states of brooding solitude and states of ecstatic agitation in public.

With "higher criticism" Weber shares distrust in the great age of much of the patriarchical legends, although he realizes that the modern trends place much greater credence in the authenticity of the Books of Moses as evidenced by William Foxwell Albright,[31] Fritz Helling,[32] and the Swedish Bible scholars following Söderbloom. Weber's "Liberalism" would seem "old fashioned" in our days of neo-orthodoxies.

---

[28] *Schillers sämmtliche Werke* (Stuttgart and Augsburg, 1855), vol. X, p. 402.

[29] "Vom Geist der Ebräischen Poesie, Erster Theil, 1782, Zweite Abtheilung, II Beruf und Amt der Propheten, Anhang: Warum waren Propheten so vorzüglich diesem Volke eigen"?, *Johann Gottfried von Herder's sämmtliche Werke* (Stuttgart und Tübingen, 1827), vol. 22, p. 151 f.

[30] "The Call of Isaiah, An Exegetical and Comparative Study," *Uppsala Universitets Arsskrift*, 1949:4, pp. 1-68.

[31] *From Stone Age to Christianity* (Baltimore, 1946).

[32] *Die Frühgeschichte des Jüdischen Volkes* (Frankfurt, 1947).

Although accepting the great age of Jewish monotheism Weber is relatively noncommittal when dealing with "origins" and speculations concerning pre-Mosaic Judaism and the early past. At this point our knowledge has been considerably extended through archeological work.[33]

We may briefly summarize some of Weber's sociological themes. For Weber the Jews enter the historical stage of Palestine as a tribal confederacy of peasants and husbandmen in quest of land. He rejects the thesis that they were either originally a ferocious "desert people" or the pacifistic partriarchs of an "idyllic oasis." Disregarding evolutionary simplifications of Jewish history, Weber conceives the Jews as socially stratified warlike peasants and small stock breeders who have nothing to do with the later Bedouin camel nomads other than to defend themselves against such raiders in the eastern deserts. The law of early Israel is not the law of the desert. The *mishpatim* of the Jews are borrowings from the Babylonian Code of Hammurabi and are more concerned with early capitalistic legal forms than camel nomadism and desert feuds.

Weber also rejects constructions of the beginnings of a Jewish state exclusively in terms of the conquest theories of Ratzel, Gumplowicz and Oppenheimer in which nomadic steppe peoples conquer sedentary agricultural populations and organize themselves politically into a ruling class. External conflict is present, but balanced by endogenous developments of state power and kingship.

The tribal confederation is unstable, integrated on the basis of guardianship of a common god. Specific historical and social reasons led early Jewry to adopt Yahwism. Yahwe is a war god. He is a jealous god, a god of anger and of mercifulness. He is ubiquitous and majestic. As the god of natural catastrophes (locust plagues, pestilence, earthquakes, floods), he is opposed to fertility deities (Baalim and Astarte) and orgiastic cults. As an invisible god he is opposed to all symbolic representations. The Jews are his chosen people on the basis of a contract with mutual rights and obligations. He is the god of the collectivity rather than the individual which is jointly responsible to him. Granted the fulfilment of special conditions, Yahwe has pledged to lift up the down-trodden and deliver them, not in the beyond, but in this world. His chosen people must show themselves worthy of Yahwe by obeying his commandments. The relation between Yahwe and his chosen people unfolds in historical time from

---

[33] William Foxwell Albright, *op. cit.* Cf. also his *Archaeology and the Religion of Israel* (Baltimore, 1942) and his *The Archaeology of Palestine* (Penguin Books, 1949).

the creation through the vicissitudes of the Exodus, from the conquest of Palestine, kingly glory to the Exile, diaspora and the fulfillment of the promise.

The first sociological theme in *Ancient Judaism* consists in tracing the powerful integral relation between <u>Yahwism and the social collectivity</u>, their inseparable mutual interaction and development.

A second sociological issue of concern to Weber is the examination of <u>social changes due to territorial organization and urbanization</u> with its reactions upon the sedentary peasantry in the Jordan river plains and mountain valleys and the quasi-nomadic stock breeders of steppe and mountain slope. A second series of social changes have their point of gravity in <u>hereditary kingship</u> which particularly under Solomon drifts toward oriental despotism. Social antagonisms generated in these changes split the kingdom. Moreover within each of the divided kingdoms social differentiation sharpens, religious leaders reorient themselves and at pressure zones the great scriptural prophets arise in whose oracles the organization of the *Old Testament* is determined.

Weber saw the civic society of Palestine as a variation of ancient Mediterranean urbanism. Leading families settled in a fortified city under a prince or oligarchy.[34] A ruling class of wealthy urban families, an urban patriciate develops. Profits accumulate from middle man trade, levies upon caravan traffic, land rents levied upon farmers on the best soil falling under the expanding jurisdiction of the armed citizenry. Urban wealth permits the patricians to become "economically expendable" and to devote themselves to politics and war. They expropriate the new military technology of chariot combat spreading out from ancient Sumner after the second millennium.[35] Only the scion of the well born family can afford costly equipment and warrior training. The ancient free peasantry is disarmed, as Weber illustrates in his comparison of the peasant summons of the Song of Deborah with the chariot cities of King Solomon.

The consequences of <u>city imperialism</u> based on the concentration

---

[34] For details see "Agraverhältnisse im Altertum," *Handwörterbuch der Staatswissenschaften* (3rd edition, 1908), reprinted in *Gesammelte Aufsätze zur Sozial-und Wirtschaftgeschichte* (Tübingen, 1924), pp. 1-288. "Die sozialen Gründe des Untergangs der antiken Kultur," ibid. pp. 289-311. Translated by Christian Mackauer: "The Social Causes of the Decay of Ancient Civilization," *The Journal of General Education*, vol. V, Oct. 1950, pp. 75-88. "Die Stadt," *Wirtschaft und Gesellschaft* (Tübingen, 1925), pp. 514-601.

[35] For a good summary of the technological aspects of chariotry see Stuart Piggott, *Prehistoric India* (Penguin Books, 1950), pp. 273-282.

of urban wealth and increasing monopoly of arms are traced by Weber in Israelite, Greek, and Roman antiquity. These urban dynamics gave rise to typical class antagonisms between city patricians and socially, militarily, and economically descending peasants. The so-called "Biblical" social evils which the prophets chastize are located in these tensions.

The process of the rise and domination of their hinterlands by the ancient cities intersects with the growth of oriental despotism. Oriental despotism is not an arbitrary phenomenon or a mere product of the strong man. It arose as an indispensable politico-economic adaptation to the problems of flood control and irrigation in the great river valleys, the Hwang Ho, Yangtze Kiang, Euphrates, Tigris, and Nile. In all the great river civilizations great bureaucratic state structures crushed or suppressed the feudal nobility, centralized the taxation of the peasantry, "collectivized" the gathering of rents and organization of labor. Their leaders became priest kings, gods on earth, or "sons of Heaven" as in China. In China the ruling class culminated in the hierarchized quasi-religious Confucian bureaucracy, representing in Mosca's terms an "organized ruling class." The bureaucracy was able to weather all political storms, Mongol invasions, dynastic cycles with peasant usurpers—beginning with strong men of crisis and ending with decadent empress dowagers and harem eunuchs.

In none of the great river civilizations were religious institutions able to oppose the princes, kings, and scribes. The emergence of independent religious leaders like the Israelite prophets was blocked, religious and political authority was combined and religious leaders like the Brahmins in India and priesthoods of Babylon and Egypt and the Confucian literati in China came to serve state power.

It is not monotheism alone which accounts for the world historical significance of Judaism. Monotheism also appeared in Egypt in unexcelled sublimity. But in neither Babylon nor Egypt was magic eliminated. The social basis for this was bound up with the course of oriental despotism in Palestine.

Palestine was territorially diversified with mountains, valleys, plains and deserts and only minor rivers. It did not provide a sufficient economic base for a despotic bureaucratic state. Rents and taxes from mountain peasants hardly compare to the yields from irrigation agriculture in the great river basins. Thus, despite the relative success of Solomon in establishing an Oriental-model state [36] his glory could

---

[36] Salo Wittmayer Baron reproaches Weber for having "overlooked a few fundamental factors, such as the exceptionally small size of most Palestinian townships, their predominantly agricultural character, their

hardly be more than that of an Egyptian vassal king. Solomon's Temple was essentially a court chapel and attempts to attach religion to the palace and establish exclusive royal prophets were unsuccessful. The emergence of "free" or "socially unattached" religious prophets and religious leaders upholding popular traditions of old opposed to despotism could not be prevented. The sociological, psychological, and ideological explanations of this constellation constitute the core of Weber's book.

The growth of the charioteering military professional at the expense of the peasant army involved the displacement of the bands of war prophets of old by the courtly prophet, promising long life, progeny, and political success to the dynasts. Other prophets established professional schools cultivating dervish ecstasy and offering their services to patrons. Some, however, developed a new conception of the prophetic role, withdrawing from social practice. In solitary broodings they received divine commandments. They did not organize bands of disciples or found religious institutions. The great scriptural prophets of doom, the "true" prophets lived for religion, opposed the ways of the world, and stood up to the kings and authorities in the name of Yahwe.

Weber characterizes them as religious demagogues out to warn and sway the people. The religious tradition hallowing them made them sacro-sanct precisely because they chanted impending doom, Yahwe's wrath, vengeance to be visited upon a disobedient and stubborn people. Prophetic oracles were remembered for generations for some of them came true and these experiences shook the entire people.

The scriptural prophets emerged during the decline of kingly power when foreign conquest threatened, in a time of mounting insecurity and intense anxiety. To explain the prophets Weber links the Levitical cure of souls and the development of prophetic messianism as an eschatological expectation for the future buttressed by Yahwism.

Weber perceived the Levites as religious specialists permeating Palestine society from South to North. The Levitical oracular tech-

---

political and economic self-sufficiency and the local popular assemblies." *The Jewish Community, Its History and Structure to the American Revolution* (Philadelphia, 1942), vol. III, p. 8 f. We cannot follow this criticism in view of Weber's characterization of King Solomon's endeavor "to establish a rigidly organized political structure out of the loose confederacy of peasants, herdsmen sibs, and small mountain cities." (p. 100, below). Elsewhere Weber refers to the type of city which "could be but a small fortified agricultural community with a market. In this case it differed only in degree from a village." (p. 14 below, see also p. 56).

nique of answering questions by yea or nay demanded a skillful preparation of questions. This led to ethical interpretations of the miraculous and increasing repression of magical thoughtways. Granted collective responsibility to Yahwe an individual's failings could endanger the community and Levitical services were increasingly sought.[37]

Weber credits the great scriptural prophets from Amos to Jeremiah and Ezekiel with the fulfillment of trends in Levitical practice, the elimination of magic and ethical sublimation of Judaism. In their roles as religious demagogues and pamphleteers the prophets expanded the features of the religious drama, magnified the stature of its protagonists to previously unknown majesty. In Weber's view the prophets were the first historically known principled men of conscience, willing and able to "rather obey God than men." He saw the emergence of conscience as a complex internal action pattern in the vicissitudes of the cultural-historical process of Jewry. It emancipated man from the "garden of magic."

While for Freud King Oedipus' and Moses' alleged fate represent only the return of primeval patricide of the brother horde and Mohammedan religion but an "abbreviated repetition of the Jewish one" [38] Weber dismisses the construction of "totemism" as the original form of religion.[39] Weber explains the prophets not by assumed racial memories but by the social context.

The prophets were supported by Yahwistic families among the rural gentry that oriental despotism in Palestine had not been able to suppress. The prophets kept alive anti-royalist attitudes, voiced the needs of the economically exploited, legally oppressed, socially descending demilitarized peasants and husbandmen. They elaborated the glorious memories of old: King David the mountaineering boy who slew the Philistine knight; the ass riding—not charioteering—popular king of the peasant militia; the charismatic leader; Moses the liberator who struck down the Egyptian slave master and led the oppressed out of the house of bondage. These were counter images to the pomp and glory of despotic kings, marrying foreign wives,

---

[37] Weber, it seems, accepts on the psychological level the translatability of deep anxieties, feelings of insecurity and impotence into religiously defined guilt feelings. See below p. 178, 300, 319 f. These psychological observations, however, do not serve to indicate ultimate origins.

[38] Sigmund Freud, *Moses and Monotheism*, tr. by Katherine Jones (Hogarth Press, 1939), pp. 91, 94, 130 ff., 148 f.

[39] He notes in passing, "Eduard Meyer, to be sure, has rightly ridiculed those who wished to find proof of 'totemism' in Israel," p. 427 below.

honoring foreign deities, establishing harems, forsaking the ways of the fathers, entering into alliances with hated Egypt.

At this point Weber, with Ernst Troeltsch, points up the political utopianism of the great prophets. For purely religious reasons, out of their trust in almighty God and his promises, in his ability to achieve what to human understanding would seem impossible, the prophets counsel political independence of the Babylonian conquerors whose frightful ways are known in Jerusalem, from the downfall of the Northern Kingdom, from the mass killings, abductions of urban skill groups, destructions of sanctuaries and cities. The universal political factitiousness and passionate excitation of the Jerusalem people made it unavoidable that the prophetic messages were interpreted in terms of their political implications, the more so as the prophets acted in public as powerful speakers. "Whether the prophets wished it or not they actually always worked in the direction of one or the other furiously struggling inner-political cliques, which at the same time promoted definite foreign policies. Hence, the prophets were considered party members." [40]

". . . according to their manner of functioning, the prophets were objectively political and, above all, world-political demagogues and publicists, however subjectively they were no political partisans. Primarily they pursued no political interests. Prophecy has never declared anything about a 'best state' . . . The state and its doings were, by themselves, of no interest to them. Moreover, unlike the Hellenes they did not posit the problem: how can man be a good citizen? Their question was absolutely religious, oriented toward the fulfillment of Yahwe's commandments." [41]

Weber rejects interpretation of the prophets as direct spokesmen of oppressed classes in their struggle against the oppressive urban patricians and the despotic state with its imposition of forced labor, heavy taxes, and other deprivations. Karl Kautsky in his analysis of "The Origin of Christianity" had advocated this thesis which comes to mind when reading the more recent interpretation of the great prophets as "revolutionary leaders" by Salo Wittmayer Baron.[42] Weber stressed the prophet's characteristic isolation from the people. He stressed the absence of any organizational endeavor and eagerness to build something resembling a political or social movement. The

---

[40] Below, p. 274.

[41] Ibidem, p. 275. See also pp. 267 ff.

[42] Cf. A Social and Religious History of the Jews (New York, 1937), vol. I, p. 71 f.

prophet of doom was typically a lone man heroically swimming against the stream, boldly shocking his hostile audiences, at best inspiring the crowd of the market place with awe. Weber emphasized the prophet's withdrawal into quasi-pathological states, his painful visions and auditions, his broodings. Occasionally the prophet, against his will, feels compelled to pronounce the divine revelations. The spirit of God comes to the prophet in his lone broodings, not in assemblies like the early Christian religious groups. Weber's analysis owes much of its impressiveness to this construction of the prophet as an outsider of his society.

A final theme requiring special attention is Weber's characterization of Jewry as a "pariah people." The term is unfortunately lending itself to misconceptions. Weber did not intend a contemptuous attitude toward Jewry. He uses the terms "pariah people" and "guest people" in a technical sense. Guest people, guest artisans, and similar terms refer to groups or individuals who as a result of invasion or conquest have been expropriated from their lands by immigrant groups and have been reduced to economic dependence on the conquerors. These may reduce the native population to the "guest status" regardless of residential seniority. Similarly, migrations of groups or individuals may result in guest-host relationships. The status relationship between the guest and host groups may vary, the guests may be legally and conventionally privileged or underprivileged. Where the status relationship is implemented by ritual barriers Weber proposes the term "pariah people."

The concepts "guest-" and "pariah people" belong to the sociological discussion of the stranger, of minority groups, of patterns of segregation and status relationships. The socio-economic situation of the guest people is determined by and dependent on the socio-economic order of the territorially dominant people. Special craftsmanship and middlemen services have frequently been the contributions of groups of "guests" to their "hosts." In ancient India as in Israel "kingly guest artisans" were to be found. Weber refers to Hiram, "a man from Tyre," the building master of King Solomon's Temple; to byssus weavers, potters and carpenters. Among the Bedouin tribes musicians, bards and smiths had such "guest status." [43]

Weber employs the concept in discussions of early Israelite tribes, of the conquest of Canaanite communities and the inclusion of the conquered into the larger community, of the place of the stranger, of *metics*, of infiltrating semi-nomadic herdsmen. The fruitfulness of

---

[43] P. 28 f. below.

his conceptional tools may be assessed from the discussion of the Levites who "represent the perfect type of 'guest tribe' in the Israelite community. . . . The Levites stood outside the association of militarily qualified landowners. They were exempt from military service. . . . Their religious services, as shown by the designation, *'eved,* was considered a liturgy of metics given to the political community." [44]

For the definition of a guest situation it matters not whether guest and host share the same religion or whether the guest is privileged or underprivileged. Nor is it necessary that guest and host visualize themselves as such. These are additional questions. Salo Wittmayer Baron's critical note on Weber's conception, we think, rests essentially on reading too much into the concept.[45] If he argues that the Jews could not be a guest or pariah people when living in the diaspora because they had a religion of their own, in contrast to guest or pariah peoples in India sharing the religion of their hosts, one might feel inclined to answer that religious differences may sharpen the distinction between guest and host. They help to maximize the social distance or mutual strangeness.

German protestant settlers came to Tsarist Russia during the eighteenth century. They received privileged guest status, were exempt from military service, and under pressure, diplomatically arranged "re-patriation" agreement and outright expulsion left the Soviet Union since the end of World War I. Their religious peculiarity probably contributed for better or worse to their "guest role." Also the question of self images and evaluations of self are irrelevant for the definition. It may well be that Russian Mennonite peasants of German descent felt "superior" to eastern Orthodox Russians, and vice versa. The same may be presumed for the relation of such sectarians to Russian communists. And even if the Mennonites were to consider themselves especially sanctified or "chosen" opposite the "children of the world" or possibly "of the devil," this would not affect their sociologically warranted characterization as a "guest people."

The same holds, in Weber's view, for Jewry in the diaspora. That even ritually segregated guest peoples, i.e., "pariah peoples," do not accept the image of the outgroup no matter how harsh the attempt of the dominant people to impose it, Weber himself has emphasized. He states: "even pariah people who are most despised are usually

---

[44] P. 172 below.
[45] *A Social and Religious History of the Jews* (New York, 1937), vol. III, footnote 6.

apt to continue cultivating in some manner that which is equally peculiar to ethnic and to status communities: the belief in their own specific honor. This is the case with the Jews." [46] In short, Weber would be the last to reject the observations which Baron directs against his conception. In fact, he demonstrates in the present work how the conception of Yahwe gains in majesty, how the perspective of an ultimate reversal of fate for His chosen people gains in grandeur precisely in the prophet's responses to suffering, to threatening disaster and Exile.

Robert Park who never displayed any particular acquaintance with Weber's work took a life-long interest in minority groups and can hardly be accused of conscious or unconscious anti-Jewish or other anti-ethnic bias. He attributed many of the so-called "race-issues" to the secularizing consequences of conquest and migration. So, for example, he urges that under urban conditions different peoples may come to "live side by side in a relation of symbiosis, each playing a role in the common economy, but not interbreeding to any great extent." Each group may maintain "like the gypsies or the pariah peoples of India, a more or less complete tribal organization or society of their own. Such was the situation of the Jew in Europe up to modern times." [47] Park has introduced into sociological literature the concepts of marginality, marginal man, etc. In substance, we think, Weber's analyses of guest and pariah situations agree with Park's more fortunate and less ambiguous terminology. Nothing would be lost were we to speak of "marginal artisans" of high or low status, instead of "guest artisans," or, with Howard Becker,[48] of "marginal traders" or "marginal trading peoples" instead of "non-resident foreign trading peoples." [49]

Weber imputes early medieval anti-semitism to the competitive hostility of the prospering resident traders. "Out of the wish to suppress such competition grew the conflict with the Jews. . . . It was in the time of the crusades that the first wave of anti-semitism broke over Europe, under the two-fold influence of the war between the faiths and the competition of the Jews. . . . This struggle against

---

[46] *Essays, op. cit.,* p. 189.
[47] Robert E. Park, "Human Migration and the Marginal Man," *Race and Culture* (Glencoe: The Free Press, 1950), pp. 353, 354.
[48] *Through Values to Social Interpretation* (Durham, 1950), pp. 109 ff.
[49] *General Economic History, op. cit.,* p. 217.

the Jews and other foreign peoples—Caursines, Lombards, and Syrians—is a symptom of the development of a national commercial class." [50]

In presenting the view that "all essential traits of Jewry's attitude toward the environment can be deduced from their pariah existence" Weber did not mean to impose the conception of the Indian caste order on Jewry. Rather he emphasized three essential differences between Jewry and Indian pariah tribes: 1) Jewry became a pariah people in a social surrounding free of castes; 2) its religious problems were not structured by a theology of birth and rebirth according to presumed merit in a world thought to be eternal and unchangeable, but rather the whole attitude toward life was molded by the conception of a God ordained social and political revolution to come, and 3) ritualistic correctness, circumcision, dietary prescriptions and the Sabbath rules combined with ethical universalism, hostility toward all magic and irrational salvation striving. The simplicity, ready understandability, and teachability of the Ten Commandments combined with the religious mobilization of the plebeian by active emissary prophets and later Rabbis living for, not off, religion, sets Judaism off from all oriental religion. Without following the Hegelian construction of the "Tübingen school" Weber nevertheless dramatizes the fork of the road between ritualistic self-segregation into a voluntary ghetto since the days of the Babylonian Exile, and the depreciation of ritualistic correctness as indicated by the prophets' emphasis on the "circumcision of the heart" or on "what cometh out of the mouth" rather than what goes into it and, finally, on Paul's victory over Peter at Antioch. It opens the road for the conception of a universal brotherhood of man and the redefinition of "the generalized order." [51]

The translation is the outcome of intimate cooperation during all phases of work, from rough draft to final version. All biblical citations of Weber's have been carefully checked and many obvious mistakes of the German text have been corrected. As in previous Weber works, we have used all of Weber's headings as stated at the beginning of his essays. We have taken the liberty of inserting additional

---

[50] *Ibid.* For an analysis of the fate of German Jewry in terms of Weber's 'guest-host' relationship we may refer to F. R. Bienenfeld *The Germans and the Jews* (London, 1939).

[51] For an excellent and thought provoking discussion of "ethics in evolution" see Benjamin N. Nelson, *The Idea of Usury, From Tribal Brotherhood to Universal Otherhood* (Princeton, 1949).

headlines for parts, chapters, and sections where advisable. The original text is divided into two essays headed, I. The Israelite Confederacy and Yahwe, and II. The Emergence of the Jewish Pariah People. A third essay on the Pharisees is added as a Supplement. The text of the first essay of the German original flows uninterruptedly over 280 pages. We realize the controversial nature of our procedure of imposing breaks upon the original text for the convenience of the reader.

We wish to thank Mr. Ned H. Polsky and the editors of *The Wisconsin Athenaean,* now *The Wisconsin Idea,* the literary magazine of the University of Wisconsin, for permission to reprint excerpts from *Ancient Judaism* published in the Autumn 1949 issue. We are grateful to C. Wright Mills and Oxford University Press for permission to quote from the essay volume *From Max Weber: Essays in Sociology* (1946); to the Jewish Publication Society of America for permission to quote from *The Jewish Community, Its History and Structure to the American Revolution* (1942) by Salo Wittmayer Baron, and to our publisher for permission to quote from Max Weber's *General Economic History* (1950) and from Robert E. Park's *Race and Culture* (1950). Professor Maurice M. Shudofsky has kindly checked all Hebraic terms and phrases. We gratefully acknowledge his aid. Thanks are due to Dr. Hedwig Ide Gerth who has assisted by checking the references, clarifying doubtful points and working on the Glossary and Index.

Hans Gerth
Don Martindale

PART I

THE NATURAL AND CULTURAL
BACKGROUND OF ANCIENT JUDAISM

CHAPTER I

THE SOCIAL STRUCTURE
AND ITS SETTING

1. Prefatory Note: the Sociological Problem of Judaic Religious History [1]

THE problem of ancient Jewry, although unique in the socio-historical study of religion, can best be understood in comparison with the problem of the Indian caste order. Sociologically speaking the Jews were a pariah people, which means, as we know from India, that they were a guest people who were ritually separated, formally or *de facto*, from their social surroundings. All the essential traits of Jewry's attitude toward the environment can be deduced from this pariah existence—especially its voluntary ghetto, long anteceding compulsory internment, and the dualistic nature of its in-group and out-group morality.

The differences between Jewish and Indian pariah tribes consist in the following three significant circumstances:

1. Jewry was, or rather became, a pariah people in a surrounding free of castes.

2. The religious promises to which the ritual segregation of Jewry was moored differed essentially from those of the Indian castes. Ritually correct conduct, i.e., conduct conforming to caste standards, carried for the Indian pariah castes the premium of ascent by way of rebirth in a caste-structured world thought to be eternal and unchangeable.

The maintenance of the caste *status quo* involved not only the continued position of the individual within the caste, but also the position of the caste in relation to other castes. This con-

servatism was pre-requisite to salvation, for the world was unchangeable and had no 'history.'

For the Jew the religious promise was the very opposite. The
social order of the world was conceived to have been turned
into the opposite of that promised for the future, but in the
future it was to be over-turned so that Jewry would be once
again dominant. The world was conceived as neither eternal nor
unchangeable, but rather as having been created. Its present
structures were a product of man's activities, above all those of
the Jews, and of God's reaction to them. Hence the world was
an historical product designed to give way again to the truly
God-ordained order. The whole attitude toward life of ancient
Jewry was determined by this conception of a future God-
guided political and social revolution.

3. This revolution was to take a special direction. Ritual cor-
rectitude and the segregation from the social environment imposed by it was but one aspect of the commands upon Jewry.
There existed in addition a highly rational religious ethic of
social conduct; it was free of magic and all forms of irrational
quest for salvation; it was inwardly worlds apart from the paths
of salvation offered by Asiatic religions. To a large extent this
ethic still underlies contemporary Mid Eastern and European
ethic. World-historical interest in Jewry rests upon this fact.

The world-historical importance of Jewish religious development rests above all in the creation of the *Old Testament,* for
one of the most significant intellectual achievements of the
Pauline mission was that it preserved and transferred this sacred
book of the Jews to Christianity as one of its own sacred books.
Yet in so doing it eliminated all those aspects of the ethic enjoined by the *Old Testament* which ritually characterize the
special position of Jewry as a pariah people. These aspects were
not binding upon Christianity because they had been suspended
by the Christian redeemer.

In order to assess the significance of this act one need merely
conceive what would have happened without it. Without the
adoption of the *Old Testament* as a sacred book by Christianity,
gnostic sects and mysteries of the cult of Kyrios Christos would
have existed on the soil of Hellenism, but providing no basis for
a Christian church or a Christian ethic of workaday life. With-

out emancipation from the ritual prescriptions of the Torah, founding the caste-like segregation of the Jews, the Christian congregation would have remained a small sect of the Jewish pariah people comparable to the Essenes and the Therapeutics.

With the salvation doctrine of Christianity as its core, the Pauline mission in achieving emancipation from the self-created ghetto, found a linkage to a Jewish—even though half buried—doctrine derived from the religious experience of the exiled people. We refer to the unique promises of the great unknown author of exilic times who wrote the prophetic theodicy of sufferance (Isaiah 40-55)—especially the doctrine of the Servant of Yahwe who teaches and who without guilt voluntarily suffers and dies as a redeeming sacrifice. Without this the development of the Christian doctrine of the sacrificial death of the divine redeemer, in spite of the later esoteric doctrine of the son of man, would have been hardly conceivable in the face of other and externally similar doctrines of mysteries.

Jewry has, moreover, been the instigator and partly the model for Mohammed's prophecy. Thus, in considering the conditions of Jewry's evolution, we stand at a turning point of the whole cultural development of the West and the Middle East. Quite apart from the significance of the Jewish pariah people in the economy of the European Middle Ages and the modern period, Jewish religion has world-historical consequences. Only the following phenomena can equal those of Jewry in historical significance: the development of Hellenic intellectual culture; for western Europe, the development of Roman law and of the Roman Catholic church resting on the Roman concept of office; the medieval order of estates; and finally, in the field of religion, Protestantism. Its influence shatters this order but develops its institutions.

Hence we ask, how did Jewry develop into a pariah people with highly specific peculiarities?

2. General Historical and Climatic Conditions

THE Syrian-Palestinian mountainland was by turns exposed to Mesopotamian and to Egyptian influences. Mesopotamian influence derived initially from the tribal community of the

Amorites, who, in ancient times ruled both Syria and Mesopotamia. The rise to political prominence of Babylonian power
at the end of the third millenium and the continuous ascendency of Babylon and its commercial importance as the area
where forms of early capitalistic business originated constituted
later aspects of Mesopotamian influence. Egyptian influences
rested on trade relations between the Old Kingdom and the
Phoenician coast, on Egyptian mining in the Sinai peninsula, and
on geographic nearness.

Because the nature of military and administrative technology
of the time precluded it, before the seventeenth century B.C.,
a lasting political conquest was impossible for either of the
great cultural centers. The horse, for instance, while not completely absent, at least, not in Mesopotamia, had not as yet
been converted into an implement of special military technique.
This occurred only during those peoples' movements which
established the rule of the Hyksos in Egypt and the dominion
of the Kassites in Mesopotamia. The technique of chariot warfare emerged only then, providing the opportunity and incentive
to great conquest expeditions into distant regions.

At first the Egyptians invaded Palestine as a source of booty.
The eighteenth Dynasty was not satisfied with liberation from
the Hyksos—among whom the name "Jacob" appears for the first
time—but pressed its conquest to the Euphrates. Its regents and
vassals, for reasons of internal politics, remained in Palestine,
even after the expansionist drive subsided. Later, the dynasty
of the Rameses had to resume the struggle for Palestine, because,
meanwhile, the strong empire of the Hittites of Asia Minor had
advanced southward and threatened Egypt. Syria was parti-
tioned, through a compromise settlement under Rameses II.
Palestine remained in Egyptian hands and so, nominally, continued till after the end of the reign of the Rameses, hence, during a large part of the period called by the Israelites the "times
of the Judges." Actually, however, for inner-political reasons,
the power of both the Egyptian and Hittite empires had declined so greatly that Syria and Palestine were left essentially
to themselves from the thirteenth century to the ninth, when
the newly established military might of the Assyrians became

important. After a first thrust in the tenth century the Egyptians stepped in again during the seventh. So did Babylonian power.

Beginning in the last third of the eighth century, Palestine's territorial independence was bit by bit lost to the Assyrians, and partially for a time to the Egyptians, and definitely to the Babylonian great kings, whose legacy was taken up by the Persian rulers. Only in the interim period of a far-reaching and general decline of all international political and commercial relations, which, in Greece, was correlated with the so-called Doric migration, could Palestine develop independently of great foreign powers.

The strongest neighbors of Palestine during the period of Egyptian weakness were, on the one side, the Phoenician cities and the Philistines immigrating from the sea, and, on the other, the Bedouin tribes of the desert, then in the tenth and ninth centuries the Aramaic kingdom of Damascus. Against the last named power, the Israelite king invited the assistance of the Assyrians. The interim period saw, if not the origin, at least the military climax of the Israelite confederacy, the Kingdom of David and, then, the Kingdoms of Israel and Judah.

While at this time the political power of the great states on the Euphrates and Nile rivers was small, one has to guard against conceiving of this epoch in Palestine as primitive and barbaric. There remained, to be sure, somewhat weakened, not only diplomatic and commercial relations, but also the intellectual influence from the culture areas. Through speech and writing, Palestine had remained in constant contact with the geographically distant region of the Euphrates even during the Egyptian dominion. The influence of Mesopotamia is in fact unmistakable, especially in legal life, but also in its myths and cosmological ideas. Egypt's influence on the culture of Palestine appears, in view of its geographic nearness, strikingly slight. This was due, first of all, to the intrinsic nature of Egyptian culture; its bearers were temple and office prebendaries who had no inclination toward proselytism. Yet in some important points Egypt probably strongly influenced the spiritual development of Palestine, although indirectly, partly by way of Phoenicia and partly as an essentially negative developmental stimulus. This stimulus can not be readily assessed, since in addition to linguistic obstacles such, apparently slight, direct influence was due to profound differences in natural environmental conditions underlying the social order.

The Egyptian corvée state, developing out of the necessity for water regulation and the construction works of the kings, appeared to the inhabitants of Palestine as a profoundly alien way of life. They detested Egypt as a "house of bondage" and "iron furnace." And, for their part, the Egyptians considered barbarous all neighbors who did not share the divine gift of the Nile floods and the royal administration of scribes. The religiously influential strata in Palestine, above all, rejected the cult of the dead, the decisive religious foundation of Egyptian priestly power, as a frightful depreciation of their own this-worldly interests. This attitude is characteristic of peoples free of hierocratic rule and comparable to the manner in which, at times, the Egyptian Dynasty itself under Amenophis IV strove in vain to escape the power of the priests even then so firmly established. Although within Palestine also, conditions of life and social relations showed considerable variation, the antagonism toward Egypt was, in the last analysis, based on natural and social differences between the two realms.

Palestine affords important climatically-determined contrasts in economic opportunities.[2] In the central and northern regions at the beginning of recorded history, grain cultivation and cattle breeding were to be found beside the cultivation of fruit, figs, wine, and oil. Date cultivation also was practiced in the oases of the bordering desert and in the territory of the palm city of Jericho.

Irrigation from springs and, in the Palestine plain, rain facilitated agriculture. The sterile desert in the south and east has been and is a place of horror and demons, not only to the peasant, but also to the herdsman. Only the marginal regions, the steppes, periodically subject to rainfall, were and are available as camel or small-stock pasture and in favorable years usable by nomads for occasional grain cultivation. All sorts of transitions from temporary to regular, settled agriculture were and are to be found. (In the book of Joshua (15:19) Calib, who had received the Hebron, gives his daughter as dowry a "south land" (*eretz ha-negeb*) and adds, at her request, "the upper springs and the nether springs." The agriculturally-useful land, in contrast to the steppe, is called "*sadeh*".) Pasturage, in particular, differs in kind. At times pastures can be utilized by a settlement in firmly delimited areas either for small stock only or for both small stock and larger cattle. Usually, however, it is necessary to change pastures in accordance with the seasonal variations of a rainy period in winter and a rainless time in summer.[3]

According to one pattern, the cattle breeders alternately use and leave empty summer and winter villages, the latter situated on mountain slopes. The equivalent is to be found among cultivators whose fields lie far apart and are subject to different periods of vegetation. In a second pattern of shifting pasturage, the grazing grounds of the different seasons may lie so far apart or vary so greatly in yield that fixed settlement is impossible. These cases concerned only small-stock breeders, who lived in tents in the manner of the camel herdsmen of the deserts and, in periodic change of pasture, drove their herds over great distances, some from east to west, others from north to south, much in the manner of similar groups in Southern Italy, Spain, the Balkan peninsula, and North Africa.[4]

Given the opportunity during the course of change of pasturage, natural grazing was usually combined with gleaning pasturage of harvested fields and the fallow land. Or again periods of village-dwelling alternated with periods of nomadism and periods of search for work opportunities afar. Some of the village-dwelling peasants in the mountains of Judah lived half the year in tents. Between fully established householding, on the one hand, and tent nomadism, on the other, were found all conceivable transitional and unstable combinations. At present, as in Antiquity, there occur transitions from nomadism to tillage caused by population increase and the concomitant need for bread and the reverse, the transitions from fellahhood to nomadism caused by sandy soil. With the exception of the quite limited lands irrigated from springs, the entire fate of the year depends upon the amount and distribution of rainfall.[5]

There are two types of rainfall. The one brings the sirocco from the South often in violent thunder storms with cloud bursts. To the fellahs and Bedouins strong lightning means strong rain. If there is no rain, today as in Antiquity, it is interpreted to mean that "God is far off" and this is viewed today, as formerly, as a consequence of sins, particularly those of the sheiks.[6] Often fatal for the agricultural top soil of Trans-Jordania, these down-pours in the steppe filled the cisterns and hence were welcome to the camel breeders of the desert. Therefore, the rain-giving God was and remained for them the wrathful God of the thunderstorm. For the date palms and trees in general, these strong rains are not detrimental but useful when not too excessive. The mild land-rains, on the other hand, make fields and mountain pastures flourish and are brought by the southwest and west wind which Elijah on Mount Carmel expected from the sea. Hence, for the tiller, most desired was this rain, in which the rain-spending God does not approach in a thunder storm—which of course often preceeded him—but "with a still, soft sound."

In Palestine proper the "Desert Judaica," the levelling off of the mountain land of the Dead Sea, formerly, as today, has been a region almost without settlements. In the central and northern Israelite mountains, on the other hand, rainfall in winter (November to March) is equivalent to the annual average for Central Europe. Thus, in good years, when strong rains set in early (in Antiquity often as early as the Feast of the Tabernacles) and continue late (until May) good harvests of grain can be expected in the valleys and luxuriant growth of flowers and grass on the mountain slopes. However, when the early and late rains fail, the absolute drought of summer makes all the grass wither and the devastation can extend over more than two thirds of the year. Then, the herdsmen, especially of sheep, had to purchase foreign grain, in Antiquity, from Egypt, or they had to emigrate. The life, especially of these shepherds, was meteorologically precarious, and only in good years was Palestine for them a land where "milk and honey flow." [7] Obviously date honey is meant, which the Bedouins knew even at the time of Thetmosis, perhaps also fig-honey in addition to the honey of wild bees.

3. The Bedouins

THE naturally given contrasts in economic conditions have always found expression in differences of the social and economic structure.

At one end of the scale stood and stand the desert Bedouins. The Bedouin proper, who in Northern Arabia, too, is quite different from the settled Arab, has always scorned agriculture, has disdained houses and fortified places, has lived on camel's milk and dates, has known no wine, has needed and tolerated no form of state organization. As Wellhausen,[8] among others, has described the situation of the Arabs in Epic times, the sib head, the sheik, was the one, normally permanent, authority beside the Mouktar, the head of the family (i.e., the tent-community). The sib comprises the complex of tent-communities which, rightly or wrongly, trace their descent to a common ancestor and whose tents, therefore, stand side by side. The sib, with its duty of blood revenge, is the most firmly and closely knit association. Communities form out of a number of sibs, through joint migration and encampment for mutual protection. Thus emerges the "tribe," which rarely comprises more than a few thousand souls. It has a permanent leader only when a man through feats of warfare or judicial wisdom has gained such distinction that by virtue of his charisma he is recognized as a *sayid*. As hereditary charisma, his prestige can, then, be transferred to the respective sheik of his sib, especially in the case of a wealthy sib.

However, the *sayid* is only *primus inter pares*. He presides over the tribal palavers (among small tribes often occurring every evening) and he has the decisive voice whenever opinion hangs in the balance, he sets the time for the departure on the march and determines the camp site. Like the sheik, however, he lacks all power of coercion. His example and verdict will be honored by the sibs only so long as he proves his charisma.

Furthermore, all participation in the war expeditions is voluntary, only indirectly compulsory through ridicule and shame. The single sib seeks adventure at its pleasure. Similarly, the sib extends its protection at will to strangers. Both, however, can react on the community, the first through reprisals, the last through revenge for the violation of guest right. The community itself intervenes only in exceptional situations, for any association more extensive than the single sib remains highly unstable.

The single sib separates from its former tribe and joins others at will. The difference between a weak tribe and a strong sib is fluid. Under certain conditions, however, the political grouping of a tribe, also among the Bedouins, can turn into a relatively firm structure. This may occur when a charismatic prince succeeds in securing for himself and his sib a position of permanent military authority. In the nature of the case, this is possible only when the warlord receives a fixed income in the form of ground rents and tribute from the intensively cultivated oases or from tolls and convoy fees from the caravans and when his income allows him to maintain a personal following in his mountain castles. (So in the land east of Byblos—where recent hypotheses locate the scene—did a Retenenu sheik hold sway over a region of wine, oil, and fig cultivation; the sheik makes the fugitive Egyptian Sinuhe his official and gives him a fief.) Apart from such situations, all power positions of individuals are quite unstable.

All notables in the last analysis have only obligations and are rewarded only through social honor, or, at best, enjoy a certain preference in judgment. Nevertheless, property and hereditary charisma can make for considerable social inequality among the sibs. On the other hand, strict duties of brotherly aid in time of need are to be found, first within the sib, and, under certain conditions, also within the tribe. By contrast, the non-brother is without rights if he has not, through table community, been received into membership in the protective association.

The grazing grounds which the loose and unstable tribe claims and defends are respected out of mutual fear of revenge. Such grazing grounds change hands, however, with shifts in power position, which is tested mainly in struggles for the most important objects, the wells. There is no property in land. War and robbery, above all highway robbery, while it is occasionally practiced as a matter of honor, stamp the typically Bedouin concept of honor. Famous lineage, personal bravery, liberality are the three traits for which a man is praised. Concern for the nobility of his family and the social honor of his good name were held by the pre-Islamic Arab to be the mainsprings of all action.

Economically the present-day Bedouin is often considered to be an unimaginative traditionalist,[9] disinclined to follow peaceable economic pursuits. This, however, is only a conditional generalization, for the tribes dwelling near the caravan routes of the desert usually had an interest in the highly profitable middleman's trade and convoy service wherever such commerce existed. The high sanctity of guest-right also rests, in part, on this interest in itinerant trade. As on the ocean, oversea trade and piracy are linked, so in the desert middleman trade and highway robbery belonged together, for the camel is unsurpassed among the animals as a carrier.[10] The foreign trader would and will be robbed, so long as no foreign power guards the routes with garrisons or the merchants fail to make firm agreements for protection with the very tribes that control the routes.

Collections of ancient Israelite laws show no trace of genuine Bedouin right, and the tradition holds that the Bedouins were the deadly enemies of Israel. Eternal feud ruled between Yahwe and Amalek. Cain, the ancestor of the Kenite tribe, bearing the "sign of Cain," that is the tribal tattoo, was a murderer condemned by the Lord to vagrancy and only the frightful harshness of blood revenge was his privilege. For the rest, Israelite custom hardly ever suggests Bedouin elements. Only one important trace exists, namely, wiping of the door posts with blood to ward off demons, a custom diffused throughout Arabia. With respect to military affairs there is the prescription in Deuteronomy (20:8) to exempt all who are "fearful and fainthearted" from army summons or to send them home. Usually this prescription is interpreted to be a purely utopian, theological construction of the time of the prophets, though it might possibly be linked historically with the strictly voluntary participation in Bedouin war expeditions. But this does not spring from borrowing from the Bedouins, but represents, rather, reminiscences of habits peculiar to tribal cattle breeders which, to be sure, correspond to Bedouin customs.

4. The Cities and the Gibborim

ON THE other end of the scale stood and stands the city (*gir*). We must analyze it somewhat more closely. Doubtlessly, its antecedents in Palestine, as elsewhere, were on the one hand, the castles of warrior chiefs established for themselves and their personal following, on the other, the refuge places for cattle and men in dangerous regions, especially those near the desert. Our tradition supplies no details about either. In his inscriptions, Sanherib speaks of King Hezekiah's numerous castles, which he claims to have destroyed. The Chronicles, also, tell of Hezekiah's castles, likewise, of numerous border fortresses of Rehoboam. The garrisons probably had castle-fiefs. Some of the cities described in the Amarna letters were obviously castles of this type. The charismatic chieftains also possessed castles, as did David and, in early times, Abimelech.

Economically and politically, the cities of the tradition represent very different phenomena. The city could be but a small fortified agricultural community with a market. In this case it differed only in degree from a village. If fully developed, however, the city throughout the ancient Orient was not only a market place, but above all a fortress and, as such, seat of the army, the local deity, his priests, and the respective monarchical or oligarchical authorities of the body politic. This clearly suggests the Mediterranean polis.

The political constitution of the Syrian-Palestine city actually represents a developmental stage of urbanism which resembles that of the old-Hellenic "polis of the gentes." Even in pre-Israelite times the sea-cities of the Phoenicians and the Philistines were organized into full cities. For the time of Tethmosis III, Egyptian sources reveal the existence of many city-states in Palestine, among them even the kind that continue to be found during Canaanite times of Israel (according to Lakisch).[11]

In the Tell-el-Amarna correspondence there appears under Amenophis IV (Ikhnaton) in the larger cities, most distinctly in Tyros and Byblos, an urban stratum beside the vassal kings and regents of the Pharaoh with their garrisons, magazines and arsenals. This urban group controlled the city hall (*bitu*) and pursued an independent policy which often was inimical to Egyptian rule.[12]

Whatever other traits may have characterized this group, it was obviously in the nature of an armed patriciate.[13] Its relations to the vassal princes and regents of the Pharaoh were apparently already similar to those we find later between the urban Israelite sibs and such military princes as Abimelech, Gideon's son. Besides, there are similarities in another respect between pre-Israelite, Israelite, and even late Judaic times. Still in Talmudic sources several categories of villages are distinguished so that a number of rural towns belong to each chief fortified city. Villages, in turn, belong to both, as political dependencies. The same or similar state is already presupposed in the Amarna letters,[14] and, likewise, in the Book of Joshua,[15] dating from the time of Kings (Josh. 15:45-47; 17:11; 13:23, 28; compare Jud. 11:27 and Num. 21:25, 32).

Obviously, this state of affairs existed throughout known history wherever the urban defense organization attained to full political and economic development. The dependent places are, then, in the situation of *periocoi* places, i.e., without political rights. The master sibs are, or are held to be, city dwellers. In Jeremiah's home town, Anathoth, there are "only small people" who lack understanding of his prophecy (Jer. 5:4), so he goes into the city of Jerusalem where the "great men" are, in hope of better success. All political influence lies in the hands of these "great men" of the capital city. When under Zedekiah, at Nebuchadnezzar's command, at times, others than the "great men" are in power and, particularly, control the office, it is held to be an anomaly. It is a possibility that Isaiah holds out as just punishment for continual profligacy of the mighty ones, at the same time, however, as a terrible evil for the community. However, the people of Anathoth are considered to be neither metics nor a special status group, but Israelites who simply do not belong to the "great men." [16]

Here the type of the prevailing polis of the gentes is developed in the very manner of early antiquity: with *periocoi* places devoid of political rights, but considered to be settlements of freemen.

The organized sib, also, remains basic in the city. However, while it has exclusive significance for the social organization of the Bedouin tribes, in the cities, the distribution of land ownership has made its appearance as the foundation of rights and has finally outweighed the former. In Israelite antiquity, social organization is usually articulated in terms of father houses (*beth aboth*). These household communities are considered to be subdivisions of the sib (*mishpacha*), which, in turn, is a subdivision of the tribe (*shebet*).

We saw, however, that the tradition of the Book of Joshua already has the tribe subdivided into cities and villages rather than into sibs and families. Whether every Israelite belonged to a "sib," might, by analogies, be questioned. The sources assume it, inasmuch as every Israelite freeman qualifies for war service. However, an increasing differentiation among the armed freemen was occurring. Occasionally tradition (in Gibeon, Josh. 10:2), expressly identifies all citizens (*anashim,* elsewhere, e.g., Josh. 9:3, *josebim*) of a city with the *gibborim,* the warriors (knights). But this is not the rule. Rather, the term *gibborim* refers regularly to the *bne chail,* the "sons of property," i.e., the possessors of inherited land called *gibbore chail* in contrast [17] to ordinary men (*'am*), the militarily trained section of whom are later (Josh. 8:11; 10:7; II. Ki. 25:4) called the warriors (*'am hamilchamah*). Boas, in the Book of Ruth, is called a *gibbor chail.*

(How inordinately expensive the armor of a *gibbor* was in the time of the writing of the Book of Samuel is indicated by the Goliath tale. He required a shield bearer, and Saul is also mentioned as having one.)

Also named *gibbor chayil* were the large owners upon whom King Menahem placed a tax levy of 50 shekels each, in order to raise the Assyrian tribute. The most important reference is II. Kings 15:20 which Ed. Meyer with justice has adduced at the time; occasionally warriors generally are so designated. However, a *ben chail* refers just as little as its literal Spanish equivalent, "hidalgo," to the possessor of any sort of land. The *bne chail* by virtue of economically inherited wealth are fully capable of equipping themselves, and hence, represent those who, economically, are fully capable of war service and war duties, therefore, from politically privileged sibs. These sibs held power when and wherever costly weapons and training were decisive in war.[18]

Also where, as so often in early antiquity, a hereditary charismatic city prince (*nasi*) stood at the head of the city, he had to share power as *primus inter pares,* with the elders (*sekenim*) of the sibs, and with the family heads (*roshi beth aboth*) of his own sib. The power of these latter could become so great and at the same time the predominance of the princely sib over all other sibs of the city and their elders could become so extensive that the city appeared as an oligarchy of the family heads of the princely sib, as we find quite regularly in Israelite history. But conditions may well have differed. In the Genesis account, Shechem is ruled by a rich sib, the *bne chamor*, the head of which holds the title *nasi* (prince) and is called "Father of Shechem" (Jud. 9:28). For important transactions, for example, for the reception of strangers into the association of citizens and land owners, this city head required the assent of the "armed" men (*anashim*) of Shechem. Alongside this old master sib there appeared after the war against the Midianites Gideon's sib as an overpowering competitor, which, in its turn, was displaced by Hamor's sib in the revolt against Abimelech.

The sibs, as in early Hellenic times, often settled interlocally; at times, a sib was predominant in several, particularly in small, towns. Thus, Jair's sib in Gilead held sway over an entire group of tent villages, which were later, also, occasionally called "cities." As a rule, actual power was in the hands of the elders (*zekenim*). These appear in all those parts of the tradition for which city constitutions are basic. Hence, they appear, above all, in Deuteronomic law as the *Zikne ha-'ir*, permanent public authorities who sit "in the gate," that is to say, administer and hold court in the market place at the gates of the city. The Book of Joshua presupposes their existence for Canaanite as well as Israelite cities. For the city Jezreel, beside the elders, "nobles" (*chorim*) are mentioned. Elsewhere, heads of the father house (*roshi beth aboth*) appear beside the elders; the family heads, also, in later times (Ezra) appear as representatives of the city beside the *zekenim* and the magistrates, differently named at the time, who are obviously identical with the latter. In the first case a permanent charismatic preference seems to have been accorded to one or several sibs constituting the magistracy, in the latter, the family heads of all arms-bearing sibs of the city are concerned. Such distinctions are also found in the older traditions. Whether and to what extent actual organizational variations corresponded to these terminological differences, however, is neither transmitted nor evident. The charismatic position of a sib of notables depends, of course, above all, on its military strength, and connected with this, its wealth. As is known from

Snouck Hurgronje's description, the place of the land-owning city sibs corresponded roughly to that of the oligarchy of Mecca. The *gibbore chayil,* the propertied hero warriors corresponded to the Roman *adsidui.* The Philistine knighthood, too, consisted of trained warriors. Goliath is referred to as a "man of war from his youth": that presupposes possessions. The ancient Israelite political leaders of the mountain tribes, however, are occasionally called "staff bearers" like the Homeric princes.

A comparison of Israelite with pre-Israelite, and with Mesopotamian conditions, shows that in Israel, never a single elder, but always several elders are mentioned in place of the single city king of the Amarna times and still later epoch of the Rameses and the one local elder of Babylonian documents.[19] This is a reliable indication of sib rule as is the plurality of *suffits* and consuls.

Conditions differed when a charismatic war lord succeeded as lord of the city in making himself independent of the aristocracy of elders by winning a personal following, or by hiring paid, frequently foreign-born, mercenaries, who constitute a bodyguard only to him. He might recruit personally devoted officials (*sarim*) from his following or from among slaves, from freedmen or the politically disqualified lower classes. If he based his rule completely on these power sources, that form of princely rule emerged which, in later inimical perspective, was associated with "kingship." The legitimate, hereditarily-charismatic "prince" of old was viewed as a kind of man who rode an ass. Therefore, the messianic prince of the future should come once again on this riding animal of pre-Solomon times.

A "king," on the other hand, is viewed as a man who has war horses and chariots in the manner of the Pharaoh. From his castles, he holds sway over the city and the dependent region by means of his treasure, his magazines, his eunuchs, and, above all, his bodyguard, which he provisions. The king installs regents over the city, probably giving his followers, officers and officials, fiefs, especially castle fiefs—such as "the men of the castle" (*millo*) in Shechem presumably had (Jud. 9:6, 20). The king imposes forced labor, and increases, therewith, the proceeds of his own land holdings. In Shechem King Abimelech has placed his castle steward (Jud. 9:26-30) in a position of authority and the ancient, hereditarily charismatic authority of the *bne Hamor* was displaced by him. The old Israelite tradition saw "tyranny" in such personal military rule of an individual. The parable of the sway of the thorn bush and the curse: that the fire from King Abimelech may consume the patricians of Shechem and, similarly, theirs him, characterizes the antagonism between charismatic tyranny and hereditarily charismatic patricians. The tyrant, like Peisistratus in Athens, rules with the support of hired "idle men" (*rekim*) and they are "rabble" (*pochazim*, Jud. 9:4)—we shall have to investigate further their social origin.

The transition between princehood and city kingship was actually quite fluid. For, throughout Israelite antiquity, even for the mightiest kings, the great land-owning sibs and their elders as a rule remained an element not to be permanently ignored. As it was a rare exception in early times to report of a harlot's son, hence, an upstart (Jephtah) as a charismatic leader, so in the time of Kings, upstart royal officials are the exception rather than the rule. To be sure, in the Northern Kingdom there were to be found several kings without father's names, hence, without descent from fully qualified sibs; Omri did not even bear an Israelite name. The priestly kings' law in Deuteronomy, therefore, deems it necessary to stress pure Israelite blood as a prerequisite to kingship. But the king everywhere has to reckon with the *gibbore chayil*, the militarily full-qualified landowners and the representatives of the notables, the *zekenim* of the great sibs, who, also, by the editors of the genuine political tradition in Deuteronomy (chaps. 21, 22, 25 in contrast to the theologically influenced places 16:18 and 17:8, 9), are considered to be the sole legitimate representatives of the people. The power situation was unstable. In an emergency, a king could dare tax the *gibbore chayil*, as Menahem did for the Assyrian tribute. And it is noticeable,[20] too, that in contrast to all other epochs, the city elders in the period between Solomon and Josiah recede more into the background in the sources. Indeed, the stewards and officials of the kings possibly displaced the elders completely, taking over their position as judges, at least in the royal residences which, after all, were fortresses. It is possible that the elders retained their old position only in rural areas as was the case in almost all Asiatic monarchies.

As soon as the power position of kingship declined, for example, through a revolution, as under Jehu, and definitively after the complete absence of kingship in post-exilic times, the elders promptly returned to their own power position in the cities. Of even greater significance was the fact that royal slaves and eunuchs only rarely played a role in office. To be sure, upstart followers of foreign or lowly birth were to be found as officers and officials. By and large they appeared during the early career or during the rise of a new prince. However, in normal times, excepting the period of David and Solomon, the most important officials, at least under the kings in the Judaic city, were from old, native, wealthy sibs. Of such, for instance, was David's field commander, Joab, and the tradition (II. Sam. 3:39) makes it clear that because of the might of his sib, King David was not in a position to punish him, and therefore, on his death bed, David recommended his revenge to Solomon. The hate of the distinguished sibs of Jerusalem cries out of Isaiah's oracle (22:15) against the foreign born *major domus,* Shebna. Normally, no king was able to conduct his government with any permanence contrary to the will of the sibs. As indicated by the context, Jeremiah considered the "*sarim* of Jerusalem" and "of Judah," of whom he speaks (34:19), as representatives of the richest families of the land.

While the early Israelite city at its height was an association of hereditary, charismatic sibs economically qualified to bear arms, quite similar to the early Hellenic and early medieval city, the composition of this association was as unstable in Israel as in the West. In the time before the kings, some sibs were accepted into the city with full rights (Jud. 9:26), others were expelled. Blood revenge and feuds between urban sibs and alliances of some sibs against outsiders, apparently, were frequent. The individual urban sib was able to grant guest rights to strangers, this, however, according to the tradition, was often precarious.

Politically these conditions suggest somewhat those prevalent in the Hellenic city of the gentes; they suggest, too, the conditions in Rome at the time of the affiliation of the *gens* Claudia with the civic association. However, the cohesion [of the Israel-ite burghers] was somewhat more loose. A formal *synoecism* occurs for the first time with the founding of a city by Ezra and Nehemiah with its fixed distribution of liturgies among the sibs, which commit themselves to move into the city. However, we know nothing concerning the distribution of city taxes and mili-tary services in early times.

In relation to the more comprehensive political organizations such as the tribe and the confederacy, the city for purposes of military draft was clearly a unit which was considered to be the equivalent of a multiplicity of tactical units, of fifty men each [21] and often comprised one thousand men.[22] The sources leave us completely in the dark concerning other relations between tribal organization and city.[23]

Presumably, the "tribe" here was an affair of those sibs eco-nomically capable of warfare, sibs which traditionally belonged to it. The plebeian freeman, on the other hand, probably be-longed merely to the place of their settlement. The manner in which the plebs were dealt with during the *synoecism* after the Exile permits this inference. Changes of military technique must have played a part in this. In any case, in the Philistine and Canaanite city organizations, the military and political dom-ination of the patricians over the surrounding countryside and its occupants rested on the summons of iron chariots of the knightly sibs; the same was doubtlessly true in the Israelite cities.

As in the ancient Hellenic and ancient Italian polis, the urban patricians held sway over the countryside, not only politically, but economically. They lived off the rents of their lands, which were cultivated by slaves subject to forced labor or tax pay-ments, or by serfs or by coloni (sharecroppers or part-tenants). In a fashion typical of Antiquity such laborers were recruited particularly from debt slaves, constantly augmented by squeez-ing the free peasants. The ancient class distinction between the urban patrician as creditor and the peasant outside the city as debtor thus, also, occurred in the Israelite cities. Here, too, the urban sibs doubtlessly gained the means to oppress the rural areas usuriously, partly directly or indirectly from commercial profits. For, as far back as we can go, Palestine was, in historical times, a middleman's country between Egypt and the region of the Orontes and Euphrates and between the Red Sea and the Mediterranean.

The significance of the caravan route for the economy is strikingly brought out in the Song of Deborah. It stresses equally that the highways were unoccupied while the travelers walked through byways because of the conflict between the Canaanite patriciate and the confederacy and that the peasants ceased work. Basically, the efforts of the cities to conquer the mountain land were attempts to gain control over the trade routes and, as elsewhere in Antiquity, the powerful sibs were interested in urban settlement for the substantial trading advantages correlated with such control of the highways and not only because they wished to share political power.

The sibs engaged either in local or interlocal trade, on the coast, in overseas trade, and, in the interior, in caravan trade, especially in the form of the *commenda* or similar legal forms of capital advance such as are illustrated by Babylonian law, which was well-known in Israel. At times the sibs had storage, marketing, or convoy rights, again, they levied fees and taxes. No details are known. In any case, income from these sources provided an essential part of the means with which to accumulate land, reduce the peasants to debt slavery through usurious lending, and to finance their own military equipment and training.

All these phenomena are typical of the polis of early antiquity. In Palestine, as elsewhere, it was of decisive significance that the city-state promoted the most highly developed military technology of the time. For the urban patriciate was the champion of knightly chariotry, which only the wealthiest sibs could afford under conditions of self-equipment. From the middle of the second millennium, this military technique was diffused from China to Ireland.

It is in accordance with our general knowledge of the Mediterranean polis that the peasant on the best soil, i.e., rent-yielding, was most exposed to the patrician's quest for land accumulation. This peasant was least able to offer military resistance. As in Attica where the fertile Pedia was the seat of patrician landlordism, in Palestine it was the plain. And, as in Attica, the *diakrioi* dwelled on rentless land on the mountain ridges which were militarily least accessible to the knights, so in Israel they were the freeholders and shepherd sibs, which the city patricians with variable success sought to subject to tax obligations.

5. *The Israelite Peasant*

CLEARLY in early times the free peasants of Israel usually lived outside all city organization. The sources say nothing of them or of their social and political organization. This, in itself, is typical. Often the lack of detailed source material concerning the free peasants has led to the assumption that, in early Roman times, there were only patricians and clients and in later times only big landlords and slaves; that in Egypt there were only officials and unfree workers or peasants on king's land. In the case of Sparta one is willy-nilly afflicted with the notion that there were only Spartans and helots. Similarly, the free peasants of ancient Israel stand in the deep shadow of mute sources which give us almost nothing beyond the fact of their existence and original power position. This, to be sure, is quite obvious in the Song of Deborah which praises the victorious struggle of the Israelite peasants under Deborah and Barak in the struggle against the Canaanite city league under Sisera's leadership. The life conditions of the peasants, however, are left obscure.

Above all, nothing is known about the political organization of the peasantry. The various ancient designations of their leaders, e.g., in the Song of Deborah, tell us nothing about the inner structure of the political organization. Similarly, they tell us nothing of the nature and extent of social differentiation which clearly also existed among the mountain peasants. Military organization into units of 1,000 men would seem to have already existed among them.[24] The round number of 40,000 able bodied soldiers in all Israel, which is named in the Song of Deborah, suggests that. However, nothing further is known.

The same lack of information applies to the economic condition of the free peasants. There is no certain trace of the open field. Some passages have been interpreted as indicative of it, and, in comparison with contemporary conditions, have been adduced where landlords who, presumably, have arisen socially from among tenants, occasionally distribute land in some regions of Palestine. These, however, are politically-determined conditions of oriental sultanism which yield no knowledge of the early peasant of Israel. Jeremiah is reported to have taken himself to the land to receive his lot among his "people" (*'am*) (Jer. 37:12). It is the one important passage, among those adduced, in support of this assumption. But its meaning is uncertain and it may well be understood to mean that the great sibs, under certain circumstances, had disposition over land, be it over permanent joint-sib property which was periodically repartitioned, be it over the heirless land of a sib member. In any case, Jeremiah was no peasant. The passage in Micah (2:5) uses the term *chelob* for the allotment of the *women* in the community (Rachel) and indicates, merely, that the landlots were measured with the cord only during settlement, but proves nothing for the periodic redistribution of land.

Whether the "Sabbath year," to be discussed later, might somehow be connected with an open field system of the past remains, as may be said in advance, more than doubtful. For the rest, the situation of the free peasants can only be indirectly determined. The Song of Deborah indicates that the ancient Israelite confederacy was, indeed, largely a peasant organization. The song has the peasants confront the Canaanite knights of the city league and extolls them for having fought "like *gibborim*." That the confederacy in historical times has at no time been only a peasant organization has also been established. Later, in the time of Kings, there is no more talk of "peasants" in the armies, at least, they are no longer the backbone of the army. It is highly probable that economic and technical military changes here played the same role as elsewhere. The transition to costly armor under the rule of principled self-equipment of the army always excludes the economically disqualified small holder from the fully equipped army. Besides, the small holder is far less "expendable" than is the landlord living off rent. The ascendancy of the *gibbor chail* over the mass of free warriors, the *'am*, is doubtlessly due to this circumstance, and it must be assumed, though it cannot be proven in detail, that the fraction represented by the stratum of economically and therefore politically fully qualified warriors diminished more and more with increasing costliness of armor. In Chronicles, revised in post-Exile times, the *gibborim* and *bne chail* are occasionally identified with all men able to "bear buckler and sword and to shoot with bow"[25] or also, simply, with "archers."[26] According to the older tradition, the *gibborim* were equipped with the lance, and, above all, with a coat of armor and apparently they were charioteers in contrast to the peasant militia. The latter, according to the Song of Deborah (Jud. 5:8), were also equipped with shield and lance, (the adduced passage would seem to indicate the opposite, Ed.). but at times only with slings, certainly, they were always essentially more lightly equipped, and, in particular, had no coat of mail. (David is unusual to mail; Goliath, by contrast, is a knight in armor). The warriors of the tribe of Benjamin, which was a peasant tribe at the time, are called "swordsmen" in the Book of Judges (20:35).

Besides having to shoulder the costs of his knightly equipment, the full warrior had to be economically expendable for military training. In the Occident similar circumstances led to a corresponding differentiation of status groups. In Israel the development was definitely similar after the great Canaanite cities had been integrated into the confederacy. To be sure, the sources never refer to a fully secular nobility as a special estate. The king could apparently marry any free Israelite inasmuch as the members of fully qualified sibs considered one another as peers. However, not all free sibs were politically equal. Naturally, there were great differences resulting from economic qualification for military service, which was a pre-condition of all political right. Furthermore, superior position in the distribution of social and political power rested on the hereditary charisma of princely sibs of various cantons (*Gau*).

Tradition always indicates the significance of a sib in pre-kingly times by the number of sib members who ride on asses. Typical, for the time of the second Book of Kings, is the use of the term *'am ha-aretz* for politically important persons alongside kings, priests and officials. Occasionally the expression means, simply, "the people of all the land" not the rural people alone. However in some places it clearly means something different.[27] It refers, obviously, to a group from which a few select men were trained militarily by a special officer of the king. Nebuchadnezzar found sixty such men in Jerusalem and carried them off. They opposed the later prophets and the submission to Babylon, as recommended by Jeremiah, and later they opposed the Jerusalem congregation of the returned Babylonian exiles.

The *bne chail* and their leaders, the *sare ha-chayalim* (II. Ki. 25:23) similarly rebel against and slay Nebuchadnezzar's regent, Gedaliah, who had been taken from the party of the prophets.

The abducted *'am ha-aretz* are not identical with the plain husbandmen who were left behind in Jerusalem (II. Ki. 25:12). Rather they may have belonged to the party of the *sare ha-chayalim* previously mentioned. Where the term *'am haarez* is intended as "plebs," this is indicated by a special addition (II. Ki. 24:14). In the light of the preceding reference to the military training of *'am haarez,* one has the choice of assuming that the king, at the time, had men from the politically disqualified plebs compulsorily drafted and drilled and that this plebeian stratum was designated *'am haarez.* Or, one may choose to view them in the main as the national "squirearchy," which, backed by their rural following, opposed the post-exilic Yahwistic Puritans, then the opponents of the rural shrines. The participation of the *'am ha-aretz* in the acclamation of kings and in counter-revolution speaks for the latter rather than the former view.

In pre-Exile times the urban sibs supplied the people who qualified fully for war service and therefore for political office. The prophetic sources speak of the "great men" in contrast to the "people" in so typical a manner that the former expression must refer to an actually exclusive, though, of course not legally, closed circle. The pre-Exile sib registers, which in Jeremiah (22:30) would seem to be presupposed at least for Jerusalem, apparently comprised only the sibs of this circle and doubtlessly served the secular sibs as an army register, indicating those qualified to serve as *gibborim. Chail,* fortune, meant also army and military ability. The "great men" of the prophetic age, hence, were those sibs which provided well-trained, fully armored and equipped warriors. Such sibs, therefore, also controlled the policy decisions of the state because they held the courts and administrative offices in their hands. Apparently, with the increasing exclusion of peasants from the army, sib organization, too, decayed among them. For this best explains the fact that in the *synoecism* of Ezra so many persons were not listed by lineage, but only by place of birth; the lineage register included only the militarily qualified sibs, in Roman terms the *classis*.

Those free men not belonging to these fully qualified sibs are identified by some eminent scholars, among them Ed. Meyer, with the *gerim* or *toshabim* of the sources: the *Beisassen* or metics.[28] But this is quite improbable. For the small-holding Israelite peasant of the Deborah army and of Saul's summons, did not qualify for service in knightly armor and can hardly have occupied the special ritualistic position, which in olden times was peculiar to the *gerim* (lacking circumcision!). And wherever we read of the "little people" in opposition to the "great" (as in the prophets, particularly, Jeremiah) they are the very Israelite brethren who are oppressed by the great and are considered champions of correct deportment and piety. The free Israelite peasants who were economically not fully qualified to serve in the army will, in substance, have occupied the place which throughout Antiquity we see assigned to the *agroikos, periokoi,* and *plebeji* and which we can plainly recognize in Hesiod. Personally free, such a peasant is legally or in fact excluded from active political rights, above all from legal office. This, indeed, gave the patricians the opportunity to exploit him usuriously, to reduce him to debt slavery, to bend the law and overpower the peasant demos. This is bewailed throughout *Old Testament* literature. This economic class-stratification Israel shared with the cities of all early antiquity. The debt slaves, especially, are typical phenomena. They are found in the tradition as the soldiers of fortune following all charismatic leaders from Jephthah (Jud. 11:3), Saul (I. Sam. 13:6, Hebrews enslaved by the Philistines), particularly David (I. Sam. 22:2) to Judas Maccabeus (I. Maccabees 3:9). Once the kernel of the army of the Israelite confederacy in the battle against the Canaanite chariot-fighting city patriciate, the free peasant with the increasing urbanization of the great Israelite sibs and the change-over to the chariot fighting technique was increasingly reduced to a plebeian within his own people.

The *metic, ger* or *toshab,* however, was something entirely different. His situation must be inferred from a combination of pre- and post-exilic sources.

CHAPTER II

THE GERIM AND THE ETHIC
OF THE PATRIARCHS

1. *The Plebeian Strata*

INCLUDED in the gerim of the cities as well as among the Bedouins of the desert were a great many artisans and merchants. To judge from Arabic conditions, the tribal organizations did not grant them full membership. The smith, for instance, the single most important craftsman of the Bedouin, is a guest artisan almost always viewed as ritually impure and usually excluded from intermarriage and commensalism. Blacksmiths form a pariah caste enjoying only traditional, usually religious, protection. This also is true of bards and musicians indispensable to the Bedouins. In agreement with this, Cain (Gen. 4:21, 22) is the tribal father of the smith and the musician and, at the same time (4:17), the founder of cities. It may, thus, be assumed that at the time of the establishment of this lineage such artisans, in Palestine as in India, were guest people, standing outside, both the *gibborim* and the general Israelite brotherhood.

Alongside the guest-status of numbers of these skill groups we encounter certain highly skilled craftsmen viewed as liberal charismatic artisans. Yahwe (Ex. 31:3 f.) "fills" Bezaleel "with the spirit of God." He is the son of Uri and grandson of Hur, of the tribe of Judah, hence is a freeman, and Yahwe teaches him to work in precious metals, stone, and wood. Alongside Bezaleel as helper appears another freeman from the tribe of Dan. They produce religious paraments, reminding us of the ritualistically privileged position of the Indian Kammalar artisans, who practiced the same art. The similarity goes farther. The Kammalar of Southern India were imported and privileged royal artisans. Dan, according to tradition, was settled in the area of Sidon and, in I. Kings 7:14, Hiram, the master builder of Solomon's Temple, is alleged to be a "man of Tyre." According to tradition, furthermore, Hiram had a Naphthali mother and was, thus, a half-breed whom Solomon called to his court. We may assume that trades important for the construction works and military needs of the king were generally organized as royal crafts.

In the post-exilic Chronicles the *byssus* weavers, potters and carpenters appear to be tribal foreigners, perhaps like the royal artisans of pre-Exile times. After the destruction of Jerusalem, Nebuchadnezzar carried off the artisans, particularly those of the king, along with the military sibs. With the return from Exile and the reconstitution of the community under Ezra and Nehemiah, goldsmiths, shopkeepers, and venders of ointments formed organized guilds outside the old kin-organizations. By this time they were divested of their tribal foreignness and were received into the Jewish confessional community-organization. However, still in the time of Jesus ben Sira, and, presumably, still later, artisans were not qualified for office, in contrast to the members of old Israelite sibs. Henceforth they constituted a specifically urban demos.

At the time of the post-Exile city-state, this plebeian stratum included, not only artisans and traders, but, as Eduard Meyer has convincingly demonstrated, other important groups. It included (1) the numerous persons in the register of peoples who returned under Cyrus and who are not listed by sib, but simply as men (*anashim*) from a certain place of the district of Jerusalem, hence as plebeian inhabitants of a rural town dependent on the capital. Furthermore, this plebeian stratum included (2) the several thousand persons who, without such statement of place of residence, were enumerated under the category "sons of bondswomen" (*bne has-senua*). Michaelis and Eduard Meyer quite rightly viewed this group as plebeian inhabitants of the city of Jerusalem. Both groups obviously are Israelite plebeians not listed in the old kin-registers of the *gibborim*. Whether they had been formerly considered to be Israelite plebeians or, like

most artisans, metics, the members of these strata, according
to Eduard Meyer's convincingly argued assumption, were now
organized with their land allotments like sibs and named after
their place of birth. They were entered into the new register of
citizens if they accepted the law.

The *synoecism* represented by the reconstitution of Jerusalem
was consummated on the basis of the old sib registers. The
families settling in the houses of the capital were considered to
be a quota representation of the old sibs. But these vestiges of
the old sib organization vanished later, apparently because it
was of no military significance in the first quite un-military
client city-state.

The official view found in post-Exile Chronicles (I. Chr.
10:2) distinguishes, beside the Israelite freeman, only the religiously privileged hereditary estates, positively, (such as the
priests and Levites) or, negatively, privileged estates (like the
Nethinim), but no secular ones. Even the David sib, which at
the time of the return from Exile is still enumerated, later fell
into oblivion. The ancestral pedigree of Jesus in the Gospels was
fabricated to conform to the old religious promises. The organization of sibs, which theoretically still existed, and the initial
liturgical organization, which did exist, in fact, recede in significance completely before personal membership in the *kahal*
or *cheber haj-jehudim*, the Jewish confessional organization.
Membership in this was now acquired either by Jewish birth and
the assumption of ritualistic duties or through personal reception. Between these categories, the Old and New Jews, there
remained only some vestiges of status difference (particularly in
connubialism with the priests). Otherwise they were equals.
Only the priestly sibs retained a special status position—to be
discussed below.

All this signifies the emergence of an urban demos in the sense
of the typical status differentiation. All artisans professing
Yahwe, though not qualifying for political office, were recognized as full Jews. The same held for peasants, whether proprietors or tenants with small holdings. This demos did not exist
before the Exile, when the principle of ritualistic tribal segregation governed these status differences. However, after the Exile
the plebeians were never organized into a true demos in the

technical sense of the classical constitution of the ancient polis. Similarly they never constituted a *popolo* or a "citizenry" in the manner of the Middle Ages. As far as is known, there was neither, as in Antiquity, an assembly by *demoi* or *tribus* or by similar local division of the defensive or voting association of all resident citizens, nor, as in the Middle Ages, a (*coniuratio*) sworn brotherhood and representation of citizens by guilds.[1] Still lacking were the political preconditions, such as the military organization of the ancient hoplites or of the medieval citizens on which the political power of occidental plebeians was based.

Despite changes in legal position, the actual social and economic situation after the Exile remained similar in principle to that of pre-Exile times. Wealthy landlords, in the main, resided in Jerusalem where they consumed their rents. Powerful sibs were also to be found residing outside Jerusalem, but they, too, were normally viewed as denizens of a city. Although its mausoleum was raised on a mountain near the coast, the Hasmonaean sib was, nevertheless, considered preeminent in the city of Modin (I. Maccabees 2:17). The distinguished secular sibs which did not settle in Jerusalem were, as a rule, opponents of the ritualistically correct Jewish community; the pious Hasmonaeans who claimed priestly descent, simply formed an exception.[2] Furthermore, economically and politically powerful families within the cities, particularly also, within Jerusalem, oppressed the plebs in precisely the same manner, through usury and perversion of justice, as formerly did the "great men," against whom pre-Exile prophets had turned. The psalmists raised frightful wails against the rich and cried out for revenge. The rich were characteristically called the "fat people," quite corresponding to the *popolo grasso* of medieval Italian terminology. And as traditionally once around Abimelech and then around David, the oppressed gathered around Judas Maccabaeus; he and his following, consisting above all of debt slaves, slaughtered the godless who were, as always in the Psalms, the "fat people" in the cities of Judah (I. Maccabees 3:9).

The economic basis of the status stratification, hence, was very stable. The only important new phenomenon in post-Exile development was that of the urban demos, the petty bourgeois increasingly became important as the champion of true piety, as the "community of the *Hasidim*." Finally, with the appearance of the Pharisee party, the petty bourgeois, although formally, it appears, without change of political rights, came to play a decisive role. Both the actual importance and the lack of formal rights of the demos were bound up with the theocratic peculiarity of the late Judaic city-state. This peculiarity, the confessional basis of the community organization, also determined the fact that the old terms for metic acquired a new meaning, namely, that of "proselyte." This occurred after the ancient tribal-foreignness of the guest artisans as opposed to the Israelites had disappeared. Before examining the implications of this we must pursue somewhat further the old, pre-Exile meaning of the term. For in spite of the constancy of the economic basis, the legal position of the demos in pre-Exile times was quite different.

2. *The Pre-Exilic Metic*

THE pre-Exile metic (*ger*) was sharply differentiated from the total foreigner, *nokri*. The latter was without rights. The *ger* was of foreign stock, but was legally protected.

A foreigner, however, was able to secure a protected relation in two ways. He could become the protégé of a single house father. In such case he stood under this man's personal protection, a protection, indeed, which a completely foreign *nokri*, such as a sojourning guest, could enjoy. Protection against the arbitrariness of the house father's tribesmen was, then, only a question of the patron's power. If his patron proved to be powerless, only the displeasure of God or the revenge of his own tribesmen could sustain the guest. The fate of the divine guests of Lot in Sodom and of the Levite in Gibeah illustrates this.

However, a metic received into one Israelite tribe from another was also considered to be without rights in this sense. This is illustrated by the example of the Levite in the narrative of the infamy of Gibeah. This also shows that a full member of one Israelite tribe settling within another, even if closely related, as Benjamin to Ephraim, was considered to be a metic rather than a full member. Like the Ephraimite in the account of Gibeah, he was able, moreover, to acquire a house, and be termed a "house father." It is not evident whether he could also acquire other land and, for earlier times, it is improbable, though not impossible; for later times, however, it is certain: it is reported of two of the patriarchs who were described as *gerim*. (The question is only: which organization, sib, local organization, or tribe had jurisdiction in the matter and what other rights went with the acquisition of land.) [3]

The norm (Lev. 25:35) probably transmitted from pre-exilic times decrees that "improverished," i.e., landless, Israelites are *ger*. Hence, and quite understandably, landlessness was a normal though perhaps not universal criterion of the *ger*. Whatever his position with respect to the ownership of land, the sources regularly mean by "*ger*" a denizen who was not only under the private protection of an individual with the religious protection of guest right, but a man whose rights were regulated and protected by the political organization. This legal situation was termed *ger asher bish'arecha* in the old legal collections, "the metic in your gates." This is to say, the metic belonged to the bailiwick of the city and stood under its regular protection.[4] Thus, unlike the *nokri*, the metic stood neither as a temporary guest nor as a permanent client under the personal protection of a single master. The sources seem to consider him qualified to appear in court, for there are warnings against oppressing him. Perhaps he required representation by a legal patron. The explicit stipulation of the holy law, that one law apply in all things to Israelite and *ger* alike, gives the impression of an innovation. The confessional assimilation of the *gerim* was underway, indeed, some categories of *gerim* belonged, as we shall see, to the main bearers of Yahwism.

Originally, however, a non-Israelite could be in the same legal situation of a *ger*, in this sense, as an Israelite from another tribe. The first was the rule inasmuch as the ritualistic prescriptions of Israelite freemen did not, originally, hold for the *ger*. Such ritualistic prescriptions applied to the entire household, but only to this circle of persons living together in the house community and sharing its religious meal. In the earliest drafts of the law books, only the Sabbath rest was held valid also for the *ger*. Presumably this prevented his labor from competing with that of the Israelites.[5]

According to the older law, circumcision was not obligatory, but optional, for the *ger* (Ex. 12:48). By the time of this statute the slave is already required to be circumcised. The slaves, therefore, could partake of the Passah-meal. This condition must have changed greatly, long before the Exile. For if priestly legislation (Lev. 17:10; Num. 9:14; 15:15, 16) established the principle that for Israelite and metic the same law and ritual were valid, this doubtlessly resulted from the fact that meanwhile many *gerim* had become circumcised and behaved with ritual correctness. We shall see how and why this occurred. In contrast to this, in pre-Deuteronomic law, slaves do not appear to have been subject to obligatory Sabbath rest (II. Ki. 4:22. The account derives from the prophetic legends of the time of the Jehu-Dynasty).

As a rule, the legal and moral commandments of the scriptures speak of the *ger* as of an isolated individual. As tradition indicates this hardly agrees with the conditions of the fully developed city-state, and certainly not with the conditions of early times. Here, those elements of the population which, as *gerim*, are not counted among the Israelite tribes, are always conceived of as organized associations just as are the politically not fully qualified Israelite peasants. The peasants are organized as villages, the *gerim* partly as local associations, partly as sibs and tribes. Tribal organization was retained even when an Israelite tribe had to affiliate with a foreign body politic. When, as in the Song of Deborah, the Danites served on Phoenician ships, this constitutes no counter-proof, inasmuch as such service probably concerns only individuals who hired out for pay as wage workers. However, the tribe Issachar, in Jacob's Blessing, is generally called a "servant." Apparently the Issachars affiliated in a body with a ruling, foreign city-state; they were politically unfree, but they retained their tribal organization. On the other hand, the tradition knows the Canaanite Gibeonites as subject to liturgies, but, also, as autonomous subjects of Israel through an alliance into which the military leaders had entered during the immigration. This relation must be distinguished from the status situation in which, according to the account of the reconstitution of Jerusalem under Ezra and Nehemiah, the watchmen of the gate, the singers and temple servants (*Nethinim*) and, also, the "servants of Solomon" found themselves. For these were hereditary, sib-affiliated, liturgy-obligated groups of Jews, but not *gerim*. The *bne Korah* whose forefather, as a rebel against the priests, already played a role in the tradition of Moses, and the *bne Asaph*, both representatives of psalmist art, were such sibs of singers who, at one time, were *gerim*, but who now had become full Jews.

The situation of the old-Israelite *gerim* was different. Whereas the free, Israelite charismatic artists of the tabernacle account are designated by kin and tribe and the foreignborn royal artisan at the construction of Solomon's Temple is mentioned without sib-designation, Genesis, as we saw, considered the iron workers and musicians as sibs of tribal foreigners bearing an eponym. Likewise the *byssus* weavers,[6] the potters,[7] and probably also the carpenters [8] among the, presumably liturgical, royal artisans, were held to be *gerim*. As such, too, were held the cattle breeders who in the pedigree of Genesis (4:20) are enumerated alongside iron workers and musicians as descendants of Cain.

In the legend of the fratricide (Gen. 4:2) Cain had just been considered to be a peasant in contrast to the shepherd Abel. Then, after the curse, Cain is viewed as a Bedouin (4:12) and in this pedigree evidently is quite generally the father of all typical guest-tribes in Israel. His brother Seth, however, is the tribal ancestor of settled wine-cultivating Israel which Noah represented. In Noah's tripartition of the tribes Canaan is considered to be an unfree tribe, doing forced labor, on the one side, to Sem, the forefather of the continental master peoples including the Hebrews, on the other to Japheth, the forefather of the northern and western coast and Island peoples. Japheth, however, "dwells in the tents of Shem," hence is doubtlessly thought of as a free metic and presumably as a merchant. The saga probably arose at a time of sharp antagonism against the rest of the Canaanites and during which friendly relations existed with the Phoenicians. The tradition traces to Solomon (I. Ki. 9:20) a general tax-liability of all Canaanites still dwelling in the country.[9]

It appears, then, that there were different kinds of *gerim:* freemen and serfs whose position cannot be ascertained in detail.[10] Whatever the actual conditions may have been which found expression or left reminiscences in all these constructions of the tradition, it nevertheless remains certain that the *gerim* were not counted among the military *bne Jezreel*, either as *gibborim* or *'am hamilchama*. They were considered to be tribal foreigners and were organized partly as settled clientele tribes, partly as unsettled guest-tribes and guest-sibs. Originally they were ritually segregated from the Israelites and thereby excluded from the connubium of peers as the account of Shechem and Dinah shows.

We are familiar with the details of ritual segregation of guest tribes from our study of India. Now the two cases of *gerim* most important to us and best evident in tradition, the small stock-breeding herdsmen and the Levite priests, correspond to this type of a guest tribe without land of its own. In tradition, both groups are characterized as not sharing in the land of the politically qualified army. Both, however, like all *gerim* had a fixed legal relationship to the settled population. In the tribal territory of Israel no agricultural land was assigned to the two groups, but they received dwelling sites, though mostly outside the city gates. They were also granted pasture rights for their animals.

3. Herdsman and Peasant

ON HISTORICAL religious grounds we shall examine more closely two groups: the herdsmen, because the tradition assigns the patriarchs to them and because they played an important historical role in the formation of prophetic Yahwe-religions, the Levites, however, as bearers of the Yahwe cult.

The territorial extent of the urban organization described above was dependent upon the political power situation and particularly upon the area where the Bedouins could be kept under control. In Roman Imperial times the city held sway far into desert areas. The Islamic invasion destroyed this, at least in East Jordan, which in contrast to the western region was occupied by the Bedouins. The onslaught of the Bedouins against the urban community organization runs through the whole of Palestine history. In the Amarna letters, the warriors, designated by the ideogram Sa-Gas (of thus far unascertained pronunciation) appear partly, and as a rule, as enemies with whom the Egyptian vassals and regents had to struggle, and, partly, as mercenaries in the service of vassals.[11] The correspondence of Hammurabi knows of the Sa-Gas as nomads on the western border of Mesopotamia, where they stood under a steward of the king. The Sa-Gas invaders of Syria and North Palestine burned the conquered cities.[12] Or they incited the local inhabitants to slay the Egyptian vassals, to make common cause with them, and "to be like Sa-Gas."[13] Again, they conquered cities without destroying them, hence, establishing themselves in place of the former Egyptian vassals and their party followings, became tribute-collecting overlords of the countryside. In all these cases it remains questionable whether these Sa-Gas[14] were really Bedouins, hence, camel breeders from the desert. They were, perhaps, something entirely different.

Midway between the settled population of the city patriciate and the peasantry, on the one hand, and the free Bedouins on the other, stood the semi-nomadic stock breeder. The peasants were partially free, partly subject to forced labor, to tax or tenancy payment. They cultivated corn, fruit, and wine and had cattle on the side. The Bedouin was a camel breeder, the semi-nomadic shepherd was a breeder of sheep and goats and represented a stratum which until recent times has been characteristic for the entire Mediterranean area.[15] The way of life of this stratum depends on the requirements of small stock, in contrast to cattle, for easy practicability of change of pastures over great distances: across the Abruzzi mountains into Apulia, or half-way through Spain, and similarly far in North Africa and the Balkans. In Spain, the so-called "Transhumans"[16] preconditions two phenomena: first, periodic migrations in common and, therefore, in contrast to the formless association of the Bedouins, somewhat firmer in-group regulation of community life; second, a firmly-regulated out-group relationship to the landlords of the traversed regions. Formal agreements must define the rights to pasturage on fallowland, stubble field as well as the migration routes if violent relations, which often occur anyway, are not to result in permanent feuds. For these shepherds are always inclined to transgress traverse and meadow rights, to allow their herds prematurely to invade fields or devastate cultivated lands along the migration routes. Jeremiah (12:10) tells of such violations of his vineyard and field.[17]

The existence and considerable importance of this itinerant shepherd stratum has been ascertained for all epochs of Palestine history. Today this pattern is also found among camel breeders who drive their herds from East Jordan for stubble and fallow in Galilee. The appearance of itinerant camel breeders, however, was not typical. The classical representatives of the small stock breeders in early Palestine antiquity were the Rechabites, a brotherhood which must have traversed almost the entire land from north to south. They were Kenites, a tribe which bordered, on the one side, on the Amalekites of the southern desert and occasionally federated with them. On the other hand, reference is made in the Song of Deborah to this tribe in the North. The basic pasture-region of the Rechabites, in Jeremiah's time, lay, apparently, in the Judaic mountains, whence in danger of war they brought their herds behind the walls of Jerusalem. Two and one-half centuries earlier, during Jehu's revolution in the northern kingdom, they were of decisive assistance. They were small stock breeders. Like the Bedouins, they disdained houses and fixed settlement, shunned fixed agriculture and drank no wine (Jer. 35). Their way of life was viewed by them as a heavenly commandment layed upon them by the founder of the organization, the prophet of Yahwe, Jonadab ben Rechab.

Other bands of small stock breeders wandered as far as the Rechabites. According to tradition, the old tribe of Simeon, which later sank into oblivion, on the one hand, entered into contractual negotiations for meadow rights in the region of Shechem, on the other, by tradition was held to have its seat in the southern part of the desert of Judah. In addition to the pure type of itinerant stockbreeder, as represented by the Rechabites, there were, naturally, numerous transitional forms. Often too, itinerant shepherds engaged in some more or less unsteady agriculture for their own needs.[18]

The transition to the settled peasant status was thus fluid. Only they could not appropriate all of the land, as land was primarily grazing ground and their property was centered in livestock. The slow movement of their small stock restricted their mobility in comparison to the Bedouins hence they were exposed to the latter's depredations. Against the Bedouins they were the natural allies of the settled peasants who were even more exposed to such depredations than the stockbreeders. There was "eternal enmity between Yahwe and Amalek." Cain, the tatooed Bedouin, was held in contrast to the shepherd Abel as cursed to eternal unrest.

Beside this, there were to be found occasional alliances of cattle breeders (the Kenites) with Bedouins, and identification with the Edomites was strong. Naturally, the transition from Bedouinhood to quasi-nomadic stock-breeding was particularly fluid, and combinations of different kinds of cattle appeared, among the patriarchs, as, for example, with Job, who is represented as owner of sheep, asses, cows, and camels, as dwelling in a house and drinking wine. The descendants of Cain, who is first considered to be a desert Bedouin, the Kenites [19] were recognized, in historical times, as an especially God-fearing, cattle-breeding tribe. The genealogy of Genesis shows this. The Midianites, at the time of Gideon, apparently had cattle other than camels. The same is true of the Edomites and doubtlessly also of the sheik who received the fugitive Egyptian Sinuhe as a guest at the time of Sesostris.—Transitions in the other direction were similarly fluid.

The relationship of the small-stock breeders (gerim) to the tillers and to urban populations normally rested on contractually-fixed meadow and traverse rights. Such relations could readily lead to full citizenship and the urbanization of wealthier sibs, be it accomplished by treaty or after violent conflict. According to the tradition the Danites had for long no fixed territory in Israel (Jud. 18:1); that is to say, they were itinerant shepherds on Judaic territory until they took possession of the city of Laish on Sidonite territory.

The social structure of the itinerant herdsman society, generally, is subject to certain developmental tendencies. Periods of peace, increasing population, and accumulation of property always signify restriction of meadow areas and the increasing use of land for tillage. This in turn necessitates increasingly intensive exploitation of the remaining grazing grounds. Both

tendencies, as a rule, led to increasing restriction of the herdsman to fixed, small grazing districts and therewith to an inescapable reduction in the size of their social units. These were
correspondingly unstable. The social organization of the small
stock breeders normally resembled that of the Bedouins: the
large family constituted an economic community, the sib guaranteed personal safety through obligatory blood revenge, the
tribe, a band of sibs, constituted the military organization protecting grazing grounds. Due to the circumstances described
above, these organizations were not necessarily more durable
among the small stock-breeders than among the Bedouins.

Among the stock-breeders tribal organization seems especially
often to have been formed by a charismatic leader. Such probably was the case for the tribe Machir which later vanished as
well as Manasseh and possibly the tribe of the "bne Jemini," all
tribes which advanced from the mountain of Ephraim to the
mountain pasturage areas of the East and South. Normally the
power of these leaders lacked stable support. Through the character of their life conditions, a tribe of pure small-stock-breeders
was much more exposed to the hazards of disintegration than
was the case in a Bedouin community, as long as it found the
economic stability of its tribal leadership either in the domination of oases or caravan routes.

An example of the instability and purely charismatic character
of warlordism among tribes of pure cattle-breeders is the view of
Jephthah's position in the tradition. The elders of the tribe
Gilead initially offered to Jephthah, an East Jordan warrior hero,
only the dignity of a "kazir," a war leader corresponding to the
Germanic duke (Herzog). This was offered for the duration of
the war of liberation against the Ammonites (Jud. 11:6). He
refused, and the army (ha'am, the men), at the proposal of the
elders, conferred to him life-long, but non-hereditary, dignity
of a rosh (chieftain, prince, headman, Jud. 11:11). The numerous ephemeral judges (shofetim) of early Israelite times,
partly mere charismatic war leaders, partly, perhaps, also endowed with the charisma of judicial wisdom were, apparently,
of the same type. Their power remained purely personal. The
East Jordan hero, Jerubbaal-Gideon, who with a purely voluntary following conducted the Midianite war, refused, according

to tradition, hereditary rule which was offered to him by some men in Israel (Jud. 8:23) and was satisfied with his share of the booty out of which he made a religious foundation (which, it may be assumed, was to yield income from pilgrims for himself and his descendants).

Enduring political structures were to be found mostly in the interstitial areas between the desert (Bedouins) proper and the mountain pastures of Palestine in the East and South. Such was the kingdom of the Moabites in Ahab's time, which has bequeathed a legacy of inscriptions. The same is true of the kingdom of the Ammonites already in the time of Jephthah, particularly, however, of the kingdom of the Edomites. This kingdom maintained stable relations with Judah, and was represented by a series of ten successive rulers before its conquest by David. The fact that the Edomite kings clearly did not succeed one another hereditarily would seem to indicate the purely personal charismatic character of the position of the rulers.

Purely political structures were highly unstable among the small-stock-breeders. Threatened by the Bedouins or, the reverse of this, the opportunity to widen their grazing grounds through war, made them join larger associations under a warrior chief. In contrast, peaceable times signified the schism of single sibs and tribal disintegration. Even in the account of the Deborah battle we find the husband of the heroine, Jael, a Kenite, mentioned as a stock-breeder who had separated from his tribe and who, by virtue of a treaty of friendship, had pitched his tents as a *ger* in the territory of a Canaanite city king.[20]

Already in the time of the composition of Jacob's Blessing, the ancient tribes of Simeon and Levi were "divided and dispersed" and in Moses' Blessing (Deut. 33) somewhat later, Simeon is no longer mentioned at all, and Levi is mentioned only as a professional priesthood. Single Simeonite sibs are known to the post-exilic Chronicles (I. Ch. 5:41, 42) as dwelling among the Edomites in Seir, the rest had received "their portion in Judah," i.e., had been absorbed in this tribe. The tribe of Reuben, once holding hegemony of the confederacy, appears, in the Blessing of Jacob, divested of its power; in Moses' Blessing it is pleaded that it not disappear completely; later it sank into oblivion. The stock-breeding sibs split off from

the Joseph tribe; in the Song of Deborah appears the tribe of
Machir, which vanished later, and later an internally subdivided
tribe of Manasseh beside Ephraim. The destruction of the tribes
of Simeon and Levi is brought about by an act of treachery and
a violent conflict against the Shechemites. In fact, the loss of
cattle in war, like the decimation of cattle through an epi-
demic, could suddenly bring about the dissolution of a cattle-
breeding tribe or its reduction by its propertied neighbors to
servant status. However, already the *de facto* pressure of expanding settlements at the expense of grazing land worked in
this direction. The process consists in the gradual transition
from quasi-Bedouin life to small stock breeding, then to settled
life and further to urbanization under the force of this pressure.
The process is mirrored in the sagas as well as in the historical
tradition. In the legend, Abraham, in addition to sheep, also has
camels and he drinks no wine, but he entertains the three men
of holy epiphany with milk. He wanders as a *ger* with contractual meadow rights between different places and only at the
end of his life does the saga have him acquire, after long transactions (Gen. 23:16), a hereditary burial ground in Hebron.
Isaac encamps, by virtue of contract, on the territory of Gerar
and digs wells there, but he has to move repeatedly. Jacob, in
contrast to the peasant Esau, is essentially considered a tent-
dwelling stock-breeder, but settling as a *ger* in Shechem he buys
land (Gen. 33:19). At the conclusion of his life it is considered
a ruse that he introduces himself to the Pharaoh as a pure
small-stock-breeder, so that he might live as a ritualistically segregated *ger* without mixing with the Egyptians. He engages in
agriculture and needs grain for food. All of the patriarchs are
described as cattle owners. Joseph finally regulates the land tax
there as vizier of Egypt.

These shifts are indicative of deep-going transitions in political organization as well as military structure. In the historical
tradition, the single Israelite tribe is to be found in all stages
of transition from quasi-Bedouinism to quasi-nomadic small-
stock-breeding and from both through the intermediary stage of
occasional agriculture (Gen. 26:12 with Isaac) to urbanization
as ruling sibs, as well as to settled agriculture as free and corvée-
rendering peasants.[21]

The almost universal transition to urbanism appears complete in the political geography of Palestine as given in the Book of Joshua. Joshua himself is compensated for his services (Josh. 19:50) with a "city" as a fief. Similarly, all the tribes, even Judah, are treated as holders of cities with villages as dependencies (Joshua, chapter 15). Their jurisdictional areas appear to cover the whole country. Even for the time in which, presumably, this passage has been written, this characterization would seem to hold only in theory. For, even in historical times, the Southern Judaic tribes were politically, like the Bedouins, mainly divided into sibs, whereas the Northern tribes in addition were organized, primarily for administrative purposes, into military units of thousand and of fifty men, in the manner of the Mesopotamian states. The contingents of one thousand as a unit for summons was, of course, also transferable to the cattle-breeding tribes. One could equate a single tribe or tribal division to one or more units of one thousand and delegate to such units the execution of a summons. This may well have taken different forms.

The Song of Deborah uses very different terms for the leaders of tribal contingents which permits us to infer variations in military structure. The kings will naturally have striven for homogeneity. As 'Fünfzigern' later became the general technical term for recruiting and summoning to war, similarly, in the tradition the leaders of the one thousand and the fifty men units were quite generally viewed as men who also in time of peace had jurisdiction in their levy districts. Doubtlessly, this was only a product of the time of kings and even then could hardly apply generally and permanently. Among the cattle-breeding sib-organized East Jordan tribes, and also among the tribe of Judah, presumably, other conditions prevailed. It appears that they did not recognize such authorities as peace-time officials, recognizing only their elders.

The confederate army summons divided into units of fifty and one thousand was, in general, not the single and, at least, not the oldest known type of military organization. Two more types are to be found. For the tribe of Benjamin, located between the Northern tribes and Judah, the account (Jud. 21:21 f.) of the events following the battle because of the Gibeah outrage—an

etiological saga for marriage by abduction which obviously must
have been known among the Benjaminites—makes it appear
quite probable that this robber tribe originally had a strictly
family-less organization of young men in the manner of the
"bachelor house." Presumably because of this, in spite of its
small territory, it attained, at times, to great power. On the other
side, as mentioned, stock breeding tribes proper, as a rule, had
the same attitude toward war as is typically found among the
Bedouins: absolutely voluntary participation, hence pure charis-
matism. This is treated in Deuteronomy as the truly classical
form. The tradition permits Gideon twice to review his levy:
first, he allowed anyone to go home who was cowardly, then, in
addition, he eliminated all those who at a ford in quenching their
thirst had forgotten their dignity as heroes and had lapped
water like dogs (Jud. 7:5).²² The first was a paradigm for the
construction of Deuteronomy (chapter 20) in agreement with
the tendencious "nomadic ideal" to be discussed below. According to this construction, not only the newly married and those
who had just planted a farm or field or vineyard, but all those
who were afraid, should remain at home. For—this is the theological argument—trust in Yahwe alone was sufficient for victory.
In the levy of Judas Maccabeus this paradigm is repeated.
Schwally has assumed that these prescriptions were not derived
from theological constructions, but from ancient magical representations. This however appears uncertain. We shall later in the
voluntary "consecration" of the crusader (Nazarite) acquaint
ourselves with religious army formations to which these ideas
could be linked. But their origin lies, rather, in Bedouin customs.

Practically viewed, this form of war was purely an affair of
warrior-followings (*Gefolgschaftskrieg*). In fact almost all Israelite battles in the time of Judges had this character. There are
actually only three cases in which tradition confirms with certainty the summons of the confederation army as a whole: the
Deborah battle, the (probably legendary) confederate execution against Benjamin, and Saul's war of liberation. These three
cases belong to the type of "holy war" (to be discussed below).
The Godpleasing king of the priestly tradition is David. However, the manner in which he won his place and conducted his

first wars, was the last example of Israelite history of a war of a charismatic warlord and his following, a fact which at once illustrates the transition to a new era.

The dualism of peasant and shepherd is also indicated in the tradition of the first kings. Saul was held to be a peasant, David a shepherd. Saul, by tradition, initiates the liberation by means of a national army summons, David by means of a partisan struggle. Certain differences in the structure of domination of both may well be recognized in spite of the tendencious character of the present tradition. Saul based his power on his own sib and on the warriors of the tribe of Benjamin. He filled his most important offices with Benjamites. Nevertheless, among his warriors, there are tribally-foreign heroes who function as his personal following.

David was sustained (I. Sam. 22:1 ff.) first by a purely personal following and this, according to tradition, consisted of 1. his own sib, 2. "oppressed persons," above all, debt slaves, hence "Catilinian characters," and 3. hired Cretian and Philistine mercenaries (Cherethites and Pelethites, II. Sam. 8:18 and repeatedly). Beside these elements there appeared with David more decisively than with Saul and his heirs 4. a following of purely personal companions, that circle of paladines and knights, whom the kingly tradition knows individually by name and whose deeds it relates. This personal following consisted, in the first place, of members of partially very powerful Judaic sibs (Joab). Beside these appeared, through defection of the paladines from Saul (Abner), also non-Judaic and several non-Israelite knights. There was a considerable number of purely personal "Hetairoi." The tribe of Judah per se, at the time of David's defection from the Philistines, was still subject to them and collectively backed David only later.

The North land joined David only after Saul's sib had been liquidated, and, indeed, by means of a special treaty (b'rith) between David and the elders of the tribes. A contract or covenant here established for the first time the national unity of all of the later twelve tribes of Israel under a national king. Only through such a treaty, that is the standpoint of the tradition, was a charismatic military leader made the legitimate monarch now entitled to summon the army. Princely following and princely mercenaries stand opposed to the legitimate militia of the *berith*-established king. The Davidian kingdom, established in the midst of Judaic stock-breeders, at first, with the help of a personal following and the might of great Judaic sibs, became, from the beginning, with the capture of Jerusalem, a city kingdom. After the revolts under the followers of Saul, then under Absalom, Adonijah, Jeroboam the old opposition of peasant tribes to city domination arose and finally split the realm; the Northern kingdom suffered the same fate with the founding of Shomrom (Samaria) under the Omrids. Jehu's revolt did not alter this fate. The Southern realm, however, after the secession of the Northern tribes, was almost identical with the boundaries of Jerusalem as was the theocratic polis after the Exile.

Through the curtailment of pasture areas these political developments were a primary cause of the disintegration of the semi-nomadic tribes and their strong decline in numbers. Most significant for our problem is that this led to the de-militarization of the herdsmen. Their scattered sibs were tolerated and weak, as against the settled peasants and even more so in contrast to the armed city patriciate. Abraham is considered by the tradition to be a politically unqualified metic of the Hethites in Hebron and other cities in whose territory he sojourns. In Salem he was considered obligated to pay tithe to its priest king. Jacob lived in Shechem, after his purchase of land, like all *gerim* before the gates of the city (Gen. 33:18). At the time of this revision of the writings certainly most of the small-stock-breeders who still remained were actually in this situation. Yet, tradition considered the patriarchs just as Job later to be very wealthy men. Most probably, however, this was no longer generally true of the later stock-breeders, for the chances for impoverishment are, in general, very great for itinerant stock-breeders. In any case, the Rechabites, according to Jeremiah, were not the owners of big herds but little men as was Amos of Tekoa of the tribe of Judah who lived on sycamore fruit and his animals. Throughout the Mediterranean basin the same basic conditions prevailed with the exception of individual and, at times, very large herd magnates.

These facts are possibly relevant to the question as to which economic categories are thought of in the legal sources by the prophets and psalmists when they speak of "the poor" (*evyonim*) as, indeed, they often do. Only in post-exilic times could the reference be to a city demos of retailers, handicraftsmen, and free contract workers. In pre-exilic times "the poor" obviously comprised, first of all, the peasants of the countryside who were squeezed by the patriciate. However, beside these, perhaps more than the sources indicate, were also the small-stock-breeders. One might think that a number of the social-ethical prescriptions for the benefit of the poor, so much discussed, especially in late Judaic times in rabbinical casuistics, originally were related to this situation. This holds, first, for gleaning rights and, later, the so-called right of the "corner of the poor." Israelite charity prohibited gleaning the stubble and reaping to the last spear, requiring that something be left for the needy. In the older wording, retained in Deuteronomy (24:19), forgotten sheafs should not be brought in later, but should be left for the *gerim*, widows, and waifs. The newer wording (Lev. 19:9 f.) ritualizes this in a manner typical of the priestly version. Land and vineyard are intentionally not to be completely harvested in order that something be left for the *gerim* and the poor at the ends of the field. The older wording of the prescription is of superstitious origin: the *numina* of the land demand a portion of its fruits, and therefore what is left belongs to them. However, the obviously later interpretation in favor of "the poor" raises the question as to who was meant originally by the poor. The *locus classicus* of this practice is the Book of Ruth. The beneficiary of gleaning is a widowed tribal foreigner who has been married to an Israelite. It was probably the original sense of the statement that she worked without being recognized on the land of her in-law, the *gibbor* Boas. Hence, the poor [23] apparently referred primarily to the coloni and farmhands of the patricians.

Conceivably the prescription in practice may have applied to the typical fraternization with landless small-stock-breeding metics, dependent on stubble pasturage and gleaning. In Arabia, where it is still widely diffused, it also benefits the landless classes. At least the question must be raised as to whether there may not have been some interrelation between the much discussed (specifically Israelite) social-ethical prescription of the religious fallow year ("Sabbath year") for the land of Palestine and such small-stock-breeder rights. In the present wording, the prescription is to leave fallow field, orchard and vineyard every seventh year in order that the poor and possibly wild creatures might benefit from the free-growing fruit. This extreme form of the prescription is found in the generally oldest collection of laws and moral exhortations, the so-called Book of the Covenant (Ex. 23:10-11). The prescription is—note this—not a legal institution. Externally it does not stand in that part of the collection which, in tolerably systematic fashion, regulates facts stated with legal precision. It is found, rather, among those prescriptions which obviously derive from religious exhortation. It is a moral prescription, not a legal regulation. The institution, doubtlessly, had no mere theoretical significance in late Judaism, but practical implications. Alongside other accounts, this is distinctly shown by the numerous responsa of the rabbis concerning behavior toward grain which has been cultivated despite the prohibition. The institution, moreover, has played a role in the contemporary Zionist endeavors to settle in Palestine.[24]

The latest collection, the priestly law in Leviticus (25:4-7) contains the prescription with detailed commentary to the effect that one should not work on the land but should let the free growing fruit be "meat" for the owner, his servant ('*ebed*), farmhand (*sakir*), metic (*toshab*), and guests, moreover, for "thy cattle and the beast that are in thy land."

This varies somewhat from the meaning it had in the Book of the Covenant. The prescription is to benefit those who stand under the personal protection of the proprietor. The construction is possible, that it originally was a corvée- and tax-remission year for the benefit of the coloni. Such an interpretation would agree well with the manner in which the seventh year is mentioned under Ezra in the resolution sworn by the community of returned exiles: "we will let fall the income of the seventh year." (Neh. 10:31). The collection of Deuteronomy, dating from the time of kings, has been interpolated, but on the whole it is transmitted in a tolerably good edition. This law book— and this is important considering its character as a compendium of religious ethics—knows of no Sabbatical year for the land, but an entirely different institution, the remission of debts on the seventh year.

Hence, it is highly probable, that the Sabbatical year was an interpolation from priestly law into the Book of the Covenant in face of the improbability of the actual execution of the prescriptions among the pre-exilic husbandmen. If, nevertheless, the prescription should go back to ancient custom, it could be based upon an institution connected with the intermittent husbandry of itinerant shepherds, hence could represent a vestige of ancient time-limits in the process of land appropriation and thus "open fields" of the community. Or, it could represent some sort of typical stipulation concerning the forms of itinerant shepherd-rights as to fallow pasturage on the land of settled sibs.

A contributing factor to the development of the prescription, to be sure, is the theological quest for consistent conclusions under the impact of the stipulation of debt-remission in Deuteronomy and the mounting importance of the Sabbath idea in the time of the Exile. Most probably the community of the Babylonian Exile ritualized this in the same manner as other late Judaic institutions and subsequently interpolated it into the Book of the Covenant. All in all, the role of the itinerant shepherd for these prescriptions remains problematical.

4. The Ethic in the Time of the Patriarchs

MORE important than these very uncertain possibilities of an economic interpretation of such individual social-ethical institutions is the general conception of popular tradition, at the time of kings, of the situation of the small-stock-breeder and which was expressed in its view of the patriarchs. This conception is, in turn, a result of characteristic conditions and it has had wide ramifications for Jewry.

The legends treat the patriarchs as thoroughgoing pacifists.[25] Their god is a god of peace-loving men (Gen. 13:8 f.). The patriarchs appear as isolated house fathers, tradition indicating nothing of political associations among them. They are tolerated metics. They are in the situation of shepherds who familywise by means of peaceful contract, secure pasturage from the settled population, and who in case of need, like Abraham and Lot, peacefully divide it among themselves. They lack all traits of personal heroism. They are characterized by trusting, devout humility and good nature admixed with a cunning shrewdness, supported by their god. The narrators expect their audiences to take for granted that the patriarchs would sooner pass off their beautiful wives as desirable sisters and surrender them to their respective protectors,[26] leaving it to god to liberate them from the protector's harem by visiting plagues upon him, rather than defending the honor of their wives. Lest the sanctity of guest-right be violated they deem it directly praiseworthy readily to surrender their own daughters, rather than to have the guest do so.

Their commercial ethic is questionable. For years an amusing play to outwit each other goes on between Jacob and his father-in-law as they haggle for the desired wives as well as for cattle which the son-in-law has earned as a servant. The tribal father of Israel gets out from under his master and father-in-law by stealth and makes his get-away. He carries off his house idol lest his route be betrayed. Even the etymology of his name is adapted to these qualities, and it seems that 'Jacob's fraud" was a proverbial turn of phrase in the time of the prophets. Moreover, it appears completely inoffensive to the saga that its hero, who is expressly described as a pious shepherd, for some food, tricks out of the birthright his hungry home-coming brother who, by contrast, is described as a thoughtless peasant [27] and hunter.[28] Then with the mother's help, the hero betrays his brother for the paternal blessing. Later, before the encounter with his brother, he addresses a quite pitiful and fearful prayer to his god (Gen. 32:10 ff.) and escapes the feared revenge by a ruse and an undignified self-abasement unworthy of a warrior hero.

The traits of the saga's preferred hero, Joseph, are priggish virtue combined with sentimental magnanimity toward the brothers who wished to kill him out of envy and who sold him into slavery because he had dreamed himself their master. His fiscal abilities in exploiting the Pharaoh's subjects in distress qualified him for becoming the Pharaoh's vizier, which did not prevent him from causing his family to give his master half-truths about their vocation.

To be sure, the pirate and merchant-adventurer ethic of Ulysses, "the man for wisdom's various arts renown'd," did not prevent him in distress from addressing uncontrolled doleful pleas for help to Athena in a manner which frequently appears to us to lie outside the realm of heroic dignity. But things such as the aforementioned are not reported of Ulysses. They characterize the ethic of a pariah people, and the influence of such traits on the out-group morality of the Jews in the time of their dispersion as an international guest-people, must not be underrated. Combined with strongly developed traits of faithful obedience, they complete the picture of the attitude of this stratum as hallowed by the tradition. It was, undoubtedly, a stratum of powerless metics who as small-stock-breeders lived among military burghers.

Contemporary analysis has increasingly isolated this stratum as important for religious history, but is inclined to regard the pacifistic character of the semi-nomads as a natural peculiarity. That is decidedly not the case.[29] Rather, it resulted from the dispersion of the defenseless small-stock-breeders with increasingly dense settlement. They lacked this pacifistic character whenever they were organized into powerful political associations.

In the mind of the Israelites the patriarchs have by no means always held the place which has been given them in the revised Torah. The older pre-exilic prophecy, indeed, did not know of Abraham and Isaac as persons. Amos knew the patriarchs Isaac, Jacob, and Joseph only as ethnic names (7:9, 16; 3:13; 6:8; 7:2; 5:6, 15). Abraham, who with Micah appears as the recipient of Yahwe's promise (7:20), appears only with Ezekiel (33:24) as the first, popular legitimate owner of the land of Canaan. The theological circles of literati, particularly the so-called "Elohist" and the Deuteronomic school seem in their revision to have placed emphasis where it still remains. The change in character of the patriarchs during the revision is obviously connected with the social descent and de-militarization of the herdsmen. In the old rank order of the tribes, expressed by seniority of the patriarchs, Reuben, Simeon, Levi, and Judah have precedence; they were all essentially semi-nomads, but at once warlike tribes, renowned for their violence. The first three were dispersed later.

After the forceful conquest of hegemony, Judah was organized
as a city kingdom. Such powerful cattle breeding tribes were
not in any way in the situation of tolerated metics. The military
tradition knows them as masters of the land and the cities dependent on them are known either as liturgy-obligated client
cities, like Gideon, or as militarily obligated, as in the Song of
Deborah, the city of Meros.

Similar things are recognized, also, in the legends of the
patriarchs. Isaac, with increasing wealth and clientele, became
too powerful for the city of Gerar of which he was a metic (Gen.
26:14, 16). In the original tradition, Jacob, too, was a mighty
hero, who overpowered a god in a nightly wrestling match. He
bequeaths to the leading tribe as primary legacy the piece of land
which he had won by "sword and bow," according to his Blessing of Joseph (Gen. 48:22). The land is Shechem, later the center of Ephraim. The pacifistic tradition (Gen. 33:19) developed
later, however, has him characteristically not conquer, but peace-
ably buy this piece of land.[30] Finally, the much discussed fourteenth chapter of Genesis [31] recognizes Abraham as a military
hero, who, with several hundred clients, took the field and recovered from the allied Mesopotamian kings, including Hammurabi, the booty which these had gathered in their fight with
the Canaanite city kings.

The contrast between the warrior's sense of honor and the
herdsman's utilitarian pacificism appears very clearly in the
diametrically opposed attitudes of the peaceable patriarch Jacob
and his warlike sons Simeon and Levi with regard to the violation of Dinah by Shechem (Gen. 34:30, 31). In such fragments
quite different traits are presumed, traits which obviously receded completely into the background in later times. For the
pacifistic tradition, borrowed or developed in agreement with
changed conditions,[32] Jacob is pious only because he stays in his
tents and, likewise, Abel is the good peaceable shepherd. Abel's
murderer, Cain, on the one hand, is a settled and violent husbandman, whose fleshless sacrifice has been scorned by God; on
the other hand, he is a cursed, roving Bedouin and, finally, the
city builder. These are the three typical opponents who oppress
the now powerless small-stock-breeders caught in their midst.[33]

Both peasants and herdsmen stood equally opposed to the

city patrician and the Bedouin; hence peasants and herdsmen developed a common interest in opposition to the latter. The Amarna tablets, the Song of Deborah, the dirge of Ephraim in Jacob's Blessing, and the traditions of Gideon, Jephthah, and Samuel express these interest-situations in various ways. Even the epoch of the first two kings reveals this situation and its political ramifications.

There were great variations in the social composition of the various tribes. Asher and Dan appear to have been urbanized first, Ephraim and the tribes Issachar, Zebulun, and Naphthali appear to have had the greatest admixture of settled peasant proprietors. Economic and political independence of these tribes, which Issachar had surrendered early, was especially threatened by Phoenician, Philistine, and Canaanite patricians. The cattle-breeding East Jordan tribes, however, were especially endangered by the raids of the Bedouins of the desert, the Midianites and Amalekites, whose attacks forced them to seek shelter in caves as in Gideon's time. Among the West Jordan tribes, Ephraim in particular, had to suffer at times from these "bowmen." The wars of Saul's peasant militia still were directed half the time against the Amelekite Bedouins. The ascendancy of settled populations over the desert tribes was only established for quite some time under David, when Edom was conquered and control was secured over the caravan routes to the Red Sea.

The city patricians, the peasants, and the herdsmen were, on the whole, equally interested in the pacification of the desert. For the rest, however, there were frequent, sharp clashes of interests. These conflicts occurred first between the peasants and cattle-breeders. Violent conflict is mentioned between the Israelite stock-breeding tribes east of the Jordan and the Ephraimites. The tradition reports especially of a war of Ephraim against the victorious Gideon (Jud. 8:1 f.) and of an arrangement which was to remove these antagonisms. The tribes of Machir and Manasseh branched out across the Jordan river to the East. Ephraim fought for hegemony, first against Gilead, then against Manasseh, as told by the saga of Jacob's Blessing of Ephraim and Manasseh. Similarly, the "younger brother" Benjamin branched off to the South and then Ephraim fought the robber tribe of Benjamin, which was taken up by later legends. All these events represent, in part, invasions by the peasants of those parts of the mountain land most suitable for cultivation and inhabited by stock-breeders. In part, they represent counter attacks and raids of cattle-breeders against peasant territory. The struggles of Judah against Benjamin and, likewise, the far earlier expansion of Judah into the territory of the Benjaminites and Danites were advances of this newly-emerged cattle-breeding tribe against the old Israelite tribes of the North. This antagonism between peasant and cattle-breeder is expressed throughout early Israelite traditions as well as in the political out-group attitude of the tribes.

In the fertile plains and on the coast, the military patrician of the cities was the enemy against whom the already settled and, particularly, the mountain peasant and semi-nomadic herdsman, at least in West Jordan, had to fight. The urban patrician sought through warfare to capture men and women slaves, to secure tribute and services, and to take as booty, according to the Song of Deborah, especially beautiful homemade textiles. In addition to this, as noted earlier, they fought for control over the caravan routes. The free peasant and herdsman of the mountains fought not only for continuation of their domination of the caravan routes and control over their profits, but to defend their freedom from tribute and servitudes to the patricians. They possibly strove, in turn, to conquer the cities, partly to destroy them, partly to establish themselves as overlords.

This antagonism corresponds, essentially, so far as such comparisons are meaningful, to the struggle of the original Swiss cantons situated along the St. Gotthard route against Zürich, of the Samnites against Rome, the Aetolians against the Hellenic city leagues and the Macedonian kings. With slight inaccuracy one might say: it was the struggle of the mountain against the plain. The natural antagonism came to an end only in the time of the Judaic kingdom. Previous to this, it runs throughout known history of Palestine. Even in Amarna times, the enemies "from the mountains," the Sa-Gas and Khabiri, threaten the cities of the plain. In the tradition of the struggle for possession of Canaan they are cities provided with iron chariots which the Israelites cannot take. All Israelite heroes of the so-called time of the Judges are members of rural sibs, who ride asses, the riding animal of the mountain, not horses. It is worthy of note that the wealth and power of such sibs is counted in terms of ass-mounted members. Saul's residence is still a village in a mountain valley and David's army commander, Joab, still does not know what to do with the booty horses and has their fetlocks paralysed. However, the peasant's and stock-breeder's opposition to the city differed in intensity. The peasant proprietor was the main champion of the battle against the urban patrician. He was most exposed to the imposition of forced labor. The Deborah war was conducted essentially as a peasant war. Praised most highly by the Song is the fact that untrained mountain footmen have fought like knights (*gibborim*) and have been victorious. On the other hand, the stock-breeding, non-agricultural, East Jordan tribes, Reuben and Gilead, had no interest in the battle. Furthermore, the confederate city Meros, and, indeed, characteristically, the coast-dwelling, early-urbanized tribe of Asher, and, similarly, the urban tribe of Dan on the territory of Sidon abstained from this battle.

The northern Israelite peasants and the Judaic mountain herdsmen, also, made common cause against the Philistines only at a late date. At first the herdsmen abstained altogether from the struggle and remained loyal to the Philistines. Tradition, therefore, confronts the Philistine knighthood first with Saul, the Benjaminite peasant, who from the plow becomes king, and then only with its favorite, the Judaic shepherd equipped only with a sling, David, as typical representatives of both categories of Israelites. Actually, of course, David started out as the leader of a mountaineer following of the usual conspiratorial nature. He was a vassal of the Philistines and made himself independent only when he became city-prince of Jerusalem: the fight of one of his heroes against Goliath took place only when he was already king.

The establishment of a unified military monarchy, summoning chariot fighting knights, decided the fate of the free peasant and herdsman militia of Israel. The Benjaminite dominion remained essentially a hegemony of rural tribes, although, according to tradition, Saul even maintained a personal following composed in part of tribal foreigners. The ass, however, was

still the characteristic animal of Saul. The old peasant regions of
Northern Israel rebelled repeatedly against David's city kingdom.

Under Solomon the royal forces were organized and furnished
with chariots and horses (unless the text is corrupt) which he
imported from Egypt to which he was bound by marriage. At
once the opposition set in which down to rabbinical times has
made for a highly ambivalent evaluation of Solomon. After his
death the non-urbanized tribes rose up against the city kingdom.
Several generations later, with the founding of Shomrom
(Samaria), they, too, formed a city kingdom which, in turn, was
repeatedly threatened by rural usurpers. The tradition and the
Assyrian inscriptions repeatedly refer to the numerous chariots
of the Omrid dynasty of this kingdom.

Social formations hitherto essentially discrete and standing
side by side as stock-breeding tribes, peasant tribes, cities, now
became fused; the capital and its ruling sibs became politically
paramount. In pre-Solomon times the actual nucleus of the old
confederacy consisted, on the one hand, of the numerically superior peasant mountaineers and the slowly decreasing stock-
breeders of the steppe regions on the other. To these must be
added various market hamlets and rural towns in the river valleys of the mountains and the mountain passes, only secondarily
—though gradually increasing—fortified cities as well. A great
increase of the stock-breeders, on the one hand, and of the urban
population, on the other, must have been brought about by the
addition of the large Judaic territory under David. Politically
and socially this benefited only patrician power, which now became paramount. However, among the plebeian strata, the old
internal antagonism between peasant proprietors, predominant
in the North, and small-stock-breeders, predominant in the
South, continued. We shall see that this had ramifications also
in the religious development.

The old stratification of Israel into armed sibs of peasant
proprietors or herdsmen, on the one hand, sib clienteles of
guest artisans, day laborers, and musicians, on the other, was
gradually displaced by a quite different stratification. Urbanized
patrician landlords as the champions of training for chivalry appear on the one hand, on the other, indebted or landless, hence,
proletarized Israelites and metic proselytes of the Yahwe ritual,

who now, in the eyes of the priest, formed a homogeneous stratum of "the poor" opposite the patriciate. The poor were not a socially or economically homogeneous stratum, but comprised all who did not belong to the military sibs.

PART II

THE COVENANT AND THE CONFEDERACY

CHAPTER III

THE SOCIAL LAWS OF THE ISRAELITE
LEGAL COLLECTIONS

1. The Laws as an Index
to Social Development

Tᴴɪs complex, unstable social composition of the Israelites gradually moved in the direction of urban patrician rule over the countryside. The development is mirrored in a peculiar manner in the legal collections which have come down to us from pre-exilic times. The social conditions are expressed more in various symptoms and the mentality (*Geist*) of this literature, more in its attitudes toward the typical antagonisms than in the formal nature and content of the collections.

These attitudes reveal the decisive influence of trade. From the beginning, Palestine was pervaded by brisk trade. Its territory was interspersed with cities, and quite exposed to the influence of the economic developments in the great culture areas. The antagonism between indebted peasants and urban-creditors existed from the beginning of recorded history. This appears already in the old collection of laws known as the "Book of the Covenant" (Ex. 21:1-22; 19). While its age cannot be determined with certainty, it is earlier than the Kings and it presents in systematic fashion primarily legal subject matter, with appendices of predominantly exhortatory character with regard to the rules of trade.[1]

Bedouin right is found as little there as in other of the preserved statutes. Neither rights of wells nor the camel or date palm appear as legal subject matter. The cistern plays a part in the Book of the Covenant (Ex. 21:33) only insofar as cattle accidentally may fall into one. However, the law of the Book of the Covenant is not that of semi-nomads or even stock-breeders. To be sure, cattle frequently appear as primary objects of moveable property, but the concern is primarily with big cattle and only secondarily with sheep. Archaism is certainly evident in that the bunting ox itself is stoned as guilty.[2]

Obviously the primary concern of this source is one of peasant property in cattle and of one peasant's protection against the cattle of the other. Damage to field and vineyard by cattle is regulated (22:5), but a peasant proprietor and not a semi-nomad is the presupposed owner of the cattle. The horse does not appear. Cows and sheep represent the kinds of live stock. The interests of village and town-dwelling peasants are almost the exclusive concern of the law. There are rulings on the breaking and entering of houses (22:7), on the liability of the landlord to the tenant (22:8). In form, too, the law is by no means primitive. For the principle of *talion* which also held for Babylon and *per se* is in no way a primitive principle, according to the Book of the Covenant (21:22 ff.) [3] holds only in the case of damage caused by a brawl, but not for bodily injury of other sorts or even generally for all crimes. This is often overlooked.

Blood revenge is found, and beside it a well developed system of *Wergeld* and amends and, in part, also, a genuine criminal law with distinctions between murder and homicide, criminal intent and negligence, with tolerably rational principles of distribution of risks. All this represents an essentially more advanced stage of legal development than the *lex Salica*. That, in matters of law, we are concerned with a culture profoundly influenced by Babylon is shown not only in the doubtless parallels in the Code of Hammurabi,[4] but, above all, in the evidence of a developed money economy.[5] Alongside the barter loan (22:14) and partnership in cattle (22:10), appeared the money loan (22:25) and the money deposit (22:7). The payment of *Wergeld* and fines was in money. The dead pledge, the purchase of slaves, particularly, the sale of one's children (21:1 f.) and doubtlessly also of one's own self into indenture existed. This is meant in Exodus 21:1 f. Otherwise the stipulation could have been circumvented through re-sale. Also, the feasting rules (23:14 f.) which are appended to the ordinances proper as part of the religious exhortation are indeed characteristic of a settled agricultural people. The great festival of the sheep breeders, the Passover, later universally diffused, is not mentioned. Instead, the feast of unleavened bread is to be found, a peasant festival which was later combined with the Passover. Also the other festivals are connected with tillage and harvest.

Especially characteristic of the "spirit" of the legal collection are the ordinances concerning trial procedures and the right of slaves and metics. These sections of the law book and its exhortatory appendices are best compared with enactments by the Hellenic *aisymnete* and the Roman *decemvir* to resolve conflicts between the patriciate and the plebs. Similar enactments were promulgated by Mesopotamian rulers in accordance with priestly-influenced welfare policies. The most far-reaching prescriptions, however, are to be found in the exhortatory parts of the collection. No gift should be taken by the judge (23:8). Judgment of the poor (*evyonim*) should not be biased in favor of the distinguished man (23:6). Nor, and this is placed first, should judgment be corrupted in favor of the pleasure of the multitude (23:2). The last was clearly possible only if the multitude (*rab*) represented a plebs of freemen who held no office. The metic (*ger*) should not be oppressed (22:21), nor be treated unjustly before the court (22:9). The Sabbath, which economically could not have made sense to pure cattle-breeders, is expressly justified as a day of rest for work-cattle, slaves ("sons of the bondswoman"),[6] and metics (23:12). It must be assumed that these metics are thought of as field workers, as *coloni* who stand outside the urban community. There was already discussion of the Sabbath year and its interpolated or distorted meaning in the present text.[7] Most radical, however, is the debt and slave right which is inseparable from debtor rights. For the slave is primarily conceived of as a debt slave, whether he had sold himself or whether his parents in need had sold him (Roman: given in *mancipium*). Indeed the exhortation to limit pawning (cf. the prohibition against the pawning of clothes, 22:26) does not go so far in the Israelite collection as in Hammurabi's Code, which forbids the pawning of work animals. In contrast, Babylonian law knows nothing of the highly significant prohibition contained in the exhortations against ruining a poor Israelite through usurious loans and against the charging of interest (*neshech*) (22:25).[8]

This, then, is the source of the distinction between in-group and out-group morality for Jewry. The prohibition against the taking of interest from in-group members derives primarily from the old ethic of brotherliness of the neighborhood organization with its duty of interest-less aid in time of need. The very general and unprecise formulation precludes the derivation of the prescription from legal practice. It was a religious commandment and formed the supplementary exhortation to those legal ordinances which, due to their great importance for the tendency of the entire collection, were placed at the head. For example (21:2 f.), it was stipulated that a Hebrew servant, hence a debt slave, must be set free after six years of service, unless he had taken a wife out of the master's household community and in order to retain her chose voluntarily to remain in permanent bondage, which then had to be witnessed through a religious ceremony involving the piercing of ears before the house idol. Second, a Hebraic bondswoman became free unless the master made her his or his son's wife and, in the first case, if he discriminated against her in favor of later wives in matters of food, clothes, or sexual intercourse. These absolutely precise prescriptions were doubtlessly old practical laws. The first of the above stipulations is found, also, in Hammurabi's Code, with an even shorter period of three years. This applied, not in the case of self-sale, but in that of the sale of married wives or children, by the housefather for his debts. The sale of wives, indeed, was unknown in Israelite law. In contrast to Babylonian law, Israelite law had ordinances for the protection of the person of the slave. Great bodily harm by the master established the claim to be set free (21:26-27); homicide (21:20) in case of instant death led to criminal punishment; otherwise, the principle applied that the master has only damaged his own operating capital and the slave was without rights (21:22). In Hammurabi's Code (No. 116) we find protective stipulations against the creditor, lest, through deprivation or arbitrary treatment, he allowed the debt servant to die. Also, here the bondsman was always thought of as a son or servant of the debtor.

All in all, this collection of laws bears the imprint of conditions which, though representative of far more restricted and impoverished circumstances of small town life than those of the old Babylonian Code, do not differ in principle. However, important contrasts are to be found. The herdsman of the Babylonian Code was a functionary of the king or an employee of a great herd owner (as Jacob in the legends was an employee of Laban), the herdsman of the Book of the Covenant, however, was a peasant. Individual land ownership was (22:5) presupposed as self-evident, for the rest, there was no treatment of real property. The peasant in Babylonia, generally, was a *colonus,* bondsman, slave, tenant or, quite often, a sharecropper of a great urban landlord. There were also *coloni* in Palestine. But the law was not interested in them, they were *gerim.* The landowner in the Book of the Covenant is no absentee owner as many a Babylonian landlord who employs a steward. Rather, he is a town-dwelling owner-operator, or a middle-sized farmer, who carries on husbandry with servants, maids, and, possibly, with bondsmen or politically disqualified *coloni.* Moreover, there is lacking the great trader and money lender of Babylon. The merchants, indeed, are conceived partially as foreigners, partially as metics; the law book does not mention them.

All these conditions differed from those of the time of the Song of Deborah principally insofar as the free peasant had now become a plebeian, standing below the developing urban patriciate. Doubtlessly the need of the codification rested on the antagonisms called forth in Israel by these developments. The conditions of the East Jordan and Southern tribes, which perhaps at the time of this legal collection were not yet counted as belonging to Israel, remained completely outside consideration. The legal collection could well have originated on Ephraimite soil, for instance, in Shechem. The term *"nasi"* for the prince, whom it was forbidden to disgrace (22:28)—the only political exhortation—like the use of "Elohim" for the godhead, would agree with what we know of the general conditions of the region about the time of the early kingship.

The revision of the Book of the Covenant which has been incorporated into the "textbook" of Deuteronomy (especially chapters 12-26) presupposes considerably changed conditions. The revision goes back to the time when the realm of Judah was in fact almost identical with the polis of Jerusalem with its small satellite towns and villages. We need not discuss, here, the extent to which this collection, composed of at least two different elements (12-19 and 20-25), from the beginning, belonged to the allegedly Mosaic *sefer hattorah*, which the priests "discovered" under Josiah in 621 and which the king, upon their suggestion, imposed as binding.[9]

In these statutes, reproduction and amendments of enforced law, didactic theology, and moral utopianism have been similarly fused as in most of the transmitted legal collections of Israel. But the relationship to the vital practice of law here is more tangible than in the later purely priestly collections of exilic times. As in earlier times, livestock (cattle and sheep) play a significant role. Neither camels nor horses—the latter came into consideration only as war horses of the king—are mentioned as objects of private business. Wealth consists primarily of surplus of grain, new wine, oil, figs, pomegranates, honey, cattle (Deut. 7:13; 8:8), but also of silver and gold (8:13). Ore mining in the country is mentioned as one of its assets (8:9). The wells in the mountains of Judah mean, indeed, much (6:11) but it is mentioned as an important difference from Egypt, also, in relation to god, that the Egyptians must sow and water the land "like a vegetable garden" (11:10), whereas on the mountains and meadows of Palestine, God sends rain and gives the harvest (11:11).

The mounting significance of land ownership appears in the heavy curse against boundary violations (22:17, cf. 19:14). The weakening of the old patriarchal position of the house-father and of the old cohesiveness and joint liability of the sib in outgroup relationships appear in the prohibition of invasion of the privileged portion of the eldest son (21:16), on the one hand, and in the elimination of the criminal liability of all members for each other's offenses, on the other (24:16). In this point the law book is comparatively modern. The practice itself, by the way, has been ascribed in a probably Deuteronomic tradition, even to King Amazia (II. Ki. 14:6). Blood revenge continued to exist (Deut. 19:6). However, trial law, including the adjudging of proofs, was relatively rationalized, especially through the requirement of two witnesses—a procedure still influential in canonical criminal law of the Catholic church.

In the Book of the Covenant and the appended exhortations the moral duty of brotherliness is repeatedly dealt with in somewhat general terms. Such general references (which, indeed, make them suspect as interpolations) are developed into far-reaching measures for the social protection of widows, waifs, servants, workers, metics, and sick persons. The curse against judges accepting gifts (27:25), against those wresting judgment against the aforementioned persons in need of protection (27:19) and the prohibition of their oppression in any form (24:17), stand beside the curse against the leading astray of the blind (27:18) and the repetition of the older commandment to return the runaway cow of one's neighbor (22:1, 3).

From the widow none at all (24:17), from the poor only restricted pawn pledges may be taken (24:10, 12). The servant may not be flayed (23:16) and—a far-reaching stipulation—a worker who has left his master may not be handed over to him (23:15). The worker, also the metic as a worker, is to be paid on the same day (24:15). The increasing significance of free day laborers appears in all these stipulations. Even now the Sabbath is considered (5:14) a day of rest in the peasant's own interest. It is said that there will always be poor people (15:11), however, there should be no Israelite beggars (15:4); this principle is basic for the social stipulations which are almost all imprecise, deriving from religious exhortations rather than from the practice of law.

The fallow-year for the land, as earlier noted, was not known to the collection, a strong proof of its later interpolation in the Book of the Covenant, on which Deuteronomy otherwise stands. But, in the interest of widows, waifs, and metics, gleaning of the field, in the wine and oil garden, was prohibited (24:19 f.) and it was permitted to still one's hunger from the fruit of the field and vineyard of another (23:24, 25). Both are vestiges of ancient neighborhood rights between landlords and serfs, perhaps, also, a reflex of the usual relations between settled peasants and non-settled small stock-breeders.

The above indicates that seizure and debt right was the genuine area of this social law code also and to an even greater extent than in the Book of the Covenant. In place of the fallow year for the land, Deuteronomy recognizes a radical law of debt which was still unknown in the Book of the Covenant. Over and above the repeatedly stipulated six year limit on Hebraic debts (15:12) already recognized in the Book of the Covenant, it stipulates the duty of providing with a *viaticum* in kind the discharged debt slave, who, after all, has produced "surplus value." Above all, it insists upon the cancellation of all debts of a fellow Israelite, in contrast to those of the foreign born, in the "year of remission" (*shnath shmitta,* more precisely *shmitta kesafim*). In late Israelite times there is proof of the actual occurrence of the Sabbath year (*shmitta karka'oth*). Yet, despite emphatic legal threats against all evasions and despite the exhortation in the *coniuratio,* under Nehemiah (Neh. 10:31), at an early time, definitely by Hillel, a form was found, the so-called *prosbul,* which permitted the contractual suspension of the stipulations of the year of remission. No certain trace of the enforcement of all debt remission can be found. It was of exhortatory religious origin and remained utopian. Even the non-exhortatory, legally enjoined freeing of debt slaves, known to the Book of the Covenant as well as to Babylonian law, was not honored under Zedekiah, despite the especially formal resolution (*berith*) to do so. This resolution had been accepted in a political emergency and the failure to honor it led Jeremiah to pronounce the gravest threats of doom (Jer. 34:8 f.). Hence, it remains a question whether and to what extent the prescriptions of debt rights, particularly those of the remission year, originally were carried out. It is not improbable that at the bottom of these formulations lay an occasional practice of the remission of debts which the theological editors then formulated as a principle and brought into relation with the idea of the Sabbath, an idea which in exilic times became increasingly important. For in substance it was a *Seisachtheia,* as was known in the Mediterranean cities of Antiquity and is represented in the resolution under Zedekiah.

With the growing accumulation of pecuniary funds through commerce, the tension between the urban patrician and the usuriously exploited peasant developed into a typical class antagonism and was viewed as such. This is indicated with especial clarity in Deuteronomy where the ordinance of the remission year is directly followed by the famous promise: "thou shalt lend unto many nations but thou shalt not borrow" with the addition of the like meaning: "thou shalt reign over many nations but they shall not reign over thee" (15:6). In the present revision, the existence of a double responsibility makes it highly probable that the general seven year remission itself and this connected paragraph represent theological interpolations of exilic times. After repetition of the promise (28:12) the exactly corresponding threat (28:43-44) is expressed for the case of apostasy from Yahwe: "the *ger* that is within thee shall get up above thee very high; and thou shalt come down very low. He shall lend to thee, and thou shalt not lend to him: he shall be the head and thou shalt be the tail."—These are announcements in agreement with those of the prophets. Because of the manner in which the *ger* is mentioned, these paragraphs are obviously pre-exilic and, at the same time, they affirm most clearly that they are based on the aforementioned class antagonism. The medieval and modern money and pawn usury of the Jews, the caricature in which this promise was fulfilled, was certainly not intended by the holy promise. No. The purport of the promise was, rather, Israel will dwell in Jerusalem and will become the patriciate of the world, while other nations will be in the political situation of underlings and indebted peasants outside the gates, exactly parallel to the relationship between city and countryside which prevailed in every typical polis throughout early Antiquity from Sumerian-Accadian times.

Still in talmudic times the situation is presupposed which is, likewise, typical for all Antiquity, namely, the indebted peasant who has to cede his inherited property to the creditor, remains as a tenant, hence, as *colonus* on the land which formerly had been his own. But this must not be the inter-relationship of Israelite tribal brothers. Such is the meaning of the social debt-right and related religious exhortations. Originally, the merchant was always a metic, and even at the time of the revision of the sources this was often the case. This is indicated by the way in which the *ger* appears in the Deuteronomic threat of doom. However, urbanization had so deeply penetrated the Israelites themselves that the class situation of the city patriciate appears as its self-evident religious promise.[10] Israelite merchants dwelling abroad (Damascus) are first mentioned in the contract of Ahab with Benhadad (I. Ki. 20:34). In the Israelite cities themselves they had, naturally, existed earlier. Even today the grain trade in Palestine is the source of great exploitation of the fellah.—Deuteronomy, indeed, treats of urban conditions, as indicated by other stipulations of the law such as ordinances to secure the roof of a house by a battlement lest somebody fall down (22:8), asylum cities for homicides (19:3), the court "in the gates" (16:18), the commandment of right measure and weight (25:14, 15). Usury must not be practiced against a poor brother (23:20), rather, one should readily lend to him (15:8). This is a feature of the duty to help in times of need which is characteristic of the typical neighborhood ethic. In case of doubt this poor brother is, however, always a man in a city (15:7), that is to say, doubtlessly and regularly an Israelite settled as a small holding peasant in a city district (which now is considered a self-evident political unit).

2. Social Law of the Israelite Collections

THE present legal norms of Deuteronomy may well have originated in the pre-exilic times of the city kingdoms, but they are certainly revised by the theologians in Exile. Presumably this also holds for the so-called "Holiness Code"[11] only that here the contribution of the Exile theologians was substantially greater. The social prescriptions[12] found in this collection like those in the so-called "Priestly Code" originated entirely in Exile. This constitutes the bulk of the material of the present day third and fourth, and parts of Book Two of Moses.

These social prescriptions are controversial both with respect to their age and their actual validity. They are a product of the theological zeal for consistency. Reminiscences of the past were employed and they were addressed to "a people holy to Yahwe," a people of "Yahwe metics" on the sacred soil belonging to them, and to which they hoped to be led back by Yahwe. Beside the prohibition of usury we meet the stipulation of the Sabbath year which was, presumably, here for the first time brought into its present form and interpolated into the Book of the Covenant.

Alongside these norms we note a further modification of the norms of debt liability. One should not treat an Israelite imprisoned for debt (Lev. 25:39, 46) as a bondsman, but as a free day laborer with respect to whom (19:13) the stipulation in Deuteronomy concerning wage payments is repeated. Israelites may possess only Gentiles or metics (25:44, 45) as bondsmen, for all Israelites are God's bondsmen (25:42). If an Israelite was forced to sell himself to a metic his sib or he himself should be allowed at any time to ransom himself (25:48). All Israelite debt prisoners, moreover, should be freed every seven times seven years in the so-called Jubilee-year. In this "freedom" year to be announced by the peal of trumpets, each piece of real estate which—it is assumed without saying out of need (cf. Lev. 25:25)—has been sold would freely revert to the seller (25:13 f.), in case the closest sib-brother had not already redeemed it (25:25), which he has the right to do. For no sale of land forever should be admissible, inasmuch as the land is the property of God, and the Israelites on it are but the metics of God. This is further proof of the fact that the absence of a right to land was considered to be characteristic of the metic. Only houses within a walled city may be permanently sold and are redeemable only within one year (25:29). A far reaching casuistry regulates the annuities to be created toward the Jubilee-year.

It has been established that the Jubilee-year itself was never realized, but was a theological construction of exilic times. The type of motivation of the other prescriptions suggests the same pattern, although possibly there might have been points of departure for this in actual legal practice. In the first place the account of the release of slaves from debt under Zedekiah (Jer. 34:8 f.) seen in connection with the prophecy of a "year of grace (*schnath razon*) of Yahwe" by Trito Isaiah (61:2) show that the public announcement of a "year of manumission" (*Freilassungsjahr*) for all debt slaves had not only occurred under Zedekiah. It was a typical event, presumably in war emergencies when all able bodied men were needed. Similar practices also occurred among the Hellenes. Moreover, the stipulation of the reversion of land possessions to the sib may be a reminiscence of ancient law. For it is striking that only in this passage of the legal collections is there mention of the sale and purchase of real estate, about which the Book of the Covenant as well as Deuteronomy remain silent. Hence, the question is whether and under what presuppositions a permanent alienation of land was admissible in ancient Israel.

In Babylonian law the sib's ancient claim of retraction was gradually overcome. As is known from the oracles of Jeremiah a sib member had at least a customarily prescribed option in the case of an intended alienation of hereditary land. The entitled person would hesitate to decline his duty of honor to buy up land lest it fall to strangers. Also, in the tradition, Naboth replied to King Ahab's offer to buy, that heaven forbid that he sell his hereditary land. This shows that land sale without sib permission at the time of this revision of the story was *per se* considered legally possible. For the rest, the numerous passages of the prophets inveighing against land accumulation by the rich are proof of this. Custom, however, disapproved of the sale of hereditary lands.

Apart from the passage already mentioned in Deuteronomy, the Priestly Code is the single legal source which discusses hereditary land rights. Indirectly such hereditary land rights played a role in the ancient institution of the so-called levirate marriage. For the right and duty to marry the childless widow of the brother to "raise up seed" to him entailed the right and duty of taking over land holdings. In the case of refusal of the closest relative they fell to the more distant candidate who assumed the marriage duty. Or, according to the view of the tradition (Ruth 4:1 f.) the very reverse obtained. Whoever in the sib wished to have the land of the childless deceased had to marry the widow. As the entire tradition shows, at least in the time of the revision of the patriarchal legends, it was considered customary that the house-father before his death or when he retired (as is mentioned in the Sirachids), settled the division of his possessions among the children with rather far reaching discretion. In so doing, he gave weight to his dispositions through solemn blessings and curses. It went without saying that here, as in all military formations of Antiquity, only sons were heirs of the land. Deuteronomy sought, as mentioned, to protect the rights of the eldest son against the molesting of his preeminent share by the father, who, under the influence of a favorite wife, could easily treat the children unjustly as found in Egyptian accounts. The Priestly Code enforced further restraints. It stipulated the daughter's capacity to inherit land after the sons (Num. 27:8) and in addition it provided that such heiresses marry only within the tribe, lest the land be alienated from it. Such maidens, in whose favor, according to the legend, Moses made the stipulation, thereupon married cousins, hence, sib members. Tribe and sib were not always sharply distinguished and it may be assumed that here the sib and not the tribe was meant. For it appears that at least according to ancient law, as we said, the tribal foreigner in general was considered a *ger* and for this reason incapable of acquiring land.[13]

There were possibly other powers beyond the ancient sib relations which fashioned the structure of landownership. These stipulations may represent survivals of such influences.[14] We find in the Hellenic cities the *"kleros"* bound partly through sib claims, partly through military restrictions on alienation. The ancient Hellenic heiress-rights stemmed, if not alone, certainly in part from military interests. The Hellenic term for *kleros* corresponded, however, as Ed. Meyer has correctly observed, to the Israelite term for landlot: *"chelek."* The term had the secondary meaning of spoils (share in booty), hence it in no way originated in agrarian communism or the institution of the sib, but in military practice.[15]

Wherever military power rested on self-equipment of free landowners, land ownership was a function of military qualification. Similarly, the desire to preserve the "name" of the sib in Israel, which was decisive for the levirate and related institutions, had in addition to religious probably also military foundations. For the family register of economically qualified military sibs was the basis of the summons. The Song of Deborah seems to indicate that the confederation army estimate (40,000) was stated in round thousands. This agrees with the later role of the thousand as the normal contingent. Moreover, from the account of the levy against the tribe of Benjamin, it may be inferred that the quotas of this estimated levy—in this case, for example (Jud. 20:10)—one in ten were summoned. As the units of thousand doubtlessly were fixed assignments of the various confederation members, the tribe responsible for the provision of such a contingent, besides being interested in its own military strength, by virtue of this confederate army structure had an interest in preserving the landlots of the warriors. Hence one may assume that the individual tribe possibly had recourse to measures comparable to those of the Hellenic cities. There, as is known, it is not easy to decide which of the residual survival of the *kleros* restraints stemmed from ancient sib rights and which sprang rather from the interests of the army organization. Partly rudimentary, partly theologically disfigured survivals of various institutions are to be found in the sources. They range from the obscure stipulations of the Sabbath year and of the *seisachtheia* to the levirate and inheritance law of heiresses, the preferential portion of the eldest (as the *kleros*-heir), and the residue of sib-retraction of hereditary holdings. All of these might have had one of their sources in such militarily-determined measures.

The following phenomena could then be interpreted similarly. For want of a physical heir, according to the Abraham story (Gen. 15:2, 3), the head servant (in this case, even a house slave from Damascus) comes into the inheritance. This conception is in the interest in having an heir for the *kleros,* not in *who* he happens to be. On the other hand, the impoverished, that is to say, he who in an emergency had to surrender his land, ceases to qualify as a full Israelite and should, according to the Holiness Code (Lev. 25:35), be treated as a *ger*. All these institutions were intended to prevent a sib from descending from the stratum of those esconomically fully qualified for military service to the mass of those unable to raise the costs of military equipment (in Roman terms, the *"proletarii,"* the descendants) or even the landless (*gerim*). Later, in connection with the Naziriteship, we will consider some other hypotheses which are related to such possibilities. Yet, all this remains uncertain.

In any case this could hardly have held universally. The above mentioned confederate army organization of the Song of Deborah and the historical literature for North Israel did not with absolute necessity suggest such institutions. For the raising of the contingent was presumably an internal affair of the individual tribe and this could proceed in varying ways.

3. The Berith

TAKEN as a whole the sequence of these legal collections signifies an increasingly theological elaboration of the law.[16] Before we examine the sources and peculiarities of this process further, we should consider the external forms in which this "theocratizing" of the Israelite social order was consummated and the driving forces of the process.

A peculiarity of the Israelite social order finds expression in the very name of the oldest law book; *sefer ha berith,* "Book of the Covenant." What interests us is the important concept of *berith.*[17]

A *coniuratio* or oathbound league of opponents of Egyptian rule was already mentioned in the Amarna letters.[18] Also the name Khabiri for the enemies of the Egyptian governors appears in the Amarna tablets, which is sometimes identified with *Ibri* (Hebrews). In view of certain linguistic difficulties, recently the term has been related occasionally to the Jewish term *"chaber,"* i.e., "comrade." In post-exilic times this term signifies the "ritually correct full Jews" as well as *"cheber,"* "confederation." On the coins of the Maccabees[19] it designated the full Jewish community and in the older tradition too (for example, Jud. 20:11), it was occasionally utilized to designate the confederation army (*loc. cit.* in a holy war because of religious crime).[20] To be sure, the derivation of *Khabiri* from this word remains improbable.[21]

The fact that various oathbound confederations under divine protection existed throughout Israelite history *per se* is not peculiar. In Antiquity every political alliance, in fact almost every private contract was normally confirmed by an oath, i.e., the curse of self. Rather, the peculiarity consists in the first place in the extensive employment of the religious *berith* as the actual (or construed) basis of the most varied legal and moral relations. Above all, Israel itself as a political community was conceived as an oathbound confederation.

An Israelite, including a member of another tribe, who stood only in the relation of a *ger* to one spoken to, nevertheless addressed him as "brother" (*achim*) even as the Swiss speaker on official occasions must address his Swiss compatriots as "*Eidge-*

nossen." And as David, according to the official tradition, through *berith,* became the legitimate king, this tradition also makes the elders of the northern tribes negotiate his recognition with David's grandson Rehoboam in the manner of an imperial capitulation. However, it is also true that incorporation of cattle-breeding sibs in a Canaanite city, or, in reverse, the affiliation of, for instance, the Gibeonites as a tributary community with Israel was always consummated through a *berith* named sworn brotherhood. All *gerim,* including the patriarchs, are in their legal situation through *berith.*[22]

According to tradition, the sworn fraternizations were ritualistically consummated by the establishment of common meals among the participants (compare Gen. 26:30 with Jos. 9:14). The collection of laws which Moses announced at the behest of God was (Ex. 24:7) named the "Book of the Covenant" (*sefer ha berith*)[23] and so, too, were called the religious prescriptions which on God's request, he wrote on two tablets (Ex. 34:28) "Words of the Covenant" (*dibre ha berith*). Likewise the Deuteronomic *sefer hattorah,* the "Book of Teaching," which as such first appeared in II. Kings 22 is called the "Book of the Covenant," its contents "Words of the Covenant" in the following account of its acceptance as law under Josiah (I. Ki. 23:2).

In the Book of Joshua a tradition is preserved in which Joshua, after the complete conquest of the land, allegedly made a covenant (*berith*) with the people and wrote down its content in the "Book of the Torah of God." It cannot be established which of the different legal collections is referred to. Against this (Jud. 9:4) it is transmitted that in Shechem at Abimelech's time there is a "house" of a "covenant-baal" (*Baal berith*), the temple treasure of which served at the same time as the city treasure. And the tradition of Deuteronomy (chiefly, Deut. 27:14 f.)[24] recognizes a solemn ceremony, which was allegedly first held with the conquest of the land. According to later versions it was held by the representatives of six tribes on the Mountain of Gᵒrizim by six others on the Mountain of Ebal (between which lies Shechem). The four or five variations of the account give the following picture. The priests on Mount Garizim pronounce a solemn blessing on those who observe the holy commandments and on Mount Ebal they pronounce a solemn curse against those who violate them. It was mentioned (Deut. 27:2 f.) that these commandments were written on whitewashed stones (proving that even then cuneiform writing no longer prevailed—otherwise their age is problematical). Tradition at several places refers still to the ceremony (Deut. 2:26 f.; Jos. 8:30 f.; 23:1 f.). It could have existed in essentially this or similar form already in early times in spite of the later (Deuteronomic) tradition. For the sanctuaries on the mountains could hardly have been acceptable to this editor, especially since, according to tradition, there were memorial boundary stones (a custom objectionable to the Puritans) and the (likewise dubious) old oracular terebinth trees. Besides, Joseph's bones rested there (tomb cult) and images of deities were buried there according to what is apparently a Babylonian rite. The transmitted curse formula (Deut. 27:15 f.), the so-called "sexual Decalogue," enumerates twelve definite sins: idolatry, cursing against the parents, boundary violation, leading astray the blind, tampering with the rights of metics, waifs and widows, sexual sins (incest and bestiality), murder (secret manslaughter), corruption of judges. Even if the age remains uncertain, in view of their interrelations with the prescriptions of the Book of the Covenant, it is still quite probable that the "Confederation Baal" was the functional deity who, through regularly repeated curses, protected these enactments which the people had solemnly accepted.[25] According to a much disfigured tradition his cult is considered to have been introduced in Shechem following a dispute and agreement between Gideon and the East-Jordan tribes with Ephraim during the Midianite war (Jud. 8:1, 33); hence the Confederation-Baal was probably the guarantor of those confederate regulations through which Israel was newly constituted.

4. The Yahwe Confederacy and Its Organs

IN HISTORICAL times the inner political history of Israel developed through ever repeated ritualistic confederate resolutions toward the establishment in Jerusalem under Joash of the pure Yahwe cult. It led, later, under Josiah to the reception of the law of Deuteronomy which, according to tradition, occurred through *berith*.[26] Likewise, it led to the resolution under Zedekiah to obey the law and release debt slaves (Jer. 34:8 f.) and then again the solemn acceptance of the congregational constitution under Nehemiah. As in the cursing ceremony, numbers of particularly important statutes were seized upon and solemnly signed and sealed by the synactic sib heads in agreement with the meanwhile usual practice of officializing documents (Neh. 10). Decisive for the context under consideration were precisely the ancient, pre-exilic and, in these cases, law-producing *berith* of the people of Israel as a whole.

In clear contrast to the *berith*-contracts among individuals or contracts with metics, they were not contracts and fraternizations among partners placed under the protection of God as a witness and avenger of perjury. But for the old conception, advanced primarily by the so-called "Yahwist," the pre-exilic *b'rithot* were confederate covenants with God Himself. Hence, in avenging the violation of the covenant He insisted on His own violated treaty rights and not only on the claims of the contract observing party placed under His protection.[27] This important conception profoundly influenced the development of Israelite religiosity. The god of the prophets based his frightful threats of disaster on the violation of the contractual good faith sworn personally to him as a contractual partner. He in turn is reminded of the pledges which he has given by oath to the forefathers (thus, first Micah 7:20). From the very beginning the entire relation even of the legendary forefathers of Israel to god, in the conception later established by the Exile priests, was consummated through ever renewed covenants; through the covenant with Noah, that with Abraham, Isaac, Jacob, and, finally, the covenant of Sinai. Meanwhile, with the change of the idea of god the anthropomorphic conception of a bilateral pact had weakened into the concept of a divine ordainment, which was merely guaranteed by a special pledge. Inherently Jeremiah's hope for the future, too, is for Yahwe to conclude another covenant with his people only under more lenient conditions than given the fathers.

Whence stems this peculiarity of the Israelite conception? Some general political conditions and a special event in religious history conjoined in its origin.

The "covenant" concept was important for Israel because the ancient social structure of Israel in part rested essentially upon a contractually regulated, permanent relationship of landed warrior sibs with guest tribes as legally protected metics: itinerant herdsmen and guest artisans, merchants and priests. An entire maze of such fraternal arrangements, we saw, dominated the social and economic structure. That the covenant with the god, Yahwe himself, became a fundamental conception for Israel's own judgment of its place among nations was bound up with the following circumstances.

As observed earlier, all political organizations among Bedouins and stock-breeders were quite unstable due to their life conditions. All these tribal organizations tended now to split into sibs again to coalesce. The fate of the tribes Reuben, Simeon, Levi, Machir on the one hand, Judah on the other, offer examples. With this instability contrasts strikingly the extraordinary stability of a definite type of organization to be found precisely among these unsettled strata: namely, the religious order or "cult" organization of similar pattern. Apparently only such a religious organization provided solid basis for permanent political and military structures. Such an organization was that of the Rechabites: for centuries, from Jehu's time to Jeremiah we see their continued existence and religious-political activities. In the Nehemiah chronicle a Rechabite is mentioned. In the Middle Ages still, Benjamin of Tudela claims to have encountered them under a "*nasi*" (leader) in the Babylonian desert. And other travelers thought even to find traces of them in the nineteenth century near Mecca. Also, the strictly Yahwistic Kenite tribe, to which the Rechabites belonged, seems to have based its cohesion on religion. For Stade has made it at least very probable that the "sign of Cain," that is to say the tribal tattoo of the Kenites [28] was no mere tribal badge, but rather a primary sign of the cult community.[29]

The Indian badges of sect would represent the analogous phenomena. The grand example of a religious quasi-order of fundamentally the same kind on the same soil was, of course, Islamism and its warrior orders, which established the numerous and, indeed, lasting Islamic states.

Now, the point at issue is not that the life conditions of the

Bedouins and semi-nomads had "produced" an order whose establishment could be considered as something like the "ideological exponent" of its economic conditions. This form of historical materialistic construction is here, as elsewhere, inadequate. The point is, rather, that once such an order was established the life conditions of these strata gave it by far the greater opportunity to survive in the selective struggle for existence against the other, less stable political organizations. The question, however, why such an order emerged at all, was determined by quite concrete religious-historical and often highly personal circumstances and vicissitudes. Once the religious fraternization had proven its efficiency as a political and economic instrument of power and was recognized as such it contributed, of course, tremendously to the diffusion of the pattern. Mohammed's as well as Jonadab ben Rechab's religious promises are not to be "explained" as products of population phenomena or economic conditions, though their content was co-determined thereby. They were, rather, the expression of personal experiences and intentions. However, the intellectual and social means which they utilized and further the great success of creations of this very type are indeed to be understood in terms of such life conditions. The same goes for ancient Israel.

As the Rechabites owed their importance to their cohesive organization as an order, so, perhaps, Judah owed its cohesive organization as a tribe, representing a powerful political structure of fraternization, to a special Yahwe covenant. The tribe appears only late in Israelite history. It is not known in the Song of Deborah. The sources, occasionally, designate it in the manner typical of cattle-breeders as a sib. At the time of Moses' Blessing it was politically hard pressed; at the time of Saul it was a tributary tribe of the Philistines. Jacob's Blessing, however, knew it in a position of hegemony in Israel, at the same time as a wine peasant, whereas Abraham in the patriarchal legend derived from cattle-breeding circles, offered no wine to his heavenly guests, although he lived in Judaic Hebron famed for its wine. Hence the tribe had—though it hardly was established only by David, as Guthe assumes—nevertheless expanded its territory under him and settled down obviously mixing with Canaanites. The sibs which the official enumerations and genealogies later counted as belonging to the tribe of Judah were, in part, probably Canaanite, in part, obviously, Bedouin in origin, thus the Kenites, the temporary allies of Amalek. The tribe of Simeon was partially received in Judah, in part it settled among the Edomites. The earliest mention of a Levite designated him as a member of Judah. Apparently also the tribe of Levi in the main was absorbed by Judah. The independent position of the tribe maintained still under Saul, continued to exist in different form also under the Davidites. Under Solomon its territory, at least the greater part, did not belong to the provinces of the kingdom, but belonged to the royal house. In any case the tribe acquired its definitive size only through David's warlordism and presumably in connection with the acceptance of the pure Yahwe cult.

One of the peculiarities of the Yahwe cult, as especially Luther assumed, was that the priests held an important position in the judicial process through trial oracles. This suggests the assumption of a specifically religious fraternization as the basis of its firm tribal cohesion. The tribe would then have been composed of fragmentary elements of diverse ethnic descent through common worship and priests. This assumption would seem highly probable if the name "Jehuda" could be considered a derivative from Yahwe.

The Israelite confederacy itself, according to unambiguous tradition, represented a war confederation under and with Yahwe as the war god of the union, guaranteeing its social order and creator of the material prosperity of the confederates, especially of the requisite rain. This is brought to expression by the name "Israel" which was meant to designate directly "the people of the fighting god" or originally to be pronounced "Jesorel," and hence to signify the god "in whom one trusts." This last is improbable. In any case, "Israel" was no tribal name but the name of an association, at that, of a cult league.[30]

The name Israel has been made the designation of an eponym only by the theological revision of the legend of the hero Jacob, hence the shadowy character of this personification.

We must examine the structure of the league somewhat more closely.

The scope of the league varied. Israel must have existed in Palestine even in the time of King Merneptah, the alleged Pharoah of the Exodus, for it was mentioned in a well known inscription [31] of the time that the attacks of the royal army had decimated Israel's manpower and possessions. The manner in which it is mentioned shows that Israel, in contrast to the small and large city states was considered to be a non-urban association. As we saw in the Deborah war, the peasants on foot and their princes taking to the field on white asses, formed the core of the army fighting against the chariot drawn knights of the city kings. The Song of Deborah recognized as confederate members the co-belligerent mountain tribes of Ephraim and its two derivative groups, Machir and Benjamin. Furthermore, Sebulon, Napthtali, Issachar, and the tribes of Assar and Dan settled near the sea were included. Moreover, it recognized the stock-breeding tribes of Reuben and Gilead from east of the Jordan, which failed, however, to come to the aid of the confederacy. The Song mentioned the city of Meros separately as violating the covenant. The two collections of Blessings recognized the usual twelve-fold number of tribes: Machir was replaced by Manasseh, Gilead by Gad, Judah and Simeon were added and according as to whether Levi was included or, as in Moses' Blessing, was counted separately as a priestly tribe, Ephraim and Manasseh were counted as two tribes or jointly as the "house of Joseph."

In the time of the Song of Deborah, doubtlessly, neither Judah nor Simeon nor Levi were considered member tribes. At that time and later Ephraim or Joseph were undoubtedly held to be the core tribes of the confederation. This is proven by its precedence in the Song, its descent from the favorite wife of Jacob, and its characterization as her favorite son (grandson respectively). The tribe recalled in the Deborah Song its battles with the Bedouins and also in Jacob's Blessing there is reference to these "arrow men" as his opponents. In Moses' Blessing express mention is made precisely of this tribe and certainly on the basis of the old tradition of a relation to the Mosaic thorn bush epiphany. Hence, Ephraim was doubtlessly important in the events which led to the reception of Yahwe as the war god of Israel. The first army leader of the confederacy to bear a Yahwistic name in the tradition, Joshua, was an Ephraimite and was buried in Ephraimite territory. It was Yahwe who from Seir in Edom drew near in the storm and destroyed the Canaanites and was praised in the Song of Deborah as war god of the confederacy standing under Ephraim's hegemony. Among the Yahwe shrines belonging to Ephraim's territory was, above all, Shechem with the confederation stone. Yet it appears that the cult place proper lay outside the city which the tradition long held to be Canaanite.

Until the foundation of the North Israelite capital of Shomron (Samaria), Ephraim in the main has obviously remained an organization of mountain-dwelling free large peasants. Israel's power once rested so much on their war power that the tribal name later came into general use for the whole of the Northern Kingdom. However there appear to have been reminiscences of Reuben, Simeon, and Levi as the core of the confederation. They received precedence in the collection of Blessings and stemmed from the elder sister Lea. Judah, on the other hand, appeared only in relatively late Blessings and won its place first after David. Abner, the warlord of Saul, held the Judaeans still as "dog's heads."

As far as can be determined this unstable Israelite confederation till the time of kings had no permanent political organs at all. The tribes engaged in occasional feuds with one another. The religious international law, which, for example, prohibited the cutting down of fruit trees, applied—if at all extending back to ancient times—presumably to such feuds as occurred within the organization. The league members in the Song of Deborah partly withheld their support. Occasionally this led to their being cursed and to holy war against the oath-breaking member. There existed no common citizenship. Such was present, apparently, only in the tribe. To be sure, grave violation of metic rights, which every Israelite enjoyed in every other tribe, under certain circumstances was revenged by the confederacy. But there existed, obviously, no unitary court or unified administrative organ of any sort in times of peace. Confederate unity found expression in that a Yahwe certified war hero or war prophet regularly claimed authority also beyond the boundaries of his tribe. People came to him from afar to have him settle their legal disputes or to seek instruction in ritual or moral duties. Such is told of Deborah (Jud. 4:5), and the present-day version of the tradition transformed all charismatic war heroes of ancient confederate times into *shofetim,* i.e., into "judges" of Israel who allegedly followed one another in an uninterrupted series and had legal authority throughout Israel. Their last representative, Samuel, during his office allegedly yearly visited Beth-el, Gilgal and Mizpeh (I. Sam. 7:15, 16) in order to "speak justice." Then, after the election of the king and his own discharge he is said to have solemnly retired from office like a Roman or Hellenic polis-official, leaving public account and the summons to raise possible complaints against him (I. Sam. 12). The Samuel tradition is without question an anti-royalist construction of Deuteronomy which presents the behavior of a Yahwe-pleasing prince as a paradigm in contrast to the kings of the present.

What fundamentally was the place of the *shofetim?* Stade maintains [32] that the later tradition simply elevated the ancient war heroes of Yahwe to the status of peaceful "judges," while Klosterman, in a spirited manner, compared the "judges" of Israel to the "law speakers" (*lögsögumadr*) of the Nordic, particularly Icelandic practice, the bearers of the oral legal tradition and the forerunners of the fixation of law in writing.[33] In this way he sought particularly to explain the origin and literary peculiarities of the pre-exilic law books, which allegedly originated in the public instructions in the law by "law speakers." The hypothesis which Puukko especially criticized in detail, according to numerous socio-legal analogies has some validity.

Law has always developed first through legal oracles, precedents, responses of charismatically qualified bearers of legal wisdom. But such charismatic law speakers have not always had the specific place of the Nordic law speakers, whose office—for office it was—was closely bound up with the organization of the Germanic judicial community. The "judges" so-called in the present revision of the tradition, had clearly quite different imprint. They were, in general, far from actual bearers of legal wisdom. Tradition placed the normal legal counsel in the hands of the *zekenim* (elders). The ordeal, on the other hand, and the regular trial-oracle were the business of the priests. And, as will be noted later, the oracle in early times was obtained purely by mechanical means (lot). For the rest, the tradition mentions very different types of dignitaries who enjoyed traditional authority within the single tribe. Hence, there could be room for a charismatic juridical procedure only alongside all these sources of legal finding.

The figures of the *shofetim* whom the present day version of the so-called Book of Judges presents vary greatly in nature. If one disregards those merely reported existing (Jair, Ebzon, Elon, Abdon), we note that Samson was held to be a purely individual hero fighting out his feuds. Ehud, too, was an individual hero, only with the difference that he killed the oppressor of Israel. Othniel, Samgar, Barak, Gideon, Jephthah and probably also Tola were considered to be successful army leaders of Israel, in truth, apparently, of their own and neighboring tribes. Only a part of them were "judges" in Israel in time of peace. And this "fact" is only quite generally noted. The whole emphasis lies rather on their accomplishment as "redeemers," that is to say, saviors in grave war emergencies.

Beside this, in a police action of the confederacy represented as a holy war (Jud. 20:28), a priest from Elide lineage (Phinehas) appeared as oracle giver of the army. Eli is a pure priest. His sons were presented as priests, but at the same time as chosen leaders of the summons against the Philistines. This last named tradition concerning the Elides is highly dubious and late, the tradition concerning Samuel, however, is completely useless. He is at one time treated as a Nabim, at another as a seer, at still others as a preacher (I. Sam. 4:1), also as a Nazarite, as priest, and, finally, as a military leader. The time in which these representations were revised clearly no longer had any certain knowledge of the actual conditions of the times of the confederacy. The most reliable source, the Song of Deborah, shows the prophetess beside the leading Naphtalite war hero, Barak, who as army leader had quite a few allied dignitaries of other tribes at his side.

The tradition expressly knows and reports of Deborah and Samuel only that they "spoke law" regularly, that is to say, gave trial oracles upon request. The same is reported in the present-day revision of the Hexateuch of Moses. The establishment of "objective," permanently valid, legal norms and their fixation in writing is reported only of Moses and of Joshua, besides Samuel, in a certain legendary case of the determination of the king's prerogative after Saul's decision. In any case there was no room with the *shofetim* for a continuously functioning "law speaking" according to the analogy of the Germanic Nordics. Political oracles, not trial oracles, were given by "prophets" like Deborah. And politico-military decisions, not legal decisions or wisdom, were the specific function of charismatic *shofetim*.

With all this it is quite probable that both proven prophets as well as war heroes, were, in times of peace, requested to settle conflicts and that the secular war heroes, as usual, took these matters in hand as their prerogatives once they had succeeded in stabilizing the rule to the extent, for instance, of Abimelech. But even the first kings were not yet considered primarily to be bearers or even creators of law, but war leaders. With David, the tradition (II. Sam. 14:2 ff.) supposes that the king, in a given case, intervenes in a blood feud. Solomon, however, was the first apparently, systematically to take the administration of justice into his hands (I. Ki. 3:16 f.). There is the account of the construction of a hall of justice under Solomon (I. Ki. 7:7). Presumably because of this innovation he was held by posterity as a source of judicial wisdom. But at first there is no mention of an official concern for the unity of law even with the kings. Still under Ahab the court could bend justice by influencing the judges.[34] However, the king does not appear as a judge. For the first time in Jeremiah (21:12) the king appears sitting in court in the morning. However, the court taking up the case of the prophet himself (Jer. 26) consisted of officials (*sarim*) and elders (*zekenim*) with the men (*'am*) as judicial assistants (*kahal ha 'am*).

The tradition simply could not be what it is if the creation of law had been a primary attribute of the *shofetim* and their successors in power, the kings, or if it had been the source of legal collections now before us. The various ambiguous statements of the tradition mentioned are evidently a later insertion of a time which—as we shall see—juxtaposed the "good old law" and the ideal pacifistic prince to the degenerate present. Also, the legal collections themselves would certainly have been different if they had derived from an originally unified and regular official judiciary of Israel. For in that case they would certainly have had a lasting practical validity. Precisely the opposite is the case, at least for the rights of debt slaves as we saw. Hence, the most important part of the entire social right will not fit such a construction.

As elsewhere, law could develop in Israel from the legal practice of ancient places of court. A legal sequence, once passed, was valid as a precedent from which there was unwillingness to deviate. *Chuk* [35] appears to have been the old typical expression for the binding custom and legal usage established through precedents (Jud. 11: 39). The leader (in the Song of Deborah also the war leader) who, according to this established custom, delivered legal wisdom was called *"chokek"* [36] in ancient Israel. In the later sources, occasionally, as synonyms Torah, *gedah,* and *mishpat* were used. Among these Torah was, in precise speech, the oracle and teaching through soul-healing Levites. *Gedah* was a stipulation recognized by a resolution of the army assembly. Finally, *mishpat* was as much a "judgment" as a legal norm, hence, the most distinctly juridical of these expressions. With respect to norms, it appears to be preferably used for rationally formulated law [37] in contrast to *chuk.* The norms of the Book of the Covenant based on Babylonian influence were *mishpat* not *chuk.*[38]

However, both legal sources agreed in employing or determining only already valid or presumably valid or fictitiously assumed law. For the deliberate creation of new law in Israel, first the verbal oracle (in the name of Yahwe or *debar* Elohim) came into consideration. The theologians of later times also clothed their social-ethical injunctions in the categorical form of such a commandment: "Thou shallst . . ." The second form of deliberate creation of new law was peculiar to Israel, it was the solemn *berith,* always following an oracle. Naturally this was utilized only in cases of special importance, including single measures such as the freeing of slaves under Zedekiah as well as the recognition of permanent norms. According to the tradition the *berith* was so put to use for the acceptance of the Deuteronomic law book. The content of the present versions is disfigured through highly contradictory interpolations and what is presumably its true core is in no way the product of a public "law speaking" or, in general, of men knowing the law. But, as the tradition indicates, it is the product of a specific theological school. We may disregard its character for the time being. It cannot be ascertained how many *mishpatim* here, (chap. 12-26) which were taken from the legal tradition, originally belonged to the published compendium. In any case, they grew on the soil of city states. They were permeated by theological constructions and represent an intense theological development of the legal norms contained in the Book of the Covenant. Also the *mishpatim* of the Book of the Covenant could only have represented the smallest part of the common law of ancient Israel. They were completely unsuited for cattle-breeding communities and were also in no way specifically peasant law. What remains after subtracting the, presumably interpolated, theological constructions represents a compromise of interests presupposing the development of the typical ancient class antagonisms.

As Baentsch and Holzinger have correctly presented it, the formal structure consists of a fairly systematically ordered code of *mishpatim* (Ex. 21:1-22:16) to which single *debarim* are unsystematically appended. These are partially legal, partially moral, and partially cultic in nature. Substantively speaking the *mishpatim* without doubt show Babylonian influence reaching into the distant past. The formal juristic technique and precision for the purely profane *mishpatim* is quite considerable, for the *debarim* in part extremely deficient. Hence the revision of the juristic parts must have been in the hands of experienced practitioners of law. As the king and his officials are out of consideration they may have to be sought only in the *sekenim* participating in law finding and constituting an important place of justice in Northern Israel where many came to seek legal counsel. This was somewhat comparable to Shechem.

The content of these legal norms proper—in contrast to the appended and inserted moral exhortations—certainly does not stem from priestly law-finding. It is indeed questionable to what extent the claims of the priests in Deuteronomy to participate in law finding and to decide disputed cases agreed with valid law in pre-exilic times. In the time of kings, in general, one has rather to assume a declining significance of the old tribal oracle as is to be observed also for Babylonia.[39]

The claims in Deuteronomy suggest the valid law in Egypt in the time of the Amon-priests. The obvious part played by reflection on the God-pleasing and reasonable nature of the law to be instituted as valid and the addition of the *debarim*, confirm the inference that Deuteronomy represents a "law book," hence, a private, not a formally authoritative work. It came into being under the influence of theologically interested circles. It was enlarged and supplemented and became a popular work in the manner of the *Sachsenspiegel* or the collection of Manu.

CHAPTER IV

WARFARE AND WAR PROPHECY

1. Holy War, Circumcision, Nazarites

D URING the old confederacy in Israel there was no authoritative place of justice. There was only the intermittent, varying sway of the charismatic war heroes, the prestige of proven oracle givers and of old shrines of the war god of the confederacy (particularly, Shiloh). There were, finally, perhaps, also some periodic amphictyonic ritualistic acts such as are possibly represented by the Shechemite prayer and curse ceremony and the repeatedly mentioned annual Yahwe festivals in Shiloh (Jud. 21:19 and I. Sam. 1:3).

The confederacy became formally active only in times of a confederate war. Then the *gedah*, as the army assembly of all Israel was preferably named, meted out justice to the offenders of the law of war or the ritualistic and social commandments of Yahwe. As the expression *gedah* for "order" indicates, the army assembly could also promulgate general decrees. In both cases the army itself participated, as is usual in such cases, through acclamation of the motions of the war leaders which the duke chose from among the elders of the contingents and who, perhaps, occasionally bore the title "Elders of Israel." These, for their part, will previously have obtained an oracle.

The division of spoils, especially the share of non-combatants, was allegedly (according to Num. 31:27) regulated by firm principles. In the story of David's division of the spoil (I. Sam. 30:26), however, these principles of division appear as his innovation. The *casus foederis* of a confederate war, its army leader, and the object of the war were always charismatically and prophetically determined through inspirations and oracles sent by Yahwe as the warlord. Yahwe himself was held to be the true leader in a war of the confederacy. The violators of the covenant had denied aid to him personally and not simply to the sworn confederates. Therefore, like Jabesh, they are eradicated. A confederate war was, thus, a holy war[1] or it could become one and certainly in emergencies always was declared to be one. The *gedah*, the army assembled, was called, in the Song of Deborah (Jud. 5:11) and in the holy war against Benjamin (Jud. 20) quite simply the "men of God" (*'am Yahwe* respectively *'am ha'elohim*).

This had, in the first place, ritualistic consequences.

According to the tradition of Samuel, in the time of the Philistines, the portable field shrine, the "Ark of the Covenant" was brought into the army camp and, according to a priestly tradition, God was ritualistically requested to arise from it as His container or as the seat of His throne and to lead the army. Likewise, after the battle He was requested to resume His seat. Also the ephod, later a priestly garment, appears occasionally in the camp (I. Sam. 14:3; 23:6, 9; 30:7). Through curses against the enemies, oracles and vows before battle, magical blessings during battle, one sought to secure Yahwe's intervention. At least in times of great war emergencies, the requisite means included also human sacrifice, as was offered for the last time by King Manasseh.

Quite apart from these special vows to be found everywhere, the army, during holy war, had to practice the prescribed asceticism, particularly fasting and sexual abstinence. David and his following, the tradition assumes, were permitted to eat holy bread, if, as warriors, they had abstained from sexual intercourse. When the results of his adultery with Bathsheba were apparent, David recalled her husband Uriah in vain from the field, to make him have intercourse with his wife and thereby cover the track. Uriah, in accordance with military discipline, refrained from intercourse. An individual's breach of asceticism, especially of fasting, threatened all with the wrath of Yahwe, necessitating death for the transgressor. Only by the sacrifice of a replacement did the army save Jonathan, the son of Saul, from this fate.

One tradition also linked universal circumcision to the preparation for the invasion of Canaan under Joshua. The Israelites practiced circumcision in common with the surrounding nations, excepting the oversea immigrant Philistines. Above all, the custom was practiced by the Egyptians, from whom, according to Herodotus, the Syrians and Phoenicians had borrowed it. Circumcision is, perhaps, the one Israelite rite diffused from Egypt. As known, its origin is controversial. Perhaps, originally, it was not universally valid for the Egyptians, but only for the genteel strata.[2] In that case it would be related either to the initiation rites of warriors or the consecration of priestly novices. The consummation of the rite in childhood is certainly a product only of later times.

Abraham circumcized Ishmael in his thirteenth year.[3] The etiological saga of Moses and Zipporah in the Exodus indicates, on the other side, that circumcision was likewise believed to ward off daimonic influence in sexual intercourse. It remains quite controversial whether the relationship of circumcision to the promise of numerous descendants, repeatedly to be found in rabbinical tradition, is old. In the peaceable post-exilic time its indispensability for proselytes, at least, was obviously not absolutely fixed. In older pre-exilic times, the army-exempt *gerim*, that is the entire unsettled population of the land, was not subject to circumcision.

This could well be a primary indication of the origin of circumcision in warrior asceticism, which hypothesis remains most probable. On the other hand, each member of the household, also the slaves, according to prescription, to be sure of uncertain age,[4] were to be circumcised. This was held (Ex. 12:48) prerequisite to participation in the domestic Passover meal. The traces of origin, thus, remain somewhat dubious. Nothing certain can be gained from the fact that the uncircumcised (*'arel*) later enter a special hades (Ezek. 31:18; 32:19 f.).[5]

In any case, the uncircumcised stranger was especially considered to be a ritualistic barbarian, and the foreskin of the enemy, as in Egypt, in the manner of the Indian scalp, was considered a trophy. By far most probable, everything considered, is, that the rite originally was somehow related to warrior asceticism and the initiation rites of bachelor warriors. Whether there were any additional relations with some sort of phallic orgiasticism, customary in the country of its origin, may well remain forever obscure.[6] In any case hygienic, rationalistic interpretations, such as still appear, are improbable here.

Alongside measures to sanctify the army, there appeared, in holy war, the ritualistic taboo of the booty: its consecration to the war-god of the confederacy, the *cherem*, which continued to exist at the time of the post-exilic transformation into a pacified confessional community as excommunication of errant fellow believers.

In Israel, too, residues of private tabooing seem to be found. The tabooing and sacrifice of the whole or a part of the living and dead booty to God was, however, universally diffused. It was especially recognized in Egypt, where the king, by virtue of ritualistic duty, slaughtered the captives. The enemy was held as godless: no trace of chivalry is to be found in either of the two cases. The *cherem* in war could go to varying lengths, and the rules of the division of booty indicate that the tabooing of the total booty, of men, women, children, cattle, houses, furniture was not the rule. Partly, only the adult men, "all who pissed against the wall," or only the princes and notables were sacrificially slaughtered. Apart from holy war, as in Islam, the ancient Israelite law of war distinguished among enemies between those who voluntarily surrendered and those who continued to fight. The lives of the former were spared (Deut. 20:11). This was a practice both within and outside Canaanite territory. Only the prophetically influenced theory of the specific holiness of the God-promised land, as it first appeared in Elijah's time, demanded the absolute expurgation of idol worshippers from the territory (Deut. 7:2, 3). And only the theory of war prophecy, and later that of the Exile and the development of Jewry into a confession inclined to the fanatical principle that one should absolutely liquidate the enemy of the country.[7]

Apart from the fact that not all wars, but only those of the confederacy, and, perhaps, not always these, were held to be holy, the relative lateness of the ultimate consequences of the *cherem* is indicated in Saul's opposition to the demands which tradition places in the mouth of Samuel. The requirements of the *cherem* were carried out with inconsiderate sharpness also in the fashioning of the tradition. This essentially theoretically bloody war code produced that peculiar connection of an almost voluptuously cruel phantasy with the commandment of mildness toward the weak and toward metics which gave its imprint to many parts of the Scriptures.

In connection with the general warrior asceticism, Israelite warfare knew the phenomena of warrior ecstasy in its two forms known elsewhere.

Warrior ecstasy occurs either as collective ecstasy of the community or as individual ecstasy of the charismatic hero. The community ecstasy is produced by the war dance and the meat or alcohol orgy of the warriors. Some traces are found in the tradition. Most distinct is—what seemed weird to the Philistines —the war orgy of the Irsaelites (*teru'ah*, I. Sam. 4:5) upon the arrival of the Ark of Yahwe in the war camp. Presumably it was a war dance around the Ark. Then there was the occasionally mentioned (I. Sam. 14:32) eating of raw flesh and drinking of blood (hence, against normal ritual) after the victorious battle.

The individual ecstasy of the charismatic hero is very widely diffused among the heroes of the type of Tydeus or Cuchullin or the "runner amuck," and is to be found in typical form above all among the Nordic "berserks." Their ecstasy makes them plunge themselves into the midst of the enemy in a frenzy of blood-lust and makes them half unconsciously slaughter whatever is around them.[8]

A typical berserk of this type is Samson of the legend whether or not he originated in a Sun myth as the name (*shamash*) suggests. When the spirit of Yahwe seized him he destroyed lions, set fire to the fields, tore down houses, and with any implement at hand slew any number of men and practiced other acts of wild battle fury. He certainly stands as representative of a type in the tradition.

Midway between such individual heroes appearing as ecstatic berserk and the acute collective ecstasy of the war dance stands the ascetic training of a body of professional warriors for war ecstasy. Such is, in vestige indeed to be found in the "Nazarites,' the "separated ones." [9] Originally they were ascetically trained warrior ecstatics who—in the single certain tradition—left their hair unshorn and abstained from alcohol and originally, also, from sexual intercourse.[10]

Samson was also so considered and in the original legend he may well have perished because he allowed himself to be seduced, breaking the sexual taboo. The Nazarites, as core of the army are to be found in the doubtlessly ancient Blessing of Moses of Joseph (Deut. 33:16) and the "long growing hair" of the men (*'am*) who consecrated themselves for battle (*hithnadeb*) appears at the beginning of the Song of Deborah.

In the later pacifistic development the Nazariteship is transformed into an asceticism of mortification by virtue of a vow to lead a ritualistically exemplary life, above all, to abstain from uncleanness. This the Nazariteship certainly was originally not, for Samson of the saga touches the carcass (of the lion) but was held to be a Nazarite. The transmitted Nazarite ritual (Num. 6) already had this character. Originally, alongside magical preparation for ecstasy, the prescriptions aimed at preserving full physical power. The old demand of Yahwe for the sacrifice of all human first-born in the old law books was replaced by a redemption fund. According to Count Baudissin's hypothesis it originally signified the obligation of the confederates to consecrate Him the eldest as a Nazarite, that is, as a professional warrior. With this one might combine, furthermore, the prescription of the double hereditary portion for the eldest, to make him economically qualified. All this remains a subjective guess which cannot be validated. More than anything else the close connection between Nazarites and "first-born" in Moses' Blessing of Joseph (Deut. 33:16, 17) might speak for it. In any case, mention of the Nazarite in both Blessing formulae concerning Joseph makes it probable that this tribe at the time of the Blessings contained a core of Yahwistic crusaders, a kind of Yahwistic war order, hence (if one will permit the expression) the depository of war power. It is impossible to know more exact details.

2. *The Nebiim*

WE CAN recognize but dimly the relation of the ancient Nazariteship to the Nebiim, another phenomenon of the time of
the old peasant army.[11] Both had close connections. In the tradition, Samuel was consecrated by his parents to Yahwe service
in a manner which suggests the Nazariteship, and a dubious
tradition considers him to be a war hero against the Philistines.
On the other hand, however, he was held also as a Nabi and
head of a Nebiim school. The Nazarite, the ecstatic warrior—
however one may evaluate this tradition—stood near the Nabi,
the magical ecstatic. That the Nazarite and Nabi shade off into
one another is in perfect agreement with what is known of other
organizations of crusaders.

The Nebiim are in no way phenomena peculiar to Israel or
the Middle East alone. Neither in Egypt (before the time of the
Ptolemies) nor in Mesopotamia is there documentary evidence
for the existence of similar forms of ecstasy. It is found only in
Phoenicia. This is certainly merely due to the discrediting of the
orgiastic cults and to the bureaucratic rules and regulations and
prebendal patterning of mantic art in the early times of the great
kingdoms even as in China. In Egypt only the incumbents of
special forms of temple prebends are called "prophets." In Israel,
however, as in Phoenicia and Hellas, and as in India, prophetic
ecstasy in the absence of bureaucratization remained a vital
force. In Israel especially, in the time of the war of liberation,
as mass ecstasy it was bound up with the national movement.
Obviously, the Israelite Nebiim did not essentially differ from
the trained professional ecstatics found elsewhere. They were
recruited according to personal charisma largely from among
plebeians as their pejorative treatment by the later tradition indicates. They apparently tattooed themselves on the forehead
(I. Ki. 20:41) like the Indian mendicants, and wore a costume
including, above all, a special kind of coat. It seems that the
leaders of the school (the "fathers") designated their disciples
or successors by throwing their magically efficacious coats over
them. They pursued their common exercises in special habitats,
apparently at times on the mountains (as, for example Carmel).

But Nebiim were also mentioned in such Israelite places as Gibeah, Rama, Gilgal, Beth-el, and Jericho. Permanent asceticism or bachelorhood is not reported of them (II. Ki. 4:1). Music and dance here, as elsewhere, were means of evoking ecstasy (II. Ki. 3:15). The Nebiim of the Phoenician Baal, which under the Omrid dynasty found entrance in Northern Israel, used a halting dance around the altar with orgiastic self-punishment as rain-making magic.

The practices of the Yahwe Nebiim included besides self-punishment (I. Ki. 20:35 f.) and the wounding of one another also the production of cataleptic states and nonsense speech without our knowing more precise details. The purpose was to acquire magical force. The miracles which (II. Ki. 4:1 f.; 4:8 f.; 4:18 f.; 4:38 f.; 4:42 f.; 6:1 f.; 8:1 f.) were told of Elisha, the last master of the guild, are quite typical of professional sorcery as found in legends of Indian and other magicians. Those magic tales, including those transmitted of Elijah, permit us to recognize that the Nebiim, like all such ecstatic sorcerers, partially were sought after as medicinemen, partially as rain makers. Partially, however, they acted, like the Indian naga and the most comparable dervishes, as field chaplains and probably also directly as crusaders.

As war prophets the Yahwe Nebiim appeared in Northern Israel with the beginning of the National wars, actually religious wars, above all, in the wars of liberation against the uncircumcised Philistines. Ecstatic prophecy obviously made its appearance then though probably not for the first time, but it appeared in all genuine wars of liberation—of which the first was the Deborah war. This prophecy at first had nothing to do with any sort of "prediction" (indeed, the oracle in the time of Gideon was purely by lot), but its business was, as with Deborah, the "mother of Israel," the incitement to crusade, promise of victory, and ecstatic victory magic. There is no certain proof of the direct connection between this ecstatic war prophecy of individuals and the later schools for Nabi ecstasy. The Song of Deborah and the Book of Judges did not know the latter.

However, there certainly was a relation between them. For the war ecstasy was in no way confined to individual ecstasy of charismatic berserks and war prophets of early times and the mass ecstasy of the dervish bands of the later times of the peasant army. Intermediary links are to be found everywhere. Not only did a considerable part if not all of the charismatic war leaders of the so-called "time of judges" have the character of warrior ecstatics, but this is especially transmitted of the first king of Israel in connection with relations to the Nebiim.

According to one tradition which no longer understood earlier conditions, Saul, after receiving his anointment and with it the "spirit of Yahwe," directly before his public appearance as king, found himself allegedly "by accident," in the company of Nebiim. He was seized by Nabi-ecstasy (I. Sam. 10). But also later when still engaged in his struggle against David (I. Sam. 19:24) upon another, allegedly accidental, visit to Samuel's Nabi-schools he was seized by ecstasy and went around naked, spoke madly and for an entire day was in a faint. At the news of Jabesh's negotiations to capitulate he was seized by holy fury sent by Yahwe; he cut up the oxen and with a religious curse against the tardy he summoned all Israel to the war of liberation. His explosive fury against David is valued by the Davidian tradition as resulting from an evil but likewise Yahwe-derived spirit. He was obviously a warrior ecstatic like Mohammed. However, even as Saul, David also frequented Samuel's Nabi dwellings. He danced before the Ark of the Covenant as it returned in triumph. From such information the precise relationship can no longer be determined in detail, but it certainly existed.

Like the ecstasies of Saul, so later tradition excused also this ecstatic act of David with some consideration. To the later tradition these acts appeared to be unkingly. Michal, David's wife, stated expressly that a king should not behave "like a plebeian." And the proverb has it: "Is Saul also among the Nebiim? Who is their father?" quite correspondingly expressing disdain for such undignified plebs.

On the one hand, the changed position of the cultured strata of later kingly times in which they were opposed to the ancient ecstatics is influential in this. On the other, the place of these dervishes meanwhile had changed because of transformations in the structure of the kingship since David established his capital in the city. The transformation was definitive with Solomon. Before his establishment as a city-king David was a charismatic prince in the old sense, who was by success alone legitimized as anointed by God. When, therefore, the Amelekites robbed the herds and wives of his following the danger was that his following might hold him responsible and make short shrift of him. That changed with the definitive establishment of the hereditary charisma of the city-dwelling monarchy and the transformation of the military organization which followed thereupon. Solomon imported horses and chariots from Egypt and created, therewith, the army of knights. The royal household provided at least for the bodyguards and for part, if not for all, of the charioteers (I. Ki. 10:26) who, under Solomon, appear quartered in special "cities for chariots." Since that time, presumably in the revision of the tradition, the army, for instance the chariot army of the Pharaoh, was called simply his "wealth" (*chail*), its royal overseer the *sar chailim*. To this were added liturgically-obligated royal artisans and forced labor of the subjects for the palace, fortifications and Temple construction and, also, for the tillage of the expanding royal desmesne. Furthermore, there were royal officials with prebends and land grants as officers and at least in the residence also as judges; a royal drill master for the army contingents; a crown treasure as a means of power and to reward the stalwart followers, and, to feed the treasure, the king's personal trade on the Red Sea. There were tributes from subject foreign territories, but also regular taxes in kind from the subjects. The territory was divided into twelve districts taking monthly turns in provisioning the royal table. Finally there were also corvées in the Egyptian manner. A regular harem appeared with kinship ties and alliances with the rulers of the great powers, above all, with Egypt and Phoenicia, affording opportunity to engage in world politics. This led to the import of foreign cults, in part only in the form of court chapels for the strange princesses; in part, however, it also led to the incorporation of strange gods into the home cult. Such were the prompt ramifications of kingly power. Thus kingship acquired the typical features of the great warpowers of the Orient.

The royal scribes, the chancellor, the major domus, the rent master and the typical Egyptian rank title "friend of the king" (*re'ah hamelech*) made their appearance. Also secular offices were filled with priests or sons of priests as expert scribes (I. Ki.

4:1 f.) and that means here, as always, the rise of schooled priests to power in place of the charismatic ecstatics. To this must be added the following. Solomon, by all these means sought to establish a rigidly-organized political structure out of the loose confederacy of peasants, herdsmen sibs, and small mountain cities. Twelve royal territorial administrative districts replaced the tribes united by the Yahwe covenant. These now became phyles as existed in all ancient city states for the repartition of the state taxes. The greatest part of the ruling tribe of Judah seems to have been exempt, sharing the royal prerogatives (*als Hausmacht*) as in most monarchical state structures. For the rest, the organization mostly employed the boundaries of the old tribes as points of departure. The division of Joseph into Ephraim and the two Manassehs is probably connected with this. The stereotyping of the twelve tribes of Israel was possibly only then brought to its conclusion. After the foundation of Samaria, the repeated defection of the northern tribes did not at all prevent both kingdoms from retaining this character henceforth. With this, however, and particularly with the increasing importance of the army of chariot fighters, the ancient ecstatic hero charisma like the confederate army summons inevitably declined in importance.

The standing army, the royal bodyguards and mercenary troops gained in importance at the expense of the old peasant summons. The old *gibborim* may well have represented *classis* (in Roman terms) capable of full hoplite duty of the confederate army. With the mounting costliness of equipment, however, they became a knighthood. The summons of the common freemen increasingly lost importance, favoring the knighthood. The basis of royal military power increasingly consisted of magazines and arsenals, which were mentioned especially for Hezekiah (II. Chr. 32:28).

This led to the demilitarization of the peasant strata already mentioned. The results of urbanization compared to those of the old confederacy are somewhat like the hegemony of the *"Grossmächtigen Herren von Bern"* to the original peasant league of the Swiss cantons. In Israel this was essentially sharpened, however, through the additional domination of the corvée kingship. One knew full well that the ancient confederacy and its army had had a different social appearance. The new taxes and kingly corvées occasioned bitter feelings.

The old fighters for freedom, the Nebiim, were hard hit by these changed conditions. They had been the religious leaders of the old peasant summons. Miriam, Deborah, according to the later (questionable) tradition, also Samuel, the old berserk heroes and the bands of dervishes were viewed in popular memories as the champions of the truly pious heroism, "inspired" by the war god of the covenant. The enemy had been the chariot fighting knights—Egyptian, Canaanite, and Philistine—against whom Yahwe through the awakening of heroic and prophetic ecstasy had led the peasant army to victory.

Now, however, the army of their own king became itself a levy of trained chariot-fighting knights and mercenaries of foreign birth among whom there was no longer room for the Nebiim and Nazarites. Hence the Nabi-ecstasy and the Nazarite-asceticism, too, were demilitarized—in religious history a very important element in inner political development. We have already seen how the disgust of court society with the ecstatic dance of David was put into the mouth of Michal. The Nabi sent by Elisha, the head of the Yahwe-Nebiim, to offer the warlord the anointment as counter king is called a "fool" by an officer of Jehu. During this Yahwistic revolt of Jehu, supported by the Rechabites against the Omrid dynasty the ecstatic Nebiim under the leadership of Elisha once more appeared as a political factor. It is striking, however, that in the accounts of the Nebiim of Elisha the ecstatic phenomena appear far more tempered than in the Saul and Samuel tradition: not vagrant delirious Dionysian bands, but resident schools stimulated by music to ecstasy are its champions. And this is the last time we hear of them as a political factor in this form. The next reference is negative: the prophet Amos under Jeroboam II protests that he is not a Nabi. This obviously meant a professionally trained ecstatic, who makes a business of ecstasy, for in other passages Amos, too, uses the term "Nabi" as a title of honor. But the scriptural prophets repeatedly complain of the mendacity and corruption of the Nebiim. And the reference is always to professional ecstatics.

The sources show clearly that professional Nabi ecstasy was

only partially politically oriented; for the rest, it was the simple trade of the magicians. Obviously these free Nebiim had no national Israelite character. Under given conditions they made their services also available to non-Israelites. Elisha went to Damascus and the enemy of Ahab, King Ben-hadad, sent for his counsel. To his captain sick with leprosy Elisha recommended a magical medicament by which he was converted into a Yahwe believer. He prophesied to the war leader of the Damascus king, Hazael, later the deadly enemy of Israel, that he was destined to wear the crown of Syria. Likewise, as an ecstatic sorcerer he was on request at the disposition of his king in the Moabite war. However, he did not enter into fixed service: tradition viewed him as the leader of a community of free Nebiim.

In Phoenicia Nebiim in kingly service were ancient. King Ahab had Baal Nebiim of his Phoenician wife in his service. But since he gave his children Yahwistic names he certainly also had Yawhe Nebiim. In a manner typical of yore in Syria, both groups were prebendaries who lived off the royal table. Apparently already at that time there was a category of Nebiim who shunned any exploitation of ecstatic charisma for profit. This standpoint is ascribed to Elisha with questionable justice. He afflicted the student who accepted compensation with leprosy. This agrees with what we find also among the intellectual strata of other lands including the Hellenic philosophers, as a matter of honor. Amos' rejection of the title of Nabi stemmed from these views.

The professional royal Nebiim as well as this stratum of free Nebiim, however, viewed themselves as guardians of the pure Yahwe tradition. With the elimination of their direct military function as crusaders through the chariot technique, there remained for the first only a sort of magical field chaplainship. Hence, they were now impelled to develop primarily the second gift peculiar to such ecstatic men, that of ecstatic prophecy.

3. *Nabi Ecstasy and Prophecy*

THE relation of Nabi ecstasy to prophecy is doubtlessly old as is suggested even by the connection of the (non-Hebraic) word "Nabi" with the name of the Babylonian oracle god. That the Phoenician city kings already in the time of the Ramassids employed ecstatics as prophets, and acted in accordance with their prophecies, like the Mesopotamian kings according to the oracles of the temple priests, is indicated for Byblos by the travel description of the Egyptian scribe and emissary of the Amon priest Wen Amon, of about the time of the Song of Deborah. One of the prophets of the king in ecstasy gave an oracle which recommended good treatment for the guest and was followed.

The old charismatic war princes of Israel had either personally asked the god directly for an omen or they bound their decision to definite signs. So, according to the tradition, did Gideon three times. Or they were incited to war by an ecstatic Nabi, as was, particularly, Barak by Deborah. For the first time with Saul does the historical tradition report a personal consultation of a "seer" (Roeh) who was at the same time a Nabi (Samuel), requiring an oracle and a magically efficacious blessing for his own, and a curse against the enemy army. The same accomplishments are then ascribed by the legend for previous times to the political charms of the Roeh Balaam. The somewhat obscure references (Num. 24:1) indicate that this Moabite or Midianite was considered to be an ecstatic. The legend introduces him as having been brought by the inimical king and compelled against his will by Yahwe to bless Israel. This, however, stemmed from later conceptions of the character of the prophetic calling. Balaam's blessings for Israel and threats of doom against Amalek, Cain, and Edom correspond to the typical prophecies of good fortune.

The historical situation presupposed corresponds to that of the times of the first kings. Hence, one may consider the sayings ascribed to him as the first certain representation of prophecy of good fortune for all Israel. The reproaches that were later made to Balaam (Num. 31:16) suggest the interrelation of the figure of Balaam with the kind of ecstacy typical for Northern Israel. This holy speech suggests some earlier prayer formulas of the collections. Thus the blessing of the tribe of Joseph in Jacob's Blessing (Gen. 49:22 f.) is to be found in the older version in Moses' Blessing (Deut. 33:13 f.). It differs, however, from Balaam's saying in that it obviously did not aim at magically influencing definite political events. It was not holy prophecy, but presumably a song of praise, which bards chanted at tribal festivals in praise of the beautiful and fertile land of the tribe, together with an entreaty for the blessing of the thorn-bush dwelling Yahwe for the brave Nazarites and first-born of the tribe. Similarly, the later prayer of Moses concerning Judah (Deut. 33:7) doubtlessly entreated the blessing of this tribe, which was held to be hard-pressed by the enemy but designated to achieve hegemony of the confederacy. Its character seems to have been essentially literary. Other tribal sayings are, in part, general songs of praise of the landed possessions or of the army of the tribe, or the reverse, censorious or ridiculing verses or, as with Reuben, Simeon, Levi, *ex post facto* justifications for their decline. All of them, however, lack true prophetic character.

Only the saying for Judah in Jacob's Blessing (Gen. 49:8 f.) bears a different imprint. Alongside the praise of the wine-blessed Judaic land it contains the affirmation that this tribe would retain the scepter and that from it the great hero of Israel would come. The speech is quite apparently a product of the great power development of David and doubtlessly *vaticinatio ex eventu.* However, it is in the nature of a prediction of good fortune in the form of a king's prophecy. In time it is presumably the oldest preserved product of this kind of Israel. In all Oriental courts, especially, also, in neighboring Egypt this kind of court prophecy of good fortune was known. Since David it was practiced by Israelite royal prophets.

Whereas the Judah speech still holds out good fortune to the king's tribe in its position of hegemony, the typical king's prophet promised good fortune to the king. The king's primary concern in this was to secure the continued existence of his dynasty through an unambiguous and efficacious oracle. The oldest transmitted prophecy of good fortune (II. Sam. 23:1 f.) of the Davidian dynasty appeared in the form of the insistence that such an oracle was given personally to David by Yahwe. Here the king's prophet put his saying in favor of the dynasty into the very mouth of the first king, whom tradition treated as a Yahwe inspired ecstatic on the throne. A later tradition is friendly to Solomon and his Temple and may well be the same which sought to sustain his doubtful legitimacy by making Nathan, viewed in the preprophetic tradition as a free "seer," into a factitious courtier who after David's death intervenes in court and priestly intrigues. This friendly tradition puts an appropriate promise of good fortune for Solomon into the mouth of this prophet promising, in connection with the Temple construction, that the Davidian throne will exist for all time (II. Sam. 7:8 f.). If great age may be ascribed to the oracle, then it would be the earliest preserved example of holy prophecy of the later type.

Of the later kings of Israel, the tradition records that Ahab especially used his apparently rather numerous courtly Nebiim as oracle givers, and thus, as givers of magically efficacious promises of good fortune. Under the strictly Yahwistic dynasty of Jehu for the first time were cases such as the following recorded (II. Ki. 14:25). Jonah, the son of Amittai of Gath in Galilea had given an oracle—doubtlessly during the arduous war against the Arameans—said to have been fulfilled. Allegedly, he had predicted that a king would appear who would restore the boundaries of the Davidian kingdom. This had been fulfilled through the war deeds of Jeroboam II who thus was the prophesied king. Hence, here the prophecy of a savior king appeared not only as a literary form—as in the Judah saying in the Jacob Blessing—but as a real oracle. Doubtlessly we here meet, too, with a king's prophet of good fortune. Their continuous employment in both part-kingdoms is also otherwise ascertained and is sufficiently well documented by the sharp words of the later independent writing prophets against the lying prophets of the kings.

4. Changing Forms of Prophecy

AS ONE may see from the above, the present day version of the tradition no longer distinguishes between "Nabi" and "Roeh." Rather it maintains, occasionally expressly, Roeh to have been the older name for Nabi. In this, tradition understands by Nabi the later scriptural prophets. This is plainly incorrect.

All the hopeless unclarity in which figures such as Balaam, Samuel, Nathan, also Elijah, today appear to us, derives not only from the fact that here, as usual, the transition of the types was fluid, but from the tendentious expurgation and obfuscation of the old contrasts. What the typical Roeh originally was is indicated by the account of Nathan's cited oracles of good fortune. He was a man who gave oracles on the basis of dream interpretations, hence successfully interpreted either dreams of his own or (like Joseph in the novelistic tradition) of others. Or, most important, in a state of apathetic ecstasy, he had visions. What differentiated the Roeh from the old Nabi was, above all, the non-employment of orgiastic frenzy and mass ecstasy. The Roeh had his visions in solitude. His patrons visited him to seek his counsel. As a general rule—though not always, as indicated by Nathan—the Roeh was believed to have magical powers. Apparently the "man of God" (*ish haelohim*) was used for such Roeh who commanded magical powers. Samuel's place in the historical tradition is, perhaps, to be explained originally from the fact that he, first, in the time of the wars of liberation, had utilized dream and clairvoyant vision for political oracles, the forms of Yahwe revelation which since were admitted as classical. Nathan and Gad (II. Sam. 24:11) under David, Ahiah of Shiloh under Solomon and Jeroboam (I. Ki. 15:19), Jehu, the son of Hanani, under Baasha appear to have belonged to this type. Later they were lumped together with the Nebiim—free or king's prophets. The giving of political oracles was apparently not the original nor, indeed, lasting form of primary activity of the "seers." On the other hand, the official oracles of the employed Yahwe priests, political and judicial, were by lot, not by dreams or visions.

Also, Roeh-ecstasy was at first private business. The tradition still recounts how everyday questions of all sorts, for example, of the finding of the she asses, were brought before the seer and how the oracles, rendered by virtue of visions, were compensated by gifts (I. Sam. 9:6, 7). To be sure, the later tradition considers the man of God and seer particularly as one who announces the will of the god of the covenant to the respective authorities: the elders or the king or to a hero whom he wishes to awaken as a charismatic war-lord. This is already represented by Samuel and Nathan. The prophetically influenced contemporary revision, particularly that of the Deuteronomic school which elevated Samuel, obviously substituted quite a different figure for the free "seer" of old.

All the types discussed belonged to the settled peasant tribes of the North. This was no accident as will be shown later. The cattle-breeding tribes and their genuine Yahwism knew, however—and again not by chance—other ways in which the godhead made known his will. The oldest is the epiphany. It is found among all the patriarchs, in the historical tradition, next in the legendary gathering of the people in Bochim (Jud. 2:1), last, however, with Gideon. Yahwe himself has already changed into a divine messenger. For in the eyes of the later tradition, only Moses had seen Yahwe face to face. What matters is that the recipient of the epiphany always hears the corporeal voice of Yahwe or his messenger and receives no more dream vision. This is again another prophetic type.[12] Its representatives claim to be the superiors of those "dreamers of dreams" whose visions were uncertain and uncontrollable.

In later times of classical prophecy this remains the same. The decisive characteristic is that one must have personal intercourse with Yahwe. One must have stood "in the counsel" of God and have personally heard the voice of the Lord if the oracle is to be valid. For this branch of the tradition dream oracles were held to be unclassical and deceptive, and the seers who merely interpreted dreams were suspect. In spite of the violent struggle against them, especially by Jeremiah, dream interpretations in later post-exilic time (Joel 3:1; Dan. 2:1 f.) regained prestige under Babylonian influence. In any case they were never completely rejected. Nevertheless, at least in pre-exilic times, the development of a priestly teaching of dream interpretation in the manner of the Mesopotamian dream books was not possible. Combinations of "seeing" and "hearing" appeared. Amos was called *choseh* by his opponents and his inspirations were combinations of "visions" with auditory interpretations of these by Yahwe. However, they were real waking visions. The prevalence of audition with him, too, is decisive for the type.

The temperament of an auditory prophet who is not inspired in apathetic ecstasy by dream visions, but is emotionally stirred by voices, is naturally far more excitable and active than that of a dream visionary. Thus the name "Nabi" came to be used also for these oracle givers. Their type left its imprint on the tradition. The "man of God" henceforth became above all one who communicates the will of the god of the covenant to the holders of political power. He did so partially in answer to questions as did the Nebijah Huldah under Josiah or Jeremiah under Zedekiah, partially, and increasingly so, without his being asked, regardless of whether the oracle would please the holders of political power or not. In fact, it was given precisely when it was unpleasant.

Tradition held Samuel to be the first prophet whose prestige allowed him to do this. In later interpretations, the possibility was emphasized that a man without office and not belonging to the priestly sibs might be seized by this prophetic spirit of Yahwe. Apparently interested parties occasionally contended this. However so important did the pattern become that it lead to the creation of a special Mosaic paradigm for this (Num. 11:26) in Eldad and Medad. In the legendary figure of Elijah this type reached its climax and at the same time inclined toward the new type of the later scriptural "prophet." Elijah differed from the old "man of God" in that he addressed his oracles, at least in part, to the politically interested "public" and not alone to the authorities: kings or elders. Elijah is the first specifically "clerical" figure of Israelite history. The biased tradition of the Nebiim brought him at least indirectly into connection with the Nabi-school of Elisha, which still retained a traditional character. Elijah has been made into a magician of the type of Elisha only by legend and by the endeavor of this epigonus of the ancient Nebiim to pose as Elijah's successor, an endeavor which even in the tradition shows as ambitious "straining."

Elijah's appearance obviously was so impressive because, in contrast to the ecstasy charms of the Baal Nebiim, he used no means other than the plain imploration of Yahwe by prayer. As we shall see, it was not by chance that tradition consider Elisha to be an independent peasant, while Elijah the Tishbite hailed from across the Jordan, hence from steppe-territory. He led a migratory life roving over the entire territory of Yahwe-worship up to Mount Horeb. He was threatened with death by the queen of the Northern Kingdom, while Elisha acted as war magician of Ahab. Elijah received his commands from Yahwe in solitude and announced them personally as the emissary of his God, as the Yahwistic view of the time usually ascribed it to the epiphanies of Yahwe's angels. His incomparable prestige rested on this and upon his hitherto unheard of lack of discretion in standing up to the political power holders. Historically he is important as the first fairly ascertainable prophet of doom. In this he is the forerunner of a series of grand figures which for our present day literary sources begin with Amos and end with Ezekiel.

They became the intellectual leaders of the opposition against kingship and all its (actual or alleged) innovations from tabooed strange and Canaanite cults to social pressure against the one time pillars of the confederate army summons. As with the apathetic-ecstatic dream visionaries, solitariness was their decisive characteristic, setting them off from the Nebiim with their orgiastic mass ecstasy. The psychological reason, however, differed greatly from those of the dream visionaries as we indicated above, and will discuss later.

The sociological reason for the prophets' solitude was, in the first place, the fact that the prophecy of doom could not be taught professionally like that of good fortune. Further, it could not be exploited for profit, for no one would buy an evil omen—and such was every oracle of doom. Moreover, all social authorities and communities would avoid the prophets of doom or would, indeed, outlaw them as destroyers of the people and of all good omens. Hence, the prophet's solitude as well as his rejection of remuneration for oracles, here first raised to a principle, were socially determined and only in part voluntary. Micah (3:5) thundered against those prophets, who predicted good fortune if paid well, and who predicted misfortune if paid poorly. (And one must remember that the oracle was held to be an omen with magical consequences.) Similar (3:11) are the denunciations against the acceptance of money by prophets in general.

This configuration, however, destined the prophets to be the greatest ideologists of Yahwism. Ideologists who knew no consideration whatsoever and who precisely for this reason accomplished their tremendous effects. King Ahab called Elijah a mischief maker and a destroyer of the people. He was, indeed, the very type of the later prophets. Tradition knows him as one

most passionately possessed by the angry spirit of Yahwe. After
the triumphant ordeal against the competing Baal priests he
girds his loins and runs down from Mount Carmel into the capital before the king. But tradition knows him also as a religious
hero, who wrestled with and scolded his God like Moses and is
held by God worthy of an epiphany, much like that of Moses.
Tradition knows him as the last great magician. He is the only
one among those whom Yahwe took into heaven whom the editors of the present revision have allowed this honor. Thus his
figure has occupied the phantasies of believers till latest times
with expectancies of his return. Along with his legendary elevation to a superhuman form, tradition presents a purely historical figure. Freed from all such supernatural features, this
figure in a decisive point corresponds to the later type of
"prophet" and is also handled in the revision of the tradition as
one of its prototypes.

Michaiah, the son of Imlah, before the campaign stands up to
the hundreds of prophets of good fortune in Ahab's service and
prophesies misfortune, which is then fulfilled (I. Ki. 22:8 f.).
This threat of political disaster, which at the same time was
magically evaluated as an evil omen, appeared to the contemporaries of Elijah (I. Ki. 21:20) as those of Micah and Jeremiah (Jer. 26:18) to be the characteristic trait of a special form
of prophecy. It was politically dangerous. However, it was also
dangerous to lay hands on the Yahwe-seized prophet of doom.
This is a carry-over from the "tabooed character" of the half-
legendary earlier "seers," projected into the future and thereby
the (alleged)) Moabite Balaam and Elisha are transformed into
prophets who against their will and intention predicted good
fortune to Israel and to Hazael respectively.

It is no accident that the first appearance of the independent,
politically oriented seers, who were succeeded by these prophets,
coincided almost exactly with that great transformation which
kingship under David and Solomon brought about in the political and social structure of Israel.

The questions of Temple construction, succession to the
throne, the private sins of the monarchs, worship, and the most
varied political and personal decisions became topics of their
oracles and their mostly undesired and extremely sharp criti-

cism. Elijah was the first also to criticize a social injustice of the
king. In tradition one yardstick is basic to this criticism: the
time-honored "law" of the ancient Israelite confederacy, as
the critics understood it. To them the source of all evil was the
transformation of the state into a liturgical state, into an Egyptian "house of bondage" in connection with chariot combat and
world politics. The whole bureaucratic apparatus was an Egyptian abomination. Censuses, even if suggested by Yahwe himself as punishment for sins, led to a pest. Popular opinion confirmed these attitudes. The Israelite peasant knew that he had
once fought for freedom from servitude against the knights. Now
he experienced the political and economic domination of the
king and the patricians and his own increasing reduction to
debt bondage. The seers and prophets independent of the king,
the popular heirs of the military Nebiim, now without commis-
sions, hence, hallowed the time when Yahwe himself as war
leader led the peasant army, when the ass-riding prince did not
rely on horses and wagons and alliances, but solely on the god
of the covenant and his help.

Initially developed in Israelite religiosity on this basis was the
high evaluation of the "belief" in the promise of Yahwe. The
name "Yahwe Zebaoth," Yahwe of the heavenly hosts [13] which
is foreign to the Pentateuch and the Book of Judges, only now
became the designation for God used by the seers and later,
following their example, by the scriptural prophets. Above all,
but not alone, the prophets of doom used it almost exclusively.
The "Zebaoth" at first were the heavenly servants of Yahwe,
above all, already in the Song of Deborah, a co-belligerent army
of star spirits (Zebah), and the angels. In the secular tradition,
however, "Zebaoth," as Kautzsch rightly emphasizes, meant the
old army summons of Israel in all those (26) places where
the word is not used in connection with the name of God. In the
eyes of these circles Yahwe was god of the confederate army,
and this is doubtlessly the reference in the prophetic title of
God, at least in part. Indeed, it is to be found in passages in
the later tradition which, as regards actual politics, stem from
pacifistic times. There is involved a subsequently idealized and
biased construction of Israel's confederate past. The Yahwistic
prophecy of doom used the expression not only because the

prophecy of good old times had been war prophecy, and was not only concerned with expressing the fact that Yahwe alone was the legitimate military leader of Israel (which was first mentioned in Isaiah 6:5 cf. also 24:21). But the term was also used because the ancient promises of God, as we shall see, had for their objective, alongside the material welfare, precisely the military glory of Israel which Yahwistic prophecy could and would not renounce.

The pacifistic form of the patriarchal legends, which had their source in the circle of de-militarized small-stock-breeders, the hallowing of the ancient social right, above all, of the social debt rights of the Yahwe confederation, dear to the de-militarized plebeians, thus were supplemented by the specific crusading legends of the actually likewise de-militarized prophets. The prophets fought in common with Yahwe only in phantasy. They were no longer military dervishes and ecstatic therapeutics and rainmakers, but a stratum of literati and political ideologists. According to the occasional observation of Amos (2:11 f.) it appears that the royal bureaucracy deliberately fought the troublesome democratic crusaders, the Nazarites and free Nibiim. According to analogies from other places this interpretation is highly probable, the more so when it is realized that in times of strong administration prophecy is silent. However, in times of decreasing power and external threat, the old democratic memories soon came to life. The utopian phantasies of their champions were saturated the more with bloody images of Yahwe's heroic feats the more un-military they had become in fact. Just as today, in all countries, we find the highest measure of war thirst among those strata of literati who are farthest from the trenches and by nature least military.

The actual stumbling block for these literati had to be the politics of the kings who had brought about all these changes in the old military and social order. The Rechabites and other Yahwe priest-led shepherds, peasants, and exemplary Yahwe believers, all joined in the sign of the hallowed good old times of pure Yahwe worship and of the free Yahwe confederacy, in opposition to all political and social change.

The external and internal independence of this criticism confronting the king was facilitated by the fact that kingship was

not hierocratic in nature. The Israelite king was no priestly dig-
nitary, although there were beginnings of such as when David
was carrying the ephod. For the rest, the king was able to hire
and to dismiss priests from the sanctuaries [14] which he sustained, indeed treating them as his officials, just as the great
landlords (Micah) did in managing their chapels. The king
could offer sacrifices as, originally, could any Israelite. But he
was not qualified to deliver oracles, to minister consecration and
grant dispensation from sins. This was a prerogative of those
charismatically qualified, of the prophets, and later of the
schooled Levites. The relatively decreasing significance of collective sacrifice in the tradition of Yahwe religion was due to
the original lack of a permanent confederate authority and to
the character of the relation of Yahwe to the confederacy. It
benefited the independence and hierocratic power position of
the free Nebiim (even as later that of the Torah teachers) over
and against the king.

The later tradition hallowed Samuel as a Roeh and Nabi and
as a representative of the ancient right. At the same time it put
into his mouth the substantive description of the hated king's
new right. Since the people, in spite of all warnings, insisted on
electing a king, Samuel allegedly (I. Sam. 10:25) set this down
in writing and thus, in agreement with the paramount conception of the *berith*, deposited it like a constitutional document in
the archives (I. Sam. 8:11 f.). The king will appoint captains
over thousands and captains over fifties. He will press the sons
of the Israelites into servicing his war chariots, others to service
as armourers and chariot builders. Their daughters will be made
into confectionaries, cooks, and bakers (for his table and army
needs). He will demand fields, vineyards, and oliveyards as
fiefs for his officials, tillage and harvest corvées, especially forced
labor, servants, maids, cows and asses for his royal demesne and
his other needs, the tenth of the yield of wine and field and small
stock for the payment of his officers and soldiers. The free
Israelites will be his "servants"—that is to say subjects instead
of members of the confederacy.[15]

The political propaganda legend turned against these things
and revised the tradition. While, for example, the genuine tradition (II. Sam. 21:19) knew that one of David's knights, El-

hanan the Beth-lehemite, had killed Goliath, the propaganda legend had him killed by the unknown and unarmed shepherd boy David with a stone in peasant manner. A great many similar features were partly selected from the genuine tradition and partly invented. To the predilection of this tradition for the old peasant army we probably owe the preservation precisely of the Song of Deborah from the old song collection, and also the form in which the conquest of Canaan and the wars of the time of the Judges have been revamped in legend. Above all, however, this predilection accounts for the hallowing of the brotherliness and plain manner of the confederates during the desert period, appropriately called the "nomadic ideal" by Budde. This bias prevailed quite obviously also in the selection of those social statutes which alone have been preserved from law collections. It determined the presumably rather extensive interpolations with utopian theological constructs.

The same bias made the representatives of the old tradition demand that the king should not "return into the Egyptian house of bondage" in order to have horses and wagons (Deut. 17:16). They spurned the splendor and glamour of the Solomon court and Temple in favor of the old peasant freedom and the old unadorned cult upon an earthen altar. Yet, in view of the important interests connected with the brilliant royal Temple cult, these demands even in the circles of pious Yahwists were not without opponents. The attitudes towards Solomon's revolutionary innovations and to kingship in general is accordingly ambiguous in the sources.

One section of the tradition recognized that in the kingless times disorder and arbitrariness prevailed and excused whatever was considered abominable from the standpoint of later ritualistic and ethical correctness. This was excused by stating that at the time there was no king in Israel and therefore "every man did that which was right in his own eyes" (Jud. 17:6; 21:25, similarly 18:1; 19:1). The great power, above all of David and also of Solomon, the builder of the Temple, naturally fostered the hallowing of these kings at the expense of the peasant prince Saul as well as of those of the divided kingdoms later. In the time of great military success in the wars of liberation and immediately afterwards kingship had enormous prestige.[16] The king

received through anointing the "spirit" of Yahwe. As yet he had
no sort of permanently effective priestly power competing beside
him. He sacrificed to God personally, in priestly garments (as
did David according to tradition) and had disposition over
priestly positions and sanctuaries almost as freely as some Mesopotamian "great kings." This tradition considered the king a
"Messiah," the "anointed" (*ha-mashiach*) of Yahwe, as, after
the Exile, the high priests. Anointment was apparently not required for the normal succession to the throne, but is found at
the occasion of the prophetic legitimation of usurpers such as
David, Jehu and probably, in agreement with this, Saul in one
of the three traditions. This practice was probably borrowed
from an old custom of native city princes (perhaps of Jerusalem)
and acquired a ritualistic significance.[17]

Another branch of the tradition, however, stood under the
influence of the declining power of the country and the mounting
prestige of the prophets. It knew, therefore, that, before Israel
set a king over itself, the god of the covenant had been the sole
and direct ruler, who had had no need of such office-tax- and
forced-labor machinery comparable to that of the contemporary
kings. He had revealed his will and intentions to seers and
heroes of the past, and if the people abided by his commandments he had always helped them.

This orientation seems to have prevailed among the Ephraimite peasants even more strongly than in the Southern kingdom, where the nearness of Jerusalem exerted its influence.
Among the prophets, Hosea was the first to give it expression.
The prestige of the Davidian Dynasty, the only one maintaining
itself permanently on the throne, in the Southern kingdom, could
hardly be directly attacked by demanding the abolition of kingship. Here, therefore, was set in motion the program of abolishing the innovations which kingship had brought about. The
political demand was, particularly, for the abolition of militarism
with its horses and chariots, the crown treasure, the harem of
foreign princesses and their cults, the kingly favorites as officials,
and the building and tillage servitudes of the subjects. Deuteronomy demanded that the king should dispense with the
haughty sultanistic airs of the "great kings," and become again a
charismatic *primus inter pares*, without many horses and chariots,

hence an ass-riding wise judge and protector of the plain people. Then Yahwe, the old god of the covenant, would be with him as once with the peasant army, against enemies regardless of how seemingly overwhelming, if only—this was prerequisite of all else—he were to renounce the pretensions to world politics which were responsible for all these innovations. We shall see how priestly power-interests and the ideologies of theologians came together in this program which the Deuteronomic law under Josiah actually sought to realize a few decades before the downfall of Jerusalem.

Kingship in Israel was no patrimonial welfare program, but was bound up with the power of the *gibborim*. The representatives of the old tradition turned against both at the same time. This current found powerful expression in the oracles of the pre-exilic scriptural prophets. Their political place and significance as a whole is to be examined in a later connection. What matters are the complaints which they took over from the popular criticism of the socio-political conditions.

Among the popular complaints reiterated by the prophets the receiving of gifts and corruption in justice head the list (Amos, 2:6; Is. 1:23; 5:3). Through such practices "judgment is turned into gall" (Amos 6:12); blood money was received (Amos 5:12); innocent blood was shed (Is. 1:15; Jer. 7:6; 22:3); the people were butchered (Micah 3:2-3); justice was perverted in favor of the godless and to the disadvantage of the poor, widows, and waifs (Is. 10:2) and of the righteous (Amos 5:12). Instead of justice, force (Jer. 7:6; 22:3) and oppression were practiced (Is. 5:7); field was laid to field and house was joined to house (Is. 5:8; Micah 2:1, 2). The poor (Amos 8:4) especially "the poor in the gate" (Amos 5:12), that is to say, the rural population were oppressed by the urban patriciate who took from them burdens of wheat (Amos 5:11). Wives and children were cast out from house and home (Micah 2:9). The poor were oppressed and the needy crushed (Amos 4:1). The rich feasted on the yield of clothing which had been pawned despite the prohibition against it (Amos 2:8). The rich were haughty (Amos 6:4 f.; cf. Is. 3:16), the *gibborim* debauched (Is. 5:22; cf. 5:11) and the cardinal vice was avarice (Amos 9:1, similarly after the Exile, Hab. 3:9).

These are the reproaches raised by plebeian strata everywhere, but particularly in the Occident in pre-capitalistic antiquity and in the early Middle Ages against the court officials or against the patrician urban sibs. In Hellenic antiquity Hesiod, for instance, was the mouthpiece of this stratum. In Israel, as we saw, kingship and wealthy military sibs were in close connection. The officials of the king were mostly taken from the patricians. These typical social antagonisms show up clearly in prophecy.

CHAPTER V

SOCIAL SIGNIFICANCE OF THE
WAR GOD OF THE CONFEDERACY

1. Uniqueness of the Relation of Israel
to its God

THE anti-royalist tradition of the urban nobles was always legitimized in terms of the old covenant which Yahwe was said to have concluded through Moses with Israel. In its special relation to God, Israel stood in contrast to all other nations, because of this very unique historical event and the unique conclusion of a covenant. Israel's special relationship to God was not merely guaranteed by God, but had been concluded with God as a party to it. The entire Israelite tradition unanimously traced its origins back to the concrete event assumed to have set the process in motion.

All prophets consider the liberation from Egyptian bondage through the miraculous destruction of an Egyptian army in the Red Sea both as a token of God's power and the absolute dependability of his promises and of Israel's lasting debt of gratitude. The uniqueness of the event was constituted by the fact that this miracle was effected by a god till then unknown by Israel and who thereupon was accepted through solemn *berith* by Moses' establishment of Yahwe worship. This reception was based on mutual pledges bilaterally mediated through the prophet Moses.

The special permanent obligations of the people to God were justified by the pledges of the people and the promises of God offered in turn. This made of him a god of promise for Israel in a sense unknown of any other god. This is the unmistakable view contained in the tradition. It is clearly presupposed in the idea of the "defection" from Yahwe as an especially fatal abomination.[1] This view, not to be found elsewhere in the surrounding world, is presupposed even in the Song of Deborah. Above all, it is the indispensable ideational basis for the incomparable importance of prophecy and for the promises of good fortune. To be sure, priests and mystagogues have always promised the believers in their gods riches, long life, numerous progeny and a good name, and the kings allowed their court prophets to give them such promises. Likewise, it was everywhere assumed that the war god of the tribe or the god of the king would assist him against enemies. This held also for Israel. People hopefully expected of the mighty god of the covenant that they would have numerous descendants, so that the people should become numerous as the sand of the seashore, and that they should triumph over all enemies, enjoy rain, rich harvests, and secure possessions, finally that the name of the legendary ancestors and that of the blessed people itself should be a blessing.

As the relationship to God rested upon a *berith* this hope gained a very firm foundation and was held to rest upon an explicit promise, a vow of God. Originally the promises were not considered to be based on special conditions. The earliest formulations in the tradition do not make them depend, for instance, on some special moral behavior of Israel. Of course, the promises were linked to the one condition: that Yahwe be indeed Israel's God and be treated as such. Then Yahwe will stick with Israel through thick and thin. This alone mattered and this was what the militaristic champions of the "spirit" of Yahwe, the Nazarites and Nebiim, the crusaders, knew full well and, as did even the Song of Deborah, impressed upon the army summons. The conception of "idolatry" as an abomination, otherwise quite unknown to religions of Antiquity, thereby gained its all-pervasive significance.

As Deuteronomy still expressly stated (7:8), it was Yahwe's vow and solely that which caused him to favor Israel before all other nations. Yahwe's favor was not awarded, for example, because of Israel's moral superiority. To be sure this was not in accordance with popular conceptions. The people knew, as do those of all nations, that other nations were not equivalent to Israel, which thus had to be considered separately by God. And as always, this differential value was based on the fact that others lived differently and did things "unknown in Israel." As Yahwe by *berith* was the contractual partner to the ritualistic and social order of the confederacy, Yahwe's reason for treating others as inferior depended simply on the fact that they didn't know his will or abide by his commandments. This negative reason for Yahwe's differentiation between Israel and other nations appears in Deuteronomy combined with the religious conception.

But the conception of the religiously minded concerning Israel's relation to its God went even further. Everywhere deities are the guardians of the social order. They sanction its violation, reward conformity to it. The believer viewing the relationship to God in terms of a *berith* had to maintain this with special ardour whenever there was occasion to inquire into the reasons for God's conduct. This occasion emerged with the decline of Israel's political power.

At times the memory of Moses and the covenant idea in general had obviously receded into the background. This occurred under the influence of the splendid power position of the kings. Later, however, shortly before the Exile and at the time of the priestly revision during the Exile, these conceptions became paramount, due to the declining prestige of the political authorities and the question as to the reason for the decline. The old right of the covenant and the importance of abiding by God's commandments as the condition of his favor forcefully reasserted themselves and stamped the hopes for the future. They were conjoined with the presupposition of abidance by the old commandments. The "covenant" idea thus became, as with no other people, the specific dynamics informing the ethical conception of priestly teaching and prophecy.

The scriptural prophets accepted as given the idea that the religious relationship of Israel to Yahwe be exhaustively characterized as a voluntary "covenant" with God himself. To be sure, threats of doom against Israel, characteristic of the prophets, are still absent from those traditions considered genuinely "Yahwistic" and "Elohistic." The promise to Abraham (Gen.

15:18-21) of domination over the land of Canaan (according to an addition: from the border of Egypt to the Euphrates river), appears to be the earliest of the great, expressly divine, promises of good fortune. This promise, too, belongs only to what Wellhausen has called the "Jehovistic" revision, that is to the time of the prophets. It was consummated through a formal ritualistic *berith* of God with the patriarch. The divine vow follows from the patriarch's faith in God who "counted it to him for righteousness." (Gen. 15:6). This is a very abstract and obviously secondary formulation. It corresponds to the form transmitted by the exilic revision (Gen. 12:2). But the conception of the significance of obedience *per se* must certainly be much older. The story of Isaac's sacrifice as the paradigm of truly unconditional faith, for instance, appears to stem from the pre-prophetic (the "Elohistic") revision, although the explicit renewal of the sworn pledge of God is for this reason considered a later addition.

The formulation of the substance of the *berith* in the form of a promise as wages for obedience thus occurs in later revisions. But the conception of *berith* was so firmly established from the beginning of the era of the scriptural prophets, that one of the first, Hosea, could immediately conceive of the religious meaning of the relation to God in terms of a marriage. Thus, every offense against Israel's duties was viewed as adultery against Yahwe. And nothing bespeaks more clearly of this ancient basis of religious conceptualization, unquestioned to latest times, than the fact that partly riotous love songs of the collection included as "The Song of Solomon" in the present canon, could attain significance as an adequate expression of the relationship of Yahwe to his people for an already strongly "pietistic-sentimental" posterity. Hence the "jealousy" (*kin'ah*) of Yahwe against other gods was one of his most firmly established traits for all prophets from Hosea to Ezekiel.[2]

The so-called "Elohist," in this case, indeed, the older of the two great source collections, quite unambiguously states that Yahwe was a newly received god [3] for the Israelite war confederacy, received through the Mosaic order of worship. According to the oldest tradition, which is also preserved in the Blessing for Ephraim, God revealed himself in an unexpected epiphany to Moses. Moses was conceived as an Israelite shepherd in Midianite service. God appeared to him in a flame of fire out of the midst of a bush in the desert near Mount Horeb. When asked for his name the god answered evasively, according to the revision of the tradition, in terms of the etymological play on words "I am that I am," but he mentions the apparently non-Israelite name of "Yahwe." [4] The god of the patriarchs, with whom he was later identified, in these older sources does not as yet have the name of Yahwe, but only the "*El*" name in various compounds. In the later priestly tradition, the compound name most highly valued was "*El Shaddaj,*" etymologically neither an Israelite word. "Moses" like "Phinehas" are Egyptian names. In one tradition Miriam and Aaron speak against Moses because of his "Ethiopian" wife. This would suggest reminiscences of old disputes among priestly sibs. In these reminiscences there also seems to survive knowledge of the fact that even later Yahwe and his priests were considered to be alien or quasi-alien to the land.

Of course, in a time of Egyptian hegemony over Palestine and the Sinai desert, the presence of Egyptian names are as little proof of Egyptian descent of the founder of the confederacy, not to mention his God, as Babylonian or Hellenic names of Jews of the later period are indicative of their descent. Yet, in contrast to Joshua, Moses originally had no designation of Israelite descent (such descent is only a late and artificial construct). The Levitical descent of the (*Elide*) priestly sib, most probably stemming from him, is also a later construction. Whatever the facts, the old tradition clearly indicates that the God had already been worshipped outside Israel at the time of his reception. Obviously he had enjoyed organized worship among the Bedouin and oasis tribes bordering on Israel to the South. From the beginning, his seat was on the mountains. However, the oldest tradition considered the oasis Kadesh, in the Sinai desert, his true sanctuary. This was where the tomb of the prophetess Miriam was located and where presumably decisive acts of Israel's self-constitution took place. The place of his organized worship most important for the origin of the Levites was at the "waters of strive" of Kadesh (Deut. 33:8), i.e., at the source of the oasis where his priests gave trial oracles. His priest [5] Jethro, according to tradition the father-in-law and adviser of Moses, was considered to be a Midianite.

Similarly, the legendary, obscure figure of Balaam, who made holy predictions in Yahwe's name, was considered a stranger partly Moabite, partly Ammonite. Correctly interpreted he was probably an Edomite or Midianite seer whom the Israelites later killed in battle. We may bypass, here, the question of how to bring the event in Kadesh into agreement with the fixed residence of the God on Mount Sinai and the conclusion of the covenant located there by a later tradition. The conquering Edomites early advanced toward the boundaries of Egypt and Jeremiah and Obadjah still considered Edom, and especially the wooded mountain of Seir, to be the ancient seat of Yahwe wisdom. Seir was the dwelling place of Esau (Gen. 32:3), the elder brother of Jacob; it was the place where dwelt the sibs of the tribe of Simeon which early fell into oblivion.

The Levitical sib of the Korahites (Ex. 6:21) originally (Gen. 36:5) seems to go back to Esau, hence to Edomite descent. In the Song of Deborah, Yahwe approaches from Seir to the scene of battle. The poet of the beautiful watchman song from the time of Exile, which chanced to appear among the oracles of Isaiah, despite the then bitter hostility against Edom, still heard from there the call "What of the night?" The Kenites who later appear as particularly zealous Yahwe believers originally did not belong to the tribe of Judah, not to mention Israel, in whose eyes Cain, in the legend of manslaughter as well as in an old Balaam saying, was an accursed man. Some doubts are raised against the assumption that Mount Sinai, later equated with Mount Horeb, was a volcano at the Northwestern shore of Arabia near the Red Sea eastward opposite the present so-called Sinai peninsula. But the saga itself has never maintained that it belonged to the territory of Israel. The same goes for Kadesh. It is also certain that the old tradition neither considered Yahwe to be the original God of Israel, nor the God of Israel alone, nor to reside in Israel. Only the final revision of the Hexateuch, which makes Yahwe a God of the universe, takes it for granted that the patriarchs, too, worshipped no other god. To the old tradition still in the Jephthah legend he is a god beside other gods, though an especially powerful and majestic one.

Moreover, he is the "God of Israel" and for Jephthah he is "my God" as Chemosh is the god of the Ammonite king.

But Yahwe was a god in a quite special sense. He was—and that remained a conception frought with consequences—a "god from afar," holding sway from his remote mountain seat near heaven and on occasion personally intervening in the course of events. From the beginning, this "distance" gave him a special majesty. To be sure, one of the old traditions maintained that the elders themselves had shared the table with him on Mount Sinai. But the predominant view of later times was that of all men, only Moses had seen him face to face (Deut. 34:10) and that after that Moses' face had shown in such supernatural radiance that he had to cover it before the people (Ex. 34:29 f.). Perhaps this is still a reminiscence of the old *teraphim* masks to be discussed at a later time. Actual opinion (Ex. 33:20 f.) held that even Moses upon his request had only been able to see him pass by backward, because anybody seeing his countenance would not live. It was no local or tribal deity familiar of old, but a strange and mysterious form which gave its consecration to the sworn Israelite confederacy.

2. *The Nature of the War God*

THE destruction of the Egyptian army to which the tremendous prestige of this god is traced by the tradition obviously occurred in the course of a sudden tide of the Red Sea raised by a storm in the wake of an equally sudden ebb-tide east of the Sinai peninsula. As indicated by the appearance of a pillar of a cloud and a pillar of fire and the fiery glow on the mountain, this may have been connected with some sort of volcanic phenomena.

Doubts have been raised against the occurrence of this catastrophe in the Red Sea as well as the Egyptian sojourn of Israel. But according to Egyptian sources it was not unusual for the stock-breeders of the steppe during times of actual or threatened drought to seek protection as metics in Egyptian borderlands. There, it goes without saying, occasional drafts of forced labor by the kings occurred and it was just as natural that, given the opportunity, they would escape the imposition of the corvée. However, the chronology of the immigration and Exodus remain quite difficult, for the border fortifications in the construction of which the Israelites claim to have cooperated seem to have been built under Rameses II, and Israel is already mentioned as an enemy in Palestine under his successor Merneptah. There is further difficulty if one identifies the "Khabiri," appearing as enemies in Palestine far earlier, under Amenophis III and IV, with the "Ibrim" the "people beyond," i.e., probably the East Jordan people as the Israelites and other tribes considered related [6] in tradition are designated in the perspective of the strangers. Apart from Abraham, who is thought of as an itinerant shepherd and who is always called the "Hebrew," this designation is only found once in the mouth of the Israelites in the Book of the Covenant [7]—otherwise only in intercourse with strangers.[8]

It has been established that the tribes which later are joined in the Israelite confederacy invaded the West Jordan land in several waves. Moreover the composition of the confederacy, as made probable by earlier discussions, underwent changes. It included Canaanites on the one hand, former Bedouin tribes on the other. It is well nigh certain that not all later tribes of Israel or their ancestors were participants in the sojourn in Egypt. The most reliable, because most natural tradition has the tribe of Judah, emerging much later, invade its dwelling place from the South and not from the East. It remains unclear whether the Phoenicians—allegedly, but hardly actually—immigrated from the Persian gulf and a part of the Sa-Gas nomads presumably from the border of Mesopotamia. It is also unclear whether elements of the Israelites, hidden behind the Abraham (or Abram) tradition, immigrated earlier, say during the time of the Amarna tablets, from the Mesopotamian steppe. This is not impossible. The name (Abiram) is frequent in Babylon. The religion ascribed to Abraham, to be sure, does not bear any traits identifiable as Babylonian. The Kedor-Laomer tradition, however, is a striking peculiarity. Also other features of the tradition suggest several waves of invasions of the country. The collections of the blessings and the priestly tradition, in any case, located the kernel of the old Israelite confederacy, as known to the Song of Deborah, in Moses' covenant with the God who had effected the Red Sea miracle, for the jurpose of conquering and maintaining the West Jordan land. There is no reason [9] to doubt the historical nature of Moses' person.[10] The question is how to evaluate his accomplishments.

It appears impossible truly to ascertain the historical course of events. The conception that a law book, such as the Book of the Covenant, or a catalogue of ethical duties, such as the Decalogue, would have been the subject matter of the *berith* rests on quite unhistorical and unpragmatic ideas, not to mention other insurmountable difficulties. According to all analogies, including the Islamite ones, and for purely objective reasons, we may assume that the substance of the fraternization, possibly not the first of its kind, consisted in the reception of rites established at places of Yahwe's previous worship. These rites were obviously very simple, in correspondence with their environment. They represented worship without images, including possibly circumcision and certainly oracles by lot. Besides, there were certain simple orders of social brotherliness which were suitable for a conquering army summons of nomads of the steppe and, last but not least, the prestige of war prophecy. The special sharpness with which the god taboos the murder of compatriots, the violation of guest right, and the strict booty taboo also fit this derivation. With due caution we may assume these (expressly or in fact) constituted the obligations which Israel assumed by *berith*. They contain no elements which do not historically occur elsewhere under similar conditions. But what of Yahwe?

He was and always remained a god of salvation and promise. What mattered chiefly, however, was that salvation as well as promise concerned actual political, not intimate personal affairs. The god offered salvation from Egyptian bondage, not from a senseless world out of joint. He promised not transcendent values but dominion over Canaan which one was out to conquer and a good life. This unbroken naturalism and ritualistic peculiarity going back to primitive socio-cultural conditions became important indeed. It became so in the fusion with ubiquitously diffused elements of a rational and intellectually differentiated civilization. The fusion began soon after the immigration. Acculturation is generally productive of entirely new and peculiar phenomena given the opportunity and compelling need of absorbing a series of as yet unsublimated ideas. If they are not yet stereotyped through priestly, official, or literary elaboration, they compel the old rationalized structures to adjust to entirely new and relatively simple conditions.

Israelite conceptions, on a Mosaic foundation, established such a necessity before the Oriental culture-elements diffused in Canaan. Through what native traits was the process consummated? The initial question is: What are the traits of the deity which, according to tradition, Moses newly introduced into the Israelite confederacy—regardless of how constituted?

A number of characteristics are attributed to Yahwe in the old tradition. With the old Hellenic and other deities of war-like peoples he shares those highly anthropomorphic traits [11] which are his precisely in the earlier parts of the tradition, especially those stemming from the South, the so-called "Yahwist" tradition. One of his traits not often to be found with similar intensity is his nearness. Obviously it is an early and later quite regular attribute. Under certain conditions even the nearness of "men of god" possessed by his "spirit" (*ruach*) is uncanny and dangerous. As we saw, the sight of him is deadly.

The "holiness" which is specific for Yahwe to an especially high degree, means, as is generally held since Count Baudissin's investigations, originally this essential unapproachability and separateness of God from all men as well as objects which are not especially ritually qualified for bearing his nearness. This aloofness follows from the danger of any contact or sight of God. This important quality is apparently partially connected with the ancient absence of images in his worship. It is, however, bound up initially with his nature and its manifestations. Yahwe resembles the Indian god Indra, for, like Indra, he is, for Israel at least, first and foremost a god of war. A variant of an ancient account calls him "a man of war" (*ish milchamah,* Ex. 15:3). He thirsts for blood, for the blood of the enemies, the disobedient, the victims. His passion is mighty beyond all bounds. In his wrath, God devours the enemies with fire or he lets them be devoured by the earth. According to the double verse of the Miriam dance, he throws them into the sea like the chariots of the Egyptians, or he mires their vehicles, like those of the Canaanites in the Deborah battle, in the rain-swollen rivulets so that the Israelite peasants could slaughter their occupants in the same way as once happened to the Latin knighthood in Greece during the late period of the crusades.

With the prophets, still, the frightfulness of his wrath and his warlike might is the preeminent trait. His mercy is of the same grandeur as his wrath. For his passionate heart is changeable. He repents of having shown good will toward men if they compensate him meanly. Then, again, he repents his boundless wrath. The late rabbinical tradition has God himself pray (!) that his own mercy may gain the upperhand over his wrath. He personally draws near in the thunderstorm to come to the aid of the army. He assists his friends, as Athena did Ulysses. He is unscrupulous also in cunning and fraud. But one can never be certain not to provoke his wrath through some unwitting oversight. Nor can one be sure of not being suddenly pounced upon unexpectedly and unasked, or threatened with destruction by a divine noumenon from among his spirits. In pre-prophetic times, the "spirit," the *ruach* of Yahwe, is neither an ethical power nor a religious state of habituation, but an acute demonic-superhuman power of varying, most frequently frightful, character. The savage charismatic warrior heroes of the Israelite tribes, berserks like Samson, Nazarites and ecstatic Nebiim, know themselves to be seized by this force. They experience themselves as his following. All war prophets and prophetesses appear in Yahwe's name. The bearers of another theophorous (Baal's) name like Jerubbaal assume a new name as warlords (Gideon).

Yahwe, like Indra, is fit to be god of war because, like Indra, he was originally a god of the great catastrophies of nature. His appearance is accompanied by phenomena such as earthquakes (I. Sam. 14:15; Is. 2:12 f.; 46:6), volcanic phenomena (Gen. 19:24, Ex. 19:11 f.; Psalm 46:6), subterraneous (Isaiah 30:27) and heavenly fire, the desert wind from the South and South East (Zechariah 9:14) and thunderstorms. As in the case of Indra, flashes of lightning are his arrows (Psalm 18:14) as late as the prophets and psalmists. For Palestine the orbit of nature catastrophies comprised also the insect, above all, the locust plague, which the South Eastern wind brought into the country. Hence the god punishes the enemies of his people with locusts and he sends swarms of hornets to confound them. He sends snakes *en masse* to punish his own people. Finally, there are epidemics (Hos. 13:14). God afflicts the Egyptians with pestilence, likewise the Philistines and others who lay hand on his holy Ark (I. Sam. 4:8; 6:5, 19). The serpent staff of his priests in the Temple of Jerusalem is probably indicative of his former role as the deity of pestilence. For as the master of disease he also could ward it off or prevent it as is always the case in similar instances. Thus all frightful and fateful nature phenomena were the desmesne of the god. He combined the traits of Indra with those of Rudra.

Besides this character of warlike-and-nature-mythological savage, he shows milder features even in the old tradition as the master of rainfall. He expressly points out to his people that in Israel, unlike Egypt, the harvest yield is not dependent upon irrigation. It is not a product of bureaucratic administration, of the king on earth and the work of the peasant, but it is the result of the rain given by Yahwe according to his free grace. The strong rainstorms, peculiar especially of the steppe territory bordering the desert, were his work.

From the beginning, Yahwe's character as rain god identified him with the individual and his economic interests and facilitated the later increasingly significant permeation of his image with the traits of a benign god of nature and the heavens. The sublimation and rationalization of the image of god into that of a wise governor of the universe was consummated above all, under the influence of conceptions of supreme heavenly deities diffused in the surrounding areas as well as in Palestine. Moreover, the belief in divine providence, a belief developed among the Israelite intellectuals, exerted a partial influence. But the features of the frightful god of catastrophes, derived from the conception of Yahwe of old, never vanished. These features played the decisive part in all those mythologies and mythological-influenced images, the utilization of which bestows an incomparable grandeur on the language of the prophets. The Yahwe-directed processes of nature are primary proof of his might, not proof of wise order until deep in exilic and post-exilic times. The connection of the qualities of Yahwe as a god of frightful natural catastrophies, not of the eternal order of nature, preserved down to the time after the Exile, was, beside the general relationship of those processes with war, based historically on the fact that God had made use of his power first in battle against the Egyptians, then, in the Deborah battle, against the Canaanites, and likewise, later against Israel's enemies. Events of nature, especially earthquakes (I. Sam. 14:15) and heavy thunderstorms (Deborah battle) provoked panic among the enemy and were ascribed to him as "divine trembling" (*cherdath Elohim, loc. cit.*). Such a volcanically determined panic (of the Egyptians) had led to the reception of the god. That remained unforgotten.

3. *Social Reception of the War God*

WHAT mattered practically was that Yahwe, despite this nature, became and continued to be a god of social organization, at least for old Israel. This must be properly understood. We must assume that, since Moses, he was the god of the covenant of the Israelite confederacy, and, corresponding to the purpose of the confederacy, he was primarily its war god. He played this role in a very special manner. He became war god by virtue of a treaty of confederation. This contract had to be concluded, not only among confederates, but also with him, for he was no god residing in the midst of the people, a familiar god, but rather a god hitherto strange. He continued to be a "god from afar." This was the decisive element in the relationship. Yahwe was an elective god. The confederate people had chosen him through *berith* with him, just as, later, it established its king by *berith*.

Yahwe, in turn, had chosen this people before all others by free resolve. This is what he constantly brings home to the people through the priestly Torah and the prophetic oracles. By free grace he has chosen this and no other people. He has given them promises as to no other people and in compensation accepted their pledges. Hence, whenever the confederate people *per se* entered a *berith*, he, the god, was an ideational party to it. All violations of the holy enactments were not merely violations of orders guaranteed by him as other gods guarantee their orders, but violations of the most solemn contractual obligations toward him personally. He who failed to accept the army summons, failed not merely to serve the confederacy, but to serve him personally and "came not to the help of the Lord" (Jud. 5:23). The members of the confederate army were called "men of God" (*'am ha'elohim* Jud. 20:1 f.).

In this manner Yahwe became not only the war god of the confederacy but also the contractual partner of its law established by *berith,* above all of the socio-legal orders. Since the confederacy was at first a stateless association of tribes, new statutes, whether cultic or legal in nature, could in principle originate only by way of agreement (*berith*) based on oracle like the original covenant. Therewith, all statutes were based on the same ground as the old contract relation which existed between the god and the people. Considered in terms of public law, the *berith,* before the advent of kingship, was no mere theoretical construction. The same holds for the religious conception. With Jeremiah (2:5) Yahwe asks "what iniquity have your fathers found in me?" And for his part, Jeremiah admonishes him not to break his covenant with Israel.

Being considered a contractual partner, this god of the covenant could be viewed in Israel neither as a mere functional deity of some process of nature or of social institutions, nor as a local deity in the manner everywhere characteristic of Oriental cities. He was no mere god of the "land." Rather, the human community of the Israelite confederate army had to be considered as his people, joined to him through common covenant. This was, in fact, the classical view of the tradition. The transfer of holiness to the political territorial holding, making it a "holy land," is but a later conception, probably suggested by heterogeneous conceptions of deity in part derived from Baal worship, in part from the localization of Yahwe as the god of the king's residence. This conception of the "holy land" is first documented for David in the time of kings in a tradition of uncertain age, then in the Northern kingdom at the occasion of Elisha's conversion of Naaman.

As guardian of confederate orders, Yahwe protects the customs and mores. That which is "unheard of" in Israel is an abomination to him. In agreement with his original nature, however, and unlike Varuna and similar deities, he was not the guardian of the confederate law and mores in the sense of sanctifying an already existing immutable order of law or a "righteousness" measurable in terms of fixed norms. On the contrary, this positive law for Israel was created through *berith* with him. It had not always been in existence and it was possible that by new revelation and new *berith* with God it could be changed again. Not only Paul, but even some individual prophets (Jeremiah and Ezekiel), occasionally believed that God had imposed some stipulations upon the people as a hard yoke or punishment, just as, according to popular myth, he had imposed the toil of work and death upon Adam.

The law was no eternal Tao or Dharma but a positive divine enactment. Its observance was jealously watched by Yahwe. On the later occasions, God's law was called "eternal" by the ethical rationalism of the Deuteronomic school (Deut. 4:2) and the original moral perfection of God's just orders was praised as peculiar to no other people (4:8). These occasional exhortatory arguments, however, do not embody the typical stand unavoidably following from the *berith* character of the law. God's ordainments come from his hand and are as *such* changeable. He may bind himself to his enactments by *berith*, but that is the result of His free resolve. Only the priestly revision knows of eternal orders. Almost all of these are cultic norms or they pertain to rights of the Aaronites who gained ascendancy only in Exile times becoming monopolists of cult leadership. Just because these norms were innovations they were designated with this emotionally changed expression (*chukath 'olam*). (Ex. 27:21; Lev. 3:17; 16:31; 23:14; 31:41; Deut. 12:1 pertain to cultic orders. Lev. 7:37; Num. 18:23 pertain to priestly law of Exile times. I. Gen. 9:14 *berith 'olam* pertains to the theological constructions of Noah's covenant.)

The only "eternal" secular order, namely the stipulation of eternal equal rights for Israel and the gerim is also a priestly innovation of Exile times. Indeed, one can recognize such new stipulations from the very use of the term "eternal." In the ancient literature of Israel, it is never maintained that this and no other social order be eternal and immutable by virtue of its intrinsic perfection, therefore guaranteed by Yahwe. Characteristically, when Job requests God to answer for the unjust order of man's condition and when God makes his appearance in the storm, he argues with not a single word the wisdom of his order of human relations, as, for instance, the Confucian would presuppose. Instead Yahwe exclusively argues his sovereign might and greatness in the events of nature. This historically determined peculiarity of God has remained fraught with consequences into times when the early Christian doctrine of natural law emerged.

From the beginning, in Yahwism there were features transcending Israel and in this sense a certain universalism was inherent in the conception of Yahwe. Rather, such elements of a potential universalism were inherent in the peculiar relationship in which, for purely historical reasons, the Israelite confederacy stood to this god. There has been recent controversy as to whether monolatry (the exclusive worship of one of several deities), henotheism (consideration of the implored god as alone mighty) or monotheism (singularity in principle) have governed the ancient conception of Yahwe. This may be a misleading formulation of the question. The conception of Yahwe has not only undergone changes, but at any given time it varied according to different social groups. The warrior knew clearly that the god whom he implored was his god and consequently that the god of the enemy was different. The gods Yahwe and Chemosh are thus treated in the Book of Judges (11:24) in the story of Jephthah and in the Book of Kings in the account of the Moabite war (II. Ki. 3:1 f.). (Apparently Chemosh was also a god common to several tribes). With regard to the king and the urban strata, especially those of the temple priests and patricians, but also of the urban masses a different conception of Yahwe obtained. The god was considered to be localized in the temple of the city and there were other gods elsewhere. One's own god stood and fell with the existence of the city. Anyone who had to leave the city (or its jurisdictional area) could not serve its god but had to serve strange deities, as did David (I. Sam. 26:19). The newcomer from a foreign land, however, had better serve the native god, because he might otherwise revenge himself as did Yahwe on the Assyrian colonists in Samaria (II Ki. 17:25, 26). This is the product of urban culture. For the Israelite of a temple city, especially Jerusalem, Yahwe resided in the Temple. The Ark of Yahwe always facilitated such localization. The transmitted ritual shows that warriors in the field conceived of Yahwe as present on this camp shrine.

Naturally, the attitude of semi-nomadic stock-breeding tribes was quite different. The tradition influenced by them takes it for granted that god is with the Israelites wherever they are (Gen. 28:20). They know full well that also non-Israelite tribes worship Yahwe, hence their legends presuppose the same not only for Laban (Gen. 24:50, 31:49), after all a relative but also for Abimelech of Gerar (Gen. 20:11; 21:23). In the Joseph legend (Gen. 41:39 f.) one can trace views typical of overseas trading peoples such as the Hellenes and the later Romans, namely, the naive identification of certain foreign deities with their own. In post-exilic Judaism this is to be found in the identification of Yahwe with the god of Nebuchadnezzar (with Daniel) and that of the Persian king. On the whole, however, this tendency was alien to early Israel because Yahwe by *berith* had become its god. In the original view, this precluded the possibility that Yahwe, as for example, Marduk and Ahuramazda, could be the tutelatory god of foreign kings in the same manner as of Israel. The professional Yahwe prophets of olden times, the Nebiim and seers, were evidently neither convinced of Yahwe's uniqueness, nor of the fact that their god had been domiciled only in Israel. In part these prophets had an international clientele. The Elijah tradition presupposes, at least in one place (I. Ki. 17:9), that also the widow in Zidon receives Yahwe's commandments. For the rest, their god was, if not the only one, naturally the strongest of them all and other gods were "nobodies." This was true also for the old Yahwistic warrior tradition (Josh. 2:9). What mattered to it most was the special position of Israel by *berith*. This tradition held that while others may worship Yahwe, Israel stands under his special protection. Yahwe was not considered to be the enemy of other nations. Only the nationalistic fanaticism of the kingly prophets of good fortune and the confessional fanaticism of the priests after the Exile occasionally approached this view. What mattered to Yahwe was Israel alone, as was, after all, expected at all times of every local god, or local saint, and every localized madonna. However, in the case of Yahwe, views leading to similar results did not derive originally from the localization but, indeed, from a (relative) universalism and the particularized *berith* with Israel.

The different conceptions of Yahwe stood side by side and

their logical contradiction was usually not perceived. In any case, one should beware of viewing the more "particularistic" conception of god as necessarily older. To some extent, the opposite holds and this was unavoidably the case with Yahwe. In the rhythmic, ancient, divine speech (Ex. 19:5) Yahwe, before announcing the substance of the covenant to be concluded which will make Israel his treasure, refers to himself as "lord of the earth." This view, alongside others, is to be found even in pre-prophetic times. The gods of other nations, after all, also make their appearance "universalistically" in this sense. This is true particularly of the gods of the great kings of the capitals of the world empires. Amon, in Egypt under the priestly rule of the later Rameses, claimed universal power of ministering grace.[12] The councillors and court prophets of the Israelite kings will have pronounced similar things of Yahwe in memory of David's kingdom.[13]

Historically the special (relative) universalism of Yahwe did not rest on this foundation, but rather on the fact of his reception. Yahwe had simply existed already and had proven his power in a manner different from other deities before Israel offered him sacrifices. This had consequences for worship. Even if he enjoyed sacrifices and these, accordingly, were considered adequate means to win his favor, nevertheless, the idea frequent elsewhere that god's existence depended upon the offering of sacrifices [14] could hardly emerge. Yahwe had his throne afar on his mountain height and had no need for sacrifices, even though he enjoyed them. Besides, note this, in the pre-kingly times during periods of peace, there existed no political or hierocratic authority whatsoever which could have offered sacrifices in the name of the confederacy. We have no knowledge of such, and its existence seems impossible. Hence, the sacrifice in ancient times simply could not gain the significance in relation to Yahwe which it obtained elsewhere. Thus, the prophets later were perfectly justified in emphasizing that not only for the time of the desert but for the Israelite confederation generally, people did not worship god by offering sacrifice. As the *berith* was the specific form through which the confederate people constantly renewed contact with Yahwe, the idea suggested itself to deem the fulfillment of his *berith*-sanctified command-

ments at least of equal or actually greater importance than occasional sacrifices offered by individuals and later by kings and
temple priests. This is asserted ever anew by part of the pure
Yahwe worshippers.[15]

During the later time of kings there was always a party in
Israel—and, indeed, it included the most powerful scriptural
prophets such as Amos and Jeremiah—who kept the memory of
this condition alive and presented any and all sacrifices as ultimately quite indifferent to Yahwe. It is understandable that
people least firmly settled at fixed places of worship, hence,
strata of small-stock-breeders, most closely adhered to this view.
Obviously, what the mighty heavenly warlord actually demanded was the precise observation of his specific rites, and,
for the rest, obedience to his revelations. This view, replete with
consequences—again for political reasons—from the beginning
remained alive among the very guardians of the old tradition.
However primitive and barbaric the ethical commandments may
have been (which today can no longer be ascertained) which
he imposed on the warrior confederacy, Yahwe was simply and
unavoidably and far more than any other deity a "jealous" god,
quite specifically securing the observance of certain ritualistic
and social-ethical workaday norms.

He was not a god—note this—who esteemed an eternally valid
ethic or who could himself be ethically judged. This last notion
emerged only gradually as a product of intellectual rationalism.
Nay, he behaved as a king, given to wrath and passion if the
obligations due him through *berith* remained unfulfilled. Duties
such as the chosen lord demands of his subject were at issue;
they were quite positive obligations. From the first people did
not and had nothing to ponder as to their absolute ethical value.
What was owed was substantially the avoidance of things "unheard of in Israel" and positive obligations fixed by *berith*.
According to an early and widely diffused opinion, these were
more insisted upon by god than sacrificial offerings. Even quite
early, the tradition presents him in a great state of rage not
only because of ritualistic, but ethical abominations. And it is
presupposed that the holy war of the confederacy could be declared to confederate members because of grave offenses, because of deeds such as had not been "done nor seen from the

day that the children of Israel came up out of the land of Egypt." (Jud. 19:30). What led the confederacy to intervene in such matters and hence led to a specifically strong ethical orientation of old Israelite confederate law, was the joint religious liability of confederate members for the offenses of each individual. This presupposition of collective liability for each offender, knowingly or unwittingly held, was of great consequence. Like the right to employ repressive measures in all international relations to this day, it was taken as a matter of course in the religious belief of people who, like Israel, stood opposite their god as an association of freemen.

Whereas in Babylonian hymns the liability of the individual for the sins of his ancestors and close relatives is to be found, joint liability of the people as a whole for each and every individual—the precondition for all prophetic prediction of doom —naturally, was ideologically undeveloped in a purely bureaucratic state. Hence, also in this the political structure played a decisive role. As the members of the collectivity are liable for one another, so the descendants are liable for the offenses of their ancestors down to remote generations. The same held for blood revenge, hence was nothing startling. With the weakening of blood revenge, changes came about. The Deuteronomic speculation considered both kinds of liability, for compatriots and ancestors, a hardship without being able actually to abolish the view. For Israel it resulted from *berith* with god himself.

A further important peculiarity results from the quality of the god as guardian of the confederate law and as war god accepted through a special contract: the god was and continued to be, in spite of all anthropomorphism, unmarried and, hence, childless. Also, the *bne Elohim* of the sixth chapter of Genesis were no *bne Yahwe*. Given the peculiarity of his position, a feminine counterpart was entirely out of the question. He lacked this supplement, just as, occasionally, certain functional deities guaranteeing the social order (Varuna, Apollo) and imported deities (Dionysus) are devoid of it for similar reasons. With Yahwe, however, this circumstance from the beginning contributed substantially to his appearance, as something unique and more removed from this world, in contrast to other divine figures. This, above all, blocked the formation of true myths which is always "theogony." Hence also this important peculiarity was probably determined through the peculiar political origin of his worship.

As we have seen, such traits of preeminence of the god of the confederacy by no means necessarily constituted a claim to exclusive recognition. The external relationship to the deities of other peoples has already been discussed. Jephthah takes for granted the reality and might of the Ammonite and later, also, Moabite god Chemosh. The view is still the same under Ahab. The Moabite king by the sacrifice of his own son was able so much to strengthen Chemosh that his anger against Israel and its god gained the upper hand. But what matters here is that *de facto* the exclusiveness of the god also did not exist within the group. It is highly probable that for the semi-Bedouins of the steppe, from the outset the great war god of the covenant was the only important deity. This monolatry is explained quite simply from the fact that they had no differentiated culture productive of functional deities and that the political community only served militarily to protect and/or conquer grazing grounds. Hence, these semi-nomadic tribes, especially in the South, were presumably from the outset the representatives of a conception of the "singularity" of Yahwe in the sense of monolatry.

This view was taken up by the professional group which was, from the beginning, peculiar to Yahwe worship: the war prophets. The oldest document which mentions with disapproval the worship of "new gods" in Israel is the Song of Deborah (Jud. 5:8). All wars against the urban patricians, Canaanite as well as Philistine, were fought in the name of Yahwe. Understandably, on such occasions, the view always emerged that exclusive worship of Yahwe who had promised military aid was a covenant duty. All non-secular, but prophetic, male or female leaders in the wars of liberation were hostile to all other deities or became so in war. For the rest,, nothing is better ascertained for the settled Israelites than the fact that they possessed "other gods" besides Yahwe. Originally this was perfectly legitimate. The possession of other gods meant merely that other cults not dedicated to Yahwe existed and that their importance quite apart from imported foreign *numina* was such that the priestly revision was unable to efface.[16]

4. *Non-Yahwistic Cults*

FROM the first, the tradition gives account of sib cults and domestic shrines. David excused himself from Saul's festive sacrifice because of a cult festival of his sib, a cult festival of which Yahwe's cult orders know nothing. Besides, not only Laban but every Israelite member of a fully qualified sib originally had a shrine in his house and a house idol (according to the stipulations covering the ceremony of hereditary enslavement in the Book of the Covenant and according to the account of David's flight from his house). From the state of the sources, one can perhaps not ascertain what, in the last analysis, were these "*teraphim*," whether possibly identical with masks or dolls which the head of the sib wore during the orgiastic mime. Here we shall bypass the question. The way, however, in which they vanish from the emended revisions of the tradition proves that they (the *teraphim*) had nothing to do with a (quite improbable) "home cult of Yahwe," just as little as the sib festivals. To be sure, the details are uncertain.

Similarly, one moves on quite controversial ground with the important questions concerning whether and what sort of death cult existed in old Israel and to what extent its complete absence later was related to the decreasing social and cultic significance of the sibs. The imaginative constructions of an original ancestor worship in Israel advanced by Stade and Schwally could not withstand the penetrating criticism especially of Grüneisen. Still, the soul of the dead appears once to have been quite a considerable power in ancient Palestinian magic. In later times, however, it is indeed a problematic form. Like a great many others, the Israelite conception of the "soul" does not necesasrily hold it to be a unit. In common with the Egyptians, the ancient Israelites ascribed at least to the king a plurality of souls. But a unitary conception of the *ka* governing even at an early time in Egyptian speculation, was not taken over in Israel and seems to have exerted no influence. The later conception going back to the fusion of heterogeneous early Israelite and several, presumably borrowed, ideas distinguished three aspects of human nature:

(1) the body (*basar*)

(2) the soul (*nefesh*) residing in the blood as bearer of the normal affects, of "individuation" (as we would say) and of all usual phenomena of life in general and

(3) the "spirit," the "breath of life" (*ruach*).[17]

Ruach is a divine breath which Yahwe has blown into man. Its presence only makes a living man out of the quite weak and merely vegetatively animated body. Yahwe makes breath come "from the four winds" through a charm word of Ezekiel in his visions. It revitalizes the dead bones dispersed on Israel's soil. Moreover, *ruach* is the special divine force, which corresponding to *mana* and *oranda*, finds expression as charisma of extraordinary accomplishments in heroes, prophets, artists and, reversely as demonic possession in grave affects and unusual psychic states. In the sources *nefesh* and *ruach* are not always sharply distinguished. Apparently the dualism of God's live breath (the "blowing" of the godhead) and dead chaos, to be found in the later revision of the stories of creation (Gen. 1) was borrowed from Phoenician ideas via speculations of intellectuals. It facilitated the conception of a dualistic *ruach-basar*. This met the anti-death cult tendencies of the priests half-way. According to the later view, namely of the *ruach* as substantially equal to the winds, it returns with man's last breath to Heaven, thus, its individuality is submerged and a realm of the dead individual souls is eliminated indeed. This did not at all agree with the old belief of the people. To be sure, the original conception of the fate of the *nefesh* while not always quite clear, obviously was that the *nefesh* continue to exist.

In one instance, with Jeremiah, the assumption, original also for Egypt, is found of a soul-sojourn in the tomb. But this concerns a heroine (Rachel) and doubtlessly was based on an ancient internment cult. The existence of a conception of an "ancestral heaven" of sib members, however, apparently cannot be ascertained. Still in late times sib tombs are to be found for distinguished individual sibs, for instance, the Maccabees, and, according to tradition of the priests and patriarchs. Such were possible only for settled tribes. Presumably the old expression "to be gathered unto their fathers" in any case signified to be buried in a common place rather than to be gathered in a special ancestral heaven, especially as the expression alternates with other turns of phrase such as "to be gathered unto his people (*'am*)," which may mean sib members as well as fellow warriors. Nor can belief in a warrior heaven be historically ascertained. In popular belief when Yahwe cut off his especially favored religious heroes they continued to exist among his heavenly hosts, that is (as in Egypt according to one view) in the shiny army of stars or perhaps also in his heavenly council, whereas the correct view may well have been that he made them softly expire in his arms like Moses. The *nefesh* of all others, however, leads a shadowy existence in Hades, *sheol*. Unlike Egyptian conceptualization, no place of blissful life of the blessed is extrapolated from this and no opportunity for rebirth is opened. Rather, all ghosts of the dead are "slack" (*rephaim*) as with the Hellenes. This, however, does not make them harmless. The stoning of a man or animal possessed with an evil spirit or seized with the *cherem* doubtlessly served the purpose of thoroughly blocking the way to its dead soul, lest it haunt the place.

Whereas in Egypt the teaching of *ka* [18] was developed from similar beginnings, the Israelite view of the "soul" remained quite contradictory. The later Deuteronomic and priestly conception occasionally enjoins strict ritualistic prohibition of the enjoyment of blood on the grounds that one must eat the soul neither of man nor animal. It would result in evil charm and possibly possession. But no teaching developed with regard to the fates of animal and human souls. The *nefesh* lives in Hades only as shadowy image of the living, for it has neither blood nor breath. According to the view, also, of the psalmists one learns nothing of Yahwe's deeds there and one cannot praise him: memory is extinguished. Like Achilles, one wishes to be preserved from this fate as long as possible, and this existence is not experienced as "continued life in the beyond." Moreover, there is no "compensation in the beyond" as represented by the judgment of the dead in Egypt as it developed out of chthonian cults under priestly influence on ethics. With the later prophets, scattered beginnings of the construction of a Tartarus for evil doers are to be found, but they are as little elaborated as with the Hellenes and Babylonians. The hazy nature of all these notions is most simply explained from the fact that *sheol* as well as *nefesh* were ancient military and folk beliefs and the champions of Yahwism bypassed both; they did not wish to recognize a soul in the beyond.[19] They employed the concept of the *ruach* probably taken over initially from the animistic idea of rebirth of warrior asceticism and later assimilated to the notion of the divine cosmic breath, the wind of Yahwe.[20] According to them, what would and should live on was something quite different, namely the good name [21] of the hero among his fellows and descendants.

As we saw, the high esteem for the name is a typical Bedouin trait. But it was dominant also in Egypt. In Israel, as in Egypt, the view was held that every name was somehow something real, of the essence of the thing or person. The fact that Yahwe will blot out the "name" of the transgressor of his "book" expresses the threat to destroy him forever (Ex. 32:32, 33 f.). The view was probably reenforced by the significance of personal charisma and the fame of the warrior hero in connection with the prevalent sib organization and the naming of distinguished sibs by the ancestor as eponym. The name of a man visibly blessed by God during his lifetime can become a "blessing" which later generations will still utilize. The supreme promise which Abraham receives from the Lord is that this will happen to his name. For, in the one old (Yahwistic) revision of the word (Gen. 12:2, 3) later refashioned (Gen. 18:18; 22:18; 26:4; 28:14), the meaning is that Abraham's name "shall become a blessing" and that sometime in the future "all generations on earth shall bless themselves by his name." By itself that meant only that he and his loved ones would lead a blessed life known to all the world. It had nothing to do with any "messianic" meaning. For the sake of the treasured name, lest it be extinguished in Israel, numerous progeny were desired (Deut. 25:6, 7, 10; Ruth, 4:5, 10; I. Sam. 24:21; II. Sam. 14:7.).[22]

It was not desired, as elsewhere, for the sake of death sacrifices,[23] though such existed. But there is nowhere an indication—at least not in the sources accessible to us—that the sacrifices be of special importance for the fate of the dead or for that of one offering the sacrifice.[24]

Although one might assume the contrary, the muteness in the

sources concerning "life after death" originally was not connected with a deliberate struggle of the priests against the power of the sibs anchored in ancestor worship. In later times priestly religion and sib power undoubtedly worked at cross purposes. Even then the contrast remained essentially latent and, in any case, did not lead to the Yahwistic conception of all death cult. Sib power and death cult go often, but not necessarily together. In Egypt the death cult in its unsurpassed intensity has by no means brought about magically or cultically bound sib associations.[25] These last were, rather, singularly absent, for the patrimonial bureaucracy of the *"corvée state"* had crushed the importance of the sibs even before the death cult received its paramount and final elaboration. The strongly-developed old Israelite sib organization, on the other hand, did not permit true ancestor worship of Chinese or Indian stamp to emerge. Nor did it allow for a death cult of Egyptian stamp. Certainly it could easily have been developed from the position of the family head as a house priest and the sib cults, and, once developed, it would have greatly enhanced the power and ritualistic prestige of the sibs thus creating serious obstacles to the diffusion of the pure Yahwe belief. The organization of guest peoples then might have possibly led to the formation of castes. Insofar, it was of no small significance that the Yahwe belief was from the beginning clearly inimical to the emergence of a death or ancestor cult.[26] For the typical points of departure for the emergence of such cults seem to have existed. A cult of actual or alleged tribal heroes is not ascertainable, but the mentioning of the tombs of several of them suggests cults as probable, which then were quite studiously reinterpreted by the later priestly revision. That the road toward the death cult had been taken is shown more by mention of the death sacrifices and mourning customs in Deuteronomy (26:14) and the residues of the death oracles, than the high valuation of piety for the corpse in the (apocryphal) Book of Tobit, which is perhaps influenced by Persia. More significant than all these residues, the quite obviously conscious and deliberate rejection of all these beginnings of a death cult by the Yahwe religion, cutting off their development, speaks for its existence.

This opposition was strikingly biased in nature. Decisive in this is not the impurity of all dead things and of everything even indirectly related to the grave, for instance, the mourning bread. The dead and everything concerning them was "impure," i.e., a source of magical defilement even where subject to a cult as in Egypt. The fact that the Yahwe priest was forbidden to participate in any way in the mourning of the dead, with the exception of his next of kin, goes, after all, beyond what might be thus determined. The same applies to the absolute ritualistic impurity of all livestock even if but parts had been used for death sacrifice or eaten at burial meals. Indeed, it was typical of the "negative confession of sin" to which the individual had to submit when "appearing before Yahwe," that the sacrifice be ritually pure in this respect (Deut. 26:14). The tabooing of death oracles has the same implication. For these were not tabooed as some form of forbidden oracular practice because they were fraudulent, but despite their efficacy and revelation of the truth, as shown, for example, by Samuel's exorcism. No, they were in competition with the oracle formulae handled by the Yahwe priests and derived from cults which obviously signified dangerous rivalry for them.

Besides native chthonian cults, above all, the Egyptian death cult in the direct neighborhood was obviously an enemy against which the tabooing of all death cult was directed.[27] As is known, the numerous scarabaeuses found in Palestine, served magically to protect the dead before the judge of the dead and suggest the probability that the Egyptian death cult was not unknown. However, nothing more clearly proves the profound discontent with which the Yahwe religion, for reasons of this all-pervasive antagonism toward Egyptian esoterics and chthonian mysteries, faced all matters of the "beyond," than the abrupt stoppage of all trains of thought [28] seeming to lead unavoidably in this direction. This is true of the whole of Old Testament literature including all prophets, psalmists, and poets of legends. For the prophets (Is. 28:15) a political alliance with Egypt means an alliance with *sheol,* that is, with the gods of death. This helps to explain their stubborn hostility against Egyptian support.

In the face of all this, one gains the impression that belief in resurrection, existing in esoteric form in Babylonia and determined through astral myths also in pre-exilic times was not unknown.[29] It appears suddenly in the book of Daniel as a ready-made conception and becomes a popular (Pharisaical) belief after the time of the Maccabees. To be sure, official Babylonian religion knows as little of this as does Israelite religion. It considers death to be an unavoidable evil of humankind. For the plant of life under the protection of evil demons is deeply hidden in the netherworld, which in Babylonia, too, is a shadowy realm. And only individual mortals, as in Israel, are removed from it by the grace of the gods into a realm of bliss. But in Israel one can sense that it is no matter of ignoring but of rejecting this afterworld. The entire realm of the dead and the fate of the soul remained uncanny to official priestly and prophetic religion. Its representatives and, indeed, the greatest of them, never employed the idea of compensation in the hereafter, an idea native to Egyptian and Zoroastrian religion. That remained the case up to the time of the Pharisees, who brought a change in this respect. Piety toward living parents is highly praised and its breach is strictly taboo, but there is never mention of a fate of ancestors in the beyond no matter how splendid they may have been. This is the case even though retribution and just compensation was what the Yahwe believers hopefully expected of their god and although there existed sib solidarity with its liability of descendants for the sins of their fathers.

In later times, as we shall see, the promises of the prophets have, by their peculiarity, co-determined this rejection of all individual compensation in the beyond in favor of collective hopes in this world. In the early period, however, this rejection of all speculation about the beyond is hardly accidental. It is equally characteristic of the law collections and the historians, and this in the neighborhood of well-known Egypt. The nearest direct opponents were presumably the orgiastic cults of the chthonian and Canaanite *numina*. General chthonian, not specifically Egyptian, traits are indicated by the tabooed mourning customs (incision of wounds, closely cropped hair, and similar phenomena) enumerated by the prophets (Amos, Isaiah, Micah) and in the Torah (Lev. 19:28; Deut. 14:1). And the prohibition (Deut. 14:2) is motivated by the relation to Yahwe, hence, in a cultic manner. As far as is known, Yahwe simply has never borne any features of a chthonian deity. He resides always on the mountains or in the temple, never in the earth. *Sheol* or Hades is never present as a creation of Yahwe; it is of all the places in the universe the one for which this is not claimed. He is never god of the dead or of a realm of the dead. The cults of chthonian deities and the gods of the dead always have quite specific peculiarities. No trace of them can be ascertained in Yahwe worship. He has just as little ever been a deity of vegetation or celestial bodies, deities whose worship is usually productive of hopes for resurrection. Undoubtedly this cultic opposition was decisive for the attitudes of Yahwe priests and Torah teachers.

Conceptions of resurrection, conjoined to death cults were probably not unknown in Palestine. However, the Yahwe priesthood had nothing to do with them nor wished to, because their own ritualistic customs agreed as little with sidereal as with chthonian cults. Besides externally opposing the priests of the dead and interpreters of death oracles, they may also have feared that any concession to speculation concerning a beyond might make them fall for immensely popular cults such as that of the Egyptian Osiris, be it the Osiris cult itself or a derived esoteric resurrection mystery. Probably favorable to this rejection of all death cults and ancestor worship was the fact that the hallowing of bookishly fixed wisdom of the ancestors, given through the Egyptian social structure, did not operate in ancient Israel. Likewise favorable was the fact that no true nobility developed with individual ancestor worship. For however little a developed "ancestor cult" occasioned the hostility of Yahwe priests against the mourning customs, the placing of the prohibition of mourning mortification by bodily incision with tattooing (Lev. 19:28)—doubtlessly a tattooing with the sib and tribal sign transmitted from the tribal father—shows that, in practice, the opposition was also directed against the cultic significance of the sib. The struggle of the pure Yahwe believers against the emergence of cult associations of the sibs, in turn, prevented the emergence of ancestor worship, which would have found its seat in sib associations. Thus, at a later time, the sib festivals vanished entirely.

PART III

PRIESTHOOD, CULT, AND ETHICS

CHAPTER VI

CULTIC PECULIARITIES
OF YAHWISM

1. The Sabbath

T HE Yahwe cult had to accommodate to the fact that in the agricultural territory of Palestine the usual sidereal and vegetation deities continued to exist. Alongside preexisting or imported Phoenician cults, particularly those of Moloch and Astarte, and Mesopotamian deities never recognized by Yahwe priests, Tammuz and the moon god Sin, the legend of Jephthah's daughter would seem to document the existence of annual wailing rites for the death of an ancient feminine vegetation deity. However, these strange gods did not have decisive significance for the formation of Yahwe religion and may be disregarded here. Their influence asserted itself in innumerable details, but not in the rites decisive for the basic patterns of the way of life. There is one exception to this. Clearly, the highly important institution of the Sabbath [1] is related to the *shabattu* day of the moon cult which also prevailed in Babylon.

The etymology of the Hebraic word for "to swear," literally, "to seventh oneself" indicates that the sacredness of the number seven found in Babylon extends back also in Palestine to olden times. The same holds probably also for the conception of the "sevenfold godhead." But the honoring of the Sabbath in both countries is hardly due to genuine borrowing, but to a common tradition. Differences appear even in the earliest mention of the

Sabbath. In Mesopotamia the *shabattu* day was strictly bound to the course of the moon: the new moon, the full moon; later it was bound up with the days of the months divisible by seven and seven times seven. In Israel every seventh day continued to be festive regardless of the phases of the moon, even though there, too, the sacredness of the new moon was ancient [2] and there are vestiges of a former sacredness of the full moon. Perhaps, as Beer assumes, the original meaning of "Sabbath" was full-moon day, only later transferred to "seventh day" (Ex. 23:12; 34:21). Israel shared with Babylon the magical conception of the number seven, but with a difference. In Mesopotamia the *shabattu* in historical times was a day of penance. In Israel, originally, the seventh day was obviously a happy day of rest from work; a day when people cared for other things than the usual occupational routine and especially visited the men of God (II. Ki. 4:23). As the Nehemiah chronicle particularly shows (13:15), it was also the day for the peasants to drive to town to the market, to the kermess,[3] just as the Roman *nundinae* and like the one day of the five-day week prevailing in some vegetable cultivating countries.

The accusation which the prophet Amos leveled against those grain sellers who deem the Sabbath too long since it disturbs their business, shows that even then the Sabbath rest was enforced at least with respect to urban and professional traders. This was necessary with regard to the *gerim* who would otherwise be advantaged in competition. Nehemiah 13:16 f. offers a close analogy. According to the prophetic legend (II. Ki. 4:23) from the time of the Jehu dynasty, slaves and cattle were apparently not yet included in the injunction to observe a day of rest. Apparently this occurred only in Deuteronomic times and only then charity seems to have been advanced as the central motive. It was only in Exile times that observance of the Sabbath, and the duty to abstain from all activity going beyond ritual prescriptions, was elevated to an importance in Israel second only to circumcision. This was brought about through the striving of the priests for insurmountable, "confessionally" discriminating duties of Israel. As the mere fact of being circumcised offered no guarantee for the truly god-pleasing life, the Sabbath became one of the chief ritualistic commandments of

Israel, one which was repeatedly and ever increasingly emphasized. It came to stand in significance beside the prohibition of murder, idolatry, and enjoyment of blood.

In the revision containing the myth of God's six days of work, the Sabbath received a cosmic explanation. The priestly position, at the time, was that violation of Sabbath rest was a capital offense (Ex. 31:14 f.).

The origin of the Sabbath is certainly not to be found among the stock-breeders of the desert or steppe—where the Sabbath is impracticable or devoid of significance and where the phases of the moon are of small significance—but it is to be found in an agricultural area. The question, then, whether the number seven refers to planetary movements or to division by four of the moon's cycle is rightly answered increasingly in favor of the latter assumption.[4] The fact that in contrast to Babylonia, the day of rest in Israel became or remained a regularly recurrent day is simply to be explained by the greater prevalence in Palestine of peasant economic interests and customs oriented around the local urban market as over against the predominance of astronomical knowledge of genteel priests among the Babylonians. In Babylon astronomical correctness was ritualistically essential. In Israel, however, during the time of the fixation of Sabbath customs, the interest of peasants and small town burghers in the regular recurrence of the market day was decisive. The regular recurrence of the Sabbath was probably established with the strengthening of the market economy. Deuteronomy, the specific law of the city-state, no longer mentions the ancient moon festivals. By themselves, the Israelites simply could not achieve sidereal correctness. One need only remember what travail a correct determination of simple astronomical facts cost even the rabbis of late Judaic times.

The Sabbath rite could readily be detached from its connection with the moon cult and could even be integrated into the Yahwe religion as one of its chief ritualistic commandments. However, there were other agricultural cults, partially taken over by the Israelites of the confederacy, partially found in their midst during their transition to fixed settlement, which posed more permanent difficulties.

The deities of the Khabiri on the Amarna tablets were called "ilani." Those of the Canaanites and of the Israelites settled in the North were called "*elohim*," a name which in some places was understood as a plural, perhaps also for the Israelite gods— the attribute often is placed in the plural—in the present revision, however, it is always thought of as a singular when the reference is to the Israelite religion. One passage in the very Book of the Covenant, however, seems to form an exception to this (Ex. 22:28). Moreover the grammatical forms in Abraham's address to the divine epiphany of the three men would seem to make it probable that the singular of the address did not preclude the possibility of polytheistic conceptions. The use of the plural to designate a preeminent and at the same time abstract supreme being seated in heavenly distances was indeed diffused in neighboring Phoenicia, and was apparently also present in Palestine.⁵ And in later Babylonian usage the plural "ilani," like "*elohim*" in Israel, is a designation of the godhead. Nevertheless it remains probable that a pantheon of some sort originally underlay the expression. However, Hehn especially made plausible that even the Israelite immigrants met with the designation as a collectivity for the "godhead" or the "supreme god." Naturally, for the Yahwe believer the supremacy of the god of the covenant was firmly established. He was for him "*elohim*," because he was simply his godhead generally.⁶

This was comparable to the position of the supreme god of heavens in Babylon and in the areas under its influence. The letter of the Canaanite Achijam (fifteenth century) designates the supreme deity as "bel ilanu," "Lord of the Gods." In the nature of the case Yahwe was fused with special ease with such supreme heavenly deities. In relatively late passages he is still called "God of gods." In the angry remarks of Isaiah against the *elim*, is continued remembrance of the fact that these were once deities opposed to Yahwe; this is suggested, too, in the names of some of them and in the clearly *ex post facto* identification with Yahwe. One tradition which in its present revision is late has the priest king Melchisedec worship the "supreme god," *El eljon* during Abraham's time in Jerusalem (?). According to other accounts this is probably a Phoenician name for the god of heavens at the head of the pantheon and Abraham then uses the same name for Yahwe.⁷ The old designation *El shaddaj* which according to Delitzsch is related to *schadu*, the Babylonian term for mountain, refers to the same.[8]

In later views other heavenly beings were considered as Yahwe's messengers and aids. Originally, however, they were themselves gods, as may be gathered from the uncertain treatment of the three figures of the epiphany with Abraham in the grove of Mamra. This also appears from the self-designation "we" often to be found in divine resolves in Genesis. "The children of the *elohim*" in the mutilated ancient titanic myth (Gen. 6) take a fancy to the daughters of man and produce with them the *Nephilim* (Num. 13:33), the giants (of the great celestial constellations) from whom stem the sons of Enak (Num., ibid.) and those knights (*gibborim*) of bygone archaic times of Canaan. The ancestors had to fight them. In the original formulation, the heavenly god destroyed them in the great flood. The starry hosts, as we saw in the Deborah Song in Northern Israel, formed the nucleus of the heavenly spirits which also, in the prophetic visions later, surrounded Yahwe. Numina, which do not appear identical with Yahwe, lay in ambush for the heroes. Such a deity is overcome by Jacob in a wrestling match.

Direct influence of Ikhnaton's sun religion on Yahwe worship is highly improbable, for propaganda for it was in any case insecure and without zeal in Palestine [9] and it occurred in remote times. However, the North Israelite abstract designation of god by "El" [10] corresponds to Babylonian usage. Moreover, the worship of the supreme god on Mount Garizim and other mountain heights suggest the Babylonian worship on gigantic terraced towers so as to be as close as possible to the god of heaven.

Almost all of these Mid-Eastern deities were astral and at the same time vegetative in nature and they closely resembled one another.[11] As is usual their personifications develop only gradually. Originally one could not separate the spirit of the star from the star itself.[12] Only functional deities of culture, as for instance, the Babylonian god of the scribes, Nabu, were from the beginning conceived quite personally. But a tendency to revert to the impersonal remained characteristic of most of them. Indeed, the supreme deities of heaven (thus Anu in Babel) always were abstract and strange to the popular cult. There was an ubiquitous bent for syncretism and for elevating the sun god as supreme, in the eyes of the intellectual the only god. In Palestine there are only scattered traces of this tendency, although the *elohim* abstraction, after all, points in this direction.

2. Baal and Yahwe: The Idols and the Ark

BAAL, the most important deity actually in competition with Yahwe was of Canaanite, Phoenician-influenced, origin and had already undergone important changes in terms of the more highly developed Babylonian religion.

As is diffused in primitive form everywhere among preliterate peoples, the original, or correctly speaking, the prevailing conception during the time of occupation was that a special god was "lord" over well defined things, events of nature, and social life. This is similar to the conception of the Indian Lord of prayer or the ancient Chinese conception of godhead. Things or events "belonged" to the respective Baal as a piece of land or head of cattle or a monopolized "vocation" "belongs" to a man. The origin of two main categories of deities is located here. First, there were functional deities, as, perhaps, was the *baal berith*, the "lord of the covenant" who had "jurisdiction" over the conclusion of covenants, protecting them and avenging their violation. Baal Zebul of Ekron, the "lord" of the pestilence carrying flies, or the "lord" of dreams, or of anger are also examples of functional deities.

Secondly, there were deities to whom fertile soil belonged, the "local deities" in this technical sense. While the Israelite confederacy god was deity of the people's community, like Bel of the Assyrian warrior people, though more in the nature of an army king, the Palestinian Baal of a place was lord of the land, of all its fruit, in the nature of a patrimonial landlord, more like the Babylonian Bel, the Lord of the Fertile Soil. Later we shall examine in greater detail the great ritualistic significance of the chthonian character displayed by most of the more important Baal cults.

To Baal were due the firstlings of all fruit of the soil, cattle, men who lived on the land, an obligation transferred by the priests to Yahwe, to whom this was originally unknown. The religious motivation of the previously mentioned duty not to harvest the land (Lev. 19:9 and 23:22) completely came from this realm of ideas as indicated by the motivation: "I am Yahwe your god." A different orientation distinguished the not entirely antagonistic conception of Yahwe from that of Baal. The former is the god of the community members, the latter that of the territorial association, the one is the god of heaven, the other god of earth. In Canaanite territory the second conception was certainly quite old; it developed on the basis of settled city life and patrician landlordism. Each city had local deities of this kind. During the Amarna time the governors complained to the king of the fact that the city deities, by whose grace the Pharaoh is lord of the city, left the city and that it, therefore, fell into the hands of the enemies.

The Israelites apparently bestowed the name of Baal upon quite a number of deities with special names: upon Hadad, who was worshipped under the image of a steer, likewise upon the Phoenician Milk or Melkart, who was imported under the Omrid dynasty. In any case, the most important competitor of Yahwe was the local Baal, because he was a functionally quite universal figure and was the proprietor of the "land" in the economic and political sense. In the case of peaceful affiliation or violent annexation of cities by Israel these Baals retained, of course, possession of the city and their shrines. In the original view, that did no harm to the great war god of the confederacy.

With the increasing prestige of Yahwe, however, his relation to the Baals had somehow to be regularized. He could, possibly, head up a pantheon as the god of heaven and something of the sort seems to be echoed in the *elohim* designation. But this brought the dangers of his fading as happened to all such supreme gods of heaven wherever they had no permanent sanctuary for workaday needs. The Baals, then, continued to be the lords of the living cults. On the other hand Yahwe was simply identified with the Baals or somehow joined to them in worship. Until post-exilic times Yahwe was worshipped by Jews without any scruples together even with entirely strange gods in one and the same temple.[13] In the case of combinations of Yahwe with the local deity, the Baal tended to become more important in times of peace and prosperity, Yahwe in great war emergencies.[14] This actually happened and explains the fact that when raising

an outcry against Baal, puritanical Yahwe prophets had most
to contend with in times of peaceful prosperity, whereas every
national war and act of foreign oppression and threat benefited Yahwe, the old god of the Red Sea catastrophe. One may
assume that there were long periods when the two kinds of
deities stood peacefully side by side and the Baals were important without being considered opponents of Yahwe. Even cele-
brated heroes of North Israel are to be found with Baal names:
especially Jerub-Baal, who as war hero of Yahwe quite characteristically received the new name of Gideon, similarly, the sons
of the good Yahwistic King Saul, whose names were also characteristically altered by later tradition.

By virtue of the frequent identification with local or functional Baals, the cult of Yahwe also adopted their cult attributes, above all, the cult images. According to tradition and
verified by excavations, the original cult of the Israelite confederacy must be considered as probably devoid of image; it
obviously was taken over in this form. Certainly this was not
the product of any ancient "high level" speculations concerning
the nature of God. Rather the reverse holds, it was the result
of primitive cult implements, which, given the great sanctity of
the ancient war ritual of the confederacy were definitively stereotyped at a particularly early time. The god remained image-less
simply because he still had none at the time of reception.

This was due to the level of material culture in the reception
area. For the same reason the oldest law books prescribe a simple altar made of earth and unhewn stones as was customary
at the time. The preservation of this image-less cult in times of
developed artistic work is, indeed, not peculiar to the Yahwe
cult. The same is ascertainable elsewhere, for instance, with
some early Hellenic and ancient Cretan cults and with the
Iranians who, like the Israelites, were influenced by Babylon.
Decisive for the retention of this feature at some of the more
important sanctuaries were doubtlessly their forms of worship
which were customary of old and esteemed as especially holy because of their age. The fear of evil charm in case of change made
the reception of icons difficult. The only thing peculiar about Israelite development was the intensity with which the negativism
toward images was carried through. It was approximated only

by Islamic development under Israelite influence and partially by Zoroastrism. Elsewhere the tabooing of images was confined to some sanctuaries or to the respective deities, and, for the rest, room was left for the practice of art inside and outside the religious sphere.

In Israel, Yahwe became the only god. Alongside the intensification of the claim of Yahwe for monolatry, the representatives of the cult without image have not only required the tabooing of Yahwe images, but also the rejection of all image-like paraments. Finally, iconoclasm was carried to an extent inimical almost in principle to the practice of all fine arts. Such was the second commandment in its definitive formulation. That had greatest bearing for the suppression of artistic practice and aesthetic sensitivity in later Jewry. This last and quite radical striving for theological consistency was but a product of the priestly quest for efficient, ritually differentiating prescriptions. It cannot be discerned in the older sources. It is even doubtful whether, in ancient times, Yahwistic Puritanism only tabooed molten images, the products of urban culture, or also (or precisely) carved images, or all images—the three Decalogues are contradictory in this. Artistic skill of the parament artisan then was considered a divine charisma.

This negativism toward all images acquired its sharpness only in the course of the quite vehement struggle which the representatives of the old image-less cult had to fight against the Yahwe images and other cult paraments. These made their appearance in the culture area of Canaan and their nature has been greatly obscured by later tradition. The *ephod*[15] especially occupies an uncertain place. As with the *teraphim* one cannot ascertain its original nature. The occasionally posited phallic nature[16] can hardly be proven. Some accounts would suggest a picture, others, something to wear with a pocket for the oracle tablets, still others a garment. Quite possibly the meaning changed under the influence of the later conception of the cult without image. If it was initially an image-like parament, it was presumably alien to the original cult of Yahwe. The account suggesting this most strongly is of North Israelite origin. Here, we may disregard the question as to whether the "tabernacle" of Yahwe was more than a later theoretical construct. The portable

"Ark of Yahwe" was far more important and represented a specific parament of the Yahwe cult without images.

It will, perhaps, never be ascertained whether this Ark, as Eduard Meyer especially assumed, originally was a fetish box and hence Egyptian in origin, or whether, as M. Dibelius [17] has made more probable, it was originally a box-like throne of heaven and hence pre-Israelite-Palestinian in origin; or whether the Ark, if nevertheless a box, originally contained a sacred stone possibly covered with runes. Or whether it was—as Schwally assumed in analogy to an Islamic military field shrine (Machmal)—from the beginning an empty box serving magically to confine the god. Dibelius, in any case, has made it very probable from the oldest accounts (Num. 10: 35, 36 in conjunction with I. Sam. 1:9 and 4:4 and the image of Jeremiah 3:16) that during the liberation wars against the Philistines, the Ark was a cherub-decorated seat upon which Yahwe sat invisibly and which, in war emergencies, was conveyed on a wagon into camp. Before battle Yahwe was summoned in a rhythmic imploration to rise against the enemies, likewise after victory to resume his seat (Num. 10:35, 36). In the later Samuel legend, Yahwe appears localized in or, probably, upon the Ark in the sanctuary. Perhaps that is the product of a later conception from the time of complete settlement—although logically incompatible conceptions of god often stand side by side.

The belief that Yahwe, during war, had his seat invisibly on the Ark was not identical, though perhaps not absolutely incompatible, with the view entertained, for instance, by the Song of Deborah of god drawing near in a storm from his seat on the wooded mountains of Seir. In any case, it is hardly accidental that the Persians, like the Israelites a mountain dwelling people neighboring on charioteering peoples of the plain, according to Herodotus (7:40) likewise carried their invisible god Ahuramazda on a wagon into war.[18] The original intention may have been to oppose the carriage riding king of heaven to the carriage riding war kings and idols of the enemies. Reichel has ascertained several instances of empty thrones of deities also in the Hellenic area.

A god, whose ancient transmitted cult was without image, plainly had to be, normally, an invisible deity. Such invisibility necessarily fed his specific dignity and uncanny mysteriousness. Here again the historically given cult form of the confederate god occasioned his spiritualization which was both facilitated and suggested by these qualities. In the tradition, the Ark is bound to Shiloh and its old Elide priestly sib, hence is North Israelite in nature. It is also quite intimately connected with the quality of Yahwe as a god of war and Lord of the heavenly hosts (*Tsebaoth*). However, the Song of Deborah and military accounts before the time of the Philistines, know nothing of the Ark and at the time its appearance is ephemeral. Thus time, occasion, and scope of its original recognition as a Yahwistic cult parament and war symbol remain uncertain. Only Deuteronomic theology made it into the "Ark of the Covenant," hence the container of the tablets of the laws. The conception of god linked to the Ark, and locating him upon it or in it, no longer had any appeal. In any case, the empty Ark and its significance was symptom and probably also occasion for the relative spiritualization of this anthropomorphic conception of god, as directly determined by the absence of images in worship. The seat of the god of the covenant on the wooded mountains of Seir naturally was without all images and temples; there is no known trace of either.

The Hezekiah annals indicate that a snake staff, the so-called "serpent of brass" belonged to the paraments of the later Jerusalemite cult. In contrast to the luxurious implements of Solomonic times it was traced back to Moses and obviously was a truly ancient implement because it was no longer understood and was interpreted in terms of etiological legends. In the tradition Moses is also treated as a therapeutic miracle maker, especially as savior from pestilence. This would well agree with the fact that epidemics also belong to Yahwe's special means of fighting his enemies. The etiological saga suggests the idea— unprovable to be sure—that the snake staff was an emblem [19] of certain later vanished medicine men who had been Yahwe priests. This completes the list of truly ancient Yahwistic paraments.

As the idolatry of the civilized country invaded the North Israelite Yahwe cult, given the intimate fusion of Yahwe and Baal, Yahwe was represented mainly as a steer, hence, probably as the fertility god of the tillers. King Jeroboam, who bears a Yahwe name and had a Yahwe prophet on his side, was credited with having put up gilded steer images in some North Israelite sanctuaries [20] for the sake of the emancipation from Jerusalem. One of these images was to be found at Dan, a sanctuary considered especially orthodox under the management of a priestly sib allegedly stemming from Moses. Not the slightest objection against the apparent employment of such Yahwe images is known of the North Israelite prophets under the Omrids: Elijah and Elishah, both relentless opponents of Baal cults which had strongly developed under Phoenician influence. The fight, also within Yahwism, against idols *per se* was set off doubtlessly by the struggle that just opened against foreign cults which were all idol cults, imported by foreign princesses and allies. The struggle could start from those sanctuaries in the country where Yahwe was worshipped without images, as was doubtlessly the practice at old non-Israelite sanctuaries of the desert. The priests of such sanctuaries necessarily were likely to regard this form the only correct one. And with mounting external pressure they could mobilize behind them the growing concern for correct Yahwe worship as known from olden time of Israel's victories. Where the Ark represented the most holy cult object, only worship without image can have existed of yore, and that was in Shiloh until the time of David. Likewise, there is no reason to doubt that since the transfer of the Ark to Jerusalem worship there also was at first entirely without image.

The tradition, however, permits us to see that the holy Ark had stood half forgotten in a private house for quite some time before David established the sanctuary in Jerusalem and after the Philistines had taken the Ark in battle and presumably had destroyed Shiloh. Hence, it means probably a first decisive turning point in favor of the power position of the image-less Yahwe cult when David made this the form of worship of the royal residence by transferring to it this very symbol of the cult without image of the confederate war god. David's alliance with the Elide priests expelled from Shiloh, presumably gave him, from the beginning, support against Saul, who, though a Yahwist, as a North Israelite was oriented to the combined Yahwe-Baal worship. This led him to institute a notorious massacre among those priests, against which the tradition reacted with a hatred still to be felt in the present revision.

With David, the South became the center of the belief in worship without image as solely correct. The Solomonic Temple, to be sure, already meant a reversal to this puritanical cult. Apparently it bore a sacred inscription which permits us to infer sun worship, a kingly cult diffused among many dynasties. Later, also, a sun carriage with horses is mentioned. And the Temple construction clearly offended against the ancient imperative of Yahwe to worship him upon a plain earthen altar without hewn stones. Doubtlessly, the Temple in many details failed to comply with the later demand for the absolute avoidance of icon-like paraments. The downfall of the Elide priest Abiathar may well be connected with these innovations of corvée kingship oriented to Egypt and Phoenicia. At the time, however, these innovations were obviously not in the center of attention. The actual fight against these innovations began only at a far later time.

No principled opposition against all images was noticeable as yet even though the most varied paraments then were suspect of alluding to foreign cults. This opposition began in the time of Hosea and attained its first success in the time of Hezekiah. At this time it did not even stop short of the ancient parament of the brazen serpent going back to Moses: it was broken into pieces by King Hezekiah. This struggle was motivated by the increasing political concern to eliminate all possible reasons for the wrath of the war god of old, who once had been worshipped without image. In addition it was motivated by the conception of god, meanwhile sublimated, in intellectual circles who cherished the very invisibility and non-representational nature of god which served their conceptualization. They now scorned the work of the artisans in foreign idolatries juxtaposing it to his superhuman majesty. Baal worship was persecuted as the source of these abominations invading Yahwe worship. Moreover, the increasing sharpness of this struggle against Baal worship was connected with profound and intrinsic pecularities of the worship of god which were inseparably bound up with the old Canaanite cult of Baal, but absolutely contradictory to true Yahwistic religiosity. In explaining this, we have to go far back and first focus attention on the priests, the managers of cult.

3. Sacrifice and Expiation

IN EARLY Israelite times there existed no generally recognized priesthood [21] of the confederacy, which could have monopolized the sacrifice to the god of covenant. This is sufficiently documented. The later sacrifice was necessarily not important in the relation between the Israelite confederacy and Yahwe. For, as stated earlier, prior to kingship, there existed no confederate authorities competent to offer regular sacrifices in peacetime. As a unit the confederacy existed only in time of war and then, according to tradition, the partial or complete tabooing of the booty was the specific ritualistic means of satisfying the god. This, to be sure, gave the god a greater stake in Israel's victory than prior sacrifice. Naturally, as to all other deities, sacrifices probably always were offered to Yahwe in order to obtain his good will. In wartime sacrifices were offered also on behalf of the confederacy, in peacetime, however, individual sacrifices were offered as warranted by the occasion. In traditional theory every meal, at least every meat dinner represented a "sacrificial feast," in the very broad sense that the deity had to receive his share by offerings. Princes and at times the heads of sibs, too, proffered sacrifices to him before battle and otherwise according to need at the old sanctuaries. According to a reliable tradition, only the sprinkling of the altar with blood would seem to be reserved to Moses, hence to professional priests. It is uncertain whether this form of worship was diffused beyond Shiloh. Its age, too, is uncertain. Later priestly theory, to be sure, represented even Saul's sacrifice without consulting Samuel (Samuel, in this, was cast into the role of priest) as a paradigm of interference in priestly jurisdiction which caused Saul's undoing. But even later this did not by any means agree with positive law. In the Book of Samuel, David wears priestly garments and gives the blessing. Under King Uzziah in the priestly revision of the kingly tradition, the same conflict occurs as allegedly between Saul and Samuel.[22] It must be taken as certain that princes and large landlords employed ritually trained priests. Originally they had free discretion in this. In the older tradition, which the Chroniclers later expurgated, David makes two of his sons priests.[23] In the Book of Judges, Micah, a big landlord does likewise, according to a tradition soon to be discussed in another connection. Shrines which princes and private persons furnished in this manner were considered their private property. They had domestic jurisdiction over them, as the North Israelite kings over Jeroboam's establishment in Beth-el (Amos 7:13). According to one tradition, they ordered their hired priests as their officials even to execute, as, for instance, in Jerusalem, the construction of altars following foreign models (II. Ki. 16:10). No collective organization of the sacrificial priests existed; this was simply due to the competition of the shrines in which, understandably, the sanctuaries of private persons in the Northern kingdom were not nearly as disadvantaged in relation to kingly foundations as were those in the centralized Jewish city-state. The main priest carried the title "the priest" (*ha kohen*); only late is the title chief priest (*kohen ha rosh*) found in Jerusalem (II. Ki. 25:18), it is not certain whether the post-exilic title "high priest" (*kohen ha gedol*) existed (II. Ki. 22:4, 8 and 23:4 is suspected as a gloss, compare II. Ki. 11:9 f., where the title *ha kohen* stands for the same superior priest Jehoiada).[24]

In any case, the cult priests of the kingly temples were enumerated as royal officials (II. Sam. 8:16 f., 20:23 f.). They accompanied the king to war and with one exception, Jehoiada under Athaliah in pre-Deuteronomic times, they played no noticeable independent political role. Least of all were they considered heads of a religious "congregation." Such did not exist. In olden times the army summons was also the religious congregation as was later the territorial community of fully qualified Israelites. The court judging Jeremiah consisted of the royal *sarim* and the *zekenim,* whose role in the verdict remains questionable. The *'am* (militia men) formed the "bystanders" of this court organization (*kahal*). The priests were the accusers but did not sit in court. The king (Josiah), not the supreme priest (Hilkiah) called the community together, also in case a religious *berith* was at issue. We may bypass here the question of ancient priest-kingship in Jerusalem suggested by the doubtful tradition of Genesis 14. In any case, according to the old tradition, the prince was legitimately and ritualistically qualified to offer sacrifice on behalf of the body politic.

Likewise, there were certainly, of yore, sanctuaries which people visited from afar and where local, hereditary charismatic priest-sibs solely conducted, according to ancient rules, solemn ceremonies for princes as well as private persons. Thus, the sib of the Elides dominated the sanctuary at Shiloh, which the prophets (Jeremiah) considered to be especially old and purely Yahwistic. The tradition concerning the ancient practice of sacrificial offerings seems to run as follows. The patrons offered flesh sacrifices in connection with individual prayers for fulfillment of certain wishes, and the priest took his share of this sacrifice. Furthermore, sacrificial feasts at which the participants got drunk were also no rare occurrence. The significance of the sacrificial meals shall concern us later and we shall ignore here the complex history of the ancient Israelite sacrifice.[25]

Here we shall first address ourselves to the sacrificial offerings. These in Israel as elsewhere were at first considered to be suitable means to reenforce supplications to the Lord. The oldest cult prescriptions, as preserved in the cultic supplements of the Book of the Covenant, required only generally that the Israelites should appear three times a year before the Lord, and should "not appear empty handed." No other unquestionably old prescriptions exist, and the practical significance of this commandment cannot be ascertained.

The significance of the sacrificial offerings first shifted quantitatively with the increasing prestige of the confederate war god as brought about by expansion and, above all, with the establishment of kingship. The Davidians and, in the North, Jeroboam, established kingly sanctuaries provided with regular sacrifices.

The change in the meaning of sacrificial offering, however, was of far greater importance. This occurred with the increasingly gloomy political prospects of the country during the further course of kingly rule. The question inevitably arose: whence this unfavorable development of the political and military situation of Israel? The answer could be only God's wrath is upon the people. The Israelite conception of sin takes its point of departure from purely objective factual data, as indicated by the old words for "sin" mostly derived from *chatah,* "to transgress."

An offense, obviously, was first and foremost a ritualistic transgression evoking God's anger. Hence, here as elsewhere fear of ritualistic mistakes and their consequences was the oldest motive for the quest of expiation. But Yahwe was also contractual partner to the *berith* with Israel, and the old social law based upon fellowship and brotherly aid in need was considered an obligation toward him. The concept of sin, thus, had to extend to substantively ethical, particularly social-ethical stipulations. Yahwistic criticism of the attitudes of the kings and of the social changes brought about by urbanism thus led to expansion of the concept of sin beyond the area of ritual to social ethics. The same occurred under similar conditions elsewhere as, for instance, is indicated by the Sumerian inscription of *Urukagina.* It seemed obvious that the mighty war god linked his grace to the observance of his commandments, solemnly adopted by *berith.* Besides ritualistic prescriptions,[26] he insisted especially upon observance of the old confederate law which he guaranteed. With failure and during times of political duress, naturally it was more widely discussed which socially relevant abomination might have caused the wrath of God and how His wrath might be assuaged. After the ninth century both kingdoms were in a chronic state of duress.

With all this, as the sources clearly permit us to see, the significance of the sacrifice as a means of expiation of guilt increasingly came to the fore. Eventually sacrifice became all important. Two out of presumably quite manifold varieties of expiatory sacrifices, *chattat* and *asham* alone became canonical through circumstances probably quite accidental.[27] This increased the necessity for having access to Yahwe priests knowing the law and ritual, in order to decipher God's will and the transgressions necessary to be expiated. With increasing rationalization of life, the demand for means of determining and expiating sins increased everywhere, including Mesopotamia, and under the pressure of its political fate this need gained an especially great momentum in Israel.

Thus, with the increasing importance of the expiatory sacrifice and instruction concerning Yahwe's will the demand increased for persons having knowledge of Yahwe and His commandments. For it was not primarily the offering of the sacrifice

itself that people sought, however important its correctness may
have been, but above all, knowledge of God's will and the events
giving offense to Him. Local and political associations as well as
individuals found themselves in this situation. The primary concern of the body politic was how to influence the fortunes of war
and produce rich rainfall, both promised by Yahwe in return
for obedience and correct behavior. To this was added the individual wish for help in all sorts of personal emergencies.
Moses, like Elijah in the tradition, performed private healing
miracles as well as political ones, especially military, rain-making, and dietary miracles. They scrutinized the will of God and
offenses against him. This last increasingly became the special
service of the professional leaders of Yahwism.

As the sources show, almost all sorts of means for determining
God's will known to the surrounding civilized world, were also
to be found in Palestine. But not all of them were considered
equally legitimate by Israelite tradition. Later only three forms
were held to be correct from the standpoint of strict Yahwe religion: (1) Yahwe's pronouncements to a true seer and prophet,
authorized to speak on His behalf. The criteria for distinguishing
a "true" from a "false" prophet will be discussed later. (2) For
certain cases oracle by lot, performed by professional oracular
priests by means of oracle tablets (*urim* and *thummin*) and perhaps originally by means of the arrow oracle, was acceptable.
(3) Finally the dream vision was considered legitimate although it met with increasing reservations. In the increasingly
prevailing view all other forms of divination of the future, be it
facts relevant for trial or otherwise, and, especially, of God's will
and intentions were considered accursed magic and, in certain
circumstances, capital offenses or simply swindles. The ordeal
until Deuteronomic times retained its place only for a few cases,
especially for testing the marital fidelity of a wife.

The oracle by lot continued to exist until late pre-exilic times.
Its ancient sacredness, like that of the image-less Yahwee cult,
rested on its very simplicity, agreeing with the primitive life
conditions of the steppe. The oracle by lot decreased in importance opposite consultation of seers, prophets, and other wise
men. The Exile tradition has it terminated by loss of the oracular
tablets. The death oracles and all other forms of divination,

despite the taboo placed upon them, continued, of course, to exist, but their importance clearly declined. The increasing consultation of seers, prophets, and experts in matters of ritual was a natural product of the increasingly complex questions to be answered. A simple "yea" or "nay" or a simple lot no longer sufficed for an answer. For genuine Yahwism there was an additional reason which sprang from the peculiar relationship to Yahwe: when Yahwe was angry and failed to help the nation or the individual, a violation of the *berith* with Him had to be responsible for this. Hence, it was necessary for the authorities as well as for the individual from the outset to ask which commandment had been violated? Irrational divination means could not answer this question, only knowledge of the very commandments and soul searching. Thus, the idea of *berith* flourishing in the truly Yahwistic circles pushed all scrutiny of the divine will toward an at least relatively rational mode of raising and answering the question. Hence, the priestly exhortation under the influence of the intellectual strata turned with great sharpness against soothsayers, augurs, day-choosers, interpreters of signs, conjurors of the dead, defining their ways of consulting the deities as characteristically pagan.[28]

The scriptural prophets and the strict Yahwistic circles close to them attacked, as we shall show, the reliability of dream interpretation which was partially connected with the specific vocational characteristics of these prophets, partly with their conception of Yahwe's peculiar nature and intentions. The struggle against magic and the irrational forms of divination waged prior to the scriptural prophets, besides the stated rational reasons, had, of course, also fortuitous historical reasons. They consisted in the manner in which the competition between the various categories of priests and soothsayers was settled and in the technical state of the oracular art as then practiced by the champions of the triumphant form.

We find the "sorcerer" described as a heretic everywhere, in China, India, and in the old Sumerian city-states. He is still the illegitimate competitor of the legitimate priesthood which often emerged out of purely fortuitous constellations. This taboo also extends to the sorcerer's practices. The oracle by lot, certainly, was no more rational than the Babylonian liver inspection, only

unlike this, it provided no points of departure for cosmic speculations. The reception of the aforementioned kinds of scrutiniz-
ing God's will, to be sure, was no mere accident. It was determined by the elimination of all practices connected with chthonian
cults and their concomitant kind of ecstasy.[29] We shall soon consider this aspect of the antagonism.

Who were the leaders in the consultation of Yahwe?

We have already considered the somewhat uncertain role of
the old "seers." Later they vanished completely. Ancient Yahwism
of the war confederacy knew the war ecstatics and emotional
war prophets and, similarly, the consultation of the apathetic-
ecstatic seer. But no official cult of the confederacy existed, consequently the priests could not raise the claim to monopolize
oracular art. From the beginning and doubtlessly not to their
liking, they had to concede that the gift of prophecying was possible and diffused beyond their circle. Nevertheless, the tension
continued to exist, at least for all those prophets who, unlike
the priests of the great residences, did not stand in kingly service. The fact that the cult was bound to the king discredited the
"sacrifice" *per se* in the eyes of circles skeptical of kingship. The
priests had to content themselves with eradicating all those practices which were sponsored by a guild-like organization in the
manner of a cult and, thereby, came to compete directly with
them. The priests sought to monopolize the regular management of Yahwe worship and all related activities. Our next question then is, who were the priests?

CHAPTER VII

PRIESTS AND THE CULT MONOPOLY OF JERUSALEM

1. The Levites and the Torah

I T IS no longer possible to ascertain the true nature of the priests of the sanctuaries of olden times. The old priestly sib of the Elides at Shiloh was transplanted by David to Jerusalem and degraded by Solomon. Zadok who became the leading priest of Jerusalem was a man who in the old tradition did not even have an Israelite patronymis name. Only the later tradition provided him with a family tree which it considered correct. The kings, obviously, had free disposition over priestly offices as well as the economic provisions for priests. At first the kings claimed the prerogative of proffering sacrifice. Still under Joash the king undertook the reorganization under state control of the prebendal provisions of Jerusalemite priests. Formally, this changed only with the Deuteronomic reform during the last days of the kingdom of Judah. The priesthood of Jerusalem then felt sufficiently strong to uphold the tithe and other tax claims of the god as applying throughout Israel, that is the Judaic Kingdom. These claims may have been the privilege of some sanctuaries, and to judge by the Melchizedek tradition, perhaps precisely in a limited area of Jerusalem. At the same time the priests tremendously strengthened their cult monopoly, which must have been preceded by a great enhancement of their prestige. The Deuteronomic law book designated the Yahwe priests who alone were considered legitimate priests of yore, as "Levitical priests."

The name of "Levi" has no Hebraic etymology.¹ Possibly Levites operated also outside Israel in the service of the Minaean tribal deity of Wadd.² The time of diffusion of these learned priests is uncertain.³ All that can be established is that originally they were not much at home in North Israel, that they spread into that direction by individual migration. Apparently they were not recognized as the sole legitimate priesthood, at least not by the dynasty of Jeroboam and, presumably, also, not in later times. All indications point to their origin in the Southern steppe bordering the desert from the oasis of Kadesh to Seir. A rather early tradition treats the Levites, first, as the quite personal following of Moses⁴ who enlisted their support against obstinate and disobedient opponents and secured his authority by a massacre among their near kin. In Eduard Meyer's plausible interpretation, this tradition, as well as Moses' Blessing, in any case, did not know the Levites as a hereditary caste. On the contrary, according to Moses' Blessing, one had to deny father and brother to be a Levite. Here, they are represented as a trained vocational status group. Their appearance later as sib organized and as a hereditarily qualified tribe would prove nothing against this. Such development was to be found repeatedly in as well as outside Israel.

Other parts of the tradition, however, know of a non-priestly, military "tribe of Levi"⁵ as a political ally of the tribes of Israel, especially of the tribes of Simeon and Judah. Jacob's Blessing does not recognize this tribe as a priestly status group or even acknowledge the existence of Levitical priests. The sources rather report military feats of violence of this tribe in common with Simeon, and Jacob's Blessing predicted Levi's dispersion because of an abomination: "they slew a man" and "houghed oxen." They shall be divided and scattered "in Jacob" and "in Israel" like Simeon.

The later priestly tradition viewed Moses as a member of the tribe of Levi. Perhaps the later tradition, which has been expurgated by bias, considered him the tribal father, or, at least, the *archegetes* of those sibs of the tribe of Levi which were or became Levites in the ritualistic sense. For clearly at the time of Jacob's Blessing there must have existed members of a tribe of Levi who were not Levites in the latter sense. One must choose between two assumptions: either a tribe of Levi was dispersed by political catastrophies or economic changes and its dispersed members devoted themselves in whole or in part to Yahwe sacrifice and Yahwe oracle and became Yahwe priests,[6] or the reverse obtains, namely there existed in the South an occupational status group first based upon personal training of members, then on hereditary charisma whose "Levite" laymen sibs were inter-ethnically diffused, hence representing sibs among which ritualistic training and tradition was extinguished. They were considered a tribe or actually constituted one and affiliated with Simeon but later disintegrated like Simeon.

With the Brahmins in India just as with the Levites we find the conflict between the personal charismatic and vocational status qualification on the one hand and the hereditary charismatic and status-by-birth qualification on the other. In that case, too, every born Brahmin is by no means qualified ritually for the privileges of the Brahmins: to proffer sacrifice, to teach the Veda, to receive prebends. Only he is qualified who has led the ritualistically prescribed way of life and has received the consecration according to orthodox teaching. In India, too, there are entire villages held in fief by Brahmins who partially, entirely, or almost entirely have renounced Veda teaching. Similar phenomena may have occurred among the Levites. The manner in which Deuteronomy combines the words Levites and priests might suggest the idea that there were at the time also untutored and ritually impure, hence disqualified, Levitical descendents who neither were nor could be priests. This assumption is practically almost irrefutable. It is conceivable then that their "divided and scattered" way of life prevented these lay-Levites from being counted among any of the other tribes, which led tradition to implicate them in common with Simeon in the Shechem crime.

In Deuteronomic times the Levitical priests were organized into hereditary charismatic sibs, representing an exclusive status group. They claimed a monopoly in the employment of certain oracular formulae, priestly teaching, and priestly positions. In this, at least in the South, they were successful. In the North, Levite priests are only mentioned twice in the Book of Judges (Chapter 17 for Dan and Ephraim). At the time of the revision of this passage of uncertain age, the Levites apparently still constituted only a vocational, not a hereditary status group. However, priestly influenced accounts of desert and conquest times and Deuteronomy, present them as a hereditary status group. This tradition treats the Levites generally as trained hereditary Yahwe priests. With this, individual Levites own private property, including houses and real estate of all sorts. The present revision of Deuteronomy in theory ascribes to them the monopoly of sacrificial offering when a priest cooperated as well as the exclusive right to give oracles by lot and to teach; the right to fees and casual payments in compensation for all this, and the right to the tithe from all yields of the land.

Legally the old tradition considered the Levites as *gerim*, as every Israelite was considered when in the territory of another Israelite tribe. Indeed, the Levites represent the perfect type of "guest tribe" in the Israelite community. They have preserved this position most clearly in the present revision of the tradition. In the account of the crime of Gibeah we find a Levite as a metic of the Ephraimites. He doubtlessly lived from casual fees. The Levites stood outside the association of militarily qualified landowners. They were exempt from military service (Num. 1:49; 2:33). Their religious service, as shown by the designation, *'eved*, was considered a liturgy of metics given to the political community. Their legal position was increasingly regulated and their group organization into father houses (Ex. 6:25; Num. 3:14 f.) corresponds to the organization of an Indian guest tribe as well as to that of Israelite tribes of the time. The prescription, in a branch of the tradition, (Num. 35:2 f.), concerning cities to be assigned to the Levites (including places of asylum) need not necessarily be fictitious, but may rest on the fact that in some cities their sustenance was secured by the assignment of dwelling sites, grazing grounds, and a share in the tax yields of certain places. Something similar for princes as for Joshua is to be found, agreeing with Indian analogies.

According to another still more questionable tradition (Lev. 25:32 f.) the fields of the Levites would be inalienable—probably because of liturgical burdens—also, their houses were not permanently alienable at will as were those of other Israelites. Their cattle (Num. 3:41, 45) were termed "cattle of Yahwe."

In any case, one may well assume that different localities made varying provisions for them. Like all *gerim* (in Joshua 14:4) they lived in the "suburbs" (*migrashim*). They received no share in plough land, which in Hebron, for instance, Caleb reserved for himself.

In some points the analogy with the Brahmins goes even further. The situation of the Levites as a guest tribe with a well defined position was not the only and presumably not the original form of their relationship to Israel. As previously mentioned, the tradition reports that princes and landlords employed lowly-born men as priests at their house chapels (*"Eigenkirchen"* in the sense of Stutz) as is disapproved in the case of Jeroboam (I. Ki. 12:31), some of them employed sons or relatives. The latter is reported in an old Danite tradition also of the landlord Micah in Northern Israel. Micah is further reported to have later entered relations with a Levite who came from Judah, entrusting him with the service at his sanctuary and, corresponding to the Indian *guru,* making him his "father."

Finally, it is reported that the Danites on their northward migration took the Levite and the image of the sanctuary along and conferred upon him the hereditary priesthood at the temple of the newly founded city in the territory of the Zidonians "until the day of the captivity of the land." This corresponds exactly to the Brahmin expansion in India. Likewise, the later Levitical court chaplains parallel the Brahmin Purohita. Here the reasons for the spread of the Levites become evident: obviously their superior ritualistic training for sacrificial services, above all, the training for "cure of souls," that is, advise how to win Yahwe's favor and ward off his wrath. The princes and landlords hired them not alone because of their personal need for such counsel, but doubtlessly also for the sake of their prestige as lords of sanctuaries and the income yielded by the repute of a sanctuary in the care of a trained priest.

We noted earlier how Gideon utilized his share in booty for the establishment of a chapel with an image. Later it may also well have happened that communities as such called on Levites and provided for their establishment in the manner of the Danites. Beyond this the Levite was free to earn income for himself.

In this manner, the Levites, by gradual expansion, attained their position as cult monopolists which in Deuteronomic times was essentially recognized in Judaic territory. Deuteronomy presupposes in every locality a resident Levite, living off sacrificial offerings. This expansion was not consummated without resistance, as shown by the curse of Moses' Blessing against those who "hate" the Levite (Deut. 33:11). The revolt of the Korachites, later appearing as degraded Levites, together with the descendants of Reuben against the predominance of the priesthood, proves in the priestly tradition that there existed a powerful stratum of men in Israel who recalled that originally nothing was known of such clerical predominance, especially not of a sacrificial and oracular monopoly of a hereditary caste. Yahwe had revealed his will through prophets and seers. Apparently it was the steppe tribe Reuben, once holding hegemony in the confederacy, that maintained this standpoint. In that case, one may perhaps ascribe the dispersal of Reuben to the absence of a firmly organized priest stratum, the existence of which made for Judah's strength. The schooling of the Levitical oracle givers and, above all, their increasing support by the kings silenced these troublesome protests. Nevertheless, it remains quite problematical for the time prior to the downfall of Northern Israel what measure of power the Levites and their oracles had there in the competitive struggle.

2. The Development of the Priesthood and the Cult Monopoly of Jerusalem

FROM the beginning the Levites, like the Brahmins, seem to have segregated themselves ritualistically from the "laity" by observing certain purity prescriptions. Of interest here is merely the strict avoidance of contact with the dead and everything connected with the cult of tombs. Clearly this priesthood was the main champion of the opposition against the neighboring Egyptian cult of the dead. Moses' Blessing (Deut. 33:8 f.) informs us unambiguously of the specific accomplishments of the Levites during the time of their universal recognition. No mention is made of a therapeutic function of the Levites, though, as noted earlier, therapeutic magic is ascribed to Moses himself

and the snake staff may possibly be a residue of former therapeutic magic. Still at a later time the diagnosis of leprosy is left
to the priests. For the rest, we hear nothing at all of therapy of
the Levites. The leper later was under their jurisdiction essentially because he was considered ritualistically impure. (The
state of medical arts in ancient Israel is quite unknown. The
recommendation of the doctor and the pharmacy by the author
of Jesus Sirach reflects conditions of Hellenistic times.) Hence,
one must assume that in historical times, truly magical therapy
was no longer vested in them. To the diseased they merely ministered "cure of souls," of which more later. Apparently they did
not use irrational therapeutic means. Put first in Moses' Blessing
(Deut. 33:8) is the memory of the oracle by a lot at "the waters
of strife" (the source of the trial oracle) of Kadesh, next (33:10)
comes the duty of teaching the *mishpatim* and Torah, and then
only follow incense and full-sacrifice.

Moses, (according to 33:8) wrested the oracle from God in a
wrestling match. The reference is to the trial oracle. The pro-
Levite Deuteronomic law admonishes the people to bring legal
disputes "before Yahwe" and the tradition has Moses, except in
special cases as magician, occupied all day long with trial
affairs until, upon Jethro's advice, he transferred them to the
sarim of kingly times, who are viewed as his subordinates. A
later tradition (Deut. 17:9; 19:17) still proposed courts of mixed
laymen and priests. These statements are indications of a tension between secular and hierocratic justice such as are also to
be found elsewhere.

In Babylon the generation preceding Hammurabi eliminated the priests from the courts in favor of laymen and restricted them to the technical execution of oracles in trial procedure instructed by lay judges. The Code of Hammurabi
mentions this in case the wife is under suspicion of sorcery and
adultery. In Israel the oracle in court verdicts was confined to
the second of such cases. Lay judges, that is the elders or royal
officials, in Northern Israel at least, decided trials alone. As indicated earlier, in Southern Israel the position of the priests in
trial procedure was apparently far more important, as may be
gathered from the significance of Kadesh and the trial oracles
in Moses' Blessing. As mentioned, it cannot be ascertained that

the priests, as sometimes assumed, actually ever functioned in the South as regular judges. They did function as arbitrators and oracle givers to whom trial parties and judges addressed questions. Their stronger position in the South is easily explained.

As the political associations of the semi-nomadic tribes usually preserved their stability only in the form of religious confederations (*Bünde*), so, with them, only the priestly oracle had a truly supra-individual compelling authority opposite the power of the sheik who depended on his personal prestige. The *mishpatim* of the Book of the Covenant stemming from North Israel and identifiable by the abstract hypothetical formulation of the facts of the case in terms of "If . . . ," as mentioned earlier, was the sediment of an ancient jurisprudence influenced by Babylonian models. Only occasionally purely mundane prescriptions assume the form of the *debarim,* "thou shallst" or "thou shallst not." This form predominates strongly, though not exclusively, in those commandments and prohibitions which are ritualistic or religio-ethical in nature and, doubtlessly, do not derive from secular jurists, but either from prophetic oracles or from priestly commandments. We shall have to discuss later the nature and origin of non-prophetic priestly prescriptions. In any case, the Levites, to whom Moses' Blessing ascribed the duty of instructing the people in the rights (*mishpatim*) as well as in the Torah have a stake in this. From the Yahwistic point of view the secular *mishpatim per se* (derived from *shafat,* "to judge"), were religiously consequential insofar as they were considered part of the *berith* with Yahwe. The Levites (Deut. 33:10) were commanded to teach the *chukim,* the (ritualistic) traditions.

The Levitical teacher had to deal, in principle, only with ritualistic prescriptions for life conduct. But the distinction between *jus* and *fas* was even less consummated here than in other hierocratically influenced social structures. In the time of Moses' Blessing, the Levites in legal disputes activated the oracle by lot (as may be inferred from the name Meribah). And after the Torah had become rational religious instruction the distinction (between *jus* and *fas*) became quite fluid. For the Levites decided by the Torah what was to be regarded as an element of the old Yahwe-guaranteed orders of the confederacy. "Torah," however, meant originally "teaching," not, as it is still at times translated, "law." To be sure, the concept is also related to the Levites' ancient oracle by lot.[7] As a rule, the concept in the sources now refers to the entire body of prescriptions to be taught by the priests. In Moses' Blessing, where Torah is distinguished from *mishpat*, it refers obviously to ritualistic and ethical, especially including, social-ethical commandments, but not legal commandments of the god of the covenant. Even if the somewhat limping verse ten in Moses' Blessing—following only verse nine and divorced from verse eight—concerning the Torah were a later insertion in connection with verse eight and the rest of the tradition, it demonstrates distinctly, nevertheless, the services underlying the expansion and power of the Levites. It rested on their responses to their "clients'" questions concerning matters other than trial procedure. From the outset the specific form of their service was here too the giving of oracles.

For private needs the purely mechanical casting of lots could be learned by the ritualistically untutored. In fact we see in the accounts of Gideon and Jonathan the use by non-Levites of omina and arrow oracles to determine the facts as well as Yahwe's will. Ritualistically correct procedure was decisive in the questioning of Yahwe. Particularly legal and political authorities had to place great weight upon this ritualistic correctness in their questions, hence, for them the Levitical oracle by lot remained of lasting importance. In spite of its prestige and official recognition, even in Ezra's time when it had long since ceased to exist, this primitive form of oracular determination could hardly satisfy the needs of the private clients in the long run.

The social conditions and therewith the questions raised became increasingly complicated. We saw that in the tradition derived from the times of the flourishing sanctuary in Dan (Jud. 17), the landlord Micah made of the Levite newcomer, allegedly a descendant of Moses, his "father," that is, he conferred upon him besides the cult of the image, above all, the instruction concerning his (the founder's) duties toward Yahwe (as in India behoves the Brahmin father confessor). We also mention that ever increasing significance was attributed to the *chattat* and *asham* sacrifices besides the ancient sacrificial offerings (supplication sacrifices). This increasing need for expiation of sins inversely corresponded to the significance of mechanical oracles by lot which gave way to rational responses to posited questions. Naturally, this increasingly rational instruction was joined to the giving of oracles to private persons.

The relation of prophecy and cultic priesthood was fluid. To be sure, Jeremiah distinguished clearly between Torah, the business of the priests, and the *debar* of God, which he claimed to be the business of prophecy. But in Isaiah (1:10, 8 and 8:16, 20) is to be found the interchange of oracle for Torah (to that extent identical in meaning with *"debar* Yahwe"), and once (8, 16) the term is used for a sealed oracle scroll which the prophet gave to the disciples. Jeremiah called Torah teachers (*Thosfê hattora,* people who "handle the Torah") besides the priests also the *kohanim,* probably the cult priests of the Jerusalemite Temple.

In any event, the Levites did not gain their prestige by their training in the proffering of sacrifices for the community, but by training in purely rational knowledge of Yahwe's commandments, of ritualistic means to amend offenses against them by *chattat, asham,* fasts, or other means, and thereby ward off threatened misfortunes and to undo already incurred ones. This was of interest to the king and the community, but, above all, to private persons. With mounting political pressure upon Israel, this very need increased generally. It became the sole meaning and intent of the Levitical Torah to satisfy this need by instruction of patrons. Instruction was given for hire (Micah 3:11). Sins were confessed to the Levite (Num, 5:6 f.) and he "reconciled" the guilty one with Yahwe (Lev. 4:20, 31; 5:10; 6:7). For the private client this was his most important service. The ascendency of this relatively rational, educative influence of the Levites—however primitive in content at first one may imagine their teaching—went hand in hand with the decline of the ancient ecstatic-irrational war prophets and Nebiim of the peasant militia.

Technical peculiarities of its oracular means tended to push the Levitical Torah toward rational method. As against the inspection of entrails, the observation of bird flight and other animal behavior, especially of any sort of mantic ecstasy, the primitive way of answering concrete questions with "yea" or "nay" by throwing lots was burdened with an absolute minimum of esoterics, emotional or mystic irrationalism. There was no occasion for the development of theories such as are represented by the Babylonian literature of *omina*.

The Levitical oracle required something quite different: the question had to be correctly put in order that the facts and God's substantive will be determined simply by lot. Everything depended on the way that the question was put, thus, the Levite had to acquire a rational method to express problems to be placed before God in a form permitting answers of "yea" and "nay." More and more questions had to arise which could not be directly settled by lot or by "yea" or "nay." Complicated preliminary questions had to be settled before they could be placed before God and, in many instances, this arrangement hardly left anything to be determined by oracle. If the patron's respective sin had been determined by interrogation, the kind of expiation was traditionally established. Only where the identity of the sinner was in question, the oracle by lot was required as the Achar story indicates like a paradigm. Particularly for private needs, the oracle inevitably became less and less important as against the rational case study of sins, until the theological rationalism of Deuteronomy (18:9-15) in substance discredited lot casting altogether, or at least ceased to mention it. As for cases where oracles had been customary and unavoidable, namely, where the traditions of Torah teachers were at a loss, the one means left was to consult the prophets.

The prestige of the Levitical Torah has undergone changes. If one may trust the respective reminiscences, this prestige begins even during the time of the old confederacy. It increased unavoidably when the Southern Judaic tribes affiliated with the confederacy. It perhaps weakened once again by the separation of the two kingdoms, but increased with the declining prestige of the Northern kings and became paramount in the Southern Kingdom.

In Egypt the expiatory sacrifice was apparently unknown. Here magicians held the place of the Levites in Israel. The cult of the dead of the Osiris priests, the most popular cult, apparently offered opportunities and incentives for rational instruction in ethical duties, at least in later times.

In Mesopotamia, however, the expiation of sins through sacrifice is to be found, particularly if occasioned by disease which was viewed as a result of divine wrath. Under guidance of the priests the sinner had to recite the ancient (partially pre-Babylonian) penance psalms in order to rid himself of ritualistic impurity (Assyrian: *mamitu*).

The process here, as in Egypt, was magical, not ethical-exhortatory in nature. The oracle by lot is mentioned by Ezekiel (21:21) for Babylonia, but it had, as far as is known, long since disappeared from priestly technique. It was not replaced by rational Torah teaching but by the collection and systematization of the *omina* and by expert priestly interpretation which has been transmitted to us in a quite scurrilous literature.[8] The reasons for this important difference in development will be discussed later.

During their rise the Levites adjusted to existing conditions. As the case of Micah illustrates, the older Levites had, without scruples, conformed to the idol cult of the Northern Kingdom; presumably they were among those who viewed the idols simply as Yahwe idols. Yet, with the opening of the icon dispute their Southern derivation, placed beyond doubt by the tradition, let newer migrants increasingly tip the scale in favor of the icon fiends. Very probably part of the Levites, later disqualified for priestly office and degraded to Temple servants, stemmed from idolatrous Levite sibs. Again the development of Brahmanism in India would offer analogies.

As with the Brahmins, the true source of the prestige of Levitical priests sprang from their knowledge of the authoritative prescriptions of Yahwe. For political reasons the cult was comparably less significant, besides, it was younger and a holy book of the character of the Veda was absent; still, Levitical knowledge concerning positive ritualistic and ethical commandments and of the manner of winning God's favor by following his commandments or by which to appease his anger. Things were what would have prevailed in India if in India there had existed only *grihyasutras* and *darmashastras* and only a few simple ritualistic prescriptions. In this consisted the great difference from the Brahmins. Furthermore, all esoterics in the Indian sense were absent. Neither magical nor mystagogic knowledge, nor book knowledge, nor astrological, therapeutic, or other secret knowledge was advanced by this wave (of Levites) slowly flooding the country from the South. Mystagogy could develop only on the soil of Nabi ecstasy and has done so as shown by the Elisha miracles. Beginning with Gen. 20:7, the tradition shows in a great many places that the "men of god" inspired shy awe and admiring faith. They intervened not only as magical aids in emergencies but also as intercessors with God and won forgiveness of sins.

Unlike the development in India, no anthropolatric worship of living redeemers developed from this. The Levitical Torah prevented it. These men of the South and their Rechabite and other allies knew only that the good old law of the Yahwe confederacy once had been established by Yahwe's *b'rith* with the Israelite militia after Moses' pronouncement, and that any violation of these enactments must provoke Yahwe's wrath. As Deuteronomy shows, the plain sincerity of the sacrificial practice stood parallel to the still simple ritualistic commandments and the rational teaching of private and social ethic.

Like the Brahmins, the Levites must have assimilated to their cult procedure all sorts of ancient methods of local priesthoods. On the other hand, intense conflicts undoubtedly occurred among the priestly sibs of various sanctuaries. Priests who engaged in rejected cults were declassed. (This, presumably, happened to the post-exilic "bards" and "*Nethinim*" deriving from orgiastic cults.) The original relationship of Levite newcomers from the South to long settled priestly sibs is problematical. The old priest sib of the Elides in Shiloh, which most probably goes back to Moses according to the Egyptian name of Phinehas in its lineage, later, to be sure, was considered a Levite sib as, also, was the priestly sib of the Danites. Originally, however, the Elides apparently were not considered Levites. The original relation to the two great priestly sibs, the Zadokites and Aaronites remains quite obscure. The first played the decisive role in Deuteronomic and early Exile times, the latter was important in the post-Exile period. The later Levitical pedigrees of both are, of course, falsifications. The Zadokites, since Solomon, were the leading priest sib of the king of Jerusalem. Deuteronomy considered its members Levites, hence, it must have even early deemed wise to fuse with the Levites, which proves that the prestige of the latter was historically established even then. The original position of the Aaronites and the form of Aaron himself remains, indeed, quite problematical.[9]

In the earliest pre-Deuteronomic accounts (Ex. 24:1, 9; 18:12) it seems that Aaron was considered the most distinguished elder of Israel, hence, not a priest. In the later, particularly exilic revisions, he is a priest and is constantly rising, first to become the speaker of Moses, who was not eloquent, then the brother of the prophetess Miriam, then the brother and, at that, the elder brother of Moses himself. And finally, in the latest revisions, he receives personal, direct revelations concerning his sib rights (Lev. 10:8; Num. 18:1, 9, 20).[10]

The Zadokites, now, were treated as part of the Aaronites. There are descendants of Moses mentioned in the old tradition. Besides the priestly sib of the Elides, the sib of Dan, especially, traced their origin to him. They were confiscated from Moses with amazing cheek and ascribed to Aaron. Aaron has been inferred to be of North Israelite origin, for the Yahwistic revision apparently knew nothing of him and linked him to the cult of the steer. The Aaronite editing of the Abraham legend (Gen. 17) has God present himself to Abraham as *"El shaddai."* Hence, the Aaronites possibly were an old sib of *El* priests and therefore placed weight upon this identification of their god with Yahwe, who during the Exile was elevated to the sole god of the universe. The note in the last verse of the Book of Joshua might suggest relations to Benjamin, the favored son in the later revision of the Jacob legend. But all this remains uncertain.

The tradition mirrors the intense conflicts among the priestly sibs also in their mutual curses besides the numerous retouchings of the composition. Opposite the presumably old lavish blessing for Phinehas, the ancestor of the Elide priest sib in Shiloh, stands, after their downfall under Solomon, the threat of disaster against this sib in the Book of Samuel. Opponents of priestly authority like the Korachites were swallowed by the earth; later they were degraded sibs of bards. Residues in the revised tradition indicate that the puritanically minded, Yahwistic priesthood and particularly those having a vested interest in the ancient Northern sanctuaries must have strongly resisted

the Solomonic Temple construction and the concomitant predominance of this sanctuary.

The secession of the Northern Kingdom was certainly essentially co-determined by these antagonisms of the priesthood and
their rules of worship, as indicated by Jeroboam's measures in
favor of Dan and Beth-El and, especially, the king's motivation.
The sharp antagonisms are most evident in the mutually biased
legends, where not even the tribal fathers of Yahwe worship
were spared. The legend of the Aaronite priests ascribe to Aaron
and the prophetess Miram grave reproaches against Moses himself, above all, for his mixed marriage. Tradition represents his
non-participation in the march into the holy land as due to his
sin. Miriam, in her turn, according to the Mosaic legend, is
therefore stricken by leprosy. Especially Aaron's position is unsettled. Besides other errors, he is particularly reproached for
his participation in steer worship—at the time of the final revision a capital crime—yet in tradition nothing evil happens to him
for this.

This struggle of the priesthoods necessarily grew in intensity
when the Jerusalemite priesthood, then the Zadokite, drew the
final conclusions after the destruction of the Northern Kingdom
and raised the quite unheard of claim, in the face of the clear
old tradition, that from now on there should exist a Temple and
ritualistically fully-qualified place of sacrifice only in Jerusalem.
The ancient worship of Yahwe on mountain heights and under
trees, at the ancient rural and provincial sanctuaries in Beth-El
Dan, Shechem, and at other places, should stop. The demand
was probably not completely novel, but presumably arose right
after the downfall of the Northern Kingdom. Apparently Hezekiah, in the grave war emergency against Sennacherib had already made an effort to achieve this. But at the time the resistance
of the ideal and material interests of peasants and landlords in
the rural sanctuaries had been too strong. There was no longer
mention of this under Manasseh who, as an Assyrian vassal, engaged in Mesopotamian star worship in Jerusalem.

Similar to the Omrids in the Northern Kingdom at the time,
his likeminded successor Amon was liquidated by a military
revolt, presumably instigated by the Yahwistic party. Strong resistance to the demands of the priests is evident, again, in the

fact that the revolution was crushed by men interested in the rural sanctuaries. These last made their appearance, for the first time, under the party name *'amme ha-'aretz,* ("countrymen"), a name occurring frequently later. However, the priests, in alliance with the distinguished noble sibs, which, in turn were friendly with the Yahwistic parties, sought to gain influence over Josiah when not yet of age. The demand reappeared when the great coalition against the Assyrian empire brought Josiah's downfall. It constituted the core demand of the Deuteronomic law book, a literary product of the stratum of intellectuals grouped around the Jerusalemite priesthood. The book was supposed to be "found" in the temple by temple employees. Obviously, the utopian hope of winning Yahwe's aid against Pharoah-nechoh, marching through Palestine, caused Josiah to fulfill the commandments contained in this find, which allegedly represented the old authentic Mosaic *sefer hattorah.* In solemn *berith* King Josiah bound the people to this law. He destroyed the ancient sanctuaries and had them ritualistically defiled through bones of the dead (621 B.C.). The defeat and death of the king at Meggiddo, however, put an end to all these hopes and generally, was a terrific blow for the Levitical Yahwe party. The obvious claim of the compendium to replace all other legal collections therewith fell down in practice for the time. However, it continued as ideal demand of the only firmly organized Jerusalemite priesthood.

The editors had prudently combined this monopoly demand with others which benefited their power position and were, at the same time, very popular. In the first place, they raised a protest against Solomonic corvée kingship. It had never been forgotten that the Davidian dynasty, of paramount prestige, also had ascended the throne by *b'rith* of the elders and that the ancient Israelite leader had been an ass-riding, charismatic prince of the people, without a train of war chariots, treasure, harem, forced labor, taxes, and airs of world leadership. This kingship was to be restored in earnest. The priestly oracle by lot was to decide the worthiness of the kings. The king was to be bound by the Deuteronomic Mosaic law, which he was to read every day. Respective accounts of the manner in which Saul allegedly had been made king by Samuel were inserted into the ancient traditions, likewise, the legend of the victory of the shepherd boy David over Goliath in place of the authentic tradition. In the revision of the kingship tradition, now, each king was graded according to his attitude toward worship on mountain heights and idolatry. For similar reasons, the ancient social law of the Book of the Covenant was correspondingly refashioned and included in the new compendium. Since the Babylonian lord-paramount of Zedekiah had an interest in weakening the prerogatives of kingship, it is quite possible that under this prince some attempt was made to realize these demands in earnest.

This compendium was the only consistent theology taken over into Exile times besides the other only partially and imperfectly unified collections and traditions. From the start, the practically most extensive demand of the Deuteronomic law was its claim for the cult monopoly of Jerusalem and its priesthood. At the same time, this demand created greatest difficulties, quite apart from the resistance of non-Jerusalemite lay interest. The question was: what was to become of those Levites and other priests who had, thus far, officiated at other sanctuaries? The later much interpolated Deuteronomic law in the present revision contains two contradictory stipulations: on the one hand, all Israelites were admonished not to leave the "Levites in their gates" without sustenance, hence they were to become rentiers without cult prerogatives. With the priests they were merely to share the right of teaching the law. On the other hand, it was stipulated that these priests should move to Jerusalem where they could participate in the cult. This stipulation had certainly not been inserted into the law by the priests themselves. And when it was executed in earnest the Jerusalemite priesthood opposed it effectively.

Meanwhile the Exile saw the abduction of all priestly sibs. It became a compelling interest of all priests to reach agreement. Ezekiel still advocated the monopoly of the Jerusalemite Zadokites and, in agreement with Deuteronomic theory, distinguished the Levites from them as second-rate priests without sacrificial prerogative. But such monopoly of the Zadokites could obviously not be enforced. Evidently the scripturally trained priest Ezra found the final compromise in Persian times, a compromise which in substance was probably also determined by the variable influence of the sibs at court. Ezra treated the Zadokites as part of the Aaronites and defined all of them as qualified for sacrifice in Jerusalem as the sole sanctuary. He subordinated to them all other Levitically recognized sibs by degrading them to inferior cult officials who were to take turns in service, certain others to liturgical "temple slaves" (*Nethinim*), singers, and doorkeepers. The tri-partition of the hierocracy into priests, Levites, *Nethinim,* still existing in the Gospels, and after the disappearance of the last into priests and Levites, derives from this regulation. It was made acceptable by means of regulating material conditions. The universal tithing of the entire sacred soil was carried through, and the yield of this and of some other—here uninteresting—taxes, was distributed among the respective hierocratic interest groups.

This manner of settling the old conflicts was determined, on the one hand, by the special conditions of the exiled community, on the other, by the nature of the political relations to the Persian court. The settlement was legitimized by interpolations of old stipulations and tradition *en masse* and by codifying the stipulations in the new so-called "Priestly Code." Ezra imposed it upon the resettled community by solemnly binding them to this Code. The details of this external regulation are of no concern here. We shall, rather, return to pre-exilic times and consider the inherent consequences and driving forces of the peculiar development.

The monopolization of the cult in Jerusalem, first, had one very important result. Domestic slaughtering and meat dinners which hitherto, at least theoretically, had been considered as "sacrifices" and "sacrificial feasts" were secularized. Henceforth they lost their sacred character, for sacrifices could only be proffered in Jerusalem. Solely the reservation was retained in, at first, questionable meaning that at least the not too distant resident taxpayers should consume their contribution as a sacrificial meal in the holy city, the others were permitted conversion into money.

This profanation of all private meals was, after the rejection of the cult of the dead, the last blow which Yahwism dealt to a possibly sacred significance of the sib. Cultic meals under the control of the sib head were henceforth impossible. The Passover meal had long ceased to be a meal of the sib, becoming, instead, a domestic family festival. The swift decline of the importance of the sib in post-exilic times is probably connected with this. To be sure, the stipulation which had to result in this was hardly intended as a deliberate measure against the sib. It was a secondary result of the establishment of the cult monopoly, as evident in the halfway measures stipulating the consumption of contributions. The cult meals *per se* had, even in pre-Exile times, been slowly but surely divested of their original meaning. We now shall focus on their original meaning and its transformation, a process intimately connected with the advance of the Levites. For here we meet profound peculiarities of the puritanical Yahwe religion which alone explain the attitude of its representatives toward other cults.

3. *The Fight of Yahwism against Orgiasticism*

EDUARD MEYER has the merit of having pointed to a characteristic ritualistic contrast in the Israelite *b'rith* between Shechem, the main sanctuary of Northern Israel, and Jerusalem. According to the Book of Joshua the covenant in Shechem was in the nature of a cult meal, hence, a communal meal, a *koinonia* with the god, as is also reported in an old North Israelite story of the Sinai covenant, where the seventy elders, likewise, were guests at Yahwe's table as he, in return, came as a guest to share the sacrificial meal of the cult members.

The transmitted rite in Judah is quite different. It is told in great detail of the *b'rith* under Zedekiah and also presupposed as valid for God's *b'rith* with Abraham. The sacrificial animal was cut up and those who bound themselves, king, priest and, as the case may be, sib elders or militia men (*'am*) all file through the pieces. In this legend Yahwe did this during the night. Hence, no sacramental *koinonia* with the god took place here. The cutting up of a sacrificial animal recurrs in another ceremony. The hero or prophet who intended to summon Israel to holy war against foreign peoples or transgressing members of the covenant, cuts up an animal and sends the pieces around the country. This was considered an admonition to dutifully follow Yahwe to war. This form is but twice reported, but precisely of the Northern tribes, of Ephraim and Benjamin. If one were to assume any sort of relationship to the Judaic form of the *b'rith,* which after all suggests itself, this form cannot have been unknown in the North. If this holds, one can assume that the *koinonia* originally customary in the firmly settled population of Shechem was the old Canaanite form of establishing a relationship to the peaceful god, whereas, with the less firmly settled peasants and herdsmen of the mountains, the other form, peculiar to the confederate war god, served the fraternization for war. This is also probably because the cutting up of the sacrificial animal may well be a ritualistic vestige of the ancient orgiastic tearing up of the sacrificial animal—with the African Bedouins a wether—as is especially to be found with mountain and steppe peoples. It was apparently eradicated among the Iranians by Zoroaster, possibly under Mesopotamian cultural influence.

One will hardly go wrong in assuming that the original meat orgy of the Judaic tribes, also to be found in the Dionysus cult, was eliminated through methodical opposition. Perhaps the later ritualistic prohibition of the enjoyment of blood indicates a step along this path. In that case, the late motivation that one "must not eat the soul of the animal" would still preserve traces of the former animistic meaning. Originally the prohibition apparently did not apply to the army in war. The development would then have to be constructed as follows: Originally, the enjoyment of blood was prohibited only in normal times, aside from the meat orgy reserved for the war god. Later, under the known demilitarizing influences discussed earlier, orgies and the enjoyment of blood were prohibited once and for all. However, this is only an uncertain hypothesis.

Finally, there is still a third form of concluding a *berith* to be found in the tradition (Ex. 24:6, 8) namely, the sprinkling of the Yahwe community and altar with sacrificial blood. This presupposes participation of the priest, for he alone could consummate the act. As this form is interwoven in the quite ancient account of Yahwe's common meal with the elders—this table community follows the conclusion of *berith* and does not establish the religious *koinonia*—the story too may be ancient and, in this case, of Southern origin. This again is uncertain. What matters for us is merely the following. In historical times the Southern tribes knew no ceremony which established a sacramental *koinonia* with the god. Therewith we arrive at an important point which determined the decisive contrast of Southern pure Yahwism with the Northern Israelite fusion with Baal and related agricultural cults and which is externally indicated by the more formal contrasts of the forms of *berith*.

Like most ancient agricultural cults, those of Baal were and remained orgiastic, specifically, of a sexual and alcoholic character. Ritualistic cohabitation on the field as homoeopathic fertility charm, the alcoholic and dance orgy with unavoidably ensuing sexual promiscuity, later tempered to sacrificial meal, singing dance, and sacred harlotry are fully ascertainable as original elements also of the Israelite agricultural cults. The residues are plain. The sexually orgiastic character of the gay Baal cults of old is shown by the "dance around the golden calf." According to the tradition, Moses raised an outcry against this, the prophets against "whoredom." The cultic dances left traces throughout. There were hierodulae (*hekdesh*) expressly documented in the legal collections, in the legends (*Tamar*) and by the prophets. This orgiasticism is also evident in explicit statements of the sources. The female companion, the *Baalat* was lacking the Baals as little as the Indian fertility deities. She was identical with Astarte, who in turn was identical with the Babylonian Istar, goddess of the sexual sphere. From the cults of Baal during his fusion with Yahwe, sexual orgiasticism invaded the Yahwe cults. The existence of hierodulae is also ascertained for the Temple of Jerusalem.

The advocates of pure Yahwism passionately fought the alcoholic, especially the sexual orgiasticism of the Baal cults and their religious influence. The fight of the Rechabites against wine was no mere conservation of old steppe habits, but mainly a struggle against the alcoholic orgiasticism of the settled population. The attitude of Yahwistic ritual and ethic to sexual life, above all, testify to this profound contrast. To serve the Baals, means, once and for all, "to go a whoring after them." The struggle left a lasting imprint on the regulation of the sexual sphere in Jewry. The religious taboo on violation of another's marriage as a capital abomination, to be sure, agrees merely with what is to be found in all prophetic and priestly controlled religions, and is only especially severe in the kind of sanction. The conception of marriage as a means for producing children and for the economic security of the mother, of course, implies neither anything specifically Israelite, but was ubiquitous. Likewise, the outspoken naturalism in the conception of sexual processes is in no way peculiar to Israel. The cultic and warrior ascetic chastity rules, taboos, and impurity prescriptions for menstruating women, etc., also were widely diffused, though in quite different ways. They were merely expressions of the conception of the sexual sphere as an area specifically controlled by demons, as suggested by sexual orgiasticism everywhere to the representatives of rational cults and religions. But the extent and manner in which Israelite ritual and legends, and precisely when under Yahwistic influence, handle this sphere is indicative of quite an extreme position. It can be explained only from the antagonistic bias against Baal orgiasticism, in the same way in which we had to attribute hypothetically the rejection of all speculation about a beyond, to a bias against the Egyptian cult of the dead.

In the sexual sphere this antagonism against orgiastic shamelessness and the Canaanites, its despised and accursed representatives, is especially evident in the strict taboo placed upon any physical divestment. The mere fact of uncovering or the mere desiring look at a relative is treated as incest (Lev. 20:10) and capital crime and the tribal father of the Canaanites is considered by Genesis as the originator of all the shamelessness which allegedly caused this people to be accursed to eternal serfdom. On the other hand (Lev. Ch. 18) every incest, any tampering with the parental harem, but also any other illicit sexual union is designated in terms of bodily divestment. In the old ritual, steps at the altar were entirely prohibited (Ex. 20:26) lest an uncovering might occur opposite the steps which belonged already to the ideal seat of Yahwe. What documents the ability of original man to distinguish between "good" and "evil," awakened after they enjoyed the forbidden fruit from the tree of knowledge, is that they are "naked." The same tendency pervades all pertinent stipulations and casuistry. Onan's sin is tabooed. According to the present tradition, it constitutes an offense against the duty of awakening progeny for one's brother. Originally, the explicit rejection was probably determined by the antagonism of Yahwists to certain Molech orgies (Lev. 20:2) in which male seed was sacrificed.

All forms of sexual intercourse, tabooed as orgiastic, incestuous, or perverse come primarily though not alone, under the Yahwistic concept of "folly" (Gen. 34:7, Deut. 22:21). And this word still in the language of the latest tradition, even in the Gospels, was the worst that could be said against an Israelite. All specifically Israelite regulations of sexual processes, therefore, are not ethical but ritualistic in nature. The substantive ethic of sexual relations in ancient Israel was no more severe than other priestly regulations. The violation of marriage in the Decalogue concerned the violation of another man's marriage, not that of one's own. Only the later post-exilic time began to taboo the husband's extramarital sexual intercourse. It did so first, in the name of prudent living, in the manner of the Confucians and of Egyptian proverbial wisdom, for instance of Ptah-hetep.

The ancient language of Israel lacked a term for "chastity" in the ethical sense. Only under Persian influence, regulation made headway and at first only in uncanonical writings (Tobit). In the old Israelite view the seduction of a girl without previous contract with her sib could call forth their revenge, as shown in the case of Dinah. The legal collections, however, require only what would amend the marriage, that is the acquistion of the girl by payment of purchase price, similar to the way in which Anglo Saxon law treats the case as a kind of property damage. The antipathy against what was considered sexually shameless has nothing to do with "special mores of purity," comparable, for instance, to those of the Bedouins. Jeremiah (3:2) reproaches the Arabs of the desert because they practice "whoredom in the ways," that is, as shown by Tamar's behavior, at places where common harlots used to stay, stood also the hierodulae of the temple whom the prophets rejected with all other residues of sexual orgiasticism. Only the homoeopathic sexual orgy was ritualistically strange to the Bedouins in contrast to the tillers.

The specifically ritualistic, not primarily ethical, character of the entire sexual casuistry, extensively preserved later, imparts a peculiar nature to it. For it is only here carried, not in kind, but to such extent with this all-pervasive bias. The ancient uninhibited naturalism in the treatment and discussion of sexual events was combined with thoroughgoing ritualistic fear of purely physical uncovering. This had no relation whatsoever to a special sense of dignity which usually implements our emotional reaction of shame as channelized through feudal or bourgeois conventions. The combination of naturalism with ritualistic fear easily appears to the modern, whose feeling of shame was influenced by feudal, bourgeois, and Christian ideas, like a caricature of the true sentiment in the sense familiar to us. The historical source of this peculiarity rests entirely on the sharp antagonism against the orgiasticism of North Israelite tillers as practiced by its priesthood. Islam displays similar phenomena, and because of its antipathy toward nudity, in all areas of its diffusion the development of the textile industry, or at least the market, has been promoted.

This opposition to orgiasticism and orgiastic ecstasy also determined the attitude of the South toward the ecstatic virtuosos emerging from both forms of orgiasticism. The ancient mass ecstatic Nebiim were, doubtlessly, an essentially North Israelite phenomenon, partially derived from Phoenician, partially from Canaanite Baal cults. Zechariah (13:5) still takes it for granted that the false prophets are husbandmen and that their allegedly self-inflicted wounds derive from the fingernails of harlots. Everywhere the charismatic ecstatics serving orgiastic mass cults have organized themselves into guilds or schools. The Nabi schools of Elisha, and those of earlier times, are local examples. The orgiasticism from which the Nabi ecstasy derived was, as shown, above all homoeopathic fertility orgiasticism. Such was unknown to the nomads and semi-nomads. If they ever knew true meat orgies, is was as a part of warrior ecstasy. To be sure, early Israel, indeed also North Israel, knew the Nazarite warrior asceticism and warrior ecstasy of the Berserks. Similarly, the ancient mass ecstasy of the Nebiim, as noted, was related to war prophecy. However, three things are obvious: In contrast to cultic orgiasticism of the Baals, the Nazarite warrior ecstatics knew indeed the prescription of alcoholic abstinence. Furthermore, classical war prophecy of the time of Deborah, in contrast to that of the Nebiim, was individual prophecy. Finally, it is noticeable that the Song of Deborah speaks of "other gods" to which Israel has surrendered. This can only refer to local deities of the region, Baalim.

Centuries later we observe again the individual prophecy of Elijah in conflict with the same "strange gods" and with orgiastic mass ecstasy. The prophet whom Jehu takes along in his wagon is a Rechabite, hence, an opponent of alcoholic orgiasticism. Repeatedly this fight is waged by men who either stem from the South or, predominantly at least, from stockbreeders. The typical individual prophet, Elijah, the deadly enemy of Baal ecstasy, hails from Gilead and is a typical migratory nomad. Elisha, the mass ecstatic, was, according to tradition, a peasant. Quite some time later, Amos, the first prophet arising against the cult practice of the North, is a shepherd from Tekoa. This leads to the following conclusion: The mass ecstatic Nebiim, under the influence of Canaanite orgiasticism and the irrational and emotional forms of magic, came from the North. The rational Levitical Torah and the rational ethical emissary prophecy come from the South. To the latter this shamelessness is an abomination of Yahwe, and cult and sacrifice, in general, mean nothing to the god of the covenant in comparison with the fulfillment of his ancient commandments.

The dualism thus ran covertly throughout Israelite history since the beginning of the invasion. It became acute with the increasingly rational character of the mentalities of the two powers opposed to the orgy: the Levites and the prophets of doom. This resulted, at least partially, from the growth of literary culture of the intellectuals. Hence we must clarify the manner in which basic elements, engaged in partly latent, partly open conflict, of the profoundly different religiosities exerted their influence upon the old Israelite literati.

CHAPTER VIII

FORMS OF ISRAELITE INTELLECTUALITY IN THE PRE-PROPETHIC ERA

1. The Israelite Intellectuals and the Neighboring Cultures

IN RICHNESS and variety the literary production of pre-exilic Israel is unsurpassed by any other literature. There are love songs of glowing, in part, with sensuousness in the temper of the warrior, in part, with courtly eroticism, or again with pastoral charm. They were recited at the gay royal court of Thirza and probably even earlier. In variations they were continued into the times of Persian influence and collected as "The Song of Solomon." Besides some inspired songs of praise for the king, contained in the Psalm collection, a number of religious hymns have been preserved which glorify with unsurpassed perfection the majesty of the Great God of Heaven in Babylonian fashion. At least in kingly times, secular as well as religious bards must have appeared as a stratum beyond the exponents of purely popular poetry. For these works are decidedly products of professional poets. And the Song of Deborah, an excellent poem written for the occasion, half religious song of triumph, half political satire against old enemies in the cities and tardy confederates, bespeaks the even greater age of this genre.

Of all means of communication found anywhere at the time, alphabetical writing was the most easily learned. According to the importation of papyrus to Byblos, documented in Wen Amon's travel account, alphabetical writing extends back to the second millennium, though we have an example of it only through the Moabite Mesha stone from the ninth century. It was probably invented to serve business interests of the merchants, and hence presumably in Phoenicia. This writing facilitated in Israel the emergence of a literature addressed to the reader, and at once an extraordinary diffusion of the arts of reading and writing. First writing benefited the kingly chancelleries. The positions of the *mazkir* (usually rendered by "chancellor" probably, at once, annalist and "advisor" of the king) and the *soferim* of David's court and at the courts of both kingdoms indicate that written administration existed at least since David. Perhaps, as suggested by a preserved record (I. Sam. 14:49 f.) beginning even under Saul. For Solomon's corvée state an estate of officials versed in writing was indispensable. Many of them were obviously recruited from among the priests, but many, too, came from secular sibs. The later pragmatically revised accounts of the kings repeatedly refer to official royal annals, and, likewise, there existed probably a Jerusalemite temple chronicalism. Furthermore, we have to assume, with Kittel, that even the first revisions of the stories of David's kingship were composed by an author who, though admitted to the royal archives, wrote independently and according to his own judgment about these affairs.

The great freedom of the tradition opposite the kings, who were at times, after all, powerful, is due to two factors. In contrast to most other monarchical states of the Orient the great military sibs in Israel had preserved a strong position. On the other hand, the seers and professional Yahwe teachers were very significant. They were personally independent and faced the kings quite critically. Because of the prestige of the old war god of the confederacy, the groups embodying his "spirit" could not be ignored by the kings.

The miracle stories included in the Book of Kings derive from the organized schools among the Northern Nebiim. Part of the Elijah accounts and, likewise, the probably pre-Deuteronomic first revision of the stories of the prehistoric seers, Samuel, above all, show that there existed circles which indeed withdrew not only from courtly but likewise from school-organized prophetic influence. There were others who maintained relations to court but also to anti-royalist Yahwists whom they systematically sup-

ported. Such circles could only be wealthy and politically influential pious laiety. Thus, during the time of Jeremiah, we meet
with distinguished sibs, which repeatedly furnish court officials
from their members, but which, obviously, at the same time
were for generations protectors of the great Yahwe prophets,
who relentlessly leveled their criticism against court and priests.
Such had to come about once the prestige of kingship became
shaky through external failure. Obviously, these independent
circles of laity and the pure Yahwe believers under their protection at an early time made it their business to gather the still-
existing old traditions concerning pre-kingly times. The occasionally cited old collections of songs, the "Book of the Wars of
Yahwe" and the "Book of the Brave" probably existed as a
collection even since early kingship. Presumably laymen turned
to the collection and selection of the popular, Yahwistically useful, not purely militaristic poetic works. The old legends, fairy
tales, parables, sayings originally were doubtlessly in the hands
of itinerant bards and story tellers to be found everywhere
among peasant and semi-nomadic populations.

To be sure, the old tradition knows only of a guest people
of musicians, the descendants of Jubal. But there were also story
tellers: the early legends of the patriarchs indeed suggest this
derivation. In contrast, the lengthy story of Joseph, for example,
in its present form, is already in the nature of an artfully composed, edifying "short story" written by an educated poet for
educated Yahwists, hence, it is a work of literary art. Thus there
were mediating links and especially, direct interrelations between exponents of the popular literature of sayings and legends
and circles of independent laity which were educated in literature and interested in political and religious policies. These
linkages are evident in the nature of some of the preserved
examples of the *mashal* (parable) category. With regard to
plastic imagination a *mashal*, such as the parable of the thorn
bush in the story of Abimelech, or the parable of the sheep of
the poor, put into the mouth of Nathan, equals the most accomplished parables of the Gospels. In this respect they differ remarkably from the typical later rabbinical *mashal*,[1] which is
mostly a product of book thinking and hence, usually, is directly
striking only in the grotesque.[2] The difference is somewhat com-

parable to that between the parables of Jesus and Paul who, as is known, occasionally daringly made use of agricultural parables making characteristic mistakes in imagery.[3]

During the time of Jeremiah (18:18) are to be found the first traces of the kind of advice given by educated men in practical workaday problems, as was later offered by the *chokma* (wisdom) teachers and their literary products. But such relationship of literati to plebeian interests in pre-exilic times is far less important than the paramount political and inseparably connected religious structured socio-political interest. The two parables, cited above, offer examples of this. Evidently, they are far from being naive products of a purely artistic nature. They stand, rather, in the service of anti-royalist Yahwistic tendencies. According to quotations and residues, it may be gathered that the whole of a quite rich and varied pre-exilic popular poetry and literature was thus worked over in the perspective of religious politics. If from this literature only that has been preserved which is included in the form of the present canon, it is the result of quite intensive intellectual work of Yahwistically interested strata of intellectuals. This was partly consummated only in exilic times but much of it was achieved in pre-exilic times and some even before the appearance of the scriptural prophets. This joint work, considering its difficulties, was quite extraordinary even though from a literary point of view we find shortcomings to which Goethe already drew attention. With regard to their biases and mentalities, there were sharp antagonisms between the various literary groups of pre-exilic times. There was an unreconciled antagonism between the groups responsible for kingly prophecy of good fortune, the national bards and historiographers on the one side, and the strata of Yahwe believers who were repressed by the kings on the other. Quite a different atmosphere pervades the residues of old erotical poetry gathered in the Songs of Solomon and preserved in a few old kingly Psalms than is to be found in the literary products of Yahwistic intellectuals. Naturally, the religiosity of the kings, when plainly expressed contrasted strongly with popular belief also in neighboring areas.

Rameses IV in his prayer to Osiris, in return for what he had given the god, asked for: food to his contentment, drink to intoxication, good health, long life, joy to body and soul, eternal rule for the descendants, joy for each day, and high level waters for the Nile. Likewise, all Babylonian kings till Nebuchadnezzar prayed for enjoyment of life and a long, happy reign. Things were probably no different in Israel. If the present tradition placed in Solomon's mouth the pious prayer mentioned, this corresponded to the often quite pious inscriptions of Nebuchadnezzar and other great kings. In both cases such pious sentiments are priestly products. The incredible megalomania of Egyptian and Mesopotamian great kings was probably also characteristic of the Israelite kings during the time of their power. In both cases, this formed a strong contrast to the plebeian need for a merciful intercessor and savior in need and to Yahwe's always especially grave anger against man's *hybris*.

Yahwe was never a god of the dynasty like Assur, Mardok, or Nebo. Rather he was always a god of the Israelite confederates. Nevertheless, the dynasties appropriated his cult and the kings had Yahwistic bards and prophets of good fortune in their service.

In circulation beside the Yahwe tradition were the most varied etiological cult sagas of native deities and heroes, numerous myths and ideas either imported from Egypt or Mesopotamia directly or via Phoenicia or already common in the area and which could not conceivably be simply eradicated. Cooperation among them was a difficult task. Besides the products of the Palestinian cultural intelligentsia proper must have played an important part. The question is: how were these products related to those of the neighboring culture area?

Nominal Egyptian rule lasted almost to the end of the time of the judges. According to the Amarna letters, however, the Pharaohs did not interfere with the religion of the country. After Rameses II they rarely employed effective political power. As in older times, opportunities for intellectual intercourse existed. An Egyptian wizard was known by repute in the time of Sesostris among the semi-Bedouin masters of the region East of Byblos. At least, the teller of the Sinuhe story could presuppose this possibility. During the time of the complete decay of the rule of the Ramases, around 1100, the city king of Byblos knew nothing of the Egyptian Amon and his power as described by his emissary Wen Amon.[4] However, his court prophets seem to have known of this. Presumably, it would explain the oracle of one of these court prophets in favor of said emissary. In any case, people in Southern Palestine were well informed about Egypt through the caravan trade. Solomon not only borrowed the chariot technique and partially, also, the manner of Temple construction (the inner sanctum)[5] from Egyptian models, but the short story of Joseph shows, after all, precise knowledge of Egyptian conditions and indicates (no matter whether for good reason) relations to the temple priesthood of Heliopolis, the main seat of Egyptian wisdom. The king of Byblos acknowledged to Wen Amon that all teaching and art came from Egypt to Phoenicia.[6]

One of the traditions concerning Moses makes him, too, an exponent of Egyptian wisdom. According to the Joshua tradition circumcision was taken over from Egypt directly, not via Phoenicia. Further traces are to be found in numerous details, partly without interest here, partly mentioned at the proper occasion. King Merneptah mentioned wars which his army allegedly fought in Palestine against Israel. But relations were by no means always unfriendly, as is evident in the following. Alongside the ethnically related Edomites, the Egyptians were expressly mentioned later as qualified for reception into the Israelite community, although the tradition presupposed not quite correctly that the patriarchs as stock-breeders were considered "impure" in Egypt.[7] As previously mentioned, the excavations in Palestine brought to light numerous scarabaeuses, which, as Erman put it, were for Egypt "as characteristic as the cross for Christendom."

In the face of all this it is striking indeed that this Egyptian rule is covered by silence in the entire tradition and that specific Egyptian elements, precisely in the early foundations of Israelite religiosity, are conspicuously absent, whereas, as we shall see, later on such asserted themselves. Eduard Meyer in explaining this silence pointed only to the youth of the Israelite tradition. But elsewhere this tradition has preserved occasional features of great age, as, for instance, the long bygone relationship to Mesopotamia. The silence about the political rule is possibly understandable as a result of the Pharaoh dealing only through his vassal princes. Even in the case of the Khabiri and the Sa-Gas during Amarna times the rule of the Pharaoh was not obvious in practice. Discounting the few raids, this held ever more for later times. For the rest, one may explain the alien character of Egyptian culture exclusively and quite sufficiently in terms of deliberate rejection by the exponents of Yahwism.

The Egyptian corvée state was indeed rejected. The taking over of its decisive features by native kings was precisely most bitterly hated by the demilitarized strata. Likewise the most characteristic feature of Egyptian piety, the cult of the dead, was rejected. As noted, alongside the radical "this-worldly" nature and orientation of the old war god of the confederacy, decisive was the fact that Yahwe, though combining different traits at different times, was never a chthonian deity, but always sharply opposed to these deities and their manner of worship. Besides, access to Egyptian sacred writing and Egyptian priestly education was not open to strangers. Egyptian teachers of wisdom (Ptah-hetep) recommended, as did Deuteronomy, popular education, but expressly excluded from this the secret teaching of the priests. Hence, the Israelite teachers neither knew nor presumably would have desired to know anything of this. The same held on the part of the Egyptians. As elsewhere defeated enemies were forced to honor the victorious deities of Egypt. But this did not make them Egyptians. Inscriptions show that there were temples of Egyptian deities in Syria and under the Rameses there were, also, temples of Syrian deities in Egypt. But this did not change the basic conditions firmly rooted in the social peculiarities of Egyptian literati culture. The individual could be integrated into Egyptian education and wisdom only *qua* individual and this meant completely to surrender his own intellectual independence. Besides, for the people as a whole, it would have meant to accept the hated bureaucracy of scribes.

The single mention of Egyptian animal worship in Ezekiel (8:10) allows us to infer that Yahwists also rejected this as an especially undignified abomination. The Egyptian priests had systematized this cult at a rather late period in the interest of hierocratic domination of the masses. Egyptian animal worship agreed in no way with the relations of free stock-breeders to their cattle and was especially strange to Yahwe's transmitted character.

This rejection of all decisive features of Egyptian culture is nevertheless proof of one thing. We have to presuppose as historical fact that independent minded and deliberate exponents of Yahwe religion existed in Palestine as well as in the oases of Edom and Midian as witnessed by the tradition. The Lybian as well as Asiatic Bedouins maintained steady intercourse with Egypt; Palestine, however, was for a long time ruled directly by Egypt. Whereas the first took over features of Egyptian religion, including even the cult of the dead, the last, at least the Yahwe believers, took over none. The actual priestly teaching, moreover, the speculative theology developed by the Egyptians already during the third millennium, remained alien to the Levitical Yahwists. Originally this theology was quite naturalistic and later pantheistic.[8] In popular religion and ethics, however, considerable affinities can be traced.

2. Mesopotamian Culture Relations

RELATIONS to Mesopotamian intellectual culture were more complex. During Amarna times cuneiform writing and the language of Babylonian diplomacy and trade were prevalent throughout the Middle East and understood by cultured Egyptians. As the Song of Deborah indicates, the idea of astral spirits and their intervention in mundane affairs was also familiar in Israel. Apparently, even Nabu, god of the scribes, had a sanctuary, and numerous details of all sorts bespeak common intellectual traits of old and mutual borrowing. Among such common features was particularly a common standard of weights and measures, including weights of coins. Much of the law and important sanctions of the cosmogonic myths were common. The closeness of the relation, however, seems to have shifted with the rise of the Phoenicians to commercial supremacy in Homeric times. Ancient Mediterranean peoples of oversea traders, pirates, and soldiers of fortune then receded into the background before Phoenician maritime dominance. Great migrations of peoples contributed to this. Phoenician alphabetical writing displaced cuneiform in Palestine and the importance of

Babylonian speech slowly declined in favor of Aramaic. Winckler has ascertained that the Babylonian language was still well known in Syria during the ninth and even into the seventh century. Aramaic attained its eventual significance as the universal language of diplomacy in the Middle East only in Persian times. Babylonia had receded into the background for quite some time.

Phoenician royal artisans worked at Solomon's Temple. Phoenician slave traders accompanied the Israelite armies profitably to dispose of prisoners of war. The cults of Phoenician Baals, Moloch and Astarte, immigrated into Palestine. The cosmogonies, circulating in Palestine, in the view of the experts were essenitally of Phoenician stamp. Individual Israelite tribes came under Phoenician suzerainty, others dispatched laborers to Phoenician ports and royal Nebiim of Phoenician type were kept in North Israel.

Only Elijah and the revolution of Jehu destroyed the Phoenician cults. The ancient ecstatic Nebiim were rejected by the Puritans. The Phoenician human sacrifices and the gnostic, sophisticated, onanist sacrifices to Moloch were tabooed by the prohibitions of Deuteronomy and the Holiness Code.

With the revival of the Mesopotamian great powers their influence waxed again. At times the Babylonian hosts of heavens, that is, the stars, were worshipped in Jerusalem by the kings, especially Manasseh, who were now paying tribute. In the circulating stories of paradise and the great flood, Mesopotamia was always considered the center of the world; the great terrace-temples of Mesopotamia were known as attempts to come close to the god of heaven. Details are of no interest here, for the main point is certain: there was no borrowing of priestly wisdom. Even the Babylonian (Sumerian) sacred language of many important pieces precluded their direct borrowing by Israelite priests. Generally we have no record whatsoever of any borrowing of elements of Babylonian sacred literature for cult purposes in Palestine. Only much later, during the time of the composition of the Psalms, are allusions to some hymnal poetry of Babylon to be found.

Yahwistic intellectuals not only failed to take over, but deliberately rejected the decisive cultic and theological foundations of Phoenician as well as Babylonian religion. Babylonian star worship and astrology in particular, were not borrowed, hence the basic pillar of what A. Jeremias termed "Babylonian *Weltanschauung.*" Presumably people in Palestine knew or understood the true secret teaching of the Babylonian priests of macroscosm and microcosm just as little as that of the Egyptians, although speculations and manipulations with sacred numbers and world periods play a role in a number of details of the present edition of the tradition. This last was perhaps only by virtue of the exilic and post-exilic revisions.

One fundamental Mesopotamian doctrine, that of astrological determinism was apparently well understood and deliberately rejected. For, what was the use of the Levitical Torah or the prophetic oracle, if the individual's fate was written in the stars? This determinism, leaving room only for the gnosis of salvation conventicles, was quite incompatible with the Levites' interests in power and soul-healing. They rejected these teachings as obstacles to a thoroughly political, Yahwistic conception of God. Even Isaiah (24:23) and Jeremiah (10:2)—for the latter one should presuppose especially close relations to the Babylonian priesthood—assured Israel, that the power of the stars would vanish before the might of Yahwe. In exilic times, Deutero-Isaiah in the very city of Babylon scorned, not only the Babylonian magicians generally, but also (47:13) their astronomical science and astrology. In post-exilic and rabbinical times, too, the sentence held: in Israel planets find no recognition.

Not that people doubted the influence of celestial bodies on the processes of the earth. The prophets did not doubt it. Nor did the priests doubt the reality of oracles of the dead and the related conceptions of a beyond. Obviously, Babylonian astrologers were occasionally consulted during the Exile, and a rabbi was still termed an astrologer in his private occupation. After all, astrological beliefs were diffused over all the earth from China to Rome and into modern Occidental times. People in Israel also believed in the stars. Rather, the following was decisive: in Israel the spirits of the stars are not the masters of human fate. Just as still in recent decades in China the president of the Hanlin Academy reproached the Empress Dowager in a memorial on the grounds that not the celestial constellation, but (Confucian) virtue of the ruler determine the destiny of the country, and as in India, karma determined fate, including the horoscope. In rabbinical times this found expression in the characteristic belief, stated in the Talmud, that all other peoples be in bondage to the astrological *Heimarmene* except Israel by virtue of being chosen by God.

In pre-exilic times the spirits of the stars were the Zebah and like all Zebaoth they were servants of the god of Israel. He alone was the governor of all fates. This was the important point and precluded the borrowing of the decisive foundation of Babylonian education. Accordingly, during the Exile we find Jews in Babylon occupying all sorts of positions, some highly esteemed, with the characteristic exception of that of the scribe. This could not be because of linguistic reasons, for the Israelites had learned the popular Aramaic language and they would have had no difficulty learning the official Babylonian language. We also find in the later tradition the supposition that Jews became influential in all sorts of court offices and in the role of eunuchs of the Babylonian kings and their successors, the Persian kings. Doubtless the exclusion from the profession of scribes was based on cultic reasons, the impossibility of acquiring the priestly imparted education without offending against the commandments of Yahwistic religion.

In contrast to its anti-Egyptian tendencies, Israelite religion remained related to those of Babylonia and official Phoenicia in one important respect. It ignored the beyond and related speculations. Specific to Babylonian religion was its syncretism, the pantheon of deities, the henotheistic absorption of divine forms to the figure at the time viewed as chief deity, the always preeminent position of the sun-god. All this remained as alien to Israelite conceptions of deity as the different though actually often similar Egyptian conceptions.

Where "monotheistic" tendencies appeared in Babylonia they were either solar in nature or they were dynastic, politically conditioned. Usually, however, they were both at once like the Ikhnaton reform in Egypt. But Yahwe happened to be neither a sun god, nor a god of the dynasty, rather, he was god of the confederate covenant. Furthermore, Yahwism had to remain alien to the tendency strong in Babylon which proceeded from the chthonian and vegetation cults toward making deliverers out of the deities of fertility and life common to man, beast and plant, and particularly toward making Ishtar into a merciful intercessor. Yahwe personally and alone is the savior.

Nergal, like Yahwe originally, was a god of certain frightful scourges of nations, above all also of epidemics. As god of the kingdom of the dead he remained strange to Yahwe. Adad appeared related to Yahwe as god of thunderstorms and warfare. His worship was indicated also in Canaan by theophorous given names, but exerted no visible influence upon the conception of Yahwe. In Israel there existed a cultured stratum of men comparable to the Babylonian priesthood, in Babylonia there existed no stratum comparable to that of the Israelite Torah teachers. No matter how many allusions in detail may be found, the rejection of the most impressive products of Babylonian astronomy is well ascertained. Again this shows clearly the great independence of intellectual culture of Palestine opposite neighboring countries.

3. *The Yahwistic and Elohistic Intellectual Traditions*

WE must beware of conceiving of Palestine at any historical time as an area lacking cultural strata of its own, as a country governed only by barbaric magic and quite primitive religious ideas. A Canaanite in a letter from about the 15th century to a prince heralds the Lord of God's grace for him, for the prince was a brother having love in his heart: hence, we may infer, he was a fellow believer. The sender then continues in almost missionary style to emphasize the importance for the king's success of the grace of him who is "above his head" and also "above the cities."

Such conceptions were certainly alien to the herdsmen and peasants of the old Israelite militia. All signs speak against assuming their complete disappearance in the more important cities. The successful rejection of the religious conceptions of great cultural areas, which evidently influenced all other spheres, and the creation of characteristically different and independent conceptions required the existence of an independent, cultured stratum which received and rationally refashioned the old oracles and promises of the surrounding world. They could not be the ecstatic Nebiim whose school tradition produced but mystery stories in the nature of the Elishah stories, nor court circles who disdained the Nebiim, nor, finally, the herdsmen and peasants and their war prophets. We have no reason to conceive of the Israelite rural people as particularly "dumb" as is occasionally done.[9] Peasants become "dumb" only where they are harnessed into and face a presumably strange, bureaucratic, or liturgical machine of a great state, or where they are abandoned as serfs to landlords, as happened in Egypt, Mesopotamia, and in the Hellenist and late Roman states. In contrast to this, the pre-exilic plebeian was at first in fact, later, in memory and aspiration, a free militia man of the confederacy, who had defeated the knighthood of the culture areas. To be sure he could never have created the rational conception of the Scriptures on his own. Others had to do this for him. But he was receptive to most of the Scriptures. One of the secrets of the development of Yahwism lies, indeed, in the interaction between an enthused stratum of intellectuals and this public composed of demilitarized and socially declassed strata under the impact of social change during the time of the kings.

Rarely have entirely new religious conceptions originated in the respective centers of rational cultures. Rational prophetic or reformist innovations were first conceived, not in Babylon, Athens, Alexandria, Rome, Paris, London, Cologne, Hamburg, Vienna, but in Jerusalem of pre-exilic, in Galilaea of late Jewish times, in the late Roman province of Africa, in Assisi, in Wittenberg, Zurich, Geneva and in the marginal regions of the Dutch, lower-German, and English cultural areas, like Frisia and New England. To be sure this never occurred without the influence and impact of a neighboring rational civilization. The reason for this is always the same: prerequisite to new religious conceptions is that man must not yet have unlearned how to face the course of the world with questions of his own. Precisely the man distant from the great culture centers has cause to do so when their influence begins to affect or threaten his central interests. Man living in the midst of the culturally satiated areas and enmeshed in their technique addresses such questions just as little to the environment as, for instance, the child used to daily tramway rides would chance to question how the tramway actually manages to start moving.

The possibility of questioning the meaning of the world presupposes the capacity to be astonished about the course of events. Now, the experiences which the Israelites had before the Exile and which gave them cause to ask such questions were the great wars of liberation and the rise of kingship, the development of the corvée state and of urban culture, the threat of great powers. Particularly, the collapse of the Northern Kingdom and the same fateful threat to the Southern Kingdom, the last remnant of unforgotten grandeur, stood before everybody's eyes. Then came the Exile. The wars of liberation established Yahwe's prestige as war god. The social degradation and demilitarization of the exponents of the old Yahwe militia created the Yahwistic history legend. The paramount questions of theodicy, however, were raised only with the threatened collapse of the kingdom.

The intellectual work which created the two great later combined revisions of the Hexateuch obviously belong essentially to the second period. They are products of two groups of religious literati, nowadays usually distinguished as the "Yahwistic" and "Elohistic" by the name they used for God.[10]

These collectors and writers apparently stood independently beside the original editors of the purely historical traditions and legends in the Books of Judges and Kings, for all attempts to carry through the distinctions between the two schools in these scriptures seem to have failed. Both collectors or schools of collectors must be viewed as highly educated men, because they advanced numerous etymologies of names and etiological stories which are quite ingenious and, in the main, cannot possibly be popular in origin. The Jerusalemite Deuteronomic school belonged to the last period. The priestly completion and revision of the preceding epochs, in the narrower sense, belonged to the time of the Exile and partially the following time, even though its beginnings may go back to pre-exilic times.

The Yahwistic and Elohistic collections[11] were not yet exposed to the grave problem of theodicy which had to come up by the decline of the national state. Their monotheism is "naive." They had, as yet, no knowledge of the struggle of the ascending priesthood with the prophetic movement and its indifference toward sacrificial worship. Likewise, as yet, they knew nothing of the later detestation of ancient rural sanctuaries, the cult paraments and images. However, these collections, one of which goes back to Solomon's time, the other to at least the eighth century, were influenced by the social problems produced by kingship. Hence, in both collections the patriarchal legends constitute an important part of the presentation. The Elohistic, indeed, begins only with these legends. And both collections then deal extensively with the Exodus from Egypt, the conquest of Canaan under Moses and Moshuah, the cultic, moral, and legal commandments which Yahwe at the time imposed on the people.

As regards the age of the material, various parts of both collections, as in the Blessings, may come from earlier times. It is not certain whether the Book of the Covenant and the ethical Decalogue originally were part of the Elohistic, nor is it certain that the cultic Decalogue was an original part of the Yahwistic collection; however, for the characterization it is not important. For, the manner of the collector's account serves as an ethical paradigm as intended by the collectors, however little they succeeded in expurgating the often quite unethical features of the old sagas. Both collections utilized nearly the same material for the time since Abraham. It would be misleading to construe an actual oppositional "bias" between them. In agreement with the mood of their public, both halo the time of the people's origin. Likewise one cannot make a case for the greater "popularity" of one of the two, or, if one wishes sometimes one, at other times the other. It was hardly unintentional when both of them conceived of the then popular promises as having been given not to a king, or to his ancestors, but to the ancient legendary tribal fathers of the people, promises such as to make Israel a great people, to bless its friends, to curse its enemies and to bequest a name which would still be a blessing to all other generations of the world at a late time.

Perhaps this conception of the ancient legendary heroes as tribal fathers of Israel as a whole was one of the contributions of these authors. In their eyes, the promises were yet unconditional, without prerequisite achievements, i.e., pledges of God's friendship for Israel through thick and thin. This ran counter to the later prophetic conception as did the prophecies of hope of the kingly Nebiim. Moreover, the glorification of Moses plays an incomparable role with them, one not found in the political, hymnic, or prophetic literature, nor, of course, in the later priestly revision, which put Aaron, the priest, as far as possible, in place of Moses. Yet, the Song of Deborah and the collection of blessings later inserted into Deuteronomy prove that Moses' prestige was absolute and ancient and no *ex-post-facto* construction. Thus, these collectors continued old popular traditions which were hardly agreeable to the kings and each of the two schools did so in a somewhat different fashion. Both viewed the patriarchs as peaceful herdsmen. The Elohistic collection, however, placed greater emphasis upon their position as *gerim* of the settled, and with them *berith*-bound population, whereas the obviously more Levitically influenced Yahwistic account (in the story of Isaac's marriage proposal) already knows the disinclination against intermarriage with the Canaanites.

To consider tillage as resulting from a divine curse is essentially the view of the Yahwist. For him paradise represented an irrigated and planted fruit garden modeled after an oasis in the steppe. The Elohist, who had included Moses' Blessing, seems to know something of the claim of the tribe of Joseph to royal dignity, whereas with the Yahwist in Jacob's Blessing, Judah, instead of Reuben and Joseph, is the champion of the promise. These and similar specific traits make the assumption of eminent scholars probable, that on the whole the Elohistic revision has been more subject to Northern, the Yahwistic to Southern influence. As regards the age of the collections, now one, then the other, has older elements, but on the whole, the Yahwistic one may be considered somewhat older. The fact that the Elohist is inclined to consider Abraham and, in general, all heroes as Nebiim, the heroes of the Joseph story as Nazarites also speaks for his, on the whole, Northern derivation. The same is shown by the fact that in the Elohistic revision the appointment of the elders in Israel is justified etiologically, whereas for the Yahwistic collection, Moses, hence the Levitical priests, are the trial judges, as was presumably largely the case or at least claim in the South. Puritanical influences are readily to be found in the Yahwistic account.

With respect to the great part played by the snake in the Yahwistic story of man's fall we may recall that staffs similar to the Mosaic snake staff in the Temple of Jerusalem were ascribed to the Egyptian magicians in the story of Exodus and that this snake staff of Moses was brought into relation with magical therapy by the Elohistic edition of the desert story. Hence, if the assumption holds that a snake cult and Levitical medicine men existed, the sharp rejection by the Yahwistic puritan tradition, under Hezekiah leading to the destruction of the idol, may here find expression in the very presentation of the snake and of its undoubted wisdom as the source of all evil. Whether, as is partially assumed, also the frequent quality of the snake as a divine animal for the kingdom of the dead played its part in this would appear doubtful.

The difference in derivation also seems to find expression in the treatment of the conception of god. The absolutely firm point of departure for both collections was the quality of the god as a personal master who by his intervention determined man's fate in the world, but since Moses was bound to Israel by *berith* and oath and guaranteed its codes and norms. That was unalterably the case. The Yahwe of Moses and of the ancient war prophets simply never was the primitive fiend into which, in the interest of a theory of unilinear evolution, attempt has been made to cast him. On the other hand he could not be spiritualized into an impersonal world power as in China and India. For reasons discussed earlier he bears certain universalist features in both collections, only in different ways. The Yahwistic collection presents him, as often noted, in occasionally quite drastic anthropomorphic form. There is no mention of the grandiose but abstract constructions of the exilic priests which made the spirit of Yahwe, brooding over chaos, strike up light by a magic word, and then day by day one thing after another was made to originate from nothingness by his mere commandment (Gen. 1). Yahwe (Gen. 2) first made water spring from the thus far desolate and barren earth, then he formed man from earth, vivified him by breathing his breath into him, and then only he allowed plants and animals to originate. He presented these to man and left to him the business of naming them, which according to the view of Moses' time and his (Egyptian) surroundings was quite important. At first he failed in offering to man an agreeable company until he fashioned out of a rib woman, whom man at once recognized as his kind. In the cool of the evening God like a sheik in an oasis promenaded in his garden Eden into which he also put man. He took him personally to task when he touched his trees against his prohibition and in punishment chased him out with a curse. In order to do so he had first to search and call man, who had gone into hiding. Likewise, in order to see the giant construction in Babylon he had to descend there. If he had to give orders or promises to man he made a personal appearance. In contradiction with the later tradition he still allowed Moses to actually see him face to face, also he dined on Mount Sinai with the elders. Hence, he is a god of corporeal epiphanies, acting entirely in terms of human motives, but, nevertheless, a god who created the universe and exerted his power also in Babylon, the center of the world.

This anthropomorphic corporeality obviously was experienced as awkward in the Elohistic view, which despite its popular nature, in this was influenced more by the ancient culture which was stronger in the North. In this view, the god of Israel is the supreme god of heaven who does not walk among men on earth. The present revision bypasses this original story altogether and begins with the patriarchal legends. It must remain an open question whether this was originally the case or whether, perhaps, the later composition did not wish to take over Elohistic conceptions which no longer agreed with the conceptions of deity of the time. In any case, the Elohistic point of view preferred to have the divine commands and promises occur in a dream, by a call from heaven, or, finally, through a messenger (*malak*) or angel of God. Occasionally (Gen. 18:2 f.), this is also found with the Yahwist. The conception of the divine messenger is ancient. The North Israelite Song of Deborah knows him at the cursing of Meroz. The Elohist, however, transforms all transmitted theophanies into the appearances of such mediating figures. This is an obvious theological construction. In the later revisions of the collections other theological constructions, perhaps taken from ancient views, are to be found beside them: such is the impersonal "majesty" (*kabod*) of God. It is used especially for the sake of reconciling the usual conception of the localization of the god at the sanctuary, especially the temple, customary with settled, particularly urban populace with the idea of the distant great god of heaven. Not God himself, but his *kabod* in the form of a radiant cloud has descended upon the sanctuary (Ex. 40:34 f.). Or another impersonal power appeared as efficacious such as the "countenance" (*panim*), the "word" (*debar*) and the "spirit" (*ruach*), most often however, in Egyptian fashion the name (*sham*) of God. The derivation of all these theological constructions is difficult to ascertain and, with the exception of the last named, shall not concern us further.

These spiritualizing tendencies were met half-way by the ancient patriarchal legends in so far as in them, as usual in theologically unreconstructed popular stories, man preferably is active and not, as in the Yahwistic story of creation, God. Some particularly ancient, because originally polytheistic epiphanies, had to be preserved. But, in general, the god of the patriarchs became a god of mysterious features recognized but indirectly in all sorts of ordainments of fate. Edifying, occasionally touching traits, such as tended particularly to be produced in the artistic elaboration of religious short stories, are most clearly evident in the story of Joseph and in that of Isaac's sacrifice. This sort of paradigm was the source of that rationalism which led to the belief in providence. On the other hand, these theological constructions show a certain preference for the development of impersonal divine powers: preferences which, as usual elsewhere, were intrinsically related to the orgiastic ecstatic nature of North Israelite divine possession.

Later this theological tendency was apparently deliberately discarded again. Whereas other theological elements were developed but in rudimentary form before the Exile, the old theological construct of the divine messenger was preserved. It implemented the increasing majesty of the god and avoided the altogether too coarse, anthropomorphic theophanies. Obviously, the reason was a purely practical one. The Levitical priestly Torah, the counseling of those pursued by hard luck, hence, by God's anger, had gained in significance, and the struggle of the puritanical Yahwists of the South had begun against the North's orgiastic communion with and possession by God. The interest in rational instruction concerning the intentions and imperatives of God, particularly about cultic and ethical sins and the warding off of their consequences had developed and this need for theodicy had to gain in intensity the more problematical the political situation. This plebeian need, however, was far better met by the corporeal, concrete god, once negotiating personally with man of the Yahwistic edition, than the more sublimated view of the Elohistic school. One needed understandable reasons for the divine judgments and hence the opportunity to refer in justification to personal, corporeal pronouncements of God. The pre-exilic prophets did not receive their commandments and oracles by messenger, but directly, although, for the rest, they are quite frequently influenced by the Elohistic conception. This resulted from the North Israelite setting of the first, lastingly influential, appearance of prophecy. Therefore, the old god of the fathers and of the covenant again made personal appearances in the integration of the old collections by the revision which, after Wellhausen, nowadays is usually designated as "Jehovistic." And, in agreement with the rational need of the intellectuals he now appeared speaking to (Gen. 13:14 f.) or arguing with his prophets. Or even his reasoning processes are literally demonstrated (Gen. 6:5 f.). The paradigm for this was offered by older Yahwistic presentations of Yahwe's reflections which caused him to punish man's fall and to destroy the Babylonian terrace tower. But the motives changed in nature. In the primitive view, still influential in the Yahwistic collection, as in all old myths, God's resolutions are guided by selfish interests, above all God's jealousy against being threatened by *hybris*, the increasing wisdom and power of man. In the later revisions, however, benevolent charity for man is the decisive motive. Thus, in the final revision of the account of the desert migration, God ponders the alternative modes of behavior of the Israelites in whose constancy he has not much trust in terms of the road on which he is going to guide them. He then decides solely for their own good. The search for purely human and understandable motives of God remains characteristic, and the account is fashioned accordingly.

It is also clear elsewhere how the intellectual attempt to sublimate the conception of god was at odds with the interest in practical cure of souls. The old sagas had Yahwe "regret," without inhibitions, his resolutions and acts. To the rational writers it appeared doubtful even at early times whether this be in agreement with the majesty of a great god. Therefore, the saying was put into Balaam's mouth that God is "no son of man that he should repent" and this was often repeated (Nu. 23:19; I. Sam. 15:29). The practical needs of Levitical exhortation, however, obstructed the consummation of this sublimation. If God's resolutions were decided once for all, prayer, search of soul, and expiation were useless. The same fatalistic consequence detrimental to the Torah teacher's interest in cure of soul had to be feared which was abhorrent in the astrological determination of man's fate. Therefore the later revisions of the Moses stories repeatedly have the prophet intercede to assuage Yahwe's wrath. Yahwe changes his mind either upon intercession or upon repentance and penance. The Nathan tradition has the same happen for David and the Elijah tradition for Ahab when they do penance. This understandable anthropomorphic god, then as today, was better adapted to the practical necessities of mass curing of souls. The Deuteronomic compendium found a resolution in that Yahwe in advance made his behavior depend upon man's conduct: "Behold, I set before you this day a blessing and a curse"; take your choice.

The attitude toward other problems, for similar reasons, remained dualistic; so with respect to the ultimate question of theodicy. Basic to the old relation of Yahwe to his people was the *berith*. Yahwe's vow to stand by this people as his own seemed constantly put into question by the disaster which continually threatened politically and partially came to pass. Occasionally the Yahwist finds succor, as in the rather late saga of the great flood, by the statement that all thoughts of man were "only evil continually." Accordingly man had, indeed, deserved all evil. But since, in spite of all, Yahwe does not wish to forgo the lovely scent of sacrifice, he resolves, precisely because of their unavoidably evil acts in the future, at least, no longer to ruin the whole world by a great flood (Gen. 8:21) which, by the way, alludes to the end of the Babylonian saga of the great flood.

The pessimistic estimation of human nature probably derived from the confessional practice of the Southern Torah teachers. It was not generally accepted. In Israel man was always thought to be weak, but not constitutionally wicked. (Only the prophecy of doom of the last days of Israel tended again to this view.) The formulation that none be innocent before Yahwe (Ex. 34:7) was more adequate and obviously amenable to the practical needs of cure of souls in the face of the suffering of the innocent.

This, however, did not as yet solve the problem of Israel's special misfortune. After all, they were Yahwe's people. The natural solution was that Yahwe had of course made prerequisite to his ancient promises the honoring of ritual and ethical obligations, which the people had failed to do. Actually, all ancient promises were refashioned from originally unconditional pledges of Yahwe into conditional pledges based on good conduct. Doubtless this again derived from the practical needs for a rational theodicy. As we shall see, it was a basic tenet of prophecy.

Difficulties, however, were inevitable. The ancient idea of joint liability of the community for the doings of each individual and of the descendants for the deeds of the forefathers, opposite the blood avenger and political enemy in a free confederacy, originally went without saying and was a useful paradigm.[12] But one had to fear that against this the question would be raised: what good would it do the individual to fulfill Yahwe's commandments if the doings of others would enmesh the innocent in misfortune just the same? For the sins of contemporaries there was the solution of dedicating them to God through *cherem* and stoning them. This was done just as people warded off an old evil against a *metic* community by surrendering the wrongdoers or their relatives, which allegedly happened under David when Saul's family was surrendered to Gibeon. At least in later times the Shechemite ceremony of curse and blessing served also the purpose of unburdening the liability of the community by transferring the curse onto the sinner's person. Capital punishment of the murderer was expressly viewed as an expurgation of the country from the joint liability for guilt against Yahwe. Special expiation ceremonies were instituted for cases in which the murderer could not be found. But this means was not available for the sins of the fathers. Here the bitter popular proverb held which Jeremiah cited: (31:29) "The fathers ate sour grapes, and the children's teeth are on edge." Hence, fatalistic consequences, detrimental to cure of soul also threatened here. For this reason, the Deuteronomic school, obviously under the influence of Levitical Torah teachers, decided completely to reject the liability of descendants for the fathers both with respect to legal practice and ethical responsibility.

However, the difficulty was that the idea of compensation for the sins of the forefathers proved indispensable for purposes of theodicy, since there was no compensation in the beyond, and since observation again and again seemed to teach that the individual simply was not punished and rewarded proportionate to his sins and good deeds. The idea of compensation was particularly indispensable for political theodicy particularly after the bitter lesson of the battle of Megiddo. Hence the prophets always employed the idea of collective responsibility of the community and of the descendants for their forebearers and the idea was never definitely discarded. In the priestly revision the assurance of God's grace and mercy still stands directly beside that of his "visiting the iniquity of the fathers upon the children unto the third and fourth generation," (Nu. 14:18). This dualism derived from the needs of pragmatic political prophecy as against the priestly interests in cure of souls and the rationalism of the educated. They all agreed, however, in the result that God was to be a god of just compensation, and this quality was indeed emphasized by the Deuteronomic school.

With this, the commandments of God as well as the expiation of offenses were more and more sublimated in the direction of ethical absolutism (*Gesinnungsethik*). What mattered to the heavenly ruler was not external conduct, but unconditional obedience and absolute trust in what, repeatedly, would seem to be problematical promises. The very idea is to be found even in the Yahwistic story of Abraham's call to move to Canaan and the promise of a son. Abraham followed the first blindly and his blind belief in the latter is "counted to him for righteousness" (Gen. 15:6).

It is no accident that the idea is first to be found in a patriarchal saga. For undoubtedly one of the pillars of the party rested on the pacifistic semi-nomads opposed to the kings and their priestly-instituted sacrificial cult. It advanced the thesis that the old god of the covenant did not enjoy sacrifices, but solely obedience to his commandments and, above all, that the very community was holy and, hence, had no need for priests. Such anti-priestly belief found its natural support in the ancient warrior asceticism and warrior ecstasy and, generally, in early conditions which knew no office-holding, hereditary, confederate priesthood. No doubt, this belief suggested itself also to the intellectual strata. Finally, in all probability the order of the Rechabites, so well liked by Jeremiah, the opponent of the Jerusalem priests, was one of the exponents of this anti-priestly belief. All those Levites who were not employed at sanctuaries, but who made a living simply by curing souls and Torah teaching, could also embrace it. It corresponded to the idea that Yahwe found decisive satisfaction in a contrite attitude per se, not sacrificial and expiatory offerings and similar acts of the sinner. This idea was probably rooted in the same intellectual circles and the editors of the tradition put it into the mouth of the old seers, first of Nathan.

Another section of the Levites, particularly those belonging to the Deuteronomic school, were too closely tied to the interests in cult and sacrifice to draw such conclusions. It was the Yahwistic tradition, which on the whole was more Southern and Levitically influenced which absorbed the prescriptions of the so-called cultic Decalogue. But as long as the priests were linked to kingship the very idea remained alive and especially in prophecy. Even the later priestly revision was unable to eradicate its traces. In the Moses stories, this revision joined Yahwe's judgment of the Korachite Levites to those heretical propositions of the sanctity of the community and the expendability of the priests, but it could not prevent it from vigorously surviving in the scriptural oracles of the mightiest prophets.

This ethical absolutism of faithful obedience to God took a plebeian turn by the manner in which the ancient mythological conceptions of God's jealousy and hatred against man's *hybris* were elaborated in the moral exhortation of the Torah teachers. Bureaucratic subordination was the source of the Egyptian sage's praise of obedience, silence, and absence of *hybris* as god-pleasing virtues. In Israel it sprang from the plebeian nature of the patronage. The Torah teachers and the circles giving rise to the prophets were devoted to the counseling and curing of souls of plebeians. Their god hated and considered as an abomination the pride, arrogance, the boastful reliance on one's own strength, as shown by the kings and their warrior heroes. Yahwe viewed with displeasure (according to Amos) the eroticism and (according to Isaiah) the gay carousing of the *gibborim*. The prophet Zephaniah knows for certain (3:12) that only the poor people have true faith in God and leave everything to his discretion and therefore alone will be spared from perishing in days to come. The failure of this arrogant caste opposite the foreign enemies in contrast to the time of the ancient peasant militia seemed proof of Yahwe's displeasure with the great. Only absolute and humble faith in him might, perhaps, lead the old god of the covenant again to be absolutely behind his people as formerly. Therewith we face again a basic motive for the utopian political ethic of the prophets and of Deuteronomy which in this stood under their influence. We shall discuss this separately at a later time. Here, we merely wish to clarify further some of the circumstances basic to the formal peculiarities of man's entire relationship to God in Israel. This concerns especially the tremendous emphasis upon rational ethical absolutism.

CHAPTER IX

ETHICS AND ESCHATOLOGY
OF YAHWISM

1. Magic and Ethics

Magic did not have its usual dominance in Israel, although it never vanished completely from popular practice. The fate of magic in Old Testament religion was determined by the systematic opposition of the Torah teachers. Though there were all sorts of magicians in Israel, leading Yahwistic circles, particularly the Levites, were not magicians, but men of knowledge. So, too, were the Brahmins, but their knowledge was basically different from that of the Israelites. When in the Yahwistic story of paradise the snake advises the woman to eat from the tree of knowledge, it holds out the promise that "your eyes shall be opened and ye shall be as gods, knowing good and evil." It told no lie, for Yahwe, after cursing man and the snake, added "man is become as one of us," hence godlike through knowledge, and he chased man out of the garden, "lest he put forth his hand, and take also of the tree of life, and eat, and live forever." Hence, one becomes a god by possessing two things: immortality and knowledge. But what kind of knowledge is meant? In both passages it is knowledge of "what is good and evil." This is the knowledge which the pre-prophetic writer believed to make man godlike, though it did not imply that this was rational-ethical, not ritualistic or esoteric knowledge.

In Egypt, too, a plebeian, uninstructed in priestly writing, is termed a man who "does not know what is good and evil." And in the story of paradise the purely ritualistic taboo on nakedness, not rational ethical knowledge, is, as far as we can see, what is imparted to man by his eating from the tree of knowledge. However, even Micah at the time of Hezekiah, emphasized (6:8) that man—hence, every man—has been "shewed what is good, namely to do justly and to love mercy, and to walk humbly with thy God." Hence what mattered was not esoteric nor merly ritualistic knowledge, but, indeed, publicly taught ethics and charity.

The Levitical Torah teacher characteristically engaged in this kind of teaching and the special relationship to Yahwe, as personal partner of the *berith* with the confederacy, first placed this strong accent upon "doing justly." Thus, preeminence was placed on obedience and ethical conduct as over against observance of purely cultic and ritualistic commandments which, given the structure of the confederacy, were necessarily almost completely absent or developed only in a few simple rules in earlier times. Since the community was jointly responsible to Yahwe for the offenses of every individual, these ethical problems were of great interest to every member of the community [1] and, above all, to the intellectuals interested in the destiny of the country. This was the point of departure for the conception of the nature of divine knowledge which became prevalent among the circles of increasingly demilitarized Yahwistic plebeians and those intellectuals who adhered to the good old law. This knowledge continually increased in importance. The early period knew divine charisma only in the form of warrior ecstasy and war prophecy. Both were decayed. As beginnings in the tradition show, there was a tendency to make a magician out of Moses whose magical charm, like that of an Indian court Brahmin, was decisive for victory. But such no longer existed. Yahwe no longer awakened a prophet to appear to him face to face. For times had changed. Elisha's war oracles represent the last echo of magical political prophecy in the tradition. The Levites were the only permanent champions of Yahwe belief and by virtue of their socially important functions felt themselves as men knowing what offenses would bring misfortunes and how to make good again. If the name of *jide' oni* (Lev. 20:27; II. Ki. 23:24) which designates the oracular spirit inhabiting certain magicians should really be equivalent to "small" knowledge, this would be characteristic of the specifically anti-magical pride in knowledge of the representatives of Yahwism. To be sure, the scriptural prophets occasionally gave advice to the kings, as did court prophets and magicians. But they did so always in the sense of the Levitical Torah: obey Yahwe and trust in him. None of them sought to help the country by sorcery.

Naturally there were tendencies to develop magical coercion of God even among Yahwists at all times and possibly until rather late pre-exilic times. Alongside other, rather secondary traces, there developed the ubiquitously diffused belief in the magical power of God's name, and were one to call him by it correctly he would obey.

It is not without reason that Yahwe, in the epiphany of the thornbush, at first avoids naming his name as did the *numen* with which Jacob wrestled. When Moses later asked Yahwe the favor of seeing him face to face, Yahwe instructs Moses to call his name. By this means Yahwe was compelled. As already noted, this widely diffused conception was native to Egypt. Yahwe's name like that of the Pharaoh, is the symbol of his power. As Jerusalem in the Amarna letters "is called by the king's name," so Israel is called by Yahwe's name (Deut. 28:10; Jer. 14:9) or Jerusalem (Jer. 25:29), or a prophet (Jer. 15:16). His name "is called, he resides" in Jerusalem, where "a house is built" for him, he "comes from far" (Is. 30:27), "is near" (Psalm 75:11). And Yahwe through his name acts in favor of all who "love his name" (Psalms 5:11; 69:36; 119:132). In part the intention may have been the previously mentioned theological attempt to eliminate anthropomorphism and personal presence of Yahwe. But in part, especially in Egypt where it prevailed, it is also a matter of the concept of the nature of the name.

It is hardly accidental that nearly all characteristic references of this kind are Deuteronomic, hence, derived from the time which generally evinces the greatest relationship to Egyptian forms of piety. The specific sanctity of God's name was also to be found in Egypt, where Isis robs Ra of his power by knowledge of his secret name, and Ptah avenges the "taking in vain" of his name. In Israel, too, the sanctity of God's name increased. Here the taboo widely diffused on use of the divine name originally did not hold. Later the attempt to compel the majestic god by means of calling his name was considered a grave offense which he was bound to avenge. The unconcern in the use of his

name, which was still prevalent in prophetic times, gave way to
specific fear to do so which must have originated at early
times. The prohibition of the Decalogue against taking his name
in vain goes back to unknown times and refers undoubtedly to
the attempt magically to compel God. This rejection may well
derive from the conscious opposition against Egypt, perhaps
specifically against the cult of the dead. For the significance of
the names of the gods is nowhere in Egypt as central as in the
125th chapter of the Book of the Dead. Their proper use is decisive
for the fate of the soul. At every gate of Hades the respective
deity demands the dead to know his name before letting him pass.
The allusions, on the one hand, the sharp rejection on the other,
are hardly fortuitous.

In practice the rejection of magic meant primarily that unlike
the process elsewhere, it was not systematized by priests for the
sake of taming the masses. In Babylonia, magic was systematized
under the pressing need for a theodicy, hence, the systematization was rational in origin. The fact that the innocent also suffer
seemed to agree with faith in the gods only if demons and evil
spirits, not the gods, caused evil. Theodicy therewith took the
path of a latent semidualism.[2] This was out of the question in
Israel. One of the fundamental theses even of the first prophet
(Amos) was that Yahwe also sent all evil. In Israel, all evil was
punishment or ordainment of the powerful god. Therefore, the
development of the magical defense against demons was confronted with that of the purely ethical Torah and with the confession of sins as genuine means of control in the hands of the
Levitical priests. This exerted an all-pervasive influence upon the
religious development of Israel.

Among the Israelites the "miracle" had a place comparable to
that of "sorcery" in Asiatic religions. The magician, the redeemer,
the god of Asia practiced "magic," whereas the god of Israel,
upon imploration and intercession, performed "miracles." The
profound contrast has been discussed before. The miracle is
more rational than magic charm. The world of the Indian remained a garden of irrational charm. Beginnings of a similar
development are to be found in the mysterious miracles (*Mirakel*)
of the Elisha stories. Their irrationality stands, indeed, on the
same level with the Asiatic charms. This mode of conception

might have readily gained the upper hand. Clearly the constant fight against all orgiastic ecstasy made for the prevalence not of magic, but of the miracle in the truly Yahwistic legends. The miracle springs from meaningful, understandable intentions and reactions of the godhead and its place, for instance, in the patriarchal legends, but also in the Moses and Samuel traditions, and in the scripture of the Old Testament generally, is comparable to that in no other holy book. Relatively economic use is made of miracles in many old sections, particularly in the patriarchal legends. In the absence of magic all questioning of the why of events, of destiny and fate was pushed in the direction of belief in providence, toward the conception of a god who mysteriously though ultimately understandably governed the world and guided the destinies of his people. The artistic Joseph legend of the Elohist had its hero give it striking formulation: "Ye thought evil against me; but god meant it unto good." Here God's will held the field opposite all human endeavor to escape it as in Indian stories fate triumphed over all tricks to outwit it. Unlike the Indian karma, the rational providence of the personal god determined destiny in Israel.

Two features were characteristic of this god of the intellectuals who despite his passionate wrath in the last analysis acted rationally and according to plan. First, as indicated, he was a god of plebeians. This has to be properly understood. In this form, Yahwe was not the god of "popular religion," nor did he accommodate the needs of "the masses." In the final triumphant conception he was always a god whom a stratum of prophets (war prophets, later Torah prophets) and Torah teachers sought to impose upon the people. Frequently they met with resistance, for the masses in need are always out for emergency aid through magic or saviors, and that was also the case in Israel. Likewise, neither the ideals nor the idealists of Yahwe religion stemmed from among "the poor."

Before the Exile, the hero of the genuine tradition of the Book of Kings, as well as of the old, fragmentary traditions from the time of the Judges, was the well-to-do and pious Israelite. In the religious legend the patriarchs, too, were quite wealthy men. In accordance with the ancient promises, here, as always, riches were the wages of piety. In all probability, the cultured exponents of Yahwe knowledge were primarily members of distinguished sibs. Yet, since the early prophets (Amos) it is evident that this was by no means always the case. The literati believed in their ability to develop and actually did develop, puritanically sincere, anti-orgiastic, anti-idolatrous, and anti-magical devoutness among circles which were largely plebeian in nature.

These strata were plebeian at least in the sense that they had no share in political power nor were they exponents of the military and corvée state or the social power position of the patriciate. That is evident in the revision of the tradition. Nowhere, except in residues of the kingly histories, does the heroism of nobles dominate. Rather the peaceful and devout peasant or shepherd is throughout the hallowed figure. And the manner of presentation and interpretation is adjusted to his horizon. Demagogic wooing of the masses, to be sure, is out of the question. As in Egypt, Levitical exhortation demanded that the judge pervert the ends of the law as little in favor of the multitude as the great. Saul's adversity is, among other things, ascribed to the fact that he obeyed the mass of foolish people. What is decisive for the worth and authority of the individual is rather the knowledge of Yahwe's commandments. But the "nomadic ideal" in the manner of the Rechabites and the memory of the peasant militia also controlled the ideals of the intellectual élite.

The Confucians just as the radical Yahwists were basically convinced that solely the fulfillment of the commandments of heaven safeguard the destiny of state. In China the virtues of a genteel, aesthetically cultured, literary stratum of prebendaries was decisive, whereas in Israel, the virtues of an ideal Israelite plebeian in town and country was increasingly hallowed. Levitical exhortation more and more took account of this conceptual horizon of their clientele. The peculiarity in this consisted in the fact that here and here only plebeian strata became exponents of a rational religious ethic.

It was likewise quite important that Yahwe remained a god of history, especially of political-military history. This differentiated him from all Asiatic deities and was due to his original relationship to Israel. For his most devout believers he always remained the war god of the confederacy. No matter whether he was also a rainmaking god or whether speculation in North

Israel elevated him to heavenly king, for truly Yahwistic and especially prophetic belief, he remained the god of political destinies. Hence he was no god with whom one could seek mystical union by contemplation, but a superhuman, yet understandable personal master whom one had to obey. He had given his positive commandments which one had to follow. One could enquire into his divine purposes, the reasons for his wrath, and the prerequisites of his mercy, just as with a great king. Beyond that, there was nothing. This presupposition, indeed, precluded the development of speculation about the "meaning" of the world in Indian fashion. For different reasons speculation with the Egyptians and Babylonians did not go beyond certain, quite narrow limits either. In Ancient Israel it had no footing whatsoever.

2. Mythologies and Eschatologies

THE rational development of the world image remained firmly channeled in one direction and thereby capable of consumation. Yahwe's peculiarities, also, set limits to his mythologization. As every other deity, the figure of Yahwe was embellished with mythological features. The grandiose images of the prophets and psalmists certainly derive from a treasure of ancient widely diffused myths. The Babylonian notions of the primeval dragon, of monsters and giants with whom God had to wrestle in producing the present world, undoubtedly were also to be found in pre-Israelite Canaan. They survived outside the cosmogony revised by the priests in the form of Leviathan, Behemoth, Rahab. And in the priestly revision the chaotic primal waters received the name of the primeval Babylonian dragon (Tehom: Tiamat). God's irrigated garden of Eden, the treatment of original man as a husbandman, the great world rivers, the Armenian mountains in the present revision of the story of creation show that none of these myths originated in the steppe or the Palestinian highland. The patriarchal planter of God's garden does not go too well with the rudiments of gigantomachy in the sixth chapter of Genesis. And the notion of God's spirit moving upon the face of the waters was received by the latest priestly revision and in turn derived from a quite different framework of ideas.

The earlier Yahwistic cosmogony did not visualize Yahwe as creating the world from a "void." Still he alone was responsible for what originated on earth. This conception, which Peisker [3] adroitly called "naive monotheism" has nothing to do with the uniqueness and universalism of God. For in almost all cosmogonies one god creates the world, no thought being given to others. But it is characteristic that a plain prose account here stands opposite the versified Babylonian saga of world origin. Moreover, the mythological imagery of the prophets, even more that of the priests, becomes increasingly abstract and less plastic. This occurs typically when theological rationalism dominates mythological elaboration. The end product, the unsurpassed, majestic, but quite unplastic story of creation in the present first chapter of Genesis is an accomplishment typical of priests. It originated in Exile times in deliberate opposition to the Babylonian environment. All the phantasms of the Babylonian primeval saga, especially the splitting of the primeval dragon, are expurgated, the monster is depersonalized into primeval waters. And creation is consummated by the mere "word" of the God, which makes the light flash and the waters divide just as it is God's word which comes to man out of the teacher's mouth. Perhaps the theogonic and gigantomachic residues were only then eliminated from the older account which was allowed to stand directly alongside the new. For here was the decisive limit to myth formation in Yahwism. Yahwe could well admit individual myths, but in the long run he could not allow for theogony, the crown of all great mythological systems. Israel, having received the theogonic myths from the outside, offered no favorable soil to them, because Yahwe remained the single god and without image. Yahwism was not a cult derived from orgiasticism and mimic demonology which could have stimulated artistic or poetic imagination and which is the normal source of all mythological systems. Moreover, the sober sacrificial cult was not the most important element in man's relation to God.

Besides Yahwe's personal traits, also, his position as guardian of the socio-legal order brought him into opposition to the divine mythologies circulating in Canaan as throughout the Middle East. This distinguished him also from the great universal deities of the surrounding culture areas. The primary field of activity for all these gods, including Ikhnaton's sun god, was the realm of nature. The political destinies usually were guaranteed by the local god of the residence, the social orders by one or several functional deities and only secondarily by the great god of heaven. Yahwe, too, was originally a god of nature. He was a god of certain natural catastrophes, which the Levitical exhortation considered expressive of his wrath against disobedience. The more important the Torah became in Israel, the more firmly was his behavior related to the individual's greater or lesser obedience and good will toward Yahwe.

Thus, all nature mythologies were subordinated to a sober, rational orientation of divine action. The reception of universalistic, cosmological myths into the Yahwe conception was unavoidable for the cultured stratum of Israel. This had far reaching ramifications for the form assumed by the myths. They were turned in ethical direction. The borrowed myths in their turn exerted but slight influence upon the conception of god and upon soteriology, at least far less than one might expect.

The cosmogonic and anthropogenic myths are of secondary importance in Yahwistic religiosity. This is most obvious in the absence of almost any allusion to the myth of the fall of man so basic to our present conception. Throughout the Old Testament it became no soteriological event decisive for Yahwe's attitude to Israel or to man. There are only sporadic and merely paradigmatic allusions to be found (Hosea 6:7). Man's fall became basic to holy teaching only through certain speculations of early Christendom. They were based upon conceptions which were undeniably derived from Oriental gnosis, but were alien to genuine Israelite piety. Adam's and Eve's fall is an etiological myth for death, the toil of labor, and the labor of birth, hostility to the snake and later, to all animals. This exhausts its significance. The rabbis later considered the worship of the golden calf an incomparable greater offense than Adam's disobedience, because in the first a *berith* was broken, not in the last. This agrees with the old familiar basis of Yahwe's attitude toward Israel, which the myths left untouched. To be sure, even Hosea (*loc. cit.*) considered Adam's offense also a violation of a *berith*. But this became no conception of consequence for Israelite reli-

gion. On the other hand, Yahwe's peculiarity exerted revolutionary influence upon myth. The Amarna tablets contain the
Babylonian myth of original man Adapa as a writing lesson for
scribes. According to this myth, Adapa forfeits immortality by
following the false suggestion of another god. For the rest he is
treated from the beginning as "impure" and hence does not
qualify for Anu's heaven. The Israelite conception fashioned
from this the very impressive paradigm of disobedience and its
consequences.

This turn was accomplished by the Levitical Torah, and was
received only in the final revision of the creation story. For with
Ezekiel (28:13 ff.) and in the Book of Job (15:7) a trace of an
entirely different conception still is evident, which conceived of
original man as a form of great wisdom and beauty. Faultless like
a cherub he lived in the (in Babylonian fashion) jewelled garden
of god on his wondrous mountain which is also known to the
Psalms and agrees with Yahwe's nature as a mountain god. But
hybris entangled him in guilt and Yahwe pushed him down.
Hence, here original man was by no means the "pure fool" of the
Yahwistic myth of paradise. As Ezekiel twice described Noah,
Job, and Daniel (14:14, 20) as three wise and pious men of olden
times, Daniel even as omniscient (28:3) the hallowing of supra-
human wisdom of the forebears was obviously in the making.
This tendency is found in the whole of the priestly tradition and
the post-Exile chokma teachers later resumed it in a different
way. It remained alien to the Torah teachers proper. With the
saga of the great flood, which experts assume to be the last received myth, the Babylonian model met the ethical need in so
far as it touched in passing, at least, upon a motive to be found
also in the patriarchal legends.

The gods reproached Enlil, who had released the great flood,
for having intended to eliminate all men regardless of whether
they did or did not sin. Only Ea's secret advice gave Noah's
Babylonian counterpart the opportunity to save himself. With
the reception of the saga, a characteristic change is Yahwe's decision not to send another great flood because man is "only evil
continually." He values man's existence and fate for their own
sake. These changes must not be explained by attributing an un-
usually "sublime" ethic to the Israelites. The ethic of old Israel

was coarse and plain. Decisive, rather, was the fact that cure of souls ministered to plebeian strata was ethical not magical in nature as a result of historically given peculiarities in the relation of Yahwe to Israel. Myths, therefore, were of interest only when functioning as paradigms. Cure of souls required for its ends divine, rationally determined miracles, proofs of divine power, punishment and reward, not tales of magical and heroic feats.

Paradise as a state of innocent peacefulness forfeited through ethical guilt was a conception of great consequence in later development. It was received together with the cosmogonic myths. The external form of paradise obviously underwent changes. In Exile times the conception of the divine mountain (Ezekiel 28:11 ff.; 31:8, 9; 36:35) served the obvious purpose of emancipating Yahwe from his localization in Jerusalem fortifying his position as universal god. The old Yahwistic conception was received from the Torah teachers. Thus far no genuine myth of paradise has been ascertained for Babylon, though there is to be found a divine magical park with trees of precious stones and a canal dug by gods. Usener [4] has ascertained widespread myths of an originally peaceful relation with the animals. Apparently such myths existed also in Babylon (Epic of Gilgamesh), and, as in Genesis, woman was responsible for the loss of this peaceful state. The myth of a god-planted and irrigated garden of peace and of man's expulsion into toilsome tillage and fight with snakes most probably originated in a country such as Mesopotamia; its age in Canaan cannot be stated. Its origin in an agricultural country is also suggested by the still transparent idea that man originally, when there was peace with the animals, lived on a vegetarian diet. There are certain indications of this, also, in the Epic of Gilgamesh. But none of the religious relevant for the borrowing seems to have known a state of ignorant innocence. [5]

In the special turn of ignorance as concerning the inadmissability of "nakedness" an inrode of the ritualistic peculiarity of Yahwism is at once evident. The central importance of the *berith* idea suggested the conception, peculiar to Israel, that man's original peace with animals rested on a special *berith* of Yahwe with the animals, and that Yahwe in the future could and would enter into another such *berith*. This idea appeared even with the first prophets (Hos. 2:18; Is. 11:1 ff.). This was what mattered in the conception. If one had once forfeited the blissful state of original peace, perhaps, if one behaved correctly it might return in the future. This eschatological conception which the prophets used was doubtlessly widespread before their time. The final state will be like Eden (Is. 51:3). There will be peace among men, the swords will be made into ploughshares (Is. 2:4) and bow, sword, and battle will remain far from the land (Hos. 2:18) and by the grace of heaven the earth will bear ample corn, new wine, and oil (Hos. 2:22). These are hopes of quite pacifistic, unmilitary peasants.

These expectations of peace were not the sole form of eschatological hopes going back to pre-prophetic times. Other hopes corresponded to different social interest situations. The warriors' popular hope for the future looked differently. Even with the first prophet (Amos) we find the expectation of a "Day of Yahwe" (*jom Yahwe*) which hitherto was usually thought of as a day of great hope for Israel. What was its original meaning? Yahwe was a war god and hence it was a day of victorious battle, as once was *jom* Midian (Is. 9:3) the day of Gideon's victory. As for Gideon, and others, the ancient oracles by lot told the hero the exact day and hour when Yahwe would deliver the enemies "into Israel's hands." This is the likely origin of this thoughtway. And the means of the old god of catastrophe were familiar: the "divine terror" through earthquakes or weather catastrophes. Hence, the Day of Yahwe was a day of frightful terror (*jom mehumah* Is. 22:5), in the eyes of the warrior, of course, for Israel's enemies, not for Israel (Amos 5:18-20). Beside this stood a pacifist conception in which the Day of Yahwe seemed a day of gay sacrificial feasting (Zeph. 1:7) to which Yahwe bid his guests.

These pacifistic or warlike hopes for the future were joined to the promises of the kingly prophecy of hope. Gressmann [6] especially has drawn attention to well established "courtly style" for such predictions at the neighboring courts of the "great kings." Each king was praised by the prophetic bards as a harbinger of blessed times, the diseased would recover, the hungry be satisfied, the naked clothed, the prisoners amnestied (thus for Assurbanipal), the poor have their rights (thus frequently in Babylonian royal inscriptions; for Israel see Psalm 72). The god (in Babylon Marduk) chooses the king (thus Yahwe, David, II. Sam. 6:21), makes him his priest (thus Psalm 110), adopts him (thus the king of Israel, Psalm 2:7) or has even produced him (*ibidem*). The king has to prove his charisma, that he is thus qualified, by bringing joy to the people (as in China and wherever genuine conceptions of charisma prevail). To certify the king's divine origin even in early Sumerian times it is told of the Sumerian King Gudea of Sargon, the founder of Babylonian power, further of Assurbanipal during late Assyrian times that his father or also his mother are unknown, that he was produced in secrecy or on the mountains, hence, by a god. Especially usurpers, though not alone, avail themselves of this means of legitimation. Apparently this conception was also known in Israel, for Isaiah made use of it when he held out the prince Immanuel whose image shows these characteristics. He is announced as a savior who would soon appear and possibly was already born. According to the more militaristic or pacifistic nature of the stratum, the savior prince then is a monarch riding in chariots and on horses (Jer. 17:25; 22:4) or a prince riding an ass in the way of the old Israelite charismatic hero of confederate times (Zech. 9:9 f.) and a prince of peace like Isaiah's Immanuel. In the kingdom of Judah this "anointed one" (*hamashiach* that is simply the king) was naturally expected to come from the tribe of the Davidians, hence from Bethlehem, who will be a "savior" (*moshuach'*) as his contemporaries conceived of Jeroboam II. The peculiarity of these hopes in Israel was politically determined.

In the great culture areas the strong, inconceivably old position of kingship linked the soteriological hopes essentially to the living king [7] and only exceptionally—as under Bocchoris—did truly messianic hopes make their appearance. In Israel, however, things were different. With the increasingly strong position of the priesthood in Egypt, too, the king (for instance, of the twenty-first Dynasty) was but the master recognized and legitimatized by Ammon, no longer a living god as, at least, officially in the Old Empire. In Mesopotamia this was always the case in historical times. However, in Israel, especially in the Northern kingdom with its constant military revolts and usurpations, the king as savior decidedly receded into the background in favor of other expectations. For Hosea there is no legitimate king at all—which agreed with the situation of the times. Elsewhere, too, the kingly prophecy of hope was confronted by the hope that either Yahwe personally would in due course take the government in hand, destroy the strange gods (Is. 10:13, 14) and fashion the world anew [8] or send a super-human miracle man to accomplish this. This man would then destroy all foreign oppressors and, not they alone, but also the wicked in Israel. Only in Israel was hope crystallized into this specific, ethical form under the influence of Yahwe's special *berith* relation to his people. No traces of a similar trend are to be found elsewhere. Such hope could not arise where magic held sway as a universal means of salvation. In Israel this hope led to the conclusion that the advent of the day of Yahwe would bring doom also to the Israelite sinner. Only a remnant,[9] *shearith*, would survive Yahwe's wrath. The very first of the prophets, Amos, operates with this idea of a "remnant" as with a fixed conception. It had fundamental importance for all the prophets. Isaiah named one of his sons *shear-jashub*, that is, the "remnant is converting." Of course, this remnant is morally qualified, so that the eschatological nature mythologies of the surrounding culture again received an ethical turn.

Two possible conceptions of the person of the eschatological hero prevailed in Yahwistic circles. Obviously, one was that Yahwe would personally take matters in hand against his enemies. The other maintained an eschatological hero would act on Yahwe's behalf. This led either on the path of kingly prophecy of hope as was mostly the case in Jerusalem where the Davidians supported it—or it led to esoteric mythologies. The savior then became an unearthly figure. In the Balaam saying (Nu. 24:17) he will rise like a "star." He is an "everlasting Father" (in the, to be sure, dubious customary reading of the passage Is. 9:6). His origin "has been from of old, from everlasting" (Micah, 5:2). These obscure hints which were further developed during the Exile into the "Servant of God" of Deutero-Isaiah, are nowhere elaborated in detail. No direct analogies are to be found in the documents thus far available from the environments of Israel. Influence of Iranian ideas is quite doubtful, and Yima and other pertinent figures of Early Iranian religion are not eschatological redeemers. The decisive passage in Micah (*loc. cit.*) presents the sib of the Davidians as the depository of the hope for salvation and the idea of a removal of great heroes of god into Yahwe's heaven was not absent in Israel (Henoch, Elijah). Therefore, the idea was probably that David would return in person. Peculiar for the Israelite expectation is the increasing intensity with which paradise, or the savior prince, were projected into the future: the first out of the past, the last out of the present. This did not happen in Israel alone, but this expectancy has never become central to religious faith with such obviously ever-increasing momentum. Yahwe's old *berith* with Israel, his promise in conjunction with the criticism of the miserable present made this possible. But only the momentum of prophecy made Israel to this unique degree a people of "hope" and "tarrying" (Gen. 49:18).

Finally, the conception that the expected catastrophe would bring good fortune first, then doom, can be found, at least in beginnings, in Egyptian religion. One used to consider it, without sufficient proof,[10] a fixed schema of the future expectation. Its borrowing by the prophets allegedly constituted the characteristic trait of the pronouncements. The schema prevails, indeed, in a considerable section of pre-exilic prophecy but it characterizes their peculiar nature by no means exhaustively. If the schema *per se* had existed, its derivation from cult peculiarities of chthonian and certain sidereal deities would suggest itself. Night and winter arrive before the deities of sun and vegetation can redeploy their strength.

It must remain an open question to what extent the conception of a god or hero suffering before their advent to power had entered popular Israelite belief. Such ideas were widespread and also were to be found in neighboring countries and stemmed from the cultic myths of the sidereal and vegetation deities. That Israel knew those childhood myths which usually go with them, is shown in the story of Moses' infancy. Pre-exilic prophecy operated with and refashioned these popular representations in its own way. So far as can be seen, the priesthood and the theological intellectuals generally avoided them and utilized instead sober promises of material prosperity, numerous and honored descendants, and of a great name to become a blessing. Presumably they avoided the popular eschatology because of its connection with strange astral or chthonian cults, or cults of the dead. Where a promise of a future personality makes its appearance, it does not hold out a king but a prophet like Moses (Deut. 18:15, 18). The hope that Yahwe in the future would personally resume government as he once allegedly ruled prior to the kingship according to the Samuel legend first appeared in prophetic times. Essentially this hope belonged only to exilic times when (with Deutero-Isaiah) the title of savior was used for Yahwe.

CHAPTER X

INTERCULTURAL RELATIONS
IN PRE-EXILIC ETHICS

1. Substantive Content of Jewish Ethics

P RE-EXILIC Torah teaching competed with prophecy for dominance of Judaism. For prophecy did not create the substantive content of Jewish ethic however important its conceptions became for its enforcement. Prophecy presupposed the content of the commandments to be familiar. The prophets alone are far from yielding an even approximately complete knowledge of Yahwe's ethical demands upon the individual. These demands received their character from quite a different area, namely, from the Torah of the Levites. They elaborated those structures which nowadays are usually considered especially significant creations of Israelite ethics, the Decalogues, to be specific, the "ethical" Decalogue [1] of Exodus 20:2 f.; Deut. 5:6 f., and the two Decalogues of Ex. 34:14 f. and Deut. 27:18 f. There have been repeated attempts to ascribe great age to these collections, possibly even Mosaic origin. The argument has been advanced that the "simple" must have stood at the beginning of "evolution." That does not always hold in this field.

Our "ethical" Decalogue, especially (Ex. 20:2-17; Deut. 5:6-18) proves its (relative) youth as a common norm by the prohibition of carved likenesses, which do not agree with early Israelite custom. Also, it speaks of the "house" of the neighbor and of testimony, thus presupposing settled houses and court procedure with witnesses. Furthermore, there is the fear of taking Yahwe's name in vain, which in pre-exilic times appears nowhere comparably strong. Finally, there is the abstract formulation of the tenth commandment, "neither shalt thou desire" even if the ethical sense of the word should only at a later time have taken the place of the originally coarser "fraudulently manipulate." And, incidentally the general prohibition of "killing" contradicts the law of the blood feud. The ethical Decalogue does not by any means comprise all prescriptions basic to old Israel. There is no mention of circumcision, nor of the ritualistic dietary prescriptions.

Apart from the emphasis on the Sabbath, the ethical Decalogue might well suggest the impression of a formula for an interdenominational ethic created by intellectuals. And this Decalogue, after all, implements Christian ethics ever anew. That does not apply to the aforementioned cursing formulae of the Shechem ceremony (Deut. 27:14-26), usually termed the "sexual Decalogue," nor to the single list of commandments preserved in Yahwistic formulation, that is the prescriptions which the text calls "words of the covenant" (*debar ha-berith*) Ex. 34:14-26 (the so-called "cultic Decalogue"). In the first, with the social security stipulations the *gerim,* characteristic for Israel, are mentioned alongside widows and waifs. In the last, however, beside the commandment of monolatry (prohibition of worshipping another "*el*") and the prohibition of molten images, there is, indeed, express prohibition of participation in Canaanite sacrifices and entering any *b'rith* with Canaanites. This is followed by prescriptions concerning the Sabbath rest and festivals, the three annual pilgrimages to the sanctuary, the firstlings due to Yahwe—all stated in rather general terms—and finally, follow three highly specialized and doubtlessly quite ancient, ritualistic, dietary rules among them one covering the Passover meal. Agricultural festivities and the Passover appear together in the "cultic" Decalogue and instances of *b'rithoth* occurred at least into Solomonic times. On the other hand, intermarriage with them, which this Decalogue did not absolutely prohibit, caused scruples first among the Yahwistic stock-breeders as suggested by the legend of Isaac's marriage proposal. Hence, the composition cannot be very old in its present form.

The same holds for the so-called "sexual Decalogue" as it presupposes that graven or molten images—an abomination to Yahwe —are put up only "in secret" which was not the case even in

Judah until late kingly times. The doubtless (relative) lateness of the present content would not preclude a great age for Decalogue-like collections of commandments in Israel. But even the differences between the present Decalogues, which all have in common the doubtlessly late stipulations (prohibition of images) make the original form problematical. Besides, one has to consider that such catechism-like moral exhortations as is Decalogue Ex. 20, according to Indian analogies, usually do not stand at the beginning of a development, but are relatively late products of pedagogical intention. Thus, in pre-exilic literature, above all, with the prophets, we find no certain traces of any special dignity and importance ascribed to the Decalogues, nor even of the presupposition that people were generally familiar with them.

In a comparison of the ethic, particularly that of the ethical Decalogue with that of the pre-exilic prophets it is remarkable that they never allude to the special dignity of this composition, as could be expected, if they then were distinguished among other norms by the prestige of deriving from Moses. First, the prophets of pre-exilic times have no idea of being economical in the use of Yahwe's name. But this could be considered the privilege of a prophet. Moreover, the enumerations by the prophets of virtues and sins have not much in common with those of the Decalogues. Apart from the specific social-political exhortation, which is uppermost in the prophetic mind, and which has no place in the Decalogue, the struggle against "other gods" and images is the true field of prophecy.

Allusions to the formulations of the "first commandment" of the Decalogue are, at best, to be found with Hosea (12:9; 13:4). For the rest, Amos lashes out against covetousness (9:1) as the cardinal sin, beside corn usury (8:5 on the Sabbath), false weight (8:5), defrauding the poor (8:6), and lechery (2:7): father and son sleeping with the same harlot. The first mentioned vices are obviously related to prophetic social ethics, the last to opposition to sacred harlotry. None of these vices emphasized by the prophets is characteristically related to the ethic of the Decalogue. Blasphemy, lying, murder, theft, adultery, are enumerated with Hosea as widespread sins. These are mentioned in the Decalogue. Besides the Sabbath and filial piety, the tenth commandment is lacking and "lying," as known, is only prohibited in the Decalogue before court. Nevertheless, until Jeremiah, this prophetic enumeration of sins comes closest to the catalogue of the Decalogue. If Hosea should have actually known the Decalogue—which remains uncertain—this might possibly suggest its North Israelite origin. Hosea calls familiarity with these divine commandments knowledge (*da'ath*) of Elohim. All of this remains quite uncertain.

With Micah (6:10, 11) false coin, weight and measure, and unjustly acquired goods are mentioned none of which are specifically related to the Decalogue.

No series of sins are mentioned in the genuine Isaiah oracles and with Zephaniah which could be related to the Decalogue. Of actually private vices, Isaiah mentions heavy drinking (5:11) which is not mentioned at all in the Decalogue, all other passages essentially expressed complaints directed against the unjust doings of the rich. One might possibly discern an allusion to the tenth commandment in Micah (2:2), but the usurious accumulation of land is a general social-ethical complaint of the prophets against the rich.

Only with Jeremiah do most of the Decalogue sins reappear: robbery and theft, murder, perjury (7:9), adultery (5:8), deceiving one's friend (9:4) violation of the Sabbath (17:22). In substance all Decalogue sins are covered except the taking of the divine name in vain and the tenth commandment. But there is no reference to the special sanctity of the Decalogue or to its characteristic formulations, or even to the existence of such a collection. This is the case for Jeremiah and, in fact, all the prophets. There is none, unless one were to relate to it, again, with Micah (6:8) a quite general emphasis on the importance of observing the *mishpatim*. This however would seem formally inadmissable, as the Decalogues represent *debarim*, not *mishpatim*. In contrast to the Decalogue, however, especially with Jeremiah, a far-going ethical sublimation and systematization of man's total moral posture is to be found. Even with Micah demands of ethical absolutism appear such as "to love mercy" besides "walking humbly" (6:8) with God, which are unknown to the Decalogue.

All in all prophecy knows nothing of a "Mosaic" Decalogue and perhaps of none at all. All of this would seem to confirm our assumption of the relative lateness and purely pedagogical purpose of the ethical Decalogue. On the other hand, the back-dating of the Decalogues too far into post-exilic times is accept-able neither for the sexual and cultic Decalogue, nor the ethical one.

Possibly the "ethical" Decalogue was even known in the time of Hosea in Northern Israel, though this is quite uncertain. In any case, there is no reason for assigning a special position to the three Decalogues, a view from which all those assumptions de-part. This is obvious for the "cultic" and the "sexual" Deca-logues. They are obviously identical in nature with the composi-tion of the sexual commandments, Lev. 18, and the collection of cultic, ethical, ritualistic, and charity stipulations of Lev. 19. This is the most comprehensive collection of all, and it includes the commandments of our "ethical Decalogue." The same holds for Lev. 20, which comprises ritualistic and sexual ethical pre-scriptions. Lev. 19, at least, goes back to a collection which in its original, though revised, content is not necessarily of later date than any of the Decalogues. The question of dating the Deca-logues, however, is related to the question of their origin.

Eminent scholars have suggested that these collections were elements of cultic "liturgies." Analogies, however, speak strongly against assuming this origin. From Egypt and Babylonia cata-logues of sins have been transmitted which have often been paralleled with the Israelite collections. What was their origin? They did not originate in cult, but in the magician's and priest's "curing of souls." The sick or unfortunate asking the priest how to soothe the godhead's wrath would be interrogated for sins which he might have committed. Doubtlesssly the priests devel-oped fixed schemata for this at an early time. In the case of Babylon a preserved catalogue of sins directly represents such a schema, and the catalogue of sins of the Egyptian "Book of the Dead" doubtless had the same origin. It states the sins which the forty-two judges of the dead will ask them for in Hades.

The Torah of the Levites pointed in the same direction. The priestly law (Num. 12:6) expressly prescribed the confession of sins and, given the case, restitution of unjustly acquired goods plus twenty percent to the wronged person, certainly based on ancient custom. The transmitted prescriptions pertaining to Levitical expiatory offerings indicate also the opportunity which occasioned this "confession" of the man proffering sacrifice. It was a private offering, no cult sacrifice. With mounting external pressure and therewith increasing pressure of general guilt feelings this very practice of the Levites gained in importance. According to Deuteronomy (26:12 f.) each Israelite had to offer the tithe every third year, and he had to declare to the Levites, *gerim,* widows and waifs that he had correctly proffered this sacrifice, violated none of Yahwe's commandments, and especially had eaten nothing of the offerings in a state of impurity or mourning for the dead and proffered no sacrifice to the dead.

This is the very form of the Egyptian declaration of freedom from sin. One need but reverse an interrogatory catalogue of sins into positive prescription to receive a list of divine commandments as represented by the Decalogues. This is their origin as of all similar collections. They derived from the confessional practice of the Levites confronting all "that labour and are heavy laden" and not from the community cult. This denied participation to those struck down by misfortune, seeing them pursued by God's wrath. The Levite in practice had constantly to deal with them as his patrons, hence the preference of the Torah for these oppressed strata and the wrath against "everyone that is proud" and shows no inclination to "humble" himself before God, i.e., before the Levite (and to compensate him for the reconciliation with Yahwe).

The community, because of its collective responsibility, too, had an indirect interest in the confession of sins. The "appearance before Yahwe" prescribed by the cultic Decalogue for all Israelites, provided a possible preventive interrogation concerning the sins of all, in order to guard them and the community against Yahwe's wrath. It was, in any case, intended to buttress the power of the priesthood. The Shechemite ceremony in the name of the community cursed those burdened by a sin (not atoned for through the Levite) lest the community suffer under Yahwe's wrath. This purpose and the cursing of sin were presumably introduced later by the Levites; the rite probably served originally only to curse demons. To the Levitical priests the task of teaching the Torah to the people, which they claimed as their rightful responsibility, served the same purpose of keeping the community free of sin in order to ward off Yahwe's

wrath. The Deuteronomic prescription to have the Torah read
in public every seventh year is as recent as the construction of
the "Jubilee year" with which it is connected (Deut. 31:10-12).
This is indicated by the fact that the *gerim* too were to hear it.
The interest of the community in the confession and cataloguing
of sins simply increased with the indications of God's increasing
wrath.

The inconsistencies in the collections and also the strange
coexistence in the present revision of "sin offering" and "expiatory offering" (*chattat* and *asham*) are due to the fact that
there was no unitary organization. Instead there coexisted numerous well-known seats of Levites and, until the triumph of
Jerusalem, also numerous Levitical sanctuaries. (One such ancient seat of Levitical wisdom to which people turned with their
questions is mentioned in II. Sam. 20:18).

In any case, the three so-called Decalogues must not be
viewed differently from other similar collections. The late legend
of the "Ark of the Covenant" as the depository of the two
stone tablets inscribed with the commandments, has contributed
to the exceptional position granted to the Decalogues in scientific analysis. Obviously the hope was to seize upon substantive
commandments traceable to Moses. But this would seem quite
vain. The reception of Yahwe as god of the covenant and the
reception of the Levitical oracle are the two contributions which
for good reasons may be traced to Moses. That is no small matter. Everything else followed from the peculiarity of the god of
the covenant as well as of the Levites in conjunction with certain historical interrelations. But the special position which the
Decalogues held, due to this vain hope, must be relinquished. If
the Mosaic *berith* should have contained substantive commandments going beyond purely ritualistic obligations issuing from
the reception, they were certainly only such as served to preserve peace among the militia and concerned the avenging of
spilt blood and perhaps "social welfare" stipulations for impoverished military sibs.

The sources show that in Ancient Israel originally as elsewhere the mores were the ultimate yardsticks of "ethics." There
is nowhere a reference to "commandments" to be found. *Nebalah*,
"wickedness" was "unheard of" in Israel. Only the Levitical

Torah began to formulate and catalogue individual commandments for confessional purposes. Among them the "ethical" Decalogue (Ex. 20) occupies a special place hardly attained elsewhere by similar collections. This is not because of its alleged
"Mosaic" derivation; it is least "Mosaic" of all. Rather, because
it probably represents the attempt to offer a summary instruction for youth, whose instruction in God's will and intention
was prescribed (Ex. 13:8, 14 and elsewhere). This was like the
Indian Decalogues which served the instruction of laity and
novices. The Decalogue owes its position to the impressiveness,
plasticity, and precision of its formulations, to the sublimation
or loftiness of its ethical demands, (which are actually quite
modest). Without doubt, the "ethical" Decalogue owes its most
important characteristics above all its separation from both
ritualistic and welfare prescription to its public. The Decalogue
aims neither at teaching the political authorities nor members
of a cultured élite, but the progeny of the broad mass of the
bourgeois and peasant middle classes, the "people." Therefore, it
contains no more and no less than what all age groups should
observe in everyday life. With us, too, the "Ten Commandments"
mainly serve instruction of youth and, particularly, popular instruction. Thus the numerous *debarim* and Torah collections,
among them, also, the Decalogues, did not by any means originate in community cult or possibly temple cult. They sprang
from the Levitical cure of souls and teaching enterprise for
which we find in Babylonian Exile the "school house," the historical antecedent of the synagogue, which originally has nothing to do with "cult."

As the Brahmins originally ascended from a group concerned
with the ritualistic and magical cure of souls ministered to individuals, so the Levitical Torah teachers attained their power
and cultural significance, not from the functions of community
worship, but from the ritualistic and ethical cure of souls, ministered to individuals (including the prince). Their participation
in worship was, perhaps, only secondary, in any case, it was not
primary. The very absence of cult centralization and of an official organ for a confederate cult in the old Yahwe confederacy
enhanced the strong influence of the ancient prophets and seers
as well as of the Levites. Even in kingly times the cult priests

proper had to take this influence into account, because broad circles of laity were exponents of the legal tradition and gave strong support to the Levites. Apparently some distinguished sibs whose members were in royal service, inclined toward a rational view of law in the way of the Levitical moral exhortation, in contrast to the sibs of the ancient *zekenim*. These distinguished sibs formed the internal opposition against the sultanist inclinations of the kings together with the Levitical Yahwistic circles, on the one hand, the *zekenim* on the other. The prophetess Hulda was the wife of such an official. The same derivation appears rather clearly in a Deuteronomic collection, for which *shofetim*, obviously lay judges of a different sort than the *zekenim*, are, together with the Levites, exponents of the judiciary whereas the old tradition always treats the *zekenim* as the truly legitimate representatives of the people.

The Levites, originally, attained their power position by giving oracular lots, later by cure of souls and therewith as Torah teachers. A strict separation of *jus* and *fas* could no longer be maintained with their increasing importance and with increased consideration given their views by the Yahwistically interested laity. The ancient, never forgotten significance of the *debarim* Yahwe for all important decisions also benefited their influence upon legal views. This cooperation of devout Yahwistic laymen with ethically reflective priests resulted in the theologizing, on the one hand, of law and the rationalization of religious ethics, on the other. Deuteronomy was the most important product of this religious cooperation. It originated under the dominant influence of the Jerusalemite priesthood after the collapse of the Northern kingdom. We have considered it earlier as:

1. the revision of the *mishpatim*
2. a compendium of Yahwistic demands for restricting royal prerogatives directed against the Solomonic corvée state and "world politics"
3. a compendium of the monopolistic cult claims of the priests of Jerusalem. Alongside these monopolistic cult claims appeared
4. the monopoly claim of the Torah teachings.

The Israelite shall act (Deut. 1.7:10) according to what is taught at the Yahwe designated sanctuary in Jerusalem.

In general, cult priests are not the usual exponents of rational ethical teachings; as a rule they are oriented to ritual. That was also the case during the time of the second Temple. At the time the great "Beth Din (was) in the stone chamber" of the Temple of Jerusalem. (Büchler has shown its position and significance in brilliant investigations). It was the central authority for deciding all ritualistic questions of conduct and at once was authorized to give expert opinions in questions of *fas* on request of secular courts. It is not transmitted in the tradition that a formally organized and recognized unified authority of this kind existed in Jerusalem in pre-exilic time. But the most cultured metropolitan priesthood of the country by this stipulation maintained the claim authoritatively to interpret Yahwe's will and intentions for courts, Torah teachers and private persons.

Deuteronomy wished to represent a compendium of Levitical teachings, the authoritative *sefer hattorah*. Later we shall have to deal with its relation to the message of the prophets. Here we are concerned with the extent to which its substance is informed by Levitical moral exhortation and theological rationalization of ethic. We may leave to the orientalist the questions whether the compendium, accepted under Josiah, originally consisted only of these exhortatory sections and the stipulations concerning the concentration of cult (and Torah teaching) and related conditions, whether not only the directly prophetic sections, in part only exilic or post-exilic, but also the *mishpatim* and the kingly law were only later fused with the exhortation. Puukko in opposition to Wellhausen maintains this. Whatever the answer, the kingly law as well as the revision of the *mishpatim* derive from the same or a closely related circle of theologians and pursue the same end. The exhortatory sections proper of Deuteronomy are the work of an individual, apparently, of a Torah teacher belonging to the Temple priesthood of Jerusalem. The nature of the "find" and the persons mentioned in this allow us to conclude that the whole was a well-prepared enterprise of a party already adhering to a corresponding view.

"Hear, O Israel: the Lord our God is one Lord,"—the opening sentence of the present Jewish morning prayer, stands at the head of the exhortation. He is a jealous god (Deut. 6:15) but he is faithful (7:9), he has sworn (7:12) the covenant with Israel, which he has chosen (7:6), and keeps it through a thousand generations; he loves his people (7:13) and if he made his people suffer toil and distress he has done so to test its sincerity (8:2, 3). For he makes his love and grace conditional upon the keeping of his commandments (7:12); if not, he will punish the sinner personally without delay (to future generations) (7:10). Above all, he hates pride and self-confidence (8:14) especially trust in one's own strength (8:17), which can readily occur once Israel will have grown rich (8:12, 13). Likewise, he hates self-righteousness (9:4), for he did not choose and privilege Israel for the sake of its virtues. It has none, for it is the least of all people (Deut. 7:7),—a quite emphatic rejection of all national pride and warrior heroism. He chose Israel because of the vices of the other people (9:5, 6) which doubtlessly refers to sexual orgiasticism (23:17) and other "local mores" of Canaan (12:30).

One shall not follow such mores of the country, thinking that one owes this to the gods of the land, but shall follow only Yahwe's commandments. All magic and interpretation of signs of all sorts (18:10, 11), all human sacrifice (18:10), but also all alliances (7:2) and intermarriage (7:3) with the Canaanites are strictly prohibited because of the danger of apostasy. Once and for all, all enemies are doomed to the *cherem*. Whoever entices apostasy and be he a prophet (13:5), one's own brother or son, must suffer death by being stoned (13:9).

As regards the relation of the pious to Yahwe one shall fear and worship him and swear only by him (6:13) and, above all, one shall love him (7:9) and have unconditional faith in his promises: Yahwe has the power to fulfill his promises to Israel no matter how much stronger the opposing nations (7:17, 18). The miracle of manna in the desert has shown that man does not live by bread alone, but by all that Yahwe has created (8:3). The power of the god is enhanced into gigantic dimensions, into monotheism. He alone is the God of heaven and earth and none else (4:39). Heaven and earth and all is the Lord's (10:14); the Lord is God, there is none beside him (4:35), these are perhaps only additions during exilic times. But God will make use of this wondrous power for Israel only when it obeys him and keeps his commandments. The following promises and curses (chaper 28), which were later augmented in Exile, may well be considered original: prosperity of all sorts will come about; when enemies approach, Yahwe will strike them down; he will give rain to the country, and make Israel the creditor of other nations, hence a patriciate. If Israel fails to obey he will reverse himself on all this.

There has been much controversy, mostly of a sterile sort— because confessional-apologetic—about the question whether for Israel "fear" was the decisive motive of moral conduct in contrast to that of other religions.[3] Realistic observation shows that this motive played a dominant role for mass religions in contrast to virtuoso religions. It stood alongside the qualitatively similar motive of hope for compensation in this world or the beyond. As the Torah teachers began the taming of the masses by a procedure for expiating sin, so did the Occidental church by penance stipulations and not by the preaching of love. The preaching of love for God and one's neighbor in the Christian church finds its precise equivalent in Israelite, above all, rabbinical teaching. They are of the same kind and sincerity of intention. Only one observation holds; the ritualistic nature of a religion determines, of course, the stronger it is, the more the worry about purely formal—for modern thought, ethically irrelevant—offenses color the religious relationship. Furthermore, it is quite correct that pre-exilic ethic developed under the pressure of fear, one is almost tempted to say of "war psychosis" in view of the frightful wars of the great conquering empires.[4] The basic mood of the Deuteronomic circle was the conviction that only a divine miracle, not human power, could bring salvation.

The utopian rules of warfare of Deuteronomy and its kingly law agree perfectly with these basic principles. In Egypt, too, in the poem of Pentaur, it is said that Amon alone brings victory and not a million soldiers. But this was not followed in practice. Also in Egypt priestly power corresponded to the claims raised by the priests in Jerusalem. But in Israel these traits had to have a far more pervasive effect. All of them rested on the prestige of Yahwe, who alone, without Israel's contribution, can and does bring matters to a happy ending if people will only trust him.

This prestige of Yahwe recalls the belief in Amon, but was

elaborated much further. In Jerusalem it resulted obviously from the salvation from Sennacherib's siege which occurred under Hezekiah, in accordance with Isaiah's prophecy and against all probability. In part, the promises of hope and threats of doom derive from the schemata fashioned by the prophecy of hope and doom. The promise concerning money loans is specifically bourgeois and Jerusalemite in nature. Strict monolatry was even an old Yahwistic demand and the in-group supplement to the monopoly claim of the Jerusalemite priests against the outside.

Essentially confessional exclusiveness against outsiders was strict even then. Partially it corresponded to priestly interests, partially to the devoutness of a civil and urban stratum of intellectuals under the hierocratic leadership of Torah teachers. The closure against the "stranger" (*nakhri*) found its in-group correlate in the religious and social ethical equality of the pious and ritualistically correct *gerim* with the Israelites, resulting from the demilitarization of the plebeians. Jeremiah, at the same time, presented the Rechabites, hence typical *gerim*, to the Israelites as exponents of exemplary and god-pleasing ways. "Plebeian" in nature is not only the complete detachment from all real political-military demands and all heroism, but the whole nature of the ethically absolutist relation to the God through humility, obedience, trusting devotion—hence the prohibition against "tempting God," that is to demand miracles from him as signs of his power (Deut. 6:16 the example refers to the events in Massah, cf. Ex. 17:2, 7).—Especially a "love" for him is characteristic which is reminiscent of pietism and appears earlier only with Hosea as a basic mood (at least can only with him be dated earlier for certain). The total attitude is characterized by pious mood and an occasional pathos in the moral exhortation and ethical sublimation of inner devotion to God. It remains free of all radical and passionate divine possession. The basic utopian presuppositions of the compendium are decisively determined by the great prophets, but the compendium is by no means their work. Experts, however, assume that the editor of Deuteronomy knew the Yahwistic and Elohistic collections and made occasional use of them, especially of the last ones. This seems quite probable.

The Deuteronomic work was probably completed near the

time of what Wellhausen called the "Jehovistic" fusion of the Yahwistic and Elohistic revisions of the ancient patriarchical legends and Levitical Moses traditions. Numerous insertions, directly reminiscent of the religiosity advanced in Deuteronomy, are to be found in these revisions which were later modified by priestly additions, interpolations and were partly reworked. The Jehovist has partly newly inserted, partly supplemented, the great promises to the forefathers. He shares with Deuteronomy the disregard for kingship. Hope is promised, not to the king, but to the pious people and addressed to its legendary tribal fathers. The promise is joined to the ancient blessings, ascribed to Balaam from the time preceding the Solomonic corvée kinship. The circles which produced both works were probably theologically interested laymen and Levites; priests contributed more strongly and directly to Deuteronomy because this is a work of moral exhortation determined by priestly interests though based upon the Torah of the Levites.

The religious attitude of the Deuteronomic moral exhortation is characterized by the strong emphasis upon the belief in compensation and providence, the edifying, soft, charitable, often contrite, disconsolate, nature of God's personal relationship to man and vice versa and the thoroughly plebeian nature of its devout humility. These traits also stood out in Egyptian popular piety of the New Kingdom and find points of departure even in the Old Kingdom. According to Ptah-hetep's teachings of wisdom, God cherished obedience above all. The memorial stones of artisans from the time of Rameses added that he is "incorruptible," shows his power to the little man and the great, that Amon especially listens to the poor when they pray to him, that like Yahwe he comes from afar to help, with the "sweet breeze" of the North wind, which people longed for there as people longed for the "still small voice" of the West wind in Palestine. One should put one's hope in Him and love Him, He will not be angry all day long. As in the Levitical Torah, man is not forever corrupt by man's fall, but foolish by nature, he does not know "good and evil." Prayer and vow—the same means as in Israel—and especially doing justly will call forth His mercy. Obviously, the belief in compensation increased strongly in the religion of the New Kingdom and disease was, of course, also there the usual form of divine punishment. Clearly this entire personal devoutness is of the same nature as that of plebeian strata everywhere. In India it has led to the belief in redeemers. In Egypt he is the Pharoah in whose intercession and mediation one places hope, essentially for political success or for rain, the sacred values for which the political organization cares everywhere. The welfare of the private individual was likewise considered dependent upon the charisma of the Pharaoh. But between him and the masses stood the bureaucracy. And personal religiosity was typically the materialistic morality of *do-ut-des*. This had no relation whatsoever with plebeian piety. And directly beside it stood the coarse magic of the priest. Man in distress turned to him for aid. To teach ethics to the masses did not enter the mind of the Egyptian priests who prided themselves upon their esoteric theology. Besides, their material interests referred them to the more profitable business of selling death book scrolls and scarabaei.

Thus, a plebeian piety existed in Egypt which was quite similar to that of pre-exilic Israel. Given the constant and direct relations, Egyptian influences are probable, though of course, not strictly ascertainable. But in Egypt this piety never became subject to systematic rationalization, be it prophetic or priestly in nature.

In Babylon, things were similar. Ancient penance psalms of the urban time of Mesopotamia are known from the library of Assurbanipal and from other sources. Their mood is substantially similar to that of the piety of the Israelite Psalms, and occasionally the thought of borrowing directly suggests itself. The piety of Nebuchadnezzar and of the early Persian kings likewise was similar to Israelite piety. The prophets of their time knew this and designated them not without reason as "servants" of God. But also here no systematic rationalization into a workaday ethic of the masses took place. Although prophecy was not entirely absent in Babylon, rational Torah teaching and the specific Israelite type of prophecy were. This was due to political circumstances.

2. The Ethic of the Decalogues and the Book of the Dead

AS THE TORAH teachers were central to the development of religious ethic we may briefly consider their substantive ethical demands and ask whether they borrowed the substance of their ethical teachings and how these are generally related to the political ethic of other culture areas.

The substantive peculiarity of the old Israelite ethic finds expression in the Decalogues and partly even more strongly in other ethical *debarim.* Comparison with the Egyptian list of sins of the 125th chapter of the Book of the Dead⁵ on the whole is of greater interest than the numerous parallels with Babylonian sin registers⁶ The latter do not yield much for ethics, in any case, hardly more than what goes without saying. The list of the Book of the Dead was available in complete form even before the Israelite confederacy was formed. Doubtlessly it stated the questions of priests in the forms in which they were stated to clients while probing for sins. There are considerable differences in detail as well as strong similarities when compared to the demands raised by the Decalogue.

The Decalogue prohibition against taking the divine name in vain, compares to the assurance never to have "adjured," i.e., magically compelled a god (B. 30). Comparable to the demand "to have no other gods" (originally "not to sacrifice to other gods") is the Egyptian demand not to disdain god in one's heart (B. 34), which has a stronger spiritual turn (*ins Gesinnungsmässige gewendet*). This was a result of the stronger pantheistic tendencies of Egyptian religion. The Deuteronomic demand to love God is not expressly stated in this general form in the Egyptian catalogues. However, even Ptah-hetep knew that God likes obedience (Pap. Prisse). (This obedience and "silence" have a strong political flavor in Egypt). The Egyptian demand for loyalty of the subjects (B. 22, 27 and chapters 17, I.3.48, and 140), is entirely absent in the ethical Decalogue and also elsewhere is reduced to the demand "not to curse the ruler of thy people" (Ex. 22:28, cf. II. Sam. 16:9 and Is. 8:21). In contrast, Deuteronomic tradition, at least, (I. Sam. 24:10; 26:9;

31:4; II. Sam. 1:14) considered regicide, including that of the Yahwe-rejected king, a grave offense, because of the magical significance of anointment. This was obviously deliberately opposed to the usurpations and massacres in the Northern Kingdom which Hosea, too, strongly disapproved, although Jehu had perpetrated the first of such slaughters at the time with the very aid and instigation of the Yahwistic party.

Parental piety of the Decalogue and, likewise, dutiful obedience to one's parents are inculcated in Deuteronomy with the threat of stoning (Deut. 21:18-21). Like the many stipulations of Babylonian legal literature against irreverent children, these passages probably refer to respect for the aged parents who sit on reserved land, and who are still topical for Jesus Sirach. This demand of the Decalogue and of Deuteronomy for filial piety and the frequently documented Babylonian threats of severe sanctions against the son who speaks irreverently to father or mother, find their correspondence in the Book of the Dead in the mere statement not to have committed an offense against the father (B. 27). For the rest, the Egyptian ethic of priests and scribes constantly inculcated respect for old age, for the teachings of parents and tradition. In Israel it is also imperative "to rise up before the hoary head, and honour the face of the old man" (Lev. 19:32). The Decalogue's prohibition of killing finds its parallel in the assurance in the Book of the Dead not to have killed nor enticed to murder (E 7 A 18). The oppression of the poor and *gerim* (Ex. 23:9) finds its correspondence in the Egyptian catalogue in the prohibition of all violence (A 14) and the instigation of harm (A 20). Numerous burial inscriptions of Egyptian monarchs and officials praise the dead for not having oppressed the poor.

The prohibition of adultery, the tabooing of incest, even in the form of looking with desire at a relative, and the prohibition of onanism, find an analogy in the prohibition of all kinds of lechery (adultery, whoredom, onanism A. 25.26, B. 15.16). The prohibition of theft and the tenth commandment of the ethical Decalogue finds expression in the Book of the Dead in the prohibition of theft (A 17) or of appropriating other people's property (A 23). The injunction against false testimony is surpassed by the prohibition of any kind of lying (E 7, A 22) and

disloyalty (A 30). The deflection of a canal (I 10) is parallel
in the Israelite curse against the moving of boundary marks, the
prohibition of false scales (E 9) belongs also to Levitical exhortation. The Egyptian confession not to have done evil to one's
neighbor (E 4), which heads all others, and the more far-reaching assurance "to have caused anguish to no one" (A 10) and
"to have made nobody weep" (A 24), "to have frightened" no
one (B 18) is paralleled in Israel in the more formal and general prescription not to wrong one's neighbor (Lev. 19:13).
This lags behind Egyptian sublimation of charity prescriptions.
As known, the general commandment to "love one's neighbor"
in Israel is identical with the prohibition of harboring a grudge
against a compatriot, which is also to be found in the Book of
the Dead (A 27).

The Egyptian catalogue lacks positive prescriptions such as
the obligation to care for the stray cattle of one's neighbor
(Deut. 22:1-4). At one place only, praise is given for showing
the right way to one gone astray. Furthermore, the commandment (Ex. 23:4-5) to bring back the stray cattle of one's
"enemy" is completely absent. In the familiar Egyptian "con-
versation of the cat with the jackal" the compensation of evil
with good is rather criticized. On the other hand, the Decalogue, as well as the old Israelite ethic generally, know none
of the rules taken from conventional properties of the Egyptian
scribes. In part these pertain to good taste, but in part, also, to
a quite sublime ethic. We mention, for instance, the prohibition in the Egyptian scribal ethic (Ptah-hetep) against shaming
the opponent by being superior in discussion and the prohibitions, also contained in the Book of the Dead, against loose
talk, exaggeration, boasting, remaining deaf to truth (B 25.29,
A 34.33, B 18.23 21.19). Such appeared only among post-exilic
Jews when the exponents of Judaistic teaching had themselves
become "*soferim*" and, later, scholarly rabbis.

3. Economic Ethic

IN economic life Egyptian ethic was distinguished by its strong
evaluation of dutiful vocational work and punctuality. This
was a natural result of the liturgy-organized bureaucratically-

managed and half state-socialist economy. Similar traits, though less distinct, are also to be found in Babylonia, where it was apparently customary, at times, to apprentice the princes too in manual construction work. In this the central significance of kingly constructions found its expression. In Egypt a strong vocational pride appears among craftsmen artists (especially masons) even during the time of the Old Kingdom just as in Israel Yahwe imparted his spirit to the craftsmen artists of the Mosaic temple paraments. The great instability of Egyptian wealth, the quite frequent ascent of plebeians into the bureaucracy (especially of the New Kingdom) at an early time pushed the conceptions of gentility of the landed office nobles into the background. Even Ptah-hetep gave praise to business activity as the sole means of preserving wealth. But the bureaucratic nature of the body politic and the strict traditionalism of the religion narrowly circumscribed the bearing of this view. The status sentiment of the scribes under the Rameses found expression in a scornful satire against all other vocations, military as well as economic. They despised all illiterate activity as miserable philistinism. Whereas no sharp distinction between personal freedom and bondage existed, the barrier between literate and non-literate man was high.

Education alone determined rank and station of the notable (*sar*). And the absolute hierarchical subordination of the bureaucracy determined man's ideals. The crown of perfection was represented by *ma,* that is loyalty, meaning, at once "propriety," "righteousness," and "dutiful devotion." It is a somewhat modified counterpart of the *Li,* the virtue of the Chinese bureaucrat. The duties of the loyal subject consisted in imitating his superior, unconditionally accepting his views, strictly observing the rank order also in the layout of burial places in the necropolis. "To bow for the rest of one's life" was considered to be man's fate. The vocational conception accordingly remained strictly traditionalist. It was forbidden to employ a worker other than in his habitual occupation. The documented strike of the workers in the necropolis of Thebes was not revolutionary but sought merely to secure the delivery of the customary income, the "daily bread" in the sense of the Christian Lord's prayer.

In Israel, prior to Jesus Sirach, no comparably strong evaluation of faithful work as in Egypt is to be found. There was simply no bureaucratic organization, and the concept of *ma* was out of place, and singularly so in religious ethic, which abhorred the bureaucratic corvée state as "the Egyptian house of bondage." Nothing bespeaks of an appreciation of economic activity as a virtue. On the contrary, covetousness is the true vice. This indicates that here the urban patricians are the enemies of the devout. "Innerworldly asceticism" was absent in Israel as in Egypt. If in Egypt man is warned to beware of woman, because a short moment of pleasure is allegedly payed for by grave misfortune, it is a rule of prudent living in the way of Confucian ethics. Analogies in Jewish literature are to be found in post-exilic times. For the rest, the supreme end of all striving in Egypt and Mesopotamia remained enjoyment of life tempered by prudence.

The Israelite attitude (*Gesinnung*) differed from this especially through the mounting fear of sin and mood of penance largely attributable to political fates. This was stronger than elsewhere, Babylon included. Ethical absolutism in its degree of sublimation was similar to that of Egypt and on the whole, at least in the workaday life of the masses, essentially more refined and developed than in the Babylonian conception of sin.[7] In practical life this was again and again magically treated and thereby deflected from its end.

Despite all similarities in detail in one important respect Israelite ethic was opposed to Egyptian as well as Babylonian ethic. It was rationally systematized to a far reaching extent. The mere existence of the ethical Decalogue and of other similar compositions indicates the contrast to the quite unsystematic registers of sins in Egypt and Babylon.

Moreover, nothing is transmitted from both these culture areas which would equal or merely resemble a systematic ethical religious exhortation of the kind of Deuteronomy. Unlike pre-exilic Israel Babylonia and Egypt knew no unified, religiously substructured ethic; Egypt had its doctrinal wisdom of life and the esoteric Book of the Dead, Babylonia had its collections of magically efficacious hymns and formulae, containing also ethical elements. In Israel this ethic was the product of the ethical Torah of the Levites continued for many generations, and of prophecy. Prophecy did not so much influence the content—which it rather accepted as given—rather it promoted systematic unification, by relating the people's life as a whole and the life of each individual to the fulfillment of Yahwe's positive commandments. Moreover, it eliminated the predominance of ritual in favor of ethics. In this the Levitical Torah gave its imprint to the content of the ethical commandments. Both jointly imparted to the ethic its simultaneously plebeian and rationally systematic character.

4. Charity

ONE characteristic element of the old Israelite ethic, shared with others, requires somewhat closer attention. The ethical prescriptions thus far discussed show, in part, striking features of the charity generally characteristic of the present revision of the Torah. Particularly noteworthy are numerous stipulations for the benefit of the poor, the *metics,* widows and waifs which are already present in the older collections, but particularly Deuteronomy. Its god is an incorruptible judge "which regardeth not persons" and "doth execute the judgment" of the prescriptions mentioned above (Deut. 10:17 f.). The formal law of debt bondage was, as noted, supplemented in the moral exhortation by far-reaching stipulations concerning payment of wages, debt remission, limitation on pledges, and general charity. The most general formulations of these duties may well be the following: "Thou shalt open thine hand wide" (Deut. 15:11), and extend aid to the needy, the poor, the robbed (Jer. 22:16), and the oppressed (Is. 1:17). The stipulations, discussed previously, respecting gleaning and a fallow year appear to be integrated into this orbit. The sources allow us to discern the steadily increasing importance of these elements of moral exhortation parallel with increasing hierocratic influence on the Israelite ethic which was originally by no means sentimental. Whence did this characteristic originate?

India and Egypt were the two areas where classically charity developed. In India, Jainism and Buddhism were its preeminent exponents. In general, Indian charity rested on the conception of all life as a unity. This was reinforced by the belief in *Sam-*

sara. Indian charity, as expressed also in the Decalogues of the Buddhists, soon adopted a formal and almost purely ritualistic character.

In Egypt charity was strongly influenced by the bureaucratic structure of the state and the economy. The kings of the "Old" and the "New" Kingdoms, and the feudal princes of the "Middle" Kingdom employed forced labor and had an interest in the preservation of the labor power of man and beast. They sought to protect them against the inconsiderate brutality of the officials and taskmasters. The Egyptian sources show clearly how strongly this contributed to the development of poor laws.[8] The officials, who were responsible to the king for the economic and demographic condition of the country, were exposed to complaints of the subjects who apparently could address complaints directly to the king. In the inscriptions the officials, even of the Old Kingdom, boast that they gave aid during famine, took no land away from anyone, did not abuse the subordinates of other officials, never settled a dispute dishonestly, neither took away nor raped anybody's daughter, violated no property, did not oppress the widows; or that they fed the hungry, clothed the naked, shipped people who had no boat across the river, filled the stables of their subordinates with cattle.[9] This always refers to the population belonging to the bailiwick entrusted by the Pharaoh to the official.

Generally the officials also express themselves as follows: they "never did evil to anybody," but rather did "what was pleasing to all." Suspicion against and tabooing of gifts for judges is almost as common with the Egyptian religious poets and moralists as with the Israelite prophets. The fear of the king, who, after all, like the Czar in Russia, was far away, was supplemented by the fear of complaints to higher authorities, that is, the gods. A monarch of the fifth dynasty said that he had not harmed anybody so that he "had complained to the god of the city." The curse of the poor was feared, directly because of the possible intervention of the god, indirectly because of the danger to one's good name in posterity, which was quite important to the Egyptian mind. The belief in the magical efficacy of a curse based on an actual wrong was obviously common in the Middle

East: hence, also, the last and the poorest could avail himself of this "weapon of democracy."

The Egyptian official, therefore, did not fail to emphasize that the people "loved" him, because he did what pleased them. Any responsibility of the great to the people was possibly still more remote to the Egyptian mind than to the Israelite. Yet an official will be "like god" if his workers trust him, if he treats them "like a crocodile" he will be cursed. Hence, Ptah-hetep's ethic of the genteel scribe emphasizes that the practice of charity will be payed for by the permanence of one's position, originally probably that of the Pharaoh, then that of god. The memorial stones of little men (artisans) of the thirteenth and twelfth centuries find comfort in the hope that Amon usually listens to the voice of the poor in his grief (in contrast to the "impertinent" great man, warrior, official). For God guides and protects all his creatures including fish and birds.[10]

In the earliest inscriptions, the kings behaved exactly like the officials, not only the Egyptian but all Mid-Eastern kings. Besides all sorts of offenses against divine property and the state, according to Urukagina, the harsh oppression of the economically weak has brought God's wrath upon his predecessors and legitimizes his own usurpation. In this case, the reference is to the hardships of the transition to a money economy in the city kingship: to indebtedness and enslavement as in Israel. The usurpers, as noted with Abimelech, always rule with the demos against the great sibs. In Egypt and the later Mesopotamian great kingdoms the usual patrimonial-bureaucratic legend of the welfare state gives its stamp to the meanwhile formalist royal charity. Rameses IV boasts of having harmed no waif and no poor man and of not having taken anybody's hereditary land. Nebuchadnezzar expresses himself similarly. Cyrus presumes that the inordinate taxation of the Babylonian people of Nabunadin caused god's wrath to come upon his king and Darius, in the Behistun inscription, takes his stand likewise on the ground of welfare policy and protectionism for the poor. These policies hence were common to all patrimonial states of the Orient and to the majority of such monarchies. In the direct neighborhood of Israel and here, probably, under Egyptian influence a Phoenician royal inscription (the oldest thus far existing) shows the very same features.[11] These ultimately formalistically rigidified, but therefore not necessarily ineffectual maxims will have probably reached from here the scribes of the kings of Israel.

This charity ethic grew out of the patrimonial welfare policy and its projection into the heavenly rule of the world. In Egypt this ethic appears to have been developed first quite consciously by the petty patrimonial princes and feudal lords of the Middle Kingdom from ever present beginnings. Later it was systematized by the scribes, priests, and priestly influenced moralists in correspondence with the general type of hierocratic welfare policy. The declaration to have coerced no one to work beyond his fixed measure (E. 5) stands at the head of all the detailed assurances which the dead in the 125th chapter of the Book of the Dead has to give in the "hall of truth." The derivation from the corvée administration is obvious. Then follow the assurances to have brought to no one fear, poverty, suffering, misfortune, hunger, mourning, not to have caused a master to abuse his slave (E. 6), not to have withheld milk from the suckling babe, not to have maltreated cattle (E. 9), and not to have harmed the sick (B. 26). At the end of the entire confession (B. 38) stands the assurance of having obliged god by one's "charity" (*mer*), "to having given bread to the hungry, water to the thirsty, clothes to the naked, and a boat to him in want of it." To this must be added the previously mentioned ethical prohibition of inflicting pain upon another or of frightening him, of doing evil to one's neighbor and the prescription of doing good also to one's enemy. The appearance of this prescription in Egyptian ethics seems, however, controversial. In substance these commandments anticipate largely the charity of the Gospels.

Presumably the development of old Israelite charity was influenced by Egypt directly or by way of Phoenicia. This influence was strongest in Deuteronomic times. Even in pre-Deuteronomic times the conviction prevailed that Yahwe protected the weak *per se*, woman against man, the concubine against the wife, the outcast son against the father (Gen. 16:5, 7; 21:14; I. Sam. 24:13). It is to be found with the Yahwist as well as the Elohist and had the same religious foundation as the Egyptian conception. The poor and oppressed "cries to Yahwe"

(Deut. 24:15) who as heavenly king may take revenge on the oppressor. In Exile the conception came to prevail in Israelite ethic that it be best to suffer oppression because such behavior would insure the revenge of God. At the time it was due to the social impotence of the oppressed classes, but it probably goes back to the significance of one's name which was to become a blessing for the descendants. For the efficacy of the curse negatively corresponds to the blessing of the poor, when treated according to the charity commandments; and it "shall be righteousness unto thee before Yahwe" (Deut. 24:13). Charity was continuously developed in increasingly systematic fashion through the moral exhortation of the Levites; the Shechemite cursing formula, influenced by them; the *debarim,* joined to the Book of the Covenant; and then Deuteronomy and the priestly law.

Despite many striking and hardly accidental similarities, the substantive demands of Israelite charity differed in tenor from Egyptian charity demands. It rested on a priestly influenced community of free peasant and herdsmen sibs, not on a priestly influenced patrimonial bureaucracy, although devout kings, following foreign example in their ethic of the welfare state, were perhaps the first to express these demands. Naturally, in Israel, too, oppressions by royal officials occurred in Egyptian fashion. Even the king might commit acts of oppression which in Egypt was officially impossible. The paradigm of the priestly revision has Yahwe react against this through prophetic pronouncements of doom. The primary evil to be fought was not oppression by a bureaucracy but by an urban patriciate, and conditions were far simpler than in Egypt. The sublimation of charity into ethical absolutism, hence, does not extend as far as in Egypt. Individual prescriptions were more in agreement with the patriarchal nature of the household and neighborhood relations than was the case with the abstractions of Egyptian scribes. Only the pacifistic, urban epoch of the Torah directly prior and during the Exile produced the abstractions of the Holiness Code. We note the injunction of replacing candid discussion by hatred and vindictiveness against one's "neighbor," that is (Lev. 19:18) against the children of one's people and, according to 19:34, against the *ger.* This is related to the principle: "thou shalt love thy neighbor as thyself" (Lev. 19:18).

This tabooing of vindictiveness might appear to be a reaction to the Levitical exhortation against the promises of some prophets strongly encouraging (political) vindictiveness. The prescription of neighborly love for one's compatriots shows however by the reenforcing addition: "I am the Lord" that this was identical with the frequently repeated prescription to leave vengeance to God (Deut. 32:35). The hope was that God would consummate it the more thoroughly. The leaving of revenge to God has no genuine ethical significance. The prescription originated in the feeling of plebeian and, at that, politically impotent strata. Obviously, the story of David and Nabal (I. Sam. 25: 24, 33) was composed as a paradigm for this even more satisfying revenge. The reservation of vengeance for God was for the Torah teachers the natural ethical parallel to abolishing blood revenge in law. The positive command to "love" one's neighbor was for them a transfer of the principles of ancient sib brotherliness to the fellow believer. Only the rabbinical interpretation made of it the positive prescription that one must not even covertly hate and pursue the neighbor with thoughts of revenge. In practice though, even in their own feeling, this proved none too successful.[12]

In Israel, as occasionally in Egyptian charity, protection of those afflicted with disease and infirmities stood alongside the protection of the poor. One shall not curse them "nor put a stumbling block before the blind" or lead them astray (Lev. 19:14). Egyptian charity, too, prescribed aid to those who had gone astray and prohibited harm to the diseased; it did not deal in detail with those afflicted with infirmities. The prophets of hope of the "great kings" usually ascribed to their ruling monarchy the defense against afflictions, disease, and similar misery. In this he proved his charisma. The peculiar saying for David (II. Sam. 5:6, 8) at the conquest of Jerusalem is probably related to the same idea of the miraculous power of a charismatic ruler.* In the Levitical Torah, however, one has to locate the

---

* In Western tradition the same miraculous healing power was ascribed to charismatic kings and heroes, including Napoleon I. See Marc Bloch, *Les Rois Thaumaturges, Étude sur le Charactère surnatural attribué à la Puissance royale, particulièrement en France et en Angleterre* (Strassbourg, New York, 1924), and the discussion of "The Charismatic Leader" in Franz

reason for the protection of the infirm in the fact that quite a few of them were numbered among the confessants of the Levites and their devoutness was too often experienced to permit unconditional retention of the ancient magical notion that the afflicted were personally hateful to God because of an offense. One could think of him as suffering for the sins of his forebears and with the deaf and the blind the assumption that they were subject to a mysterious divine verdict, could readily lead to the conception that they might also command forces which others lacked, as indicated by the widespread esteem for the blind. To hurt them seemed in any case apt to provoke the wrath of God.

Finally, there are a number of stipulations for the protection of animals to be found in Deuteronomy like the one protecting the mother bird (22:6, 7) and the famous prohibition (25:4) not to "muzzle the ox when he treadeth out the corn," whereas on Roman plantations the slaves at the millstone wore muzzles. To this must be added the evaluation of the Sabbath as a day of rest also for cattle and of the Sabbath year as giving animals the opportunity to feed freely. The Israelite sources do not permit discernment of the extent to which these theological constructions hang together with the ubiquitous Mid-Eastern belief in an original and hoped-for paradisical state of peace between man and beast or whether they are related to some sort of ancient ritualistic vegetarianism which perhaps sprang from local agricultural cults, or whether they simply resulted from the commandment of love. Balaam's talking ass was simply an animal of popular fable to be found elsewhere like the prophetic lamb under Bocchoris in Egypt. In Egypt the prohibition against the ill-treatment of cattle probably originally goes back to the interest of the king in its labor power. With Rameses II we find the characteristic promise to the horses having saved him from the battle of Kadesh that they shall be fed, henceforth, in his presence in the palace just as he promised his workers correct payment of their wages. This resulted from the typical relation of the rider or stable master to his animals. The

---

Neumann, *Behemoth*, The Structure and Practice of National Socialism, 1933–1944 (New York, 1944), especially pp. 92 ff. [Ed.]

priestly systematized, popular animal worship and the ability of the souls of the dead to assume animal forms was hardly the source of this friendly attitude toward animals. But these conceptions naturally promoted charity toward animals.

As its absence in the legend (II. Ki. 4:23) indicates, in Israel the Sabbath rest for cattle, as for slaves, was only a product of late kingly, presumably Deuteronomic times. Possibly the kindness toward animals, at least its general direction, was due to Egyptian influence. All in all it is quite probable that Israelite ethics and charity in late pre-exilic times have been influenced in many details by the example of the great culture areas, especially by Egypt, directly or by way of Phoenicia. The decisive features of this sort of charity have also developed without borrowing wherever priestly interest in physically afflicted or unfortunate patrons were strong enough to promote a rationalization of welfare work for the weak. The Israelite Torah has independently refashioned the commandments even where the assumption of external influence suggests itself.

More important than all individual differences is the previously emphasized fact that magic formed no substitute for fulfillment of the commandments. Egyptian priestly teaching, for instance, might raise ethical or charity commandments of whatever content. What reenforcement could it provide, if simple magical means were at hand allowing the dead to hide his sins in the decisive moment before the judge of the dead? This, indeed, was the case. The plea to one's own heart in the Book of the Dead (ch. 30, L. 1) not to testify against the dead was later reenforced by providing the dead with a consecrated scarabaeus, which enabled the heart to resist the magical power of the judges of the dead and to conceal sins. Hence, one outwitted the gods. Things were not as crass in Babylon. But in neo-Babylonian times, magic of all sorts was the specific, popular means of influencing the invisible powers. With increasing rationalization of the culture feelings of sinfulness became also more intensive in Mesopotamia particularly among the pacifistic bourgeois population. Later, however, the expressive Sumerian and old Babylonian penitential psalms were used purely as magical formulae and often without regard to their meaning. This happened after the evil spirits as cause of all evil in popular belief had taken the place of the great deities. In ancient Yahwism this kind of magic was absent and therefore the once-accepted ethical commandments necessarily had greater practical importance. This was due to the different turn given to the problem of theodicy and to the frequently adduced circumstance that each and every individual in Israel had to fear the vengeance of god if violation of his commandments were tolerated in their very midst. For Israel was an association of free compatriots who, by virtue of *berith*, were jointly responsible for keeping the commandments of the god of the covenant. Hence, in Israel people reacted against sin by means of casting out the unreconciled sinner, by banning and by stoning him.

Capital punishment without mercy was obligatory for certain serious offenders, because it was the one and only means of expurgating the community. This motive was indeed absent in bureaucratic monarchies and especially where professional magicians were present. It is analogous to the responsibility of the early Christian and puritan communion of the Lord's Supper for removing the obvious reprobate from the table of the Lord in contrast to Catholicism, Anglicanism, and Lutheranism. The specific ethical turn of the Levitical Torah was necessarily greatly reenforced by the steady pressure of this interest. The attitude of the Levites, however, originated in relation to their private clientele. Moses' establishment of the ancient *berith* and the assumption of the oracular functions gave the first impetus to all this. Hence to this extent Moses is rightly considered the founder of this important ethical development. The religion of Israel developed into a structure able to resist all disintegrating influence from the outside, and it lived in this form through history. This entire development would have been impossible without the intervention of prophecy. We shall now consider this unique phenomenon of great consequence.

PART IV

THE ESTABLISHMENT OF THE
JEWISH PARIAH PEOPLE

CHAPTER XI

SOCIAL PSYCHOLOGY
OF THE PROPHETS

1. Political Orientations
of Pre-Exilic Prophecy

AFTER the lull in the conquest policies of the great states which had facilitated the emergence of the Israelite Confederation, in the ninth century, the great kings of Mesopotamia, like those later of Egypt, once again resumed their expansionist policy. Syria became a theatre of hitherto unprecedented military events. Never before had the world experienced warfare of such frightfulness and magnitude as that practiced by the Assyrian kings. Blood fairly drips from the cuneiform inscriptions. The king, in the tone of dry protocol, reports that he covered the walls of conquered cities with human skins. The Israelite literature preserved from the period, above all, the oracles of classical prophecy, express the mad terror caused by these merciless conquerors. As impending gloom beclouded the political horizon, classical prophecy acquired its characteristic form.

The pre-exilic prophets [1] from Amos to Jeremiah and Ezekiel, viewed through the eyes of the contemporary outsider, appeared to be, above all, political demagogues and, on occasion, pamphleteers. Isaiah, for example, directed a pamphlet against Shebna (22:15 f.) with a postscript against Eliakim who in the first draft had been mentioned honorably. In the same category belongs the written curse which Jeremiah placed upon Semachiah. This characterization of the prophets (as demagogues and pamphleteers) can indeed be misleading, but properly understood it permits indispensable insight. It means that the prophets were primarily *speakers*. Prophets as writers appear only after the Babylonian Exile. The early prophets addressed their audiences in public.

Except for the world politics of the great powers which threatened their homeland and constituted the message of their most impressive oracles, the prophets could not have emerged. They could not have arisen on the soil of the great powers for the simple reason that "demagogy" was impossible there. To be sure, the "great king" of Assyria, Babylonia, and Persia, like the Israelite king and every ancient overlord, permitted his oracle to determine his political resolutions, or at least allowed for the oracular determination of the time and particulars of his measures. The Babylonian king, for instance, before nominating a high official, consulted the oracle priests as to the candidate's qualifications.

This, however, was strictly an affair of court. The political prophet did not speak in the streets nor address the people directly. The political preconditions for doing so did not exist, nor would it have been tolerated. There are indications that public prophecy was expressly forbidden, which prohibition is consistent with the conditions of the bureaucratic states, particularly in the time of the Jewish Exile when sources indicate that there were probably sharp repressive measures. Nothing is known of the existence in the great states of political prophecy comparable to that of the classical period in the Near East and in Egypt. Things were different in Israel and especially in the city-state of Jerusalem.

The old political prophecy of the time of the confederacy had addressed itself to the collectivity of the confederates. Such prophecy, however, was sporadic, for the confederacy had no fixed and common oracular sanctuary like Dodona or Delphi. The priestly oracle by lot, the only form of consulting the deity recognized as classical, was technically primitive. Under the rule of the kings free war-prophecy became obsolete and the confederate oracle decreased in significance in proportion as the court prophet's rose.

Free prophecy developed only with the rising external danger to the country and to the royal power. According to the tradition, Elijah had publicly stood up to the king and his prophets, but was forced to flee the country. This held also for Amos under Jeroboam II. Under strong governments or under governments supported by a "great power," as for instance, Judah under Manasseh, prophecy, even after Isaiah's appearance, remained silent—or rather was reduced to silence. With the decreasing prestige of the kings and the growing threat to the country, the significance of prophecy again increased and the scene of the prophet's activities moved closer and closer to Jerusalem.

Among the early prophets Amos made his appearance at the sanctuary of Beth-el, and Hosea in the Northern realm. Even Isaiah identified pasture and wasteland (5:17; 17:2), in the manner of an outright Jerusalemite. Apparently Isaiah preferred the public courtyard of the Temple as a scene for his appearance. Finally Yahwe commanded Jeremiah: "Go thou into the streets of Jerusalem and speak in public."

In a time of distress a king like Zedekiah would secretly send for the prophet requesting a divine word. As a rule, however, the prophet personally confronted also the king and his family in the street, spoke in public, or—though this was unusual—dictated his word to a disciple and had it circularized. This last is illustrated by Isaiah who had his disciples seal one of his oracles (8:16) and by Jeremiah's written oracular curse against Babylon (51:59 f.). Occasionally individuals or deputations of elders requested and received oracles from the prophets, Jeremiah included (21:2 f.; 37:3; 38:14; 42:1 f.).

However, usually the prophet spoke on his own, i.e., under the influence of a spontaneous inspiration, to the public in the market place or to the elders at the city gate. The prophets also interpreted the fates of individuals, though as a rule only those of politically important persons. The predominant concern of the prophet was the destiny of the state and the people. This concern always assumed the form of emotional invectives against the overlords. It is here that the "demagogue" appeared for the first time in the records of history, at about the period when the Homeric songs threw the figure of Thersites into relief.

2. Hellenic and Judaic Prophecy

IN the early Hellenic polis, however, the assembly of notables as found in Ithaca was one in which the people, as a rule, listened and at best participated through acclamation. There was orderly debate; the floor was granted by handing over the staff to the speaker. On the other hand, the demagogue of Periclean times was a secular politician, leading the demos through his personal influence and speaking before the sovereign ecclesia.

In Homeric times the seer was recognized and consulted in the midst of the assembly of knights. Later this practice decayed. Figures such as Tyrtaeus and the demagogic war poetry of Solonic times enjoining the conquest of Salamis come closest to the ancient free political prophecy of the Israelite confederacy. However, the figure of Tyrtaeus was bound up with the development of the Spartan army of disciplined hoplites and Solon, for all his piety, was a secular politician. Solon's mind was lucid and clear and his profoundly "rationalistic" spirit fused the knowledge of man's insecure fate with the firm faith in the value of his people. Temperamentally he was a preacher of genteel and pious custom.

Orphic and Israelite prophecy and religiosity were more closely related. Tyranny, friendly to the plebs, particularly that of the Peisistratids, sought contact with these plebeian theologians. The same was true, at times, for the politics of the Persians, at the time of the attempts at conquest. During the sixth and early part of the fifth century, "chresmologists," itinerant vendors of oracles, and vaticinating mystagogues of all sorts wandered through Greece and gave consultations for a price. They were consulted by private citizens as well as politicians and especially by exiles. On the other hand, nothing of religious demagoguery in the manner of the Israelite prophets is known ever to have intervened in the politics of the Hellenic states.

Pythagoras and his sect gained very considerable political influence, and ministered spiritual guidance to the nobility of the Southern Italian cities, but the Pythagoreans did not constitute prophets of the street. Genteel philosophers of the type of Thales not only predicted solar eclipses and formulated rules for prudent living, but actively engaged in politics in their cities, at times in dominant positions. However, they lacked the quality of ecstatic men. The same holds for Plato and the academy—their political ethic was, in the last analysis, utopian—which were of great influence upon the fateful development (and disintegration) of the realm of Syracuse. Ecstatic political prophecy, however, remained hierocratically organized at the official oracle places which answered the official questions of the citizenries in well-turned verses. The firm military structure of the city was averse to free emotional prophecy.

In Jerusalem, on the other hand, the purely religious demagogue was spokesman and his oracles highlighted obscure fates of the future like lightning out of somber clouds. Such prophecy was authoritarian in character and averse to all orderly procedure. Formally, the prophet was strictly a private citizen. For this very reason, he was, naturally, by no means an indifferent figure in the eyes of political authority. Jeremiah's collected oracles were brought before the council of state and the king by distinguished citizens in the king's service. For each such oracle was an event of public significance. This was so, not merely because the oracle influenced the mood of the masses, but also because as an anathema, a good or evil omen, it could exert magical influence upon the course of events.

3. Established Authority versus the Prophets

THE holders of established power faced these powerful demagogues with fear, wrath, or indifference as the situation warranted. Sometimes they sought to draw the prophets into their service. Sometimes they behaved like King Joiakim who, sitting in his winter garret with ostensible composure, listened to the collected oracles of doom and as they were read to him by court officials threw them sheet by sheet into the fireplace. Or, again, the power holders took action against the prophets.

As the lament of Amos indicates, under strong governments, like that of Jeroboam II, prophecy was forbidden. When this prophet (Amos) proclaims God's wrath over Israel because of the attempts to suppress prophecy, his complaint is quite comparable to the demand of the modern demagogue for freedom of the press. Actually, prophetic words were not restricted to oral communication. With Jeremiah they appeared in the form of open letters. At times friends and disciples of the prophets wrote down the spoken word and turned it into a political pamphlet. Later on, at times simultaneously (as was also the case with Jeremiah), these sheets were collected and revised. They constitute the earliest known example of political pamphlet literature directly addressing itself to contemporaneous events.

The form and tenor of pre-exilic prophecy was in accordance with this phenomenon and the entire situation in which it appeared. Everything was calculated to loan word-of-mouth demagoguery a timely influence. Micah introduced the opponents of the prophets as speakers. The prophets were personally attacked and pilloried, and frequently we hear of violent conflicts. All the recklessness and frantic passion of the party struggles, e.g., of Athens or Florence, was equaled and, at times, surpassed in the angry addresses and oracular pamphlets, particularly of Jeremiah. Curses, threats, personal invective, desperation, wrath, and thirst for revenge are to be found in them. In a letter to the Babylonian exiles Jeremiah slandered the counter-prophets for their alleged dishonorable way of life (29:23). Jeremiah's curse brought death to the counter-prophet, Hananiah. When, despite all abomination, Yahwe left unfulfilled the threats against his own people which he had put in the prophet's mouth, Jeremiah fell into a rage and, in view of the derision of his enemies, demanded that God let fall the day of prophesied doom (17:18), that he avenge him on his persecutors (15:15), that he let stand his opponents' sin against him (18:23) without expiation, in order that Yahwe deal with them the more terribly in the time of his anger. Often he appears actually to revel in the representation of the frightful doom of his own people which he prophesied as certain.

However, in contrast to the party demagogues in Athens and Florence, after the disaster at Megiddo and later, after the catastrophe prophesied for decades had befallen Jerusalem, there is no trace of triumph over the fact that the prediction was correct. Also, there is no longer, as previously, sullen despair. But alongside grave mourning there appears hope for God's grace and better times. And in his passionate wrath over the impenitence of the listeners he allows Yahwe's voice to warn him not, through ignoble words, to forfeit the right to be Yahwe's mouthpiece. He is to speak noble words, then Yahwe will turn the hearts of men to him (15:19). Indeed, unconfined by priestly or status conventions and quite untempered by any self control, be it ascetic or contemplative, the prophet discharges his glowing passion and experiences all the abysses of the human heart. And yet, despite all these human frailties, characteristic of these titans of the holy curse, it is not their private motives but the cause of Yahwe, of the wrathful God, that reigns supreme over the uproar.

The prophet's vehement attack was countered by an equally vehement reaction of the public. Numerous verses, particularly again of Jeremiah, occasionally might suggest monstrous delusions of persecution mania and describe how the fiend now hisses, now laughs, now threatens and mocks. This was actually the case. In the open street the opponents of the prophets engaged them, insulted them, and struck them in the face. King Joiakim caused Egypt to surrender the prophet of doom Uria to him and had him executed. And when Jeremiah, who was repeatedly taken into custody and threatened with death, escaped this fate, it was due to the fear of his magical power.

Always the life and honor of the prophets were in danger and the opposition party lay in wait to destroy them by force, fraud and derision, by counter-magic and especially by counter-prophecy. After Jeremiah went for eight days with a yoke on his shoulders, to illustrate the unavoidable subjection to Nebuchadnezzar, Hananiah opposed him, seized and broke the yoke, to destroy the evil omen before all people. Whereupon Jeremiah, at first quite taken aback, left to return with an iron yoke and scornfully demanded that the opponent try his strength upon it and prophesied his early death. These prophets were torn in the midst of a snarl of party antagonisms and conflicting interests, especially with respect to foreign politics. This could not be otherwise. The question for the national state was to live or be crushed between the Assyrian world power on the one hand, the Egyptian on the other. No one could avoid taking sides and no man active in public could escape the question:

whose? As little as Jesus was spared the question whether it be right to pay the Roman tribute!

Whether the prophets wished it or not they actually always worked in the direction of one or the other furiously struggling inner-political cliques, which at the same time promoted definite foreign policies. Hence, the prophets were considered party members. After the second fall of Jerusalem, Nebuchadnezzar, in his relation to Jeremiah, took into account the fact that the prophet had promoted faithful allegiance to the king. When we see the sib of Saphan support the prophets for many generations [2] as well as the Deuteronomic movement, we may well infer that foreign-political party interests played a part. But it would be a grave error to believe that political partisanship of the prophets, for instance, for Assyria by Isaiah or for Babylon in the case of Jeremiah, determined the content of the oracles, by which they advised against alliances with these great powers. Under Sennacherib the same Isaiah [3] who had previously seen Assur as the tool of Yahwe, turned sharply against the "great king" and against capitulation in opposition to the faint-hearted king and his aides. As, in the beginning, he almost welcomed the Assyrians as executors of well-deserved punishment, so he later cursed this godless, overbearing, inhumanly cruel royal sib and people determined only to overpower and destroy others. He prophesied their downfall. When, later, this occurred it was jubilantly hailed by the prophets.

Jeremiah, to be sure, had incessantly preached submission to the power of Nebuchadnezzar to an extent which we would nowadays call high treason; for, what else is it when he (21:9), in the face of the approaching enemy, holds out grace and life to those who will desert and surrender and destruction to the rest? However, the same Jeremiah who still in his last oracle from Egypt occasionally referred to Nebuchadnezzar as the "Servant of God" (43:10) and who, after the capture of Jerusalem, receives gifts from the king's representative and an invitation to come to Babylon gave the travelling marshal of King Zedekiah a sheet with a prophetic curse of Babylon to take along on his journey with the commandment to read it there aloud and then to throw it into the Euphrates (Jer. 51:59 ff.) in order, through this magic, to secure the downfall of the hated city.

As all this indicates, according to their manner of functioning, the prophets were objectively political and, above all, world-political demagogues and publicists, however, subjectively they were no political partisans. Primarily they pursued no political interests. Prophecy has never declared anything about a "best state" (disregarding Ezekiel's hierocratic construction in the Exile) nor has it ever sought, like the philosophical *aisymnete* or the academy, to help translate into reality social-ethically oriented political ideals through advice to power holders. The state and its doings were, by themselves, of no interest to them. Moreover, unlike the Hellenes they did not posit the problem: how can man be a good citizen? Their question was absolutely religious, oriented toward the fulfillment of Yahwe's commandments.

Certainly this does not preclude the fact that at least Jeremiah, perhaps consciously, assessed the actual power relations of his time more correctly than did the prophets of grace. Only this was not decisive for his attitude. For these concrete power relations were what they were only through Yahwe's will. Yahwe could change them. Isaiah's admonition to stand fast against Sennacherib's attacks ran counter to all realistic estimate of political probability. To seriously maintain that, even ahead of the king! he had had news concerning the circumstances which caused Sennacherib to move away, is rationalism, indeed, equivalent to those attempts to explain the miracle at the wedding of Cana by means of liqueur which allegedly Jesus secretly brought with him.

Quite unconvincing is one suggestion as to the relationships of the Yahwe prophets to inner-political parties—a "priest and citizen-party"—of the world empires, especially the Mesopotamian, relations which some pan-Babylonians have tracked down with ingenuity. There is no doubt that the respective foreign-political relations, also partisanship, almost always had internal religious ramifications. Egyptian partisans practiced Egyptian cults, those of the Assyrians, Babylonian ones, and Phoenicians also had their special cults and, in the case of a political alliance, worship of the respective gods was an almost indispensable affirmation which a great king, however tolerant otherwise, probably demanded as a sign of political obeisance. Furthermore, there are sufficient records to indicate that, e.g., Nebuchadnezzar was not disinclined after the first as well as the second conquest of Jerusalem and the abduction of the Egyptian partisans to use the influence of the Yahwe believers similarly as a support of his domination as, later, did Cyrus and Darius. Also Necho's policy after the battle of Megiddo, already appears to have pointed in a similar direction [4] without thereby winning the prophets for Egypt. As the beginning of this important maxim, deviating from old Assyrian ways, namely, to rule with the help of native priests, one may well consider the reported way of the Assyrians of meeting the religious needs of Samaria after the destruction (II. Ki. 17:27 f.).

With this turn of religious policy of the great states, for the prophets their foreign domination lost much of its religious terror and it may well be that this fact has co-determined Jeremiah's attitude. However, the causal significance of such factors is obviously incomparable with respect to the importance which "church-political" reasons presumably had for the behavior of Hellenic oracles, particularly of the Delphic Apollo opposite the Persians. Also here the attitude of the oracles basically presupposed that fate was with the Persians, since the miraculous rise of Cyrus and Darius. However, the flattering devotion of the king and of Mardonius and the substantial gifts which they proffered combined with the justified expectation that, in case of victory, the Persians would also here manage to tame the disarmed citizenry with the help of the priests. Such were the quite substantial props to the attitude. No such material considerations existed for the prophets. Jeremiah evaded the invitation to come to Babylon, and it seems quite some distance from his correct assessment of the power situation to the assumption of some pan-Babylonians that there existed an international party-following of priests and burghers on the one hand and military nobles on the other. Such assumptions are quite unacceptable and we shall see that the prophets' stand with respect to foreign alliances generally and particularly their constant disinclination against the alliance with Egypt was determined by purely religious motives.

4. *Status Orientations and*
Inner-Political Attitudes

THE attitudes of the prophets toward internal affairs were, however pronounced, just as little primarily based on political or social-political considerations as their views on foreign policy. In status origin the prophets were diverse (*uneinheitlich*). It is out of the question that they were, for the most part, derived from proletarian or negatively privileged [5] or uneducated strata. Moreover their social ethical attitude was by no means determined by their personal descent. For they share the same attitude despite their very diverse social origins.

Throughout they argued passionately for the social-ethical charity-commandments of the Levite exhortation for the benefit of the little people and hurled their wrathful curses preferably against the great and the rich. However, Isaiah, who among the older prophets was most vehement in this, was the descendant of a genteel sib, closely befriended by distinguished priests, had intercourse with the king as his councillor and physician and in his time was, without doubt, one of the preeminent men of the city. Zephaniah descended from David and was a great-grandson of Hezekiah; Ezekiel was a distinguished Jerusalemite priest. These prophets were, thus, wealthy Jerusalemites. Micah stemmed from a small town, Jeremiah from a village. Jeremiah came from a landed sib of rural priests, perhaps the old house of Eli's descendants.[6] He bought land from impoverished relatives. Only Amos was a small-stock-breeder: he called himself a shepherd who had lived on sycamore fruit (the food of the poor) and he came from a small town of Judah, but was obviously well educated. It is Amos, for example, who knew the Babylonian Tiamat-myth. However, like Isaiah, with all his grave curses against the great, he yet pronounced the rule of the uneducated, undisciplined demos as the worst of all curses. So, also, Jeremiah despite his more democratic descent and still sharper language against the outrages of the court and the great was just as sharp against the plebeian ministers of Zedekiah. He took it for granted, too, that little people understand nothing of religious duties. Of the great one might expect it and therefore they deserved the curse. A personal factor might have played a part with this prophet in his particularly sharp opposition to the Jerusalemite priests, if he really were a descendant of the priest Abiathar whom Solomon once had exiled to Anathot for the benefit of Zadok. But even this played, at best, an aggravating part in comparison to the substantive reasons.

In any case, no prophet was a champion of "democratic" ideals. In their eyes the people need guidance, hence, everything depends on the qualities of the leaders (Is. 1:26; Jer. 5:5). Moreover, no prophet pronounced any sort of religious "natural law," even less a right to revolution or self-help of the masses suppressed by the mighty. Anything of the sort would undoubtedly have appeared to them as the very pinnacle of godlessness. They disavowed their more violent forerunners. Hosea condemned Jehu's revolution, a work of the school of Elisha and the Rechabites, with the sharpest curses and he prophesied Yahwe's revenge. With the characteristic exception of Ezekiel's theological construction of an ideal state of the future during the Exile, no prophet proclaimed a social-political program. The social-ethical demands which they rather presuppose than raise, suggest the Levite exhortation, the existence and knowledge of which all prophets treat as self-evident. Hence, the prophets were not, for their part, champions of democratic social ideals. But the political situation, the existence of strong socio-political opposition to the corvée exacting kingship and the *gibborim*, these provided the sounding board for their primarily religiously determined message and also influenced the content of their conceptual universe. This however was mediated by those strata of intellectuals who were devoted to the old traditions of pre-Solomon times, and whose social position was close to that of the prophets.

5. *Social Context of the Prophetic Message*

ONE important principle united the prophets as a status group: the gratuitous character of their oracles. This separated them from the prophets of the king, whom they cursed as destroyers of the land. And it distinguished the prophets from all groups that made an industry of prophecy in the manner of the old seers or dream-interpreters whom they despised and rejected. The complete inner independence of the prophets was not so much a result as a most important cause of their practice. In the main they prophesied disaster and no one could be sure whether on request, like King Zedekiah, he might not receive a prediction of doom and therewith an evil omen. One does not pay for evil omens nor expose oneself to them. Primarily unbidden and spontaneously impelled, rarely on request, the prophets hurled their frequently frightful oracles against their audience.

However, as a status principle this gratuitous practice is, indeed, characteristic of a stratum of genteel intellectuals. The borrowing of this principle, later, by the plebeian intellectual strata of the rabbis and, from them, by the Christian apostles form exceptions of great importance for the sociology of religion. Moreover, the prophets did not by any means find their "community," so far as that term applies (of which more later) either solely or primarily in the demos. On the contrary, if they had any personal support at all, it was from distinguished, individual, pious houses in Jerusalem. Sometimes for several generations such served as their patrons. Jeremiah was supported by the same sib which also took part in the "finding" of Deuteronomy. Most sympathetic supporters were found among the *zekenim,* as the guardians of the pious tradition and, particularly, the traditional respect for prophecy. Such was the case for Jeremiah in his capital trial; it was also true of Ezekiel, whom the elders consulted in Exile.

The prophets never obtained support from the peasants. Indeed, all prophets preached against debt slavery, the pawning of clothes, against all violation of the charity commandments, which benefited the little man. In Jeremiah's last prophecy, peasants and shepherds were the champions of piety. However, this form of prophecy was true only for Jeremiah. The peasants belonged as little to his following as the rural squirearchy; in fact, the *'am ha-aretz* were among the more important opponents of the prophets, especially of Jeremiah who was opposed by his own sib. Because they were strict Yahwists, the prophets declaimed against the rural orgiasticism of the fertility cults and the most tainted rural places of worship. Above all the prophets declaimed against the shrines of Baal, which meant much to the rural population for economic as well as ideal reasons.

The prophets never received support from the king. For the

prophets were champions of the Yahwistic tradition opposing kingship which was compromised by politically necessary concessions to foreign cults, intemperate drinking, and by the innovations of the Solomonic corvée state. Solomon was not of the slightest importance for any of the prophets. When a king is mentioned at all, it is David who is the pious ruler. Hosea viewed the kings of the Northern realm as illegitimate, because they had usurped the throne without the will of Yahwe. Amos mentioned the Nazarites and Nebiim among the institutions of Yahwe, but not the kings. Indeed, none of the prophets denied the legitimacy of the Davidians. However, respect even for this dynasty, such as it was, was only conditional. Isaiah's Immanuel-prophecy, after all, may well be considered as the prediction of a God-sent usurper. Yet it was for Isaiah that David's age represented the climax of national history. Relentless attacks against the conduct of the respective contemporary kings grew in intensity. Such raging outbursts of wrath and scorn as those of Jeremiah against Joiakim are rarely to be found. Joiakim shall go to earth like an ass (22:19) and the queen mother who apparently participated in the Astarte-cult, shall have her skirt pulled over her head that all might see her shame (13:18 ff.). But even Isaiah called his woe down on the land the king of which "is a child and is led by women" and he stood up boldly to the grown-up king in a personal encounter.

With obvious intent the prophetic tradition preserved the account of Elijah's conflicts with Ahab. The kings returned these antipathies in kind. They tolerated the prophets only in uncertain times, but, whenever they felt sure of themselves, they had recourse, like Manasseh, to bloody persecution. Beside the politically conditioned worship of foreign deities or incorrect cults, the wrath of the prophets against the kings was, above all, directed at world politics *per se,* the means and presuppositions of which were unholy. This applied particularly to the alliance with Egypt. Although fugitive Yahwe prophets, such as Uria, sought refuge in Egypt, and although Egyptian rule was lenient and certainly religiously non-propagandistic, the prophets rebelled with especial bitterness against this alliance. The reason is made obvious in Isaiah (28:18).

Dealings with Egypt are an "agreement with Sheol," that is to say with the chthonian gods of the realm of the dead which they loathed.[7] Obviously in this the prophets rest their political attitudes solidly on the priestly tradition; their political stand is throughout religiously conditioned. As against the king, so the prophets declaimed against the mighty, particularly the *sarim* and *gibborim*. Along with the injustice of their courts, the prophets cursed, above all, their impious way of life and debauchery. But obviously the opposition of the prophets was independent of such single vices. The king and political-military circles could make no use whatever of the purely utopian exhortations and counsels of the prophets.

The Hellenic states of the sixth and fifth centuries regularly consulted oracles but in the end and precisely in the days of decision, as, for example, during the Persian war, they failed to honor the advice of their oracles even though they were politically oriented. As a rule, it was politically impossible for the kings of Judah to heed the advice of the prophets. And the knightly sense of dignity which here as elsewhere is aloof from prophetic belief, necessarily made them reject as beneath them Jeremiah's advice with respect to Babylon. They disdained these screaming ecstatics of the streets.

On the other side, the popular opposition against the distinguished knights and patricians of the time of the kings which the intellectual strata had nourished played its part in the attitude of the prophets. Avarice is the preeminent vice, that is to say, usurious oppression of the poor. The prophets are not interested in the royal army. Their future kingdom is a kingdom of peace. In this they did not by any means represent something like "Little Judah" pacifists. Amos promised to Judah dominion over Edom and over those people which are called by Yahwe's name (9:12). The old popular hope of world domination recurred repeatedly. Increasingly, however, the idea gained currency that the political aspirations of Israel would only be realized through a miracle of God, as once at the Red Sea, but not through autonomous military power, and, least of all, through political alliances. Ever anew the wrath of the prophets turned against such alliances. The basis of the opposition was again religious. It was not simply because of the danger of strange cults that such antipathy was felt. Rather, Israel stood in the *berith* with Yahwe. Nothing must enter competition with the *berith*, especially not trust in human help, which would bespeak of godless disbelief and evoke Yahwe's wrath. As Jeremiah saw the matter, if Yahwe had ordained the conquest of the people by Nebuchadnezzar, one must accept the fact.

Defensive alliances against the great kings were offenses against God so long as the great kings were executors of his will. If they were not and if He wished to help Israel, He would do so alone, Isaiah taught. Probably he was the first for this reason to preach indefatigably against all and every attempt to work out an alliance. Clearly, the whole attitude toward internal as well as foreign affairs was purely religious in motivation, nothing bespeaks of political expediencies. The relationship to the priests also was religiously conditioned.

No prophet before Ezekiel spoke favorably of the priests. Amos recognized, as noted, only the Nazarites and Nebiim as Yahwe's tools, but he failed to mention the priests. The very existence of their type of free prophecy was, from the time of its appearance, a clear symptom of the weakness of priestly power. Had the place of the priest been like that in Egypt, or even in Babylon, or in Jerusalem after the Exile, free prophecy would doubtlessly have been suppressed as dangerous competition. Since originally, in the confederate time, there was no central shrine and no official sacrifice, this was impossible. Meanwhile the prestige of the old royal prophets and seers and then of Elijah and the Elisha-school was firmly established. Powerful sibs of pious laity backed the prophets. Therefore, the priests had to tolerate them despite frequent and sharp antagonisms. But, they were by no means always antagonistic to the priests. Isaiah had close relations with the priests of Jerusalem and Ezekiel was throughout priestly in outlook. On the other hand, we find the sharpest conceivable personal conflicts with the cult priests, first with Amos in Beth-el and last with Jeremiah in Jerusalem. The latter's trial (Jer. 26) suggests almost a prologue to what was to happen in the same place six hundred years later. Tradition of the events possibly exerted some actual influence later.

Jeremiah was charged with a capital crime because he had prophesied for the Temple the fate of the shrine in Shiloh which the Philistines once had destroyed. He was dragged before the court of officials and elders, and the priests and prophets of salvation acted as his accusers. However the difference of the times is evident in the result. Jeremiah was acquitted on advice of the elders, in spite of the complaint of the priests, on the ground that there existed the precedent of Micah's case. Micah, they said, had prophesied under Hezekiah similar events.[8] The occurrence indicates that prophecies against the Temple itself were rare. Above all such oracles in the last analysis implied no doubt in the Temple's legitimacy. Later, to be sure, Jeremiah readily comforted himself and others for the loss of the Ark of the Covenant under Nebuchadnezzar. His prophecy, nevertheless, deals with the destruction of the Temple as a grievous misfortune which was only conditionally held out as a punishment for sins in case of failing conversion (26:13).

In fact, no prophet attacked the Temple proper. Amos called the sacrifice in Beth-el and Gilgal transgressions (4:4; 5:5) presumably meaning by this only the cult practices of the peasants. Such cult practices were deeply hated by all representatives of shepherd piety. The people should not frequent these places, but "seek Yahwe" (ibid.). Amos knew Zion as the seat of Yahwe in the same manner as Hosea acknowledged Judah as the one undefiled seat of Yahwe. Isaiah's trust in the invincibility of Jerusalem in his late oracles doubtlessly rested on the presence there of the Temple. It was in a temple vision during his youth that he had seen the heavenly court. For Micah, despite his oracle of doom, Mount Zion remained the future place of the pure Torah and prophecy of Yahwe. The prophets preached only against the impurities of the cult practiced there, particularly against defilement by sacred courtesans. In the case of Hosea almost the whole strength of the prophet was absorbed by the fight against the worship of Baal, a fight which runs through pre-exilic prophecy. But they never preached for the correct priestly cult.

Jeremiah has evidently at first welcomed Deuteronomy and thus the centralization of the cult in the Temple of Jerusalem (2:3), but later (8:8) he terms it the product of the lying "pen of the scribes" because its authors held fast to false worship (8:5) and rejected the prophetic word (8:9). The implications of this are clarified elsewhere (7:4; 11 ff.), namely, the Temple in itself is useless and will suffer the fate of Shiloh unless the decision is made to change conduct. What is particularly stressed here,

alongside single social ethical wrongs, is trust in "unprofitable lying words" (of Zion priests) (7:8). This was the one decisive
thing, the failure of the priests to heed those divine imperatives
which the prophet announced as directly inspired by Yahwe.
Besides the prophet criticized their personal sinfulness.

Thus, in characteristic fashion, the bearer of personal charisma
refused to recognize office charisma as a qualification to teach if
the priestly teacher is personally unworthy. For, the prophet who
did not participate in the cult naturally considered the teaching
of God's word (*dabar*) as he received it as religiously all important, hence also in priestcraft the teaching (*torah*) not the
cult (Jer. 8:6; 18:18). This held also for Jerusalem (Micah 4:2).
Likewise the prophet naturally considered as important for the
people only obedience to the *debarim* and the *torah* and not the
sacrifice nor ritualistic prescriptions like observance of the Sabbath and circumcision which later in the Exile obtained such decisive significance. Even with Amos, a shepherd, Yahwe is impatient
of the Sabbath of the disobedient people,[9] and Jeremiah opposes
to external circumcision the "circumcision of the foreskin of the
heart" (9:24 ff.) as the only truly important fact.

This does not necessarily imply a denial but, rather, a strong
devaluation of all ritual. The prophets, here too, have accepted
the intellectual's conceptions which grew out of the *torah*. Yahwe,
at least according to the postulate, was a god of just ethical compensation and they considered the mundane fortune of individuals
—of which Isaiah speaks (3:10)—just as much as the direct "fruit
of their doings," as that of the people. The older prophets at least
juxtaposed this massive ethical righteousness of deeds to the
equally massive ritualism of the priests. The opposition to the
priestly evaluation of the sacrifice increased until, with Amos and
Jeremiah, it was completely depreciated. Sacrifice is not commanded by Yahwe and therefore it is useless (Jer. 6:20, 7:21).
Even Amos (5:25) argued that no sacrifice was offered in the
desert. If the people are rebellious and their hands bloody, then,
according to Isaiah (1:11 f.) their sacrifices and fasts are an
abomination to Yahwe. Considering Isaiah's relationship to the
priesthood and his esteem for the fortress-Temple, it is safe to
assume that such words imply no unconditional rejection of cult
and sacrifice. The same may well be true of the other prophets.

Nevertheless the attitude toward sacrifice in the oracles is cold to the point of enmity.

Through all prophecy sounded the echoes of the "nomadic ideal" as the tradition of the literati idealized the kingless past. To be sure, the shepherd Amos who promised Judah riches in wine (9:13) was as little a Rechabite as Jeremiah. And Jeremiah was the one prophet who entered into personal relationship with the order and upheld its piety as exemplary for Israel. But in his old age, Jeremiah bought an acre of land. Compared to the luxurious and therefore haughty present which was disobedient to Yahwe, the desert times remained to the prophets the truly pious epoch. In the end, Israel will again be reduced to a desert and the Messiah king as well as the survivors will eat the nourishment of the steppes: honey and cream.

The total attitude of the prophets has often been described as "culture hostility." This should not be understood to mean their personal lack of culture. The prophets are conceivable only on the great sounding board of the world-political stage of their times. Similarly, they are conceivable only in connection with extensive cultural sophistication and a strong cultured stratum, though, for the reasons previously discussed, only in the frame of a small state somewhat similar to Zwingli in a single canton. They were all literate and on the whole obviously well informed as to the peculiarities of Egyptian and Mesopotamian culture, especially, also, in astronomy. The manner in which the prophets used sacred numbers, for example Jeremiah's use of the number "70" may well permit us to infer that they had more than a hazy knowledge of Babylonian astronomy. In any case, tradition records no trait that would permit the inference of any attempts at flight from the world or the denial of culture in the Indian sense.

In addition to the *torah*, the prophets knew also the *chokma* or *'ezah* (Jer. 18:18) of the teachers of prudent living (*chakamin*). However, the educational level of the prophets may well have been more comparable to that of the Orphics and folk prophets of Hellas than to that of the genteel sages as represented by Thales. Not only all aesthetic and all values of genteel living in general, but, also, all worldly wisdom was viewed by them with quite alien eyes. These attitudes were sustained by the anti-chrematistic tradition of the puritanically pious in their environment who were suspicious of the court, the officials, the *gibborim* and the priests. In its inner structure, however, these attitudes of the prophets were purely religiously conditioned by the manner in which they elaborated their experiences. To these we must now turn.

6. Psychological Peculiarities of the Prophets

PSYCHOLOGICALLY viewed most pre-Exile prophets were ecstatic men. At least, Hosea, Isaiah, Jeremiah and Ezekiel professed to be and undoubtedly were. Without gross carelessness, one may safely assume that all were ecstatics, though of various kinds and in different degree.

As far as we know, the way of life of the prophets was that of peculiar men. Jeremiah, upon Yahwe's command, remained solitary, because disaster was anticipated. Hosea, upon Yahwe's command seems to have married a harlot. Isaiah, upon Yahwe's command (8:3) had intercourse with a prophetess whose child he then named as previously ordained. Strange, symbolic names of children of prophets generally were found. The prophet's ecstasy was accompanied or preceded by a variety of pathological states and acts.

There can be no doubt that these very states, originally, were considered important legitimations of prophetic charisma and, hence, were to be expected in milder forms even when not reported. Some prophets, however, expressly recount such states. Yahwe's hand "fell" upon them. The spirit of the Lord "took" them, Ezekiel (6:11; 21:14) smote with his hands, beat his loins, stamped the ground. Jeremiah was "like a drunken man," and all his bones shook (23:9).

When the spirit overcame them, the prophets experienced facial contortions, their breath failed them, and occasionally they fell to the ground unconscious, for a time deprived of vision and speech, writhing in cramps (Is. 21). After one of his visions, for seven days long Ezekiel (3:15) was paralyzed. The prophets engaged in strange activities thought to be significant as omens. Ezekiel, like a child, built himself out of tile stones and an iron pan a siege play. Jeremiah publicly smashed a jug, buried a belt and dug the putrid belt up again, he went around with a yoke around his neck, other prophets went around with iron horns, or like Isaiah for a long time, naked. Still others, like Zachariah inflicted wounds upon themselves, still others were inspired to consume filth, like Ezekiel. They screamed (*karah*) their prophecies aloud to the world, partly in indistinguishable words, partly in imprecations, threats, and benedictions with saliva running from their mouths (*hittif* "*geifern*" means to prophesy), now murmuring or stammering. They described visual and auditory hallucinations and abnormal sensations of taste and feeling of diverse sorts (Ezek. 3:2). They felt as if they were floating (Ezek. 8:3 and repeatedly) or borne through the air, they experienced clairvoyant visions of spatially distant events like, allegedly, Ezekiel in Babylon at the hour of Jerusalem's fall, or of temporally distant events to come, like Jeremiah (38:22) of Zedekiah's fate. They tasted strange foods.

Above all, they heard sounds (Ezek. 3:12 f.; Jer. 4:19), voices (Is. 40:3 f.) both single ones and dialogues, especially often, however, words and commands addressed to themselves. They saw hallucinatory blinding flashes of light and in it the figures of superhuman beings, the splendor of heaven (Is. 6, also Amos 9:1). Or they saw actually indifferent objects: a fruit basket or a plummet and suddenly to them, most usually through a voice, it was plain that these objects signified fateful decisions of Yahwe (especially Amos). Or they fall, like Ezekiel, into auto-hypnotic states. One meets with compulsive acts, above all, with compulsive speech. Jeremiah felt split into a dual ego. He implored his God to absolve him from speaking. Though he did not wish to, he had to say what he felt to be inspired words not coming from himself. Indeed, his speech was experienced by him as a horrible fate (Jer. 17:16). Unless he spoke he suffered terrible pains, burning heat seized him and he could not stand up under the heavy pressure without relieving himself by speaking. Jeremiah did not consider a man to be a prophet unless he knew this state and spoke from such compulsion rather than "from his own heart."

Such ecstatic, oracular prophets have not as yet been demonstrated in Egypt and Mesopotamia or pre-Islamic Arabia, but only in the neighborhood of Israel (as kingly prophecy like in Israel), in Phoenicia and, under rigid priestly control and interpretation, in the oracular establishments of the Hellenes. But nowhere is there a tradition of free demagoguery and prophesying ecstatics in the manner of the Israelite prophets. This could hardly be due to the lack of the respective states of mind. Rather it is because in bureaucratic kingdoms, such as the Roman empire, the religious police would have intervened. Moreover, among the Hellenes in historical times such psychic states were no longer viewed as holy, but as sicknesses and undignified and only the traditional priest-regulated oracles were generally acknowledged. In Egypt, ecstatic prophecy made its appearance only under the Ptolemies and in Arabia only in Mohammed's time.

This is not the place to classify and interpret, as far as that is possible, the various physiological, psychological, and possibly pathological states of the prophets. Attempts made thus far, especially with respect to Ezekiel, are not convincing. It affords, furthermore, no decisive interest for us. In Israel, as throughout antiquity, psychopathic states were valued as holy. Contact with madmen was taboo still in rabbinical times. The royal overseers appointed over the prophets (Jer. 29:24 f.) were called "overseers of madmen and prophets." And tradition reports that even Jehu's officer, at the sight of the prophet's disciple offering the ointment to the king to have asked "Wherefore came this mad fellow to thee?" But our concern here is with something very different.

Of interest, in the first place, is the emotional character of prophetic ecstasy *per se*, which differentiates it from all forms of Indian apathetic ecstasy. As noted earlier (p. 107/3) the pre-eminently auditive nature of classical prophecy, in contrast to the essentially visual apathetic ecstasy of the ancient "seers," was purely historically conditioned by the contrast between the Southern Yahwistic conception of Yahwe's revelation and the conception of the North. The corporeal "voice" of God appears in place of the old corporeal epiphany, which the North, with its different representation of God, theoretically rejected and which did not agree with the psychic quality of Northern piety which had sublimated orgiasticism into apathetic ecstasy. With the increasing recognition of the auditive character of the inspiration as the sole badge of authenticity was correlated the intensification of the political excitement of the listeners. This corresponded to the emotional character of prophecy.

A further important characteristic is that the prophets interpreted the meaning of their own extraordinary states, visions, compulsive speeches, and acts. Despite their obviously great psychological differences their interpretations always took the same direction. The act of interpretation *per se*, however close it seems to us today, could by no means be taken for granted. A prerequisite was that the ecstatic states were not valued for themselves, as personal and sacred possessions, but an entirely different meaning was ascribed to them, that of a mission. This is still more obvious in the homogeneity of interpretations, a point which deserves more detailed elucidation.

Only at times did the prophets speak out of direct ecstasy (Is. 21:3, 4; Jer. 4:19 f.). Usually they speak about their ecstatic experiences. The typical oracle begins with "Yahwe said unto me. . ." There are diverse shades. Ezekiel, on the one hand, squeezes whole treatises out of some of his visions although he was an apparently quite pathological and ecstatic character. On the other hand, there are numerous short verses of pre-Exile prophets which were thrust into the addressee's face in supreme passion and apparently in a state of ecstasy. The most ecstatic and timely pronouncements were forthcoming without the prophet being asked [10] but solely inspired and pressured by Yahwe. The prophet was then carried away in the face of an especially dangerous situation of the country or under an especially shattering impression of sin.

In contrast we find among the classical prophets those relatively rare cases in which the prophet had been previously asked to prophesy. He seems but rarely to have answered at once. Like Mohammed he brooded in prayer over the case; Jeremiah once did so for ten days until the ecstatic seizure occurred (Jer. 42). Even then, as a rule, the visionary or auditory experience was not at once broadcast among the tarrying listeners, for such experience was often obscure and ambiguous.

The prophet then pondered in prayer about the meaning; only when he possessed the meaning would he speak out. Some of the prophets used the form of divine speech—Yahwe spoke through them directly in the first person—other prophets used the form of reporting about Yahwe's words. Human speech predominated with Isaiah and Micah, divine speech with Amos, Hosea, Jeremiah, and Ezekiel. Finally, all prophets were given to the interpretation of events including those of their workaday life, as significant manifestations of Yahwe. (cf. especially Jer. 32).

Characteristic of the typical dicta of the pre-Exile prophets in general is that they have been spoken or, as is once said of Isaiah (5:1), chanted, in tremendous emotion. To be sure, one may find occasional verses which were perhaps left deliberately ambiguous, as was the well-known *kroisos* oracle of the Delphian Apollo and individual intellectual elaborations such as those of Ezekiel. But this was not the rule. Moreover, it is probably justifiably held that one may discern the conscious adherence to certain stylistic rules of prophetic poetry. For instance, usually the name of the person thought of is not mentioned unless it is to be cursed.

These rules did not alter the timely and emotional nature of prophecy. The conception of deity, though, delimited the content of experience. The corporeality of Yahwe's voice for the prophets meant that the prophet on the one hand felt decidedly "full of God" and on the other that the traditional nature of Yahwe's majesty precluded a true "embodiment" of God in the creature. Therefore, the euphemisms for the corporeally inaccessible were chosen.[11]

All Hellenic oracular dicta known to us were delivered on request. In their tempered and "perfect" form they do not remotely attain the emotional forcefulness of the spontaneous prophetic verses of Amos, Nahum, Isaiah, Zephaniah, and Jeremiah. In the partly fragmentary tradition, the great power of rhythm is yet surpassed by the glow of visionary images which are always concrete, telling, striking, concise, exhaustive, often of unheard of majesty and fecundity; in this regard they belong to the most grandiose productions of world poetry. They only lose in articulateness when the great acts of the invisible God on behalf of Israel had to be fashioned out of a vague vision of fantastic but indeterminate images of the future.

Whence did this emotion come if the truly ecstatic and pathological excitement was already dated and had faded out, as was often the case? The emotion simply did not flow from the pathos of these very psycho-pathological states, but from the vehement certainty of successfully having grasped the meaning of what the prophet had experienced. The prophet, unlike ordinary pathologically ecstatic men, had no vision, dreamed no dreams, and heard no mysterious voices. Rather he attained clarity and assurance through a corporeal divine voice of what Yahwe had meant by these day-dreams, or the vision, or the ecstatic excitement, and what Yahwe had commanded him to say in communicable words.

The tremendous pathos of prophetic speech in many cases was, as it were, a post-ecstatic excitement of in turn semi-ecstatic nature which resulted from the certainty of truly having stood "in Yahwe's council," as the prophets put it—to have said what Yahwe had told them or to have served as a mouthpiece, through which Yahwe literally spoke. The typical prophet apparently found himself in a constant state of tension and of oppressive brooding in which even the most banal things of everyday life could become frightening puzzles, since they might somehow be significant.

Ecstatic visions were not required to place the prophets in this state of tension. When the tension dissolved into a flash of meaningful interpretation, coming about in the hearing of the divine voice, the prophetic word burst forth. Pythia and the interpretative priestly poet were not separated here. The Israelite prophet united both in his person. This explains his tremendous élan.

Two further circumstances are important. First, these psychic states of the prophet were not connected—as, for example, was the ecstasy of Pythia—with the use of traditional ecstasy means of the Nebiim, nor, generally, with any external mass stimulation, hence, an ecstatic community. We find nothing of the kind among the classical prophets of our collection of scriptures. They did not seek ecstasy. It came to them. Besides, not one of them is reported to have been received into a guild of prophets through the laying on of hands or some such ceremony or to have belonged to any sort of specialized community. Always, rather, the prophet's calling came directly from Yahwe, and the classical prophets among them told us of their visionary or auditory "call." None of them used any intoxicants, the use of which they cursed on every occasion, as idolatry. Similarly, we hear nothing of fasting as a means of ecstasy evocation among the pre-Exile prophets, though tradition once recounts of Moses (Ex. 34:28) fasting. Thus, emotional ecstasy does not appear among them in the form of the early Christian community (and its possible antecedents).

In the apostolic age the spirit did not come upon the solitary individual, but upon the faithful assembly or upon one or several of its participants. This, at least, was the rule and the form of experience which the community evaluated as typical. The "spirit was poured out" to the community when the Gospel was preached. Speaking in tongues and other gifts of the spirit including, also, prophecy, emerged in the midst of the assembly and not in a solitary chamber. All these things obviously resulted from mass influence, or better, of mass gathering and were evidently bound up with such, at least, as normal precondition.[12] The culture-historically so extremely important esteem for the religious community as depository of the spirit in early Christendom had, indeed, this basis. The very community, the gathering of the brethren was especially productive of these sacred psychic states.

This was totally different for the ancient prophets. Precisely in solitude did the prophetic spirit come. And often the spirit first drove the prophet into solitude, into the fields or desert, as happened, still, to John and Jesus. But when the prophet was chased by his vision into the street among the multitude, this resulted only from his interpretative construction of his experience. Be it noted that this public appearance of the prophet was not motivated by the fact that the prophet could experience holiness only in public under the influence of mass suggestion like the early Christians. The prophets did not think of themselves as members of a supporting spiritual community. On the contrary. Misunderstood and hated by the mass of their listeners they never felt themselves to be supported and protected by them as like-minded sympathizers as did the apostles of the early Christian community. Hence, the prophets spoke at no time of their listeners or addressees as their "brethren." The Christian apostles always did so.

Indeed, the pathos of solitude overshadows the mood of the prophets. Before the Exile it was preponderantly hard and bitter—or again, as in the case of Hosea, it was soft, melancholy prevailed. Not ecstatic crowds, but one or several faithful disciples (Is. 8:16) shared their solitary ecstasy and their equally solitary torment. Regularly and obviously they were the disciples who recorded the prophet's visions or they had the prophet dictate his interpretations to them as Baruch, the son of Neriah, did for Jeremiah. On occasion they collected the prophecies in order to transmit them to those concerned. Once the pre-exilic prophet stepped forth and raised his voice to speak to the multitude he regularly had the feeling of facing people who were tempted by demons to do evil, to engage in Baal orgiasticism or idolatry, to commit social or ethical sins or the worst political blunder by rebelling against Yahwe's ordainment. In any case, the prophet felt himself to be standing before deadly enemies, or to face men whom his God intended to make suffer terrible misfortunes. His own sib hated him (Jer. 11:19, 21; 12:6) and Jeremiah hurled forth an anathema against his native village (11:22, 23). The prophet of doom emerged from his solitude after having experienced his visions and born out his inner conflicts. He returned to the solitude of his home viewed with horror and fear, always unloved, often ridiculed, threatened, spit upon, slapped in the face.

The sacred states of the prophets were in this sense truly personal [13] and were thus experienced by them and their audiences, and not as the product of an emotional mass influence. No sort of external influence, but his personal God-sent condition placed the prophet in his ecstatic state. And during the very epoch of the prophets the tradition and high esteem of ecstasy *per se* as holy, clearly receded into the background. After all, both prophecy and counter-prophecy confronted one another in the street. Both equally claimed ecstatic legitimation and cursed one another. Where is Yahwe's truth? everybody had to ask. The conclusion was, one cannot know the true prophet by ecstasy alone. Therewith the substantive significance of ecstasy declined, at least with respect to its manner of communication. Only exceptionally and only as a means to an end is it mentioned which emotional states the prophet has experienced in his ecstasy. For, in contrast to Indian counterparts, this did not count. Ecstasy did not guarantee genuineness. Only the hearing of the corporeal voice of Yahwe, the invisible God, assured the prophet that he was Yahwe's tool. Hence, the tremendous emphasis upon this point.

This, the hearing of the voice of Yahwe, is the prophet's self-legitimation, not the nature of his holy states. Hence, the prophet abstained from gathering a community about him which might have engaged in mass ecstasy or mass-conditioned ecstasy or ecstatic revivals as a path to salvation. Nothing whatever is known of this with regard to classical Yahwe-prophecy. The nature of its message contradicted it. Unlike the possession of pneuma in the early Christian sources, the prophet's attainment of a state of ecstasy or his ability to hear Yahwe's voice is nowhere said to be a prerequisite also for his audience. Prophetic charisma rather was a unique burdensome office—often experienced as torment. Unlike early Christian prophets, the Yahwe prophets never aimed at allowing the spirit to come over the audience.

On the contrary, the prophetic charisma is their privilege. It is a free gift of godly grace without any personal qualification. In the accounts of their ecstasy of calling, this first ecstasy, giving the prophet his "call," is never presented as the fruit of asceticism or contemplation or moral attainments, penances, or other merits. On the contrary, it was always in agreement with the endogenous nature of the psychic state, a sudden unmotivated occurrence. Yahwe called Amos away from the flocks. An angel of Yahwe laid a glowing coal upon Isaiah's mouth, Yahwe himself touched with his hand the mouth of Jeremiah and thus consecrated them. At times, the prophet resisted, like Jeremiah, with anxiety, this charisma which was laid on him as a duty; at times he offered himself joyfully to the God in quest of a prophet, like Isaiah.

And, in contrast to Indian as well as Hellenic prophets of the type of Pythagoras and the Orphics and, also, the Rechabite Puritans, no Israelite prophet ever thought of taking to a ritualistic or ascetic path of salvation superior to workaday ethic. Nothing of the sort. This shows the great importance of the *berith*-conception, which unambiguously established what Yahwe demanded of his people in connection with the Levite Torah, which had fixed the divine imperatives as universally binding. Here it came to fruition, that the Torah did not develop out of the personal quest for salvation of literary stratum of genteel thinkers, but out of the cure of souls by practitioners, ministering the confession and atonement of sins. Without regard to this circumstance the entire development remains completely incomprehensible. It found its expression also in the qualification of the prophecy.

We noted that ecstasy as such no longer served as legitimation, but solely the perception of Yahwe's voice served this function. But what assured the audience that the prophet had actually, as he maintained, heard the voice of Yahwe? This question was answered in part historically, in part religiously and ethically. Historical conditions and Yahwe's ominous nature determined Jeremiah (23:29) to present as criterion the traditional opposition to the kingly prophets of good fortune. The explanation is to be found in the social struggle against kingship and its servitudes and the *gibborim*. The true prophet held out no good to the great ones.

Commitment to Yahwe's commandment as known to all (23:22) was ethically conditioned. Only the prophet who morally exhorted the people and sanctioned sins (through threats of doom) was not a lying prophet. Yahwe's commandments, however, were generally known through the Torah. Thus the Torah is always the completely self-evident presupposition of all prophecy. It is seldom explicitly referred to because it went without saying.

The Hellenic teachers of wisdom of the sixth century, too, preached the unconditionally binding character of the moral law. Substantively this law was similar to that of the prophets—as the social ethic of the Hellenic *aisymnete* enactments is intrinsically related to that of the Book of the Covenant. But the difference was that in Hellas as in India the specifically religious saviors and prophets joined salvation to special prerequisites of a ritualistic or ascetic nature, indeed that they were bringers of "salvation" and especially of salvation in the beyond. In the precise reverse, the Israelite prophets annunciated doom, at that, in the here and now and this in retribution for sins of Israelites against the universally binding law of their God. By upholding abiding adherence to this workaday ethic as a special duty of Israel by virtue of the sworn *berith,* the mighty pathos of eschatological threats and promises worked for adherence to these plain commandments which all were able to follow and which, in the view of the prophets, also non-Israelites would abide by at the end of time. The great historical paradox was that the later official workaday ethic of the Christian West, which substantially differed from ancient Hellenic and later Hellenist theory and everyday practice only in sexual matters, here was raised to a special ethical duty of a people chosen by its God, the mightiest of all, and exhorted by utopian promises and punishments. The special promise of salvation held out to Israel made morally correct action and the abidance by everyday ethic all important. However banal and self-evident this may seem, here alone it was made the basis of religious prophecy. Highly special conditions led to this result.

CHAPTER XII

THE ETHIC AND THEODICY
OF THE PROPHETS

1. The Prophetic Ethic

By virtue of their calling the prophets laid claim to special qualities. The expression "spirit" (*ruach*) of Yahwe was rarely applied and only by one of these pre-exilic prophets (Is. 30:1; Mic. 3:8) for their special endowment, although occasionally (Hos. 9:7) the expression "spiritual man" (*ish haruach*) is employed by a scriptural prophet. The expression first appears frequently with Ezekiel, then with Deutero-Isaiah and the post-exilic prophets. Apparently the opposition to professional Nebiim led the older prophets to avoid the term, or use it but rarely. Besides *ruach* in linguistic usage denoted essentially the irrational and transitory states of ecstasy, whereas the prophets located their sense of dignity precisely in the habitual possession of consciously clear and communicable interpretation of Yahwe's intention. For the first time with Ezekiel was *ruach* viewed again as a mysterious divine power, which to disdain was sacrilegious like in the Evangels. First in the Exile (Deutero-Isaiah 40:13; 42:1; 48:16), "*ruach*" became a transcendant, and finally (Gen. 1:2) a cosmic entity which Trito-Isaiah first termed "holy spirit" (63:10 f.).

However, if the prophetic charisma first means the ability rationally to understand Yahwe, it nevertheless contains quite different irrational potentialities. The first of these is magical power.

Isaiah is the only scriptural prophet mentioned as medical

consultant during a sickness of King Hezekiah. In a politically difficult situation he asked King Ahab to demand from him confirmation of his political oracle by a miracle. The king was evasive and Isaiah thereupon spoke the famous words concerning the "young woman" who was already expecting with the savior prince Immanuel. As the situation indicates, this was not only a prophecy, but the pronouncement of a decision of Yahwe. This pronouncement effected the promised good and resulted from the king's lack of faith. The prophets had the power to kill through their words (Hos. 6:5; Jer. 28:16, 17). Jeremiah gave a messenger a curse formula to take along to Babylon in the expectation that its reading and drowning in the Euphrates would effect the predicted doom. But wonders are never effected by any sort of sympathetic or other magical manipulation; only by simple (spoken or written) word. Above all, this magical power—so important in Jesus' image of self—receded completely into the background in the prophets' revelation of self.

They never mention it as proof of their divine legitimation and actually do not claim it personally. Certainly Jeremiah knew himself to have been set by Yahwe over all nations (1:10) to destroy them or to offer them the "cup of fury" (25:15 f.). However this self-awareness always changed into the consciousness of being no more than a tool. Not the prophet's own will but the decision of Yahwe imparted by his corporeal voice, his "word" (Jer. 23:29) will effect the prophecy. The prophet claimed only to know these decisions, Yahwe's miraculous power and its workings. "Yahwe does nothing," Amos assured, "without first revealing it to his prophets." This was the source of their self-assurance. To some extent the prophets also claimed the ability to influence the decisions of Yahwe. Already with Amos the prophet occasionally appears as intercessor, as the tradition ascribes this function to Moses and also to Abraham. But Yahwe would not always listen to pleas. Occasionally he declared himself unwilling to change his mind, even if Moses or Samuel would come before him. And the prophet did not even reckon with the possibility of influencing Yahwe by magic. On the contrary, that would be a mortal sin before this frightful god. The prophet turned just as little into a redeemer, were it only in intent, nor into an exemplary religious virtuoso. He never claimed the right to be worshipped in the manner of hagiolatry, he never claimed to be free of sin.

The ethical demands which the prophet placed upon himself were no different from those of all. Of course, there appears as a sure sign of the lying prophets, beside their failure morally to exhort the people and to threaten disaster, also their own failure to be converted and obey the divine imperatives, a permanently important characteristic, rich in consequences. But Jeremiah, for instance, never claimed to be morally infallible. At Zedekiah's instigation he told a falsehood in order not to expose the king to the partisans of Egypt (38:14 ff.). This was in agreement with the ethic of the patriarchs and, by the way, with the fact that Yahwe himself put the "lying spirit" to his service—the duty of truthfulness of the ancient Israelite (also of the Decalogue) as well as the Homeric ethic is not so absolute as that of the Indian and is surpassed by the demands, for example, of the Sirachid. In any case, it indicates that the prophet who as such claimed unconditional faith, separated his office from his personal behavior. The Torah would hardly have approved of the tremendous excesses of hatred and wrath against opponents typical of some prophets. To be sure, Yahwe occasionally seemed to join the effect of his words upon the hearts of the people to the condition that the prophet speak pleasing "noble words." For the rest, Jeremiah considered himself "impure" and weak. No prophet judged himself in possession of holiness. He was nothing but a means for the communication of divine imperatives. He always remained a tool and servant of his respective mission.

The emissary type of prophecy had never been more completely developed. More even than in the ancient Christian community. No prophet belonged to an esoteric "association" like the later apocalytics. No prophet thought of founding a "congregation." It is a sociologically decisive difference as over against early Christian prophecy, that there were no pre-conditions for this and given the mentality of the prophets it eliminated the possibility of a communal cult as represented by that of *Kyrios Christos*. The prophets stood in the midst of their people and were interested in the fate of its political community. They were interested in ethics, not in cult, in contrast to the

Christian missionaries who offered, above all, the Lord's Supper as a means of grace. At this point an element of the early Christendom is indeed evident, which stemmed from the mysteries of late antiquity and which was completely alien to the prophets. All this, in turn, is connected with the peculiar nature of the Israelite relation of the deity in whose name the prophets speak, and with the meaning of their prophecy. Both, however, provided them their religious climate of opinion which had been prepared by the Israelite intellectuals, particularly the Levite Torah. As can be discerned, they neither announced a new conception of God, nor new means of grace, nor even new commandments. At least, they had no intention of doing so. It is presupposed that God is known to all and that "He hath shewd thee, O man what is good" (Mic. 6:8). This was: to abide by those commandments of God which are known from the Torah. Isaiah called also the Torah of God his own prophecy (30:9). The prophets throughout refer to transgressions of these well-known commandments.

Similarly, their environment furnished the problems central to their prophecy. The popular fear of war surged up to them with the question as to the reasons of God's wrath, for means to win his favor, and the national hope for the future in general. Panic, rage, thirst for vengeance against the enemy, fear of death, mutilation, devastation, exile (even with Amos), enslavement, and the question whether it be correct to resist, submit to, or seek alliance with Egypt or Assur, or Babel—all these agitated the people and reacted upon prophecy. The social unrest influenced the inner core of their representations, even when they appeared in public by their own volition.

The question for the why of the misfortune was answered from the beginning thus: Yahwe, their own god, willed it so. Simple as that appears it was anything but self-evident. For, however many single traits of universalism the conception of god had absorbed, at least in the mind of the intellectuals, it would have better corresponded with popular opinion to assume either that the foreign deities, for the time being, were for some reason stronger or that Yahwe didn't care to help his people. Prophecy, however, surpassed the latter possibility and maintained that he willed misfortune on his people. Amos asked "shall there be evil in a city, and the Lord hath not done it?" (3:6).

Opinion differed as to whether such godly decisions were temporarily determined, as most oracles presupposed, or whether Yahwe of ancient times had ordained doom as Isaiah (37:26) maintained. Judgment differed according to the circumstance, particularly whether the wrathful god of the confederacy or the sublime world-monarch stood more in the foreground. In either case, however, Amos' contention, so horrible for popular opinion, grew out of the special historical basis of Yahwism. Decisive in this connection was what Amos (4:10) elaborately recalls, namely that Yahwe was of yore primarily a god of natural catastrophes who could and often did send pestilence and frightful misfortunes of all sorts against those who evoked his wrath. He had repeatedly visited military disaster on the enemy and rescued Israel; often, however, this was only after having let his people suffer such misfortune for quite a time. Therefore, and for this reason alone, the prophets became politicians. Now political disaster stood ominously at the gate, doom that pertained to Isaiah's true sphere of activity. Initially, political misfortune was second to the expected cosmic catastrophes of nature, but its significance steadily mounted in the prophecy of doom. It must be ascribed to Yahwe and no other god. He was, however, on the other hand, the god who had known only Israel of all families of the earth. "Therefore," Amos (3:2) with deliberate paradox had him say, "I will punish you for all your iniquities." Israel alone stood in *berith* to him the breach of which Hosea, perhaps the first to have here fixed the opposition of the Lord's people to the impure "nations" (9:1 f.), compared to adultery. Yahwe had made certain promises to the forefathers and given an oath. He had kept his promises and had brought immeasurable blessing to the people in war and peace. The prophets admonish him not to break his covenant and he, in turn, asked (Jer. 2:5) what iniquity—i.e., what deviation from his covenant—had the forefathers of Israel found in him?

The fulfillment of the promises was conjoined to the condition not only that they remain contractually faithful only to him as their single god and not turn to others, but that they also and

above all abide by his commandments and especially those
which he had laid on them alone. This is the view of most of
the prophets of Amos, Micah, Jeremiah, but also Isaiah. According even to Amos there were iniquities for which Yahwe
as world monarch also punished other nations, especially, the
neighbors of Israel. To this belonged (Amos 1:3 ff.) the violation
of a form of international religious law which was presupposed
as valid among Palestine peoples. Of course, Yahwe above all
punished violations against Israel, the barbaric devastation of
Gilead by the Damascenes, kidnapping and sale of prisoners,
to the Edomites by Gaza and Tyrus, the pitilessness of the
Edomites in war, the ripping up of pregnant women by the Ammonites. In this there was nothing special. However, Yahwe
also punished the injustice of a third people against another,
such as the burning of an Edomite kingly corpse by Moabites.
In this is revealed the culture community of the Palestine peoples, which is interpreted as a tribal relationship. Perhaps it
signifies also a relationship of international law.

The Edomites are reproached for the violation of "brotherly"
relations to Israel; Tyrus is even charged with having disregarded a "brotherly league," hence, presumably a sworn military agreement of international law concerning the treatment of
prisoners of war. It appears possible that similar agreements also
existed with other neighboring peoples, agreements which caused
Yahwe's vengeance. The purely ethical turn was consummated
with the rise of the universalist conception of god. Opposite
the Mesopotamian great kings, Isaiah sees the reason for
Yahwe's wrath in their excessively cruel warfare, and the *hybris*
of these world monarchs aroused Yahwe's jealousy.

In contrast to this, according to Amos, Israel itself was punished because of all guilt. It draws his wrath upon itself particularly through the violation of "righteousness" and that meant
violation of its peculiar social institutions. Most of the prophets,
thus, considered the imperatives of brotherliness which the
Levite exhortation had developed in connection with the ancient
legal collections. Amos characteristically posed alongside one
another (2:6 f.) the seduction of the Nazarites to the breaking
of their ritual duties and the oppression of the Nebiim and the
breaking of the commandments of the Book of the Covenant

concerning the treatment of imprisoned Israelite debtors and concerning the pawning of clothes, hence, elements of the ancient military and social organization, which during the times of the confederacy stood under Yahwe's protection. The special position of Yahwe to Israel as contractual partner of the confederacy is especially obvious in this. In their oracles other prophets, besides gross private sins (essentially the sins of the Decalogue), adduce chiefly unbrotherliness in all its forms, especially, however, as in all Mid-Eastern and Egyptian charity ethics, the oppression of the poor in court and through usury. In all these motivations of Yahwe's wrath, even in the deliberate paradoxes of Amos, may be discerned the impact of an intensive culture of intellectuals.

Social ethical motivations of godly punishment are also to be found elsewhere. The patrimonial bureaucracy of the neighboring great kingdoms always had given rise to the patriarchal and charitable ideal of the "welfare state," and there it was universally believed that precisely the curse of the poor against the oppressor be the harbinger of evil. This idea apparently through Phoenician mediation, also appeared in Israel. The kings of Mesopotamia in their inscriptions reproach their conquered opponents of having visited social iniquities on their subjects (already Urukagina, also, Cyrus). And in Chinese sources, with the change of dynasties or with the conquest of a single state of another ruler, frequent reference is made to illegal treatment of subjects and unclassical deportment. In all such cases this argument is the product of priestly or ritualistic strata of intellectuals in bureaucratic states. Israel was unique, in the first place, only in that the claim on the charity of ruling strata, above all, the royal officials, were borrowed demands which elsewhere usually followed the development of a national bureaucratic machine and a corresponding cultural stratum.[1] Whereas this development of patrimonial kingship as such was rejected by pious Israelite intellectuals in favor of the ancient ideas of district princes. And further, it is unique that the motivation is to be found in the threats of disaster of prophets and that they hold out punishment not only personally for the rulers, but the people as a whole which out of the *berith* solidarity is jointly responsible for the sins of the kings and the great. This was connected with the peculiarity of the political and religious constitution of Israel.

Also elsewhere with the prophets we discern the intellectual accomplishments of the Israelite administration of justice and the teaching of wisdom. Besides their own oracles, the *debarim Yahwe*, the prophets name as authoritative sources of morality, *chuk*, that is, as noted, ancient custom as determined through legal oracles of the *chokekim* and *torah*, the rational Levitical teaching (Amos 2:4; Is. 24:5) and finally *mishpat*, the law proclaimed in verdicts (Is. 16:5) and statutes of the *sarim* and *sekenim*. The binding nature of these norms was not contended and the *chokma*, the rules of prudent living taught by teachers of wisdom was not rejected in principle despite the prophets' occasionally sharp opposition against the judges, especially the *sarim*, the *chokekim* and also the teachers of the Torah, who speak merely vain words. To be sure, the prophets' attitudes differed. As noted, none of them raised the claim to annunciate new commandments as Jesus on occasion emphatically did: "It is written, but I say unto you. . . ." But the falsification of the long-revealed true will of Yahwe through the "lying pen of the scribes" and the "unrighteous decrees" which the *chokekim* gave to the disadvantage of the poor (Is. 10:1 f.) are sinful just as the repeatedly branded injustice of bribed judges. Occasionally, the prophets drawn into the counsel of Yahwe, out of his sovereignty completely reject the value of both the *chokma* and the commandments (*mitzwot*) which the teachers honor with their lips (Is. 29:13, 14). Jeremiah's personal scepticism of the teachers was still greater. But this did not change the fact that the positive commandments of the Levite Torah in substance were identical with those of the prophets.

The significance of the Torah for the prophets went beyond the substantive presentation of the commandments. The fundamental prophetic idea that Yahwe ordains terrible misfortunes for moral and especially social-ethical trespasses originated in the Levitical practice of confession and expiation and its development through rational moral exhortation. Also, the transfer of the idea of God's vengeance of sins and failings of individuals to the people as a unit is certainly pre-prophetic no matter how old the priestly ritual of penance for entire communities as stated in our version of the scriptures may be. For this important idea developed out of the never-forgotten nature of Israel as by the *berith* jointly liable association of freemen. The oracles of Amos presuppose this theodicy of misfortune. But like every theodicy it probably first was an idea shared only by intellectual strata. Probably then unheard of was its forceful pronouncement in public by a visionary such as Amos in explanation of the disaster at hand. This explains the tremendous impression he made, which is attested to by the fact that the oracles of this prophet were the first to be preserved. An additional factor, of course, was the actual advent of the disaster which had, indeed, been prophesied in the time of political and economic prosperity under the rule of Jeroboam II. We have emphasized above that the place of classical prophecy was determined by the waning power of and mounting threat to both kingdoms. This should not be misunderstood. These factors did not cause prophets of doom *per se* to arise. Even Elijah stood up to the king as a prophet of disaster and prophecies of misfortune were directed against the people possibly even before Amos.

The prophets' visions of doom were "personally" ("endogenously") determined. Reading their scriptures, one sees at a glance that the hard, bitter and passionately stern temperaments in most of these personalities were pre-formed dispositions without concern for the situation of the moment. They viewed the world as doomed precisely at the height of seeming happiness. Amos did not mention Assur by name. It is called "the enemy" and the prophesied exile was to take place "beyond Damascus." That was plain enough. As the reason for seeing the advent of disaster thence the prophet stated the worship of Mesopotamian deities (5:27). The prophets based their somber forebodings not on the world situation but on the all round corruption. Such presentiments also recurred to Isaiah precisely after Sennacherib's retreat in contrast to his previous trust in victory (22:14). The actual advent of misfortune seemed rather to relieve the prophets. The corruption which they saw around them at long last seemed to find its compensation and therewith exoneration.

It remains, of course, more than questionable to what extent one may therefore speak of a specific "personality type" of the prophet in the sense of ascribing to him an unambiguous predisposition for this emotional state. For, the fragmentary remains of their oracles themselves permit us to discern basic differences in temper such as the impetuous, burning, unbroken passion of Amos, the tenderness and warmth of the wooing of Hosea, the steely noble and self-assured élan and the strong and profound enthusiasm of Isaiah. Jeremiah's tender soul suffered grievously from emotional depressions and *idées fixes,* but he disciplined himself by force of his calling to a desperate heroism. This contrasts with the ecstatically excited but inwardly cold intellectualism of Ezekiel. All these contrasts may be grasped and still they change nothing in the prophecies of doom. The following circumstance constitutes striking proof. With the definitive fall of the temple the prophecy of doom came to an end and the consolation and prediction of hope began. Hence, the prophecy of doom resulted from the horror of the abominable desertion of Yahwe and his commandments and from terrible fear of the consequences, from the unshakable faith in the promise of Yahwe and the desperate conviction that the people had forfeited or were about to forfeit it.

Obviously, the prophet of doom entertained changing views concerning the degree of probability with which the frightful disaster impended. At times, especially for Amos and Jeremiah, occasionally also the youthful Isaiah, all hope seemed vain. At times there was the possibility, probability, even certainty of salvation or—that is the rule—the return to better times after the doom. No prophet absolutely and permanently opposed this hope. And he could not have done so if he wished to exert any influence on his audience. This influence, however, was to the prophets, in spite of the personal nature of their ecstasy, no matter of indifference. They felt themselves to be "watchmen and testers" appointed by Yahwe. Jeremiah considered a true prophet only one who lashed the sins of the people and—in connection therewith—prophesied disaster. But misfortune must not be absolute and definitive, but conditional through sin.

The prophets, already Isaiah, still more Jeremiah, wavered in their attitudes. Where they would act pedagogically they portrayed Yahwe as a god who would repent his decisions. When they spoke under the direct impression of corruption, all appeared vain and hopeless. The pedagogical objections of the practitioners of cure of soul, especially the teachers of Torah had quite some weight with the prophets. This is shown by the paradigmatic story of Jonah as over against Isaiah's incipient conception of a predestination of destructive fate. The story of Jonah stemmed obviously from intellectual circles and its actual theme is to preclude the unchangeability of the prophecy of doom and instead to justify the changeability of Yahwe's decisions.

The ecstatics, of course, given to their visions, have not expressly engaged in such considerations which could be decisive for the Torah teachers, concerned with the curing of souls, and this was still more the case for the priestly editors. On the other hand, this is no reason to assume that only the priestly editors had put the prophecies of good into the mouth of the prophets. For one recognizes distinctly how the pedagogical intent enters with the prophets, with Amos only once (5:15), with Hosea several times, and still more often with Isaiah, and, despite his pessimism, most strongly and as a matter of principle with Jeremiah (7:23). Besides, against acceptance of the interpolation speaks the presence of certain definite categories of salvation such as that of the timely converting "remnant" even with the first prophets (Amos). Rather, the traditional hope of the supplementary exhortations to the covenant code proper and the recurrent spontaneous thought that the misfortune could hardly be the end of Yahwe's plans for Israel, made for the constant revival of hopeful promises, however vague in form and held out only to that "remnant that shall stay upon the Lord." The pedagogical intention was increasingly helpful even if the single prophet in anguish visualized nothing but gloomy fate. In any case one can hardly assume an unambiguous psychological determination for "political hypochondria" to be the source of their attitudinal position.

The prophecy of doom can largely be traced to the psychic dispositions of the prophets, as conditioned by constitution and experience. It is no less certain that it was indeed the historical fate of Israel, which provided this prophecy with its position in the religious development. Naturally tradition has preserved the very oracles of prophets which came true or appeared to have come true or the coming true of which could still be expected.

The increasingly unshakable prestige of prophecy in general rested on the few, but for the contemporaries tremendously impressive cases, which unexpectedly bore the prophecy out as right. This applied, first, to Amos' oracles of disaster concerning the then mighty Northern Kingdom, then to Hosea's oracles of doom for the dynasty of Jehu and for Samaria. Then there was Isaiah's oracle of good fortune for Jerusalem, during the siege of Sennacherib. Despite all probabilities to the contrary, with the sureness of a sleep walker, he admonished the citizenry to hold out. And although the final result was a veiled submission of the king, it appears certain that the siege of Jerusalem did not lead to a capitulation, for Sennacherib himself did not maintain this in his account. Above all, the conquest and destruction of Jerusalem confirmed the frightful oracles of disaster of the youthful Isaiah, of Micah and especially of Jeremiah and Ezekiel. Apparently the prestige of prophecy had suffered a decline after the disappointing battle of Meggido. With the predicted return from the Exile, however, the authority of the prophets became unshakable. People completely forgot that the greater number of oracles, even those included in the scriptures, had not been fulfilled.

In the face of this is benefited prophecy that from the beginning, even by Amos, the changeability of Yahwe's resolves had been expressly retained. This permitted the followers of the prophets to retreat behind it. After all, the penance practice of the Levites likewise presupposed this changeability, since forgiveness of sins guaranteed the warding off of threatened disaster. Therefore, for the prophets Yahwe is ever again a god of grace and forgiveness, however much he remained in their eyes a god of wrath and revenge and however severely, in single cases, he exercised his wrath. That he was such, distinguished him in the eyes of the prophets from all other deities. An element of tenderness runs through such prophecies of grace to be found especially with Hosea and Jeremiah, but also in some oracles of Isaiah. Yahwe woos the faith of Israel like a lover.

On the whole Yahwe's features, even where this benevolent aspect was emphasized, had to assume incomparably greater majesty than in the literary products of circles of Torah scholars, as represented by Deuteronomy. God could use the great kings as a means of punishing a sinning Israel and manipulate them at his pleasure. The universalism and majesty of such a god had to rise to new heights over that of the old god of the Israelite confederacy and the bourgeois dispenser of grace of the Levites. All prophets preferred, without doubt in deliberate continuity with the ancient heroic age, the name "Yahwe Zebaoth" hence the designation of the war god of the confederacy. But now his features are fused with those of a god of the whole great heaven and world. The royal court of the great kings played for Israel a role similar to that of the Persian *basileus* for the Hellenes, as, for instance, in Xenophon's *Cyropaedia,* although he was also an enemy of the country. This court supplied the image of the heavenly courtly state, where the ancient warlord no longer was surrounded by his following, the "sons of god," but had at his service a host of heavenly spirits, whose very attire was fashioned after Bablyonian and Egyptian models. Seven spirits corresponding to the seven planets surrounded his throne. Among them was one with a pen dressed in linen corresponding to the god of the scribes. His spies rode horses in colors of the four Babylonian wind gods, roving through the world and reporting the news. The king of heaven, in supernatural splendor, rode a wagon with cherubs, clearly comparing to the Babylonian hieratic figures. Nevertheless it still happened that he called out the spirits of nature to bear witness against treaty-breaking Israel as in a trial. But, as a rule he is the sovereign lord of the entire world of creatures. The mild benevolence which occasionally is available to him in no way prevented that he was in turn, like the secular kings, characterized by quite amoral traits. As the Indian patrimonial kings sent their *agents provocateurs,* so he sent his "lying spirit" to blind his enemy. His own prophets occasionally shuddered before him. Isaiah called his judgment against Assur "barbaric," a power which he himself had called upon as a tool. Ezekiel (20:25) was not at all shocked by Yahwe's similar plans to destroy the enemies of Israel whom he had called himself. But he also believed that Yahwe had given laws for the destruction of his own people.

Scriptural tradition takes for granted that Yahwe deliberately sent false advice to disobedient Israelite kings. Only Hosea (11:9) took offense at such traits and if the version, which is controversial between Wellhausen and others, is correct, he let Yahwe say that nothing was done "from passion" because he was "holy and no destroyer." The experience that Israel would reject and disregard the clear prophetic word just the same convinced also Isaiah that Yahwe himself did not wish it otherwise, that he even hardened the people in order to destroy it. This idea, also important in the New Testament and later in Calvinism, originated here. For Yahwe remained quite different through his traits of actual-passionate behavior from the Hellenic world-god, for instance, of Xenophanes. Thus, all in all, he remained a fearful god. Often, the ultimate purpose of his acts appeared to be solely the glorification of his own majesty over all creatures. This he had in common with the mundane rulers of the world. Therefore his total image remained uncertain. One and the same prophet saw him now in super-human holy purity and again as the ancient warrior god with a changeable heart. If he thus retained highly anthropomorphic features, the most sensitive of the prophets, unlike the ancient Yahwistic narrators, no longer dared to endow his visions of heavenly splendor with realistic traits, at least, not with regard to the person of the invisible god of yore. What they see is "like a throne," however no real throne. Also, Isaiah saw only the flowing robe, not God himself.

The abode of Yahwe remained as ambiguous as his nature. Even Amos said that he had created heaven and earth and had assigned to the celestial constellations their places. This, however, did not prevent him, according to the same prophet from "roaring from Zion." Isaiah had his vision of divine majesty as a Temple vision. This localization had to endanger the prestige of Yahwe at the downfall of the Temple. Innumerable sanctuaries had been seen devastated by the conquerors and their idols dragged off unable to defend themselves.

Could that also happen to Yahwe? The prophets were uncertain. In contrast to his previous threats, Isaiah, after Sennacherib's leave, was firmly convinced, according to many late oracles, that Jerusalem as the seat of Yahwe could never fall. However, after Amos and Hosea had predicted the downfall of the Northern Kingdom as Yahwe's intention, the downfall of Jerusalem itself was conceived as a god-ordained fate even in Isaiah's early oracles, since Micah and definitely since Jeremiah. The ultimate advent of this fate, hence, did not only not diminish but enhance god's prestige. The deities of the victorious great kings could not be the authors of this catastrophe. They were besmirched with the abomination of temple harlotry and idolatry or even with the despicable animal worship of the Egyptians. Hence, all such deities of other nations could at best be viewed as demons and were "nobodies" against Yahwe. With Hosea appeared the scorn and ridicule of idol worship and the intellectuals argued with increasing consistency that the idol was man-made, hence religiously meaningless, least however the seat of a god.

The thesis that other deities did not exist at all has not even been maintained by Deutero-Isaiah during the time of Exile. Meanwhile, through the prophets' theodicy of misfortune Yahwe actually ascended to the rank of the one god deciding the course of the world. Especially important in this, first, was that he retained the old features of the frightful god of catastrophe. Moreover, the theodicy of misfortune was brought into relation to the confessional practice of the Levite Torah. And finally, in connection with both of the above, Amos gave a turn to the *berith* idea which made Yahwe himself the cause of all misfortune.

The consequence of all this was that to the prophet's mind, there existed no demons of any sort besides Yahwe. No independent or anti-Yahwe demons were necessary to bring misfortune to individuals and to Israel. Yahwe alone determined the details of the world. As we have seen, this monism was the most important presupposition of all prophecy. The universally diffused folk belief in demons only penetrated the religiosity of the intellectuals of post-exilic Jewry. This penetration was completed only under the influence of Persian dualism. The prophets were certainly not unacquainted with the Babylonian belief in demons. However, it remained as irrelevant for their conceptions as the astrological, mythological and esoteric doctrines of the surrounding world. Yahwe had been the god of a political association, namely, the old confederacy and retained this role in the puritanical conception. This made him preserve one indelible characteristic throughout the adopted cosmic and historical universalism, namely, he was a god of action, not of eternal order. This quality was decisive for the character of the religious relationship.

Even the direct experiences of the prophets were fashioned by their conception of the immutable qualities of this god. The imagination centered always around the image of a heavenly king of frightful majesty. This concerned, first, their visual experiences. The role of vision, as we saw, differed with the various prophets. It was most important for the oldest prophet, Amos, who, therefore, was also called "seer" (*chozeh*). Visions, however, were not absent with the other prophets, particularly Isaiah and Ezekiel. And the prophet saw also other things than simply the heavenly splendor. Clairvoyantly, he saw in the distance an advancing army on a mountain pass. Or, from Babylon, he saw a man, mentioned by name, die in the Temple of Jerusalem. Or the prophet was seized by his hair and a being consisting of fiery brilliance removed him from Babylon to Jerusalem. But always it was a matter of his realizing the direct intervention of the divine and royal Lord. Or, when the prophet saw an almond bough or a basket with fruit this had some sort of meaning and was a symbol fashioned by God. Sometimes it was in dreams, but particularly often it was in a waking dream that these visions pressed upon the prophets.

Acoustic experiences of the prophets, as has been discussed in another connection, in characteristic fashion much surpassed such visual experiences. The prophet either heard a voice which spoke to him, commanded him, and charged him with a mission to communicate, possibly also to perform, or, as we saw in the case of Jeremiah, a voice spoke out of him, whether he would or not. The superior importance of these auditory experiences to visions, as indicated, was no accident. It was bound with the tradition of the invisible god, which precluded the telling of anything about him or his appearance. But it also resulted from the one way open to the prophet of realizing inwardly a relationship to this god. Nowhere do we find the prophets mystically emptying their mind of all thought and perception of sense matter and structured objects, a process which initiates apathetic ecstasy in India. Nowhere do we find the tranquil, blissful euphoria of the god-possessed, rarely the expression of a devotional communion with God and nowhere the merciful pitying sentiment of brotherhood with all creatures typical of the mystic. The god of the prophets lived, ruled, spoke, acted in a pitiless world of war and the prophets knew themselves placed in the midst of a tragic age. Above all, several of the prophets themselves were deeply tragic men. Not all were, and not always, but often and precisely in the moment of greatest nearness to God.

Among the pre-Exile prophets Hosea experienced the state of being seized by Yahwe's spirit as a fortunate possession. Amos experienced as the support of proud self-assurance the knowledge of being initiated into all his plans. Isaiah craved the honor of prophecy. However, even he felt, at times, weighted down by his office in view of the frightful severity in some announcements of God and his resolutions. For Jeremiah, finally, the prophetic commission meant an unbearable load. At least he never experienced the presence of Yahwe as a blissful incumbency of the godhead, but rather always as a duty and command, mostly as a hectic stormy demand. Jeremiah felt raped by Yahwe like a maiden by a man or overpowered like a surmounted wrestler. This important religious-historical fact is basically different from all Indian and Chinese prophecy, it resulted only partly from psychic preconditions of the prophet, and partly from the necessity meaningfully to interpret his experiences. He was constrained by the nature of the belief which was inescapable. It stood as an unshakable *a priori* to all their experiences and determined the selection of such psychic states as could qualify as truly prophetic. The unexampled force, as well as the firm inner barriers, of this prophecy rested on this ground. Because of this *a priori* the prophets could not be "mystics." Their god was—to Deutero-Isaiah—quite understandable by man and had to be. For he was a ruler of whom one desired to know how to obtain his grace. Neither the prophets nor (so far as we know) their public ever raised the question as to the "meaning" of the world and especially of life in the attempt to justify its fragmentary, woeful, and guilty transitoriness and its contradictions. Such questions gave the decisive motive of all holy knowledge in India.

In connection with this the prophet or his public had never in any way been driven to seek God out of the need for salvation, redemption, and perfection of the soul as against this imperfect world. Moreover the prophet never felt himself deified by his experience, united with the godhead, removed from the torment and meaninglessness of existence, as happened to the redeemed in India, and for him represented the true meaning of his religious experience. The prophet never knew himself emancipated from suffering, be it only from the bondage of sin. There was no room for a *unio mystica,* not to mention the inner oceanic tranquility of the Buddhistic *arhat.* Nothing of the sort existed. Finally there was no thought of a metaphysical gnosis and interpretation of the world. The nature of Yahwe contained nothing supernatural in the sense of something extending beyond understanding. His motives were not concealed from human comprehension.

On the contrary, the task of the prophet as well as the Torah teacher was, indeed, to understand Yahwe's counsels in terms of justifiable motives. Yahwe was even prepared to represent before the court of the world the justice of his cause. Isaiah (28:23-29), in a parable taken from farm life presented the nature of Yahwe's world government plainly and obviously exhaustively. This sufficed as a theodicy just as fully as the quite similar parables of Jesus who, in this respect, proceeded from quite similar presuppositions. Like prophecy itself, world events are rational in character; they are determined neither by blind chance nor magical forces. They have understandable reasons. Also, later Jewry felt it to be specific of their prophets that their oracles in contrast to gnostic esoterics could be understood by everybody. "Inscrutability" in principle was out of the question, however incomparable Yahwe's horizon was to that of the creature. This principled understandability of the divine counsels precluded any question as to the meaning of the world possibly going beyond Yahwe. Likewise his personal majesty as a ruler precluded all thought of mystic communion with God as a quality of man's relation to him. No true Yahwe prophet and no creature at all could even have dared to claim anything of the sort, much less the deification of self.

The prophet could never arrive at a permanent inner peace with God. Yahwe's nature precluded it. The prophet could only discharge his internal pressure. The positive, euphoric turn of his emotional state had to be projected by him into the future as a promise. That determined the selection of prophetic temperaments. There is no reason to assume that apathetic-mystic states of Indian stamp have not also been experienced on Palestinian soil.

One cannot even say for sure whether or not prophets like Hosea and perhaps also others might not have been receptive to such emotional experiences. Emotional ecstasy of the Israelite type in India would presumably either have taken the path of passionate asceticism and mortification or, had its representatives acted as demagogues, they would have been considered not saintly men but barbarians. They would have had no influence. In Palestine, on the other hand, the apathetic-ecstatic states of Indian type had to suffer the same fate. They were not interpreted by the Yahwe religion as holy and were therefore not bred through formal training as in India. Finally ecstatic possession of God, leading to *anomie,* was sharply rejected. According to Jeremiah, anyone is a lying prophet who disregards the law of Yahwe and does not seek to lead the people to him.

Thus mystic possession of otherworldly godliness was rejected in favor of active service to the super-natural but, in principle understandable, god. Likewise, the speculation concerning the why of the world was rejected in favor of plain devotion to the positive godly commandment. No need was felt for a philosophic theodicy and where the problem which the Indians elaborated ever anew, still arose, it was settled with the simplest means conceivable. The thought of the pre-exilic prophets of the time of Ezekiel did not extend into the past beyond the Exodus from Egypt. Not only did the patriarchs—in contrast to Deuteronomy —play a most modest and occasional role, but also the "original man" of Ezekiel (28:17) points to a version of the Adam myth which greatly differs from the later borrowed version.

The legend of the golden calf was apparently unknown to Hosea. For him the outrage of the Baal-Peor played the corresponding role. Yahwe's wrath is always traced to the sole motive of Yahwe's covenant with Israel as a confederate association, whose members are jointly liable for one another and also for the deeds of their ancestors. His wrath was not attributed to qualities resulting from original sin nor Adam's fall. Man appeared entirely qualified to fulfill Yahwe's commandments, although actually he did it unfortunately not constantly and hence repeatedly was in need of Yahwe's mercy. Also the prophets were not primarily concerned with the question of the moral qualification of individuals, but with the consequences which could and must be brought over the collectivity by the impious acts of the qualified representatives of the people, the princes, priests, prophets, elders, patricians and only secondarily by all other members of the nation. Ezekiel (chaps. 14 and 18) first expressly posed the problem as to why the righteous should be made to suffer with the wicked and where there be a compensation for this. Jeremiah (31:29) held out only for the kingdom of the future that everyone would have to suffer only for his own misdeeds and that one would no longer say "The fathers have eaten sour grapes and the children's teeth are set on edge." Deuteronomy had, as noted above, broken with the principle of joint liability. It characterizes the peculiarity of prophecy which is entirely concerned with the collective fate of the people, not with that of the individual, that it remained more conservative in just this point.

From the beginning, however, the expectation, even of Amos, was that the pious "remnant" would be spared doom and that, in the end, they would share in the state of bliss. Also the question of the theodicy was answered, or actually not answered, by Ezekiel. He held that Yahwe would spare on the day of doom the righteous, regard those who had not practiced usury, who had returned pawned goods, and had practiced charity, and all who had been converted in good time would not die. The sinful people would not be saved for the sake of no matter how pious individuals (14:18). There was but the hope that God, when the time of vengeance was past, would permit better times to come for the "remnant of Jacob" who would keep faith. Meanwhile the prophets viewed the relation to Yahwe as in the case of blood revenge, feud and war, that the individual was responsible for what his tribal and sib companions did or his forefathers had done and left without expiation. Violations of the confederation duty had repeatedly occurred and were also easy to demonstrate in the present. Consequently God was simply always right and there were no problems for a theodicy. Expectations of a beyond, finally, ensued least of all from such problems. The representation of the eschatological event as a day of "judgment" made its appearance, but was nowhere developed.[2] The "wrath" of the God sufficed to motivate everything.

The shadowy realm of Hades was held by all pre-exile prophets quite in the same manner as the Babylonians as the unavoidable abode of all the dead which Yahwe did not, like some of the great heroes, take to Himself. Death *per se* was considered an evil, and premature, violent, unexpected death was viewed as a sign of divine wrath. Sheol throws wide its mouth, according to Isaiah (5:14) and salvation from Sheol, of which Hosea (13:14) speaks, is not the saving from a "Hell," but simply from physical death.

The prophetic horizon remained, in this, like the official Babylonian one, completely this-worldly in contrast to the Hellenic mysteries of the Orphic religion which operated throughout with promises of the beyond. There was, indeed, concern with individual salvation. But, in contrast to the Levites' curing the souls, Israelite prophecy while taking this as a point of departure was concerned only with the fate of the people as a whole. In this the political orientation of the prophets is always obvious. Prophecy also bypassed completely the Babylonian and other myths of journeys to Hades. They had nothing to do with the future fate of the pious community and did not fit into Yahwe belief. Only in a poem of Exile times falsely ascribed to Isaiah are to be found traces of a distinction in the fate of the dead in Hades, doubtlessly this was under the influence of late-Babylonian representations. And even there Hades still remained quite in keeping with the Homeric character. All, including the great kings, are powerless shadows, only certain great criminals receive special punishments (Isaiah 14:9 f., 19 f.). Yahwe's commandments like his ancient promises were quite concrete and positive and purely this-worldly. Only timely problems of a concrete inner-worldly conduct could merge and demand answers. All other problems were precluded. One must fully realize the tremendous economy of psychic resources conditioned thereby, to assess the importance of this state of affairs. For Bismarck the exclusion of all metaphysical rumination and in its stead the psalter on his night table was one of the preconditions for conduct unbroken by philosophy. Likewise the Jews and the religious communities influenced by them were affected by this barricade against pondering the meaning of the cosmos. This barrier was never entirely eliminated. Conduct according to the commandment of God, not knowledge of the meaning of the world behoved man.

An ethic does not receive its peculiar nature through the special character of its commandments—the Israelite workaday ethic was not dissimilar from that of other nations—but through the underlying central religious mentality. Israelite prophecy has greatly influenced its framework.

The decisive religious demand of the prophets consisted not in the demand to observe particular rules, however important this was and however much the true prophet felt himself to be a guardian of morality, and however great importance was given, for example by Isaiah (3:10) to righteousness based on good works. Decisive was faith. Not to any similar degree, love. To be sure, love constituted with Hosea (3:1)—who was of North Israelite orientation—the basic relationship of God to his people, and also other prophets, particularly Jeremiah (2:1 f.) described in lyrical mood Yahwe's loving relationship of previous times to Israel, his bride. But that was not predominant. Moreover, the specifically holy state was never a loving communion with God. We have examined the reasons for this above.

Presumably the demand for faith within Israel was first raised and emphatically stressed by the prophets, and, indeed, by Isaiah (7:9). This agreed with the nature of the prophetic inspiration and its interpretation. They heard the voice of God which required in the first place nothing from them and the people other than faith. The prophet had to demand faith of himself and this faith had to be devoted to the missionary messages which his god laid on him. Hence, the faith which the Jewish prophets demanded, was not that internal behavior which Luther and the Reformers intended. In truth, it signified only the unconditional trust in Yahwe's omnipotence and the sincerity of his word and conviction in its fulfillment despite all external probabilities to the contrary. The greatest prophets, especially Isaiah and Ezekiel, indeed, based their stand on this conviction. Obedience and particularly humility were the ensuing virtues and both were especially appreciated by Yahwe, especially humility, the strict avoidance not only of *hybris* in the Hellenic sense, but in the last analysis of all trust in one's own abilities and all self-renown. This representation was of great consequence for the development of later Jewish piety.

The ancient fear of arousing the jealousy of God by excessive good fortune and drawing revenge for proud self-confidence permeates the prudence of Homeric and still Solonic and Herodotic times. In Israel this fear was confined in its effects by the barriers of an intelligent and sober view of man's fate. The demand of "humility" in the sense of the prophets would have been shocking to the hero's sense of dignity, and a genuine belief in providence with its demand to honor God alone and abject submission to his counsels could attain supremacy only in the neighborhood of world monarchies, not in free states. With the prophets, however, this humility became absolutely dominant. The great kings fail and their kingdoms perish because they claim the honor for their victories and do not give it to Yahwe. And the great, in the prophet's own country at the peril of destruction, act no differently. Whoever, on the other hand, walks in humility and complete obedience in Yahwe's paths has his assistance and, indeed, need fear nothing. This also constituted the foundation of prophetic politics. The prophets were demagogues, and anything but practical politicians or political partisans. Therewith we return to what was said at the beginning.

The political stand of the prophets was purely religiously motivated through Yahwe's relationship to Israel. Viewed politically, their stand was quite utopian. Yahwe alone would ordain everything according to his will. And for the immediate future his intents, in view of the behavior of his people, were threatening and terrible. The great kings and their armies were, as indicated, his instruments. Insofar as their acts were God-ordained and Isaiah found Yahwe's will to destroy those whom He had called near, "barbaric." For Jeremiah, Nebuchadnezzar is "God's servant" and in the late post-exilic book of Daniel because of this designation he became a convert to Yahwe.

The nature of this conception and particularly its reception into Israelite piety shows again the special position of Israel. In a very similar situation, that of the impending attack by the Persians, the Delphian Apollo, too, gave oracles of doom to his people. He counseled the Greeks to flee to the ends of the earth. That, however, was destiny, not the consequence of religious guilt. Yet throughout Antiquity the idea was diffused that an enraged deity, even the god of the polis might visit misfortune on his people and especially in war. This also is to be found prominently in early Hellenic poetry. Also the quite specific idea is not peculiar to Israel that a universal god should punish the guilt of the people by leading the enemy against the city thereby bringing it either close to destruction or actually having it destroyed. It is found in Plato, in the Critias fragment and in Timaeus °— writings which may well have been influenced by the terrible experience of the downfall of Athenian power after Aegospotami. Here as there similar things are considered vices, namely, mammonism and *hybris* cause divine intervention. But these theological constructions of the head of a philosophic school remained without historical-religious consequences. The streets of Jerusalem and the grove of Academos were indeed different sites for religious annunciations. The unrestrained demagogy of the prophets was quite alien to the genteel thinker and political pedagogue of the educated youth of Athens and—occasionally—of Syracusian tyrants or reformers. Despite all divine demonism and emotional excitability the orderly procedure of the Athenian *ecclesia,* a rationally organized council, still would have been no scene for ecstatic oracles.

Above all, the specific Israelite conception of the catastrophic nature of Yahwe as well as the special *berith* of the people with God was indeed unavailable. This only infused the entire conception with the resounding pathos of punishment for the breach of a covenant with this fearful god. Hence, whatever important role oracles and omina played in Hellenic antiquity for various political decisions, they developed into no such prophetic theodicy as the scriptural prophets used from the outset in interpreting their tragic history. The vision of misfortune, though, did not result from this way of interpreting history. Jeremiah had Yahwe confirm to him that he had not called for, but rather predicted the day of doom for Judah. To his torment he had been commanded to do so. Likewise Isaiah, as noted, resisted inwardly certain threats of disaster against Assur. But once misfortune for Israel had come to pass its interpretation followed the course which the conceptions of the Israelite intellectuals and particularly the Torah teachers had shown on the basis of the ancient *berith*-idea.

Israel upheld the commandments of the Holiness Code. Yahwe intervened against other nations if his majesty was insolently of-

---

° Jowett, vol. 4, pp. 370 f., 397 f. [Ed.]

fended. Isaiah's well-known curses against Assyria, according to the reasons given, are solely motivated by the fact that the prophet in view of the behavior of these kings deemed it impossible, that Yahwe could permit it indefinitely. Hence, considerations of practical politics played no part in the seeming change of the prophet's attitude to Assur. With regard to Jerusalem he changed his position likewise, for purely religious reasons. Initially, the corrupt city seemed destined to fall. Zedekiah's faith in Yahwe suggested to him the view that Jerusalem would never fall. Despite the confirmation of this opinion by Sennacherib's withdrawal, he was so impressed by transgressions which continued to exist without change, that, in the end, he turned pessimist again. This could never be forgiven! For the other prophets, too, the religious behavior of the ruling strata is always decisive. At times it appears as if almost each of them seemed to despair of all hope. For Amos, Isaiah, and Jeremiah this must have been the case at times. But this state of despair has been definitive for none of them.

2. Eschatology and Prophets

PROPHETIC expectation of the future was as utopian as prophetic politics. Such expectations dominated the prophets' intellectual orientations and gave coherence to their ideas. The prophetic mind was saturated with warlike and partially cosmic horrors to come. In spite, or better because, of this they all dreamed of a kingdom of peace to come. Already for Hosea, and similarly for Isaiah and Zephaniah, this kingdom assumed the usual Babylonian, Mid-Eastern features of Paradise. To be sure, it has been maintained without justification that one could find with the prophets Babylonian astrological doctrines of the earth's revolution as determined by the precision of the equinoxes.[3] The prophets, rather, adjust representations of an original state and hopes for the future to the special presuppositions of Israel's relationship with Yahwe. Such representations are by no means necessarily related to Babylonian astronomical teachings. They are wellnigh universally diffused, and, in Antiquity, Virgil still in his fourth Eclogue makes use of such representations in the typical form of the return of the golden age following the iron age.

Yahwe will establish a new *berith* with Israel, but also with their enemies and even with the wild animals.

Ever since then the pacifistic hope recurred alternating with expectations of revenge on the enemies. The wondrous eschatological Prince Immanuel, who eats cream and honey, is for Isaiah a prince of peace, whose sway extends to the end of the earth. No prophet has dared to promise that death will vanish again. But, says Trito-Isaiah (65:20) everybody shall "fill his days." Such conceptions were clearly the result of the transposition of popular myths of an original state into intellectual speculation. Besides these we find gross expectations of the future of the burghers and peasants. They expected, above all, external prosperity of all sorts and, in addition, revenge on the enemy. After its consummation the horses and chariots and all apparatus of kingship, its pomp and palaces of its officials, will vanish. A savior prince riding an ass in the way of the ancient cantonal prince will make his entrance into Jerusalem. Then the military machine will be superfluous and the swords beaten into ploughshares.

In what was this now civically, now paradisically represented holy time related to the pre-exilic prophet's prediction of doom? It has often been believed possible to determine a unified "schema," first frightful calamity, then exuberant bliss as the constant type of prophecy. The assumption was that this type was borrowed from Egypt. However, such a unified schema for Egypt would not seem sufficiently corroborated by the evidence. Thus far, actually only two instances have been adduced. Besides it would be equally suggestive to point to the influence of fertility and celestial cults and their myths as the source of such peripeties. Such cults were doubtlessly diffused also in Palestine. (cf. especially Isaiah 21:4 f.). For such myths the rule was that it must first be fully night or fully winter before the sun or the spring could return. Undoubtedly this could have influenced man's imagination beyond the circle of the cult member proper, although it is not certain whether the prophets have been so influenced. For, in the first place the alleged schema cannot be demonstrated for all the prophets. Precisely with the early prophets those oracles which would correspond to it are in no way the rule.

With Amos but one example of the peripety is to be found

(9:14). Otherwise there is only the hope that, perhaps, though not for certain, the remnant who are converted will survive by Yahwe's grace and only the sinners will die (5:15;9:8,10). Most of his oracles contain sole threats of disaster. In Hosea's view the fate of the Northern kingdom would seem to differ from that of Judah. In Isaiah one finds oracles of disaster without prophecy of good and the promise of the boy Immanuel is not connected with an oracle of disaster. A true peripety from misfortune to good fortune is to be found particularly in one of his oracles (21:4 f.) where Jerusalem sinks into Hades and then is saved. This certainly recalls cult mythologies.

Otherwise one finds with wellnigh all prophets the Deuteronomic type of alternative which differs entirely from said schema. The alternative of either fortune or misfortune, according to the conduct of the people, is rather frequent (in pre-Deuternomic times: Amos, 5:4-6; Is. 1:19,20, in post-Deuteronomic times: Jer. chaps. 7 and 18, Ezek. chap. 18). Generally correct only is the fact that no prophet exclusively pronounced oracles of misfortune. Furthermore in some cases prophecy of good was joined to the threat of evil as the peripety after the appeasement of Yahwe's wrath and as compensation for the pious "remnant." In many oracles calamity appeared quite unavoidable and must occur under any circumstance as a long impending fate. Finally, when considering the oracles of a prophet as a whole, one must get the impression that both evil and good and, of course, evil first, must unavoidably occur. The unavoidability of misfortune appeared as a consequence of sins even of the forefathers who for no reason broke the covenant (Jer. 2:5). But most prophets have retained this fatalistic idea just as little as did the Torah teachers. People can amend their way and avoid evil, although only a "remnant" will do so. A unity, in the sense of a schema, exists, if comparing the single oracles, not even in one and the same prophet. Rather, what was prophesied changed according to the state of sin and the world situation.

Prophecy knew not of the Hellenistic *moira* and the Hellenistic *heimarmene;* it knew Yahwe whose decisions varied according to man's conduct. Only the two following conceptions were essentially held in common. First, that there would come "The Day," the "Day of Yahwe." In popular expectation it was viewed as a day of horror and doom, particularly military disaster for the enemy. For Israel, however, it was conceived as a day of light. It was also viewed as a day of calamity for Jewry, at least for the sinners. The way in which Amos proclaimed this seems to indicate that this important conception was actually his intellectual property. To be sure, the interpretation of it as a day of good fortune for Israel continued. But the idea that at the same time or previously a severe calamity as a punishment of sins would occur remained the common property of prophecy. Similarly, the conception of the "remnant" to whom good fortune would be imparted, is to be found even in Amos, and is clearly developed by Isaiah, who named his son accordingly. Since both of these representations together formed the schema: calamity for the people (or for the sinners), good fortune for the rest, a peripety from evil to good or a combination of both actually represents the type toward which the prophetic promise constantly gravitated. This, however, was hardly due to a borrowed schema, but simply in the nature of the case, as soon as the character of the "Day of Yahwe" as (at least, also) a day of evil was accepted. For, a simply hopeless threat of disaster would not have made pedagogical sense. Hence the type of peripety must have had its way at least in the selection of scriptures by the collectors.

For the prophets themselves, of course, one should, in general, not assume primarily pedagogical purposes as informing the threats of disaster. They prophesied their visions and voices. They were not true "preachers of penitence" as appeared during the time of the Evangels and in the Middle Ages. Naturally, they did not fail to call to repentance and penitence. On the contrary, Jeremiah, indeed, considered the denunciation of sin as one of the characteristics of the true prophet, this important principle differentiates the prophets from all mystagogues. Hosea, at the very beginning, most passionately raised the call for penitence and it is especially to be found in Jeremiah (chap. 7). As a rule, however, the content of the great visions and auditions consists simply of what good and evil Yahwe had decided already and possibly why. The people were in hard and clear terms without any admonition, expected to assume the responsibility for their own or their ancestors' guilt.[4] The genuine exhortatory scolding and penitence speeches and admonitions of the prophets personally, in contrast, are introduced as a rule, not as the *debarim* of Yahwe, but as personal speeches of the prophets, commanded by God. In any case the schema, first evil, then good, was given in the nature of the case and can be understood so without the assumption of borrowing.

The passionate vigor of the prophetic accusation and threat and the mostly general turns of phrase of the admonition stand in contrast to the style of the Torah. Deuteronomy is more edifying in tone; the older moral exhortation was forceful but matter of fact in its enumeration of special demands. This is not only determined by differences in temperament. On the contrary. The prophetic temper is, rather, conditioned by the timeliness of the prophet's expectations. The expected evil or good is but rarely placed in the distant future. Mostly it can come to pass at any time. As a rule, however, it is likely or certain to be directly at hand. Isaiah saw the young woman already expecting the eschatological boy king. Every military move of the Mesopotamian rulers, especially events such as the invasion of the Scythians, could mean or initiate the approach of the "Enemy of the North" —presumably a figure of the popular-mythological expectation. In Jeremiah's eyes, especially, this was the harbinger of the end. The fateful peripeties of the contending states kept alive these expectations.

This timeliness of the final hope was indeed decisive for the practical-ethical significance of prophecy. Obviously eschatological expectations and hopes were popularly diffused in the neighboring states. But, their vague indefiniteness failed, as in all such cases, wellnigh completely to affect conduct in practice. The story teller, the actor in a cultic masquerade, and possibly the intellectual gnostic in his esoteric conventicle knew how to exert temporary or personally limited influence. Nobody considered these expectations as timely and as factors which one had to take into account in one's whole way of life. The prophecy of the royal prophets of good fortune evoked timely expectations as did the itinerant chresmologists among the Hellenes. But, in the first case, they were narrow courtly circles, in the other discrete private individuals who more or less took their expectations into account.

In Israel, however, due to its political structure and geographical situation everybody—as shown by Jeremiah's capital trial—at least among the elders knew even after a hundred years of an oracle of doom such as that of Micah. And the whole populace was agitated when a prophet arose to proclaim striking threats. For, the predicted misfortune was timely indeed, threatening everybody's existence and necessitating the question as to what could be done to ward it off. Moreover, the threats were backed by a prophecy which was legitimated by the most striking confirmation of several unforgotten oracles of misfortune. And the prophets, in turn, were supported by the strong ancient opposition to kingship. Such timely expectation was nowhere else represented by a ruthless public demagoguery and at once joined to the traditional idea of old of Yahwe's covenant with Israel.

For the circles of true believers in Yahwe, of course, precisely this timeliness of the final expectations was decisive. We know from the Middle Ages, the time of the Reformation, as well as the early Christian community, the powerful impact of such expectations. In Israel, too, they have indeed been decisive for the way of life of such pious circles. In the last analysis they alone explain the utopian world-indifference of the prophets. When they counselled against all treaties, when they ever-again turned against the vain arrogant doings of this world, when Jeremiah remained single, it was for the same reason that led Jesus to counsel "Give unto Caesar what is Caesar's." It is like the opinion of Paul, that each should remain in his calling, that one should remain single or married, as before, and have wives as if one had them not. All these affairs of the present after all are completely irrelevant, for the end is directly at hand.

This sense of the timeliness of the final expectation gave its stamp to the personal attitude of the prophets and their adherents as to the early Christians. It gave the prophet's announcement power over their audiences. And in spite of the delay of the Day of Yahwe for a millenium unto Bar Kocheba's fall, each new prophet received the same passionate belief though restricted to a narrow circle before the Exile. Here, too, the unreal proved to be effective and left traces in the most profound reaches of the religion and established its power over life. The unreal alone imparted the hope that made life bearable. Above all, the complete renunciation of all hope in a beyond and of any kind of true theodicy—despite the constant quest for reasons of misfortune and the postulate of just compensation—could be borne most readily in a time when everybody expected the eschatological event during his lifetime.

These men of most passionate temper produced by Israel lived in a constantly tarrying mood. Immediately after the outbreak of disaster one expected good fortune. Nothing indicates this more clearly than Jeremiah's attitude in the face of the impending fall of the city. He buys land, because the hope for new times will soon be realized, and he admonishes the exiles, to mark their route in order to find the way back.

The expected good fortune itself was gradually sublimated. The final hopes stood side by side: partly these were chiliastic expectations in a cosmic sense of a final paradisical state with Hosea and Isaiah, partly the burgher's robust material hopes of Deuteronomy that Israel would constitute a nation of Jerusalem patricians, other nations would be bondsmen and tributary peasants. Both hopes more and more receded into the background until they revived in post-Exile times, the first with Joel, the second with Trito-Isaiah (6:15,6). Alongside the political expectation of a military victory and Israel's sway over other nations, as found especially in Micah (4:13), and alongside the ancient peasant promises of rich harvest and external prosperity (Amos) there appeared with the prophets the far more idealized pacifistic hope of a future kingdom of peace. The temple fortress was to be in the center (Isaiah), as the single seat of the Torah, and wisdom, and teaching for all nations (Micah). The hope, to be found even in Hosea (2:19) that Yahwe in times to come would, in a new *berith* with Israel, guarantee righteousness, judgment and lovingkindness is deepened in the sense of ethical absolutism by Jeremiah (31:33, 34) and Ezekiel (chap. 36).

The hope is that Yahwe would form a more benevolent *berith* with his people than was the old hard covenant with its severe laws. He would take away the stony heart and replace it with a heart of flesh, he would put a new spirit within them and cause them to walk in his statutes. "I will put my law in their inward parts, and write it in their hearts." Then "they shall

teach no more every man his neighbor," for they shall all know
Yahwe. So long as the cosmic order will remain, they will never
cease to be his people. Here we meet at least an allusion to the
fact that sin *per se* can be a problem of theodicy. The whole,
however, represents a high degree of ethical sublimation of
hopes as once elaborated in a poem which is questionably
ascribed to Amos (9:11 f.). The idea of this "new covenant"
resting on pure belief was still significant for the development
of Christianity. Sin itself, the removal of which through Yahwe
is hoped for, also for its part is greatly internalized and conceived as a unitary god-estranged mind, the circumcision of the
"foreskin of the heart" is for Jeremiah decisive, not anything
external. Also that is very similar to the well-known evangelical
pronouncements. No longer a social but a purely religious utopia
is here visualized. For Jeremiah this internalization and sublimation of expectations went hand in hand with the formation of
quite modest external hopes. Deuteronomy presupposes the city
state and the patrician position of the pious and prophecy, for
the rest, where touching upon these hopes, viewed the Jews at
least as the spiritual master people of the earth, as teachers and
leaders.

With Jeremiah this, too, has disappeared. He mentions Zion
but once (31:6) as the seat of Yahwe worship. He also knows
the master people ideal in its sublimated form. But with increasing age he becomes more moderate. In the future Yahwe
will bless pious herdsmen and peasants (31:24). It is sufficient
for him that people will sow and harvest the land again in the
future. A kind of idyllic happiness threatens to displace the
great eschatological expectations of world domination. We now
stand in the midst of all the misery of consumated devastation
and Jeremiah's prophecy toward the end of his life concluded
with renunciation. He counselled submission to this Yahwe
ordained fate, continued stay in the land, obedience to the
Babylonian king, and then to his viceroy. He warned against an
exodus to Egypt. And while at first he had expected the early
return of the exiles, later he advised them to make themselves
at home in their new place of dwelling. After the assassination
of Gedaliah and his own abduction to Egypt he clearly stood
at the end of his hopes as is indicated by his moving deeply

resigned testament to his loyal disciple Baruch: "Behold, I will bring evil upon all flesh, saith the Lord: but thy life will I give unto thee for a prey in all places wither thou goest." (45:5). According to a late Judaic tradition Jeremiah was stoned in Egypt.

This completely pessimistic and docile attitude could not possibly serve as a support of the community under exilic conditions. Already his advice to the exiles, to make themselves at home in Babel, sufficed to provoke a sharp conflict with the counter-prophet Shemaiah, as the irritated letters to Babylon indicate. Especially Ezekiel, preeminent among the prophets, carried away into the Exile, opposed him sharply and maintained the timeliness of the hope for return. It was indispensable for the very cohesion of the community. The final hopes which were decisive for the powerful impact of the prophets, were, of course, not the sublimated, but the crude forms which continued to coexist with all prophets. According to all experience, eschatological ideas which fail to hold out the Day of Judgment and Resurrection as timely, have had strong effects just as seldom as any purely secular hope for good fortune in the distant future. Decisive was precisely that here the "Day of Yahwe" was predicted as an event that everybody could hope or fear to experience here and now and that big revolutions in this world were in sight.

Various representations of the savior personality corresponded to the different cast of the final hopes. Amos did not know of a savior, he emphasized extensively the saving of the "remnant." With the other prophets, however, the expectations of good fortune were saturated with images of saviors in the form known to the tradition of ancient heros of the confederacy, the *shofetim*, the "redeemers." These images were linked with the eschatological representations offered by the environment.

Of course, the image of the redeemer ultimately did not offer what might have been useful. Among the possible images of a redeeming savior for the prophetic mind incarnation as well as divine generation and apotheosis proper were precluded as all of these were incompatible with the traditional peculiarity of Yahwe. That the role of savior would go to a foreign king (Cyrus) is only a conception of the time of Exile (Deutero-

Isaiah). In Israel the figure of the savior had to be related to the "Day of Yahwe," hence, to a very specific eschatological event the nature of which, as we saw, ensued from the traditional peculiarity of the god of catastrophe. The cultural religions and cults of the surrounding world (including, by the way, Iranian religion), in this special sense, knew of no "eschatological" figure of a savior king. At best one could borrow from them speculations concerning a pre-existent redeemer of astral character (in the Balaam dirge Num. 24:17) or in the nature of the first man (most distinctly possibly in Job 15:7 f., allusions could, perhaps have been borrowed Is. 9:5, Micah 5:1 and Ezek. 28:17). Even if at times such cult legends and/or speculations of intellectuals are echoed in mysterious hints of the prophets none of them resolved to take his stand on the basis of such conceptions which necessarily lead to mystery esoterics. They were prevented from so doing out of fear thereby to damage Yahwe's sole majesty.

The figure of the redeemer must retain the nature of a creature. Hence there remained either the Barbarossa hope, which, as far as is known, was not diffused in the environment, but could easily be derived from the prophecy of the redeemer king, which in Israel would have meant hope for the return of David. Or there was the hope for the appearance of a new Israelite savior king, either as a scion of Davidian lineage or as a miraculous child of somehow supernatural, hence primarily fatherless generation. In Mesopotamia especially such traits were ascribed to kings, during their lifetime, especially to usurpers. All these possibilities are to be found: the first with nearly all prophets, the last especially with Isaiah in the prophecy of the child Immanuel, the son of the "young woman."

The legitimacy of the Davidians was doubted by none of the prophets, also, not by those appearing in the Northern Kingdom, Amos and Hosea. For Amos, Zion is the seat of Yahwe, for Hosea Judah is not defiled by the sins of Israel, particularly, not by the shame of usurpers. Apparently he did not at all believe in the downfall of Judah. Also for Isaiah, the "remnant" appears to have originally meant Judah. For Micah the savior king would come from the seat of the Davidian sib, Beth-el Ephrat. For Isaiah it is quite probable that the figure of the holy child Immanuel signified defiance of the impious royal family.[5] And for Jeremiah and Ezekiel the hopes for the ancient dynasty strongly receded into the background. Alongside the Davidians there is to be found in Ezekiel (21:32) also the hope for him "whose right it is and I (Yahwe) will give it him." The promises of the prophets were anti-royalist only in the sense of the popular opposition which the intellectuals supported. The savior prince was not expressly a warrior king who for his part fulfilled Israel's revenge on the enemy, although, of course, this representation too occasionally appeared. The rule was, rather, that Yahwe himself would execute the punishment.

That the figure of the savior assumed the traits of a prophet and teacher was already prepared in pre-Exile times through the strong emphasis of the Torah upon everything which in the end, Zion would have to offer to the world, and through the Deuteronomic prediction that Yahwe would awaken in Israel "a prophet like unto Moses." Since Hosea (12:11) it was Moses, and since Jeremiah (15:1) and Deuteronomy it was Samuel besides Moses whom prophets have stamped as the *archegetes* of their own vocation. An essentially pure religious character could be preserved for these figures in contrast to the rulers and leaders of armies—they are councelors and admonishers—not mass leaders. This made both, Moses and Samuel, appear suitable for this role. The legendary figure of Elijah was quite naturally joined to them. He was the first prophet known to have stood up to the king as a prophet of doom in the later sense. The traditional representation of the "Day of Yahwe" as one of political and natural catastrophe made it difficult to displace the popular savior king by a purely religious figure. The genuine eschatological conception of a savior teacher belongs, therefore, first to the time of the Exile; and the hope for the return of Elijah, the anti-royalistic magician, won popularity only in later times, as we know from the *New Testament*. For the prophets, speculation over the nature of this eschatological figure evidently played a quite minor role. Foremost on their mind was that Yahwe, by stupendous action, would soon bring about a tremendous revolution. This distinguished the prophets from the Deuteronomist who, in the manner of a moral preacher, arranged a sequence of all sorts of promises of good and evil in exhortatory fashion.

In the last analysis the prophets were not interested in man's action during this revolution; their views of this varied. The absolute miracle is the pivot of all prophetic expectation without which its specific pathos would be lost. Therefore the image of the Messiah did not become absolutely lucid and constant— usually not even for one and the same pre-Exile prophet. Also the role of such predictions varied in each case, sinking to a low point with Jeremiah. Like Amos, he placed all emphasis on the converted remnant of the people, and with him we find but one truly "messianic" prediction. The same applied to Ezekiel, his contemporary. The prestige of the Davidian dynasty was plunged deeply into the shadow. We find ourselves already in the course of a profound transformation which made out of the "Israelite people" the community of the "Jews." Judah came to the fore as the bearer of the promises even since the decay of the Northern Kingdom, with Hosea, and increasingly so with the later prophets although the hope of a final reuniting of the entire people was not surrendered.

Before we examine this development of the people of Israel into Jewry a question must be briefly posed: what influence was worked by the pre-exilic prophets in relation to other active powers in the development of ethics?

They took over, as noted, all substantive commandments of the Levite Torah. The idea of Yahwe's *berith* with Israel and the essential features of their specific conception of god were also taken over from previous times. Social strata, which, like the prophets, confronted kingship and the material and aesthetic culture of the preeminent, had appeared before. And the sceptical attitude toward sacrifice has most probably always existed, also outside Rechabite circles. The question is whether one has to ascribe to the prophets alone the powerful stimulus of the divine plan of evil and good underpinning the ethic and the extensive sublimation of sin and god pleasing behavior into ethical absolutism or whether one has to consider this as a cultural product of the pre-prophetic intelligentsia. All intrinsic evidence suggests that these conceptions developed out of the cooperation of prophecy and the gradual rationalization of the Levite Torah and the thoughtways of pious, cultured lay-circles.

The increasing coincidence of the prophetic register of sins with the commandments of the Decalogue, indeed, suggests this.

The prophets were, in terms of their time, cultured men and maintained friendly, though sometimes strained, relations to those circles which led up to the Deuteronomic school. The Torah teachers will have contributed to the systematic ethical casuistry; prophetic inspiration will have contributed the lead and watchword for the ethical sublimation and concentration. One need only compare the Deuteronomistic edifying way of thought and expression, characteristic of the burgher, with Isaiah's oracles in order to reject the (seriously advanced) idea that Isaiah composed this exhortatory work himself and transmitted it "sealed" to his disciples. This is simply unthinkable and whereas the alternative, "blessing or curse according to conduct," indeed agreed with the folk pedagogy of Torah teaching, it was alien to the visions of impending doom precisely of Isaiah and the later prophets. Decisive, here, was the pressing timeliness of the fearful expectations of the prophets, who addressed themselves throughout to the political catastrophes.

This stood in contrast to the individual retribution of sins and the piety of the Torah teacher's patronage. Besides there were somewhat philistine hopes and fears of the burgher advanced in the exhortatory tone of the detailed moral preaching of Deuteronomy. Yet Deuteronomy is, of course, inconceivable without the prophets. For precisely Deuteronomy placed its hope on the prophet of the future. And the naive rules of war in Deuteronomy are purely utopian in the prophetic manner and can be explained only in terms of the assimilation of the conception of faith which the prophets experienced directly. Only everything is transposed into everyday life and breathes the atmosphere of genre.

Similarly—what cannot be here pursued further—the entire present revision of the tradition and the Torah, so far as they may be considered pre-Exile works, were prophetically influenced though to different extent. But they were doubtless not elaborated by prophetic editors. Without the tremendous prestige of these demagogues, known and feared by all the people, it is difficult to see how the conception of Yahwe as the god of the universe, the destroyer and rebuilder of Jerusalem could have become authoritative. This conception was equally remote from all popular and priestly conceptions of the relationship of Israel to its god. It is completely inconceivable that without the profound experiences of a confirmation of the prophetic words of doom uttered in public and still remembered after a hundred years (Jer. 26:18) the belief of the people was not only unbroken by the fearful political fate, but in a unique and quite unheard of historical paradox was definitively confirmed. The entire inner construction of the Old Testament is inconceivable without its orientation in terms of the oracles of the prophets. These giants cast their shadows through the millennia into the present, since this holy book of the Jews became a holy book of the Christians too, and since the entire interpretation of the mission of the Nazarene was primarily determined by the old promises to Israel. Again, the internal Israelite development from a political to a religious association would have been inconceivable without the grandiose constructions of Yahwe's intentions and the firm trust in his promises in spite of all, yea, precisely because of all the visitations which he ordained for his people in accordance with the uncanny predictions. Solely the internal transformation of the people of Israel facilitated the continued existence of the Yahwistic community after the destruction of Jerusalem.

The pressing emotional timeliness of the eschatological expectation was all-decisive. There was indeed great need for it in Exile. Nothing much could have been done with the mere Torah and the edifying exhortations and consolations of the Deuteronomic intellectuals. Thirst for revenge and hope were the natural mainsprings of all conduct of the believers, and only that prophecy which offered hope to all to see these passionate expectations still fulfilled during their lifetime could give religious cohesion to the politically destroyed community. The new religious association, by ritualistic incapsulation, could consider itself as the direct continuation of the old ritualistic folk community precisely because the prophets had offered no means for the formation of a new religious community, and because, in practice, the substance of the eschatological message consisted solely in sublimation of the traditional religion into ethical absolutism. This definition of the new association as a continuation of the old ritualistic folk community was not possible for Christendom in the long run.

CHAPTER XIII

THE PARIAH COMMUNITY

1. The Development of Ritualistic Segregation

P ROPHECY together with traditional ritualism of Israel, brought forth the elements that gave to Jewry its pariah place in the world. The Israelite ethic especially received its decisive imprint of exclusiveness through the development of the priestly Torah. Egyptian ethic, too, was exclusive insofar as, like all ethical codes of Antiquity, it ignored the foreigner as a matter of course. Apparently the Egyptians knew no bar against intermarriage with strangers nor the assumption of their ritualistic impurity. In contrast to Israel, the Egyptians, like the Indians, seem to have avoided contact with the mouths and dishes of beef-eating peoples.

In Israel, originally, ritualistic segregation from strangers was totally absent and exclusiveness according to type received its special accent only in connection with the development into a confessional association. This transformation of the Israelite community began, to be sure, under the influence of the Torah and prophecy even before the Exile. Its first expression was the increasing inclusion of the metics (*gerim*) into the ritualistic order. Originally, the *ger*, as we saw, had nothing to do with ritual. Circumcision was not an exclusively Israelite institution. Among Israelites it was obligatory only for the army. The Sabbath was a day of rest diffused, presumably, among full Israelites and perhaps beyond the circles of Yahwe adherents. Gradually it attained the status of a rigid command of the religious ethic. That the *ger* was permitted to be circumcised and then admitted to the Passover meal (Ex. 12:48) was doubtlessly an innovation determined by the pacifistic transformation of the pious circles of Yahwists. This became (Num. 9:14) a duty of the *ger*. The enjoyment of blood (Lev. 17:10) and the Moloch sacrifice (Lev. 20:2) had probably earlier been forbidden to the *gerim* by threat of capital punishment and, above all, he was required to observe the Sabbath. The Deuteronomic and finally exilic priestly doctrine (Num. 9:14; 15:15, 16) destroyed all ritualistic differences between full Israelite and *gerim*.

Hereafter, one law shall be for the Israelite and the stranger for all time to come. (The obviously late addition Ex. 12:49 agrees with this.) According to Deuteronomy 29:11 the *gerim* belong to the union with Yahwe, and in the Book of Joshua 8:33 this is even incorporated in the Shechemite curse and blessing ceremony. (The late prescription, Deut. 31:12 hence expressly stipulates that the Torah should be publicly read also to the *gerim*.) The driving forces in this process were the demilitarization of the Israelite peasants and town farmers in connection with the interest of the priests in the patronage of the *gerim*, among whom such exemplary pious people were to be found as the Yahwistic stock breeders—while the "preeminent," in the account, figure together with the Korahites in the latter's insurrection as opponents of the priests. The politically disqualified or less qualified strata were here, as often elsewhere, an increasingly important field of work for the Levites, and in the Exile, for the priests.

The prescriptions concerning the reception of total strangers, first of the Egyptians and Edomites, into full ritualistic communion, as found in the present revision of Deuteronomy (23:8) derive probably only from Exile times. In place of the ancient organization of settled warriors with the *berith*-bound guest tribes of affiliated *gerim*, there increasingly appeared now a purely ritualistic organization, a territorial organization at least in theory, with Jerusalem as the postulated capital.

Originally there was no common attitude toward the future form of the Yahwe community. Soon after the first abduction, Jeremiah advised the exiles to make themselves at home in Babylon. After the destruction of Jerusalem, he urged, on the other hand, that those left behind should remain in the land.

In that case, a rural community with Mizpeh as its center would have emerged under Babylonian suzerainty. But Ezekiel opposed this very sharply (according to the presumably correct interpretation of 33:25). Jerusalem was to him, the priest, the only legal place of worship and without retaining the promises for Mount Zion there was no hope for the future. Practically he was undoubtedly right. The commandment of ritualistic homogeneity of the people, including the *gerim,* was brought into a new relation with the specific ritualistic purity of the land, as maintained even at the time of Amos. Yahwe had given this to Israel in contrast to other lands. The increasing confessional zeal of the exilic priests hence demanded theoretically that no ritually impure persons be tolerated as permanent residents of Palestine.

Thus, almost at the moment when Israel lost its concrete territorial basis the ideal value of the political territory was definitely and ritually fixated for the henceforth developing internationally settled guest people. Only in Jerusalem could sacrifice be performed and only the ritually pure must be permanently settled in the territory of Israel. All ritually pure adherents of Yahwe, however, whether they be Israelites or *gerim* or new converts were now confessionally of equal value.

The purely religious nature of the community, resting on the prophetic promises, determined the substitution of this confessional and essentially sharpened segregation for the political separation from the outside. We may trace this first in the development of substantive ethics.

Originally, as was always the case, the duties of the Israelite differed naturally with respect to a tribal brother as over against a tribal stranger. The ethic of the patriarchs considered as inoffensive fraud the deception even of ethnically close tribal strangers such as the Edomites (Esau) or the nomads of the East (Laban). Yahwe commands Moses to lie to the Pharaoh (Ex. 3:18; 4:23; 5:1) and helps the Israelites in the embezzlement of Egyptian goods during the Exodus. Also, within Israel itself, there were, as we saw, tribal differences with similar consequences. The *ger* was legally protected by the framework of the *berith* with his community; ethically he was protected only through the Levitical moral exhortation. However, any sort of "xenophobia" was lacking in older times. Among the *gerim* there were to be found, as the tradition indicates, also Canaanite communities in agreement with the paradigm of Gibeon. Only Yahwistic Puritanism posed against Canaanite sexual orgiasticism and Solomon's national kingdom, sharpened the opposition to the Canaanites including the Canaanite *gerim*. In the exilic view, all Canaanites were held to be enemies, and destined by Yahwe to bondage for their sexual shamelessness and later on to be liquidated because of the holiness of the land, and lest they tempt Israel to godlessness (Ex. 23:23 f.; 34:15). According to this view no *berith* with them was admissable unless, in accordance with the reservation of the Shechem-tradition they enter the ritual community through circumcision. In view of the doubtless prevalence of circumcision among the Canaanites, already observed, this was a later interpolation. For in early times the relation of Israel to the non-Israelites had been rather politically determined, also, with regard to worship and ritual. Originally, there was neither exclusion from commensality, nor, in this connection, the incompatibility of strange sacrifice. The table community with the Gibeonites was, of course, as the text indicates, no "sacrificial meal," but simple commensality by virtue of the *berith*. Just the same, on ritual occasions the Israelites accepted strange food. The account of the meal of Joseph and his brothers and the Egyptians (Gen. 43:32) indicates that the denial of commensality with strangers by the Egyptians at the time of the origin of this tradition characterized them in contrast to Israel. Under the influence of Yahwistic Puritanism, common sacrificial meals with strangers (Ex. 34:15; Num. 25:1 f.) were prohibited with increasing severity. These prohibitions would hardly have been necessary, unless such meals had not originally existed among the Israelites as among others. It remains questionable whether the treaty-bound sacrifice of Jacob and Laban (Gen. 31:53) was considered by the Elohist as such. He considers Laban as the servant of other gods. However, the histories of Elisha still bear out that an adherent of Yahwe, who found himself in foreign service, like Naaman, in the view of the time was permitted to participate in worshipping the god of his king, doubtlessly because this was a political act. Later confessional Judaism would have viewed this conception as an abomination. Rather than submit to the demand for king and emperor worship, it chose martyrdom. The full conclusions of strict monolatry, as determined by the *berith* were simply drawn only in the time of the confessionalization.

Also connubium with the stranger is mentioned without scruples. A captive, and indeed, in this connection a captive Canaanite, could be taken for wife. That she was considered a concubine and that it was stipulated that the son of the bondswoman should not inherit in Israel, was here, as elsewhere, only the developmental result of an epoch in which the propertied sibs endowed their daughters with a dowry at marriage and thereby claimed for their children a monopoly of legitimacy. Perhaps this led, first, to scruples against intermarriage with non-members. In the time of the marriage of princesses these scruples were soon intensified among the pious for confessional reasons. True prohibitions against mixed marriages, however, appeared only during the Exile. David's lineage, as indicated by the tale of Ruth, still includes a stranger.

The inner relation to the non-Israelites is most clearly reflected in the development of Yahwe's attitude to them.[1] First, purely political motives were decisive for Yahwe's stand. Non-Israelites *per se* were indifferent to him. If war broke out, he stood, naturally, on the side of Israel. But, strangers, even when worshipping other gods, were not hideous to him. If they assisted Israel in war or were otherwise helpful (Hobab as leader through the desert, Num. 10), moreover, if they betrayed their people to Israel (Rahab and the spies in Josh. 2) they received the privilege to dwell as *gerim* in Israel. It is out of the question that foreigners should be fought because of their foreigness. On the contrary, Yahwe obviously disapproved of harming them in politically imprudent and above all treacherous fashion (as in the case of Shechem). And the pacifistic god of the patriarchs was clearly glad about Abraham's generosity to Lot in the peaceable division of land (Gen. 13) and honored Abraham's intercession for Abimelech. Occasionally Yahwe views with displeasure the decency of treatment of strangers to Israel repaid by ill. Never, in the ancient tradition, are other nations reproached in the name of Yahwe for worshipping their own gods. On the other hand, the legitimacy of other gods for them was recognized only exceptionally (in the Jephthah account and the original account of the sacrifice of his son by the King of Moab). All these are usual attitudes slightly modified only by the special *berith*-relation of Yahwe to Israel. However, according to the patriarchal legend (Gen. 27:40) Yahwe had also given Edom, an ancient sanctuary of Yahwe, a promise, though a more modest one, and likewise to Ishmael who also was considered to be inclined to worship Yahwe.

A universalist rationalization of these representations began with the theological need for a theodicy, which derived from the *berith* of Yahwe his right to punish Israel for disobedience in order to explain the political threat and the defeats. Yahwe remained, as before, indifferent to other nations. However, he used them as "scourges of God" (Peisker) against disobedient Israel, and as soon as his people had again improved, he had them crushed again by Israel.

This is the typical action pattern of the present version of the Book of Judges. Israel alone matters for Yahwe; the others are but means to an end. For this end, Yahwe had to have the power to use them at his discretion. Hence, he must also, at least in part, determine their fate. He did that by no means only to their disadvantage. To be sure, the boundaries of the dwelling site of Israel, which was his work, were not established in the interest of other people, but they still were to their benefit. The then existing peaceable state with Moab and Edom found a clear expression in the explanations of Deuteronomy: that Yahwe had given Seir as a dwelling to the children of Esau, and Moab to the children of Lot (Deut. 2:4, 9) and upon this rested the prohibition military to contend them. His disposition with respect to strangers became, in many ways, increasingly similar to those over Israel. In the priestly revision of the Exodus legend it is Yahwe who hardened the heart of the Pharaoh (Ex. 7:3)—which corresponded to the Deuteronomic mentality—in order to be able so much the more to glorify in his power. Subjectively, indeed, the strangers as e.g., the Pharaoh, did not know Yahwe (Ex. 5:2, Elohistic), however the belief, that it was Yahwe, who brought the Philistines with the Arameans from afar, must go back to a time even preceding the first prophets, since they presuppose this belief. Only with the increasing universalization of the con-

ception of god the special position of Israel through Yahwe became the paradox, the motivation of which was sought through
renewed emphasis on the ancient *berith*-conception (now in the
form of a one-sided divine promise from love without reason and
conditioned by obedience or on account of the god pleasing unconditional faith of the forefathers or because of the—cultic—
abominations of other nations). From a historically conditioned
social form of the body politic, the *berith* was transformed now
into an implement of theological construction. Only when Yahwe
had increasingly become the heavenly sovereign of heaven and
earth and of all people, Israel became his "chosen" people. As we
see in the case of Amos, the special ritual and ethical duties and
rights of the Israelites were based upon their belief of being the
chosen people. The general and primorial dualisms of in-group
and out-group morality now received this supporting pathos for
the Yahwe community.

In the field of economics it found its striking expression first
in the prohibition of usury, then in the stipulations of social protection and brotherliness of the charity exhortations. For originally it rejected only (Ex. 22:25) the oppression of the poor
doubtlessly (cf. Lev. 25:36) the impoverished brother, and pertained only to full Israelites (*'am*). Deuteronomy expressly permitted usury toward confessional strangers (*nakhri*). Originally,
it was usury toward the *ger* as is evident in the related Deuteronomic promises and the parallel threats of disaster (the latter still
mention the *ger* instead of the *nakhri*). Usury, indeed, remains
usury. But according to the correct interpretation of Deut. 23:20,
Yahwe will also bless this usury with success like all other ven-
tures of the Israelite unless he practiced it against brothers.
Similarly, all other social-ethical prescriptions: the Sabbath Year,
the unharvested edge of the field for the poor, gleaning, were
restricted to the *gerim* and the *evyonim* of one's own people. The
"neighbor" is always the compatriot, or now the co-believer. This
applies no less to the moral imperatives of the exhortations of
one's own people toward the members. One shall bear no hate
in his heart, but "love him as one's self," the "enemy," whose cattle one should not permit to go astray (Ex. 23:4) is no foreigner
in the political sense, but, as Deut. 22:1 indicates, a compatriot
with whom one is on inimical terms. Good will and righteous

behavior of an Israelite toward a stranger can indeed add to the good name of Israel and therefore be pleasing to Yahwe. But the moral commandments of the exhortations are restricted solely to the "brethren." Guest right remained sacred as of yore. Otherwise, only great abominations toward strangers endangering Israel's reputation were disapproved also by Yahwe.

2. The Dualism of In-Group and Out-Group Morality

THE separation of economic in-group and out-group ethic has remained permanently significant for the religious evaluation of economic activity. Rational economic activity on the basis of formal legality never could and never has been religiously valued in the manner characteristic of Puritanism. It was prevented by the dualism of the economic ethic which stamped as adiaphorous certain forms of behavior toward the outsiders which were strictly forbidden with respect to brothers in belief. This was decisive. It posed difficulties for Jewish ethical theorists.

Maimonides was inclined to view interest taking from strangers as indeed religiously commanded. Besides the historical situation of the Jews at the time this was doubtlessly co-determined by the disinclination against the admission of such adiaphorous acts which endangers all ethical formalism. The late Judaic ethic disapproved of usury in the sense of an inconsiderate exploitation, also of non-Jews. The success of such disapproval had, however, to be precarious in the face of the robust words of the Torah and the social situation which meanwhile had developed. In any case, the dualism in the interest question remained.

The theoretical difficulties of ethical thinkers are naturally matters of secondary importance. Practically, however, this all-pervasive ethical dualism meant that the specific puritan idea of "proving" one's self religiously through "inner-worldly asceticism" was unavailable. For this idea could not rest on a basis which was as such objectionable, but "permissible" toward certain classes of people. Thus the religious conception of "vocational" life of ascetic Protestantism was absent from the outset. The exceptionally high (traditionalistic) esteem for religiously pursuing one's daily work which we will find (with Jesus Sirach) could not alter this. The difference is plain.

To be sure, the rabbis, especially in the time of the proselytizing propaganda, greatly stressed righteous and honorable behavior of the Jews toward their host nations. In this point, the talmudic teaching is in no way different from the ethical principles of other religious communities. Especially early Christendom (Clement of Alexandria) [2] has, with respect to economic ethics, inclined to the same dualism which confined the law of usury of the *Old Testament.* The puritanical crusader faced non-Puritans with the same abhorrence—in part fed on the *Old Testament* mood—as did the priestly law of Israel the Canaanite. Moreover, no Puritan could ever have said that an unbelieving king could be a "Servant of God" as Israelite prophecy expressly declared, for example, of Nebuchadnezzar and Cyrus. In the area of economic ethics, however, the Christian sects of the seventeenth and eighteenth centuries (particularly the Baptists and Quakers) pointed with pride to the fact that precisely in economic intercourse with the godless they had substituted legality, honesty, and fairness for falseness, overreaching, and unreliability; that they had carried through the system of fixed prices, that their patrons, even when sending only their children, would receive always real value at a fair price, that deposits and credits are sure with them, that precisely therefore, the godless prefer to patronize their stores, their banks and their workshops before all others: in short, that their superior, religiously-determined economic ethics gave them superiority over the competition of the godless according to the principle "honesty is the best policy."

This is in complete agreement with what could be concretely discerned in the United States during recent decades as characteristic of the middle class way of life. It held, similarly, for the Jains and Parsees in India—only here ritualistic fetters firmly delimited the possible extension of rationalization of economic enterprise. As little as the correct Jain or Parsee would a pious Puritan ever place himself at the disposition of colonial capitalism, of the state purveyor, ancient tax- and custom-farmer, or monopolist. These specific forms of ancient, non-European and pre-bourgeois capitalism to him were ethically objectionable and God-disapproved forms of brutal accumulation of money.

Jewish economic ethic was quite different. First, it was impossible that the ethic of precisely the patriarchs was without effect which implied with respect to "non-members" quite distinctly the maxim: *"Qui trompe-t-on?"*. In any case, there was no soteriological motive whatever for ethically rationalizing out-group economic relations. No religious premium existed for it. That had far reaching consequences for the economic behavior of the Jews. Since Antiquity, Jewish pariah capitalism, like that of the Hindu trader castes, felt at home in the very forms of state- and booty-capitalism along with pure money usury and trade, precisely what Puritanism abhorred. This was held in both cases as unobjectionable on ethical principles. Although whoever practised usury as a tax farmer in the services of a godless Jewish prince or, worse, of a foreign power against one's own people was deeply objectionable and held by the rabbis as impure. However, against foreign peoples this way of acquisition was ethically adiaphorous. The moralists, naturally, made the reservation that outright deception was always abominable. Thus, economic pursuits could never furnish the setting for "proving" one's self religiously. If God "blessed" his own with economic success, it was not because they had "proven" themselves to be pious Jews in business conduct, but because he had lived a god-fearing life outside his economic pursuits (so, already, in the Deuteronomic usury teaching). As we shall see later, the area of proving one's piety in practice, for the Jew, lay in quite a different area than that of rationally mastering the "world" and especially the economy. The elements of the religiously determined way of life which enabled the Jews to play a role in our economic development will be considered later. In any case, the oriental and South and East European regions where the Jews were most and longest at home have failed to develop the specific traits of modern capitalism. This is true of Antiquity as well as of the Middle Ages and modern times. Their actual part in the development of the Occident rested essentially on their character as a guest people, which their voluntary segregation imposed on them.

This place as a guest people was established through ritualistic closure which, in Deuteronomic times, as we saw, was diffused, and during the time of the Exile was carried through by Ezra's and Nehemiah's enactments.

The downfall of the national state and the Exile meant different things for Northern Israel and for Judah. In Samaria, the Assyrian kings, in exchange for the abducted warriors, had settled Mesopotamian colonists, who, as the tradition shows, very quickly accommodated themselves to "the gods of the land," hence, the forms of Yahwe worship found there, allegedly induced through frightening miracles of Yahwe. Apparently Nebuchadnezzar had thoroughly destroyed Jerusalem—though this was done only very reluctantly and after long considerations for he would have preferred to use it as a stronghold against Egypt. By means of repeated deportations he had abducted the urban patrician and official families, that is, the court nobility, the trained warriors and royal artisans, the hierarchy and probably also the rural notables. There remained, essentially, the small peasants in the land and, as Babylonia already had had no strong peasant population for a long time, no settlement with Mesopotamian or other colonists occurred.[3]

The fate of the exiles in Babylon appears to have varied. It is certain that a large part of them—though hardly all—were settled near the capital in the countryside. In agreement with what we always find in inscriptions of the Mesopotamian great kings they had doubtlessly to dig (or repair) canals, hence they lived together in settlements of their own paying taxes to the king from the reclaimed land and rendering corvée upon demand. Forced labor was mentioned by the prophets (Is. 47:6; Jer. 5:19; 28:14; Lamentations 1:1; 5:5). Need, in one case particularly, hunger was complained of (Is. 51:19). An increase of oppression under King Nabu-nadin, in contrast to the treatment under Evil-Merodach, as Klamroth deems, would not be surprising, since Cyrus' inscriptions indicate, that said king had also increased forced labor for his own people. Individual imprisonment, which according to prophetic passages appear probable, may well have been due to resistance and this, in turn, to the activities of the prophets of hope (Jer. 29:21) who arose at least until the downfall of Jerusalem under Zedekiah.

As a rule the oppression can, objectively, not have been very severe, for already in Jeremiah's letter to the heads of the Exile community, it is presupposed that the exiles were occupationally free and able to establish themselves in Babylon at their pleasure.

Thus we find increasing numbers of exiles in the very capital and, according to the Murashu-Documents, discovered and published by the Pennsylvania expedition, in the most varied occupational positions with the sole exception of purely political offices. Access to these was dependent on education as a Babylonian scribe, and this education obviously was denied to Jews as to other non-Babylonians.[4]

The number of Jewish names in Babylon increased especially in Persian times and one finds, at that time, Jews as land-owners, rent collectors, employees of Babylonian and Persian notables. Finally, and doubtless increasingly, Jews were found in trade and particularly money exchange, which, indeed, in Babylonia, first in Hammurabi's time, had permitted the "financier" to emerge as a type. The slight ethnic and—after the exiles had accepted the Aramaic folk idiom—linguistic differences have prevented, from the beginning, the development of persecutions such as those in Egypt. It prevented, too, ghetto-like existence, as is indicated by the contemporary Assuan papyri. The community increasingly prospered. Among all foreign peoples, it seems to have played the most important role second only to the Persians. A considerable part of the exiles had, indeed, become wealthy, as indicated by the significant contribution to the Temple construction with the return from Exile. And there was no small number of wealthy men who preferred to remain behind in Babylon, lest they lose their possessions. This occurred, of course, under Persian rule, which was outspokenly friendly to the Jews and witnessed Judaic eunuchs, like Nehemiah, as personal confidants of the king. A systematic oppression, precisely of the exiles, by the Babylonian administration is indeed improbable. Religious intolerance cannot be ascertained. However much, in the given case, the great kings saw to it that the defeated pay deference to their gods, like all overlords of Antiquity, they intervene only when necessary for reasons of state.

Meanwhile, all these Oriental monarchies knew no true emperor worship in the manner of later Rome. To be sure, the ruler demanded the prostration and unconditional obedience, but he stood, nevertheless, under the gods. This circumstance facilitated tolerance. Yet hatred against Babel was very strong, as the jubilant prophecies of doom in Deutero-Isaiah indicate with the approach of the Persian war. The result was that the community in the course of the Exile gained great cohesion. This was the work, above all, of the priests, who were abducted *en masse* only with the last deportation at the destruction of Jerusalem. Previously Nebuchadnezzar had obviously hoped to utilize them as a support.

Authority was held among the exiles first by the "elders" whom Jeremiah's letter (Jer. 29:1) mentions at the head and before the "priests and prophets." Officially they remained, perhaps, the permanent representatives responsible to Babylonian administration. King Evil-Merodach, to be sure, after long captivity had shown mercy to the penultimate Judaic King Joiakim and received him at his court table. The Davidians as the royal sib therewith must have gained an honorific preference in the community of exiles, though, at first, hardly more.

Actually, the priests came increasingly to the fore, alongside some prophets of whom more below. The Christian bishops during the time of the great migration of peoples developed their power for similar reasons. One recognizes the great importance of the priests even in the early period, in the Book of Ezekiel. Ezekiel was of priestly descent. His plan for an Israelite state of the future indicates the disrepute of kingship. The prince (*nasi*) is basically but a patron of the church for the theocratically constructed community. The "highpriest" of the Temple of Jerusalem appears first with him (Ezekiel) as the central figure of the future hierocratic order. The utopian and at once schematic details of his project are of no interest here. Besides the figure of the high priest, it was of practical significance that here for the first time the status differentiation of the cult priests was carried through: a differentiation which separated the *kohanim* from the rest of the "Levites" not qualifying for sacrifice. Here, naturally, difficulties arose. For Ezekiel the Jerusalem Zadokites still play the decisive role as the sole *kohanim*.

On such a basis the unification of the diverse priestly families was not possible. Only the further developmental course must have brought about the settlement with the non-Zadokite priests, the Aaronites. With the beginning of the Persian domination the priests became paramount. This was connected with the quite consistently pursued policy of the Persian kings, always to place the priesthood in the saddle as a useful tool for taming the dependent peoples. Already Cyrus paid reverence on the one side to Babylonian gods, on the other, however, boasted of having reinstated at their old sites all those deities which the Babylonians deposed and whose images and treasures they had carried off to Babel.

In agreement with this policy he, also, permitted the Israelites to return to their homes. For all that, he was still not as consistent in his use of the priests as Darius. Persian policy sought first to win the legitimate Davidian dynasty for a support. Two Davidians, Sheshbazzar and Zerubbabel were found succeeding one another as *nasi* of the returned exiles. But the project had to be abandoned presumably because the position of the David sib, in the confusion of the false Smerdis, had proved to be of doubtful political value. The prophet Haggai, then, had prophesied to Zerubbabel, the swift restoration of the crown of David. Whether Zerubbabel made a corresponding attempt is uncertain. But he disappeared thereafter and his sib was no longer relevant for the Persians. As a matter of general principle, Darius' policy took for its point of departure the alliance with the national priesthoods. For Egypt there is documentary evidence of his restoration of the old priestly schools. The quasi-ecclesiastic organization of Egyptian religion with its synods and its national power position dates first from this. For the cults of Apollo in Asia Minor something similar is to be found. It is established for early Hellas that the Persians had the Delphic Oracle and all sorts of plebeian prophets on their side. It was the result of the battles of Marathon, Salamis and Platea which preserved Hellenic culture which was free from priestly domination, from becoming subjected to the Orphic teaching of metempsychosis or other mysteries and priestly domination under Persian protection. Persian policy toward the Israelite priests after Darius and even more in principle since Artaxerxes followed this course with smashing success.

The priests had no interest in seeing the Davidians restored to royal power and preferred to assume decisive authority in all social and internal affairs, if need be under foreign regents, who therefore stood aloof from the concerns of the community. This was agreeable to the interests of Persian policy. The figure of

"high priest," completely unknown before the Exile, was fashioned to make him the representative of the hierarchy by raising
the demand for purity, bestowing upon him the privilege of entering the inner sanctum of the Temple and qualifying him alone
for performing certain rites. This creation resulted from the
cooperation of the priestly influenced Exile prophecy and the
priestly revision and interpolation of the ritualistic commandments. The priestly revision of the *mishpatim* and the Torah
mentions "the prince" (*nasi*) only in the prohibitions against
cursing him, for the rest, they disregard him completely. All
this was in perfect agreement with Persian policy. The priests
had also otherwise done preparatory and very consistent work
toward an understanding with Persian kingship as consummated
under Artaxerxes. This work entailed first a zealous registration
of the priestly sibs with a claim to full priestly office and of
the now separate Levites and religious functionaries disqualified
for such office and, likewise, of the community members.

At that time the comprehensive sib registers have been fabricated which partly contradict obviously the older tradition. They
represent a considerable part of the present priestly revision of
tradition and for the future were to serve as the sole certifica-
tion of ritualistic qualification. The further work consisted in
determination and written fixation of the rules of worship as well
as prescriptions for a ritualistic way of life. Besides, the entire
written tradition then existing and the Levitical Torah were
correspondingly revised. In the main the tradition has then,
during the fifth century, received its present form.

After this preliminary work had been accomplished the priests
succeeded through their contacts at the court under Artaxerxes,
to attain the following: (1) A Judaic eunuch and favorite of the
king, Nehemiah, with full power of a regent reorganized the
Jerusalem community and secured its continued existence by
walling of the city and by synoecism. (2) A priest, Ezra, proclaimed a "law" which had been drafted by the priests in the
Exile community in Babylon, as binding for Jerusalem by force
of royal authority. He bound the representatives of the community to honor it by means of a solemn document. What interests
us here is primarily the consummation of the ritualistic segregation of the community. It was carried out in Exile after the

North Israelites, deported by the Assyrians, had been almost completely absorbed by the environment. This absorption taught the priests and Torah teachers the decisive importance of such ritualistic protective barriers for their own interests.

The absolute prohibition of mixed marriages was practically the most important point. Ezra put it over by quite theatrical means and it was at once enforced with all relentlessness including the dissolution of the existing mixed marriages. The previous irrelevance of this prohibition is indicated in the old sources (Gen. chaps. 34:38; Jud. 3:5, 6; Deut. 21:10 f.) and the mixed blood of the Davidians (Ruth!). Furthermore, among those settled in Israel, alongside the distinguished sibs and quite a few priests and Levites, the family of the high priest was guilty of the abomination (Ezra 10:18 f.). In the priestly revision this struggle against mixed marriages has found expression in a whole series of theological constructions. So in the objection to the use of mixed seeds in the field, mixed threads in weaving, and bastard animals. It is possible that these prohibitions were at least partially linked to ancient superstitions of unknown origin. But generally it is more probable that one and all of the prohibitions represent late theological constructions of formalist minded priests occasioned by the tabooing of "mixture" with Gentiles. For example, the use of the mule as a matter of course is established for pre-Exile times.

Next to connubium we have to consider the role of commensalism for the caste-like closure against outsiders. We saw that commensalism was readily practiced also with ritualistic strangers, but as is natural elsewhere only within the circle of either permanent *berith* affiliates or temporary affiliates by guest right. At the separate meal of the Egyptians and Hebrews in the Joseph story the denial of commensalism is laid at the door of the Egyptians in contrast to the Israelites. Only the extraordinary stress in the priestly law on dietary prescriptions created tangible difficulties in practice.

The cultic Decalogue contained a highly specialized dietary prescription which was later extended with important consequences, namely, the prescription not to cook the kid in the milk of the mother. But neither here nor in other certainly pre-exilic statutes were the later and most characteristic dietary prohibitions of the Israelites carried or mentioned, except the prohibition of numerous and, in part, very important animals (Lev. 11). Such prohibitions pertain to (1) the hip nerve which in its later specialization almost precluded all enjoyment of the hind quarters; (2) fat (Lev. 3:17; 7:23, 25) which prohibition in later interpretation was restricted to four-footed animals, forcing the Israelites to use goose fat; (3) blood, this necessitated the salting and watering of meat; (4) fallen and lacerated meat, which in combination with no. (3) determined the ritualistic regulation of slaughtering.

Some of these prohibitions (Lev. 3:17) are already characterized by their form as amendments of priestly enactments. The enjoyment of meat of the ass is presupposed in II. Kings 6:25. The prohibition of fallen and lacerated meat is presupposed by Ezekiel (4:14, compare with 44:31) as holding only for the priests, and in Trito-Isaiah (66:3) only the sacrifice of sow's blood is mentioned as an abomination. Some features of these prohibitions must go back to ancient times, in part as general taboos, in part as sacrificial taboos for the benefit of God,[5] in part as priestly purity taboos. This holds, presumably, for the objection to pork and hare's meat and the prohibition mentioned in the tradition of Samuel (I. Sam. 14:33 f.) against the enjoyment of blood. The etiological saga, generally a certain indication of great age, is to be found only for the usage not to eat the hip-nerve, a metaphysical, hence relatively late, interpretation (from the belief in souls) of the blood prohibition.

In later Judaism the prohibition of the Decalogue against cooking young kids in their mother's milk was extended to any joint cooking of meat and milk. This seems to derive from a local taboo of the Shechemite cult and is found there without motivation as a positive statute. The denial of enjoyment of fallen or lacerated cattle may be related to sacrificial prescriptions. There is nowhere to be found an etiological legend for the prohibition of certain kinds of animals. In its place appears, rather, a kind of scientific distinction, certainly not old, but a product of priestly schematization. It is similar and partially equivalent in manner to that in Manu (V. § 11 ff.) and presumably has considerably extended the range of prohibited meats.

To trace the grounds for establishment of individual prohibitions would seem to be a vain endeavor. It is ascertained for the time of the Evangels that the pig was still raised, also as a herd animal, in Palestine. Even later the bristles were not held to be impure, only the eating of the meat. All small-stock-breeders, including goat breeders, once representative of pious Yahwism, were considered impure only in talmudic times though not because of pork eating, but for their Levitically impure way of life. The most likely reason would be that here, as in the case of the church taboo of horse meat in Germany, the sacrificial feats of strange cults were forbidden. The rather widespread prohibition—also diffused in India and Egypt—can, however, also have been borrowed from the outside.

The prohibition of the enjoyment of blood and the increasing anxiety of avoiding all cattle not specifically killed by slaughtering had to be more incisive for possible commensalism than this rejection of a number of elsewhere quite favored meat dishes. This inhibition of commensalism had to be especially effective when the necessity was deduced of introducing a ritually controlled and regulated special method of butchering (*shachat*) for all animals, as occurred in post-exilic times. All cattle incorrectly slaughtered were considered carcass (*nebelah*) even when the mistake was due, for instance, to a notch in the knife (because then it had been torn) or some other oversight of the butcher, who could learn his art only after long practice.

The difficulty for correct Jews of living isolated or in small communities resulted from the indispensability of *kosher* neighborhood butchers. This has promoted, to this day in the United States, the dense concentration of orthodox Jews in the great cities (while the reform Jews in isolation were able to pursue the very profitable business of usuriously exploiting the rural Negro.) The casuistic elaboration of this dietary and butchering ritual falls only into late antiquity, but basically goes back to the exilic priestly teaching.

This ritualization of dietary habits made commensalism very difficult. No true prohibition of commensalism was ever known to official Jewry. The admonition of the (apocryphal) Jubilee Book (22:16) to separate from the Gentile and not to eat with him has been accepted as little as a general impurity of the houses of Gentiles or of their personal touch. Only the Jew going to enact a religious rite, in later times was placed under the commandment of rigid segregation from all things pagan (John 18:23). All the same, the reports of the Hellenic and Roman authors bear out that correct Jews naturally had considerable scruples in the face of any commensalism with Gentiles. Undoubtedly this is primarily responsible for the reproach of the *"odium generis humani."* [6]

In Exile times the strict observance of the Sabbath came to the fore as one of the most important "differentiating commandments," for, in contrast to mere circumcision, it furnished a sure and generally visible sign that the respective person actually took his membership in the community seriously, then, because the religious festivals were bound up with Jerusalem as the place of worship and the Sabbath represented the one festival independent of all cultic apparatus. Naturally, the Sabbath rest rendered cooperation with non-members in the workshop quite difficult. This, besides the high visibility of Sabbath observance, actually contributed greatly to segregation.

The majestic account of creation in the priestly revision sanctioned the Sabbath with a very impressive etiological myth by means of the six days of divine work. The ritualization of the Sabbath found expression in comprehensive insertions in the text of the Decalogue. The commandment to cease all field work, stemming from the Yahwist (Ex. 34:21) and the Elohistic general prescription of rest from work (Ex. 23:12) now became a prohibition of all activity, a prohibition of leaving one's home (Ex. 16:29), later softened through the delimation of the Sabbath way with all sorts of possible evasions—of lighting fire (Ex. 35:3) so that one had to cook already on Friday—for the lamp tempered by possible evasions—of carrying loads and burying beasts of burden, of going to market, of contracting any sort of business, of fighting and loud speech (Jer. 17:19 ff.; Trito-Isaiah 58:13 f.; Neh. 10:31; 13:15 ff.). The performance of war service, in Seleucid times, was declared impossible essentially because of the Sabbath and dietary prohibitions. This sealed the definitive demilitarization of the pious Jews, except in case of crusades when according to Maccabean view the end justifies the means.

There are indications of incipient creation of a special costume, as the late *"tefillin"* presented in similar manner for the exemplary pious, but, at first, these beginnings were not further developed.

CHAPTER XIV

THE EXILE

1. Babylonian and Egyptian Exiles

I N LATE Judaism as well as in early Christendom, considerations were raised against all participation in activities which might only indirectly benefit pagan sacrifice, and against any social intercourse which might entail the danger of an indirect participation in pagan worship. The most important practical objections were first developed by the rabbis, but prophecy and the Torah furnished their basis.

This refusal of participation in any sort of sacrificial meal was unique in Antiquity and, indeed, decisive for the political pariah situation of Jewry. The characteristic feature of this tendency toward segregation was that it was promoted by the Babylonian Exile community and, under its influence, by the organizers of the community of those who had returned to Palestine.

The Egyptian Exile community was according to the prevalent names, strongly recruited from Northern Israelites, who continued the syncretic tradition of Northern Israel. In contrast, the Babylonian community was Judaic and strictly Yahwist in origin. This is also borne out by the numerous name creations during the Babylonian Exile; they all were formed on the root *"jah,"* not *"el."* Above all, the Babylonian community was centered around the continuity of the prophetic tradition in contrast to that of the exiles in Egypt, where the Jewish opponents of prophecy had turned and dragged Jeremiah away by force. A political alliance with Egypt had always been rejected with special sharpness by the prophets.

One can assess the supreme importance of prophecy and its hopes for the formation and preservation of Jewry by considering that on the whole the situation of most Babylonian exiles was much more favorable than that of the Egyptian exiles. Above all, the former were far less rejected by the Babylonian environment than were the latter. Nevertheless, actually the Babylonian and not the Egyptian Jews were in the lead in establishing the decisive ritualistic barriers against the outside, in organizing the internal affairs of the community even as they were later the representatives of talmudic education. Naturally, there were also priests in the Egyptian community. But the prophetically influenced priesthood in Babylon, which kept the Deuteronomic tradition alive in their midst was the sole nucleus of further development.

In Palestine the urban population supported the puritanical tradition in opposition to both the wealthy rural sibs and the rich priests. The consequential social antagonisms of post-exilic times appeared right away. The Samaritans, from the outset, opposed the returned exiles. According to the tradition (II. Ki. 17:24) the population represented a fusion of settlers, coming from Mesopotamian and Aramaic cities, with the native Israelites. Under the guidance of Northern Israelite priests they worshipped Yahwe, but often in community with other godheads. Their most influential strata were, on the one side, the officials and other interest groups adhering to the court of the regent, who always remained in Samaria, and, on the other side, wealthy rural and small-town sibs, which were interested in the rural cults. When, apparently first under Darius, the Temple construction in Jerusalem was begun, they offered their cooperation, but as Rothstein[1] has made probable, Zerubbabel, in consequence of an oracle of Haggai (2:10 f.) rejected them (Ezra 4:3). Whereupon they, in turn, enforced the discontinuation of the Temple construction. Their enmity to the Jerusalemites continued and, especially, they hindered every attempt to fortify the city. The opponents who caused the Jerusalemites constant anxiety (Ezra 3:3) were named *amme ha-'aratzoth*.

As conditions under Nehemiah indicate a considerable part of the propertied strata of the city of Jerusalem and rural environs, laity, officials, and priests, including the very family of the high priest, were related by marriage with the opponents of Babylonian Puritanism, and partly were in agreement with the opponents, partly wavering in attitude (Neh. 5:1; 6:17 f.). So it remained. Still in Hellenistic times (as appears according to Josephus) a brother of the high priest was related by marriage to a Samaritan governor and moved thither. (Perhaps this occurred even in the time of Nehemiah.)

Only the royal prerogatives, bestowed upon Ezra and Nehemiah caused, apparently, the preeminent groups to obey at all. The plebeian Thekoites, to be sure, cooperated in constructing the walls, but the nobles (*adirim*) of the city Thekoa did not (Neh. 3:5). Also the strata of propertied Jerusalemites exacted usury from the small owners exactly as before the Exile, so that a sharp conflict developed (Neh. 5:7). Nehemiah, for his part, supported himself along with an escort by his apparently great personal money holdings and those of the Babylonian exiles; for the rest, he had mass support. In order to force the wealthy Jerusalemites to remit debts, he called for (Neh. 5:7) a "great assembly" (*kahal hagedolah*). Similarly Ezra (10:8), in order to force the dissolution of mixed marriages assembled the "congregation of those that had been carried away" (*kahal hagolah*), at that, under the threat of spiritual sanctions, namely excommunication from the *golah* and the *cherem* of the possession of those who failed to appear. Whether, in this case, the *cherem* meant only tabooing, hence, boycott, or effective destruction, must remain uncertain: feuds developed in the land as Nehemiah's presentation indicates. In the annals of Ezra (6:21) the term "*nibdalim*" ("those who separated themselves") is to be found, for the congregation of the ritually correct exiles and those who joined them. This congregational organization was doubtless first the work of Nehemiah.

Formally the efforts of Nehemiah were directed to two things: (1) synoecism of sibs and a redeemed part of the rural population in the now fortified city of Jerusalem; (2) formation of a congregation which assumed definite minimal duties by means of a sealed and sworn covenant signed by Nehemiah, the representatives of the priests, Levites and "heads" (*rashim*) of the people (*ha'am*). These obligations were (according to Neh. 10)

(1) suspension of connubium with the *ammê haarezoth*, (2) boycott of all market traffic on the Sabbath, (3) remission of all debts every seventh year, (4) a head tax of 1/3 shekel per year for Temple needs, (5) delivery of wood for Temple needs, (6) firstlings and/or redemption of firstlings according to the priestly law, (7) deliveries in kind to the Temple priests and Levite tithes, (8) maintenance of the Temple.

The Chronicler made the account of this fraternization follow the imposition of the Mosaic law, that is the Exile-priests' revision of the cult and ritual prescriptions. However, despite the eminent cultic place of the high priest envisioned in this very law he took no part in the act and his signature did not appear among those of the trustees of Nehemiah's newly organized congregation. The singularly ambiguous position of the new foundation appears in all this and continued throughout Jewish history. On the one side, it was a matter of a formally voluntary religious association. On the other, this community of exemplary righteous persons claimed to be, in the last analysis, the sole heir of the sacerdotal and therefore also of the political position of Israel. Actually, however, the political prerogatives rested always in the hands either of the Persian satrap and later of the Hellenistic regent and their officials or in those of a special commission of the king, as Nehemiah was *de facto*.

Ezra's position, likewise, rested formally solely on the authority invested in him by the Persian king. We may bypass the question whether the written order of the king, reproduced by the Chronicler, was authentic, and whether he was commissioned to carry out the law of the "God of heaven" (Ezra 7:23) if need be by use of force (*ibid.* 26). But Ezra's position, opposite the high priest, is inconceivable without far-reaching royal authorization. Obviously, the king granted no secular prerogatives whatever, especially no judicial prerogatives, to the functionaries of the new community. At the time of Nehemiah's arrival in Jerusalem, the governor, residing in Samaria, appears to have administered justice whereas Jewish district officials administered local affairs. Neither this, nor the tax obligations to the king, appear to have been permanently revised. Only the priests, Levites, and temple servants became tax exempt by the (alleged) letter of the king. However, we hear nothing about a right of the community to self-government. Likewise, the priestly and Levite-tithe, probably, were actually compulsory only in the intervening epochs in which ritually correct Jewish princes ruled and so far as their power extended. Religious means of coercion, the ban from Nehemiah's organization, later the ritualistic declassification of the non-tithe payers as *'am ha-'aretz*, must have guaranteed income. The ambiguity of this situation, the source of recurrent conflicts, is clearly discernible in the documents.

Jewry was a purely religious community organization. The tax delegations which they took upon themselves appear formally to have also been voluntarily assumed. The written petition of the upper-Egyptian Jews of the year 408/7 for the reconstruction of their Yahwe temple was addressed to the governor in Samaria as well as to the governor in Jerusalem, after they had previously—without receiving an answer—written to "the high priest and the priests in Jerusalem, his colleagues." Apparently, they were not quite certain who was actually the proper authority. Besides, it is not astonishing that they failed to receive an answer from the Jerusalemite priests.

For, the organization of the Jewish congregation signified the ritual separation from the Samaritans and from all Israelites or half-Israelite inhabitants who had not been formally received into the community. Above all, it signified separation from the Samaritans, although these had accepted the entire Torah in the revision of the Exile priests and had Aaronidic priests. The monopolistic position of Jerusalem as the place of worship was the decisive point of discord. Characteristically, the Babylonian exiles had placed decisive importance on this cult monopoly. They were the only ones to do so. The Egyptian community of exiles had, as the documents from Elephantine indicate, built their own temple, and the high priest Onias, who in the confusion of Maccabean party struggles had escaped to Egypt, still had not scrupled to build a temple there. The thousand year long dominant influence of Babylonian exiles appears in nothing more clearly than that their principle, cherished from the beginning, won out. For this result, it was of greatest importance that the leading priestly families and eminent prophetically influenced circles which had produced the Book of Deuteronomy, had been deported thence and maintained the continuity of the tradition. This was more important than the economic preeminence of the Babylonian exiles, which was later, at least, equaled by that of the Alexandrian community.

In addition, we have to consider ethnic and especially linguistic conditions. The Babylonian Jews, on the basis of common Aramaic speech, remained in full community with the mother land, the Jews in Hellenistic territories did not—a fact which exerted a characteristic influence on the fate of the Christian mission with the twofold proselytes. For the first time, and exclusively, the sacrifice took on the character of a community sacrifice. This was of capital soteriological importance through the establishment of the monopoly of sacrifice of Jerusalem in connection with the Diaspora of Jewry. Daily sacrifice in Jerusalem was paralleled by the fact that the individual henceforth ceased to sacrifice at all, that *chattat* and *asham*, at least for the Diaspora Jew, continued to exist only in theory. The individual paid a fixed tax to Jerusalem instead of sacrificing by himself. In practice, however, the victory of these Babylonian conceptions was very advantageous for the international diffusion of Jewry. It was essential for the Diaspora Jew that worship in Jerusalem was ministered as commanded by Yahwe. However as a guest people in foreign lands they naturally won uncommon freedom of movement, if they were not burdened with the duty to construct temples of their own in foreign lands.

According to principle, the *gola* rejected any other temple as illegal. Henceforth the opposition to the Samaritans gained increasing sharpness. Even in the times of the Ptolemies we find Jews and Samaritans in Egypt bitterly competing against one another. We shall not be concerned here with the fate of the Samaritans. In religious history they are, nevertheless, quite interesting in that one may study their fate in comparison with that of the Jews in order to establish negatively what the exclusively Torah oriented religion of the Israelite priests lacked for becoming a "world religion." The *bne Yisrael*, as they called themselves, remained pure ritualists. They lacked (1) the linkage to Judaic prophecy, which they denied; their hope for a Messiah remained, therefore, the hope for an inner-worldly prince, the *ta'eb* (second coming) without the tremendous pathos of the prophetic theodicy and social-revolutionary hope of the future. (2) Despite the existence of synagogues they lacked the development of the law through this plebeian stratum of popular authorities as represented by the rabbis, and they lacked their contribution, the *mishna,* the significance of which we shall examine later. They failed to develop Pharisaism which gave birth to the Talmud. They rejected the hope for resurrection. In this, too, they were related to the party of the Sadducees in Jerusalem, with whom they also shared friendly relations to Hellenism. Thus, one may say they lacked the confessional development which was anchored to the content of prophetic and rabbinical soteriology and the particular Pharisee rationalism. They experienced revivals still during the Middle Ages (fourteenth century) and still in the seventeenth century they had colonies diffused in the Orient (to India); but they failed to develop a national religious ethic which could have won the Occident. They exist, to this day, as but a tiny sect (and notoriously as the sharpest cheats of the Orient, whose falsifications have even victimized serious scholars).

We may state the result of the development as follows: the "Jews" as the community henceforth was also officially named, became a ritualistically distinct confessional congregation which was recruited by birth and the reception of proselytes. For ritualistic segregation was paralleled by the ready reception of proselytes. The true prophet of proselytism was Trito-Isaiah (Is. 56:3, 6).

While the priestly code speaks only of equality for the *ger* and old stock Israelites, but expressly excludes the "foreigner" (*nechar*) from the Passover (Ex. 12:43), Trito-Isaiah summons the foreigner (*nechar*) who above all things observes the Sabbath and the other commandments of Yahwe, to join the "covenant" and therewith share the good fortune of Israel. Proselytes were, apparently, made even during early Exile times. Proselytism must have increased during Persian times when the Jews ascended to court offices. The story of Elisha and Naaman appears to have been included in the revision of the kings' legends as a paradigm for what was, at the time, a presumably permissible (later in reaction against the Roman and Hellenistic emperor worship a strictly tabooed) and very lax practical attitude

toward the gods of foreign kingdoms on the part of Jewish cour-
tiers. The admission of previously excluded eunuchs in Trito-
Isaiah was perhaps tailored to suit the personal case of Nehemiah. Post-exilic times then imported into the Torah the general
principle that foreign sibs, through accepting the duties of the
law, after three generations would be fully equal to the old
Jews and might only not have connubium with priests. As later
to be discussed, one applied the old principles for handling of
gerim to those strangers who attached themselves as friends to
the community without assuming the full obligations of the
law. Within Jewry the Chronicler recognized only the status
group of the *kohanim* (priests), that is to say, the descendants
of the Aaronites, the Levites, and the later vanished caste-like
declassed *Nethinim* (temple servants alongside other categories
of menial temple service). The privileged status groups stood
in full connubium and full commensalism with all other Old
Jews; they were originally only required to observe relatively
simple and specific purification duties which were expanded for
the high priest. It must be reserved to a later discussion how the
distinguished priestly sibs became socially differentiated from
the ordinary Aaronites and how ritually the concept of the *'am
haarez* changed its meaning. After the Exile, it was identified
first with inhabitants standing beside the *kahal hagolah*, the
community formed by the observance of ritual duties, above all,
the Samaritans. All in all, the Jews by virtue of the imposition
of the ritualistic law, as brought about by the Babylonian community of exiles and by the formation of the *gola*-community
became a pariah people with a cult center and a central congregation in Jerusalem and with international affiliated congregations.

Its most consequential social peculiarity from the beginning
was found in the fact that a truly correct observance of the
ritual was made extremely difficult for the peasants. Not only
because the Sabbath, the Sabbath year, the dietary prescriptions *per se* were difficult to observe under rural conditions.
But above all, because the increasing casuistic development of
the practically important commandments made instruction in
ritual indispensable for correct conduct. The priestly Torah,
however, naturally, extended only slightly into rural areas. Be-

sides, we shall see later that the observance of the true Levitical purity commandments which the exemplary pious propagated increasingly were well nigh impossible for the peasants in contrast to the city people. This impediment for the peasants was not balanced by a compensatory appeal. The calendar of festivals of Exile priests, which Ezra imposed, had robbed the old festivals of their earlier relation to the cycle of work and harvest in rural life.

Moreover, Jews living among foreign peoples could hardly maintain a ritually correct way of life in rural areas. The center of gravity of Jewry had to shift increasingly in the direction of a transformation into an urban pariah people—as, indeed, came to pass.

2. Ezekiel and Deutero-Isaiah

WITHOUT the promises of prophecy an increasingly "civic" religious community would never voluntarily have taken to such a pariah situation and gained proselytes for sharing it with world-girdling success. It is a stupendous paradox that a god does not only fail to protect his chosen people against its enemies but allows them to fall, or pushes them himself, into ignominy and enslavement, yet is worshipped only the more ardently. This is unexampled in history and is only to be explained by the powerful prestige of the prophetic message. This prestige rested, as we saw, externally on the fulfillment of certain predictions of the prophets, or more correctly, on the construction of certain events as the fulfillment of prophecies. The stabilization of this prestige can clearly be recognized in the very midst of the Exile community of Babylon. While the Egyptian party abducted Jeremiah by force and hated him—allegedly, stoned him—in spite or, perhaps, because of the frightful fulfillment of his oracles, the Babylonian community in the beginning had ridiculed Ezekiel as a fool, but with the shattering news of the fall of Jerusalem, changed its attitude completely. Whoever did not despair completely, hereafter found in him an advisor and comforter and sought his advice. And while the Samaritans understandably rejected a prophecy which consistently predicted only disaster for the old kingdom of Samaria and had an exclusive concern for Jerusalem, prophecy within the Exile community won its definitive place through the fulfillment of those predictions which annunciated the return from the Exile, to which one clung during the Exile in Babylon, and which were considered fulfilled by the establishment of the *gola* congregation in Jerusalem. This congregation appeared as the "remnant," the saving of which, since Amos and, above all, since Isaiah, was promised. Its future in Exile had become the topic of prophecy which no longer held out doom, but hope for salvation.

Immediately after the fall of Jerusalem, the complete fulfillment of the frightful threats of Yahwe, this transformation of prophecy into that of hope was consummated by Jeremiah and, above all, by Ezekiel. And if for melancholic Jeremiah warmhearted consolation and modest hope for another opportunity peacefully to till the soil of the homeland, basically constituted the substance of all expectation, the ecstatic Ezekiel indulged in dreams of a frightful doomsday of the enemy, unheard of miracles and a glorious future. He could not dare to proclaim threats against Babel as ecstatic prophets of hope still had done up to the very fall of Jerusalem. Such threats had called forth the sharp intervention of the government, and Jeremiah's admonition for patient obedience.[2]

The Persians had not yet made their appearance. Hence, Ezekiel was engrossed in obscure intimations of hope. Oracles of disaster against the neighbors who maliciously enjoyed Israel's misfortune, namely, Tyros, Sidon, Ammon, Moab, Edom, the Philistine cities and against Egypt, which had proven to be an undependable ally, made room for hope to see Israel restored through the power of Yahwe alone. The threats against Egypt utilize mythological themes of a world catastrophe. Gog would seem to represent the figure of a barbarian king, a construct departing from the person of a petty prince of the interior of Asia Minor (of Tubal and Meshech 38:2), fantastically built up into an overlord of the Northland, the ancient source of all migration of peoples. In days to come he would lead all savage people against the restored holy people of Yahwe. And Yahwe would prepare doom for him and for all enemies of Israel, whom Yahwe himself has called near, in a horrendous massacre, leaving to Israel but the task of mopping up the holy land which has been turned into a defiled field of corpses (chaps. 38 and 39). And then what?

Originally, Ezekiel had thought of a second coming of David or of a Davidian (34:33). But the incorrigible behavior of the royal sib and the knowledge that priestcraft alone could keep the community together, transformed his ideals. He was himself a Zadokite and thus after twenty-five years of captivity, his final hope turned to the image of the aforementioned rationally ordered theocracy. The hope for a king was buried but those who remained faithful are assured of great prosperity in this world and—as already with Jeremiah—Yahwe will conclude a new eternal covenant with the people, endow it with a new and living heart of flesh and blood instead of stone that leads them to ruin (36:26, 27) and secure them a high place of honor before all nations in honor of Yahwe's name.

The wild ecstatic visions and auditions of his earlier years have died away. Ezekiel paints a panoramic image of the good society and with artful, pedantic skill mints his visions into an intellectually constructed utopia (chaps. 40 ff.); he is the first prophet who has turned into a writer.[3]

Ezekiel was, as mentioned, not only a writer but a priest engaged in cure of souls. He was also, so to speak, a "religious-political" counsellor of the individual exiles as well as the elders who in Exile were the prominent representatives of the faithful. He saw himself as a "watchman" of the people (3:17). And in the experiences of his curing of souls, the questions of "guilt" for the disaster of Israel were certainly brought home to him. Above all, he faced the question of collective guilt and joint liability, which had been a concern of Torah teaching. One may observe, plainly, how he seeks to define his stand. In the torment of his pathological impediments he felt himself (4:5) occasionally destined to atone for the old collective guilt of the people. On the other hand, like his predecessors, he often in the frantic wrath of his oracles of doom accused the people as a whole of hopeless corruption and seemingly prophesied general and final doom. But this to him was unbearable and, in view of the at least partially undeserved suffering of the exiles, in contrast to the political incorrigibility and economic selfishness of the Jerusalemites, the *gola* was the exclusive vessel of all hope and future welfare (11:16) while those at home were responsible for all the disaster. After the downfall of Jerusalem this too was superfluous for the needs of theodicy, however greatly this conviction has since supported the determined religious self-consciousness of the Exile community.

Among the exiles economic differentiation existed and sharply increased and, on the one hand, the well situated were inclined to greater indifference and adaptation, on the other, the resentment of the pious poor mounted. The thought of having to atone collectively for the sins of the fathers in bygone times proved unbearable and insupportable. There was an urgent demand for seeing faith in Yahwe rewarded. Like the school of the Deuteronomists before him, Ezekiel, too, resolutely made a clean break with the old idea of joint liability (chaps. 18 and 33) and at the same time with the idea, presumably suggested by Babylonian astrolatry, that Yahwe inexorably brings home to us that "our sins be upon us" (33:10) like a fate. This view necessarily led on to magics or to mystagogics or to fatalistic conclusions detrimental to cure of souls. The individual is not at all irretrievably burdened with guilt, neither with his own nor with hereditary guilt of the fathers. Yahwe forgives the individual according to his conduct. The righteous, who abide by the *mishpatim*, the charity commandments, and *chukkot* of Yahwe will live; sincere conversion washes away even severe guilt. This furnished a religious support for the mood of penitence, since prevalent in the *gola*. At the same time it prepared the difference between the solely chosen humble "pious" in contrast to the frivolity of the rich and mighty which later stamped Jewish religion, above all, in the Psalms.

However, the need for distinguishing signs in order to retain the community firmly in the hands of the priests to whom Ezekiel himself belonged turned Ezekiel's positive demands for good conduct in the direction of cult and ritual, as has been shown above. Thus ethical absolutism—the beautiful image of the transformation of the stony heart into a heart of flesh and blood—and priestly formalism apparently stand unmediated side by side: the first a legacy of the old prophecy, especially that of Jeremiah, besides being the fruit of the personal religious experience; the last representing the prescription of the practical interests of the priest.

Among the prophets first in post-Exile times the case was similar. Haggai and Zechariah, the prophets of hope of the short period of hope under Zerubbabel, orient themselves once more quite nationally to kingship and Temple. The night visions of Zechariah, a cultured priest, are artistic compositions: the planetary spirits in seven eyes (3:9) the "accuser" and the angels in heaven show Babylonian influence, the citing of old prophets (1:6) as authorities and the angel of Yahwe as bearer of the divine imperatives, in place of the direct inspiration, correspond to the derivative nature of the writing and he shies away from the old naturalistic corporeality. In substance everything is centered around the Temple construction after the completion of which the day of hope will be fulfilled.

The very reverse is to be found in the oracles of Trito-Isaiah (66:1 f.). The Temple is rejected since heaven itself be Yahwe's temple which represents a modified reminiscence of the relative indifference of the early prophets to cult, likewise the strong emphasis upon social and humanitarian duties (58:1 f.) as more important than all fasting. Idolatry and foreign cults are, as before the Exile, the decisive sins. On the other hand, it is precisely this prophet who placed strong emphasis on the fulfillment of the external codes of the ritualistic way of life which now became the single sign of community membership. He once more gave expression to the hope of a day of Yahwe (66:12 f.) as the day of consolation for Israel, of misfortunes for the enemy; and frightful thirst for revenge against the enemy dwells in the grandiose image of the God who like a vintager reddened with the blood of the Edomites bestrides the mountains (63:1 f.). Similarly there is found in Joel (2:20) the by now stereotyped appearance of the enemy of the North and a fantastically elaborated judgment of all nations (3:1 f.).

But on the whole the shift has been consummated which was determined by the situation of the petty bourgeois congregation opposite the inimical or indifferent patriciate. For Trito-Isaiah as for other prophets of the time such as Malachi (3:18) the pious in contrast to the godless were the champions of hopeful promises and God is a God of the humble (Trito-Isaiah 57:15). According to Deutero-Zechariah (9:9 f.) the future king rides upon an ass, because he is a prince of the humble and the poor. The justice by faith with Habakkuk (2:4) corresponds to the Isaiahic conception, without attaining to its timely utopian grandeur. For all is transposed into petty bourgeois terms. A severe locust plague gives Joel (2:12) occasion for a peculiarly conceived penitential sermon which after all ends in mere sacrifice and a day of fasting and prayer. Whereas Malachi attributes Yahwe's wrath to mixed-marriages. Indeed, Yahwe loves his people (Mal. 1:2); however, the pious expects pay (Trito-Isaiah 58:6, 9) and Malachi (3:16) borrows the Persian idea of divine bookkeeping of the acts of men. One the other side, Deutero-Zechariah would seem (11:4 f.) to have borrowed the theory of the four kingdoms of the world. With Joel the old even pre-prophetic utopian hope of a final paradise is quite realistically portrayed as luxurious prosperity in the manner of the old popular expectations.

Large parts of this latter-day prophecy represent predominantly the peculiar mixture of literary education with at times impressive religious warmth, but on the other side adjustment to the homespun mores and needs of the bourgeois members of a congregation which on the whole lived a peaceful and comfortable way of life in, to be sure, modest circumstances. Expressly documented is public political activity of prophets for the time of Nehemiah, who fought hard against the prophets of hope of his time. Many oracles and prophetic poems of this epoch are purely literary in nature as already in Exile times since the late period of Ezekiel and like numerous Psalms which often by mere accident are not counted among the prophetic songs (and vice versa). This is not to say that they were unimportant for religious development, though not always for that of their own time.

Literary Exile prophecy had, above all, produced the most radical and one may say the one truly serious theodicy of ancient Jewry. It represents at the same time an apotheosis of sufferance, misery, poverty, humiliation, and ugliness which in its consistency is not even second to New Testament prophecy. The author named at present Deutero-Isaiah (Isaiah 40-55) [4] who created these conceptions obviously wrote anonymously in view of Babylonian censorship [5] which he certainly had to fear because of his exceedingly passionate (and vain) hopes of seeing Cyrus destroy Babel.

The religious attitude of Israel toward poverty and suffering in general went through various stages although the later never completely displaced the earlier. As elsewhere it was originally assumed that the well-to-do, healthy, esteemed man stood in the full grace of God. The patriarchs as well as Boas, Job, and other pious men were wealthy people. Loss of wealth, sickness, misery were held to be signs of divine wrath. This is self-evident to Job's friends. The prophets also hold out this fate as divine judgment. We saw, however, a shift in attitude to the various social strata in agreement with the transition to urban culture. The military Israelite peasant and herdsman increasingly became a pacifistic *periocoi* and poor man (*ebjon*) threatened with debt bondage, pious seers displaced the war prophets, the king, forced labor, the knight, the patrician creditor and landed rentier took the place of the patriarchal rural princes. Charity ethic of neighboring kingdoms influenced the religious exhortation of the Torah teachers. Obviously, the way of life of the rich and eminent was neither ritually nor ethically immaculate. Moreover, their prestige decreased with the waning power of the state. Even in Zephaniah the poverty of the remnant of the people after judgment day is connected with their piety.

The attitude of pre-exilic ethic entailed no such positive esteem for the poor as the pious. The poor, sick, infirm, the waif, widow, metic, wage worker were objects of dutiful charity, but not themselves representatives of a superior morality or a specific religious dignity. Plebeian rule was held as a punishment. Nevertheless, under the influence of the Levitical exhortation, Yahwe was increasingly viewed as the god who helped the miserable and oppressed to get justice without, of course, any overtones of natural law demands for equality.

To be sure, the prophetic and Deuteronomic conception of Yahwe as a god who, above all, hated arrogance, hence the specifically plebeian virtue of humility was increasingly made the exclusive value. Departing from these representations, Deutero-Isaiah, in the misery of Exile, drew the final conclusions from his consistently universalistic conception of God. With him the wealthy man *per se* in one place (53:9, to be sure, of uncertain reading) is so completely identified with the godless, that the Servant of God is simply said to have died "like a rich man" in spite of his righteousness. Precisely the pious of the Exile were often the people whom enemies oppressed and abused. As the explanation in terms of ancestral deeds was no longer accepted, Deutero-Isaiah formulated a new theodicy. Yahwe is for him the god of the universe. The existence of other gods is not absolutely denied, but Yahwe will call them before his seat and destroy their arrogated worth. Yahwe alone is the world creator and governor of world history, the course of which fulfills his hidden designs. The ignominious fate of Israel is one, and indeed the most important, means for the realization of his worldwide holy plan. For Israel itself it is a means of purification (Is. 48:10). Yahwe does not purify his faithful "as one refines silver" but he makes them his "chosen people" "in the furnace of afflictions." This, however, not for the sake of Israel alone, as in all other prophecy, but also for the sake of the other nations.

The theme is developed in the much discussed songs of the "Servant of God" (*'eved Yahwe*). The peculiar conception of this figure obviously vacillates—at least in the final textual version—between a single figure and a personification of the people of Israel or, rather, of its pious core. Besides all sorts of unacceptable personalities the figure has been interpreted as that of King Joiakim who as a youth was abducted to Babylon, pardoned after long years of imprisonment, and invited to the royal table; the Book of Kings concludes with his liberation from captivity. But, unless one wishes to relate the various songs to distinctly different representations qualifying as Servants of God, neither this nor any other assumption is truly compelling, and also the question whether an individual person or collective personification cannot be consistently answered. The author would seem to have linked fates and woes, well known to his public as a matter of course, above all, the "pierced" ankles of the prisoners, with features of an eschatological figure of unknown derivation. Obviously it is deliberate art form when he moves to and fro between the personal representative of fateful suffering and the suffering collectivity in such a manner that occasionally it is hard to tell even in a single instance which possible meaning was guiding the artist. Israel is the Servant of Yahwe, it is said (49:3) and even before (48:20) it is said, that Yahwe redeemed his servant Jacob. However, immediately after the first passage (49:5, 6) the Servant of Yahwe is called upon to convert Jacob, to restore the tribes of Israel. For Yahwe had given him the tongue of a disciple to speak in time to the weary (50:4) and further (53:11) (to be sure, in an uncertain reading) his knowledge is viewed as the source of hope. This was the customary way of speaking of prophets or Torah teachers, hence one may be inclined to see in the Servant of God a personification of prophecy. This the more so as the predictions of the author who knows and rejects the magic and astronomy of the Babylonian sages, issues in the statement that the Servant of God be destined to be "a light to the Gentiles" and "salvation unto the end of the earth" (49:6). That it was the powerful self-confidence of the prophet who, in view of the coming fulfillment of the old promises through Cyrus, experiences prophecy as a supernational universal power, is suggested also by other passages and by the very nature of case. On the other hand, some passages sound undeniably as if a ruler, not a prophet, were speaking. But Moses, the archetype of prophet, had also been a hierocratic and popular leader, and precisely in exilic times one had unearthed again the figure of the wise priest-prince, Melchisedec.

With the universalism of God went the world mission. Although Deutero-Isaiah is not concerned with it in detail it is no accident that the later compiler of the present Book of Isaiah directly joined to his writings those of the post-exilic anonymous writer (Trito-Isaiah), the most energetic advocate of the religious world propaganda and of the religious equality of all proselytes who accept Yahwe's order. (Is. 56:6, 7). The task and honor of the world mission is in fact already argued by Deutero-Isaiah and among the prophets of hope it is he who speaks relatively least of a social super-ordination of the Jews over other nations as the goal of salvation or promises of revenge on the enemy as does Trito-Isaiah (60:10, 14, 15) who holds out the subjection of the Gentiles in compensation for the long shame of Israel. Deutero-Isaiah, too, proclaims in detail the judgment of Babel (chap. 47) and the humiliation and retribution against the enemies of Israel (49:23, 26 and elsewhere). This, however, is not the core of his prophecy of hope. Also for him, God has hidden his countenance before Israel because of the godlessness of the fathers, and he admonishes the seeking of the Lord, the return from godless ways and thoughts (55:6, 7).

However, this evalution of misery as punishment for sins as well as the, only occasionally indicated, admonitions to do penance, are far surpassed by an entirely different and positive soteriological meaning of suffering *per se*. Precisely blameless suffering is valued in sharpest contrast to pre-exilic prophecy. Again the manner of expression oscillates, now Israel, now prophecy, now a single eschatological figure seems to be thought of as the vessel of significant suffering for salvation. People who know righteousness and the doctrine (Torah) are admonished not to fear the abuse and threats of the world (51:7). The prophet extols in the first person that he who has been endowed by God with the gift of teaching (50:4) has given his "back to the smiters and his cheek to them," that he has "plucked off the hair," that he does "not hide his face from shame and spitting" but "set (his) face like a flint" (50:6, 7) since he knows the Lord was with him and would not let him perish. Evidently the Servant of God here is meant to represent prophecy *per se*.

In further songs, however, the figure receives again a plainly personal and soteriological turn. Many are horrified by the Servant of Yahwe because he is uglier than others (52:14 by many scholars viewed as a gloss). He is the most "despised and rejected of men," full of pain and suffering, one, before whom one hides one's face, because one counts him for nothing (53:3, 4) and because one holds him "stricken, smitten of God, and afflicted." "We considered him thus" it is said—so that here, either scorned Israel or its prophets, abused by their own people, might be personified. It is no new thought for prophecy that the Servant of God (53:11) pleads on behalf of the wicked. (Jer. 15:1; Ezek. 14:14). That he gives his life for "bearing the sins of many" might possibly though with great difficulties, still border on what was also believed of the early Israelite Men of God, such as Moses who offers his own life, if his people not be forgiven (Ex. 32:32).

Substitute sacrifice for sins in itself was also a native concept in old Israel. For Ezekiel's ecstatic states of convulsion already the representation once (4:5) is to be found that the many years of

shameful deeds of Israel must be atoned for by an equal number
of days of lameness for the prophet on behalf of his people,
which will be exposed to the taunts of the Gentiles (5:15).
Deutero-Isaiah, however, places all emphasis (53:12) on the fact
that the Servant of God, for the sake of his sufferance, was numbered with the transgressors and buried with the wicked although
he did not belong to them. Thereby he bore the sins of many; he
was "pierced and bruised for our iniquities"; and Yahwe "laid
on him the iniquity of us all" (53:5, 6) and his redemptory accomplishment was found in the fact that under torment "he
opened not his mouth." "He is brought as a lamb to the slaughter"
and he made his soul, that is, his life, an offering for sin (53:7, 10).

As later for Job, the climax of suffering is not that he was a
sacrifice or sacrificed himself, but that in addition he was considered a sinner under the rage of God. In the light of the intellectual context once taken up by Deutero-Isaiah, these conceptions are in no way so heterogeneous that one were somehow
compelled to assume foreign derivation. They appear in themselves only as the consistent summary and rational reinterpreta-
tion of already existing points. The purely external descriptions,
especially the "piercing" *per se,* suggest only the thought of a
Jewish martyr type. But it can surely not be deemed impossible
that an eschatological figure of a popular myth was involved. If
that were the case it would be derived from one of the broadly
diffused cults, be it of Tammuz (as is often assumed) be it of
another dying god such as Hadadrimmon of Meggidon, who is
mentioned in Deutero-Zechariah (12:10, 11) in connection with
the same image of the "pierced one." But if actually such borrowing or influence were the case, which remains quite doubtful, the
fundamental change of meaning would only be the more impressive.

After all, the dying deities lacked all relation to sins of a community and to the soteriological end of their expiation. Quite
otherwise here. The god or son of god who dies for mythologically
constructed, cosmic or theogonic reasons has, in agreement with
the nature of Yahwism, become a Servant of God who offers himself as a redeeming sacrifice. The redeemer is not the dying
Servant of God, but Yahwe himself (Is. 54:8) who now, in agreement with the promises of other prophets, concludes a covenant

of peace with his people, more lasting than the mountains (54:10), renewing the mercies of David (55:3). The guiltless martyrdom of the Servant of God is for Yahwe the means allowing to do this. This is indeed strange to the traditional conceptions. Why is this means recognized? "My thoughts are not your thoughts, neither are your ways my ways" (55:8). Hence we face a mystery understandable only to the circle of initiates which is in turn based on the assumption that the prophet's imagination has been influenced by some sort of eschatological myth.[6]

As has been often maintained, however, the ethical turn of this soteriology was lacking in all known mythologies of the dying and resurrected vegetation or other deities and heroes. Usually they were quite unethical. Hence, to the best of knowledge this turn was the spiritual property of the prophets. Its form and nature must be rightly viewed. It was not or only quite secondarily implied in the function of suffering as a punishment for previous sins. In agreement with the prophetic tradition this function is also mentioned by Deutero-Isaiah. Rather, the more the figure of the Servant of God appeared in the foreground, the more it is expressly emphasized that his suffering was unmerited. In fact, the other nations and the godless were certainly not superior to Yahwe's suffering, chosen people. Besides, this very prophet places less weight on the breach of the old *berith* than others. In contrast he used the promises for Abraham (51:2) and Jacob as points of departure which the earlier prophets did but seldom. But this, too, is peripheral. His problem is neither the promises nor the *berith*, but the theodicy of Israel's suffering in the universal perspective of a wise and divine world government.

Granting such questions, what constitutes for him the meaning of his glorification of sufferance, of ugliness, and of being despised? Of course, it is not an accident but design that the prophet makes the eschatological person repeatedly shift from a personification of Israel into one of prophecy and *vice versa*, and that Israel consequently appears now as the champion, now as the object of salvation. The meaning of it all is plainly the glorification of the situation of the pariah people and its tarrying endurance. Thereby the Servant of God and the people whose archetype he is, become the deliverers of the world. Thus, should the Servant of God even have been conceived as a personal savior, then he qualified only by voluntarily taking upon himself the pariah situation of the Exile people and by suffering without resistance and complaint misery, ugliness, and martyrdom. All the elements of the utopian evangelical sermon "resist no evil with force" are here at hand. The situation of the pariah people and its patient endurance were thus elevated to the highest station of religious worth and honor before God, by receiving the meaning of a world historical mission. This enthusiastic glorification of suffering as the means to serve world deliverance is clearly for the prophet the ultimate and in its way supreme enhancement of the promise to Abraham, that his name in days to come shall be great and that he shall be "a blessing."

The specific ethic of meekness and non-resistance revived in the Sermon on the Mount and the conception of the sacrificial death of the innocent martyred Servant of God helped to give birth to Christology.[7] To be sure it was not this conception alone, but in connection with later apocalyptics, the teaching of the Son of man [8] of the Book of Daniel and other mythologies. Nevertheless the words of the cross "My God, my God, why hast thou forsaken me" form the beginning of the twenty-second Psalm, which from beginning to end elaborates Deutero-Isaiah's thesis of meekness and the prophecy of the Servant of God.[9] If actually not first the Christian community but Jesus himself should have applied this verse to himself, this would certainly allow us to infer not intense despair and disappointment—a strangely frequent interpretation of the word—but on the contrary, messianic self-reliance in the sense of Deutero-Isaiah and the hopes expressed at the end of the Psalm.

In Jewish canonical literature, however, this Psalm is the one product which is completely oriented to Deutero-Isaiah's soteriology, while single quotations from the allusions to him occur repeatedly in the Psalms. The mood of Deutero-Isaiah, the worm feeling (41:14) and the positive evaluation of self-abasement and ugliness, has had broad ramifications in Jewry as well as in Christendom up to Pietism. Whereas the conception of the innocent Servant of God offering himself voluntarily for the sins of others at first fell into complete oblivion in Judaism. This was due to events. According to Deutero-Isaiah's opinion, redemption or compensation for suffering obedience was near at hand. He was

(45:1) the anointed of the world god, Cyrus, before the gates of Babel, which he would destroy. But Babel remained standing and Cyrus behaved like its legitimate king. To be sure, the return from Exile was realized. But conditions did not permit to experience the return as a redemption. Besides this intellectual theodicy could not become the common property of a believing congregation, no more than could the redemption conceptions of Indian intellectuals. Certainly the unjustly "pierced" righteous one, who at the end of days is rewarded is to be found as an image of Israel in Deutero-Zechariah and in the Psalms. The Book of Daniel (11:33 and 12:3) and especially the apocryphal Book of Wisdom made liberal use of Deutero-Isaiah. According to the authors' status position, the predictions of suffering and the recurring elevation of the Servant of God, here were related to the Torah teaching or the righteous people of Israel. But the adaptation is quite imperfect. In particular, nothing indicates the acceptance of a martyr who by his voluntary and uncomplaining sufferance expiates the sins of the people of Israel, not to mention those of the whole world.

Job is totally ignorant of the Deutero-Isaiahic form of theodicy of suffering and its god-pleasing nature. Moreover, the naïve Messiah hope of folk belief has never taken this as its point of departure. The same holds for early rabbinical literature. It, indeed, visualizes a Messiah dying in combat, but not one suffering as a redeemer. Only in the Talmud is such a figure (b. Sanh. 98b) to be found and only since around the third century A.D. the teaching of the suffering Messiah and of suffering *per se*. These came to the fore again under severe oppression.[10] Until then only the substantive mood of Deutero-Isaiah toward silent suffering exerted lasting influence. This mood was transmitted and reenforced by several Psalms; Deutero-Isaiah's attitude was well known as evident in repeated quotations. The lasting pathos of the pariah situation and the peculiar perspective of the Jews had, in this extraordinary book, their strongest inner support, until this product of the Exile constituted one of the strongest influences in the emerging belief in Christ.

Not only the stylistic form, but also the conception of prophetic charisma have been influenced by the fact that the Exile prophets and many of the post-Exile religious writers were no longer demagogues oriented toward contemporary religious politics. Older prophecy generally [11] did not employ the terms of the old North-Israelite ecstatics concerning Yahwe's "spirit" (*ruach*) taking possession of the prophet. This was an alien conception. The corporeal voice of God spoke to them, or out of them as it were, through them as instruments. They could not resist his words. Where God himself is called a "spirit," this serves to emphasize his great distance from men. The "hand" of Yahwe directly grasps the prophet and he speaks, like Isaiah, the "Torah of God." They were characterized, in variable degrees to be sure, by an emotional-ecstatic attitude and addressed themselves to timely events. Their interpretations, of course, were controlled by definite ideas concerning man's interrelation with God. With the elimination of contemporary political concerns a change occurred. Even in his late oracles, Ezekiel has lost all original ferocity. There is no trace of emotional ecstasy in Deutero-Isaiah. With Trito-Isaiah (61:1) the prophetic "spirit of the Lord" (*ruach adonai* Yahwe) is "upon" the prophet as a lasting condition and impels him to teach.

Actual emotional states always recur when it mattered: exerting an influence on timely political decision, or expressing and discharging the thirst for revenge against political enemies—as in Trito-Isaiah's vision of the vintager. But even in the prophecy of timely hope of the Zerubbabel time, prophetic style differs from that of the pre-Exile period. Night or dream visions, denied by that latter as, at best, inferior, came to the foreground as with the old "seers"; Zechariah simply was a priest rather than a demagogue. And the "spirit," which again played a role for Haggai, Joel, and Deutero-Isaiah, has become in part a prophetic hope, in part a theological construction, avoiding the old corporeal representation felt to be embarrassing. Above all, the congregation is the vessel of this "spirit."

Yahwe's explanation in Ezekiel (39:29)—perhaps to be ascribed to the revision—that he has poured out his spirit upon the house of Israel and therefore in the future after the advent of salvation will no longer turn away, this explanation with Deutero-Isaiah (44:3) is transformed into a promise for the future. God will pour out his spirit, that is to say that of prophecy (as 42:1 states) upon the seed of Israel. The entire "people in the land" is the vessel of the spirit. Trito-Isaiah (63:10, 11) speaks of the "holy Spirit" imparted by Yahwe to the people in Mosaic times, as being vexed by its transgressions. Even Haggai (2:5) promises the return of the spirit of Yahwe with reference to Yahwe's pledge during the Exodus. According to the text there is no thought in all this of the seventy elders being seized by the spirit of ecstatic prophecy (Num. 11:25), but of the specific holiness of the covenant-abiding people (Ex. 19:5) as a lasting state of mind. To be sure, the anti-priestly (Korahite) theory of pre-exilic times had deduced from this the equal holiness and charismatic qualification, not only of the priests, but of all members of the congregation.

With the prophets of post-Exile times, Joel (2:28 f.) and Deutero-Zechariah (12:10) the conception of the spirit assumed again essentially different forms. Deutero-Zechariah, indeed, held out only the spirit of prayer for the Day of Yahwe to the community, to the citizens (*josheb*) of Jerusalem headed up by the Davidians. This spirit, however, should manifest itself in the passionate bewailing of the "pierced one" modeled after the laments of the vegetation cults. Thus the eschatological figure of the pious Servant of God and martyr of Deutero-Isaiah appears again in ecstatic outbreaks of penance. With Joel, however, it is the old ecstatic emotional prophetic spirit. Before the advent of that "Day of Yahwe," when only those will be saved who appeal to Yahwe's name, this spirit will be poured upon all community members, their sons, daughters, servants and bondswomen; it will evoke dreams among the elders, visions among young men, and prophecies among children. Doubtlessly here the prophet goes back to old traditions of lay ecstasy and the final hope is linked to the universal return of the gift of prophecy.

The conception became important for the development of Christianity. The Pentecost miracle is reported with express reference to this passage which is quoted at length (Acts 2:16 ff.). Obviously the Christian mission placed great weight on this miracle only for the sake of this return of universal prophecy, because afterwards the advent of the (Christian conceived) Day of the Lord as Joel had prophesied, seemed certain. For early Christendom, the spirit as a phenomenon of mass ecstasy, a characteristic feature of it in contrast to pre-Exile prophecy, was legitimized by this and only this passage in Jewish prophetic literature.

3. The Priests and the Confessional
Restoration After the Exile

IN the development of Judaism such passages indicate only that the genuine "spirit" of the old prophecy was in eclipse. It did not disappear because of an "immanent" psychic law of mysterious sort. It vanished because the priestly police power in the Jewish congregation gained control over ecstatic prophecy in the same manner as did the bishopric and presbyterian authorities over pneumatic prophecy in the early Christian congregation.

The charisma of ecstatic prophecy lived on among Jewry. The visions ascribed to Daniel and Henoch were ecstatic in nature as were many experiences of other apocalyptics, even though the psychic states as well as their interpretation, differ sharply from those of ancient prophecy. Above all, literary art forms won dominance over actual emotional experience. However, of all these later writings only the Book of Daniel won official recognition and compelled inclusion in the canon. All others were tolerated, but were considered unclassical private works or even heterodox. The activities of these seers became therewith an affair of sects and mysteries. Likewise, prophecy of timely religious policies lived on into the last period of the second Temple.

Popular opinion firmly upheld the divine nature of the gift of prophecy and all prophets were popular figures. The priests always opposed them. The representatives of political prophecy sharply opposed the priestly reform of Ezra and Nehemiah. Nothing has been preserved of the oracles of such prophets: the priests accepted only what furthered the priestly organization of the congregation. A certain disparagement of prophetic charisma was facilitated by the mutual contradictions of the oracles. The contrast of the oracles of Isaiah and Micah, Isaiah and Jeremiah, and Jeremiah and Ezekiel must have already shaken the belief that each prophetic ecstasy *per se* offer the intrinsic guarantee of being the vehicle of divine pronouncements. How then were one to recognize true prophecy?

According to experience false prophets too (Deut. 13:3) had miraculous powers. Since the Deuteronomist (18:12) this question was answered by reference to the fulfillment of the prediction. But that was no criteron for the meantime, hence the time which mattered. Therefore Jeremiah (23:22) offered a second criterion, the prophet was a true prophet only when he criticized the sinners, hence, bound the community to Yahwe and his law, otherwise he was a false prophet. This again is paralleled by the increasing role of the ethical criterion in the early Christian community. The firmly structured respect for the accomplishment of the Levite Torah here bore its fruit in the Jewish congregation as did later the reception of the Old Testament in the Christian congregation.

In the post-exilic congregation the priests succeeded completely in destroying the prestige of the ancient Nabi ecstasy. We see the result in Deutero-Zechariah's scorn for the prophets as representatives of the spirit "of uncleanness" (13:1 ff.). In the day of Yahwe the prophets would be driven from the land with the idols. Whoever conducted himself as such, will be debunked and stabbed by his parents as a betrayer, he will be ashamed of his dream visions, no longer wear the rough garment (prophetic mantel), will admit that he is a peasant and that his alleged stigmata were caused by the fingernails of harlots. In the form of this contemptuous self-ridicule of prophecy the priestly revision compelled this dangerous competitor to take his own life. As in the Christian office church, so in official Judaism, the age of prophecy was held to be closed, the spirit of prophecy was extinct.

This development always sets in with the complete unfolding of priestly hierocracy in defense against religious innovators. The expression "*ruach ha kodesh*" (in the LXX πνεῦμα τὸ ἅγιον "holy spirit") appeared first in one of the most emphatic sermons of penance of Trito-Isaiah (63:10, 11). It is similarly conceived in a profoundly pessimistic Psalm of penance (51:11) as a state of mind of man standing in Yahwe's grace. The dove, the symbol of persecuted Israel (Psalm 74:19) was, at the same time, utilized by the rabbis as a vessel of this attitude. Inwardly it differed as profoundly from the Christian emotional pneuma as from the prophetic spirit of old which, according to later teaching, since Malachi has been imparted to no one. Yet if God wills it a mysterious heavenly voice (*bath kol*) can be heard as a loud call or a soft whisper. But it is no prophetic gift to hear it. For it speaks, according to the circumstance, to the wicked as well as to the righteous and teacher, announcing good or evil and greatness or summoning to conversion quite in the manner also to be found in the New Testament. To hear it is no privilege of an individual; for one cannot "possess" it or be possessed by it, as the prophets were once possessed with the spirit of Yahwe. To hear the voice is (Yoma 9b) indeed a gift of grace for Israel but inferior to that of the ancient prophetic spirit.

The increasing bourgeois rationalism of the people integrated in the relatively pacified world, first of the Persian kingdom, then of the Hellenic, had given the priests the opportunity to suffocate prophecy. To this must be added the fixation of the standard tradition in writing and the ensuing change in teaching and moral discipline. Hence, when the political events of the Maccabean period again called leaders of the demos to the fore against the genteel priesthood and the Hellenistic indifference of the rich and learned, these demagogues were of a stamp quite different from the prophets of old.

As the Nehemiah account permits us to see the social structure again substantially co-determined the form of piety of the Jewish community, which then was stripped of prophetic charisma. The "pious," the *Hasidim* as they were called especially in early Maccabean times, the *'anawim* as they were also named in the Psalms now became the main champions of a newly developing Jewish religiosity. They represent primarily an urban demos of town-farmers, artisans, traders, and as typical of Antiquity, often stand sharply opposed to the wealthy urban and landed sibs both secular and priestly. This was not in itself new. New was only the form and intensity of the struggle. This was essentially due to the urban character of the demos. Whereas the pious in pre-Exile prophecy still represented a mere object of charity as preached by the prophetic and Levitical and especially Deuteronomic circles, they now became vocal and came to feel themselves to be the chosen people of Yahwe in contrast to their opponents. In our sources their religious mood is brought to clearest expression by the Psalms.

PART V

SUPPLEMENT: THE PHARISEES

CHAPTER XV

SECTS AND CULTS OF THE POST-EXILE PERIOD

1. Pharisaism as Sect Religiosity

SINCE Maccabean times Pharisaism developed significant characteristics which left their eventual imprint on Judaism. The forerunners of the Pharisees appear even during the national uprising of the Maccabees. The core motive was found in a reaction against Hellenism [1] to which the upper strata succumbed.

The Psalms mention the *Hasidim* as the "pious," i.e., those who adhered to the customs of the fathers. They were the followers of Judas Maccabeus. On the one side, contrary to the strictest interpretation of the law, they even fought on the Sabbath; on the other, they emphasized especially the old abidance by the law. It seems a mistake to see in the "saints of old times" (*Hasidim-ha-rishonim*) as they are named in the Talmud, a specially organized sect, though some passages suggest this.[2] Probably the συναγωγή Ἀσιδαίων* of the Maccabean Books is, simply, the *kahal Hasidim* of the Psalms, the gathering of the pious, anti-Hellenistic people who supported the movement. It does not matter whether their direct military contribution was slight as Wellhausen assumes.

Beside the *"Zad 'kim"* the *Hasidim* are thought of in the eighteen blessings, a fact which already speaks against their character as a sect. Certain peculiarities such as the practice of

---

* Synagoga Asidaion = Hasidic synagogue.

meditating for an hour before ritualistic prayer is ascribed to them. The movement died—usually its end is dated with Joshua Katnuta—when the Maccabean rule out of necessity accommodated itself to the needs of a small secular state, borrowing the traits of a petty Hellenistic kingship. The realization that this was politically unavoidable had, indeed, led the pious to the conviction that foreign rule was preferable to an allegedly Jewish king who enjoyed national prestige but invariably failed to abide by the law. This conviction was still expressed by the pious after Herod's death in their request to Augustus not to make the Archelaos the ruler. Since that time the Pharisee movement took the place of the *Hassidic*.[3]

A man was called *perusha* (plural *perushim;* Aramaic, *perixhaya* and its Hellenic derivation Φαρισαίοι) when he segregated himself from impure persons and objects. This was the meaning also of the old *Hassidic* movement. However, the Pharisees gave the movement the form of an order, of a "brotherhood," *chaburah,* which one could join only by formally obligating one's self to most rigid Levitical purity before three members. Not everyone, of course, who actually lived as a "Pharisee" joined the order as a *chaber.* But the order formed the kernel of the movement. It had branches in all cities where Jews lived. Since they lived in the same purity as the priests, its members claimed holiness equal to those who lived correctly and superior to that of incorrect priests. The charisma of the priest was depreciated in favor of personal religious qualification as proven through conduct. Naturally, this was brought about only gradually. As late as the second century in the time of the composition of the Book of the Jubilee, the scholars and teachers were the religious leaders of the citizenry and, as a rule, belonged to priestly and Levitical sibs. The behavior of the aristocracy radically transformed the situation. In the face of the national and religious attainments of the pious, its attitude was vascillating and often scandalous, for it was both inclined and forced to political compromise.

The aspect of the brotherhood movement decisive for Jewry was that they segregated themselves not only from the Hellenes, but also precisely from non-observant Jews. There developed the contrast between the Pharisaic "saints" and the *'am ha-'aretz*,[4] the "countrymen," the "ignorant" who did not know nor observe the law. The opposition was greatly intensified, bordering on ritualistic caste segregation. The *chaber* (brother) had to obligate himself not to have recourse to the services of a priest or Levite unless he be a ritualistically observant Jew, hence no *'am ha-'aretz*. He obligated himself not to share the table with pagans or *'am ha-arez,* to avoid connubium and association with them and, in general, to minimize all intercourse with them. This rigidity was an innovation. Of course, frequently a deep hatred resulted between the *chaberim* and the *'am ha-arez*. The wrathful speeches of Jesus of Nazareth against the Pharisees are sufficient evidence.

Thus, we are faced here with the sect, indeed the inter-local sect. It permitted the *chaber* coming to a strange place with testimonials of his brotherhood at once to become a denizen in a community of like-minded persons. The community favored him socially (and unintentionally though actually, also, economically) as sects have always done (most strongly in the area of the Puritan and Baptist sects in modern times). Paul learned the technique of propaganda and of establishing an indestructible community from the Pharisees. The powerful rise of the Jewish Diaspora since Maccabean times and the complete unshakability of its communities by the foreign environment from which they segregated themselves was largely the work of their brotherhood movement. Its historical significance precisely for the Diaspora and for the peculiarities of the Jewish religion will become clearer when we examine the accomplishments of the Pharisees.

The opponents of the Pharisees were the great patrician aristocratic sibs and, above all, the priestly nobility, the Zadokites ("Sadducees") and their connections. This opposition did not express itself in form and outer bearing. Indeed, the pious Pharisee insisted precisely on everything being tithed in accordance with the priestly law. In actuality, however, the opposition is already evident in the demand that the priest live correctly in the Pharisaic sense if he is to serve his function.

To this picture must be added the community institutions partly created by the Pharisees in their official capacity as a brotherhood, partly created under their influence. For the "community" now became the bearer of the religion; this was no longer the function of hereditary charisma of priests and Levites. Apart from a series of small ritualistic differences this appeared most clearly in the following innovations.

The brotherhood instituted its eucharists ("love feasts") which were quite similar in nature and certainly models for the later Christian institutions of the same type. Even the blessing of the meal had a similar form. Moreover, the Pharisees instituted the very popular water-procession, similar to the procession of *charitonite gurus* of India. They created, above all, the synagogue, the central institution of late Judaism, which for the Diaspora Jew substituted the priestly cult. Finally they created high and low instruction in the law, which was to make a permanent impression on Jewry. Slowly, but profoundly, they transformed the interpretation of the Sabbath and the festivals. In place of the priestly temple festival appears the domestic or synagogical festival and therewith an inevitable devaluation of sacrifice and priesthood even before the fall of the second Temple. The process compares to the same symptoms of emancipation from the Brahmins in India. Above all, now one consults the teacher learned in the law rather than the priest if one is in external or inner need or in doubt concerning ritual duties. The decision of the *soferim*, educated in Pharisaic terms, are held by the Jews as law—death is the consequence of its transgression. However, the *sofer* also claims the right, in the given case, of granting dispensation from law and vow, an understandably highly popular function.

The manner in which the Pharisaically learned *sofer* rendered his decisions accommodated itself—for all the rigidity of ritualistic purification requirements—quite essentially to the interest of the civil strata, especially to that of the petty bourgeois. The brotherhoods here, as always, were primarily rooted among these. Philosophical speculation, naturally, was rejected as dangerous and quite Hellenistic. The reasons for ritualistic prescriptions were not to be pondered, but they were simply to be observed, for "the fear of sins surpasses wisdom." However, the rejection of philosophical rationalism was correlated with a practical-ethical rationalism characteristic of petty bourgeois strata.

Practical everyday needs and "common sense" dominate the discussion and resolution of controversial issues.

During the time decisive for the formation of Jewry, i.e., in the two centuries before and the two after the beginning of our era, the issues were hardly "dogmatic" in nature, so that the existence, the very possibility and religious permissibility of Jewish dogmatics has remained controversial in principle until today. Rather, the controversies occuring were bound up with questions of everyday life. As, in the Talmud, the prophets are highly valued for their "understandability" by everyone, so all talmudic teaching is directly understandable, adjusted to the mind of the average burgher and, in this sense, "rational." Sadducee practice always clung to the letter, for example, the literal fulfillment of the talion "an eye for an eye"; Pharisaic practice, however, as represented, for instance, by R. Simon ben Jochai, dealt with the "ratio" of the prescriptions and eliminated senseless prescriptions or reinterpreted them (for example, penance after an agreement instead of the talion was admissible).

In practice the Pharisees met the economic interests of the pious halfway—who adhered to them as representatives of a more inward piety. The reception of the *ketubah*-prescriptions and other protective measures of the law of family property appeared to have been their work. Ethical rationalism is obvious in the handling of tradition. The "Book of Jubilees," a specifically Pharisaic work,[5] retouched the entire story of creation and the patriarchs, expurgating what was shocking. On the other hand, adaptation was made to the original belief in spirits found everywhere in the world. The common oriental angel-and-demonology, partly subject to Persian influences and also known to Judaism in late antiquity was accepted essentially under Pharisaic influence and completely contrary to the educated genteel strata. Besides accommodating to the given mass belief this occurred also on "rational" grounds: the supreme god was thereby at least partially absolved from responsibility for the imperfection of the world. The enhancement of the belief in providence [6] and strong emphasis on the "mercy" of God stem from similar though redirected motives and correspond to the ubiquitous religious tendencies of plebeian strata.

The civil character of the strata primarily supporting the religiosity explains, also, the significant intensification which the expectations of a "savior" and a beyond reached under the influence of the Pharisees. The messianic hope and belief in the resurrection of the dead to a better life were throughout borne by the Pharisees. This last, at least, was absolutely repudiated by the distinguished Sadducees.

To be sure, the demands of the Pharisees on pious Jews were considerable. The "heavenly kingdom" was to appear and whoever wished to share it had to shoulder the "yoke"[7] (*ol malkas shamajim* of the "yoke of the commandments" *ol hamizwoth*). This is possible only through strict training, characteristic of the endeavor of Pharisaic rabbis in the teaching institutions of late Judaism. "Holiness" of life was demanded. Solely for God's sake his commandments should be observed, not for pay and advantage. Above all, those laws should be observed which served strictly to separate the pious from the Gentile and "quasi-Jews." Circumcision and Sabbath rest were considered central for this special character of differentiating the pious from all others. Judging from the severity of its violation, the Sabbath obviously became much more strict.

Obviously, in our context, it is important to assess the direction of these demands.

Phariseehood was primarily urban in nature. Of course, this is not to say that all Pharisees were urban burghers. On the contrary, quite a few of the leading talmudic rabbis were land owners. But the form of holiness which they practiced and the weight given to education (Hebraic, hence increasingly foreign-language education)—as we shall see below, not alone by authorities, but everyone—increasingly prevented the point of gravity of its adherents from being found among peasants. It is no accident that *'am ha-arez*, the non-Pharisees, originally were "the countrymen" and that, also, small Judaic towns could not be important: "what good can come out of Nazareth?" The *chevra*, the Pharisaic order was indeed a substitute for the rural neighborhood for landless city dwellers and as such it corresponded to their external and inner interests. The transformation of Jewry into an inter-local, essentially urban, landless (at least, no longer predominantly firmly settled) guest people was essentially consummated under Pharisaic leadership.

This strong shift in Jewish religiosity was brought about by the Pharisees, only in part by virtue of their control of traditional forces. Under John Hyrcanus they constituted a powerful party; Salome Alexandra (78-69) delivered the Sanhedrin up to them; Aristobulus expelled them again; Herod sought to win their good will. Their final rule began with the fall of the Temple: then all Judaism became Pharisaic, the Sadducees became a heterodox sect. Even before this the transformation of religious authority had begun, a transformation decisive for their rule. The hereditary aristocracy had to give way before the aristocracy of the learned. Descendants of proselytes often have been the best leaders of the Pharisees. Above all the rise to power of the rabbis was a product of the urban Pharisaic development of Jewry. The rabbis were, in the decisive time of the development of Jewry, a stratum to be found again in primitive Christendom and in the Christian sects; the similarity, to be sure, is but remote.

2. *The Rabbis*

THE rabbis were not in any way a "Pharisaic institution." Formally they had nothing to do with the brotherhood. Only in the initial stage of their development, they had the closest relation to that movement. The eminent teachers of the epoch in which the Mishna developed were Pharisees in spirit if not in form, and the "spirit" of Pharisaism informs their teaching. It may be noted in advance, the name "rabbi" (from rab, great, hence rabbi, "my master"), so far as Jewish sources attest became a fixed title [8] only after the fall of the Temple.[9] Previously the *sofer* was a man learned in scripture, a designation with fixed content. The "teacher" however was the person of respect. Nevertheless we need not scruple to use the term even for the time before the downfall of Jerusalem, for the scriptural authorities of the community, even at that time, this appellation was applied, though not exclusively. What, then, are the rabbis?

Formal legitimation as "rabbi" appears only with the establishment of the patriarchate after the fall of the Temple. At the time, the rabbi was required to be formally ordained, the development of the Mesopotamian and Palestinian academies established a fixed curriculum. All this was previously out of discussion. As far as it known, there existed no official legitimation of "rabbis" whatsoever.

The tradition of the *soferim* was the sole criterion. They were distinguished and recognized for their religious learning and their accepted interpretations of scripture. Hence their personal disciples and their's in turn were primarily considered as qualified scholars. The personalities, quoted for wisdom of the Talmud, are by no means only *soferim* or trained rabbis. On the contrary, with a certain studiousness tradition occasionally places especially subtle interpretations of Torah and moral teaching in the mouth, for example, of a rabbi's ass driver (Jonathan) and makes learned rabbis seek counsel with a pious, hence acknowledgedly wise, field worker (like Abba Chilkijat). To be sure, this was viewed as something quite special. It proves that the separation was not sharp, but said ass driver was expressly distinguished from the rabbi as an "ignorant man." He is no rabbi.

The conditions presupposed by the Gospels indicate, likewise, that at the time no firmly exclusive organization existed, but one consulted men who actually legitimized themselves through charismatic knowledge of the law and the art of interpretation. Intervention, obviously, was only negative repression, be it on the part of the priests, be it by self-help (lynch law) of the masses under the leadership of individuals, or (and most likely), the Pharisaic community when the manner of interpretation was offensive and found sufficiently strong opposition. The accounts of the Gospels indicate what great consideration was given to the popularity of a teacher. The authorities are hesitant to intervene even against the obviously false doctrine, if "the people" adhere to the person of the teacher.[10] The formally charismatic authority of the rabbinical teacher was supported solely by education and schooling and found its analogies in many similar phenomena from the Roman jurisconsul (before the time of the obligatory license) to the Indian *gurus*. There were, however, important differences between these types. It is the peculiarities of the rabbis that we must now consider.

In the main they were a stratum of plebeian intellectuals. There were, of course, genteel and wealthy men among them.

But, even a glance at the personalities recognized in the Talmud as authorities or exemplary rabbis indicates that the plebeian down to the day-laborer in the field is the spokesman and that among the rabbis themselves the wealthy and genteel men form a small minority. This holds without doubt for the time of the composition of the Talmud and before. As we have seen, numerous mystagogues and sect leaders of other religions were also "plebeians." However, the (old) rabbi differed from them particularly in exercising his function as advisor and counsel in matters of ritual avocationally, that is, alongside his secular occupation. That was no accident, but a consequence of the rigid prohibition against teaching (and interpreting) the law for compensation.[11] This prohibition—which found its sequel in the Pauline—"if any would not work, neither should he eat"—from the beginning, completely prohibited the development of the rabbis into mystagogues of Indian imprint. It explains also in quite important points some peculiarities of their teaching.

The occupational positions of leading rabbis have often been listed. Understandably one finds numerous land owners among them. Certainly many land rentiers, for these had the leisure to devote themselves to study. It is striking, however, that among the preeminent older Talmud authorities—hence before the time of the fall of the Temple—one finds, besides a few merchants, especially artisans: blacksmiths, sandle makers, carpenters, shoe makers, tanners, architects, boatsmen, wine testers, woodmen. Also, the first two famous founders of schools and sharp controversialists, Hillel, the elder and Shammai, were artisans. Thus, they are men of the same social stratum which produced Paul and the personalities mentioned in his letters.

It is quite correct that the Jewish municipal law of talmudic times privileged the rabbis [12] by granting them exemption from taxes and from most (not all) corvées and by giving them the right of selling their products in the market before others.[13] But apart from the question as to whether these privileges already were in effect in the time of the second Temple, it was also later considered in order, that the rabbi earn his livelihood through work. He should work a third of the day, study the rest. Or he worked in summer and studied in winter. Later there were all sorts of circumventions. It was permitted, at least for judges, to receive compensation for "lost time" (lucrum cessans) and gifts naturally always existed. Nevertheless, until about the fourteenth century, the Jewish rabbis fulfilled their obligations in principle without payment, originally as a "secondary occupation." "To earn money by working with one's own hands is better than the wealth of the *rash galut*"—the head of the church!—"who lives off other people's money," held for the old rabbis as a maxim. Thus, we meet here as intellectual champions of a religiosity, gainfully employed persons and among them a considerable number of artisans. Aside from the few beginnings in medieval India we meet this phenomena here for the first time. We assess its significance by a comparison with other strata.

The rabbis [14] were, first of all, no magicians or mystagogues. This differentiated them from the Indian and the East Asiatic plebeian soul shepherds of all types. The rabbis worked through teaching as speakers and writers, the mystagogues through magic; the rabbis' authority rested on knowledge and intellectual schooling, not on magical charisma. This resulted in the first place, from the place of magic in general in post-prophetic Jewry. The idea that one may coerce the deity through magic is radically eliminated from Jewry. The prophetic conception of God, once for all, precluded this. Therefore, magic in this primitive sense was indeed held by the Talmud as abominable and blasphemous. Ultimately, all forms of sorcery were considered dubious or suspect.

This requires qualification. Magic continued to exist in two forms, exorcism and healing through word magic. Partly it was tolerated in practice, partly it was even viewed as legitimate. Here not coercion of God, but of demons was involved and the latter, as noted, played an acknowledged role in Pharisaism. This management, however, did not belong to the normal occupation of the rabbis.

For the rest Judaism, including Pharisaism, did not deny the charisma of the miracle. The Gospels had the Jews and also, expressly, the scholars and Pharisees, demand a "sign" from Jesus. However, miraculous power is attached to the prophet who legitimates himself as god-sent, namely, if he actually has this gift from God and not from the demons.

With prophecy, however, the scripturally learned rabbis naturally lived in a state of tension, which is characteristic of any stratum of learned men who are ritualistically oriented to a law book as against prophetic charismatics. Indeed, the possibility of the appearance of prophets was not denied, at least, not originally. With this admission, the more urgent were the warnings against false prophets. Decisive for this was the fact that Jewish prophecy was once for all committed to be emissary, pronouncing its message at the order of a super-worldly god, not by virtue of a godliness of its own or divine possession of the prophet. Such a prophet is one who teaches and speaks "without commission." How can one tell this? What is the sign of the falseness or truth of a prophet?

Above all, Jeremiah's (23:9 ff.) criterion was authoritative for rabbinical interpretation. Not only is the prophet self-evidently false if he teaches false gods or whose prophecy remains unfulfilled,[15] but every prophet is bound by the law and its commandments and whoever seeks to estrange men from them is a false prophet. Hence only one who converts men from their sins can be truly god-sent. Not visions or dreams, but devotion to God's commandments as laid down in the law is proof for truth of the prophet, for his being no "dreamer." Visions and dreams had already been discredited by the old priestly tradition, because it was obvious that there were also (and precisely) visions which had turned the people to orgiastic Baal-service.

Likewise, miracles could be performed in the name of demons. Therefore mere miraculous power is no proof of genuine prophetic charisma. And even if the prophet in his teaching seemed to bear the signs of a divine mission, the charisma of working miracles *per se* offered no definite proof of its actual truth. On the basis of mere miraculous power, the true prophet could, at best, be granted power of giving dispensation from the law in single cases—as also claimed by the rabbis—no more. What interests us essentially here is that the conservatism of the correct legal ethic and the struggle against sins was the ultimate and unconditional standard for measuring the authenticity of prophecy.

The rabbis did not derive their authority from mysteries practiced in their circles. A whole series of cosmological, mythical, magical views and practices were borrowed from Babylonian and here and there perhaps from Egyptian priests. These borrowings were more or less refashioned for ritualistic calendar purposes. However, decisive is that the supreme, esoteric substance of Babylonian priestly wisdom was not borrowed: neither astronomy and astrology nor divination (by means of livers of birds). The last was expressly forbidden,[16] though it certainly occurred among the populace. Once astrology was to be found among talmudic occupations, and horoscopes occasionally were cast here as elsewhere. However, rabbinical teaching expressly prohibited the consultation of the Chaldeans, "for Israel there are no prophets." The Jewish priesthood had successfully eliminated these competitors and the old rabbinical group decidedly rejected this pagan science, particularly astrology, at least in old talmudic times as insults to the majesty and freedom of decision of God. Neither the scientific traditions nor implements were available for the rabbinical pursuit of such learning.

The rabbis were not magicians, prophets, esoteric philosophers, astrologers, or augurs. Neither were they bearers of an esoteric salvation doctrine, a gnosis. The special form of Mideastern gnosis with its demiurges and normlessness (*Anomismus*) was rejected and forbidden. Furthermore, at least in classical talmudic times all gnosis in general was forbidden. Decisive was the fact that gnostic-mystic pursuit of salvation tends to devaluate law and ethically correct conduct. Suspicion was cast on every sort of purely mystical pursuit of salvation, not only forms of mysticism characteristic of genteel intellectual strata. All mysticism was held as "dreaming" that implied the danger of being led astray by demons. This held particularly for states of god-possessed ecstasy and corresponded to the old struggle of the prophets against orgiasticism.

As the Talmud considers "understandability" of the prophets as an index to their value, so the rabbinical interpretation tacitly, but consistently, denied all enthusiasm and the use of irrational means to achieve God. This is not to be explained by "class situation," for the great mass of mystagogues in the Orient and Occident had as their public precisely the small burghers whose predisposition for mystical-ecstatic religiosity has always been ambiguous. It resulted rather from the character of the Jewish tradition established through priestly law on the one hand, through prophecy on the other. This held, in any case, for the Jew who did not wish to renounce the attachment to the law, hence for the Pharisee. The dutiful and continuous study of the law, *per se*, deflected him from the irrational forms of seeking salvation. This was due to the ethical rational content of the Torah and the prophets. Moreover, the Scriptures compensated for the deficiency, if he experienced it as such. The tremendous pathos of the great prophets, the inspiring forcefulness and enthusiasm of the national historiography, the plain but passionate earnestness of the myth of man and creation, the strong emotional content of the Psalms, and the legend of Job and others, and the proverbial wisdom—these provided a framework for religious experience of almost all conceivable emotions. And in its way it is second to nothing.

The uniqueness did not rest in the substance of the experiences *per se*. For their elements and problems one can undoubtedly find parallels in the most varied writings of the world. Its uniqueness, rather, lay in the compression of this content in such narrow compass, and especially in the popular character and absolute understandability of the holy text for everyone. What matters is not that Babylonian mythical and cosmological themes have been borrowed in Biblical accounts, but that they have been transposed from priestly back to popular tradition. It was the directly understandable and, at the same time, heaven soaring prophetic conception of God which determined also this aspect of the "specific understandability" not only of the related events, but above all of their ensuing morale, understandability for everybody, even for a child.[17]

Understandable to the Hellenic child (as to any child) were the Homeric heroes; to the Indian child the related parts of the Mahabharata. But the ethical content of the Bhagavadgita will not be comprehensible to any child, not to the Indian child either. The same applies to the true salvation teaching of Buddha and also to Indian cosmology and anthropology, which are products of intensive thought. Against this, the Jewish Scriptures represent a "rationalism," moralistic as well as pragmatic-cosmological, which is immediately popular and precisely in the most decisive parts addressed to child-like understanding as no other holy book in the world, with the possible exception of the stories of Jesus of Nazareth, or—for quite different reasons— the Chinese teaching of youth.

The paradigm of the one super-worldly god constructs him in part as a father, in part as a now gracious, now ungracious king controlling the vicissitudes of the world. To be sure, he loves his people, yet when it disobeys he punishes it sternly, but can be won again through prayer, humility, and moral conduct. Among all cosmogonic and anthropological mythologies this construction makes all of the events of the world and of life rationally understandable in agreement with the naive, philo- sophically unsophisticated mind of the masses and children. This rational understandability was characteristic of the reli- gious pragmatism of the myths, hymns, and prophets as known to the community through teaching, preaching, and reading. It forced rabbinical thought in its course.

An esoteric gnosis of aristocratic religious virtuosi could not readily grow on such soil, or, if it developed secondarily, it could not easily expand. Esoterics could emerge at best when joined to the visions of the prophets which partly were obscure and the original contextual meaning of which had been partly forgotten and which promised a better future to His stricken people. Religio-philosophical speculation in fact took this as a point of departure. Of this later.

Two things, however, belong to our present context. First, there were speculative eschatologies proper. They originated in connection with the Daniel and Henoch literature and through borrowing of Persian and Babylonian speculations about the re- deemer. The teachings of a "Son of man," of Matathron and similar figures were generally known in circles of Pharisee rabbis proper, but remained strange to them. These doctrines were extensively elaborated, though not exclusively, in the conventi- cles of the *'am ha-arez.* Also Jesus or his followers doubtless took their Son of man representations therefrom, not out of Pharisaic and rabbinical teaching. For these, the Messiah re- mained an earthly king of the Jews promised for the future. This king, with the help of the reconciled god, was to raise his people to its exalted place of old, either destroy its enemies, or—as in the Psalms—reduce them to servants, again finally turn them to the belief of Israel. Or, in connection with the resurrection, the idea was that a king would emerge in the kingdom of whom the resurrected pious persons would again lead a new and pure life.

But all these hopes which so readily led to metaphysical, hence esoteric, speculation, were simply hopes, expectations of the future. It is clear that these expectations whenever they came to mind had to impart a tremendous pathos to the piety of the Jews. One of the basic differences from all Indian savior religion rests in the presence of such expectations of a last day. Moreover, if in view of unusual signs and revolutions, or under the influence of eschatological prophets, these expectancies seemed to come true they could and did lead to the mightiest and under certain conditions wildest enthusiasm. But, in workaday life or when circumstances deflected attention from them they were inevitably reduced to a soulful longing to be saved from suffering and distress. The order of the world, the Jewish people and the pious alike were accused as insufficient and such longing contented itself again and reconciled itself with its fate. This benefited the character of Jewish religion as a "religion of faith." This was especially true in talmudic times after the fall of the Temple under Hadrian when messianic hopes were postponed to faraway times. Conduct could be influenced in practice only by the question what kind of behavior might entitle men to expect the timely advent of the redeemer and to enter personally the resurrection. The rabbis answered in terms of the priestly paradigm of the holy history and the prophets, and, naturally, the law. Its emotional significance was thereby greatly enhanced. The sins of the community, of the authorities (the falling away from God particularly) were, in the eyes of the rabbis, doubtlessly also the severest of all sins, because they forfeited the coming of the Messiah for future times and thus betrayed all the pious and their hopes. On the other side, the universal promises of the Torah and the prophets, according to which all nations were to be brought to God and to Israel, certainly became one of the decisive motives for proselytism, as we shall show below. For the individual only the law and its fulfillment came into consideration. Indeed, there was no other holy path. The prescribed path, however, was open to every man, for, in the last analysis, the rabbis rejected asceticism as well as the intellectual mysticism of a salvation aristocracy.

3. *Teaching and Ethic of*
Pharisaical Judaism

PHARISAIC and older Judaism were unfamiliar with the dualism of "spirit" and "matter," or "spirit" and "body," or "spirit" and "flesh," or divine purity and the corruption of the "world," dualisms which Hellenistic intellectualism had elaborated. Neo-Platonism developed this into the idea that the body be the "dungeon" of the soul, a *pudendum*. Individual circles of Hellenist Judaic intellectuals (Philo) took it over, Paul's Christian teaching made it the fundamental conception of his ethical world image.

All this is alien to Pharisaic-talmudic Judaism. Certainly God is creator and Lord of the world and men are his creatures, not his shoots or emanations. He has created them, including his chosen people, not generated them. For prophetic Judaism this followed from God's universalism and, interconnected with this, his mighty power, which gave him sovereignty also over his own people. He is the god of world history. This dualism has been alleged to be characteristically Jewish or "Semitic" respectively in contrast to those other conceptions. For practical ethics, however, a decisive accent rests upon it only insofar as it dispensed with all theodicy. Besides the absolute weakness of men against God had to be realized, above all, magic compulsion of God was absolutely excluded, and "faith" inevitably received the specific coloring of childlike "obedience" to the world monarch. That was certainly important enough. However, "rejection" or "devaluation of the world" followed in no way.

The Jewish god is a patriarchal monarch. He proves to be the merciful "father" of the children, who were created in his image. The world is not evil but good, as the creation story indicates. Man is weak, as a child, and therefore inconstant in his will and amenable to sins, that is to say, to disobedience against the fatherly creator. It is not only the individual—this is stressed —but precisely, also, the collectivity, the people. And thereby the individual as well as the people as a whole spurn his love and mercy for themselves and their descendants and often for long times, and in some respects, permanently. Thus Adam and Eve through disobedience have caused for all their descendants death, the pain of birth, the subjection of woman to man, and the necessity and fatigue of work. But precisely the rabbinical outlook was inclined to judge more strictly than Adam's fall the disobedience of the people, the worship of the golden calf and of Baalim which were responsible for the downfall of the Jewish people. However severely the disobedient people are scolded there was no thought of "original sin" or creatural corruption or depravity of the sensuous. Moreover, the idea was quite remote that withdrawal from the world be prerequisite to religious salvation.

The prohibition of "pictures and likenesses" was certainly a highly important source of the negative relation of Jewry to sensuous artistic culture. Like the horror of pronouncing the name of Jehovah, this prohibition was magical and anti-idolatrous in origin, then it was placed into the context of the ideas of the majesty of God and His omnipresence in his creation and Pharisaism experienced it as a significant and, above all, distinctive characteristic over and against the idolatry of foreign peoples. But this, for its part, was no result of "anti-sensuousness" or withdrawal from the world.

Pharisaic Judaism was also far from rejecting wealth or from thinking that it be dangerous, or that its unqualified enjoyment endangers salvation. Wealth was, indeed, considered prerequisite to certain priestly functions. For the rest, the prophets and Psalms had chastised the unbrotherly exploitation of economic power as shattering the old neighborhood ethic sanctioned by Yahwe's commandments, and the brotherliness of the compatriots. In this, the petty bourgeois ethic of the Pharisees of course agreed. As we shall see, the old stipulations against usury and in favor of debtor and slave and the priestly construction of the week of the Sabbath year and of the debt remission in the Jubilee year were casuistically elaborated.

However, there was lacking precisely any point of departure for an economically ordered methodic or inner-worldly asceticism as well as for a sexual asceticism. To be sure, occasionally the question was posed whether it be not better for the rabbi to remain single to allow him to devote himself untroubled to his studies. But this had nothing to do with "asceticism." However, it is noteworthy that the duty to work, important for the good of the community was here sufficiently strong to shatter the old commandment to produce progeny. However, otherwise the cultic and magical purity duties known from Jewry and outsiders betrays no scruples against sexual intercourse and against the enjoyment of women. Candid openmindedness is evident in the injunction that one should leave the old Israelite warrior "time to enjoy his wife." This would also hold for the talmudic Jew. The relentless struggle against "whoredom"—besides murder and idolatry considered the third greatest sin—stemmed from the old priestly struggle against Baal-orgiasticism, and the strict confinement of sexual intercourse to legitimate marriage corresponds throughout to Indian and similar commandments; the sharp struggle against every form of onanism (including *onanism matrimonialis*) corresponds to the Biblical curse which was determined by the struggle against the onanist Moloch-orgiasticism.[18]

The quite emphatic recommendation of early marriage—delay beyond a certain age made one a sinner—as with Luther, springs from the conviction of the frankly sensuous people that otherwise sins are unavoidable. Sexual phenomena continued to be considered plainly natural. The old taboos against exposure and all nakedness may well have emerged from the struggle against orgiasticism and were perhaps sharpened through the opposition to the Hellenic gymnasium. These taboos went hand in hand with blunt speech and (later) regulation of sexual behavior in the interests in part of Levitical purity, in part of hygiene. As is known, both phenomena are also to be found in Islam and other "purity" oriented religions. Judaism, in this respect, goes further than Catholic confessional literature and practice and is shocking and often disgusting to modern erotic feeling and to a sense of dignity of a feudal or intellectual aristocracy. To be sure, such dignity was foreign to Jewry as well as Catholic chaplainocracy. Abstinence from alcohol and meat, as upheld by the correct Hindu and practiced, indeed, by the genteel strata, was unknown to the rabbis and pious Jewish laymen. Obviously, the old Baal-orgiasticism, contested by priest and prophet, was mainly sexual, hence fertility and not alcoholic orgiasticism.

As women and wine please the human heart, so wealth and all ritually permissible enjoyments of this world. On the whole the basic attitude of the old rabbis toward the world may well find its expression in the talmudic saying that paradise belongs to him "who makes his companion happy." In any case we must by no means seek a principled, ascetic way of life at the basis of Pharisaic Judaism. It required strict ritualism as did the official religion of India. For the rest, Judaism was a religion of faith based on trust in God and his promise of living in fear of sin as disobedience toward him and in fear of its consequences.

Judaism certainly did not represent an ascetic way of life. To be sure in one point its way of life resembled the rational ascetic principles: in its commandment of vigilant self-observation and absolute self-control. The indispensability of the first unavoidably resulted from constantly measuring one's correct deportment by the law with its innumerable ritual commandments, and especially prohibitions to be observed. Six hundred thirteen prescriptions were counted as given by Moses and rabbinical casuistry multiplied them greatly. The second was partly connected with this, partly bound up with the old opposition to orgiasticism. While the old Israelite Jehovah was a god of passionate wrath, more than any other, the rabbis, as happened in China, considered any excitement as of demonic origin and as dangerous to salvation, hence as sin. The dominant attitude of the Talmud, at least externally, differs greatly from and contrasts to the religiosity of the Psalms which, as we have shown, often are permeated by passionate wrath and hatred or to the sharp resentment toward the godless who are well off, to the reveling in fantasies of revenge in the Book of Esther, and also to the Ebionite hatred of riches of the Gospel of Luke as it appears, for instance, in the prayer of Mary. Such religious rationalization of the need for revenge of the enemy or fortunate ones assigns second place to one's own revenge against injustice, because God will then consummate it the more sharply in the here and now or in the beyond. A still further sublimation unreservedly forgives the enemy in order to shame him and scorn him before others or, and above all, before himself. These rationalizations were not only known to the Talmud, but their nature was distinctly recognized and sharply rejected by the rabbis. For nothing is more impressively emphasized than the commandment: not to will the "shaming" of others.

In family relations great praise is given to the most beautiful act of piety, namely, to have avoided the shaming of the parents who have wronged the child. However, the same applies to the wrongdoer, particularly in the course of quarrel and discussion. The hopeless downfall of Jewry through the destruction of the Temple clearly led the rabbis to focus attention upon the ethical problems of the resentment of repressed and sublimated revenge. Early Christendom was less sophisticated and has given less thought to these facts. As is known, it shows some examples of a rather open ethic of resentment which was fought in talmudic Judaism.

To be sure, the struggle of the rabbis against the religious internationalization of revenge is ethically impressive and indicates, indeed, a strong sublimation of ethical feeling. But it proves essentially that it did not remain hidden to them how strong a factor the need for revenge, condemned to impotence, actually was in Judaism of late antiquity.

CHAPTER XVI

JUDAISM AND EARLY CHRISTIANITY

1. *Essenism in Relation to the Teachings of Jesus*

As indicated above, alert self-control was strongly developed by the Jews even in Antiquity. However, it was not founded in an ascetic way of life.

Certainly ascetic institutions are to be found among the Jews. Aside from cult prescriptions of abstinence and purity for priests, there were, in particular, the ritualistic fasts prescribed at definite times. But they were throughout cult prescriptions, intended primarily to appease God's wrath. The same is true of individual fasts. In fact anyone fasting was without further ado considered to be a sinner. Undoubtedly asceticism might have found a point of departure here: the thought and the sermon of the need for penance is indeed specific to ancient Judaism as important consequence of its conception of god. With the increasing devaluation of priestly sacrifice, the individual readily came to view a life of penitence as a path to salvation. The few great fasting men of Jewish religious history (properly authenticated only by R. Zaina) must doubtlessly be viewed as great penitents. Vows such as those of the old Nazarites persisted as a means of pleasing God or of warding off His wrath. Paul, too, as is known, made a vow (for a certain time) and redeemed it when he was a Christian. Presumably it was intended as a means of preventing his epileptic attacks.

An ascetic sect developed on similar foundations only much later among the "mourners for Zion," the followers of Korah. This is of no interest to us here. Seeming "ascetic" phenomena among Pharisaic Jewry actually stemmed from the pursuit of Levitical purity decisive for Pharisaism. This pursuit of purity could vary in intensity. Normally it led the Pharisees to become increasingly exclusive and systematically ritualistic. This correctness as mentioned did not require separation from workaday life. But the principle could also be pushed beyond the demands of inner-worldly morality. This was the basis of Essenism which, from this point of view, was merely a radical Pharisaic sect.

The Essenes extend back to the second century B.C., but their age and possible interrelation with the Rechabites is doubtful. Moreover some important questions concerning their teaching are only hypothetically answerable. Nevertheless, the striving for absolute Levitical purity, externally and spiritually, can be plainly recognized as a fundamental element. The Essenes were, like the larger Pharisaic brotherhood, an order. But their affiliation prescriptions were far stricter and comprised, above all, a solemn vow, a novitiate, and years of probation. The organization of the order was quite strict and monk-like. The head (*mishmer*) of the local chapter had unconditional authority. Excommunication lay in the hands of a council of one hundred full members. The apostolate among the Essenes, as with the official Jewish community, presumably served mainly to raise funds on behalf of the order. The fact that the apostles always wandered in pairs—as did the early Christians—probably served the purpose of controlling ritualistic correctness.

The Essenes segregated themselves from the less pure by excluding not only connubium and commensality but all contact. They, too, rejected incorrect priests and this led them, not only to a devaluation, but to strong distrust of priests in general, a fact which was certainly co-determined by their special attitude toward the sacrifice.

Besides the strong accent on baptism of novices and on purity baths, constantly repeated on all conceivable occasions, the radical striving for purity was ritually expressed in the strictness of the specifically Pharisaic commandments. The fear of ritualistic defilment and all purity prescriptions were extremely intensified. All study, except of the law and scriptural cosmology, was held to be pagan, hence dangerous; and purely secular enjoyments were objectionable, hence had to be avoided. The Sabbath, for the Essenes, was no day of joy, as for the ordinary Pharisee, but a day of absolute rest. Copulation was restricted by the Essenes to Wednesday, allegedly lest the child come into the world on the Sabbath. Dress prescriptions (*tsitsit*) were held to be absolute. The morning prayer was preceded by a period of contemplation. Not only killing, but any injury to the neighbor, even out of negligence, was held to be severely self-defiling. The commandment not to steal was tightened, one was not to burden his conscience with any sort of gain. The legitimacy of all gain seemed problematic. The Essenes, therefore, shunned trade even as war; they rejected the possession of money and slaves; they restricted permissible possessions to the necessities of a handicraft or tillage livelihood. Correspondingly, they pushed the old social commandment of brotherliness to the length of an unworldly love communism of consumption. In this connection is mentioned not only the *agape*, the love feast the means of which were furnished by the propertied, but Philo also reports common houses and magazines, and a common "treasure." Presumably surpluses over personal needs were deposited there for the sake of a highly developed charity.

Whether complete communism actually developed and whether even these institutions were actually fully developed among all Essenes is uncertain. For the Essenes lived mainly in Palestine, but apparently did not always possess settled places for meals. Besides the support of the poor, the obligation to receive and support travelling brethren (hence, probably journeyman artisans) was one of their basic institutions. The common treasury probably served primarily this purpose.

The Essenes considered rage and all passions as demonically instilled states. They viewed them as more dangerous even than did the ordinary Pharisees. Presumably from this point of view the pious were expressly exhorted to use prayer as a radical counter means toward those who had wronged them; that is, to "love one's enemy." The holiness of the name of God led them not only to reject the oath, but to develop a secret doctrine and Arkan-discipline. This discipline required ritualistic chastity for those interested in the promised gifts of grace, hence strict sexual continence and a strong disinclination toward marriage, which was controversial for them insofar as it led to complete rejection of marriage. Marriage, as we saw, was also considered undesirable by some of the Pharisaic rabbis. The true motive for the special Essenian way of life is apparently to be found in the gift of grace conveyed by the secret teaching and the quest for this reward. For this contains an element which can be distinctly recognized as alien to Pharisaism and Judaism generally.

The secret doctrine, according to Josephus, was contained in carefully guarded holy writings. In the reception as full member, the individual had to obligate himself by oath to silence toward outsiders, but to candor with brethren of the order. The substance of the secret doctrine appears to have consisted of an allegorical re-interpretation of the holy legends, a pronounced faith in divine ordainment, and a more than usually explicit angelology, various acts of sun worship—the most striking foreign element—and in place of the Pharisaic belief in resurrection was posited a promise of immortality with conceptions of heaven and hell. With regard to rituals the rejection of animal sacrifice is characteristic of the Essenes. Therewith they excluded themselves from the Temple cult, but they retained the relationship to the Temple through sending of gifts. The charisma which the Arkan-discipline was to provide was, to all appearances, the gift of prophecy which Josephus ascribes to them, probably it correlates with their belief in ordainment. Besides this, their therapeutics is praised, especially their knowledge of the powers of minerals and roots. Their religiosity, essentially, was one of prayer characterized by intense devotional attitudes.

Evidently these elements of Essenian doctrine and practice were no more than an extreme extension of Pharisaic purity-ritualism and did not stem from Judaism. The angelology also of the Pharisees, was of Persian origin. The sharpened dualism in the doctrine of body and soul points in the same direction—though here Hellenistic influence is conceivable. Quite Persian (or Persian Babylonian) is the veneration of the sun which—in contrast to the former—appears indeed to be non-Jewish and its tolerance by correct Jewry seems strange. The inclination toward celibacy, the ranks of the order, and the rejection of animal sacrifice may represent Indian influence—through some sort of mediation—but, like washings and sacraments, these elements could also stem from Hellenistic-Oriental mysteries. Probably the elaboration of secret doctrine was derived from the same source. In fact, the order of the Essenes represents a fusion of sacramental mystery religion with Levitical purity ritualism. It was differentiated from the usual Mid Eastern savior mysteries in the lack of a personal savior as an object of worship. The intense messianic hope for the Essenes as for the Pharisees was a hope for the future. Thus the sect, in rigorous judgment, should have been heterodox.

Judaism, however, by virtue of its ritualistic character, circumvented this as did Hinduism in similar cases. The Jewish congregation overlooked the obviously heterodox inroads because communion with the Temple was retained and the Mosaic law was observed to which Pharisaism attached the greatest value. Observance of the law in the sense of the Pharisees was even especially emphasized. The sect was tolerated like a Jewish fellowship which was specialized by indifferent special vows and teachings, in the way followed as long as possible in the face of the similarly conditioned Nazareean community of Jewish Christians who adhered to the Jerusalem Temple and observed the law.

The boundary between Pharisaism and Essenism, however, was fluid at least with regard to way of life. No closed corporate organization of this form with the prohibition of profitable pursuits is known to have existed on the basis of ordinary Pharisaism of the time. On the contrary, the Gospels represent the Pharisees as "covetous." However, numerous phenomena suggest a similar mentality. First, the acosmism of love. Well-to-do people were designated as "*hasheina*" (the "secret ones") who on principle and in a grand manner gave secretly to the poor, who likewise accepted them in secret without their persons being known, and not only occasionally and in an unorganized fashion but out of a common treasury established for the purpose. According to the Talmud such funds would seem to have been established in almost all cities. In this the characteristic trait of talmudic *caritas* finds expression in agreement with the rabbinical commandment to shame "no one" and the later principle stressed by Jesus "let not thy left hand know what thy right hand doeth," because only then can the gift merit heavenly reward which otherwise would be preempted. This trait is also characteristic of modern Jewish philanthropy, in contrast, for example, to the Puritan but also to the usual Christian charity.

The striving for absolute purity motivated the withdrawal from all worldly pleasures, as practiced by the *"kadosh"* ("saint") in the manner of the Essenes and also hermits, *"barnaim"* ("peasants," of hermitages), are occasionally to be found. These phenomena of an actual rejection of the world were, however, just as alien to ordinary Pharisaism as were the respective rules of the Essenes and in turn may well be explained by non-Jewish influences. Ritualistically there are certain overtones of old *Hasidic* and Essenian practice to be found with the *"Watikim,"* who regulated the morning prayer with formal strictness so that its end coincided with the sunrise—to mention but one of many similar phenomena. Despite all its ritualistic correctness and strict segregation from paganism, Pharisaic Judaism remained exposed to the most varied invasions of heterogeneous ritualism (for example to sun-cult ritualism). Although the development of a genuinely secret teaching was quite alien to Pharisaism, it could not possibly hinder the diffusion of apocalyptic, eschatological, Messiah expectations and prophecies. In the nature of the case these functioned similarly and were in the air, as is indicated most plainly in the environment of the Gospel stories and myths.

The organization, religious conduct, and ethic of the Essenes have often been related to original Christian practice, especially by Jews. The Essenes, like the Christians, had baptism, the love feast (*agape*), the communism of acosmic love, the support of the poor, the apostolate (in the Jewish sense of the term), the aversion toward marriage (for the sanctified members), gifts of grace, above all prophecy desired as a holy state. (Also the expression ἐκκλησια was used for their community meetings.) Their ethic, like the early Christian, was strictly pacifistic, commanding love of enemies, it gives a favorable estimate of the hopes for salvation of the poor, an unfavorable one of the rich even as the Ebionite elements of the Gospels. To this come the elements of common Pharisaic ethic which are related to the Early Christian. Essenian ethic like the Early Christian in many points represents Pharisaic ethic intensified. The nature of this intensification, however, differs between the cases. For precisely with regard to ritualistic (Levitical) purity, even Jesus' message took quite a different course. The monumentally impressive lordly word, "not that what goeth into the mouth defileth a man; but that which cometh out of the mouth" and out of an impure heart, (Math. 15:11, 18 f.) meant that for him ethical sublimation was decisive, not the ritualistic surpassing of the Jewish purity laws. And the anxious segregation of the Essenes from the ritualistically impure is contrasted by his well-ascertained unconcern in having intercourse and table community with them.

The ethical conceptions to be found on both sides, however, were diffused in most varied forms in the original area of both communities, and the identical institutions were shared partly already by the Pharisaic *chevra*, partly, as must be assumed, by manifold cult communities. What matters more than all else is that the epiphany of a present personal savior and his cult, as well as the tremendous and specifically early Christian significance of the "spirit" πνευμα as far as known, remained alien to the Essenes.

The pneuma, as charisma and indicative proof of an exemplary state of grace, was indeed no strange concept to Jewry, nor to the teaching of Pharisaism. The "spirit of Yahwe" as berserk-charisma came over the hero (Samson) and king (as a fierce wrath over Saul), and particularly as the charisma of vision and prophetic pronouncement, possibly of miracles over the seers, prophets, and miracle-workers. The highpriest is in need of Yahwe's spirit in order validly to expiate the people, the spirit leaves him (Phinehas), it forsakes the king or hero if he is sinful, and it is also mighty in every teacher: as the prophet sees and hears through the spirit, so the teacher teaches through it. In the Talmud it is called *ruach-ha-kodesch*, in the *Septuagint* translation of Psalm 51:11, and Isaiah 63:10, 11 πνεῦμα τὸ ἅγιον. Its daemonic counterpart is the teaching of the "impure spirit." In the Gospels the scribes call it the spirit of Beelzebub, the "prince of the devils" [Math. 12:24]. The rabbis, for fear of using the name of God, use instead of "holy spirit" often the name "*shekina*." There developed the doctrine that the "divine spirit," which in the beginning of creation "moved upon the face of the waters," was created on the first day. The dove, the symbol of persecuted Israel, was also in the Talmud occasionally treated as the harbinger of the spirit.

Also in talmudic literature is to be found the representation that the holy spirit intercede with God for men as *"synegor,"* that is to say "paraclete," [1] intercessor and helper. The teaching of the closure of the prophetic age, however, led to the assumption that the holy spirit, since Malachi had vanished from the world. One can no longer obtain it, but only *"bat kol,"* the spirit which the rabbi requires for the correct interpretation of the divine law. On the other hand Joel (2:28 f.) had conceived the purity and holiness of the select after the coming of the Messiah in this manner. The holy spirit would be imparted to all, it would permit the sons and daughters to prophesy, the elders to have dreams, and the young to have visions and the spirit would be poured out, also, upon servants and maids. The revival of the holy spirit in all men accordingly would be a sign of the advent of the Messiah and of the kingdom of God at hand. This representation has been decisive for the early Christian conception of the Pentecostal miracle. The "spirit" in this specific sense of an irrational godly prophetic gift, the rabbis could neither claim for themselves nor could they consider it a sign of the state of grace of the community members.

The rabbinical teacher, however elevated his authority, could never think of claiming the place of a spiritual "superman." His authority always rested on the word scripturally fixed in the Torah and the prophets. All development in the direction of the worship of the soul shepherd, in the manner of *guru*-worship in India, in Asia and in Christendom was completely precluded. Also, it was excluded by the nature of the Jewish conception of god which compelled the rejection of all deification of creatures as pagan abominations. Neither did the rabbi come into consideration for veneration as a saint or mystagogue in the manner of Christian or Asiatic phenomena of this sort. He pursued a religious calling, but did not dispense grace. To do this, originally within limits, was the charisma of the priest and remained characteristic only of the *kohanim* qualified by *ceramitic* descent, but essentially formalistic—as they alone were qualified to say the "priestly blessing."

First the *Hasidic* movement in Eastern Europe created in the *tsadik,* the virtuoso of *Hasidic* mysticism, a form corresponding to the Asiatic type of helper in need and mystagogue. Therefore the *tsadik's* claims stood sharply opposed to the authority of the rabbi, and were rejected by the latter as heresy. The Jewish rabbi dispensed neither sacramental grace, nor was he a charismatic helper in need. His special religious possession was "knowledge." This, however, was extraordinarily cherished. His honor surpassed that of his seniors and even of the parents, "knowledge above all." His personal authority rested above all in serving as a model by leading an exemplary way of life. Its characteristic, however, was merely the strict orientation to the divine word.

Also in his workaday's duties, the rabbi was a servant of the "word," no "preacher," to be sure, but a "teacher." He taught the law in the closed circle of his disciples and did not publicly exhort the community through preaching. Indeed, he taught also in the synagogue. However, in ancient Judaism, so far as is known, he taught publicly only on the Sabbaths before the great festivals and on the *Kallaben* days. Then the purpose, too, was to teach the pious community the ritual duties in those times, just as, in case of doubt, he assisted the individual by advising him in matters of ritual duties. Besides the systematic education of the disciples in the law the professional work of the rabbi consisted mainly in giving *responsa* in the manner of the Roman jurist; besides, he functioned as an arbitrator and the rabbis called especially in the *"Bet Din,"* functioned as judges proper. The public religious ethical sermon on Sabbath afternoon was, in Jewish antiquity, quite unorganized. As far as preaching existed—which may well have been the case to a considerable extent—the sermon, then as later, was handled by personalities other than the local rabbi, namely by the "magyr." This rabbinically schooled itinerant teacher of later times is certainly a very old phenomenon. A wandering sophist, guest of the well-to-do community members, he journeys from one community to the other exactly as did Paul who preached throughout in the synagogues. Certainly, not only itinerant speakers appeared. But the very extensive freedom to teach and preach allowed anybody to preach who thought himself qualified and was thus considered by the community. Also the "scribes" did so who actually presupposed evangelism ritualistically though obviously not as part of their normal vocational duties. On the other hand, the rabbi was concerned only with tasks of a non-priestly and purely technical ritualistic nature. In ancient Judaism this meant, above all, the conduct of the ritual bath (*mikweh*) and *shehitah*, the ritual butchering ("*schächten*") which he had to supervise and perform personally under certain conditions. In all this the authoritative interpretation of the law was and remained the main business.

The technical nature of legal interpretation corresponded to the social nature of the petty bourgeoisie. This stratum to which the early rabbis largely belonged was its main champion. As emphasized above, "common sense" and that practical-ethical rationalism, an attitude always close to bourgeois strata has strongly influenced the way in which the rabbis handled the law. Thus the "*ratio*" of the stipulations instead of the letter on the one side, the compelling needs of everyday life, above all, of the economy, on the other, came into their own. But there was no opportunity at all for genuinely "constructive" rational thought, hence, "juristic" thought proper, as has been practiced by the Roman responding jurists and by them alone. In practice, this means capacity for the formation of rational concepts. The rabbis were no exclusively secular and above all no status group of genteel jurists like the Roman jurisconsuls, but plebeian teachers of religious ritual. The rabbi was inwardly not only more strictly bound to the positive divine commandment than the jurist can ever be to positive law, but there were also the typical forms and limitations of all petty bourgeois rationalism. Word interpretation and descriptive analogies take the place of conceptual analysis; concrete casuistry takes the place of abstraction and synthesis.

The *responsa* of the early rabbis were, after all, largely oriented to practical rational needs, but they were addressed to the concrete individual case. This practice underwent a sort of "theoretical" broadening when, after the fall of the Temple, the great rabbinical schools in Mesopotamia and Palestine became organized centers of *responsa* practice, a position which they retained for the entire civilized world till the end of the Carolingian times. Meanwhile the position of rabbi was tied to ordination (laying on of hands) by the patriarch or his legitimate representatives, and a regular academic curriculum was prescribed with lectures, questions, and discussions with the teacher, with study prebends, and boarding schools.

The special organization of the Pharisaic brotherhood had apparently disappeared, *chaber* later referred to a man who studied the law with particular zeal, the typical late Jewish notable, and *"perushim"* is found as a designation for students. The "spirit" of Pharisaism was all dominant in Jewry. But it was no longer the spirit of an active brotherhood, but the spirit of literary study *per se*. According to occasional notions, God Himself "studies" the timelessly valid law in order to abide by it, somewhat in the way in which the Indian world creator practices asceticism enabling him to create the world.

Now systematic thought detached from the single case could develop. Its peculiarity, however, was in part determined by its ties to the tradition of the early rabbis and in part by the social structure of Jewry.

Pharisaic purity ritualism brought about higher ritual barriers against both outsiders and in-group members. The barriers precisely against in-group members were important. The Essenian community segregated itself out of fear of defilement from intermarriage, commensalism, and any close contact with the rest of the Jews, and it is questionable whether they were the only conventicle of this kind. The Pharisaic brotherhood segregated itself likewise from the *'am ha-artez*,[2] Jerusalemite Jewry and those influenced by the Jerusalem priesthood segregated themselves from the Samaritans and all other survivals of the old Yahwe faith, anchored to local shrines and not influenced by the prophets and the Jerusalem priesthood after the Samaritans had been formally excluded from the sacrifice in Jerusalem which they were inclined to honor. Thus there emerged a firm and, due to its ritualistic condition, a caste-like structure of the old Yahwe believers. Alongside this the hereditary privileges of the priest and Levite sibs continued to live on within Jewry. They were not completely excluded from intermarriage with other Jewish sibs, but were, indeed, under the commandment of hypergamy. To this was added the ritualistic rejection, in part tabooing, in part <u>disapproval of certain occupations</u> as an element of religious status formation.

As <u>despised and despicable w</u>ere held, alongside ass and camel drivers and pottery dealers, freight carriers on land and sea and warehousemen, all of these doubtlessly because a ritualistically pure way of life seemed impossible for them. The first category, naturally, also because they were <u>originally foreign-born guest workers</u>. To this came the Deuteronomically accursed occupations of sorcerers and soothsayers of all sorts. But the ritually pure considered as dubious also trades such as those of peddlers, barbers, veterinarians, certain stone workers, tanners, milkers, wool-combers, weavers, and goldsmiths. The reason given for some of these trades is the fact that their pursuit brings one in <u>ever dubious contact with women</u>. Besides traditional social evaluations, the decisive factor was <u>the general distrust in the possibility of combining the occupation with ritualistic correctness</u>.

In addition the descent of some of them from immigrants (thus the goldsmiths) may have mattered. A high priest may not be taken out of a family which has dedicated itself to these trades. However, not all of these trades seem to have stood outside the Pharisaic order, or, at least, not during the entire talmudic period. At least, a tanner is to be found among the better known rabbis (R. Jose) and, as already noted, even an astrologer. <u>Special synagogues</u> for some of the old royal handicrafts, for coppersmiths and cashiers, are mentioned in talmudic literature. <u>Separate seats according to trade</u> in the common synagogue were frequent. Actually the occupations precisely of the <u>royal artisans</u> (beside these, also, others) were to a large extent <u>hereditary sib-professions</u> and the <u>artisans</u> were <u>tribal foreigners</u>, imported by the king, which may well explain their special position. Among the suspect occupations were also to be found those the Jews largely followed later, in the Middle Ages. The rejection of these trades does not bespeak a genuine caste-like segregation in ancient Jewry. Nevertheless its internal structure shows important features of such segregation.

2. Increasing Ritualistic Segregation
of the Jews

TOWARD the outside world Jewry increasingly assumed the type of a ritualistically segregated guest people (pariah people). And indeed Jewry did this voluntarily and not under pressure of external rejection. The general diffusion of "antisemitism" in Antiquity is a fact. Likewise, this only slowly increasing rejection of the Jews precisely kept step with the increasingly rigid rejection of community with non-Jews by the Jews themselves.

The ancient aversion to Jews was far from constituting a "racial" antipathy. The tremendous scope of proselytism, soon to be discussed, is sufficient evidence against this. It was, rather, the negative attitude of the Jews themselves which was decisive for the mutual relation. Deviant and absurd appearing rites were known in Antiquity in richest measure. The reason was certainly not there. The pronounced indifference toward the polis deities whose guest rights they enjoyed, must, of course, have been felt to be godless and insulting. However, that also was not decisive. The "misanthropy" of the Jews was, if one goes to the root of the matter, always the ultimate and decisive reproach, the principled refusal of connubium, commensality, and every sort of fraternization or closer community even in business life.

And what is not to be underrated—this went together with the opportunity, offered by the *chevra*, for every Pharisaical Jew to fall back on the strong support of the brotherhood. The economic effect of this factor could not escape the attention of pagan competitors. The social isolation of the Jews, this "ghetto" in the intimate sense of the word, was, indeed, primarily self-chosen and self-willed and this to a constantly increasing extent.

First the influence of the *soferim* was decisive, then that of the Pharisees. The former, as shown, endeavored in principle to preserve the pure faith of the Jews. Quite otherwise with the Pharisees! They advocated, first and foremost, a (ritualistic) doctrine; a confession, not—at least not primarily—a nationality. For them proselytizing, the most zealous propaganda endeavor on behalf of their community went hand in hand with the inconsiderate segregation from the ritualistically impure. Jesus called to them ". . . hypocrites, for ye compass sea and land to make one proselyte . . ." (Mat. 23:15). The most zealous Pharisees considered it indeed as god-pleasing possibly to make a proselyte each year.

3. *Proselytism in the Diaspora*

IN the main, Jewish propaganda, like early Christian of post-apostolic times, advanced through voluntary and private endeavor, not through official authorities. The attitude of the latter and also that of official literature was vacillating.

The old tradition of the law (Ex. 12:48) still bore the traces of the time when the Yahwe-religion of the confederacy expanded through the reception into full citizenship of neighboring tribes and sibs of *gerim,* that is metics and clients, who dwelt as protégées within Israel. The legal position of the metics was regulated and it was also defined which ritualistic rights they could win only through circumcision.

Prophecy (Is. 14:1) predicted of the strangers who came to Israel restored to its landed possession and would "cleave to the House of Jacob." This passage, in connection with the promise to Abraham and the numerous references which held out the coming of all peoples on earth to Israel to worship its God appeared to prove propaganda as pleasing to God, possibly as a very means to prepare the time for the coming of the Messiah. However the views of the holy literature differed in this point.

The Ruth and Jonas legends were decidedly favorable to proselytism, an authority as significant as Ezra, however, was averse to propaganda. The familist organization of the priesthood as well as of the newly constituted polis of Jerusalem, for which he deserves credit, stood in the way, at least, of individual affiliation, and Ezra placed decisive importance upon purity of blood for the sake of the desired segregation of the holy people.

All this was quite different for the Pharisaic petty bourgeois and tipped the balance again in favor of propaganda among its representatives, especially those in the Diaspora. Most teachers considered it as decidedly meritorious to bring a pagan into the *shekinah* ("Divine Presence"). Soon so much so, that by use of the old metic concept also such propaganda was held as valuable, which under certain conditions renounced the demand for the prompt and complete assumption of all ritualistic duties, above all, circumcision, through the proselytes and promoted the provisional affiliation as mere "friends," i.e., half-Jews. For the demand of circumcision was understandably a very serious handicap for the propaganda among adult men. Women, therefore, were far more numerous among the full-proselytes than men. Three (not only two) steps of affiliation were distinguished, (1) the *"ger-toshab,"* the "friend" (the half-convert). He accepted the monotheist belief in God and the Jewish ethic (of the Decalogue), but not Jewish ritual; his ritualistic behavior remained quite uncontrolled and he had no formal relation to the congregation. (2) The *"ger-sha'ar"* ("proselyte of the gate") was, according to theory, the old metic under Jewish jurisdiction. He vowed before three members of the brotherhood to honor no idols. The seven *Noachidic* commandments, the Sabbath, the taboo against pigs, the ritualistic fasts were binding on him, but not circumcision. He was a passive member of the community with limited rights of participation in festivals and celebrations of the synagogue. (3) The *"ger-zadek"* or *"ger-berith"* ("proselyte of righteousness") who after circumcision and assumption of ritual duties was received into full community. His descendants became first fully qualified Jews in the third generation.

The expectation in this practice was that the *ger-toshab* and still more the *ger-sha'ar,* even if personally avoiding circumcision, still might decide to have his children circumcised and thus become full Jews, and in a great many cases the expectation certainly came true. For this practice met more than halfway the interests of the environment, above all, of the Hellenes. What attracted them to Judaism was, of course, not its ritual. According to the whole character of Hellenistic religiosity, this could have been the case only if Judaism had offered sacramental or magical means of redemption, and promises in the manner of the mysteries, hence irrational holy paths and states, and precisely these were out of the question in Judaism. What was appealing were the conception of God which appeared as grandiose and majestic, the radical elimination of the

cult of deities and idols felt to be insincere, and, above all,
Jewish ethic, appearing as pure and vigorous, and besides the
plain and clear promises for the future, hence rational elements.
Jewry attracted people who found their religious satisfaction
with the purity of the ethic and the power of the conception of
God. The fixed order of life *per se,* offered by the ritual, exerted
a great appeal which must have been especially strong in times
which after the collapse of the national Hellenic states witnessed
the decay of the traditional militarist structuring of the citizens'
way of life in the polis. The age of intellectual rationalism
with its increasing "bourgeois" rationalization of Hellenic religiosity, especially during the last centuries of the Roman Republic
was also the great epoch of Jewish proselytism. Whoever by
nature or experience was disposed to irrational mystical quest
for salvation will have remained aloof, and the age of an increasing pursuit of irrational holy states did not benefit Judaism,
but the mystery religions and Christianity. The full Jewish ritual
was presumably adopted mostly by persons on their own behalf
or on behalf of their children among strata interested in affiliat-
ing with the Pharisaic brotherhood. The available evidence
shows that this was indeed the case among the petty bourgeoisie,
especially the artisans and retailers. Although the Jewish belief
was *religio licita* still, according to Roman administrative law,
the full convert forfeited the *jus bonorum* and the Jewish law
disqualified him for office, because it would not permit him to
take part in the state cult.

The Jewish Diaspora, on its side, was greatly interested not
only in increasing its membership but also in winning "friends"
on the outside, especially among influential and office-qualified
circles; hence, from its standpoint, too, the way of meeting the
problem was quite expedient. In practice it signified a compromise between confessional loyalty and ethnic exclusiveness.
The born Jew and those observing the law for three generations
enjoyed privileged status in the community before converts,
their children and grandchildren. The non-circumcised, but
oath-bound proselytes and mere "friends" stood outside the
community, somewhat in the manner of the "laity" over and
against the *Bhikshu* in India. The ritual was absolutely binding
for the Jewish born and the circumcised converts, in part for

the oath-bound proselytes, not at all for the "friends." Occasionally, however, far more liberal views were to be found. Doubts were even raised as to whether circumcision prescribed for the Jewish people actually was indispensable for the conversion of the non-Jewish born and whether a ritualistic purity bath (hence: baptism) would not suffice. Mixed marriages with (non-circumcised) proselytes appear to have occasionally been legitimized by rabbinical *responsa*. These views, however, were isolated opinions.

4. Propaganda of the Christian Apostles

THE conditions actually prevalent came out in the struggles which the Pauline Mission unleashed in the Early Christian community as well as in Judaism. In this the New Testament accounts bear the stamp of full trustworthiness in the decisive points. They show that it was not the beginning of the mission among the pagans (and non-circumcised proselytes)—as is still widely held—which called forth storm and strife. The leaders of the Jerusalemite congregations which strictly adhered to the ritual and the Temple cult had taken quite a realistic stand and at the same time favored the traditional handling of non-circumcised proselytes. They had formulated a minimum ethic for these and had sent it through two emissaries to the missionary community in Antioch (Acts 15:23 ff.). They were admonished to "abstain from idols, from blood, and from things strangled, and from fornication," but should otherwise not be bound by the ritual. If they observe this they are what the cited writing calls them "Brethren which are of the Gentiles." That was quite inoffensive also from the Pharisaic standpoint. Then, however, the news reached Jerusalem that Paul was also engaging in missionary work among full Jews and misleading them not to observe the ritual. With reference to this letter James and the elders, on behalf of the congregation in Jerusalem, made him answer for this (Acts 21:21 ff.). They demanded that because of this suspicion he undergo the usual purity probe in the Temple and that four oath-bound penitents be called in. Paul accepted this. However the numerous Diaspora Jews present got sight of him in the Temple and sought to lynch him because he (1) allegedly agitated against the law and Temple cult, hence, preached apostasy toward the law (among Jews!) and because he (2) had brought a non-circumcised (Trophimus) into the Temple (which Luke disputes).[3]

The uproar over this occasioned his arrest. Missionary work among the Gentiles or uncircumcised proselytes was not utilized to reproach him, but rather was expressly praised by James and the elders (Acts 21:20). Almost without exception Paul preached in the synagogues and it is clear and often emphasized that the mass of uncircumcised proselytes formed the core troupe of his missionary congregations. Judaism had through them feathered the bed for the Christian mission. To be sure, the proselyte compromise of the Jerusalemites did not solve even externally all difficulties of the Christian mission. Both sections, the Jerusalemite elders as well as Paul, veered and took uncertain steps. The question of commensality with uncircumcised proselytes had apparently been settled affirmatively between Peter and Paul in Antioch, then, however, under James' influence Peter retracted (Gal. 2:11 f.) Paul, for his part, in contrast to his behavior in the case of Titus (Gal. 2:3) circumcised Timotheus [4] in order to secure for him the commensality of the Jews in Asia Minor. The Jerusalemites accceded to Paul's standpoint only step by step and in part, Peter, apparently after the death of James. The old Ebonite congregation of Palestine, however, which continued to observe the law, treated Paul as an apostate. The decisive reason which compelled the leaders of the Jerusalemites to meet Paul halfway was, as the sources indicate (Acts 10:45-7) the experience that the converts from the Gentiles were just as well seized by the spirit and showed the same symptoms as the Jewish Christians. According to Peter's view during whose preaching in Caesarea this occurred, one therefore could not deny them baptism and equality. Regardless of the historical value of the details the basic fact is certainly correct and highlights the great transformation. In Judaism the prophetic spirit would have been controlled by measuring its predictions by the law and rejecting or accepting it accordingly. For Early Christianity, the spirit, its signs and gifts for their part, were standards determining the requisite extent of the ties to Jewish ritual. Obviously this "spirit," the pneuma had an essentially different dynamic than the *ruach-ha-kodesh* of correct Jewry.

The competition of Judaism and Christianity in their proselytizing mission came to an end with the first and definitively with the second destruction of the Temple under Hadrian, after, particularly in the last war numerous proselytes had perpetrated treason against the Jews. Doubts against the making of proselytes had never been completely silenced among the Jewish congregations. Now they increasingly won the upper hand.

The reception conditions for proselytes were regulated and the reception bound to the consent of a full quorum of a rabbinical court. The opinion emerged that the proselytes were "as troublesome for Israel as leprosy." The number of conversions diminished under the pressure of anti-Jewish sentiment. The emperors intervened; as conversion disqualified from office it could not be tolerated. Dio Cassius relates of severe laws even under Domitian. Circumcision of non-Jews was forbidden and treated like castration. Not only full conversions but likewise and perhaps still more the half-conversions quickly declined: already in the third century the *ger-toshab* seem to have been rare and later the assumption held that their existence had been in agreement with the scriptures only so long as Israel had been a state. It goes without saying that under the Christian emperors the propaganda (398 A.D.) even as the holding of Christian slaves (exposing these to the temptation of making proselytes) were strictly forbidden. The prohibition laws of Domitian must certainly have benefited Christian propaganda which everywhere entered on the heritage of Judaism. The strongly increasing tension of Jewish Christian relations, as shown by the different attitudes of the Gospels in accordance with their time of origin [5] and still more by the later literature, has first and essentially been brought about on the part of Jewry.

The Jews, as *religio licita*, exploited the precarious situation of the Christians who unlike the privileged Jews were not exempt from obligatory emperor worship by denouncing them in order to mobilize public authorities against them. Hence the Christians considered them the originators of the persecution. The barrier raised by both sides now became insurmountable:

the number of Jewish converts to Christianity swiftly declined and about the fourth century was practically nil, above all, among the broad strata of the petty bourgeoisie, even before the financial interests of the medieval princes made the conservation of the Jews desirable in their eyes. The goal of the conversion of Jews has been pronounced very often by Christendom, but, as a rule, it was mere lip service. In any case the missionary endeavor as well as the compulsory conversions have always and everywhere remained equally inconsequential. There are the promises of the prophets, the horror and disdain for Christian polytheism, above all, however, the exceedingly stable tradition created by an incomparably intensive education of youth for a ritualistically quite firmly structured way of life.

And there is the strength of the firmly structured social communities, the family, and the congregation, which the apostate lost without the prospect of finding equally valuable and certain affiliation with the Christian congregations. All of this makes the Jewish community remain in its self-chosen situation as a pariah people as long and as far as the unbroken spirit of the Jewish law, and that is to say, the spirit of the Pharisees, and the rabbis of late antiquity, continued and continues to live on.

NOTES

List of Abbreviations

BWAT—Beiträge zur Wissenchaft vom Alten Testament
JQR—Jewish Quarterly Review
JQRNS—Jewish Quarterly Review, New Series
MDOG—Mitteilungen der Deutschen Orientalischen Gesellschaft
MNDP—Mitteilungen und Nachrichten des Deutschen Palästina-Vereins
SBAW—Sitzungsberichte der Berliner Akademie der Wissenschaften, Philosophisch-historische Klasse
SMAW—Sitzungsberichte der Münchner Akademie der Wissenschaften, Philosophisch-historische Klasse
ZAW—Zeitschrift für die Alttestamentliche Wissenschaft
ZDMG—Zeitschrift der Deutschen Morgenländischen Gesellschaft
ZDPV—Zeitschrift des Deutschen Palästina-Vereins

I. The Social Structure and its Setting

1. It would require more than a lifetime to acquire a true mastery of the literature concerning the religion of Israel and Jewry, especially since this literature is of exceptionally high quality. For ancient Israelite religion, modern Protestant, especially German, scholarship is acknowledged to be authoritative to this day. For talmudic Judaism, on the whole, the considerable superiority of Jewish scholarship is unquestionable.

From the outset, in our attempt to present developmental aspects of Judaic religious history relevant to our problem, we entertain but modest hopes of contributing anything essentially new to the discussion, apart from the fact that, here and there, some source data may be grouped in a manner to emphasize some things differently than usual. Our questions may, of course, vary in some points from those which *Old Testament* scholars legitimately raise.

Actual harm has been done to purely historical inquiry into Judaic religious history, as elsewhere, only where value judgments have been allowed to interfere with detached analysis. No strictly empirical, historical, or sociological discipline can ever answer questions such as whether the Mosaic conception of God or the Mosaic ethic, assuming them to be reliably ascertainable, are superior to those of the surrounding world. Such questions can only be raised on the basis of given religious premises. Religious premises have strongly influenced the methodology of some relevant part of purely empirical research into Israelite religious history.

One may, of course, ask whether, as measured against developmental stages of religion to be found elsewhere, Israelite religious forms are 1. more or less ancient ("primitive"), or 2. more or less intellectualized and rationalized (in the sense that magical representations have been eliminated), or 3. more or less consistently systematized, or 4. more or less ethically absolute (sublimated) than comparable conceptions found in the surrounding world. One may, for example, compare the ethical demands of the Decalogue with those of corresponding units and, as far as both follow a parallel course, determine what demands are raised by one and not the other and *vice versa*. It is possible, likewise, to examine the conception of God, to determine the extent of universalism in relation to God, to ascertain the extent to which anthropomorphic traits have been eliminated and so forth, in the one case and compare it to the unity and ethico-intellectual direction of the other.

Such comparison readily shows, for example, that the Israelite conception of God is less universalistic and anthropomorphic than the older Indian conception. It shows that, in important respects, the ethic of the Decalogue raises more modest demands not only than do the ethical systems of India (particularly Jainism) and of Persia (Zoroastrism), but also of Egypt. Moreover certain central problems (for example, those of theodicy) in Israelite and precisely in prophetic religion appear only in relatively "primitive" form.

However, a faithful Jew (or Christian) would with justice emphatically deny that such propositions have the slightest bearing on the religious value of such conceptions. Empirical research, of course, treats the data and sources of Israelite-Jewish-Christian religious developments impartially. It seeks to interpret the sources and to explain the facts of the one by the same principles it applies to the other. Hence it has as little use for "miracles" and "revelations" in one case as in the other. But, in either case, it is out of the question that empirical research could wish or even be able to deny anybody the opportunity to evaluate, as "revelations," facts which science seeks to explain empirically as far as the sources permit.

Even when deviating widely from its conclusions, all *Old Testament* study today is based on the splendid work of J. Wellhausen, *Prolegomena zur Geschichte Israels* (Berlin, 1882; Eng. Trans., 1885); *Israelitische und Jüdische Geschichte* (1894, 4th ed. 1901); and his other works, especially, *Die Komposition des Hexateuchs und der historischen Bücher des Alten Testaments* (1889, 3rd ed. 1899). Wellhausen brilliantly utilized methods which he brought to highest systematic perfection. Since the work of de Wette, Vatke, Graf, these methods have never been abandoned and were further developed by Dillman, Reuss and others.

Wellhausen's central conception of Jewish religious history may best be termed "immanent evolutionary." The developmental course of Yahwe religion is determined by its unique, intrinsic tendencies, though, of course, under the influence of the general fate of the people. The striking passion with which Wellhausen defended his thesis against the brilliant work of Eduard Meyer, *Die Entstehung des Judentums* (Halle, 1896), even though this largely did justice to Wellhausen, is to be explained in terms of Wellhausen's presuppositions which in the last analysis were religiously determined.

As could be expected of a universal historian of Antiquity, Eduard Meyer places the concrete historical fate and event into the foreground of causal ascription (in this case a certain policy measure of the Persians). He has, thus, a preference for an explanation which is, in a sense, "epigenetic." In the controversy with Wellhausen general expert opinion, apparently, deems Eduard Meyer to be right.

An "evolutionary" interpretation of Israelite religious history is especially apt to employ biased presuppositions if it dogmatically applies the findings of modern ethnography and the comparative study of religions to the religious development of Israel. This, to be sure, does not hold for Wellhausen. In such dogmatic evolutionism it is assumed that magical and "animistic" representations, observed everywhere among "primitive" peoples, must also stand at the beginning of the religious development of Israel and that these must have been displaced only later by "higher" religious conceptions. The writings of Robertson Smith and the partially brilliant work of *Old Testament* scholars, as well as that of others, established analogies to be expected beyond doubt at every step of the way particularly between ritualistic prescriptions, myths and legends of Israel and the numerous magical and animistic representations to be found elsewhere. (Eduard Meyer, to be sure, has rightly ridiculed those who wished to find proof of "totemism" in Israel.) Occasionally, however, it has been forgotten that Israel entered upon its historical life as a confederacy of peasants, but (like Switzerland) found itself surrounded by countries with highly developed literary cultures, urban organization, overseas and caravan trade, bureaucratic states, priestly knowledge, astronomical observations and cosmological speculations. Ethnographic evolutionism, hence, was most radically opposed by the culture-historical universalism of the Assyriological scholars, in particular, and most radically by the so-called "pan-Babylonians."

The representatives of this view went far in this direction. They include scholars of the stature of Eberhard Schrader (cf. especially his *Die Keilinschriften und das Alte Testament*, 1872; 3rd ed. Eng. Trans. by O. C. Whitehouse, 1885–88), Zimmerman and Winkler (1901–1902) and H. Winckler (especially his *Geschichte Israels in Einzeldarstellungen*, 2 vols.) and Jensen, who is even more radical, and, in a more cautious manner, occasionally also, the far more moderate A. Jeremias, who, nevertheless, adheres to the "principle" of this conception (in addition to the "*Handbuch der altorientalischen Geisteskultur*, 1913, see, especially, *Das Alte Testament im Lichte des alten Orients*, 2nd ed. 1916). There have not been lacking attempts to prove the astro-theological origin of most of the Pentateuch stories or to convert the prophets into partisans of an international mid-eastern priestly party.

The lectures and essays of Fr. Delitsch popularized, at the time, the so-called "Bable Bible controversy." Today, a serious scholar would hardly attempt to deduce the religion of the Israelites from Babylonian astrological cults and secret priestly knowledge. (As an extreme parallel of such excesses on the side of Egyptology one might name, for example, something which seems to be quite a failure: D. Völter, *Aegypten und die Bibel* (Leyden, 1905), which should be compared with the very cautious works of W. Max

Müller, particularly, *Asien und Europa* and the monographical literature to be cited below.) If, in the following presentation, there is little mention made of those results of the "pan-Babylonian" studies which must be accepted as established, this is not due to a lack of respect but to our central concern in the practical ethic of Israel. The important cultural-historical relations which are of interest to the pan-Babylonian scholars are not the decisive ones, as will be shown, for the interpretations of this ethic.

The theses of the pan-Babylonian scholars have exerted considerable influence on research. They impressed the idea that Israelite religion was a modification of the religions of neighboring civilizations. This was bound, in turn, to react upon the questions posed by the *Old Testament* scholar. Inasmuch as one cannot possibly deny the strong cultural influence particularly of Babylon, but also of Egypt, on Palestine, *Old Testament* research in turn, particularly under the leadership of Gunkel, had, meanwhile, considerably corrected Wellhausen's developmental scheme. The actual permeation of Israelite religion with magical and animistic elements, on the one hand, the interrelation with the circles of great neighboring cultures, on the other, was brought out more clearly, and work was concentrated upon the question, which is actually decisive, as to what, after all, constitutes the indubitable peculiarity of Israelite religious development in comparison with those which were, in part, universally diffused, in part, common traits specifically culturally determined. Moreover, what are the determinants of this peculiarity?

However, entanglements with the religious value positions of the scholars soon reappeared. The "uniqueness," for some scholars, turned once again into a "unique value" and briefs were made for such theses as: Moses' accomplishment had been a creation "unsurpassed" in religious and moral substance by anything in the surrounding cultures. (This is perhaps best illustrated by some works of Baentsch, who, otherwise, has great merits. Budde, in particular, has criticized such works of Baentsch.) If, in this manner, research has occasionally in detail been deflected by valuations from the purely historical-empirical assessment of facts, the brilliant work of *Old Testament* scholars has led to conclusions critical of the tradition which even the most conservative scholars could not escape.

For the non-philologist, it is difficult to arrive at flawless positive statements. He cannot, as a rule, check the controversies concerning the textual sources. Frequently the text is corrupt and, at that, at the most important part, or it has been interpolated and amended at unknown times. Often the decision as to interpretation depends, moreover, on the more or less radical doubt as to the authenticity of those reports which, in ferentially speaking, priestly editors might have been somehow interested in falsifying. On the whole, the non-specialist will do well to examine, first of all, those reports which philological authorities agree, for linguistic or substantively compelling reasons, not to doubt as falsifications. He will ask, hypothetically, whether they are useful implements of historical interpretation. The extent to which the various *Old Testament* scholars follow such "conservative" use of the sources varies greatly and recently, in reaction against extreme scepticism, a possibly too fargoing liberalism is on the increase. An extremely conservative standpoint is to be found, for instance, in the otherwise excellent and most detailed works of Kittel, *Geschichte des Volkes Israel* (2 vols., 2nd ed. 1900 and 1902, respectively). Among other modern works we may mention the short introductory *Geschichte des Volkes Israel* by H. Guthe (2nd edition 1904), the outline by Valeton in Chantepie de la Saussaye *Lehrbuch der vergleichenden Religionsgeschichte* (1897) [a fourth edition appeared 1925 ed. by Alfred Bertholet and Edward Lehmann, Ed.].

The work of C. F. Lehmann-Haupt, *Israel, Seine Entwicklung in Rahmen der Weltgeschichte* (Tübingen, 1911), gives a very lucid presentation of foreign political developments. Besides Kayser Marti's work one will gratefully use Smend's *Religionsgeschichte*. Especially indispensable for research in the field of early Israelite history despite all criticism is Ed. Meyer's work (with *addenda* by Luther) *Die Israeliten und ihre Nachbarstämme* (Halle, 1906). For internal affairs and cultural conditions, useful is, also, Frantz Buhl, *Die Sozialen Verhältnisse der Israeliten*, besides the compendia of Hebraic archeology by Benzinger (1893) and Nowack (1894).

For religious history we mention B. Stade, *Biblische Theologie des Alten Testaments* (Vol. I, 1905, II, ed. by Bertholet, 1911) which in detail is often disputable but exceptionally substantial and dense. In addition to this the posthumous work of E. Kautzsch, *Die Biblische Theologie des Alten Testaments* (1911) is likewise remarkable for very concise formulations.

The collection for the comparative study of religion edited by Gressmann in association with Ungnad and Ranke under the title *Altorientalische Texte und Bilder zum Alten Testament* (1909) was unfortunately not available during the revision of the manuscript. Among the numerous commentaries on the *Old Testament* is that edited by K. Marti in association with Benzinger, Bertholet, Budde, Duhm, Holzinger, and Wideboer. Its use is especially agreeable for the non-specialist. Highly meritorious and in part excellent is the modern annotated translation of the *Schriften des Alten Testaments* by Gressmann, Gunkel, Haller, H. Schmidt, Stärk, Volz (1911–?). It aims at broader circles, hence the translation is partly too free and especially (still) incomplete; it is organized according to scriptural sources, topics and chronology.

Single quotations of other works are referred to at the respective place. The literature (including literature of highest quality) is so extensive, that, in general, we quote only when a special substantive reason warrants it. For once there seemed little danger to me that an omission might give the appearance as if I were claiming to present "new" facts and views. That is out of the question. Somewhat new are some of the sociological viewpoints and questions which we address to the data.

2. Concerning the natural conditions of Palestine one has to consult the numerous publications of the *Zeitschrift* and the *Mitteilungen und Nachrichten des Deutsche Palästinavereins*, besides general works on Palestine. On the climate of talmudic times cf. H. Klein, *Zeitschrift des Deutschen Palästina Vereins*, vol. 37 (1914), pp. 127 ff.

3. On this point see particularly the observations of Schumacher in his travel account of Transjordania, *MNDP* (1904 ff.).

4. See the excellent work by R. Leonhard: "Die Transhumanz im Mittelmeergebiet," *Festschrift für Lujo Brentano* (Munich, 1916).

5. For the best meteorological observations see F. Exner, ZDPV, vol. 33 (1910), p. 107 ff.

6. *Fellachensprichwörter und Gebete* gathered by Dr. Canaan, ZDPV, vol. 36 (1913), pp. 285, 91.

7. It is controversial whether the land of Canaan could have merited this designation and what it means. See, on the point, for instance recently Kraus, ZDPV, vol. 32, p. 151. He wished to interpret, from talmudic sources, the "flowing" literally as the coalescence of goat milk and fruit honey from dates, figs and grapes. Against this cf. Simonson, *ibid.*, vol. 33, p. 44, who rightly views it as figuratively intended. Likewise, Dalman (*MDPV* 1905, p. 27) states: "cake is sweet as honey" following the interpretation of contemporary Palestine Jews, he believes Palestine always to have been poor in cattle. Against this, see what, to my knowledge, is the best treatise, by L. Bauer (*ibid.*, p. 65). He refers to the richness in milk still in the present (butter and milk the most important means of subsistence) and interprets the honey to mean honey of grapes, which latter assumption Dalman, however, proves to be erroneous for Antiquity (*ibid.* 1906, p. 81). Häusler (ZDPV, vol. 35, 1912, p. 186) doubts whether there was ever wealth in honey. But in the Amarna letters too (No. 55 of Knudtzon's edition) honey is found as an allowance of an Egyptian garrison. The honey which the fugitive Egyptian Sinuhe at the time of Sesostris I mentions as plentiful in Retenu land, besides the cultivation of figs, oil and wine, was perhaps likewise date honey. Manna tasted like bread "made with honey" (Ex. 16:31). Isaiah (7:22, 23) announces that when Palestine after its devastation by the Assyrians shall have reverted to steppe where briars and thornes will stand in the place of vines, then the pious left in the land shall eat butter and honey as before. Therefore, the Holy child Immanuel also shall eat cream and honey (7:15). This recalls the nourishment of the Zeus boy from Crete: cream and honey. Therefore, the purely eschatological meaning of the term as the food of the gods is preferred by Gressmann, *Die israelitische Eschatologie*, p 207. Cf. also the literature cited there. After all the food of the gods is the ideal food of the wealthy in a steppe region.

8. Wellhausen, Julius, "Ein Gemeinwessen ohne Obrigkeit," *Göttinger Kaiser-Geburtstagsrede* (1900).

9. J. Hell, in *Beiträge zur Kunde des Orients*, vol. V, pp. 161 ff.

10. "Ismaelite," hence, Bedouin traders buy Joseph from his brothers. Gen. 37:25.

11. Cf. W. Max Müller in JQRNS, vol. IV (1913/14), p. 65.

12. The Bitu of Tyros is distinguished (Knudtzon No. 89) from that of the regent, the appointee of the Pharaoh. The correspondent draws the attention of the Pharaoh to the fact that, not the regent, to whom he always addresses himself, but the circles in control of the city hall determine the politics of Tyros. The regent later was slain.

13. If (in Knudtzon No. 129) "the Great" of a city are mentioned it remains questionable whether officials or patrician sib elders are meant;

in any case, the urban populace has political influence. The people of Dunip (cf. No. 50) request from the king a certain man for regent. The city dwellers of Byblos, in common with the regent's renegade brother, close the city gates on the regent, a Canaanite. Elsewhere, city people made common cause with the advancing foreign invaders: death threatens the regents. The city is lost when the Egyptian garrison withdraws or rebels because provisions fail to arrive or because people refuse corvées on the official fiefs of the regents and the military. This seems to me the inescapable interpretation of conditions touched upon in Nos. 117:37; 138; 77:36; 81:33; 74:125 and more often. This is, in part, deviation from O. Weber's excellent interpretation in Volume II of Knudtzon's edition. It seems to me quite improbable that the people who leave for lack of provisions refers to "peasants." To be sure, the same term is used which in Mesopotamia designates the "colonus" in contrast to the patrician freeman. But the μάχιμοι of the Pharaoh were in the main invested with very small fiefs (enfeoffed foot soldiers), and thus the "huubshtshi" mentioned in the documents are probably liturgically enfeoffed military prebendaries as are typically found in the Middle East and in Egypt. In No. 74 the field, that is the fief of the regent, has remained untilled because people have refused to render the corvée; therefore he is in need. The garrison fares similarly and that is why it is disloyal. Obviously, the garrisons are numerically very small: occasionally the regents put through new requests for 50 or less men. Petty conditions prevail generally: a tribute of the prince of Meggido amounts to 30 head of cattle.

It is improbable that the people who (No. 118:36) surrender the city to the enemies are meant to be peasants: how, of all people, could they do it? They are the city dwellers who in Byblos and elsewhere manage the defection.

Similarly, I cannot accede to O. Weber's view (*loc. cit.*, p. 117-8) that in Tyros and other cities the aristocracy allegedly was Egyptian, the demos, however, hostile to Egyptian rule. At the time a powerful demos has hardly existed even in the larger cities. They were, rather, the patricians, that is city-dwelling wealthy sibs engaged in trade, who felt the liturgies and taxes of Egyptian rule to be burdensome. The records bear witness to considerable money payments.

14. Knudtzon No. 290: a rural town in the territory of Jerusalem has revolted. In No. 288 it is mentioned that the viceroy of Jerusalem, at earlier times, had ships on the sea. On which? My guess is on the Dead Sea in the south. (The revolt of Seir in Edom is mentioned.) The ruling princes of Jerusalem had always sought to secure control over the caravan routes to the Dead Sea. Hence, the sway of the city extended far into the desert.

15. Aside from Josh. 15:45-47 only villages (*zerim*) are listed as dependencies of cities. Where, however, "Daughters" are mentioned, dependent cities are meant, not villages. For the entire matter cf. Sulzberger, "Policy of the Ancient Hebrews," *JQRNS* (1912/13), p. 7. For the cattle breeding East-Jordan tribes (Reuben) it is characteristic that there is always talk of "Gentes, Cities, and Daughters." Here, at the time of the Bible revision this organization was not yet completed.

16. It seems to me, the only shortcoming in Eduard Meyer's excellent presentation cf. *Die Israeliten und ihre Nachbarstämme* and *Enstehung des Judentums* is that this distinction running throughout early antiquity to the time of establishment of "democracy" is not emphasized. Not all free land-owners in ancient states, especially the city-states, are full citizens or political peers, but only those economically qualified for war service; that is, in Israel, the *gibbor chail*. There are, in the fully developed Israelite city-states, certainly, also free Israelite land owners, who do not belong to these and who therefore like the Hellenic *periocoi* and the Roman plebs stand outside the full citizenry.

17. The indiscriminate use of "*'am*" and "*gibborim*" beside one another is to be found in a somewhat corrupted passage in the Song of Deborah (Jud. 5:13). If one accepts Kittel's reading and at the end reads *kaggiborim* as Gressmann proposes, the meaning is clear. This presupposes, however, that *'am* and *gibborim* were two different groups, the latter the Israelite knights, the former the Israelite peasants who fought "like knights" but simply were not knights, (cf. verses 11 and 14). Against this, the city of Meros (according to verse 23) seems to have had the duty to come to the aid of the confederacy with knights (*gibborim*). The victory song characteristically curses this city, hence deems it deserving to be outlawed and destroyed in holy war, but not the peasant tribes who likewise had broken the covenant.

As a rule the *gibbor* is the knightly hero as in *Genesis* 6 or in the lists of David's paladines. Colorless is the term used especially in the Book of Joshua, but also in the Book of Kings, *'am hamilchamah* meaning "warrior people." In Joshua 10:7 it is used beside *gibbore chail*, *gibbor* and *'am hamilchamah* appearing beside one another in Isaiah 6:22, and the fighters *per se* are by no means all *gibborim*, cf. Jeremiah 5:16, where the foreign nation, approaching to punish Judah, is said to be all *gibborim*, which, in this case, means trained warriors.

18. It appears impossible that the "40,000" in Israel (Jud. 5:8) were considered *gibbor chail* as Ed. Meyer assumes. In the Song of Deborah the *gibborim* are, indeed, not mentioned in Israel, but near the city of Meros.

19. The contrast is not absolute. In the Babylonian myth of the flood the fold and "elders" of a city are presupposed (translated by Gunkel, *Schöpfung and Chaos*, p. 424, line 33). And, on the other hand, Hamor means the "father" of Shechem, of course, only as a kinship-eponym. A single elder already occurs in the old texts from Ur; N.d. Genouillac, "Textes juridiques de l'époque d'Ur," *Revue d'Assyriologie*, Vol. 8 (1911), p. 2.

20. On this point and on the elders in general see the good Leipzig Dissertation of Seeseman, *Die Ältesten im Alten Testament* (1891). The antagonism in Deuteronomy was first referred to by A. F. Puukko, "Das Deuteronomium," *BWAT*, p. 237.

21. Luther's term *Fünfzigern* means to recruit, Ex. 13:18; Jud. 7:11; Josh. 1:14; 4:12 cf. Ed. Meyer, *loc. cit.*

22. Units of one thousand men are equated to settlements, such is Ophrah (Jud. 6).

23. Concerning the *shebatim*, *mishpachot*, and *alaplim* see Sulzberger, *loc. cit.*, with several disputable assertions.

24. Units of a thousand men also appear to have been native to the Edomites in East Jordan. Gideon speaks of his "thousand men," Abimelech and Saul, however, of their *mishpacha* (Cf. Ed. Meyer). However, the Gideon tradition has been notoriously revised and the military organization of the charismatic kingdom of the Edomites would be no certain proof of the original organization characteristic of the nomads and seminomads. Ed. Meyer, himself, links the "thousand men units" to the cleros (*chelek*) which is an urban phenomenon.

25. The Chronicles, however, are (politically) biased in favor of the pious plebs and the editors interpret their materials accordingly. Reference is thus made to the then long-vanished tribes of East Jordan, I. Chr. 5:18.

26. So for Benjamin I. Chr. 8:40.

27. In opposition to Klamroth's assumption in his "Die Jüdischen Exulanten in Babylonien," *BWAT*, Vol. 10 (1912), digression pp. 99 f., I cannot believe that *'am haarez* originally referred to either mere local residents of the "subjects" partly in the "pejorative sense," partly in opposition to king, priests, and nobles, hence to the "plebs." It is true, they are distinguished from the priests, the king (and the princes) and the officials and officers. They are the fighting men and, indeed, landowners, originally armed men. Among them, apparently, also, the fully-qualified rural sibs, the rural gentry, if one wishes to use the term. For they are the people—and not somehow leaderless "peasants"— who (Cf. Ezra 4:4) hinder construction in Jerusalem and who (*ibid.* 3:3) are mentioned as *ammê haarezoth*, as men from various rural regions. The pre-exilic and exilic meaning is not easily ascertainable, given the lack of terminological precision in the sources. In the mouth of the Pharaoh, in what is presumably a later edition to the Yahwistic description of the flight from Egypt (Ex. 5:5), the expression simply means "the people" (Israel). In the older literature the term is used mainly in the second Book of Kings, in Jeremiah and Ezekiel. Both of these prophets have a decidedly unfriendly attitude toward the *'am haarez*. Jeremiah shall be brasen walls (1:18) against king, official priest and *'am haarez* if they should turn against him says the promise of Yahwe in the course of his calling. In Ezekiel (22:29) the *'am haarez* oppress the "poor" (*ebjon*) and the *ger*, hence, they are conceived of as men of social power. In the II. Book of Kings 25:19 an officer of Zedekiah is mentioned who has to drill *'am haarez*, and the Babylonians find 60 of these in the city and take them along to Babylon. Immediately before, at the siege of Jerusalem, it is said, II. Ki. 25:3) that the *'am haarez* had no more to eat—like the garrison of the Amarna letters—and concluding (25:20) that the *'am hamilchamah*, the warriors, had fled the city. One is tempted to view them as the free militia-men recruited from and trained by the country as over against the king's men (especially mercenaries provisioned by him). That remains, of course, uncertain. However, according to the account of Jeremiah 34:19 "the entire *'am haarez*" alongside the princes, officials and priests participated in the berith under Zedekiah because of the emancipation of the debt-slaves. Hence it would seem that there were

slave holders among them as the Ezekiel passage would suggest. "All the *'am ha-aretz"* rejoice to King Jehoash (II. Ki. 11:14), destroy the shrine of Baal, slay Amon's murderer (*ibid.* 21:24), and, after Josiah's death, make Jehoahaz king (*ibid.* 23:30). The order of propitiatory sacrifice begins with that for the community as a whole, then follows that for the king and finally that for an *'am haarez* (Lev. 4:27). Hence, usage is doubtlessly unprecise. Often *'am haarez* is actually intended to mean merely "the people." But originally *'am haarez* is by no means the "subject" or plebs in contrast to the nobles or even the "foolish peasant." The stupid peasant is called by Jeremiah (5:4) *dallim* and by Isaiah (2:9) the peasant is called *adam* in opposition to the "*ish*," the "man" in the sense of *ish hamil chammah*, the warrior. But the *'am ha-aretz* are fully qualified Israelites, apparently, in essentials, the old rural militia (from whom the urban landowners are not distinguished). Theory considered them now, as before, bearers of military might and hence of political rights. In the reaction against the presumably Yahwistic revolt against Amon they were obviously men having vested interests in the rural sanctuaries.

28. *Beisassen,* or metics are the usual translations of the terms. Ed. Meyer has suggested the rendering of "*toshab*" by "client." The client, however, presupposes a relation to a single master, and the sources leave that open for *toshab*. In the law books the client of a single house, apparently, is called *ger* (Ex. 23:12). Abraham is repeatedly named *ger we toshab* without being thought of as the client of an individual. The *toshab* of a priest is to partake of sacred food as little as his worker (Lev. 22:10). This ritualistic prescription might suggest the inference of a client. But *toshab* here seems to refer precisely to a man who does not belong to the household like the *sakhir*, a free day-laborer over against the *'ebed*, the servant, who is mentioned together with the *toshab*, here probably the *inquilin*. In Leviticus 25:47 the *toshab* is mentioned with the *ger*, the free metic who had grown rich. The original legal meaning of the two terms often used cumulatively in the sources can apparently no longer be ascertained.

II. The Gerim and the Ethic of the Patriarchs

1. It has been thought possible to view the Jewish *'am haarez* as a sort of ancient Hebrew parliament. Sulzberger and particularly Sloush ("Representative government among the Hebrews and Phoenicians," *JQRNS,* Vol. 4 (1913), p. 302 ff.) adduce for this the analogy of the *'am Zor, 'am Zidon* and *'am Karthachdeshoth* on Tyrian, Sidonian, and Carthaginian coins and the eras counted from the beginning of the rule of the *'am*. The latter are, in these cases, family heads, but doubtlessly representatives only of the urban patrician sibs. As in Jerusalem, according to Nehemiah 10, the signatories of the religious covenant, they formed apparently a closed circle, which suggests that the *'am* consisted of an oligarchical army as was known also in Hellenic cities in pre-democratic times.

2. Considered ritualistically, from the beginning the Hasmonaean heroes behaved rather incorrectly. In contrast to the pious folk who (I. Macc.

2:29) fled into the desert and allowed themselves to be butchered on the Sabbath (verse 38), Matthatias decided with his following to fight on the Sabbath (verse 41). Soon after the liberation the truly pious considered the Hasmonaeans to be objectionable Hellenists.

3. So far as this concerns peasant and not warrior allotments, which possibly occurred, it might well have been considered an affair of the individual village. We may recall that Hesiod's family, too, came to Boetia as tribal foreigners, yet the poet became a landowner there—technically a *periocoi*.

4. The place of the priestly tribe of Levi in the Levite cities of the tradition is perhaps the best indication of how the normal situation of a metic was traditionally viewed.

5. In terms of the kind of argument advanced for the Sabbath commandment in Nehemiah's time, where the prohibition of weekly market-traffic is the main point of the ordinance, the prohibition was doubtlessly in the interest of Israelites and not strangers. It was directed against unfair competition by non-Jews. Similar cases are to be found with Amos and Jeremiah. In older times when rest from field work was the decisive and only reason for the Sabbath prohibition this could, of course, have been otherwise.

6. I. Chr. 4:21: "house of byssos-work." They were organized into sibs and, along with others, held to be descendants of a son of Judah. Characteristically, however, without their own eponym. The descent from Judah, hence, may well represent a post-exilic fiction.

7. I. Chr. 4:22-23. Joash and Saraph were the family heads (*ba'alim*) at Moab and, according to old accounts, they lived in Lachem. "They were potters and dwelt in fenced gardens with the king, to do his work." Hence, they had service-fiefs.

8. Joab, Seraiah's son is called I. Chr. 4:14 "father of the valley of carpenters," a district of Jerusalem. Hence, the carpenters appear to dwell as *coloni* on Joab's real estate, or (and more probably) Joab was held to be their patron and they held this patronage as a kingly prebend. In this case, no statement concerning sib organization appears.

9. The tradition is highly questionable. The note in verse 22, that in contrast to the Canaanites, he had employed all Israelites only as warriors (*anshe hamilchamah*), officers or officials, is biased in the interest of the Israelite plebeians. That freeborn persons, also, were subject to forced labor is evident from I. Ki. 5:13 where the Israelites have to supply 30,000 workers. The note indicates, however, that, at the time, men not qualified for war service and free land holdings, once for all, were not Israelites, but *gerim*.

10. According to I. Chr. 23:1 David allegedly recruited stone masons from among all the *gerim* of the land for temple construction. Probably stone masons were rather royal artisans and, therefore, *gerim*.

11. Knudtzon No. 196.

12. *Ibid.*, No. 185.

13. *Ibid.*, No. 74.

14. That the Khabiri belonged to the Sa-Gas is, according to the Bogazköi-discovery, no longer questionable.

15. The significance of the "sheep nomads" for the Yahwe cult is discussed by Luther in Eduard Meyer, *Die Israeliten und ihre Nachbarstämme*, p. 120 f.

16. Recently R. Leonards "Die Transhumanz im Mittelmeergebiet" in the *Festschrift für Brentano* for the first time deals with them comprehensively in a meritorious manner.

17. Also in Jer. 6:3 the enemies who are prophesied to come are compared with shepherds who pitch their tents roundabout and select grazing grounds.

18. The East Jordan hero Jerubbaal-Gideon is threshing wheat (Jud. 6:11).

19. See Num. 24:21, 22 for this identification which occasionally has been contested for no good reason.

20. Jud. 4:17. The last lines of the verse may well be an insertion as some scholars assume. In that case, it is clear proof for the conditions at the time of the insertion.

21. According to the tradition, Dan (Jud. 18:1) for a long time had no fixed dwelling place in the land. In the Song of Deborah the Danites hired out to the Phoenicians as oarsmen. Often, the tradition calls this tribe only a "sib." In Jacob's Blessing it is a robber tribe which lies "like a serpent on the caravan routes and bites the heels of the horse." In Moses' Blessing it is "a lion's whelp: he shall leap in Basam," hence in Hauran. Probably at the time of the first advance of the Philistines, probably even before the Deborah battle, the Danites had not been able to maintain their tent encampments, the "camp of Dan" in the Judaic Mountains, with their military forces (according to tradition 600 men)—presumably the Philistines against whom the Danite hero Samson fought were the opponents; yet the places concerned were later in Judaic possession—they wandered therefore to the north and settled down in the Sidonite mountain city Laish after conquest and liquidation of the Sidonites. Dan was later restricted to this city community named after it and as a tribe was only a fiction. That the city of Dan was viewed as particularly correct religiously, makes it probable that the account of the tradition of the wandering life was true. For religious correctness is presupposed for all ancient herdsmen tribes. From a second saying in Jacob's Blessing it has been rightly concluded that Dan temporarily has been deprived of its political independence. The same is expressly stated in Jacob's Blessing of Issachar which is only briefly mentioned in Moses' Blessing as a tent dwelling tribe, in consequence of the transition to permanent settlement: "And he saw that rest was good, and the land that it was pleasant; and bowed his shoulders to bear, and became a servant unto tribute" (Gen. 49:15), hence doubtless a settled peasant. Issachar was settled at least in part in the fertile plains of Jezreel. The tribe Naphthali is called in Jacob's Blessing "a hind let loose," hence was probably a semi-Bedouin tribe (if no simple pun on the name was intended). According to the Song of Deborah it had its seat on the mountains, whereas in the Moses' Blessing it is mentioned as

blessed by Yahwe on the seashore and in possession of a city (Merom). The similar case of the sea-coast dwelling tribe Asher, whose wealth from oil making was proverbial appears in Jacob's Blessing as paying tribute to a Phoenician city king's kitchen. In Moses' Blessing however Asher's fortifications (bars of iron and brass) and its strong army are praised. The tribe Zebulun in the time between the origin of the respective saying in Jacob's Blessing and the Song of Deborah reading must have changed its dwelling place (the reading in Moses' Blessing verse 18 appears to have been falsified). In Jacob's Blessing it appears on the sea coast and "leans on Sidon" i.e., probably is dependent on the Sidonians, while in the Deborah Song it is a warlike mountain tribe. The tribe of Benjamin is a robber tribe in Jacob's Blessing "ravaging as a wolf; which in the morning devours the prey and at night divides the spoil." In Moses' Blessing it has peacefully come to rest. The tribe of Gad appears later (in Mesa's and Ahab's time) to have been a Moabite tribe. Its name was probably that of an old fortune god.

22. Somewhat distorted in the present-day reading.

23. Cf. v. Gall, "Die Entstehung der humanitären Forderungen des Gesetzes," ZAW, vol. 30 (1910) p. 91 f., who exclusively emphasizes the (in itself undoubted) superstitious origin. The question is, however, why was here the stipulation, which disappeared in other culture areas, retained?

24. The rabbis of Jerusalem had spoken for the commandment. If I remember correctly, German Jewish authorities had done likewise. The Eastern Jewish rabbis, however, declared allegedly the settlement of the land to be such God-pleasing work that one might dispense with the old prescription.

25. On the Patriarchal legends see (in part against Ed. Meyer) Gressmann, "Sage und Geschichte in der Patriarchensage," ZAW, 30 (1910) p. 91 f. He places most of them in the category of "fairy tales" which in view of the old shrines with which they are connected and by which they are localized, may well go too far. But he rightly opposes the opinion that the names necessarily either must be heroes' or tribal names.

26. This is thrice told, cf. Genesis 12:13; 20:2; 26:7.

27. "Ish sadeh" ("man of the ploughing field" Gen. 25:27) is to be translated by peasant rather than by "vagabond of the steppe" as repeatedly it has been falsely rendered.

28. As Abel to the peasant Cain so the smooth Jacob was contrasted as a pious shepherd dwelling in tents with the hairy peasant Esau. And as Cain on the other hand became a Bedouin, so Esau for his part a covetous hunter.

29. The following should not be misunderstood. The origin of the various patriarchical accounts in their present form is probably correctly ascribed to ancient times. There is much to indicate that they have originated partly under the dominion of the Cheta in the steppes between Syria and Mesopotamia, partly under Egyptian domination in the Southern Judaic steppes. Of course, there were always cattle breeders in the specifically weak and pacifist situation, which the stories presuppose. But the decisive feature, their relation to the tribal fathers of the Yahwe confederacy of Israel must

of necessity be late because it can in no way be reconciled with the events to be assumed as ancient history. Precisely if one believes in the "conquest" of Canaan by Israel. Some of the accounts of the Patriarchs make unhistorical presuppositions such as Pharaoh's gift of camels to Abraham, for then the camel was still unknown in Egypt. The Patriarchs could be the tribal ancestors of Israel as a whole only after the unification of the realm, hence after David. Above all the originally local nature of the patriarchical accounts seems with certainty indicated by connection of each with a specific place of worship.

30. Late Jewish tradition deemed to recognize this lot of Genesis (48:22) in a village near Samaria with "Jacob's well" (St. John, 4:15). The revised tradition knows nothing to report of the land conquests by Jacob. Hence, this trait has been extinguished.

31. The present-day wording of this very late chapter composes old reminiscences into a historical fable. However, that it be a state novel fabricated for high-political reasons of legislation (so Asmussen *ZAW* vol. 34, 1914) appears to me very improbable. The Israelites of the Exile could hardly engage in studies of archives in order to ascertain the use of names of Elamite kings. And the name-form Kudur (Kedor) Laomer is genuine.

32. On the Patriarchs and the immigration question see: Weinheimer in the *Z.D.M.G.* (1912). Not all his theses appear acceptable, but noteworthy is what is said of the succession of the stages of the three Patriarchs from the "nomad" Abraham to the "peasant" Jacob.

33. Luther (in Ed. Meyer, *Die Israeliten und ihre Nachbarstämme*) assumes that the Yahwist only has intentionally transformed the Patriarchs, originally described as settled husbandmen into semi-nomads, for the sake of what Budde has called the "nomadic ideal" of the times of the prophets. Although such a transformation *per se* is not impossible, it is improbable because many characteristic features of the stories, especially their ethic, have obviously originated in the midst of as yet quite unsophisticated herdsmen. The husbandry of Isaac in Gerar is described as "cultivation in the manner of nomads." The much discussed mentioning of the names of the patriarchs Abraham and Joseph in Egyptian inscriptions appear rather doubtful. Cf. W. M. Müller, *M.D.V.A.B.* (1907) vol. I, pp. 11 and 23.

III. The Social Laws of the Israelite Legal Collections

1. Cf. the well-known publication of Baentsch on the Book of the Covenant and the popular presentation of Adalbert Merx in the *"Religionsgeschichtliche Volksbücher."*

2. Residues of similar conceptions are found in the Old Roman *actio de paupere.*

3. It is different in the later legal collection with its characteristic deviations.

4. The manner of formulation of the principle of *talion* (Hammurabi

196), the case of endangering a pregnant woman (210), particularly the handling of bunting cattle (251) are so similar to Hammurabi that accident is precluded. Also the treatment of the concubine, given the husband by his childless wife (145), agrees exactly with the Hagar account.

5. However, against Baentsch, it must be held that in the Book of the Covenant there is no mention of coined money. Money metal was weighed in natural form. That is no "primitive" state as Procksch opines. Apart from the overseas trade agreements of the old commercial city of Rome long antedating Roman coinage of money one should recall the fact that, e.g., a trading city such as Carthage adopted coinage only with the transition to the recruitment of mercenary armies abroad. The entire Phoenician trade expanded without coined money.

6. This definition is juridically quite correctly formulated as the legal claim to the mother is decisive.

7. The ordinances concerning the Sabbath year in the present text, in contrast to those concerning the Sabbath day, speak much more abstractly of poor fellow-tribesmen (*evyonei 'am*—in the oldest sources, *'am* is the expression for the fighting men) who should benefit by the fruit. This and the doctrinaire stipulation that possibly wild game should eat the fruit suggests later theological constructions as probable.

8. The later term that became usual for interest, *ribbith*, obviously has been borrowed from Babylonia. There it had penetrated the sphere of private law from the conceptual sphere of "tax" or "tribute," presumably because the original interest in private law also here, as a rule, was not fixed interest but a share of the harvest yield or profits; Leviticus 25:36-37 mentions *marbit* for usury.

9. Cf. especially A. F. Puukko, "Das Deuteronomium" (*BWAT*) who would exclude precisely these parts. For political reasons, this assumption seems to me so improbable for part of the legal statutes, especially for the characteristic king's law that also other parts of the section seem to me very likely part of Josiah's *Sefer hattorah*. Wellhausen, indeed, considered chapters 12-26 as the original nucleus of Deuteronomy. Cf. his *Komposition des Hexateuch* p. 189 f.

10. Israel shall become a *city* of righteousness according to Isaiah's promise (1:26).

11. This name for the collection Lev. 17-26, as is known, stems from Klostermann. It is pre-exilic because its basic stock apparently does not differentiate between priests and Levites. It was revised in post-exilic times, for (Lev. 21) there are references to the high priests, with special cultic purity obligations, and because repeatedly a small cultic community is presupposed. (See in this respect Puukko, *Das Deuteronomium*, p. 49).

12. The priestly writing shows quite unmistakable relations to Ezekiel. However, it was the Aaronites, not the Zadokites (see below) who bore it on their scutcheon. It is certainly earlier, standing nearer to Ezra than to the prophecy of Ezekiel.

13. According to Ruth 4:3 at the time of the revision of this legend a mother also inherited from her childless sons. The whole account, to be sure, lacks legal precision.

14. Sulzberger, *loc. cit.*, so far as I know, is the only one to assume similar interrelations. However, in my opinion he holds a highly improbable view of the power of the Israelite confederation to control its members. After all it acted only intermittently and had no administrative agencies.

15. Precisely the derivatives of the verb *nachal* meaning "to inherit," "to get possession" and *hiphil* meaning "to make hereditary," "to divide the inheritance," "to give in possession" were used with reference to Canaanite lands; "inheritance" as well as "possession" were called *nachalah*.

16. It is remarkable that even so eminent a scholar as Procksch has still made the attempt, at least with respect to Deuteronomy in relation to the Book of the Covenant to defend precisely the opposite thesis (*Die Elohimquelle*, p. 263 ff.).

17. The work of Kraetzschmar, *Die Bundesvorstellung im Alten Testament,* (Marburg, 1896) differs in many ways from what follows and was not available to me during the conclusion of this work. Stade, who maintains that the idea of the confederacy appears only late, in the last analysis wishes to say only that the *berith* of Moses did not have the form of a legal enactment, which is certainly correct. However, the paramount significance of the *berith* idea will be witnessed ever anew.

18. Knudtzon No. 67.

19. The coinage inscription of the Maccabean priest-princes reads "*kohen ha gedol w cheber hajjehudim,*" "high priest and confederation of the Jews."

20. In the war against Benjamin because of the offense of Gibeah. Otherwise the word occurs with Isaiah (47:9, 12) for the confederation of magicians and robbers; with Hosea (6:9) for the confederation of priests; Proverbs 21:9 and 25:24 for the house community; in the Psalms (119) for the brothers in belief. The word was, at the time, utilized somewhat as an equivalent to the expression of the oldest tradition for friend, neighbor, "*rea'*," which characteristically is derived from *ra'ah,* "to graze," Piel: *re'ah,* "to choose a companion," hence it is probably derived from the camp-community of the Bedouins or the cattle breeding sibs.

21. See the discussion of Böhl, "Kanaanäer und Hebräer," *BWAT,* Vol. 9, 1911, p. 85. The identification with "*'Ibrim*" appears possible and probable. In any case the concept of the "brother in belief" was not absent in pre-Israelite times as a later to be mentioned letter of a Canaanite from the 15th century indicates. When addressing a fellow Israelite, however, the expression *chaber* was not used but apparently always "*ach*" (brother).

22. Abraham through *berith* became a *ger* in Beer-Sheba (Gen. 21:31, 34). Isaac formed a sworn bond with Abimelech of Gerar (Gen. 26:28). Abimelech appears despite verse 31 which emphasized the reciprocity of the obligation just as lonely as the one who makes the *berith* (26:8) as later Yahwe over and against Israel, because in both cases the side of the weaker is less privileged (Israel as Yahwe's *ger!*). Similarly, Israel over and against Gibeon (Jos. 9:6 ff.). In the Deborah tradition the husband of Jael fixed his tents by virtue of *berith* as a *ger* on Canaanite royal terri-

tory. King Asa sent by power of *berith* tribute to Ben-hadad (I. Ki. 15:19). Ahab and his prisoner Ben-hadad concluded a *berith* (I. Ki. 20:34) as Jonathan did with David (I. Sam. 18:3; 20:8); David with Abner (II. Sam. 3:12). Jabesh asked Nahash for one (I. Sam. 11:1). In all these cases, as between Yahwe and Israel it is a matter of a *feodus iniquum* among unequals; in contrast the *berith* between Jacob and Laban is a *feodus aequum* (Gen. 31:44). The international law, which supported Tyros, was called (Amos 1:9) "brotherhood" (*berith achim*). Already from these examples follows in any case that *berith* is rightly rendered through "confederation" and Kautzsch (*Biblische Theologie des Alten Testaments* p. 60) is quite wrong in denying this meaning which is the absolutely central point for the whole of ancient Israelite religion. David (II. Sam. 5:3) became king of Israel in the same sense through *berith* with the elders as previously Yahwe became its God. That the Septuaginta translated *berith* with διαφήχη, not with συνφήχη agrees with the ideas of its time, not with those of early history. The conception of God of the priestly revision ("P") as expressed, for instance, in the account of God's promise to Noah, Abraham, Phinehas (Num. 25:12) agrees, however, with the conception of the *berith* as a one-sided pledge of God in the nature of a privilege (Gen. 9:9) which is merely guaranteed by special solemnity and external signs. Cf. Holzinger's Commentary on the Book of Genesis, *loc. cit.* p. 129 f. and above all the quite detailed studies of linguistic usage by Valeton, ZAW XII. X(1892) p. 1 f., 224. For the eschatology there was also a *berith* with the animals (Hos. 2:18). *Berith* is used in the sense of "privilege" Num. 18:19, in the sense of "prescription" (*salt berith*) Lev. 2:13. "P" refers never to the Sinai law as *berith,* whereas for the Yahwist ("Y") the Horeb confederation and the *berith* on the fields of Moab are typical bilateral *feodera.* According to Isaiah 24:5 Israel has broken the "eternal covenant" (*berith golam*). The expression "*karah berith*" corresponds, as often noted, quite to the *feodus icere,* ὅρκιατέμνειν of the Romans and Hellenes. With Nehemiah this linguistic usage has faded and *amanah* is used instead of *berith* (10:1).

23. With regard to the Book of the Covenant as well as to these words of the covenant it remains, of course, questionable to which parts the terms of the earliest tradition referred. The previously discussed legal collection which at the indicated place is now called Book of the Covenant, is never so designated in its own text, where the word "covenant," indeed, does not appear, while the ritual prescriptions Ex. 34 are expressly introduced as *berith,* and, through the bilateral nature of the pledges, agree better with the character of a covenant than do the other collections which essentially contain unilateral prescriptions (*mishpatim*). The "words of the covenant" Ex. 34:28 are identified by the presumably later addition of "the ten words" with the Decalogue. But originally the expression referred obviously to the just mentioned directly preceding ritualistic prescriptions. (See on the whole question Baentsch, *loc. cit.*)

24. The respective chapter (27) of Deuteronomy is held to be a recent compilation and insertion. But its original material could hardly be of recent origin. The great contradictions of the account and the representation of

the twelve tribes by one man each may well be credited to the editor, likewise the unclear change of place references (on the Ebal or below in the valley of Shechem). Probably the fragment is held rightly as of Elohistic origin.

25. The difficulty that the confederation Baal had a temple, whereas the ceremony apparently proceeded from the grove (or godly tree) Moreh is not insuperable. The connection with the cult in groves and on mountains speaks for the age and the significance of the ceremony, which, although in the time of Deuteronomy it could have persisted only as a reminiscence, yet was not completely eliminated by the editors who were inimical to all such cults. It is possible that their significance meanwhile had been transformed in correspondence with the spirit of Deuteronomy. Originally, there may have been a solemn curse against demons in connection with the imploring of God's blessing. For the conception of those times the purpose may have been solemnly to transfer the religious and joint liability of the people for the sinners to them alone by their solemn curse.

26. In these cases the *berith* was concluded "before" Yahwe, not "with" Yahwe. This is readily explained from the fiction that this *berith* represented only a renewed vow of one party to the contract, namely the people, to fulfill the obligations of the old covenant with the God. Allegedly they had failed to honor it.

27. The one-sided loyalty oath of the people under Nehemiah was not called *berith* but *amanah* (Neh. 10:1).

28. How old the Yahwe piety of the Kenites was remains an open question. König (*ZDMG* 69, 1915) draws attention to the fact that the first well ascertained Kenite Yahwe name is that of Jonadab ben Rechab. Hence this prophet perhaps played the role of Moses.

29. "Das Kainzeichen," *ZAW*, vol. 14, 1894, p. 250 f.

30. In the myth Jacob received the name Israel after his *berith* with God (Gen. 35:10).

31. Spiegelberg in *Berichte der Berliner Akademie der Wissenschaften* 1896. Steindorf in ZAW vol. 16.

32. Stade, *Biblische Theologie des Alten Testament* (1905), p. 285 f.

33. Klostermann, *Der Pentateuch* (1907) has been criticized in detail by Puukko, *Das Deuteronomium* pp. 176-202. K. sought through his hypothesis to render understandable the peculiar literary character of Deuteronomy. He maintains that it was an eschatology lecture on religious laws. The comparison of the story of the "find" with the "law" of Numa can hardly be called fruitful.

34. Also Micah (7, 3) declaimed against the fact that the judge made decisions according to the arbitrariness of the prince.

35. *Chuk* (and *chukah*) signifies besides traditional law and custom also law of nature (in Job and Jeremiah). Priestly language particularly in Lev. and Num. used it for the divine order often with adjectives in the sense of "eternal" unchangeable. *Chuk* and *torah* were named together by Amos (2:4) and Isaiah (24:5).

36. The *chokek* makes false judgments (*chuk*) Jer. 10:1.

37. In pre-exilic prophetic language this significance is maintained in rather pure form (Amos 6:11 and later often).

38. Occasionally there is to be found beside *mishpat* and *chuk* also *mishmereth* (Gen. 26:5). The word designates originally "function" in the sense of assigned work and "order," hence stems from bureaucratic ideas.

39. Ancient Babylonian civil justice developed out of temple justice. Concerning this and the cooperation of the priests in recent Babylonian times see E. Cuq, "Essay sur l'organisation judiciaire de la Chaldée," *Revue d' Assyriologie,* vol. 7 (1910).

IV. Warfare and War Prophecy

1. The individual phenomena bound up with these circumstances have been treated in excellent manner by Schwally, *Semitische Kriegsaltertümer,* vol. I *Der Heilige Krieg im alten Israel* (Leipzig, 1901).

2. Yet Gunkel recently has advanced good reasons against Reitzenstein for the universality of circumcision in Egypt (*Archiv für Papyrus Forschung,* vol. II, Sect. 1, p. 13 f.). The late comment of Origin to the effect that the priests were allowed to teach the hieroglyphs only to the circumcised, is hardly usable. Joshua 5:8 shows clearly that the author considered circumcision an affair of the army. Joshua carried it out allegedly in order to escape the scorn of the Egyptians.

3. Circumcision in Egypt according to the monuments was not carried out in childhood but in boyhood.

4. The circumcision of slaves was certainly an innovation, which can also clearly be recognized in the late account of the covenant with Abraham (Gen. 17:12).

5. Without motivation, as a covenant sign to be performed in childhood, circumcision was introduced by the pacifistic patriarchal legends through the simple command of God to Abraham.

6. The possibility that the Passover originally represented a meat orgy of Bedouin warriors is too uncertain to be taken into consideration. Naturally it would be conceivable that the transformation into a domestic festival resulted only from the earlier portrayed splitting of the tribes of cattle-breeders with increasing settlement (Similarly, Ed. Meyer, *Die Israeliten* pp. 1-38). However, the smearing of the posts with blood and the prohibition of the enjoying of blood appear to indicate that the meat orgy was eliminated even in ancient times, if it ever existed.

7. This is naturally no contradiction to the humane guest-right of the older legal collection, for this concerns the *ger,* not, however, the complete stranger. Ritualistically segregated metics simply should no longer exist at all.

8. Some such nordic savages were kept in Constantinople still at a late time in about the manner as earlier war elephants. The question whether the warrior ecstasy of the berserker was carefully planned and induced by poison, is now usually denied.

9. The Talmud indicates that "Nasiroth" and "Perishot" (wherefrom Pharisee) at the time were viewed as identical.

10. The assumption that the omission of the haircut and abstention from alcohol represented two different forms of warrior asceticism, as Kautzsch partly maintains, seems uncertain.

11. For the etymology usually the Arabic *naba'*, to announce, and the Babylonian Nabu, the scribe and announcer of the decisions of the council of deities is adduced. Note the significance of Mount Nebo, the name of which probably hangs together with Nabu. Moses as well as Elijah were carried off by Yahwe from Mount Nebo or its neighborhood. For the prophecies of the time before the scriptural prophets see Sellin, *Der alttestamentliche Prophetismus* (Leipzig, 1912) p. 197 ff. and G. Hölscher, *Die Propheten* (1914) cf. Part II.

12. Visions and auditions are naturally not strictly separated but related in various ways. Of Hosea, the first prophet, it is merely said that the "word of Yahwe" (*debar* Yahwe) came to him. Amos tells of all sorts of images which Yahwe then interprets for him (1:1; 7:1; 4:7; 9:1). Similar accounts occasionally are still to be found with Jeremiah and, in a somewhat different manner, with Ezekiel. Isaiah by contrast does not see images to be interpreted, but he sees and hears what he shall proclaim; or he sees the splendor of God and then receives his commandments. In any case, audition becomes all important. As seer, the prophet was called *choseh* (derivations from *chasah* later signified "night vision"). For details see Part IV.

13. Wellhausen and after him Hehn (*Die biblische und die Babylonische Gottesidee*) interpret the much disputed concept of heavenly hosts relatively universalistically. Yahwe is the lord of all those spirits who are in the world. Yet, the relation to the military is quite unmistakable.

14. Amos 7:10, 13. The priest of Bethel accused the prophet before King Jeroboam for having incited rebellion, then expelled him from "the king's sanctuary (*mikdash*) and house (*beth*)."

15. Yahwe has given the king to Israel "in anger" (Hosea 13:11). To be sure, here the illegitimate usurpers of North Israel are meant.

16. See K. Budde, "Die Schätzung des Königstums im Alten Testament," *Marburger Akademische Reden* No. 8, (Marburg, 1903).

17. Schwally's derivation of the word *nadib* for "prince," "noble" from the self-consecration for war is very questionable. *Nadib* means prince here as everywhere in the sense of "giver," "giver or gifts"; only the *hithpael* could have as in the Song of Deborah (Jud. 5:1 f.) the meaning of "to offer oneself" as in a questionable reading in another place (Jud. 5:9) of the Song of Deborah.

V. Social Significance of the War God of the Confederacy

1. Hehn justly draws attention to the fact that this conception does not recur in any other Mideastern religion (*Die Biblische und die Baby-*

Ionische Gottesidee, p. 272). Indeed, it can be understood only in terms of the old *berith* relationship.

2. Cf. Küchler, *ZAW,* vol. 28, 1908, p. 42 f. Küchler shows at the same time how, since the destruction of Jerusalem, with Ezekiel, Yahwe's "jealousy" is no longer turned against other deities, and thus against Israel, if it should serve them, but against Israel's enemies.

3. Budde, especially, has emphasized this point. Cf. his "Das nomadische Ideal im alten Testament," *Preussische Jahrbücher,* 1896, vol. 85 and *Die altisraelitische Religion.*

4. The etymology of the tetragrammaton Jhwh has remained just as controversial as the question as to whether it has been contracted into Jahwe from Jah (occurring in given names) and Jahu (or Jao, the name used in Jewish congregations in Elephantine during the sixth century and also appearing in theophorous given names) or whether, in reverse, Jahu and Jah were abbreviated forms of Jahwe. On this point and the Masoretic vocalization see besides the usual literature also J. H. Levy in *JQR,* vol. XV, p. 97. The derivation from the Babylonian Ea (see A. H. Krone, *ibid.,* p. 559) appears fantastic. On the whole it is quite improbable that the names of ja in the Amarna tablets or the similar elements of Babylonian names should have something to do with Yahwe. (Cf. Marti in *Theologische Studien und Kritiken,* 1908, vol. 82, p. 321, and W. Max Mueller, *Asien und Europa,* p. 312-13). It seems impossible to follow Hehn (Cf. his *Biblische und Babylonische Gottesidee*) in assuming the name to be a theological construct of Moses ("he is present") as Yahwe was worshipped not only in Israel.

5. Jethro sacrifices to Yahwe as his priest and Aaron and the elders of Israel have commensalism with him.

6. Since Winckler's find in Boghazköi (*MDOG,* vol. 35, 25) most scholars, thus Böhl (Hebräer und Kananäer) accept the identity of Sa-Gas and Khabiri as ascertained. Nevertheless, it is hardly by accident that the Khabiri obviously attack from the Southeast, the Sa-Gas from the North and Northeast and that only the latter are mentioned in Mesopotamia.

7. The Book of the Covenant designates the debt slave as a "Hebrew servant" (Ex. 21:2, similarly in Zedekiah's resolution of debt remission Jer. 34:9-14, and Deut. 15:12). Perhaps the term stood here in memory of language usage of old debt remission contracts of the urban nobles with the peasants in opposition to the non-Hebrew, that would mean, in this case, urban patricians. The remarkable distinction of tribal fellowmen in Philistine bondage as "Hebrews" from Israel (I. Sam. 14:21) may perhaps have similar reasons.

8. Eber is the tribal father also of the tribes in Arabia all the way to Yemen (Gen. 10:21, 24 f. Yahwistic). The instances in which Ibrim is used and which go back to times earlier than the priestly revision (Gen. 39:17; Ex. 1:15 f. 2:6 f. I. Sam. 4:6 f.; 13:3, 19; 14:11; 29:3) always concern relations to the Egyptians or Philistines. See Böhl, *loc. cit.* p. 67. It is striking that (Num. 24:22 the Balaam saying) misfortune is prophesied to "Eber" together with "Asshur."

9. Disregarding the internal improbability of the invention of what is,

in the tradition, a purely human figure, its historical authenticity is made the more probable through some highly remarkable features of the tradition which permit us to infer as unrecognized residues of ancient antagonisms. The name ("Mushi") recurs among the Levitical lineages (Ex. 6:19; Num. 26:58 and elsewhere). An old tradition knows of Moses' children (Ex. 2:22; 4:20) and the Danite priesthood was genealogically derived from him. The entire later priestly-revised genealogy, however, knows nothing of descendants of Moses. According to Ex. 18:2 f., Moses sent his children with his wife to Jethro, who then brings them after him into the desert. In I. Chr. 6:1, 16, 17 respectively 3 the Gershom and Eleazar who were called children of Moses in Ex. 2:22 are counted as children of Levi or Aaron respectively, Eleazar likewise already in Num. 26:1 and elsewhere. To stamp Moses an absolutely pure Levite, his father Amram is given his aunt Jochebed for wife (Ex. 6:20 f.). The confusion in the Levitical family trees is especially evident in Num. 26:57 in comparison with 58. Moses is reproached for having an Ethiopian wife. The Zadokites and Aaronites simply were interested in seeing to it that there be no pureblooded Levitical sib going back to Moses. Egyptian names such as is "Moses" itself, are to be found among their chief competitors, the sib of the Elides (Phinehas). In the entire historical tradition and with the prophets as well as the prophetically stylized chronicles Moses, to be sure, plays a remarkably small part, which is possibly connected with the original relationship of only the North Israelite tribes (Ephraim) to the epiphany of the thorn bush.

10. On Moses cf. Volz, *Mose* (Tübingen, 1907) and Gressmann, *Mose und seine Zeit* (Göttingen, 1913). Against his interpretation as "medicine man" see Koenig, *ZDMG*, 1913, vol. 67, p. 660 f.

11. The various parts of the body of Yahwe, eyes, ears, nose, lips, hand, arm, heart, breath are in part named, in part presupposed.

12. Wen Amon (according to Breastead, *Records* vol. IV, p. 80) presents to the king of Byblus that the Pharaohs (whose shipments of silver the king of Byblus misses) were unable to accomplish what god Amon could accomplish (who for this very reason sends no material gifts) namely give him long life and good health (this, to be sure, does not agree with the courtly style of the Old Kingdom). Also the king of Byblus is said to "belong" to Amon, whom to obey allegedly brings good fortune to everyman.

13. The differences in the deities of the surrounding world especially of Mesopotamia, are excellently presented by Hehn in his *Die biblische und die babylonische Gottesidee* (Leipzig, 1913).

14. In contrast, the gods in Egypt require nourishment through man's sacrificial offerings just as do dead souls. (v. Bissing, *SMAW*, 1911, No. 6.)

15. For this entire context see, especially, Budde's cycle of lectures on ancient Israelite religion. He may well have most clearly seen and emphasized the determination of the ethical nature of the religion of Israel by the character of the godhead as elective.

16. Against the very pronounced view of Eerdman (in the *Altestamentliche Studien*) to the effect that some parts of the *Old Testament* do not

at all know Yahwe, that they were in fact specifically polytheistic, see Steuernagel in the *Theologische Rundschau,* 1908, p. 232 f.

17. Intelligence resides in the heart, the affects in the kidneys.

18. In Egypt the *ka* was "life power," also "soul" and at the same time nourishment which the soul needs to exist. It corresponds to the *nephesch* insofar as it goes to the realm of the dead (v. Bissing, *loc. cit.*)

19. Thus the later trichotomy would have developed from a fusion of the two dichotomous conceptions. Also Kautzsch, who takes a decided stand against the trichotomy, cannot help as a matter of fact to grant its later existence.

20. Nevertheless Yahwe gives a vow by his *"nephesh."*

21. Giesebrecht, *Die altestamentliche Schätzung des Gottesnamens and ihre religionsgeschichtlichen Grundlage* (Königsberg, 1901).

22. Job, in setting his hope in the fact that his "blood avenger lives," means that Yahwe will restore his good name which has been damaged by the suspicions of friends. Trito-Isaiah, in contrast to the older prohibition based on the opposition against the royal eunuchs, announces to them their admission to the community (56:4, 5) and in so doing he holds out to them "a better name" than through sons and daughters if they abide by God's commandments.

23. Also in Egypt it is the name which must live on, not the descendants of the dead. For the wealthy, the cult is not a matter of the descendants but of the prebend-endowed priests of death. The continued existence of the name, however, determines the continued existence of the soul in the beyond. This close relationship of the conception of the value of the name in Israel with that of Egypt, indeed, throws a strong light on the biased rejection of all expectancies for a hereafter and death cults. The abuse of the name of Yahwe finds its correspondence in the sanction of blinding, which Ptah according to an inscription (in the British Museum) has imposed on the vain use of his name. See Erman, *SBAW,* 1911, p. 1098 f.

24. Eduard Meyer has frequently expressed the one-sided view that the death sacrifices are not offered because of the power of the dead, but that they rather presuppose the impotence of the dead, who could not exist without them. In general, it is quite correct that deities as well as the souls of the dead are in need of the sacrifices as the Homeric shadows in Hades are in need of blood. But for Egypt the inscriptions even of the old Empire bespeak of the power of the dead. The dead holds out revenge to him damaging his good fortune, intercession with the great god or other blessing to him who offers prayers and sacrifices to him. And the whole of Chinese ancestor worship, especially the mourning rites the meaning of which is entirely forgotten, presuppose the power of the soul of the dead. Thus the power relationship is a mutual one: the dead is in need of sacrifice, but like the gods, he also has the power of compensating for them or for their omission. Absolutely correct is only that "ancestor worship" *per se* is no universal developmental stage of religion. This holds already for the reason that—as Egypt shows—death cult and ancestor worship need by no means necessarily coincide.

25. Even the dead of the Old Kingdom in the tomb inscriptions do not

turn to the descendants, but to anybody approaching their grave for the sake of prayers and sacrifices and they promise intercession to anyone who does their bidding. The death cult, however, is secured by priestly prebends, not by religious obligation of the descendants.

26. The rejection of the Egyptian death cult followed by no means from the tribal strangeness and the differences in conditions of life. The likewise tribally strange Lybian Bedouins had taken over the entire death ceremonial of the Egyptians (cf. Breastead, *Records,* vol. IV, p. 669, 726 ff.). Like Lybian chiefs, also Semitic Bedouin sheiks are often to be met with in Egypt and also at court. There were also Syrians with Egyptian-theophorous names.

27. The explicit prohibition of self-mutilation during mourning (Lev. 19:28) however, is directed against ecstatics and their magic. The technique of embalming, however, was known in Israel (cf. Gen. 50:2, 3).

28. Thus in the vision of Ezekiel of the bones of the dead, their revival by word magic is exclusively valued as proof of the power of Yahwe. Also only a glorious life in the future is held out to the 'Ebed Yahwe of Deutero-Isaiah, in which this form wavering between eschatological personality and personification obviously comes into focus in the second quality.

29. The whole question has been dealt with by Beer in his beautiful treatise on the biblical Hades (*Theologische Abhandlungen für H. Holtzmann,* 1902).

VI. Cultic Peculiarities of Yahwism

1. On the Sabbath, see the very precise treatise of G. Beer, "Einleitung in die Übersetzung des Mischna-Traktats Schabbath," *Ausgewählte Mischnatraktate,* ed. by P. Fiebig, No. 5 (Tübingen, 1908) p. 10 f. Furthermore, Hehn, "Siebenzahl und Sabbat bei den Babyloniern und im Alten Testament," *Leipziger Semitische Studien,* vol. II, 5, 1907.

2. The early prophets considered new moons and the Sabbath as festive days of Yahwe.

3. Meinhold's idea (last in *ZAW,* vol. 29, 1909) that the Sabbath allegedly became a weekday only in Exile therefore seems unacceptable. Precisely those who had remained in Palestine obviously knew the fixed weekly Sabbath as a market day. For this very reason I cannot share Beer's assumption that the Sabbath indeed had become a regular day of the week only in the Exile in Babylon.

4. As a matter of fact Budde refers to Amos 5:26, i.e., the Assyrian names of Saturn. König has come out against the belief in the great significance of the moon cult (the names of Mount Sinai and Abraham's women) for the Yahwe religion. Cf. *ZDMG,* vol. 69 (1915) p. 280 f.

5. Baumgärtel in his "Elohim ausserhalb des Pentateuch," *BWAT,* vol. 19, 1914, has shown that *elohim* as a name for God occurs with decreasing frequency from the Book of Judges through the Books of Samuel and on to Kings. It is used throughout in the second and third Psalm complexes and in the Book of Koheleth; it is almost never used by the prophets.

The obviously proverbial turns of phrase with *elohim* represent old Canaanite language usage. The use of *elohim* in late writings is of course due to shyness opposite the tetragrammaton.

6. Hehn, *loc. cit.*, formulates this somewhat differently and to my mind not without being open to controversy.

7. Late sources, such as Jesus Sirach and occasionally the Psalms and the Book of Daniel know again the "supreme" god, probably with regard for an environment of proselytes. (Hehn, *loc. cit.*)

8. In Job (5:17; 8:5) it is translated by παντοκράτωρ. The priestly revision of Genesis uses it for the purpose of identifying the ancient ephraimite *El* cults with the later Yahwe cult.

9. That King Ikhnaton "has placed his name forever upon the land" (of Jerusalem) (Amarna tablets) does not mean, as has been believed, that solar monotheism existed there, but rather political dominion of Ikhnaton.

10. Gressmann (in *ZAW*, vol. 30, 1910, p. 1 f.) holds the view that the "Elim" were the deities of the semi-nomadic tribes in contrast to the Baalim, the deities of the settled husbandmen. Much, indeed, is to be said for this assumption. First, the name of Baal never occurs in the patriarchal legends, nor, generally, in the Book of Genesis. Furthermore, the nature of the case makes Baal appear to be "lord" of the ploughland and the undoubted relationship to the Baalim of the coastal cities, above all, of Phoenicia. Whereas *El* points eastward where the nomadic tribes moved to and fro between Mesopotamia and Syria. The designation of the Khabiri deities as the *"ilani,"* however, may be rather adduced for the contrary, hence, the name must have been known also to the settled inhabitants. Likewise *El eljon* is after all the god of a civilized people. In any case the thesis seems worthy of the attention of the experts, as it would do justice to the construction of the priestly code concerning the pre-Mosaic worship of God among the patriarchs (*El shaddaj*).

11. Luther, with Eduard Meyer (*Die Israeliten* etc.) assumes that in David's time the Baal cults were Canaanite peasant cults, hence were orgiastic in nature, that the *El* cults were attached to trees and groves, and that the Yahwe cult in Gibeon (?) and Shiloh was a cult of the war god.

12. This is the opinion of Hehn, *loc. cit.* which agrees with that of Dhomme, *La Religion babylonienne et assyrienne*.

13. According to the papyri this was the case in the Jewish congregation in Syene whose many Ephraimite names allow the inference that they stemmed from Northern Israel (Bacher, *JQR* vol. XIX, 1907, p. 441). For details see Margolis, *JQR, New Series*, 2, (1911–1912) p. 435 where it is stated that the sacrificial offerings were distributed between the god of Jasu and a goddess.

14. Given the national character of Yahwe as fixed by *berith,* Baal seems to have played the main part in the mixed godhead for the foreigners. W. Max Müller has shown that Baal is to be found in Egypt as a warlike foreign god residing on mountains, hence with traits which certainly do not derive from his but from Yahwe's image.

15. Among the more recent studies we refer to Sellin's work in the *Nöldeke Festschrift* (1906).

16. Foote, *Journal of Biblical Literature*, 21, 1902.

17. "Die Lade Jahwes," *Forschungen zur Religion und Literatur des Alt-Testamentlichen Judentums* (Göttingen, 1906). Concerning the imageless cult on Crete see *Archiv für Religionswissenschaft*, vol. VII, p. 117 f.

18. The supreme Babylonian deities apparently were neither placed upon their thrones in the form of idols but symbols of the latter, such as Anu and Enlil.

19. Eshmun, the Phoenician god of healing, too, had a snake symbol.

20. The alleged wrath of the prophet Ahijah (I. Ki. 14) over this recognition is a later legend. The true reason of the Levites' opposition is clearly shown in I. Kings, 12:31, they were against the employment of plebeians as priests.

21. See the basic work of Graf Baudissin, *Geschichte des altestamentlichen Priestertums* (Leipzig, 1889). Some hypotheses, above all, that the priestly codex was prior to Deuteronomy have been relinquished today.

22. Uzziah's sacrifice is treated as a serious sin only by the (post-exilic) annalist (II. Chr. 26).

23. II. Samuel, 8:18. *Ibidem* 20:26 a Jairite is mentioned as his archchaplain besides the priests Zadok and Abiathar. The post-exilic chronicle subsequently eliminated David's sons.

24. See Struck, "Das Alttestamentliche Priestertum," in *Theologische Studien und Kritiken*, 81 (1908) p. 1 f.

25. A short but not uncontroversial sketch of the history of sacrifice in ancient Israel is to be found in Stade.

26. It is highly questionable whether there existed any generally valid rites beside circumcision and the prescriptions for the warriors (especially for the Nazarites).

27. *Chattat* and *asham* in the present revision are completely intertwined and yet treated as two separate things. They are first mentioned with Ezekiel as firmly established, common Israelite institutions. Earlier there is no mention of them, neither in I. Sam. 3:14 (where *sebach* and *mincha* sacrifices are mentioned as means of expiation) nor in Deut. 12, where sacrifices are mentioned in detail. The last shows clearly that the two kinds of sacrifice do not derive from the Jerusalem Temple cult. The conclusion of some, however, (for instance, of Benzinger) that, therefore, they must have been developed only in Exile times or shortly before, would certainly be wrong. Ezekiel may have been first to consider them as common Israelite institutions. The concept of *asham*, however, is to be found even in the Samuel tradition (the penance of the Philistines). As it were, the two kinds of sacrifice belong simply to Levitical private practice in which Deuteronomy had no particular interest. According to the prescriptions of the priestly law, *chattat* would be the more comprehensive of the two sacrifices.

28. Deuteronomy 18:10, 11, 14; Lev. 19:26, 28, 31; Num. 23:23.

29. The remark Lev. 20:6 shows that the opposition against the ecstatic magic also here played its part. See below.

VII. Priests and the Cult Monopoly
of Jerusalem

1. Schneider,"Die Entwicklung der Jahwereligion und der Mosessegen," *Leipziger Semitische Studien*, vol. 1, 1909, claims to be able to derive "Levi" from the word for "snake" and also adduces Adonijah's move to the snake stone and the name of one of David's forbearers.

2. This is maintained by Ed. Meyer. See the inscription in D. H. Müller, *Denkschrift der Kaiserlichen Akademie der Wissenschaften Wien*, Philosophisch-historische Klasse, vol. 37 (1888).

3. Jacob's Blessing knows no Levitical priests. Only Moses' Blessing knows the Levites, as teachers of Torah and as priests (cf. Ed. Meyer, *Die Israeliten* etc. p. 82 f.).

4. *Isch chasidecha*, i.e., "men of thy holy one" (of Moses) is used in Moses' Blessing for Levite (Deut. 33:8).

5. Perhaps also the inscription of the Ramassidian times which appears to recognize *"lui-el"* as a tribal name.

6. Ed. Meyer (*Die Israeliten* etc.) holds it for certain that the "tribe" of Levi was settled in Meribah (the "Prozesswasser") (hence represented a type of Pandit sibs of the Indian type.)

7. The name "Torah" is derived from "to throw lots." See Ed. Meyer, *ibid.*, p. 95 f.

8. Cf. Ungnad, *Die Deutung der Zukunft bei den Babyloniern und Assyrern* (Leipzig, 1909).

9. Cf. Westphal, "Aaron und die Aaroniden," *ZAW*, vol. 26 (1906).

10. Schneider, *loc. cit.*, wishes to derive the Aaronites from the Ark of the Covenant which would suggest itself as such. But they are nowhere connected with Shiloh as he assumes.

VIII. Forms of Israelite Intellectuality
in the Pre-Prophetic Era

1. For a collection of examples see, for instance, Fiebig, *Altjüdische Gleichnisse und Gleichnisse Jesu* (Tübingen, 1904).

2. Some of the older mashals, from the times of the Tannaites in Palestine, form, indeed, mostly exceptions to this, especially a few in the treatise *Pirke 'aboth*. Besides this judgment is, of course, meant to apply only relatively.

3. Cf. Romans 11:17 for the completely wrong parable of grafting.

4. For Wen Amon's travel account see Breastead, *Records*, vol. IV, p. 563 ff.

5. The Egyptian inner sanctum, too, is dark and must only be entered by the king as later in Israel only by the anointed high priest.

6. Travel account, see Breastead, *loc. cit.*, p. 579.

7. According to Herodotus the ritualistic strangeness of the Egyptians

opposite the Hellenes rested on the fact that these ate cow meat which made it impossible for Egyptians to kiss them or to use their eating utensils. This rather than the quality of stock-breeders *per se* may be back of the conception of the account of Gen. 43:32.

8. Erman, *SBAW*, p. 1109.

9. See for instance Klamroth, *loc. cit.*

10. Since de Wette generations of scholars have investigated the distribution of the material of the Hexateuch between the two collections and later (Deuteronomic, priestly, and other) insertions. The basic results are not controversial among the great majority of scholars; however, many details remain doubtful. Only the attempts to analyze the great collections into ever more layers have boomeranged into the seemingly vain attempt to dispute against the ascertained results. [For a recent and fundamental attack upon the "critical modern school" see Fritz Helling, *Die Frühgeschichte des Jüdischen Volkes* (Frankfurt, 1947) Ed.]

11. The relationship of both collections has been beautifully treated by Procksch, *Die Elihomquelle* (Übersetzung und Erläuterung), (Leipzig, 1906). Procksch assumes that Elijah had a certain influence on the revision and ingeniously seeks to explain thereby (p. 197) the use of the Elohim name as due to the intention to emphasize his unique value. The question of an originally rhythmic nature of the story is important, but cannot be answered by the non-expert. See for this, Sievers in *Abhandlungen der Königlich Sächsischen Gesellschaft der Wissenschaften*, vols. XXI-XXIII (1901, 1904, 1906) and Procksch's discussion of Sievers, *ibid.*, p. 210 f.

12. On the development of the idea see Lohr, "Sozialismus und Individualismus im Alten Testament," *ZAW*, 1906, supplement 10. The treatise is good, only the title is somewhat misleading.

IX. Ethics and Eschatology of Yahwism

1. Especially with Hehn, *loc. cit.*, p. 348 I find indications concerning the significance of what he calls the "democratic" character of Israel for the peculiarity of Israelite ethic.

2. J. Morgenstern in *Mitteilungen des Vereins für Alte Geschichte*, vol. 3, (1905) hinted at demonology as resulting from a need for theodicy.

3. Peisker, "Die Beziehungen der Nichtisraeliten zu Jahwe nach der Anschauung der altisraelitischen Quellenschriften," *ZAW*, vol. XV, Supplements (1907).

4. Usener, *Religions-geschichtliche Untersuchungen* (Bonn, 1899) p. 210 f.

5. For the Babylonian myth of original man Adapa is by no means in a state of innocence, he is, rather, an "impure" man whose entrance into Anu's heaven is dubious (cf. verse 57 of the translation in Gunkel, *loc. cit.*). Otherwise, original man, as mentioned, is usually endowed with great wisdom by the gods.

6. Cf. Gressmann's excellent treatise, "Der Ursprung der israelitisch-

jüdischen Eschatologie," *Forschungen zur Religion und Literatur des Alten und Neuen Testaments* (Göttingen, 1905) vol. 6. For criticism see Sellin, *Der alttestamentarische Prophetismus* (Leipzig, 1912) p. 105 ff.

7. The Pharaoh (Rameses II) appears as intercessor for procuring rain, see Breadstead, *Records*, vol. II, p. 426 (even for the land of the *Chetahl*)

8. The old hope of the Red Sea song, Ex. 15, is that Yahwe once shall become lord of the world, not that he already is, as Schön, *loc. cit.* interprets it. What people expect is also, not as Sellin assumes, a "judgment" of Yahwe, but the kindling of his wrath. The idea of a "judgment day" proper is never actually elaborated and where it is suggested, it is Yahwe who, as partner of the *berith*, has a trial with the inhabitants of the country. He is party not judge. (Thus with Hosea and in Deuteronomy.)

9. The conception of the "remnant" is discussed by Dittmann in *Theologische Studien und Kritiken*, vol. 87 (1914) p. 603 f.

10. J. Krall has discussed the Egyptian prophecies of good and evil in the *Festgabe für Büdinger*. A speaking lamb prophesies before a man called Psenchor under King Bocchoris first evil, coming over Egypt from the North East, then a time of good fortune; then the lamb dies. Furthermore we may mention von Wessely, "Neue Griechische Zauberpapyri," *Denkschriften der Königlichen Akademie der Wissenschaften,* Philosophisch-historische Klasse, No. 42, and finally von Wilcken, in *Hermes*, 40, the so-called "Prophezeiung des Töpfers," which predicts misfortune from the East and the destruction of Alexandria apparently, possibly this follows an older paradigm. Eduard Meyer in *Sitzungsberichte der Akademie der Wissenschaften*, vol. 31 (1905) assumed, among other things because of a papyrus commented upon by Lange, that the prophecy of a savior king also had been ascertained for Egypt. Gardiner's new reading, however, shows that this holds as little for this case as for the papyrus Golenisheft, which has been similarly interpreted. Rather in the one case a god, in the other a living king is meant. The prophecy to Mykerinus mentioned by Herodotus and the Amenophis prophecy mentioned by Manetho (Ed. Meyer, *loc. cit.* p. 651) represent traditions of insufficient authenticity. All in all they prove that prophecies of good and evil also existed in Egypt but they do not provide sufficient verification for the thesis that Israelite prophecy had borrowed from Egypt a fixed "schema."

X. Intercultural Relations in Pre-exilic Ethics

1. Concerning the Decalogue see Matthes, *ZAW*, vol. 24, p. 17.

2. Connubium is presented as dangerous only to loyalty to Yahwe. The formulation seems to indicate that connubium of peers existed only where a *berith* had been established which would correspond to conditions elsewhere, for instance Roman conditions, and would agree also with the presuppositions of the Dinah story.

3. For pre-exilic times see, on this question, the essay of Schultz in *Theologische Studien und Kritiken* (1896) vol. 63, which is good in its way.

4. Despite this, such fear of sin as, for instance, that of Alphons von Liguori or of some pietists is nowhere to be found in Israel or among Jewry.

5. We cite in the following the translation of Pierret (*Le Livre des Morts*, Paris, 1882). "I" refers to the introduction, "E" to the end, "A" and "B" to the two halves of Chapter 125, 21 Confessions.

6. The Babylonian list of sins, edited by Zimmern (*Beitr.* 1) and also quoted by Sellin, *loc. cit.*, p. 225 is the one most closely related to the ethic of the Decalogue. Disdain for one's parents and insulting one's older sister, adultery, killing, entering the neighbor's house, taking away the neighbor's clothes come closest to the sins of the Decalogue. The removing of landmarks, retention of prisoners or refusal to free them (doubtlessly bondsmen), loose and obscene talk, lies and insincerity belong to the offenses which, though not in the Decalogue, are prohibited in the Levitical exhortation, whereas no direct parallels are to be found for causing quarrels among parents and children or siblings and the wrong of "giving in small but refusing in big matters." The fact that purely ritualistic errors are placed on the same footing with this corresponds to the "cultic" and "sexual" Decalogue of Israel. Otherwise there are thus far no striking parallels between the two ethics. In contrast to the Egyptian and Levitical exhortations, Babylonian ethic apparently did not place stress on "loving one's neighbor," which presumably was due to the much stronger development of business life in metropolitan Babylon. Again, in contrast to Egypt, there is no sublimation in the direction of ethical absolutism (*Gesinnungsethik*), as in the suppression of "desire" of the 10th commandment. In Egypt the greater emphasis on "moral intention" (*Gesinnung*) was presumably first occasioned by the special significance attributed in the judgment of the dead to the "heart" as the seat of knowledge of one's own sins.

7. For the conception of sin and its development in Babylonian religion see Schollmeyer, "Sumerisch-babylonische Hymnen und Gebete an Samas," *Studien zur Geschichte und Kritik des Altertums,* Supplement (Paderborn, 1912), and J. Morgenstern, "The doctrine of sin in the Babylonian Religion," *Mitteilungen des Vereins für Alte Geschichte* (Berlin 1905) vol. 3.

8. See, for instance, the prohibition against depriving a poor man of his position during his corvée service for the king (nineteenth Dynasty). Breadstead, *Records,* vol. III, p. 51.

9. Breastead, *Records,* vol. I, 239, 240, 281, 328 f., 459, 523. All these inscriptions stem from the time of the Old Kingdom and begin with the first Dynasty.

10. For documents of Egyptian popular piety of the time of the Rameses see Erman, *SBAW*, vol. II, p. 1086 f. For the growing belief in compensation in the New Kingdom see Poertner, "Die ägyptischen Totenstelen als Zeugen des sozialen und religiösen Lebens ihrer Zeit," in *Studien zur Geschichte und Kritik des Altertums,* vol. 4, No. 3 (Paderborn, 1911).

11. On Kalumus' inscription see Littmann, *SBAW*, Nov. 16, 1911, p. 976 f.

12. In his polemic against Protestant scholars Büchler presents R. Chanina as a model of Jewish morality. Chanina died wrapped in a Torah scroll, because he believed that way to be better assured of God's vengeance on his tormentors.

XI. Social Psychology of the Prophets

1. G. Hölscher's work *Die Propheten* (1914) deserves special mention. It has great merit although various theses are controversial in detail. Hölscher is informed by modern psychology and presents the entire historical background. For single prophets see the modern commentaries.

The ecstatic proclivities of the prophets are discussed with his usual brilliance by H. Gunkel, "Die geheimen Erfahrungen der Propheten," (lecture, "*Suchen der Zeit*," vol. I, 1903). The *Schriften des Alten Testaments*, vol. II, 2, contain excerpts of this besides translations and partially excellent single commentaries by H. Schmidt on Amos and Hosea (vol. II, 1) and a very useful introductory analysis of the literary peculiarities. Of other literature see Giesebrecht, *Die Berufsbegabung der alttestamentlichen Propheten* (Göttingen, 1897); Cornill, *Der israelitische Prophetismus* sixth ed. (Strassburg, 1906); Sellin, *Der alttestamentliche Prophetismus* (Leipzig, 1912). Further literature will be mentioned at the respective places. Ernst Troeltsch makes many correct observations on the "ethos" of the Old Testament prophets in "*Logos*," vol. VI, p. 17 and justly places greater emphasis than is usual on the utopian nature of their "politics." Here we shall not go into details.

2. See for Jeremiah 26:24; 29:3; 36:11; 40:6.

3. For Isaiah's political position see especially Küchler, *Die Stellung des Propheten Jesaja zur Politik seiner Zeit* (Tübingen, 1906). Cf. also the observations of Procksch, *Geschichtsbetrachtung und Geschichtsüberlieferung bei den vorexilischen Propheten* (Leipzig, 1902).

4. This is suggested by the fact that the king placed on the throne by him was given a theophoric (Yahwe-) name.

5. This has been maintained especially for Amos (for example by von Winckler). Küchler, *loc. cit.*, disputed this for good reasons.

6. For this obviously unprovable assumption speaks his way of repeatedly mentioning Shiloh as the first place of pure Yahwe worship and the manner in which he compares the destruction of Jerusalem with the undoubtedly half forgotten devastation of Shiloh centuries ago.

7. It is a conjecture of Duhm that, at another place, it is Osiris presumably who is named among the deities whom Yahwe will destroy.

8. The present version of the text, Micah 1:55, is not entirely correct in this.

9. It has been generally assumed, and rightly, that Jeremiah is not the author of Jer. 17:19 f.

10. Ezekiel, however, was once seized by ecstasy in the presence of the elders who consulted him (Ezek. 8:1).

11. Sellin, *loc. cit.* p. 227 rightly observes that the form in which the divine word reaches the prophet as a rule is not stated in detail. What was decisive was that the prophet had given an interpretation of his intentions which was evident and therewith conclusive to him.

12. This holds for all "speaking with tongues" and also for the "prophecy" which then addressed itself to the present. Similarly it reappeared among the Anabaptists and Quakers of the sixteenth and seventeenth centuries, today it occurs most characteristically in the American Negro churches (also of the Negro bourgeoisie, for example, in Washington, where I witnessed it).

13. Consideration must always be given the fact that all contrasts are linked by transitions and that similar phenomena are to be found also with the Christians. Among them, too, individuals are the psychic "centers of infection."

XII. The Ethic and Theodicy of the Prophets

1. For the charity commandments of the Torah were of course no longer a sublimation of the ethic of the peasant neighborhood as such; like all peasant ethics it was remote from such sentimentalism. These commandments belonged to the ideology of Mid Eastern Egyptian kingship and its literati of priests and scribes.

2. Cf. Sellin, *loc. cit.*, p. 125.

3. Yahwe's "great" day as stated by Zephaniah (1:14) might best recall the great world days. But it is at once obvious that such is out of the question. Before the Exile only very general knowledge of all such matters had reached Israel.

4. With Amos (except in one passage) and even with Hosea in one place (5:4) the calamity is presented as inescapable, clearly because the content of the vision led to this. The same recurs with Isaiah, and, again, quite preponderantly with Jeremiah.

5. Strangely enough, also Hölscher (p. 229, note 1) believes the child Immanuel could not represent an eschatological but rather an actual and known figure (possibly: Isaiah's own wife and son!) because otherwise "nothing would be proven" by the miraculous sign. But there is no question of "proving" anything, rather the disbelief of Ahab results in the envisioned event, expected timely, namely, his rejection in favor of the savior child.

XIII. The Pariah Community

1. On this point see the good work of Peisker. The significance of international rules of warfare among Palestinian nations can not be ascertained in detail and has been mentioned earlier.

2. [For a recent discussion of the entire problem see Benjamin N. Nelson, *The Idea of Usury* (Princeton, 1949) p. 3 ff. Ed.]

3. This is rightly emphasized by Klamroth, "Die Jüdischen Exulanten in

Babylonien" (*BWAT* vol. 10, Leipzig 1912). The valuable writing is repeatedly used below. Its single weak aspect is, perhaps, that at times it seeks to find more data concerning the actual conditions of the Exile community in the prophetic passages than is warranted and that it believes too literally in the description of the misery of the exiles.

4. Cf. S. Daiches, *The Jews in Babylon in the Time of Ezra and Nehemiah according to Babylonian Inscriptions,* Publ. Con. No. 2 (London, 1910).

5. Jud. 13:4 appears to suggest that the prohibition of eating "unclean things" originally held for laymen only by virtue of a vow.

6. Correct Jews in general did not, due to dietary rules, hesitate to extend hospitality to non-Jews, but on their part declined that of the pagans and Christians. The Frankish Synods declaimed against this as against a humiliaton of the Christians and in their turn exhort the Christians to decline Jewish hospitality.

XIV. The Exile

1. "Juden und Samaritaner," *BWAT* 3 (Leipzig, 1908). At Jeremiah's time (41:5) people came from Shechem and Samaria to participate in the Temple sacrifice.

2. Concerning Ezekiel cf. Herrmann, *Ezechielstudien* (Berlin, 1908).

3. Nothing speaks for the frequent assumption that these sections have been added later as the doomsday fails to agree with the later church political projects of the Exile priests and their elaboration by Ezra and Nehemiah. The turn from semi-pathological and eschatological apocalyptics of the ecstatic to the subtleties of a projected future state of the intellectual is indeed nothing singular.

4. While it has been ascertained that this chapter of the present Book of Isaiah originated in Exile times and also the non-identity of its author with that of the following pieces (Trito-Isaiah) is increasingly recognized, the question remains, whether the chapters ascribed to Deutero-Isaiah should be ascribed to a single author or the so-called 'eved-Yahwe songs to another. The songs of the "Servant of God" remain now as before a crux of interpretation. Besides Duhm's Isaiah commentary we may refer to Sellin, *Die Rätsel des deuterojesajanischen Buchs* (1908) and to Gressmann's discussion in his aforementioned *Eschatologie* (1905), to Laue's essay in *Theologische Studien und Kritiken* (1904), as well as to Giesebrecht, *Der Knecht Jahwes des Deuterojesaja* (1902). We mention especially Rothstein's very penetrating review of the older presentations of Sellin (in the first volume of Sellin's *Studien für Enstehungsgeschichte der Jüdischen Gemeinde nach dem babylonischen Exile* (1901) *Theologische Studien und Kritiken* (1902) vol. I, p. 282. See also Staerk in *BWAT,* vol. 14 (1912). Staerk distinguishes between the four songs of Isaiah (42:1 f.; 49:1 f.; 50:4 f.; 52:13 f.) and the other Servant of God songs and deems it certain that the 'eved represents the people of Israel.

In these four songs God's Servant is held to be a personal figure, in the first three a partially heroic figure, partially that of a martyr, conceived as a preexisting universal savior, in truth a transfer of the hope for the Davidians to prophecy. The criticism of Sellin is often convincing. Nevertheless Sellin's theses in important points have enduring value. Sellin is the main proponent of the Joiakim-hypothesis and at the same time of the homogeneity of the Book of Deutero-Isaiah. The sympathetic and unbiased reader will increasingly be impressed by this homogeneity of authorship. The book originated piece by piece under the impact of enthusiastic hopes for Cyrus and then the pieces were gathered into a book.

Against this the interpretation of the Servant of God as referring to Joiakim appears hardly acceptable, especially because he is a man with the gift of Torah teaching, hence a prophet not a king. The book impresses one as the religious poetry of an intellectually outstanding enthusiastic thinker writing for a small circle of likeminded men. The assumption is therefore admissable that the shifting emphasis between individual and collective interpretability is the intentional art form of this prophetic theodicy. For us the decisive point of Sellin's hypothesis lies in the fact that the author allegedly transferred the songs originally referring to an individual (Joiakim) after Joiakim's death to the people of Israel and therefore integrated them with the pieces which originated only then under the impression of Cyrus' approach. With this Sellin accepts, in the end, the contention that Deutero-Isaiah in the final revision no longer considered Joiakim but the people of Israel or its pious core respectively as the repository qualities originally assigned to the king. Only philological experts could say the decisive word about the spirited construction. In any case the here presupposed ambiguity was also then what the author of the final revision intended.

5. Besides Duhm, Hölscher, curious to relate, has come out for non-Babylonian origin (because of Is. 52:11 and 43:14) and suggests Egypt as a guess (especially Syene because of 49:12). This however seems unacceptable already because of the timely interest in Cyrus not to mention the strong interest in things Babylonian.

6. The call "from the womb" (Is. 49:1) on the one hand agrees with Babylonian royal terminology, on the other, with the providential call of Jeremiah in the womb (Jer. 1:5). Sellin (loc. cit. p. 101 f.) has convincingly demonstrated strong overtones of Babylonian hymns and laments in the author's diction. (By the way Kittle had already suggested this in his Cyrus und Deuterojesaja, ZATW (1898).

7. The pericope of the Servant of God is used especially often by the Synoptics and the Acts, next in the Letters to the Romans and the first Letter to the Corinthians, but also with John. I. Cor. 15:3 shows that the tradition furnished Paul the idea of the Savior dying as expiatory sacrifice. Jesus refers to the prophetic prediction Mat. 26:24 (equals Is. 53:7, 8). Often it is stated literally parallel to Deutero-Isaiah that Jesus was the chosen one (Acts 9:15 equals Is. 42:1) to the pleasure of God (Mat. 3:17 equals Is. 42:1) free of sins (John 8:46 equals Is. 53:5) the Lamb of God (John 1:29, 36 equals Is. 53:4 f.) the light of the people (John 1:5 equals Is. 42:6 f. called to give rest to those that labor and are heavy

laden (Mat. 11:28 equals Is. 55:1 f.) lived lowly (Phil. 2:7 equals Is. 53:2, 3) was despised (John 1:10 equals Is. 53:2, 3) misunderstood (Acts 8:32 f. equals Is. 53:7, 8) accused (Mat. 26:63) and scourged (Mat. 27:26) suffering silently like a lamb, interceding for the wicked (Luke 23:34 equals Is. 53:5 f.), gave his life a ransom for many (Mat. 20:28 equals Is. 53:10 f. thereby effected remission of sins (Luke 24:47 equals Is. 53:5 f.) and was glorified by God (John 13:31; 14:13; Acts 3:13 equal Is. 49:5; 55:5). Especially characteristic is Romans 4:25 (equals Is. 53:5, 12) where Paul makes use of the quite ambiguous translation of LXX. Occasionally, also, the role of the apostles is characterized by images drawn from Deutero-Isaiah. (Acts 13:47 equals Is. 49:6) All passages are conveniently compiled in E. Huhn, *Die Messianischen Weissagungen des israelitsch-jüdischen Volks*, Vol. II (1900).

8. Frequently instead of the "Servant of God" simply "Son of Man" is used, which indicates borrowing via mysteries.

9. The reading of verse 16 is corrupt where "hands" and "feet" are mentioned. Hence, it may be questionable whether lacing or piercing of ankles as in the case of captives is meant. But the translation of the LXX seems to prove already that that is the case. The same is indicated in the following verses, where the distribution of garments by drawing lots is mentioned. The Christian community however must, perhaps in consequence of LXX, have understood that verse as absolutely referring to a crucifixion for the whole presentation of the Evangels is clearly influenced by the twenty-second Psalm. Consequently it is quite probable that the "pierced" one of Deutero-Isaiah was on the author's mind, in any case, that Psalm twenty-two usually was thus understood. The Christian congregation has also otherwise made promiscuous use of the Servant of God songs and this Psalm as predictions referring to Christ and has fashioned the representation of the passion accordingly.

10. Cf. Dalmann, "Der leidende und sterbende Messias der Synagogue im ersten nachchristlichen Jahrhundert," *Schriften des Inst. Jud.* vol. IV (Berlin, 1888). Representative suffering in itself was a quite familiar idea in rabbinical times (4 Macc. 6:29; 17:22).

11. For Hosea the prophet is the "man of spirit."

XV. Sects and Cults of the Post-Exile Period

1. The severe danger of Hellenization is probably meant by Psalm 12:2. [Weber interprets the passage as a reference to Sophistry. Ed.].

2. See Macc. 7:12.

3. Cf. Elbogen, *Die Religiösen Anschauungen der Pharisäer* (Berlin, 1904).

4. The name *'am ha-artez* since the revision of the Book of Ezra (9:1) and Nehemiah (10:31) is technical. As a religiously inferior "mass," however, they developed in opposition first to the *Hasidim* then to the Pharisees since the Maccabean times.

5. Written toward the end of the second century B.C. Cf. Charles, *The Book of Jubilees* (London, 1902).

6. Always, at least the orthodox pagan predestination has maintained *behirah,* the ethical freedom of will, the freedom of choice between good and evil. Rather than touch this freedom God's omniscence was occasionally represented as conditional.

7. This is the term also in the daily prayer, the *shema.*

8. First for Gamaliel the elder.

9. Jewish authorities therefore declare Mat. 23:7, 8 to be an "anachronism."

10. In general this was, of course, only the case if the person concerned was no mere teacher, but a prophet endowed with miraculous power.

11. Not infrequently the primary occupations of Indian *gurus* also were in trade, landowning, or acting as rentiers.— However, the Jewish rabbi of early times necessarily sought his living from sources other than his "spiritual" calling. The Indian *guru,* as a rule at least, lived primarily by fees and donations yielded by his spiritual functions. In (eastern) Jewry not the rabbi but the new *Hasidic* charismatic mystagogue corresponded to the *guru,* as will be discussed below.

12. In the Talmud that means the ordained rabbis.

13. B.B. 22a.

14. Unless otherwise qualified reference is always *a priori* to the rabbis of the epoch under discussion, that is the time which has furnished the material for the composition of the Talmud.

15. Deut. 13:2, 3; 17:20 f.

16. Deut. 18:11.

17. Where such "application" was actually not self-evident, as in the case of the problem of Job and occasionally elsewhere it at least seemed to be self-evident.

18. Lev. 18:21.

XVI. *Judaism and Early Christianity*

1. Philo uses the term "synegor" for the "logos" which sustains the high priest.

2. The Gospel of Luke, in a striking manner (7:36; 11:37 ff.; 14:1) has Jesus repeatedly eat with a Pharisee (the last time even with a chief of the Pharisees—meaning, as the parallel passage indicates a "ruler of the synagogue"). Both of the older Gospels know nothing of this. This might be tendencious as Luke emphasizes also in the Acts the conversion of "Pharisees," and as the table community of Peter with the Hellenes of Antioch was so important for Paul. Strictly observant Pharisees would have denied commensalism to an *'am ha-arez* or incorrectly living man. According to Joh. 8:48, the Jews called Jesus a "Samaritan."

3. Acts 21:28 f. Only the passage Acts 22:21 f. takes an apparently somewhat different standpoint. (It reports indignation of the crowd over the fact that he represented himself as savior sent to the Gentiles). If any version is authentic obviously the account of James' attitude and the motivation of the attempted lynching is. Naturally the Jews could hardly be happy about the attempt to alienate their uncircumcised proselytes. However, no attack upon the law is to be found in this.

4. Acts 16:3. Timotheus had, to be sure, a Jewish mother, while his father was a Greek (Acts 16:1).

5. Cf. especially the Gospel of John. There, not only the "scribes" and "Pharisees" as opponents of Jesus are very often replaced by the "Jews" generally, but above all, the extent to which the Jews persecute him is increased to the extreme over and against the other Evangels. With John the Jews almost incessantly are after his life which is not the case to the same extent with the Synoptics. (Even with Luke in several instances, (11:14 f.) the "Pharisees" as opponents of John and Jesus are replaced by "the people" or "several").

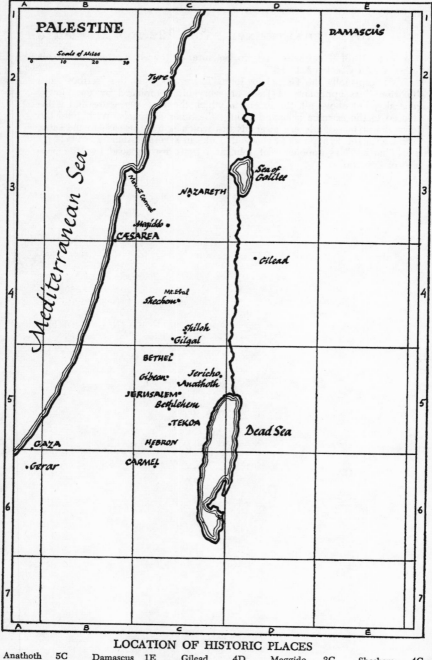

PALESTINE

DAMASCUS

Scale of Miles
0   10   20   30

Tyre

Mediterranean Sea

Sea of Galilee

NAZARETH

Mount Carmel

Megiddo
CÆSAREA

Gilead

Mt. Ebal
Shechem

Shiloh
Gilgal

BETHEL

Gibeon
Jericho
Anathoth

JERUSALEM
Bethlehem

TEKOA

Dead Sea

GAZA

HEBRON

Gerar

CARMEL

LOCATION OF HISTORIC PLACES

Anathoth	5C	Damascus	1E	Gilead	4D	Meggido	3C	Sheshem	4C
Bethel	5C	Gaza	5A	Gilgal	4C	Mt. Carmel	3C	Shiloh	4C
Bethlehem	5C	Gerar	6A	Jericho	5C	Mt. Ebal	4C	Tekoa	5C
Caesarea	4B	Gibeon	5C	Jerusalem	5C	Nazareth	3C	Tyre	2C
Carmel	6C								

GLOSSARY AND INDEX[1]

1. SUBJECTS

Academos, local heroes of Attica to which the ancients traced the name of the Academy, 320

Acculturation, 126

Achar story, 179

Achim (Hebr.), def., 75

Acosmism, denial of the reality of the world opposite the sole reality and importance of God, hence devaluation of the world, 409

Adad, Babylonian deity, 189

Adam and Eve, 132, 227 f., 315, 401

Adapa, Babylonian original man, 228

Adiaphorous, indifferent, 343

Adirim (Hebr.), the great ones, nobles, 358

Administration, city, 17 f.; kingly, 18 f., 99 f., 113, 195; post exilic, 359 f.

Adsidui, 18

Agape, def., 407, 410

Agroikos (Gr.), def., 27

Ahuramazda, Persian deity, 134, 158

Aisymnete (Gr.), council of Greek city states, 63, 275, 295

Alcohol, *see* Orgiasticism

Altar, 156, 161, 163, 188, 190

'Am (Hebr.), def., 16; 24, 86

Amarna age, the age to which Biblical writers ascribe Abraham and the beginning of Hebrew religion, c. 1400 B.C., 155

Amarna letters, letters addressed by the petty kings of the land to the Egyptian Pharaohs (Amenophis II and IV), 15 f., 36, 75, 198

'Am ha-aretz (Hebr.), def., 25 f., 184; 387, 390

'Am haelohim (Hebr.), def., 131

'Am hamilchamah (Hebr.), def., 16

Ammê haarezoth (Hebr.), 359

Ammonites, 41, 123, 302

Amon, Egyptian deity, 135, 231, 246, 248, 257

Amorites, 6

Amphictyony, league of Greek states allied for the protection of a centrally located sanctuary. Among the temple associations that of Delphi was of special importance. Amphictyonic, 90

Anashim (Hebr.), def., 16 f.; 29

Anathema, a solemn religious curse, 271, 293

Ancestors, 228

Ancestor worship, 139, 143

Angelology, 389, 408

Anglicanism, 263

Animals, berith with, 229, 322; eating of, 351 ff.; protection of, 261 f.; sacrifice of, 187 f.; worship, 200 f.

Anomie, Anomismus, devaluation or rejection of the world and its norms, 315, 396

Anthropogenic, man-derived, 227

Anthropolatry, the worship of a human being as divine, 181

Anthropomorphism (anthropomorphic), ascription of human traits to deities and/or things non-human, 137, 210 ff., 310

[1] Def. stands for definition. The chronological data were taken from Sigmund Mowinckel, "Die Chronologie der Israelitischen und Jüdischen Könige," *Acta Orientalia,* vol. X, 1932, p. 271 and from William Foxwell Albright, *From Stone Age to Christianity,* Baltimore, 1946.

Anti-chrematistic, against wealth, 285

Antisemitism, 417 f.

Anu, supreme god of the heavens in Babylonian religion, 153, 228

Apocalyptics, 376, 380

Apollo, a Greek and Roman deity; god of light, health, music, poetry, prophecy, 137, 276, 290, 319, 349

Aramaic, *see* Language

Arameans, inhabitants of Aram which designates nearly the same districts as Syria, 341

Archegetes, leader, guide, 170, 331

Arhat, a Buddhistic saint of the highest rank, 314

Ark of the Covenant, 91, 94, 98, 133, 158 f.

Arkan-discipline, esoteric teaching, *see* Discipline

Art, artists, 35, 199, 253; bards, 28; dance, 97; legends, 212; literature, 194 ff., 366, 369, 397 f.; music, 28, 35, 97, 196; poetry, 194, 196, 290; and religion, 401

Artisans, 29, 202, 253, 393, 416; Bedouin, 28; byssus weavers, 29, 35; guest, 28, 202; guilds of, 29; Indian, 29; Israelite, 28; royal, 29, 35, 416; scorned, 161. *See also* Bezaleel

Asceticism, methodical denial of sleep, food, sexual gratification, etc. Weber distinguishes two main types of asceticism, the other-worldly asceticism of the monk, and the inner-worldly asceticism of the Puritan who lives among the worldly without being of them, 254, 343, 401 ff., 410

Ass, 25, 54 f., 82, 106, 113, 115, 261, 280, 352; ass-riding, *see* King

Assuan papyri, 347

Assur, supreme god of Assyria, 305, 309, 320

Astarte, Phoenician deity, 149, 189, 202, 280

Astral spirits, 203 f.

Astrolatry, star worship, 367

Astrology, astronomy, 203 ff., 285, 396

Avarice, 116, 237, 281

Baal, title of numerous local deities among ancient Semitic people, typifying the productive forces of nature, 77, 154 ff., 161, 189, 279, 283, 293, 401, 402; Baal Peor, 315; Baal Zebul, 154

Baalam's saying, 103, 123

Baalat, female companion of Baal, 189

Baptists, 344

Barbarossa hope, 330

Basar (Hebr.), 140

Barnaim def., 410

Basileus (Gr.), king, 309

Bathkol, (Hebr.) def., 412, 382

Bedouins, 10 ff., 36 ff., 142, 188, 191; Cain, 35, 52; Egypt, 201; Notables, 12; Sib, 11; and Yahwe, 122

Beelzebub, 411

Behistun Inscription, 257

Bel, Assyrian and Babylonian deity, 154

Berith (Hebr.), covenant, treaty, 45 f., 75 ff., 78, 118 ff., 126, 130 ff., 184, 214, 294, 303, 305, 332, 341 f.; new, 327, 366; violations of, 165 ff., 301, 320

Berserks, ecstatic Nordic warrior heroes, 94, 97, 101, 128, 192

Beyond, the, *see* Hereafter

Bhagavadgita, 397

Blessings, Jacob's and Moses', 41, 82, 95, 103 f., 170, 174 f., 209

Blood revenge, 62, 137

Bne Asaph (Hebr.), def., 35

Bne chail (Hebr.), def., 16, 25 f.

Bne Korah (Hebr.), def., 35

Body, 400, *see also Basar*

Bodyguard, 18, 100

Book of the Covenant, 48 f., 61 ff., 70, 75 f., 88, 164, 295, *see sefer ha berith*

Book of Daniel, 319, 376 f., 380

Book of the Dead, among the ancient Egyptians a collection of religious texts, magical spells, etc., for guidance of the soul on its journey to the next world, 239, 250 ff., 262

Book of Esther, 403

Book of Joshua, 15 f., 43, 76, 187

Book of Jubilees, 353, 389

Book of Judges, 97, 133, 341

Book of Wars of Yahwe (Num. 21:14), 195

Book of Wisdom, 377

Brotherliness, 64, 67, 126, 302, 407

Buddhism, 255, 314

Bureaucracy, 96, 143, 256, 303

Calvinism, 310

Camel, 8, 11, 13, 37 ff., 42, 61, 66

Canaanites, 35, 236, 339, 340; city, 21, 155; cults, 109

Capitalism, refers to different modes of profit making. Weber distinguishes modern industrial capitalism with its rational capital accounting from various universally diffused and ancient types of political capitalism oriented to booty, fiscal, colonial, etc., profit opportunities, 345

Cassites, tribe, 6

Caste, a hereditary status group in India. Its special way of life is not only legally and conventionally but also ritually sanctioned (Max Weber, *Essays in Sociology,* tr., ed., and with an introduction by H. H. Gerth and C. Wright Mills, Oxford University Press, New York, 1946, pp. 396 ff.), 3, 143, 170, 416

Casus foederis (L.), a case within the provisions of a treaty, 90

Catholic Church, 5, 263, 402

Chaber (Hebr.), def., 75; 386, 415

Chaburah, chevra (Hebr.), brotherhood, def., 386, 390; 411, 417

Chail (Hebr.), def., 99, *see* Wealth

Cherem (Hebr.), def., 93 f., 141

Chthonian cult, earth cult, belief in earth and under-earth spirits, 144 ff., 204

Chaldeans, inhabitants of Chaldea, district of Babylonia, 396

Chariotry, 6, 22, 27, 82, 99 ff.

Charisma, originally it is conceived to be a magical quality of an extraordinary person, leader, ruler who claims authority and leadership on its basis. Where leadership and group-cohesion is based on the belief of the followers in the alleged, presumed, or actual extraordinariness and irreplaceability of the leader, Weber speaks of charismatic leadership, charismatic authority, etc., 11, 17 ff., 40, 98 f., 157, 395; prophetic, 294, 395; hereditary: the belief in the transfer of extraordinary and exemplary endowments of a religious, political, or military leader to his descendants may secure a special prestige position to his kin. Weber uses also the term "gentile charisma" with reference to preeminent families, 18 f., 9&, 388

Charity, Christian, 258; Egyptian, 258; Israelite, 47, 255 ff.; *hasheina* (Hebr.), def., 409

Chastity, 191, 407

Chelek (Hebr.), def., 73

Cherem (Hebr.), def., 358; 93, 215, 245

Chiliastic expectations, expectations that Christ will return, 327

Chokek (Hebr.), def., 87; 304

Chokma (Hebr.), def., 197; 285, 304; teachers, 228

Chorim (Hebr.), def., 17

Chresmologists, def., 270; 325

Christians, 292, 299 f., 326, 328, 334, 348, 410, 421 ff.

Christology, teachings regarding the Christian Savior, 376

Chuk (Hebr.), def., 87, 304

Circumcision, 27, 34, 92, 150, 199,

284, 336, 339; and proselytes, 419 ff.

City, a dense settlement of a large number of households without mutual acquaintance of the inhabitants. Regular exchange of goods in a local market is essential for their economic life. (Max Weber, *Wirtschaft und Gesellschaft*, Tübingen, 1925, pp. 514 f.), 13 ff., 21, 155, 353

Class: "We may speak of a 'class' when (1) a number of people have in common a specific causal component of their life chances, in so far as (2) this component is represented exclusively by economic interests in the possession of goods and opportunities for income, and (3) is represented under the conditions of the commodity or labor markets," (Max Weber, *Essays*, p. 181)

Class antagonism, 31, 54, 56 f., 68, 88, 382

Classis, 100

Colonus (L.), (a) a member of a Roman colonial settlement (b) a Roman sharecropper or tenant farmer, since the fourth century tied to the land, 21, 63, 65, 69

Commandments, 165 ff., 236, 242, 245, 300, 304; second, 157; tenth, 236

Commenda (medieval law), the trust in which goods are delivered to another for a particular enterprise, as to market abroad, 22

Commensalism, table community, 76, 186 f., 339, 351, 353 f., 387, 406, 411, 415, 417, 422; with Gentiles, 353 f., 356; with Yahwe, 124, 211

Communism of consumption, 407

Compensation, 216, 246, 305, 372

Confederacy (Israelite), 81 ff., 90 ff., 125, 131, 136 f., 162

Confucian, 132, 224, 254

Congregation, 163, 299, 358, 360, 362, 376, 380 f.

Coniuratio (L.), def., 31, 68, 75

Connubium (L.), 36, 340, 387, 406, 417

Covenant, see *berith*

Corvée: servitudes, taxes in the form of forced labor (such as construction work or repair of roads) exacted by public authorities, 8, 200

Cosmogony: speculation about the origin of the universe, 202, 226; Cosmogonic myths, 201

Creation, story of, 226, 228, 354

Critias fragment, Plato's, 320

Cult, 79 ff., 115, 139 ff., 202; imageless, 114, 127, 156 ff., 401; monopoly of Jerusalem, 186, 360; of Dead, 8, 144, 174, 179, 200 f.

Culture borrowing, 199, 374 f., 408, 410; from Babylonia, 149 ff., 396; from Egypt, 92, 198 ff., 322; influence of Babylon and Egypt, 5, 7, 62, 262; Mesopotamia, 201 ff.

Culture traits, fusion of, 126 f.

Cure of soul, 173, 175, 214 f., 229, 239, 294 ff., 306

Cyropaedia, political and philosophical romance by Xenophon, 309

Davidians, 164, 280, 330 f., 348, 349, 351, 366

Day of Yahwe, def., 230; 324, 329 ff., 368, 379

Death, 143 ff.; cult, *ibid.; see also* Hereafter

Debar, pl. *debarim* (Hebr.), the word, commandment, 87 ff., 212, 238, 242, 250, 259, 284, 304, 325

Deborah, Song of, 55, 80, 82 ff., 91, 95, 97, 103, 111, 114, 119, 123, 125, 138, 158 f., 176, 178, 192, 194, 201

Decalogue, cultic, 351 f.; ethical, 235 ff.; origin of, 235, 237, 239; sexual, 77, 236

Decemvir (L.), member of an elected

ten men committee in ancient Rome. They had special authority e.g., in matters of land distribution or sacrifices, 63

Deity, functional: the personification of some natural or social process. Gods of storm, of rain, of growth, etc. Social functional deities are exemplified in the gods of crafts, the god of blacksmiths in Greece, the gods of scribes in Egypt and Babylonia, 154; foreign, 311, 363, 417; local, 154

Demagogy, *see* Prophet

Demons, 311

Demos, the people, 30 f., 382

Dervish, member of an Islamite ascetic order distinguished by violent dancing, pirouetting, chanting or shouting, 97 f., 101

Deuteronomy, 68 ff., 76 f., 84, 87 f., 119, 179, 184 f., 202, 209, 243, 247, 333, 360; find of, 184, 244; Deuteronomic reform, 169

Darmashastras, metrical law books of Hinduist India, 180

Diakrioi, (Gr.), poor peasants, 23

Diaspora, 420 f.

Dietary prescriptions, 141, 351 ff.; kosher, 353

Dionysus, Greek deity, 137, 188

Discipline: "The content of discipline is nothing but the consistently rationalized, methodically trained and exact execution of the received order, in which all personal criticism is unconditionally suspended and the actor is unswervingly and exclusively set for the carrying out the command," (*Essays,* p. 253) Arkan, 407, 408; Essenian, 406 ff.

Dove, 381, 411

Dream, 106 ff., 167, 211, 290 f., 379, 395

Ea, in Assyro-Babylonian mythology the god of the ocean and subter-

ranean springs and of wisdom, 228

'ebed (Hebr.), def., 48

Ebionites, ultra-Jewish party in the early Christian Church, 403, 410, 422

Ecclesia, an assembly. Originally that of the freemen of Ancient Athens. In Christian usage, a congregation, a church, 320

Eclogue, Virgil's, 321

Ecstasy, *see* Prophets, Mass; apathetic, 106 f., 109; China, 96; India, 288; types of warrior, 94; orgiastic: euphoric states often induced by means of music, dance and toxics, and leading to sexual orgies, 106, 109, 212

Edomites, tribe, 39, 41, 123, 199, 302, 339, 368

Education, Egyptian, 200, 253; Levitical, 242; talmudic, 357

El. El eljon, El Shaddaj (Hebr.), 122, 152, 182, 356

Elders, *see Sekenim*

Elohim (Hebr.), def., 152 f., 155

Elohistic collection, 121, 207 ff., 247 f.

Emperor worship, 362

Enak, sons of, descendants of the *Nephilim,* 153

Enlil, deity, 228

Ephod (Hebr.), def., 157; 91, 113

Epiphany, manifestation of a deity, 107, 109 f., 121 f., 124, 153, 211 f., 221, 310

Eponym, a person, real or mythical; the name of such, 35, 81, 142

Eschatology, the doctrine of the last or final things as death, 230 ff., 334, 398 f.; intellectualist, 233, 321 ff.; popular, 233, 374; and class situations, 230

Esoterics, designed for and understood by select circle of initiates, 398

Essenes, Essenism, 406 ff.

Ethical absolutism (*Gesinnungs-ethik*), 216 f., 332, 335, 367; plebeian, 247

Ethics, 250 ff., 318 f., 410, 420; dualist, 342 ff.; economic, 345; Israelite, 47 f., 219 ff., 254 ff.; Jewish, 4, 235 ff.; understandability, 396 ff.; workaday, 249, 294 ff., 403; *see also* Commandments, Neighbor

Etiology, the ascription of a cause or reason, adj. etiological, 159, 207

Eucharist, def., 388

Eunuch, 20, 204, 347, 350

'eved Yahwe (Hebr.), *see* Servant of God

Evyonim (Hebr.), *see* Poor, the

Exile, the, 328 f., 346, 356 ff.

Exiles, 204, 346 ff., 357 ff.

Exodus, 82, 92, 124, 338

Exorcism, conjuration of an evil spirit, 144

Expiation, 165, 177 f., 179, 216, 246, 295

Faith, 318, 399

Family, *see* Marriage

Fanaticism, 134

Fas (L.), moral or customary norm, 244

Fasts, 405

Fear and Hope, 246

Feasting rules, 62

Feuds, 37, 83

Filial piety, basic for belief in patriarchical domestic authority, internationalized during childhood through dependence on primary domestic group. "Paternal authority and filial piety are not primarily based upon actual blood ties, however normal they may be." (Max Weber, *Wirtschaft und Gesellschaft,* p. 680), 251

Folly, 191, 251

Function, objective and subjective intention, 274

Fünfzigern, def., 90 f.

Gens, 20

Ger, pl. *gerim* (Hebr.), the resident alien. Comparable to the Greek metic, 27, 32 ff., 46 ff., 63, 69, 73 f., 92, 336 ff., 342, 363, 418

Ger-toshab (Hebr.), def., 419, 423

Ger-sha 'ar (Hebr.), def., 419

Ger-zadek or *ger-berith* (Hebr.), def., 419

Ghetto, 3, 5, 417

Gibbor, pl. *gibborim* (Hebr.), knight, hero, 16, 18, 24 ff., 47, 100, 116 f., 153, 218, 278, 281

Gibbore chayil (Hebr.), propertied hero warriors, 16, 18 f., 24

Gibeonites, 339

Gigantomachy, adj. gigantomachic, a war of giants, or of gods and giants, 226

Gir (Hebr.), *see* city

Gnosis (Gr.), salvation religion making knowledge of God, of the meaning of the world, and man's estate a prerequisite of salvation, hence, speculation, scholarly mythology utilizing allegories, symbols, and degrees of initiation, 227, 314, 396, 398

God, *see* Yahwe

Gola (Hebr.), diaspora community, 358, 361, 363, 365 f.

Gospels, 258, 297, 324, 392, 410, 423

Great Flood, 202, 214, 297

Grihyasutras, Brahmanical writings concerning domestic rules, 180

Guest people, 28, 143, 338, 345, 361, 390

Guest right, 13, 32, 50

Guest tribe, 173

Guilt feelings, 240

Guru, Indian term for venerable teacher and father confessor, 173, 412

Hadad, Hadadrimmon, Syrian deity, 155, 374

Hades, *see* Sheol

Hagiolatry, worship of saints, 299

Hair, 95
Ha kohen (Hebr.), the priest, 163
Hammurabi, Code of, 62 ff., 347
Harlot, harlotry, 192, 237, 251, 286, 311, 402, see also Hierodulae
Hasheina (Hebr.), see Charity
Hasidim (Hebr.), def., 32; 367 ff., 382, 385, 386, 412
Hasmonaens, Maccabean dynasty in Judea, 31
Heimarmene, "allotted destiny," concept of Hellenistic stoicism, 204, 323
Hellenism, 5, 349, 385
Henotheism, def., 133, 204
Herdsmen, 36 ff., 51 ff.; demilitarization, 51; piety, 283
Hereafter, 140 ff., 144, 316 f., 327, see also resurrection
Hero, see warrior; lack of heroism, 50
Hetairoi (Gr.), companions, 45
Hexateuch, 123
Hidalgo, Spanish noble, 16
Hierocracy, adj. hierocratic, rule of religious leaders, 113, 186, 381
Hierodulae, (hekdesch, Hebr.), sacred harlots, 189, 283
Historical materialism, 80
Hittites, an ancient people alluded to in the Old Testament, 6
Holiness Code, 70, 74, 202, 259, 320
Holy land, 131, 338
Honey, 10, 285
Hoplite, heavily armed footsoldier of Greek antiquity, 31, 100
Horse, 6, 18, 55 f., 62, 66, 99, 114 f., 261
Human nature, 215
Humility, 247, 318 f.
Hybris (Gr.), crime to provoke the wrath of the gods by arrogance and overweening pride, 198, 213, 218, 228, 302, 318, 320
Hyksos, earliest invaders of Egypt, 6
Hypergamy (Gr.), marriage of women into a higher caste or status group, 415

Ibri (Hebr.), def., 75, 125
Iconoclasm, 157
Idolatry, 119, 180, 311, 368, 401
Ilani, def., 152
Immanuel, prophecy of prince, 231, 280, 298, 322, 325, 330 f.; see also Messiah, redeemer
Indra, Indian deity, 127, 128
In-group and out-group morality, 64, 342 ff., 415
Intellectuals, 161, 194 ff., 220, 233, 247, 278 f., 303, 392; see also Literati, Rabbi
Interest taking, see Usury
Ish haelohim (Hebr.), def., 106
Ish haruach (Hebr.), def., 297
Ishtar, Babylonian deity, 205
Isis, Egyptian deity of fertility, sister and wife of Osiris, 221
Islam, 37, 79, 93, 157, 158, 192, 402

Jainism, one of the Religions of India, 255
Jehova, 401, 403
Jehovistic, 121, 213, 248
Jewry, ancient, 3 ff.; and capitalism, 345; international diffusion, 361; and sex, 189 f., 402 ff.; world image of, 4; see also Pariah people, Resentment
Jews, 332, 362, 401; in United States, 353
Joint liability, 215, 303 f., 316
Jom Yahwe, see Day of Yahwe
Jubilee year, 71, 241, 401
Judah, see Tribe
Judaism, post-exilic, 134; and early Christianity, 400 f., 404; world historical significance, 4
Jus bonorum (L.), 420
Jus et fas (L.), right, law, 176, 243
Justice, social, 111, 116, 237, 255 f., 342 f.

Ka, Egyptian term for soul, life power, 139
Kabod (Hebr.), def., 212, 214
Kadosh (Hebr.), def., 410

Kahal (Hebr.), def., 163
Kahal hagedolah (Hebr.), def., 358
Kahal hagolah (Hebr.), def., 358
Kallaben days, 413
Kammalar, 28 f.
Karma, 204, 223
Kazir (Hebr.), def., 40
Kedor-Laomer tradition, 125
Ketubah prescriptions, 389
Khabiri, enemies of the Egyptian governors in the Amarna letters, 75, 125, 151, 200
Kingdom, Northern, 19, 82, 183, 207, 231, 310, 356; Southern, 115, 207
Kings, 18 f., 25, 41, 231 f.; anointment, 115; ass riding, 18, 116, 184, 322, 368; great kings, 7, 115, 267 f., 275, 282, 319; and law, 84 ff.; and priests, 113, 169; religion, 197 f., 249; religious demands, 275
Kleros (Gr.), def., 73 ff.
Kohanim (Hebr.), def., 178, 348, 363
Koinonia, def., 187; 188
Korahites, followers of Korah, 123, 174, 182 f., 217, 337
Kosher, 353
Kroisos oracle, 290
Kyrios Christos, 4, 299

Labor, 67; despised, 416; forced, 55, 99, 115, 124, 346; legal status, 67; and man's fall, 227; in Egypt, 256
Land, 24, 71 ff.
Landlords, landlordism, 66, 113, 155, 163, 173
Land owners, ownership, 65, 73
Language, 202, 204, 361, 390
Law, 84 ff.; debt remission, 68 f., 71, 358, 401; development of, 84; Icelandic, 84; International, 83, 302; Israelite, 61 ff.; Mosaic, 359; natural, 278, 370; and rabbis, 414; rational, 66; Roman, 5, 370; slaves, 63 f., 71; marriage, inheritance, 72 ff.; written, 86. *See also* Mishpat, Chuk, Shofetim
Leprosy, 102, 175, 183, 423

Levirate, def., 72
Levites, 30, 113, 170 ff., 193, 203, 217, 219, 220, 240, 243, 261, 263, 350, 416; gerim, 36, 172 f., *see also* Priests
Lex Salica, the Salic law, 62
Lex talionis, law of retaliation
Li (Chin.), def., 253
Literati, 112, 193, 207 ff., 224; contemporary, 112; Elohistic and Yahwistic, 207 ff.; *see also* Intellectuals
Liturgy, public expenditure defrayed by wealthy citizens out of their private fortunes. Weber classifies states according as to whether state finance is based upon tax collection or liturgies, 34
Lord's Supper, 263, 300, 388
Lucrum cessans (Roman law), gain forfeited by delay, 394 (The German text would seem to be corrupt at this point)
Lutheranism, 263

Ma, def., 253 f.
Magic, 179 f., 219 ff.; compulsion, 400; of Elisha, 97, 102; Elijah, 110; lack of, 4, 97, 166 f., 210, 262, 394; rejection of, 222, 245; *see also* Prophets
Magyr, def., 413
Maccabees, distinguished Jewish family in Jerusalem in the 2nd century, 75, 140, 145, 354, 382, 385; *see also* Hasmoneans
Mahabharata, one of the two chief epics of ancient India, 397
Malak (Hebr.), def., 211 f., 153
Mana, in the primitive world widely diffused conception of a spiritual potency, or force, or principle in animate and inanimate things, 140
Manu, Collection of, 88, 352
Marduk, deity, 134, 230
Marriage, 50, 121, 190, 336, 402, 415; by abduction, 44; mixed, 183, 209, 236, 340, 351, 358, 369, 421;

of Moses, 183; of Prophets, 286; sexual relations, 189 ff.; *see also* Levirate

Martyr, 374, 377

Mashal (Hebr.), def., 196

Mass ecstasy, 98, 192, 379

Massacre, 160, 170, 365

Matathron, 398

Mazkir (Hebr.), def., 195

Medicin, 175

Megalomania, delusion of grandeur, 198

Men of God, 131, 181, 373

Mercenaries of David, 45

Merchant, 65, 70

Mesha stone, a slab of black basalt bearing an inscription in Phoenician-Hebrew characters, recording the victories of Mesha, king of Moab (II. Kings, 3:4). In 1868 this stele was recovered from the Arabs by Clermont-Ganneau. The Mesha stone is not the only example of early writing. The so-called Gezer-Calendar indicating the seasonal agricultural operations in awkward writing on a limestone tablet today is ascribed to the late tenth century and considered the oldest preserved Israelite inscription, 195

Messiah, 377, 398, 412, 418; king, 18, 115, 285, 398 f.; image, 331; *see also* Immanuel, Redeemer

Messianic hope, 361, 390, 409

Metempsychosis, transmigration of souls, 349

Metic (Gr.), resident alien of Greek city states, 70 f., see *Ger*

Midianites, 17, 123; war, 77

Military organization, 21 f., 43 ff., 55 f., 73 f., 113; 241; *see also* Warfare, Warrior

Milk or Melkart, deity, 155

Miracles, 22 f., 246, 298, 365, 411; Cana, 275; charisma of, 394 f.; Elijah, Elisha, 97, 166; Moses, 166; Pentecost, 379, 412

Mishpat, pl. *mishpatim* (Hebr.), def., 87 f., 176, 238, 244, 304, 350

Moabites, 41, 123, 302; war, 102, 133

Moira (Gr.), fate (cf. Plato, Republic X), 323

Moloch, deity, 149, 202; and *ger,* 337; orgiasticism, 402

Money economy, 62

Monolatry, def., 133; 138, 157, 247, 340

Monotheism, def., 133; Babylonian, 204

Moon cult, 151

Moshuah (Hebr.), def., 231

Mountain vs. plain, 54

Mule, 351

Murashu Documents, 347

Mystagogue, exponent of mystery cult, 119, 180, 324, 393 f.

Mystery, in ancient pagan religions certain secret rites to which only the initiated were admitted, like the Eleusinian mysteries. In Christian religion a sacramental rite, the Lord's Supper, 300, 317, 349, 408

Mysticism, 225, 313, 396

Myths, 198, 226, 229, 322, 375; astral, 144; *see also* Tiamat

Mythology, 225, 232, 398

Nabi, pl. Nebiim, professionally trained magical ecstatic, 96 ff., 101 f., 108, 113, 128, 134, 192, 195, 202, 206, 280, 282, 291, 302

Nabu, Babylonian god of scribes, 153, 201

Nakedness, 192, 219, 287, 402

Nakhri (Hebr.), def., 247, 342

Name, 6, 102, 122, 142, 212, 221 f., 286, 343, 376

Nasi (Hebr.), def., 65, 79; 16, 349 f.

Natural law, see Law

Nature catastrophes, 128

Nazarites, def., 94 f.; 44, 101, 128, 192, 209, 280, 282, 405

Nebalah (Hebr.), def., 241

Nebiim, *see* Nabi

Necropolis, cemetery, 253

Nefesh (Hebr.), def., 140 ff.
Neighbor, 70, 246, 252, 259 f., 342
Neo-Platonism, 400
Nephilim (Hebr.), cf. Genesis, 6:1 ff., def. 153
Nergal, solar deity in Babylonia, presiding over nether-world, 205
Neshech (Hebr.), def., 64
Nethinim (Hebr.), def., 34, 186; 363
New Testament, 310, 331
Nibdalim (Hebr.), def., 358
Nobility, 118
Nokri (Hebr.), def., 32
Nomadic ideal, 44, 114, 224, 285
Nomadism, 9
Nomads, *see* Sa Gas
Noumenon (Gr.), 128
Numen, Numina (L.), spirits, ghosts, 47, 138, 145, 221
Nundinae (L.), the ninth day marking the Roman week, 150

Obedience, 121, 136, 216, 220, 250 f., 318 f., 400 f.; Egyptian, 250 f.
Odium generis humani (L.), hatred of mankind, 354
Officials, 20, 195; *see also* Sarim
Old Testament, 4, 27, 334, 344, 381
Omen, omina (L.), foreboding, 179 f.
Onanism, sexual self-gratification, masturbation (Genesis, 38:9), 190, 202, 402
Oracles, 85, 90, 97, 106 f., 116, 166 f., 175 f., 177 ff., 243, 276; Delphi, 349; Hellenic, 281; of prophets, 271, 307 f., 320, 357, 364 f., 380
Oranda, *see* Mana
Ordeal, 84, 166
Orgiasticism, pursuit of ecstasy through intoxicants, dance, music, etc., 93, 188 f., 191 ff., 212, 226, 245, 402 ff.
Oriental monarch, monarchy, 19 f., 231, 257, 302, 330, 347
Orphism, a Greek mystery cult of Dionysus ascribed to Orpheus as founder, Orphic teaching, 349; orphics, 285, 294
Osiris, Egyptian deity, brother and husband of Isis, 146, 179

Pacifism, 281, 322; of patriarchs, 49, 52, 112; prophecy, 270; religion, 317; *see also* Peace, Paradise
Panim, def., 212
Paraclete, 412
Paradigm, a model or pattern, 108, 121, 212, 213, 363, 398
Paradise, 209, 211, 219, 228 ff., 233, 261, 321, 369
Parament, 157, 159, 161
Pariah or guest people, def., 3; 51, 363 f., 375, 417, 424
Pariah situation, 336 ff.; 356, 376 f.; cf. Max Weber, *Essays*, pp. 189 f., 399
Parties: represent voluntary associations within corporate groups seeking power for their leader and ideal and material advantages for the members, 274
Passover, 62, 92, 187, 236, 337
Patriarchs, 36, 42, 46, 52, 370, 389; legends, 49 f., 80, 208, 223
Patricians, 15, 19, 27, 31, 53, 69 f., 117, 281; urban, 56 f., 21; military, 54
Patriciate, 14, 47, 57, 116, 259
Patronymic name: a name derived from that of a father or male ancestor, 169
Pauline mission, 4 f., 393, 421 f.
Pawning, 63
Peace, paradisical and final, 230
Peasant, 21 f.; "dumb," 206; Israelite, 23 ff., 26 f., 53 f., 64 f., 82 f., 96, 111, 346, 370; pacifist hopes, 230; and ritual, 363 f.; summons, 26 f., 100, 111
Penance, penitence, 246, 367, 381, 405; preachers of, 324
Pentaur, Egyptian poet, 246
People's movement, 6
Periocoi, def., 15; 27, 370

Peripety (Gr.), a change from one state of things within a play to its opposite (Aristotle, *Poetics*, ch. 9, 11); a turning point, 322 ff.

Persians, 158, 276, 311, 319, 349 f., 365, 382, 408

Petty bourgeoisie, 31 f.; and rabbis, 414; and religion, 388

Pharisaism, pharisees, 386 f., 396 f., 400 ff., 417 f.; urban, 390

Philistines, 55, 92, 97, 128, 138, 158, 160, 282, 341

Philosophers, Hellenic, 102, 275, 294 f.

Phyle (Gr.) tribe, 100

Pietism, 247, 376

Pious, *see* Hasidim

Plebeian strata, 21, 29 f., 223 f., 389; composition of, 29 f.; reproaches of, 116 f.; and religion, 198, 224; teaching of, 242

Plebeji, 27

Pneuma (Gr.), spirit, term used especially in the New Testament, 381, 411, 423

Pochazim (Hebr.), heedless, rash, "rabble," 19

Polis (Gr.), city state of Antiquity, 14 f., 21 f., 31

Polytheism, 152, 155 f., 212, 414

Poor, the, 47, 57, 63, 116, 218, 223, 256 f., 370

Popolo grasso, 31

Power, 79

Prayer, 197 f., 407 f.

Preaching, 413 f.

Prebend, adj. prebendal, right of an officeholder to yields from state or church lands or from other public income, 169

Prestige, of landlords, 173; of Levites, 178, 179, 182; of political authorities, 120, 85; of priests, 169; of prophets, 282, 326, 333 f., 381; of Yahwe, 246, 310

Priesthood, a special circle of cult leaders officiating at regular recurrent times at fixed places according to definite norms on behalf of religious communities worshipping God or gods, 174 ff., 183

Priestly Code, 70 ff., 186

Priestly sibs, 164; Aaronites, 181 ff., 348 f.; Danites, 173, 181 f.; Elides, 122, 164, 169, 181 f.; Zadokites, 181 f., 185 f., 348, 362, 366, 387, 389, 390; conflicts among, 181 ff.

Priests, 30, 99 f., 160 f., 162 f., 239, 348 ff.; exilic, 348; high priest, 350, 351, 359, 360, 363, 416; of Jerusalem, 185; opposition to, 217; and prophets, 380, 382; *see also* Levites

Primus inter pares, first among equals, 16, 115

Proletarii, def., 74

Prophets, origin of, 46, 108, 193, 277 f.; of doom, 109 f., 279, 295, 305 ff., 322; of hope, 103 ff., 109 f., 230, 232, 295, 372; types of, 108, 116, 120 f., 193, 270, 297, 299 f., 320, 395; false, 287, 293, 295, 299, 306, 381, 395; auditory, visionary, 106, 107 f., 287 ff., 294, 305, 312; psychology of, 109, 272 f., 286 ff., 293 f., 305 f., 325; solitude, 106, 109, 292; demagogues and pamphleteers, 267 ff., 271 f., 275, 320, 377 f.; language of, 129, 289 ff.; pacifistic, 112, 281, 322; complaints of, 116; expectancies, 321 ff., 365; public of, 109, 134, 205 f., 273 f., 279, 281, 292 f.; and politics, 273 ff., 300 f., 316 f., 319; and Egypt, 144, 280 f., 356; and culture, 285; and ethics, 235, 237 f., 304, 318; and democracy, 278; and magic and mysticism, 298, 313 ff.; and orgiasticism, 193; and remuneration, 109, 278 f.; and king, 109, 195, 280 f., 326; and peasant, 279, 328; and priests, 178, 282 f.; 380 ff.; and rabbis, 395; and Temple, 283; coat of, 96, 381; *see also* Asceticism, Dream, Ecstasy,

Eschatology, Nabi, Oracles, Seer, Torah, War prophecy, Yahwe
Prosbul, rabbinical device for evading the provisions of the law, 68
Proselytes, 32, 92, 417 f.; Paul and, 421 f.
Proselytism, 362; appeal of, 419 f.; and circumcision, 419 ff.; and Egypt, 7
Protestantism, 5
Providence, belief in, 129, 212, 223
Psalms, 202, 249, 367, 376 f., 398, 403
Ptah, Egyptian deity, 221
Puritanism, 263, 343, 345
Purity commandments, 364, 390, 402, 406, 415 f., 421; and peasants, 363 f.
Purohita, Indian term for house priest or house chaplain. Model situation of the Brahmin, 173

Quakers, 344
Qui trompe-t-on? (Beaumarchais, *Barbier de Seville*, III, 11), 345

Ra, sun god of Egypt, 221
Rab (Hebr.), def., 63, 391
Rabbi, 391 ff., 411 f.; and astronomy and astrology, 151, 203; and Christian teaching, 246; occupation, 393 f.; and prophecy, 395; and remuneration, 279; and ritual, 414
Rain, 9 f., 66, 97
Rational, Rationalism, 136, 178, 205, 212, 213, 214, 226, 243, 254, 314, 388, 389, 397 f., 420; bourgeois, 382, 414; economic, 343; Pharisaical, 179, 193, 362, 389
Rationalization, of charity, 262; of image of God, 129; of life, 165; of magic, 222; of religion, 167, 243, 249, 403
Rechabites, 38, 46, 79, 101, 112, 181, 189, 217, 247, 278, 285, 294, 332, 406
Redeemer, 4 f., 85, 329 ff., 377; *see also* Immanuel, Messiah

Red Sea crossing, 118, 124, 156, 281
Rejection of the world, 410
Religio licita (L.), tolerated religion, 420, 423
Religiosity, Israelite, 78; Jewish, 382; plebeian, 247 ff.
Religious innovations and cultural marginality, 206 f.
Religious order, 79 f.
Religious promises, 70, 80, 118 ff., 166, 208, 215 f., 233, 296, 301; Jewish vs. Indian, 3 f.; of prophets, 379
Remnant, def., 232; 307, 316, 323 f., 330, 365
Resentment, 367, 404
Responsa (L.), legal advice, 413, 421
Resurrection, belief in, 144 f., 362, 390, 399, 408
Revenge, 259 f., 368, 378, 403 f.; blood, 62, 66, 137, 191
Rites, 126, 151, 187, 354
Ritual, Ritualistic, 33, 177, 191, 219, 220, 246, 334 f., 353, 363, 414, 419; fasts, 405; ritualistic segregation, 336 f., 353 f., 362
Ritualism, 410
Ritualists, 361 f.
Robbery, Bedouin, 12 f.
Roeh (Hebr.), *see* seer
Rosh (Hebr.), 40
Ruach (Hebr.), def., 140; 127, 142, 212, 297, 378 f., 411
Ruach ha kodesh (Hebr.), def., 381
Rudra, deity, 129

Sabbath, 149 ff., 336 f., 354, 363, 390; and cattle, 48, 150; and *ger*, 33; rest, 34, 63, 67; year, 48 f., 363
Sachsenspiegel, 89
Sacrifice, 113, 135 f., 142, 162 ff., 186 f., 217, 284 f., 336 f., 361; *chattat* and *asham*, 165, 177 f., 241, 361; collective, 113, 135; human, 91, 95; of Isaac, 121; and Levites, 177 f., 239 f.; opposition

to, 285; Phoenician, 202; secularized, 186; substitute, 373 f.

Sadducees, see Priestly sibs

Sa Gas, warriors mentioned in the Amarna letters, 37, 172, 200

Sakir (Hebr.), def., 48

Samaritans, 361, 363, 364, 416

Samsara, doctrine of transmigration, 255

Sanctions, 216, 239 f., 263, 358

Sanctuaries, 77, 113, 115, 156 f., 160, 164, 183 ff.; of Dan, 160; Levitical, 241

Sanhedrin, Greek name of Council of State, 391

Sar (Hebr.), def., 253

Sarim (Hebr.), def., 18; 86, 163, 175, 281, 304

Satrap, governor of a satrapy, a province of ancient Persia, 359

Savior, 390; images of, 231 f.; king, 105, 231 f., 330 f.

Sayid, chief, 11

Scarabeus, 144, 199, 249

Scythian invasion, 325

Sect, 344, 362, 409

Seer, 103, 106, 110, 195, 288, 312, 381, 387

Sefer ha berith (Hebr.), def., 75 f.

Sefer hattorah (Hebr.), def., 76; 66, 184, 244

Segregation, 387, 416 f.; confessional, 338; of Essenes, 406; voluntary, 345

Seisachtheia (Gr.), remission of debts, 68, 74

Sekenim (Hebr.), def., 16 f.; 19, 84, 86, 88, 279, 304

Sermon of the Mount, 376

Servant of God, of Yahwe, 5, 232, 344, 371 ff.

Seven (sacred number), 149, 151; Seventy, 285

Shabattu, def., 149 f.

Sham (Hebr.), def., 212, see Name

Shamash, Babylonian sungod, 94

Shame, 192; to shame, 403 f., 409

Shearith (Hebr.), def., 232, see Remnant

Shekina (Hebr.), def., 418

Shepherd, see Herdsmen

Sheol (Hebr.), hell, Hades, 141 f., 144, 280, 317

Shofetim (Hebr.), def., 40; 84 ff., 243, 329

Shrines, domestic, 139; private, 163; rural, 26, 183; Yahwe, 83

Sib, "gentile charismatically outstanding agnatic descendants of charismatic chieftains" (Max Weber, The Hindu Social System, tr. by Hans Gerth and Don Martindale, University of Minnesota Sociology Club Bulletin No. 1 (1950), p. 66; German text p. 56, Fn. 1). As Weber rejected "the Irish term clan as ambiguous" we felt constrained to render Sippe by sib rather than by "clan" which since Baden-Powell has become the usual term for large kinship groups in English literature. Old Testament kinship terms are still controversial. (For a recent discussion see Fritz Helling, Die Frühgeschichte des Jüdischen Volkes, Frankfurt, 1947, pp. 34-48.) 16 f., 20 ff., 24 ff., 30 f., 73 f., 195 f.; and cult, ancestor worship, 139, 146; Bedouin, 11; decline of, 187; military, 195; and prophets, 196, 282; joint liability, 66; registers, 73, 350; see Priestly sibs

Sidereal, pertaining to celestial bodies, 146, 149, 151, 233, 322

Sin, moongod, 149

Sins, 77, 165, 237 ff., 250 f., 328, 368, 401; confession of, 222, 239 f.; see also Expiation

Slaves, 34, 54; Christian, 423; debt, 21, 27; kingly, 20; Roman, 261

Snake, snake staff, 128, 129, 159, 161, 174, 210, 219, 227

Social antagonism, 56, 116 f., 357 f.; see also Class antagonism

Social stratification, social structure, 56 f., 79 f., 382

Sofer, soferim (Hebr.), def., 391 f.; 194, 252, 388, 417

Song of Solomon, The, 121, 194, 197

Sorcerer, sorcery, 97, 102, 167

Soteriology, adj. soteriological, religious teaching of salvation and a redeemer, 227, 345, 361 f., 373

Soul, -body dualism, 400; Israelite conception of, 139 f., 145; *see also* *Nefesh*, Cure of soul

Spirit, holy, 411 f., 423, see *Ruach*

Star worship, 183, 203

Status, status group, the latter comprises people who enjoy the same degree of the same kind of deference, honor, respect, or prestige. This may rest on military, political, or sacerdotal power, education, wealth, office, rank, etc. Status groups usually follow a conventional style of life, 17 f., 25, 30, 170, 171, 172, 363

Steer worship, 183

Stockbreeders, 8 f., 62, 66; and Sabbath, 151; social organization of, 39 ff.

Stranger, 93, 337 ff., *see also Nakhri*

Sublimation, 328, 332, 335; of conception of god, 214; of ethics, 238, 259

Suffering, 373 ff., 377; *see also* Servant of God, Theodicy

Suffits, 18

Sultanism, oriental, 24, 99

Sungod, 153 f.

Sunworship, 161

Synactic, acting together, 78

Synagogue, 242, 362, 388

Syncretic, syncretism, the (attempted) union of conflicting parties or principles, 153, 204, 356

Synegor, 412

Synoecism, process of settling in a city. The Hellenic term refers to the founding of cities by noble families, 21, 26, 29, 350, 358

Tabernacle, 157

Talion, principle of, retaliation (Levit. 24:20), 62

Talmud, 204, 362, 377, 393 f., 396 f., 411, 412

Tammuz, Babylonian deity of spring and vegetation, 149, 374

Tax, 359, 361

Teacher, 392, 413; see also *Sofer*

Tefillin (Hebr.), 355

Temple, 408; construction of, 110, 161, 183, 357, 368; destruction of, 283, 310, 391, 404, 423; of Solomon, 99, 114; *see also* Jerusalem cult monopoly

Teraphim (Hebr.), def., 139; 124, 157

Theocracy, government of a state by experts in divinity, 366

Theodicy, a vindication of divine attributes or actions, particularly holiness and justice in the face of existing evil, 207, 213 ff., 222, 305, 315, 316, 327, 341, 370, 376; of sufferance, 5, 369

Theogony, adj. theogonic, the origin of the gods or an account of it; a genealogy of the gods, 137 f., 226, 374

Theophany, a manifestation or appearance of a god to man, 211

Theophorous names, 205

Tiamat, the dragon in an old Babylonian myth (cf. Jastrow, Morris, *Religion of Babylonia and Assyria*, Boston, 1898, p. 428), 277

Timaeus, Plato's, 320

Tobit, the Book of, 143, 191

Torah, 87, 179, 193, 212, 239 f., 284, 300, 304, 350; and prophecy, 284 f., 294 f., 300, 307, 332; teachers, 113, 146, 176 ff., 214, 218, 220, 242, 247, 366

Toshab (Hebr.), def., 48; 27

Trade, 61, 99; and finance, 347

Trade-routes, 12 f., 22, 53, 199

Trades, despised, 416

Trading peoples, 134

Tradition, genuine, 113 f.
Traditionalism, 343; Bedouin, 12; Egyptian, 253
Transhumans, 37
Tribal organization, 40
Tribe, 41 ff., 51 ff., 73 f., 125, 209; Assar, 82; Benjamin, 43 f., 82; Dan, 82, 28, 173; Ephraim, 42, 53, 82 f., 100; Gad, 82; Gilead, 40, 82, 302; Issachar, 82; Joseph, 42, 82, 100; Judah, 28, 43, 46, 79 f., 82 f., 103 f., 170, 330, 332; Kenites, 38, 79, 123; Machir, 40, 42, 79, 82; Manasseh, 40, 42, 82, 100; Reuben, 41, 79, 82 f., 103; Simeon and Levi, 38, 41, 79, 81 ff., 103, 170 f.; Zebulun, 82
Tsadik (Hebr.), def., 413
Tsebaoth, def., 159; 111

Unio mystica, communion with God, 314
Urbanism, urbanization, 42, 43, 56, 69 f.
Urim and *thummim*, oracle tablets (Exodus 28:30), 166
Usury, 68, 70, 237, 316, 342 f., 358, 401
Utopianism, 319, 326, 376; of Ezekiel, 365; Platonic, 271; of prophets, 369; theological constructs, 114

Varuna, Indian deity; in early Hindu mythology with Indra the greatest of the gods of the Rig Veda, 131, 137
Vaticinatio ex eventu, prophesying from the unfolding event, 104
Viaticum in kind, allowance in kind, 68
Village, 14 f.
Virtuoso and mass religion, 246, 298
Volcano, 123, 124, 128, 130

Wadd, Minaean deity, 170
War, warfare, 21, 90 ff., 267; Bedouin, 11, 13; booty, 54, 90, 93; finance, 22, 100 f.; followings, 44; holy war, 44, 83, 85, 90 f., 93; Israelite, 13, 82; objects of, 54; and Sabbath, 354; summons, 43, 73 f., 100 f.; trophy, 92; voluntary participation, 11, 13, 44
War prophecy, war prophets, 83, 128, 138, 178, 192, 268
War psychosis, 246
Warrior, 16, 18, 25, 83 ff., 100, 128, 142; asceticism and ecstasy, 90 ff., 94, 97, 217; *see also* Bodyguard, Nabi, Nazarite
Waters of strife, 122, 175
Wealth, 238, 370, 401, 403; of exiles, 347; patriarchs, 293; mammonism, 320
Welfare state, 303
Wergeld, a fine for manslaughter and other crimes against the person, payable to the relatives of the deceased in the case of manslaughter, or to the injured person in the case of a wound, 62
Writing, 84, 194 f.; cuneiform, 201

Xenophobia, hatred of foreigners, 339

Yahwe, name, 122, 221; conception of, 137, 210; god of the covenant, 115 f., 118 ff.; wargod, 82 f., 91, 111, 127; invisible, 158 ff.; voice, 288 ff.; majesty of, 308 ff.; universalism, 123, 133 ff., 210, 371, 372; traits of, 121, 126 ff., 136, 146, 159, 210, 224 f., 245, 300 ff., 308, 312, 314; and rain and thunder, 10, 129; and catastrophes, 128 ff., 300 ff.; not chthonian, 145 f., 200; demands of, 136, 215 f.; wills misfortune, 300, 311; offenses against, 110 ff., 130, 165 ff.; father image, 400; and plebeians, 223; and strangers, 340 f.; abode, 122 f., 124, 133, 310; and Baal, 154 ff., 159 f., 189; also *Berith*

Yahwism, development of, 301 ff.; image of, 400
Yahwist, Yahwistic collection, 121, 134, 207 ff., 247 f.
Yima, Indian deity, 232

Zidonians, inhabitants of Phoenician city of Zidon, 173
Zionism, 48
Zoroastrism, 145, 157

2. PERSONS

Aaron, 122, 182 f., 209
Abba Chilkijat, 392
Abel, 35, 39, 52
Abiathar, the priest, 161, 278
Abimelech, son of Gideon, 14, 17, 18 f., 31, 76, 86, 134, 196, 257, 340
Abner, Saul's general, 45, 83
Abraham, patriarch, 42, 46, 49, 51, 52, 74, 80, 92, 121, 125, 142, 152, 153, 182, 216, 298, 340, 375, 376, 418
Absalom, son of David, 46
Achijam, 15th century Canaanite, 152
Achilles, 141
Adonijah, son of David, 46
Ahab, king of Israel (c. 875–852 B.C.), 58, 70, 72, 86, 102, 105, 108, 109, 110, 138, 214, 280, 298
Ahia, the prophet, 106
Amaziah, king of Judah, 66
Amalek, Esau's grandson (Ex. 17: 8 ff.), 13, 39, 81, 103
Amenophis III (c. 1415–1380 B.C.), 125
Amenophis IV, see Ikhnaton
Amon, king of Judah, 183
Amos, the prophet, 46, 51, 101, 102, 136, 145, 193, 218, 223, 230, 232, 237, 267, 269, 271, 277, 280, 281 ff., 284 f., 290, 294, 298, 300 ff., 303, 305 ff., 308, 310 ff., 316, 321 ff., 324, 327, 328, 330, 332, 338, 342
Archelaus, son of Herod, 386
Aristobulus, son of Herod, 391
Artaxerxes, 349 f.

Assurbanipal, king of Assyria, 230, 231, 249
Athaliah, queen of Judah, 163
Athena, 51, 128
Augustus, 386

Balaam, half legendary seer, 103, 105, 110, 123
Barak, army leader, 85, 103
Bar Kocheba, leader of revolt against Hadrian, 326
Baruch, son of Neriah, disciple of Jeremiah, 293, 329
Bathsheba, wife of Uriah, 91
Benjamin of Tudela, medieval traveler, 79
Bezaleel, artisan (Ex. 31:1 ff.), 28 f.
Bismarck, Otto von (1815–1898), German statesman, 317 f.
Boaz (The Book of Ruth), 16, 47, 370
Bocchoris, Egyptian king, 231, 261
Buddha, 398
Büchler, 244

Cain, 13, 28, 35, 39, 52, 79, 103, 123
Caleb (Josh. 14:6 ff.), 173
Chuchullin, chief warrior in the older heroic (Ulster) cycle of Ireland, 94
Clement of Alexandria, 344
Cyrus, king of Persia, 29, 257, 276, 303, 329, 344, 346, 348, 370, 372, 377
Czar of Russia, 256

Daniel, central figure of The Book of Daniel, 134, 145, 228, 319, 376, 377, 380, 398

Darius, king of Persia, 257, 276, 349, 357
David, king of Israel (c. 985–955 B.C.), 14, 20, 25, 27, 31, 44 f., 53, 55, 76, 81, 86, 90, 91, 98, 104 f., 110, 114, 115, 131, 139, 160 f., 162 f., 169, 185, 195, 214, 215, 233, 260, 277, 280, 330, 340, 349, 351, 366, 375
Deborah, the prophetess, 86, 97, 101
Delitzsch, 152
Deutero-Isaiah, the prophet, 232, 234, 297, 311, 313, 329, 348, 369, 370 f., 372, 374, 375, 376 ff., 379
Deutero-Zechariah, the prophet, 368 f., 374, 377, 379, 381
Dibelius, M., 158
Dinah, Jacob's daughter (Gen. 34), 36, 52, 191
Dio Cassius, 423
Domitian, Roman emperor, 423

Ehud, judge, 85
Eldad (Num. 11:26 ff.), 108
Elhanan, knight of David, 113 f.
Eli, high priest, 85, 277
Eliakim (Joiakim), son of Josiah, (II. Ki. 23:34), 267
Elijah, the prophet, 97, 105, 108, 109 f., 111, 134, 160, 166, 193, 195, 202, 214, 232, 268, 280, 282, 305, 331
Elisha, the prophet, 97, 101, 102, 108, 110, 131, 160, 181, 192, 193, 206, 220, 222, 278, 282, 339, 362; see also Nabi
Erman, Adolf, Egyptologist, 199
Esau, 42, 123, 338, 341
Evil Merodach, king of Babylon, 346, 348
Ezekiel, the prophet, 51, 109, 121, 132, 140, 180, 185, 200, 228, 261, 277 f., 282, 286 f., 288, 289, 290, 297, 306, 308, 309, 312, 315, 316, 318, 327, 329, 331, 332, 338, 348, 352, 364 ff., 369, 373, 378, 380
Ezra, the scribe, 21, 27, 29, 34, 185, 346, 350, 358 f., 364, 380

Gad, seer of David, 106
Gedaliah, governor of Judea, 26, 328
Gideon, judge, 17, 40, 44, 85, 103, 107, 119, 128, 155, 173, 230
Goethe, 197
Gog, 365
Goliath, Philistine warrior, 16, 18, 25, 55, 114, 185
Gressmann, 230
Grüneisen, 139
Gudea of Sargon, Sumerian king of Lagash (c. 3000 B.C.), 231

Habakkuk, the prophet, 369
Hadrian, Roman emperor (A.D. 117–138), 399
Haggai, the prophet, 349, 357, 368, 378 f.
Hammurabi, Babylonian king, 52, 175
Hananiah, false prophet, 272
Hazael, war leader, 102, 110
Hehn, Viktor, 152
Henoch, prophet, 232, 380, 398
Herod, king of the Jews, 386, 391
Herodotus, Greek historian, 92, 158, 319
Hesiod, Greek poet, 27, 117
Hezekiah, king of Judah, 14, 100, 159, 161, 183, 210, 220, 247, 277, 283, 298
Hilkiah, high priest under Josiah, 163
Hiram, king of Tyre, 29
Hillel (c. 30 B.C.), Jewish scholar and sage at Jerusalem, 68, 393
Hiram, Solomon's master workman, 29
Hobab (Num. 10), 340
Homer, 319, 397
Hosea, the prophet, 115, 121, 161, 231, 237, 239, 247, 251, 269, 278, 280, 283, 290, 301, 306, 307, 308, 309, 310 f., 313, 315, 317 f., 321, 323, 324, 327, 330, 331, 332
Huldah, the prophetess, 108, 243
Hyrcanus, high priest, 391

Ikhnaton (Amenophis IV), (c. 1380 B.C.), he undertook strenuous though shortlived religious reforms in Egypt, viewing the sun as the source of all power and life, 8, 14, 153, 204, 227

Isaac, the patriarch, 52, 121, 209, 212, 236

Isaiah, the prophet, 15, 20, 123, 145, 152, 178, 203, 218, 231, 238, 247, 267, 269, 274, 275, 277 f., 280, 282 f., 284, 286, 290, 294, 298, 300 ff., 305, 306, 307, 308, 309, 310, 312, 313, 314, 317 ff., 320 ff., 323, 324, 325, 327, 330, 333, 365, 378, 380

Ishmael, son of Abraham, 92, 341

Jacob, the patriarch, 6, 42, 46, 50, 52, 65, 81, 82, 123, 182, 221, 339, 372, 375, 418

Jains, Indian Hindu sect, 344

James, 421 f.

Japheth, son of Noah, 35

Jehoiada, high priest, 163

Jehu, king of Israel (c. 843–821 B.C.), 20, 38, 46, 101, 105, 106, 114, 150, 193, 202, 251, 278, 288, 308

Jephtah, judge, 27, 40, 85, 123 f., 133, 138, 341; daughter of, 149

Jeremiah, the prophet, 15, 20, 24, 26 f., 38, 46, 68, 72, 78, 86, 107, 108, 110, 123, 131, 132, 136, 140, 163, 164, 178, 191, 196, 203, 215, 217, 238, 247, 267, 269, 271, 272 f., 277 f., 279 f., 281, 282 f., 284 f., 286 ff., 289, 290, 293, 294, 295, 298, 299, 302, 304 f., 306, 307, 308, 310, 312, 313, 315, 316, 317 f., 319, 320 f., 324, 325, 326, 327, 328, 329, 331, 332, 337, 346, 348, 356, 364 ff., 367, 380 f., 395

Jeroboam, king of Israel (c. 930 B.C.), 46, 101, 106, 163, 164, 170, 173, 183

Jeroboam II (c. 790–749 B.C.), 105, 231, 268, 271, 305

Jerubbaal, 128, see Gideon

Jesus of Nazareth, 30, 197, 274, 275, 314, 326, 334, 376, 387, 394, 398, 409, 411, 418; charisma of, 304; self image, 298; solitude, 292; see also Servant of God

Jesus ben Sira, 29

Jesus Sirach, 175, 251, 253, 299, 344

Jethro, Moses' father-in-law, 122, 175

Joab, David's general, 20, 45, 55

Joash, king of Judah, 77, 169

Job, central figure of the Book of Job, 39, 46, 132, 228, 370, 374, 377, 397

Joel, the prophet, 327, 368, 378 f., 412

Joiakim I, king of Judah, 348

Joiakim II, king of Judah, 271, 273, 280, 371

Jonadab ben Rechab, 38, 80

Jonah, the prophet, 105, 307

Jonas, 418

Jonathan, ass driver, 177, 392

Jonathan, son of Saul, 92

Joseph, Jacob's son, 42, 77, 106, 134, 196, 199, 209, 212, 223, 339, 351; traits of, 50 f.

Josephus, Flavius (c. 37–95), Jewish historian, 358, 408

Joshua, successor of Moses, 43, 76, 83, 86, 92, 122, 172, 208

Josiah, king of Judah (640/38–609 B.C.), 66, 76, 77, 116, 163, 184, 244

Jubal, ancestor of musicians (Gen. 4:21), 196

Judas Maccabaeus, 27, 31, 44, 385

Klamroth, 346

Kautzsch, 111

Korah, leader of rebellion against Moses (Num. 16), 405

Laban, patriarch, 65, 134, 139, 339

Lot, nephew of Abraham, 32, 49, 340, 341

Luther, Martin, 318, 402

Maimonides, Moses (1135–1204), Jewish philosopher, 343

Malachi, the prophet, 368 f., 382, 411

Manasseh, king of Judah, 91, 183, 202, 269, 280

Medad (Num. 11:26 ff.), 108

Melchisedek, priest king of Salem (Gen. 14:18), 152, 169, 372

Menahem, king of Israel (c. 749–737 B.C.), 16, 19

Merneptah, king of Egypt, 82, 125, 199

Meyer, Eduard, 16, 27, 29, 73, 158, 170, 187, 199

Micah, landlord, 113, 163, 173, 177

Micah, the prophet, 24, 51, 109, 145, 180, 220, 232, 238, 272, 277, 283, 290, 302, 308, 310, 325, 327, 330, 380

Michaiah, son of Imlah, 110

Michal, David's wife, 98, 101

Miriam, prophetess, called the sister of Aaron, 101, 122, 127, 182 f.

Mohammed, 5, 80, 98, 289

Moses, 73, 76, 92, 107, 110, 118, 120, 121 f., 124, 125 ff., 159, 161 f., 166, 170, 175, 181 ff., 189, 199, 208, 209 f., 211, 217, 220 f., 233, 237, 241, 263, 291, 298, 331, 338, 372, 373, 403

Naaman, Syrian commander-in-chief, cured of leprosy by Elisha (II. Ki. 5:14), 131, 339, 362

Nabal, man of Carmel, 260

Naboth, 72

Nabunadin, king of Babylon, 257, 346

Nahum, the prophet, 290

Nathan, the seer, 104, 105 f., 196, 214, 217

Nebuchadnezzar, king of Babylon, 15, 26, 29, 134, 198, 249, 257, 273, 282, 319, 344, 346

Necho, king of Egypt (c. 600 B.C.), 276

Nehemiah, governor of Judea, 21, 29, 34, 68, 78, 150, 346, 347, 350, 357 ff., 363, 369, 380, 382

Noah, 35, 228

Obadjah, prophet, 123

Omri, king of Israel (886–875 B.C.), 19, 46, 56, 101, 155, 160, 183

Onias, high priest, 360

Parsees, Zoroastrian sect in India, 344

Paul, 132, 197, 326, 387, 393, 400, 405, 421 f.

Peisistratus (c. 605–527 B.C.), tyrant of Athens, 19; Peisistratids, 270

Peisker, 226, 341

Pentaur, Egyptian poet, 246

Peter, 422

Pharao, 14, 18, 42, 50, 99, 184, 198, 199 f., 221, 249, 256, 257, 338, 341

Philo Judaeus (c. 20 B.C.—A.D. 50), Hellenistic Jewish philosopher of Alexandria, 400, 407

Phinehas, high priest, 85, 122, 181, 182, 411

Plato, 271, 320; Neo Platonism, 400

Ptah-hetep, Egyptian teacher of wisdom, 191, 200, 248, 250, 252, 253, 257

Ptolemies, 288, 361

Puukko, 84, 244

Pythagoras, 270, 294

Pythia, 291

Rachel, 140

Rahab (Jos. 2), 340

Rameses, 6, 18, 135, 200, 248, 253; Ramses II, 125, 198, 261; Ramses IV, 197, 257

Rehoboam, king of Judah (c. 930–914 B.C.), son of Solomon, 14, 76

Reichel, 158

Rothstein, 357

Ruth, central figure of The Book of Ruth, 47, 340, 351, 418

Salome Alexandra, queen of Judea (78–69 B.C.), 391

Samson, judge (Jud. 13 ff.), 85, 94, 95, 128, 411

Samuel, prophet and judge, 84, 85, 86, 93, 96, 101, 105 f., 108, 113, 144, 158, 162, 182, 184, 195, 234, 298, 331, 352

Saul, king of Israel (c. 995–985 B.C.), 16, 27, 45, 53, 55, 86, 93, 98, 101, 115, 139, 156, 160, 162, 184, 195, 215, 224, 411

Schwally, 44, 139, 158

Sennacherib, king of Assyria (II. Ki. 18:13), 14, 183, 247, 305, 308, 310, 321

Sesostris, name of a legendary king of Egypt, 39, 198

Seth, brother of Cain, 35

Shammai, founder of school, 393

Shebna (Is. 22:15), 20, 267

Shechem (and Dinah, Gen. 34), 52

Shem, Noah's son, 35

Shemaiah, counterprophet (Jer. 29: 30 ff.), 267, 329

Sheshbazzar, prince of Judah, leads return to Jerusalem, 349

Simon ben Jochai, Torah teacher, 389

Sinuhe, fugitive Egyptian, 12, 39, 198

Snouck Hurgronje, 17

Solomon, king of Israel (c. 955–930 B.C.), 19, 20, 29, 35, 56, 86, 99, 100, 104 f., 114, 161, 169, 182, 195, 199, 280, 339; see also Song of

Solon (c. 638–558 B.C.), Athenian sage and lawgiver, 270, 319

Stade, 79, 84, 139

Stutz, 173

Tamar, wife of Er (Gen. 38), 189, 191

Tethmosis III, king of Egypt, conquers Palestine 1459 B.C., 14

Thales, (c. 640–546 B.C.), Greek sage and philosopher, 270, 285

Thersites, in Homer's Iliad the most vindictive and impudent of the

Greeks before Troy (Iliad II, 212), 269

Timotheus, 422

Titus, 422

Tydeus, warrior in Greek legend (Iliad, XIV, 114–132), 94

Tyrtaeus, Spartan poet, (c. 7th century B.C.), 270

Ulysses, 51, 128

Uria, prophet, 273, 280

Uriah, a captain in David's army, husband of Bathsheba, 91

Urukagina, (c. 2450 B.C.), last prince of Lagash lineage of city of Ur, 165, 257, 303

Usener, 229

Uzziah (Azariah), king of Judah (c. 776–735 B.C.), 162

Virgil, 321

Wellhausen, 11, 121, 244, 247, 309, 385

Wen Amon, Egyptian scribe, 103, 194, 199

Winckler, 202

Xenophanes, Greek poet and philosopher (c. 536 B.C.), 310

Xenophon, Greek historian and philosophical essayist (c. 430 B.C.), 309

Zadok, chief priest of Jerusalem in the time of David (II. Sam. 24 ff.), 169, 278

Zaina, R., 405

Zechariah, the prophet, 192, 287, 368, 378

Zedekiah, the last king of Judah (598–588 B.C.), 15, 71, 78, 185, 187, 269, 277, 279, 287, 299, 321, 346

Zephania, the prophet, 218, 238, 277, 290, 321, 370

Zerubbabel, successor of Sheshbazzar, 349, 357, 368, 378

Zipporah, Moses' wife, 92

Zoroaster (Zarathustra), Persian religious teacher, 188

Zwingli, Swiss Protestant reformer at the time of Luther, 285

3. PLACES AND COUNTRIES

Aegospotami, battle of, 320
Alexandria, 361
Ammon, 365
Anathot, 15
Antioch, 422
Arabia, 287 f.
Assur, Assyria, 274, 300, 305, 309, 320
Athens, 19, 128, 272, 320
Attica, 22 f.

Babel, 153, 300, 329, 365, 370, 372, 377
Babylon, Babylonia, 77, 102, 145, 149 ff., 151, 153, 156, 167, 175, 179 f., 202, 204, 211, 225, 239, 249, 250, 254, 262, 281, 282, 298, 309, 311, 316 f., 321, 328, 329, 337, 346 f., 350, 368, 396; Exile community, 356 f., 360 f., 363, 365
Beth-el, 84, 96, 163, 183, 269, 282
Bethlehem, 231
Bochim, 107
Byblus, Syria, 12, 14, 103, 194, 199

Canaan, 17, 114, 121, 126, 153, 204, 208, 229, 245
Caesarea, 422
China, 22, 96, 143, 154, 203, 210, 224, 231, 303, 313, 398, 403

Dan, 183
Delphi, ancient Greek town, where was located a temple and oracle of Apollo, 268, 290
Dodona, ancient town of Epirus, with sanctuary and oracle of Zeus, 268

Edom, 83, 103, 123 f., 201, 281, 341, 365

Egypt, 6 ff., 23, 93, 96, 99, 180, 198 ff., 200, 206, 219, 221 f., 231, 239, 247, 249, 250 ff., 257 f., 280, 287 f., 300, 322, 328, 349, 353, 365; charity, 256, 259 f.; education, 253; Exile community, 356 f.

Florence, 272

Gibeah, 32, 97, 172
Gibeon, 215, 339
Gilead, 17, 193, 302
Gilgamesh, epic of, 229

Hebron, 42, 46, 80, 173
Heliopolis, 199
Hellas, 295, 349

India, 3, 28, 79, 96 f., 143, 171, 173, 177, 180 f., 204, 210, 249, 255, 295, 312 ff., 315, 345, 353, 362, 388, 394, 403, 412, 420
Iran, 232, 330
Ireland, 22
Israel, 25, 56, 81 f., 87, 90, 96, 118 ff., 134, 138, 150 f., 175, 215, 219, 221 f., 223, 224, 232 f., 245, 250 ff., 263, 281, 285, 287, 290, 295 f., 301, 302, 303, 305, 307, 309, 310, 318, 319, 320, 325, 327, 331, 332, 334, 336, 338, 339, 340, 341, 342, 343, 370 f., 373, 375, 377, 378, 381 f., 412, 418
Ithaca, 270

Jabesh, Transjordania, 91, 98
Jerusalem, 15, 26, 29, 46, 114, 160, 169, 221, 241, 243, 244, 279, 282, 283, 308, 310, 321, 323, 327, 334, 337 f., 346, 350, 357, 358, 360, 365, 367; cult monopoly, 174 ff., 183, 185 ff., 360 f.

Jezreel, 17
Judah, 38, 231, 277, 283, 285, 320, 323, 330, 332, 346

Kadesh, 122 f., 170, 261

Laish, 39

Marathon, battle of, 349
Massah, 247
Meggido, battle of, (609 B.C.), 184, 216, 272, 276, 308
Meroz, cursing of, (Jud. 5:23), 212
Meshech, (Ezek. 38:2), 365
Mesopotamia, 5 ff., 96, 150, 180, 206, 229, 231, 287, 330
Midian, 201
Mizpeh, 84, 338
Moab, 365
Modin, 31
Mount Carmel, 96, 110; Ebal, 76 f.; Garizim, 76, 153; Horeb, 108, 122, 123; Seir, 123, 158 f., 170, 341; Sinai, 123 f., 211; Zion, 283, 310, 328, 330, 338

Nazareth, 390

Palestine, 5 ff., 8 ff., 21 f., 28, 149, 322, 338, 357

Phoenicia, 35, 96, 99, 102, 149, 152, 201 f., 257, 287
Platea, battle of, 349

Rome, 23, 54, 348

Salamis, battle of, 349; conquest of, 270
Salem, 46
Samaria, 100, 308, 346, 357, 359, 364
Shechem, 17, 18 f., 36, 38, 42, 46, 52, 76, 77, 83, 88, 90, 183, 187, 339, 340, 352; ceremony of curse and blessing, 215, 236, 240, 259, 337
Shiloh, 90, 106, 159 f., 162, 164, 169, 181 f., 282, 283
Shomron, Samaria, 46, 56, 83
Sidon, 365
Sparta, 23, 270
Swiss cantons, 54, 75, 100
Syracuse, 271, 320
Syria, 5 f., 102, 200, 202, 267

Thekoa, 193, 358
Tubal (Ezek. 38:2), 365
Tyrus, 14, 302, 365

United States, 344, 353